THE EU ACCESSION TO THE ECHR

Article 6 of the Treaty on European Union (TEU) provides that the EU will accede to the system of human rights protection of the European Convention on Human Rights (ECHR). Protocol No 9 in the Treaty of Lisbon opens the way for accession. This represents a major change in the relationship between two organisations that have co-operated closely in the past, though the ECHR has hitherto exercised only an indirect constitutional control over the EU legal order through scrutiny of EU Member States. The accession of the EU to the ECHR is expected to put an end to the informal dialogue, and allegedly also competition between the two regimes in Europe and to establish formal (both normative and institutional) hierarchies.

In this new era, some old problems will be solved and new ones will appear. Questions of autonomy and independence, of attribution and allocation of responsibility, of co-operation and legal pluralism will all arise, with consequences for the protection of human rights in Europe.

This book seeks to understand how relations between the two organisations are likely to evolve after accession and whether this new model will bring more coherence in European human rights protection. The book analyses from several different, yet interconnected, points of view and relevant practice the draft Accession Agreement, shedding light on future developments in the ECHR and beyond. Contributions in the book span classic public international law, EU law and the law of the ECHR, and are written by a mix of legal and non-legal experts from academia and practice.

Volume 48 in the series Modern Studies in European Law

Modern Studies in European Law

Recent titles in this series

Empowerment and Disempowerment of the European Citizen
Edited by Michael Dougan, Niamh Nic Shuibhne and Eleanor Spaventa

Legal Reasoning and the European Court of Justice
Gunnar Beck

Lawyering Europe: European Law as a Transnational Social Field
Edited by Antoine Vauchez and Bruno de Witte

Services and the EU Citizen
Edited by Frank S Benyon

The Accession of the European Union to the European Convention on Human Rights
Paul Gragl

Normative Patterns and Legal Developments in the Social Dimension of the EU
Edited by Ann Numhauser-Henning and Mia Rönnmar

The European Neighbourhood Policy and the Democratic Values of the EU: A Legal Analysis
Nariné Ghazaryan

EU Security and Justice Law: After Lisbon and Stockholm
Edited by Diego Acosta Arcarazo and Cian C Murphy

EU Environmental Law, Governance and Decision-Making
Maria Lee

Shaping the Single European Market in the Field of Foreign Direct Investment
Philip Strik

Nationalism and Private Law in Europe
Guido Comparato

EU Asylum Procedures and the Right to an Effective Remedy
Marcelle Reneman

The Constitutionalization of European Budgetary Constraints
Edited by Maurice Adams, Federico Fabbrini and Pierre Larouche

For the complete list of titles in this series, see
'Modern Studies in European Law' link at
www.hartpub.co.uk/books/series.asp

The EU Accession to the ECHR

Edited by
Vasiliki Kosta
Nikos Skoutaris
and
Vassilis P Tzevelekos

·HART·
PUBLISHING

OXFORD AND PORTLAND, OREGON
2014

Published in the United Kingdom by Hart Publishing Ltd
16C Worcester Place, Oxford, OX1 2JW
Telephone: +44 (0)1865 517530
Fax: +44 (0)1865 510710
E-mail: mail@hartpub.co.uk
Website: http://www.hartpub.co.uk

Published in North America (US and Canada) by
Hart Publishing
c/o International Specialized Book Services
920 NE 58th Avenue, Suite 300
Portland, OR 97213-3786
USA
Tel: +1 503 287 3093 or toll-free: (1) 800 944 6190
Fax: +1 503 280 8832
E-mail: orders@isbs.com
Website: http://www.isbs.com

Hart Publishing is an imprint of Bloomsbury Publishing plc.

British Library Cataloguing in Publication Data
Data Available

ISBN: 978-1-84946-523-6

Typeset by Compuscript Ltd, Shannon
Printed and bound in Great Britain by
CPI Group (UK) Ltd, Croydon CR0 4YY

Foreword

It is a privilege to introduce this book on accession of the European Union to the European Convention on Human Rights. Accession would be the culmination of many years of debate about the relationship between the EU and the ECHR—a debate in which it is not always easy to weigh the pros and cons of accession. What is not open to debate, however, as this book brilliantly demonstrates, is that, contrary to first impression, accession of the European Union to the ECHR raises issues of the greatest importance.

My own interest in the subject goes back to the first stages, and I had the good fortune to act, over the years, in a variety of capacities,[1] and I can attest that the debate has developed in ways which were totally unforeseeable.

The earlier debates were provoked by the European Commission's bold proposal for accession, issued as early as 1979. In the early stages of consideration of this idea, views were divided on the significance, the import, of accession. On the one hand, accession could be seen as something of a constitutional revolution. That was part of the background of Opinion 2/94, in which, long before the Lisbon Treaty amendment expressly providing for accession, the European Court of Justice ruled in 1996 that the then European Community had no implied competence to accede to the ECHR.

On the other hand, accession could, and can, be seen, more modestly, as simply filling a gap in the protection of human rights. The nature of the gap can be simply stated. In the absence of accession of the EU to the ECHR, in every instance where Member States act directly, or where they give effect to EU measures, their acts can be challenged before the Strasbourg Court. Yet, where the EU, its institutions, or its 'bodies, offices and agencies' act directly on individuals, groups or corporations, no such challenge is possible. The suggestion that the gap can be filled by proceedings brought against the EU Member States collectively must be rejected; the EU certainly has a separate legal personality, and has its own responsibility for its acts.

The potential gap in the protection of human rights under the existing law is well illustrated whenever a new Member State joins the EU, with the result that many competences exercised by that Member State are transferred to the EU. All measures taken prior to joining the EU, are subject to challenge before the Strasbourg Court; after that State joins the EU, the exercise of those competences by the EU, if exercised directly, may escape such challenge.

The size of this gap in the system of protection is hard to quantify. On the EU side, it sometimes seems difficult to maintain that the gap is large, because to do so would be to

[1] I was involved in various aspects of the relationship between the EC/EU and the ECHR, inter alia, as a barrister, introducing before the ECJ one of the earliest cases in the area: Case 130/75 *Prais v Council* [1976] ECR 1589; as a professor, lecturing annually in a course on European Integration at the Europa Institute, Amsterdam on the European Community and the ECHR (at a period when there was less to say on the topic); as a special adviser to the House of Lords Committee reporting on the Commission's proposal, launched in 1979, for Community accession to the ECHR; as an Advocate General at the ECJ, hearing the request by the Council for the Court's Opinion on accession to the ECHR, Opinion 2/94 [1996] ECR I-1759; again as Advocate General, delivering my Opinion in the *Bosphorus* case, Case C-84/95 [1996] ECR I-3953; and in various capacities since then.

accept a serious deficiency in the existing system. So it is sometimes argued that the case for accession is primarily symbolic. But it can be maintained that, on the contrary, the gap is substantial, and could be significantly filled by accession. True, the European Court of Justice has in recent years developed a body of case law which enables it to review EU measures for breach of fundamental rights; and the ECJ now follows closely the Strasbourg case law. But there has been, in the past, criticism of the ECJ for, as it seemed, giving high priority to the goal of European integration, sometimes at the expense of fundamental rights. And there are some areas where the ECJ lacks jurisdiction: eg where the measure is outside its jurisdiction.[2]

The answer perhaps is that the size of the gap will become apparent only after accession. One good reason for that view is that it will depend on how the Strasbourg Court exercises its new jurisdiction in cases brought against the European Union. Which in turn raises the question: Will it continue to apply the '*Bosphorus* presumption'[3]?

This is one of the many key questions discussed fully in this book. In the *Bosphorus* case, after the ruling of the ECJ, the European Court of Human Rights decided in effect that, so long as the EU offered equivalent protection to the ECHR, there was a presumption that a State had not departed from the ECHR when it did no more than implement the obligations flowing from membership of the EU.

It seems unlikely that, after the accession of the European Union, the Strasbourg Court will treat the EU more favourably than the Contracting States by giving the EU the benefit of this presumption. After all, accession is predicated, very reasonably, on the notion that the European Union and the Contracting States will be treated on the basis of equality. However, could a modified version of the *Bosphorus* presumption be applied to both the EU and the Contracting States? Discussion of this question gives, as they say, food for thought.

Two other key issues may be singled out for mention, simply by way of illustration: both issues are of a technical character, but both raise important issues of principle.

The first is the mechanism for prior involvement of the ECJ: the objective here is to enable the ECJ to rule on the interpretation or validity of the EU provisions arising before the Strasbourg Court, if the ECJ has not already had the opportunity to do so. Although there was agreement of principle between the two Courts on the desirability of such a mechanism, both the principle and its mode of implementation remain controversial.

The second is known as the 'co-respondent mechanism': What is the procedure to be followed where it is unclear, at least at the outset, whether the EU or its Member State is responsible for a particular alleged violation of the ECHR? To resolve that question may involve difficult questions on the allocation of competence between the EU and its Member States. How, and by whom, are such questions to be resolved?

Another question of great general importance is raised in this book. Currently the ECHR has a varying legal and constitutional status in different Contracting States. When, as a result of accession, the ECHR is fully integrated into EU law, it may be expected that the ECHR will have the same status as other EU law, applied uniformly in all EU Member States, and benefiting from the principle of primacy, at least in cases where EU law is in

[2] For instance, the Act on direct elections to the European Parliament was not a measure which could be challenged before the ECJ

[3] See the *Bosphorus* case, above, n 1.

issue. Will the same hold true, in due course, in all cases where the ECHR is invoked in national courts, even where EU law is not in issue?

A further large question which deserves to be asked is what the effect of EU accession will be on the Strasbourg Court itself, apart from some addition—hard to quantify in advance—to its excessive case-load. Is accession likely to strengthen, or to weaken, the Court? This question assumes all the more importance at the present time, when the Court is in some quarters being undermined—most notably, and most regrettably, by the United Kingdom, inter alia by deplorable delay in the execution of the Court's judgments.[4]

If the Court is not seriously damaged by current developments, EU accession might be seen as strengthening its position. It will become the final arbiter on human rights for the European Union as well as for the States Parties to the Convention. And the acceptance by the European Union of the Court's jurisdiction—acceptance of supervision by an external court—should also strengthen the Union. First, it may lead to some genuine improvement in human rights protection by the Union institutions and other entities. Second, the willingness of the Union to accept the jurisdiction, and to respect—it is to be hoped—its outcomes, may redound, rightly, to the credit of the Union.

There could be further, long-term advantages for Europe, including those resulting from a closer relationship between the Union and the Council of Europe. It is not altogether far-fetched to see, one day, those Council of Europe States which do not aspire to join the Eurozone as an outer ring of the European Union. It is, after all, not very long since it was almost unthinkable that States in the former Soviet empire would join the Council of Europe, still less the European Union. The possibility should not be excluded that the remaining European States which are not in the European Union, including a future reformed Russia, might join such an outer circle of the European Union.

The progress of accession has not been smooth. After complex negotiations, the current phase includes further proceedings before the ECJ on the Commission's request for an opinion on the question whether the Draft Agreement on the Accession of the European Union to the Convention is compatible with the Treaties. Further negotiations might be necessary to comply with the Court's opinion, when delivered (Opinion 2/13).

To return to this book: many aspects of the issues mentioned above are fully discussed in the following pages. But the contributions also raise, and explore, a host of other fundamental questions. This book will be essential reading for all those interested in the future judicial and legal organisation of Europe. The editors, the contributors and the publishers are to be warmly congratulated on a splendid achievement in legal scholarship.

February 2014 Francis G Jacobs

[4] For the most recent developments in this miserable saga, see the report of the Joint Committee (House of Lords and House of Commons) on the Draft Voting Eligibility (Prisoners) Bill (HL Paper 103, HC 924, published on 18 December 2013) dealing with the United Kingdom's reaction to several judgments of the Strasbourg Court on prisoners' voting rights. The executive summary contains the following significant statement: 'Underlying our inquiry is a far-reaching debate about the United Kingdom's future relationship with the European Court of Human Rights, the Convention system as a whole, and our attachment to the rule of law.'

Acknowledgements

The chapters of this book are based on papers presented at a two-day workshop organised by the University of Hull McCoubrey Centre for International Law and the Faculty of Law of the University of Maastricht on 16–17 November 2013 at the University of Maastricht in Brussels. The organisation of this workshop has been possible thanks to the funding provided by the British Academy and the European and National Constitutional law project (EuNaCon) directed by Professor Monica Claes, and funded by the European Research Council. Mr Carmino Massarella, PhD candidate at the University of Hull, provided valuable academic and clerical support to both the workshop and the book. Last but not least, Dr Nikolas Kyriakou, Dr Andreas Scordamaglia-Tousis and Ms Alexandra Theofili, PhD candidate at the University Panthéon-Assas (Paris 2), provided insightful comments when designing the workshop and throughout the editing process.

Acknowledgements

[illegible]

Contents

Table of Cases

Chronological

France

General Court (EU) (formerly Court of First Instance (CFI))

Table of Legislation

Table of Conventions and Treaties and Agreements

1

Introduction

The EU Accession to the ECHR Ante Portas: *Questions Raised by Europe's New Human Rights Architecture*

I. SETTING THE SCENE

THE QUESTION OF the accession of the European Union (EU) to the European Convention on Human Rights (ECHR) is rather old. The first academic debates regarding this date back to the early years of integration.[1] These have been regularly recurring, with landmark events in the evolution of fundamental rights protection in Europe triggering renewed academic reactions. This was so when *Opinion 2/94* was pronounced,[2] after the *Bosphorus* ruling[3] and when the EU Charter of Fundamental Rights emerged.[4] The Treaty of Lisbon evidently brought the debate again to the spotlight to an even greater degree than before.[5]

[1] See, for example, H Schermers, 'The European Communities under the European Convention on Human Rights' (1978) *Legal Issues of Economic Integration* 1; P Pescatore, *The Court of Justice of the Communities and the European Convention on Human Rights, Mélanges Wiarda* (Cologne, Karl Heyman Verlag, 1988); JP Jacqué, 'The Convention and the European Communities' in J McDonald, F Matscher and H Petzold (eds), *The European System for the Protection of Human Rights* (Leiden, Martinus Nijhoff, 1993).

[2] J Kokott and F Hoffmeister, 'Opinion 2/94, Accession of the Community to the European Convention for the Protection of Human Rights and Fundamental Freedoms' (1996) 90 *American Journal of International Law* 664.

[3] See, for example, S Douglas-Scott, 'Case Comment on Bosphorus Hava Yollari Turizm Ve Ticaret Anonim Sirketi v. Ireland' (2006) 43 *CMLR* 243; C Costello, 'The Bosphorus Ruling of the European Court of Human Rights: Fundamental Rights and Blurred Boundaries in Europe' (2006) 6(1) *Human Rights Law Review* 87, 94.

[4] F Jacobs, 'The European Convention on Human Rights, the EU Charter of Fundamental Rights and the European Court of Justice—The Impact of European Union Accession to the European Convention on Human Rights', available at www.ecln.net/elements/conferences/book_berlin/jacobs.pdf; HC Kruger, 'The European Union Charter of Fundamental Rights and the European Convention on Human Rights: An Overview' in S Peers and A Ward (eds), *The European Union Charter of Fundamental Rights* (Oxford, Hart Publishing, 2004) xvii.

[5] See, for example, J Jacqué, 'The Accession of the European Union to the European Convention on Human Rights and Fundamental Freedoms' (2011) 48 *CMLR* 995; G Gaja, 'Accession to the ECHR' in A Biondi et al (eds), *EU Law after Lisbon* (Oxford, Oxford University Press, 2012), 180; O De Schutter, 'L'adhésion de l'UE à la Convention européenne des droits de l'homme: feuille de route des négociations' (2010) 83 *Revue trimestrielle des droits de l'homme* 535; T Lock, 'Walking on a Tightrope: The Draft Accession Agreement and the Autonomy of the EU Legal Order' (2011) 48 *CMLR* 1025; X Groussot, T Lock and L Pech, 'EU Accession to the European Convention on Human Rights: A Legal Assessment of the Draft Accession Agreement of 14th October 2011', *Fondation Robert Schuman, European Issues*, No 218, 7 November 2011, available at www.robert-schuman.eu/en/doc/questions-d-europe/qe-218-en.pdf; A Potteau, 'Quelle adhésion de l'Union européenne à la CEDH pour quel niveau de protection des droits et de l'autonomie de l'ordre juridique de l'UE?' (2011) 115 *Revue générale de droit international public* 77.

Yet, things are different this time. For the first time, the Treaty on European Union (TEU) provides not only for an express legal basis for accession in its Article 6(2), but also for a legal obligation, evidenced in the phrasing that the Union *shall* now accede to the Convention. Protocol No 8 of the Treaty of Lisbon sets the 'red lines' that the EU is not allowed to overstep when acceding to the Convention system. Also on the ECHR side, there was a treaty amendment in order to allow for EU accession. Under Article 59(2) ECHR,[6] the EU *may* accede to the Convention. Indeed, after more than two years of negotiations (the modalities of which are very eloquently presented by Drzemczewski in the very first chapter in Part I of this volume), an agreement at the negotiators' level has been reached on a number of draft documents,[7] forming a 'package' that is necessary for accession.[8] The key document is the draft accession agreement,[9] which has been given the form of an international treaty. This aims to add one extra party (ie, the EU) to the system of Strasbourg. For that reason, it shall equally modify the text of the ECHR in parts. The draft agreement is currently being reviewed internally by the contracting parties. On the EU side, the European Commission requested an Opinion on the draft agreement from the Court of Justice of the European Union (CJEU) on the compatibility of that instrument with the Treaties on the basis of Article 218(11) TFEU.[10] The European Parliament and the Council, along with the national parliaments of the contracting parties, will then be asked to consent to the instrument. The agreement will not enter into force until all[11] contracting parties have consented to be bound by it, in accordance with their respective constitutional provisions.

The process is still ongoing and its fate is uncertain. In particular, it is not clear when and under what specific terms the Member States of the Council of Europe (CoE), some of which are also Member States of the EU, and the EU itself will agree on the latter's accession to the Convention system. What is certain, however, is that once this materialises, we will witness a landmark moment in post-war European history: a dynamic supranational entity with integrational ends will be included in a normative and institutional framework that has been equally designed to promote integration,[12] albeit by different means. Undoubtedly, this is not a trivial change of context for the relations of these two regional regimes that share common historical origins and, ultimately, serve contiguous purposes as well. The CJEU in Luxembourg and the European Court of Human Rights (ECtHR) in

[6] As amended by Protocol No 14 of the Convention, which entered into force on 1 June 2010.

[7] All five documents are contained in the appendixes of Doc 47+1(2013)008rev2 (10 June 2013, *Council of Europe, Fifth Negotiation Meeting between the CDDH ad hoc Negotiation Group and the European Commission on the Accession of the European Union to the European Convention on Human Rights: Final Report to the CDDH*), which is available at www.coe.int/t/dghl/standardsetting/hrpolicy/Accession/Meeting_reports/47_1(2013)008rev2_EN.pdf. Not all of them create legal obligations as such (see, for instance, the draft explanatory report); one of these documents aims at modifying the internal rules of the CoE (draft rule to be added to the Rules of the Committee of Ministers for the supervision of the execution of judgments and of the terms of friendly settlements in cases to which the EU is a party) and another looks like a unilateral act by the EU (draft declaration by the EU to be made at the time of signature of the accession agreement), which, inter alia, will be expected to ensure that it shall request to become a co-respondent or accept an invitation to that effect when the conditions established by Article 3(2) of the accession agreement are met.

[8] Doc 47+1(2013)008rev2 (n 7) 3, para 9.

[9] Ibid 4, Appendix I.

[10] Pending Opinion 2/13. Application lodged with the CJEU on 4 July 2013.

[11] Article 10(3) of the draft Accession Agreement, Doc 47+1(2013)008rev2 (n 7).

[12] Preamble and Article 1, Statute of the Council of Europe.

Strasbourg have been (at least in the relatively recent past) interacting relatively closely,[13] despite their institutional disjunction. The role of human rights within the EU is well known and does not need to be discussed here. Despite the EU's initial economic focus, the evolution of fundamental rights protection in the EU has been spectacularly dynamic.[14] It has contributed to the constitutionalisation of an entity presenting quasi-federal features. Human rights, including the ECHR's 'constitutional'[15] public order,[16] form part and parcel of the EU's system, which is increasingly moving towards the establishment of a proper, full *état de droit*.[17]

One may suggest that the ECtHR appears to appreciate this—especially if one adopts a rather 'innocent' reading of *Bosphorus*, that is, if one chooses to see no other motivations behind its famous presumption of equivalent protection[18] than genuine comity—under conditions reminiscent of *Solange*.[19] Before *Bosphorus*, but also now in cases falling outside the presumption's ambit,[20] especially when states enjoy discretion in the way they implement EU law,[21] the ECtHR is only exercising an indirect 'constitutional' control over the EU legal order through scrutiny of the common Member States' practice in instances of implementation of EU law within their domestic legal order. If one wants to draw the big

[13] S Douglas-Scott, 'A Tale of Two Courts: Luxembourg, Strasbourg and the Growing European Human Rights *Acquis*' (2006) 43 *CMLR* 629. See also C Timmermans, 'The Relationship between the European Court of Justice and the European Court of Human Rights' in A Arnull et al (eds), *A Constitutional Order of States?* (Oxford, Hart Publishing, 2011); A Rosas, 'The European Court of Justice in Context: Forms and Patterns of Judicial Dialogue' (2007) 1 *European Journal of Legal Studies* 1; FG Jacobs, 'Judicial Dialogue and the Cross-fertilization of Legal Systems: The European Court of Justice' (2003) 38 *Texas International Law Journal* 547, especially 550–52; G Harpaz, 'The European Court of Justice and its Relation with the European Court of Human Rights: The Quest for Enhanced Reliance, Coherence and Legitimacy' (2009) 46 *CMLR* 105.

[14] S Douglas-Scott, 'The European Union and Human Rights after the Treaty of Lisbon' (2011) 11(4) *Human Rights Law Review* 643; G de Búrca, 'The Evolution of EU Human Rights Law' in P Craig and G de Búrca (eds), *The Evolution of EU Law*, 2nd ed (Oxford, Oxford University Press, 2011) 465.

[15] The literature on the constitutional functions of the ECtHR is voluminous. Among others, see L Wildhaber, 'A Constitutional Future for the European Court of Human Rights?' (2002) 23(5–7) *Human Rights Law Journal* 161; W Sadurski, *Partnering with Strasbourg: Constitutionalization of the European Court of Human Rights, the Accession of Central and Eastern European States to the Council of Europe, and the Idea of Pilot Judgments*, EUI Working Paper Law No 2008/33, available at http://cadmus.iue.it/dspace/handle/1814/9887; R Harmsen, 'The European Court of Human Rights as a "Constitutional Court": Definitional Debates and the Dynamics of Reform' in J Morison, K McEvoy and G Anthony (eds), *Judges, Transition, and Human Rights* (Oxford, Oxford University Press, 2007), especially 41 et seq; and the more critical contribution by L Favoreu, 'Cours constitutionnelles nationales et Cour européenne des droits de l'Homme' in L Condorelli (ed), *Libertés, Justice, Tolérance* (Brussels, Bruylant, 2004), especially 796 et seq.

[16] See, for instance, European Commission of Human Rights, *Chrysostomos, Papachrysostomou and Loizidou v Turkey*, decision on the admissibility (4 March 1991) [20].

[17] See, eg, L Pech, 'The Rule of Law as a Constitutional Principle of the European Union', Jean Monnet Working Paper 04/09.

[18] *Bosphorus Hava Yolları Turizm ve Ticaret Anonim Şirketi v Ireland*, App No 45036/98, ECHR 2005-VI, [149] et seq.

[19] Among others, see N Lavranos, 'Towards a *Solange*-Method between International Courts and Tribunals' in Y Shany and T Brouder (eds), *The Shifting Allocation of Authority in International Law: Considering Sovereignty, Supremacy and Subsidiarity. Essays in Honour of Ruth Lapidoth* (Oxford, Hart Publishing, 2008); G Gaja, 'The Review by the European Court of Human Rights of the Member States' Acts Implementing European Union Law. "Solange" Yet Again?' in PM Dupuy et al (eds), *Common Values in International Law: Essays in Honour of Christian Tomuschat* (Kehl, Engel, 2006).

[20] Lock gives the example of EU primary law: T Lock, 'Beyond Bosphorus: The European Court of Human Rights' Case Law on the Responsibility of Member States of International Organisations under the European Convention on Human Rights' (2010) 10 *Human Rights Law Review* 529, 531 and 538. See also *Matthews v UK*, App No 24833/94, ECHR 1999-I, especially [31] et seq.

[21] *Michaud v France*, App No 12323/11, 6 December 2012 [103].

picture, the tale of the two European courts contains elements of both complementarity[22] and fragmentation,[23] that is, institutional co-operation and competition.[24] The accession of the EU to the ECHR is expected to usher in a new chapter in terms of their interaction. The European system for the protection of human rights will be centralised and formal (both normative and institutional) hierarchies will be established. This will frame within a new structure that story of pluralism, informal judicial dialogue but maybe also implicit 'hegemonic struggle'[25] between Europe's two judicial authorities. In this respect, the future[26] of the *Bosphorus* presumption is a key question. It is discussed in this book by Judge Timmermans and especially by De Schutter, who finds in it inspiration to present a thought-provoking scenario/suggestion. De Schutter envisages the expansion of the *Bosphorus* doctrine, which could be redeployed to redefine a more horizontal relationship between the ECtHR and the states parties to the Convention. This would work to the detriment of the hierarchy and the model of full scrutiny that currently exists.

Yet, irrespective of the fate of this presumption or the intensity of scrutiny more generally, the draft accession agreement makes it clear that, even if questions of final judicial authority are not fully settled,[27] the post-accession order will be structured on a vertical basis. This will lead to a recalibration of power given that the system's ultimate judge will be sitting in Strasbourg. The EU will be submitted to the external control of the ECtHR, which will have the last word. It may choose to exercise self-restraint on its powers or to fully exercise them, but this is its own choice to make.

II. SCOPE AND LIMITS

A new era is to begin. Some old problems will be solved and new ones will appear. This is the starting point of this book, which has a rather forward-looking focus. The aim is threefold: first, to critically evaluate major features of the accession, such as the famous co-respondent mechanism and the prior-involvement procedures; second, to look beyond the modalities of the accession and identify new questions that may arise from it; and, finally, to investigate the impact that accession may have on human rights protection within the EU, but also beyond it, in the Europe of 47. Outside the institutional dimension of the questions faced by the EU and the CoE, or the more technical legal issues, like those of attribution of conduct and allocation of responsibility between the EU and its Member States, the accession

[22] See above n 13. See also J Callewaert, 'The European Convention on Human Rights and European Union Law: A Long Way to Harmony' (2009) 6 *European Human Rights Law Review* 768.

[23] One only needs to compare *Behrami* (*Agim Behrami and Bekir Behrami v France and Ruzhdi Saramati v France, Germany and Norway*, App No 71412/01 (2007) 45 EHRR SE10) with *Kadi I* (CJEU, Case C-402/05 P *Yassin Abdullah Kadi* and Case C-415/05 P *Al Barakaat International Foundation* (3 September2008)). *Cf Nada v Switzerland* [GC], App No 10593/08, ECHR 2012.

[24] See, for instance, I Canor, 'Primus Inter Pares. Who is the Ultimate Guardian of Fundamental Rights in Europe?' (2000) 25 *European Law Review* 3.

[25] The term used by M Koskenniemi ('What is International Law For?', in MD Evans (ed), *International Law* (Oxford, Oxford University Press, 2003) 110) to refer to one of the causes of fragmentation in international law.

[26] See, among others, T Lock, 'The ECJ and the ECtHR: The Future Relationship between the Two European Courts' (2009) 8 *Law and Practice of International Courts and Tribunals* 375.

[27] Which, as Halberstam demonstrates, is one of the features of heterarchy, but is also a commonality that the European and the American systems share. D Halberstam, 'Constitutional Heterarchy: The Centrality of Conflict in the European Union and the States', *University of Michigan Law School, Public Law and Legal Theory Working Paper Series*, Working Paper No 111, 2008.

invites us to examine the impact this may have on the substantive level of human rights protection in Europe. Moreover, it dictates the examination of the way in which the various actors involved, including the national legal orders and their judiciaries, will interact or will be affected by the accession. Is (constitutional) legal pluralism going to recede in favour of the order posited by the accession agreement? How will the relations of the two European regimes evolve after accession? What will be the role of their respective courts and also of the national courts in that respect? More generally, how can multiple legal orders be co-ordinated under the new architecture and how can this shape a new, common space of human rights protection in Europe? Is this new model going to bring more coherence in the protection? What will be the interplay between the ECHR and the Charter of Fundamental Rights, and how will this affect the *effet utile* of fundamental rights in Europe?

However large this list of questions already is, it is not exhaustive. To attempt such an exhaustive analysis in an area that involves as many actors, themes and parameters as the EU accession to the ECHR would be over-ambitious. The scope of this book is therefore inevitably *limited*. Certain questions could not be addressed here, even if they were central to the topic of the accession. To name but a few examples, questions relating to inter-party cases,[28] positive obligations of the EU[29] and responsibility (and allocation of competences) for execution and compliance with judgments[30] have not been included in this book. The topic's complexity and size also explain why more than one classification of the questions discussed in the book may be equally pertinent. There is an inevitable overlap between these classifications that points to the multidimensional nature of the EU's accession to the ECHR. An attempt has been made to classify the chapters into various themes in order to provide for a structured analysis. However, this is neither the sole nor a perfectly comprehensive taxonomy. The paragraph that follows presents the structure that has been finally chosen. Two other strands around which the chapters in the book centre are presented in section IV.

III. THE BOOK'S CONTENTS

As already mentioned, a structured analysis of the EU's accession to the ECHR necessitated the compartmentalisation of the book into six distinct but interrelated sections.

Part I refers to the institutional arrangements, with emphasis being given to the prior involvement mechanism, which aims at protecting the EU's autonomy. However, it also moves beyond this question and discusses more generally certain aspects of the modalities of the accession, such as how the EU will be represented before the CoE, especially with regard to the matter of the election of its judges.

Part II is devoted to questions of responsibility, involving the other 'enfant terrible' of the accession agreement, that is, the co-respondent mechanism. The idea is not only to

[28] P Gragl, *The Accession of the European Union to the European Convention on Human Rights* (Oxford, Hart Publishing, 2013) 174–208.

[29] Judge Gaja, who refers to the EU's omissions, and especially de Witte, in his forward-thinking epilogue, explicitly address the question. However, admittedly, the issue of positive obligations could have been further analysed in the course of the present edited volume. See T Lock, 'Accession of the EU to the ECHR. Who Would Be Responsible in Strasbourg?' in D Ashiagbor, N Countouris and I Lianos (eds), *The European Union after the Treaty of Lisbon* (Cambridge, Cambridge University Press, 2012) 129 et seq and especially 131. See also Doc 47+1(2013)008rev2 (n 7) 24, para 47.

[30] Referring to the means that will be used or developed by the EU and/or its Member States to remedy a breach and guarantee non-repetition in accordance with Article 46 ECHR.

discuss the mechanism as such, but also to place it next to the case law of the ECtHR on the responsibility of Member States for conduct linked to their membership of international organisations. At the same time, the chapters in this part focus on the interrelationship between the mechanism and the rules of international law on the responsibility of international organisations.

Part III attempts to zoom out from the accession agreement and bring into the picture an often-neglected part of the system, that is, its 'basis', the national legal orders of the Member States and their institutions, and in particular their courts. These will continue to implement and interpret both EU law, including the Charter, and the ECHR on the basis of subsidiarity. Therefore, they will be expected to adapt to the post-accession environment, their responsiveness to the new system being one of the preconditions for its success.

Part III is also linked to Part IV, which aspires to offer a universal overview of the post-accession environment from the perspective of pluralism and the co-existence of the various elements, segments and units of what will continue to be a Europe of 47. The discussion on pluralism is linked with suggestions about reforms of the system. This is so given that some of the authors in this volume see accession as an opportunity still to be seized, and others as one that has been missed already.

This leads to Part V, which focuses on substantive issues of human rights. In addition, it sheds light on one of the most important tools, namely interpretation aiming to inquire about the existence of the so-called European consensus as a justification for dynamism in human rights protection. Regarding the first aspect of Part V it goes without saying that the list of the rights discussed here could not be exhaustive by any means, making selectiveness unavoidable. As will be explained further below, the choice has been made to focus not on specific rights but on three areas of economic activities within/of the EU. These are trade, competition and procurement, which, unlike other areas, including the four freedoms, appear to be relatively neglected in scholarship and not to benefit adequately from the 'humanisation' of the EU. Next to these areas, one of the chapters in this part of the book is devoted to a principle, ie, equality, that (should) underpin the policies of the EU, including those with an economic dimension.

Part VI offers certain concluding observations and has the privilege to host the views on the accession of two former judges of the European courts, as well as of the former Special Rapporteur of the International Law Commission (ILC) that codified the Articles on the Responsibility of International Organizations (ARIO) (who is currently a judge at the International Court of Justice). Rather than being an epilogue, the very last chapter critically touches upon the main questions covered in the book with a view to shaping the EU's future human rights agenda.

IV. BEYOND THE BOOK'S CATEGORIES: TWO FURTHER TAXONOMIES

A. Intra-disciplinary Analysis

Notwithstanding the division of the book into six parts, the aim throughout the volume has been to offer an intra-disciplinary[31] approach to the topic of accession. The book does this

[31] Although certain authors in Part V of the book, such as Hoekman and Mavroidis, also employ a multidisciplinary law and economics methodology next to a classic analysis of the law in their chapter.

by looking at it from three perspectives: EU law, public international law and constitutional law. The reason for opting for such an intra-disciplinary approach is to facilitate dialogue and avoid a monothematic analysis. The latter could be understood as a demonstration of zealot fidelity or 'patriotism' to the primacy, autonomy and/or self-sufficiency of a particular area of law. So, the book aims at comparing and juxtaposing, but also building bridges between the various areas of law and orders involved, which after all is the ultimate goal of the accession itself as well.

Evidently, some questions cannot be answered in the absence of a certain expertise. For example, the question of the preservation of the autonomy of the EU legal order (a genuine concern explicitly raised by the aforementioned Protocol 8 of the Treaty of Lisbon) is of course a question to be posed primarily to EU and constitutional lawyers. At the same time, the issue of the co-respondent mechanism and the allocation of responsibility between Member States and the EU (as a *sui generis* type of international organisation) requires engagement with the ILC's recently finalised ARIO.[32] This clearly falls within the expertise of international lawyers. However, this is a rather evident allocation that reinforces the book's primary aim, namely to promote pluralism in the voices, approaches and areas of expertise it hosts. In other words, the project compares the questions raised above from several different yet interconnected points of view.

More importantly, however, such an intra-disciplinary approach is dictated by the fact that the accession of the EU to the ECHR is a case study that allows us to debate the impact this may have on the relevant areas of law. This is, for instance, the question as to whether, post-accession, the ECHR case law on the responsibility of the EU and its Member States can contribute to the development of a *lex specialis* (especially regarding attribution) vis-a-vis the ARIO and the very interesting, although not necessarily fully converging, observations in that respect made by d'Aspremont and Sarvarian. The accession requires the accommodation of multiple actors within a centralised system of international human rights protection. This relates to the EU's external relations,[33] but also to another thorny question, namely responsibility of international organisations and especially the attribution[34] and allocation of responsibility between Member States on the one hand and a *sui generis*, regional economic integration organisation that progressively grows quasi-federal features on the other.[35] The question of the applicable law is of practical importance for the accession itself. The starting point is of course the accession agreement and its co-respondent mechanism, which is discussed in the book, for instance, by Judge Gaja, De Witte and especially Delgado Casteleiro. Yet, as always happens with (allegedly) self-contained regimes, especially in the case of secondary rules regulating responsibility,[36] the

[32] A/66/10, para 87. *Yearbook of the International Law Commission, 2011*, vol II, Part Two.

[33] M Cremona, 'External Relations of the EU and the Member States: Competence, Mixed Agreements, International Responsibility, and Effects of International Law' (2006) 22 *EUI Working Papers, Law* 2 (including the particular questions raised by mixed agreements).

[34] PJ Kuijper and E Paasivrita, 'EU International Responsibility and its Attribution: From the Inside Looking Out' in M Evans and P Koutrakos (eds), *The International Responsibility of the European Union* (Oxford, Hart Publishing, 2013); E Cannijjaro, 'Beyond the Either/or: Dual Attribution to the European Union and to the Member State for Breach of the ECHR' in M Evans and P Koutrakos (eds), *The International Responsibility of the European Union* (Oxford, Hart Publishing, 2013).

[35] See, among others, S Talmon, 'Responsibility of International Organizations: Does the European Community Require Special Treatment?' in M Ragazzi (ed), *International Responsibility Today: Essays in Memory of Oscar Schachter* (Leiden, Brill, 2005) 414. For a comprehensive collection of papers on this topic, see M Evans and P Koutrakos (eds), *The International Responsibility of the European Union* (Oxford, Hart Publishing, 2013).

[36] B Simma and D Pulkowski, 'Of Planets and the Universe: Self-contained Regimes in International Law' (2006) 17 *EJIL* 483.

law may need to expand beyond the accession agreement as well, which raises the question of the pertinence of the principles emanating from the case law of the ECtHR and of the ARIO itself, both aspects being discussed here by Judge Gaja, Sarvarian and d'Aspremont.

A second example to be given, this time from the point of view of constitutional law, is the number of questions raised by the accession with regard to the well-known debates on the concepts of 'intertwined constitutionalism',[37] 'multi-level constitutionalism'[38] and 'constitutional pluralism'.[39] Here the main inquiry is whether, post-accession, the idea of overlapping and non-hierarchical constitutional orders as developed by MacCormick[40] remains a pertinent conception for understanding the relationship between the EU and the ECHR legal orders. It might seem obvious that the new structure favours hierarchy, perhaps to the detriment of more pluralistic dynamics and the consequent cross-fertilisation. However, this is only the case if one limits one's approach to the part of the structure that concerns the EU and the ECHR order alone. Yet, the system remains multi-level, now having an even more complicated basis. Some states will remain entirely disconnected from the EU's order; some others will in certain cases (of reserved competence) directly refer (beyond their national constitutions) to the ECHR, whereas in other cases these states will refer to the EU order, having simultaneously to comply with the ECHR[41] and ultimately falling, together with the EU, under the jurisdiction of the ECtHR. In their contribution to this volume, Claes and Imamović shed light on this new 'geometry'. They draw attention to the fact that, as things stand now, the national courts[42] are first in line when it comes to fundamental rights protection, both in the context of the EU where individuals usually do not have direct access to the European courts in Luxembourg, and in the context of the ECHR, which requires domestic remedies to be exhausted first, with the Strasbourg Court offering only subsidiary protection. National courts are key actors in the complex web of fundamental rights protection in the EU. Even if it is more centralised than is currently the case, Europe's post-accession constitutional space will rest on an equally wide, varied and entangled basis.[43] This is the reason why this book contains a number of contributions discussing the role of national authorities, once again from various perspectives. These include the viewpoint of EU law in the chapter by Morijn, who discusses in a critical manner the use of the EU Charter in national policy practice. Equally, the practice of national authorities is seen through the prism of *sensu lato* European constitutional law in the chapter by Claes and Imamović, but also of comparative constitutional law, which is the method Martinico employs. In fact, Martinico demonstrates that the national courts have already

[37] J Ziller, 'National Constitutional Concepts in the New Constitution for Europe' (2005) 1 *European Constitutional Law Review* 247 and 452.

[38] I Pernice, 'Multi-level Constitutionalism and the Treaty of Amsterdam: European Constitution Making Revisited?' (1999) 36 *CMLR* 703.

[39] N Walker, 'The Idea of Constitutional Pluralism' (2002) 59 *MLR* 517.

[40] N MacCormick, *Questioning Sovereignty: Law, State and Nation in the European Commonwealth* (Oxford, Oxford University Press, 1999).

[41] This may lead to dilemmas for states when EU law violates the ECHR. On this question, see the brief but pertinent comments made on the occasion of the CJEU *Melloni* judgment (C-399/11, 26 February 2013) by Weiler in his editorial note: JHH Weiler, 'Human Rights: Member State, EU and ECHR Levels of Protection' (2013) 24 *European Journal of International Law* 471.

[42] See also O'Meara, who in her analysis on the role of national courts also refers to the *erga omnes* nature of the obligations stemming from the ECHR. N O'Meara, 'A More Secure Europe of Rights? The European Court of Human Rights, the Court of Justice of the European Union and EU Accession to the ECHR' (2011) 12 *German Law Journal* 1813, 1829–31.

[43] On the interaction between courts in this complex environment, see P Popelier, C Van De Heyning and P Van Nuffel (eds), *The Interaction between the European and the National Courts* (Mortsel, Intersentia, 2011).

played a major role in the approximation of the reception of the regimes of the ECHR and the EU within national legal orders, and the effect that these two are given domestically.

In similar terms—and this is further proof of the circularity between the various disciplinary perspectives and the (case) study of the accession—the idea of constitutional pluralism[44] allows Harmsen to highlight about another aspect of the new scheme, which appears to neglect the continued reform of the ECtHR as a remedy to its workload, and to point to the direction of a primarily 'formative' jurisprudential approach focused on the fostering of dialogue. Central to this process is the role of judges and of the hermeneutic tools they use, such as the aforementioned European consensus. This interpretative method has been created by the ECtHR itself and is discussed in the chapter by Dzehtsiarou and Repyeuski, who argue that the increasingly mathematical and rigorous approach of the ECtHR to the European consensus will turn the EU with its 28 Member States into a key player in European human rights law after its accession. This very same concept of European consensus occupies an essential place in Judge Rozakis' conclusions too. Judge Rozakis evidently departs from the presumption that the ultimate goal of accession is to safeguard and maximise unity in the European protection of human rights, as well as to avoid the emergence of two strong poles (one in Strasbourg and one in Luxembourg) that would be only loosely linked via Article 52 of the Charter of Fundamental Rights. Instead, he resorts to the idea/means of the interpretative method of European consensus as a foundation for an evolutive interpretation of the living instrument that is the Convention, also in accordance with the standards of protection offered within the 28 Member States of the EU, as these will be identified by the CJEU also on the basis of the Charter.

Undeniably, one of the goals of accession is to act as a catalyst for unity and coherence and, thereby, also further integration in Europe in the area of (and by the means of) human rights. This might be a desirable potential outcome, but it is to be greeted with reservations, such as that raised by Harmsen, who draws attention to the 'two Europes' within the ECHR system, ie, the group of the EU member States, as opposed to the other group of the remaining 19 non-EU European states. That the accession will centralise one of the two 'geopolitical entities' in Europe shall not discharge the ECtHR from having to maintain a balance between the different 'tempos' of evolution in human rights protection that will stem from each group, only one of which may be echoed by the case law of the CJEU. There is a concern that the ECtHR may tilt the balance in favour of the EU's 'tempo', given that a common human rights standard across the EU Member States will be readily available to the Strasbourg Court. Besides, this critique may be seen as something that reinforces Lixinski's argument, which emphasises the potential of the accession outside of the judicial arena, defending the idea of a more 'pluralistic' understanding of pluralism that would go beyond courtrooms.

B. Institutional Arrangements and the Substance of Human Rights Protection

A second basis of taxonomy would be the rather straightforward idea of the distinction between the substantive protection of human rights and the institutional arrangements for that protection—and, in our case, the modalities of the accession.

[44] It is worth noting that the term 'constitutional pluralism' is defined/used by the different authors of this book, with different areas of expertise, in a rather varied way.

Starting with the latter aspect, the focus is of course on the two inter-linked innovations that the accession agreement establishes exclusively for the EU, namely the procedural guarantees for prior involvement of the CJEU and the co-respondent mechanism. Yet, before referring to them in further detail, it is necessary to make two points. First, as the chapters by Vogiatzis and especially Drzemczewski (in his contribution discussing the election of the EU Judge to the Strasbourg Court under Article 22 ECHR) show, the modalities of the accession extend well beyond the named two special arrangements for the EU. For instance, Vogiatzis explains that the question of prior involvement may also come into question outside the courts if the applicants opt for avenues of extra-judicial redress. The analysis concludes that, in the case of ombudsmen, prima facie, no gap appears to exist for prior involvement and the relevant provisions of the accession agreement suffice to cover this scenario too. Yet, this does not mean that the agreement is in a position to cover each and every aspect of the accession or that it is impossible for lacunae to appear. In this respect, Delgado Casteleiro, for instance, discusses the Common Foreign and Security Policy[45] from the perspective of the co-respondent mechanism. At the same time, Drzemczewski gives the example of the European Parliament's participation in the Parliamentary Assembly of the CoE whenever the Assembly exercises its functions relating to the election of judges. The necessary arrangements that have to be made in this respect go beyond the accession agreement and require action within and by the institutions themselves (which, in turn, raises a number of other very interesting questions about the legal nature of those acts).

Second, it is obvious that the ECHR has not been initially designed with a view to hosting legal persons other than states, such as the supranational EU. Therefore, for its system to effectively accommodate the EU, it needs to change. The obvious question to be raised at this point is what these changes should be. The answer to this depends on yet another (preliminary this time) question. What needs to be addressed first is what the criteria are for deciding these changes. From the standpoint of international law, the parties to an agreement (such as that for accession) are free to opt for any terms they like (provided that they do not breach *jus cogens*, which seems to be irrelevant to the question at issue). Therefore, the contracting parties have no particular restrictions from this perspective. They may consent to give the EU an entirely privileged position within the new structure or may ask it to limit changes to the current agreement to the extent that these are absolutely necessary for the participation of a non-state entity within the intergovernmental regime of the ECHR. Between these two extremes, a variety of (more or less legitimate) factors may come into play. One preoccupation could be to safeguard the autonomy of the EU (prior involvement) and to allow it to rely on its quasi-federal elements rather than treating it as a 'conglomerate' of sovereigns (as revealed by the logic of joint responsibility and the co-respondent mechanism). These objectives can be juxtaposed to ideas such as effectiveness (and rapidness) in human rights protection and equality (as Harmsen and De Schutter, for instance, argue in this book), or more generally the absence of disparity between the parties to the ECHR system. Apparently, these preoccupations involve a degree of ideology, which then translates into preferences. Depending on what one's priorities are, one should only allow a conflicting objective to be fulfilled to a limited extent, that is, to the degree that this will not (disproportionately?) undermine one's prioritised objectives. Accordingly, for those giving greater weight to human rights, some of the provisions of the accession agreement that

[45] See also R Wessel, 'Division of International Responsibility between the EU and its Member States in the Area of Foreign, Security and Defence Policy' (2011) 3 *Amsterdam Law Forum* 42.

grant a special status to the EU will be thought to be unnecessary and therefore illegitimate. Seen from this angle, the 'existential anxieties' of the EU are nothing more than the 'capriccio' of Europe's 'spoiled child'. They simply undermine human rights protection. Likewise, for those giving merit to the EU's sensitivities, its special status and what this entails will be seen as a fully justified cause, that is, a necessity that ought to be addressed.

The question of the balance that needs to be maintained between these (from the standing point of this introductory note equally legitimate) preoccupations and objectives is very apparent in the case of prior involvement. Apart from the pertinent comments made by De Witte, this book hosts the dialogue between Judge Timmermans and Torres Pérez. Torres Pérez challenges[46] the double rationale of the procedural privilege of the EU (ie, the preservation of the autonomy of EU law on the one hand and respect for the principle of subsidiarity under the ECHR on the other). She also puts forward proposals for ensuring that its operation will not hinder the protection offered to individuals. From his side, Judge Timmermans accepts that the case law of the ECtHR does not threaten the monopoly of the CJEU to assess the validity of EU acts, but defends prior involvement on forceful grounds, mainly on the basis of subsidiarity from the perspective of the Convention. Yet, to a certain extent, Judge Timmermans also gives merit to the argument that there may be alternatives within the EU's order to address the problem that the dual system of legal protection within it creates for subsidiarity under the Convention, without necessarily having to establish a special status that will only apply for the EU.

The very same question regarding the 'necessity' of special treatment in favour of the EU equally applies in the case of the co-respondent mechanism (the logic and function of which are discussed in detail by Delgado Casteleiro in this volume). The difference here is that, as the chapters by Judge Gaja, d'Aspremont and Sarvarian reveal, this relates to a debate that has already taken place within the ILC, when the Commission was discussing the speciality of regional economic integration organisations for the purposes of the codification of the law of international responsibility of international organisations. Delgado Casteleiro explains that the rationale behind the co-respondent mechanism is unity in the representation of the EU. One could, of course, argue that this goal can be reached through different avenues. For instance, the EU could bear the sole responsibility, absorbing the conduct of its Member States (as proper federations do), rather than being jointly[47] responsible with them. Yet, the fact is that its members are called to give effect to its acts and the absence of devices like the co-respondent mechanism would compel the ECtHR to proceed with attribution and allocation of responsibility. Besides, this is the reason why the co-respondent mechanism is linked[48] with the procedure of prior involvement in proceedings to which the EU is a co-respondent. This gives Judge Gaja and Vogiatzis the opportunity to criticise the limitations that currently exist in the extent of the application of this procedure. Such limitations also exist due to the asymmetry in the co-respondent mechanism between the EU and its Member States, with the latter group only being able to join a procedure against the EU if primary law is involved.[49] Both authors suggest that prior involvement should be expanded to all cases where the EU would be a respondent.

[46] Among others, see also T Lock, 'EU Accession to the ECHR: Implications for Judicial Review in Strasbourg' (2010) 35 *European Law Review* 777, 793.

[47] Doc 47+1(2013)008rev2 (n 7) 26, para 62.

[48] Ibid 27, para 66.

[49] Ibid 24, para 49.

However, there is another aspect that could be critically discussed here. Joint responsibility means an absence of causality. Under the co-respondent mechanism, in principle,[50] the EU and its Member States will jointly share responsibility, without the ECtHR being able to diagnose causality (who has done what or who has failed to do what) and proceed to attribution. In a sense, both the EU and its Member States are hidden under a common artificial 'veil'. This is the function of the co-respondent mechanism. The Court will identify wrongfulness stemming from the actors behind the veil, but will not allocate responsibility individually to each of them.[51] All actors will be treated as one and as jointly responsible. Attribution may be excluded, yet the other side of the same coin is competence/power to comply with a judgment. In practice this means that the actors behind the veil who are found to be jointly responsible will have to proceed with their own 'domestic' arrangements with regard to compliance. They will also have to decide between them with whom the powers lie to adopt measures of compliance such as changing case law, amending legislation or even developing policies of compliance and taking executive/administrative measures. This is in absolute conformity with the idea of the preservation of the autonomy of the EU, which requires it to deal with these matters and shape its strategy for compliance internally, without having an external agent empowered to assign tasks and attribute wrongfulness, but also—intrinsically—competences and responsibility for compliance too.[52]

However (and this is where the scheme becomes very interesting), because of subsidiarity and prior involvement (linked to the co-respondent mechanism), when the ECtHR will be diagnosing a violation (for which the EU and the respondent states will be held jointly responsible), ipso facto, the breach at issue will also involve a violation of the Convention because of incompatible case law by the CJEU, owning to the mere fact that the Court of Justice will have failed to remedy the violation internally before the case reached the ECtHR. This will equally imply that, for the purposes of compliance, apart from any other pertinent measure (depending on the nature of the particular issues raised by a case), the CJEU too will always have to change its practice in this respect. Particularly in the case of a diagnosed breach owing to the implementation of EU law by a Member State, the CJEU will be proven to have failed to remedy a violation suffered by the victim because of the conduct of the state authorities. It is not the place here to enter into the debate about whether and when the conduct of state authorities (which, as observed by de Witte, enjoy various degrees of discretion, also depending on the degree of harmonisation of an area or policy) is attributable to the EU or to discuss the distinction between factual and normative[53] control as a criterion for attribution. Nevertheless, causality and the relevant criteria would be pertinent for qualifying the EU's breach as either a violation of a negative obligation or a violation of a positive obligation, which implies lack of due diligence (ie the EU failing to prevent/remedy a human rights violation). In a nutshell, there appears to be circularity regarding negative and positive human right obligations. This is inherent to human rights. It cannot but apply within the EU's system as well, that is, behind the veil used as a metaphor earlier. The co-respondent mechanism will prevent (to the extent

[50] Ibid 4; Article 3(7) of the draft Accession Agreement.

[51] C Eckes, 'One Step Closer: EU Accession to the ECHR', *UK Constitutional Law Group*, available at http://ukconstitutionallaw.org/2013/05/02/christina-eckes-one-step-closer-eu-accession-to-the-echr; De Schutter (n 5).

[52] Doc 47+1(2013)008rev2 (n 7) 26, para 62.

[53] Among others, see C Martín, 'European Exceptionalism in International Law? The European Union and the System of International Responsibility' in M Ragazzi (ed), *Responsibility of International Organizations: Essays in Memory of Sir Ian Brownlie* (Leiden, Martinus Nijhoff, 2013) 189 et seq.

that this applies) the ECtHR from proceeding with determining which legal person has breached which dimension in the dipole of positive and negative aspects of a human rights obligation. Yet, this question will return at the stage of compliance, where, apparently, the analysis of the ECtHR and its rationale for diagnosing a violation will be of pertinence. Judgments may be delivered in compliance with the co-respondent mechanism and the amalgamation of the EU and its Member States that this envisages. Thus, they will abstain from naming the author of a breach. However, they will identify its source and *ratio* ...

Having discussed the modalities of the accession and the particular institutional arrangements made for accommodating a supranational entity into a by and large intergovernmental regional human rights system, a few words should be noted on the substantive issues of the protection offered. As mentioned above, Part V of this book is devoted to certain dimensions and areas of substantive protection. However, aspects of this discussion can be found in other chapters of the book as well. This is the case, for instance, in the chapter by Vogiatzis, who, for the purposes of his enquiry about subsidiarity and extra-judicial redress, thoroughly compares Articles 6 and 13 of the ECHR with Article 47 of the Charter. This is of course also linked to the question of Articles 51 and 52 of the Charter, which are central to the argument built by Judge Rozakis. More generally, it is linked to the new 'ethos' of human rights protection within the EU, according to the arguments put forth by de Witte, but also by Georgopoulos in what he identifies as the subtler potential impact of accession in the area of procurement law.

Given the space constraints within which any book operates, a choice had to be made regarding the aspects of substantive human rights protection to be included in this volume. With that in mind, the idea has been to focus (apart from the European consensus method of interpretation, which is peculiar to the ECtHR) on the economic dimension of human rights protection, as this forms part of the 'core' of the EU's raison d'etre. It is in this context that Kapotas' discussion of the distinction between full as opposed to formal equality (also on the basis of negative and positive obligations in the context of discrimination) acquires its full meaning for the purposes of this book. The conception of equality defended by the author could justify pro-active protection in labour/employment as well as in socio-economic rights and welfare state policies.

The reference made to the 'core' of EU integration brings to mind the four internal market freedoms. However, this is a topic that has been extensively discussed in the literature. For that reason, this book chooses to navigate new seas and discusses three other areas of economic policy, namely trade (Hoekman and Mavroidis), competition (Sanchez Graells) and procurement (Georgopoulos). The EU exercises different competences (in terms of both type and degree) in each of these areas. However, what these three areas have in common is that, thus far, they all have raised issues of respect for human rights, albeit to different degrees. This is especially so with regard to the protection of property, but also to the guarantees of access to justice and procedural fairness. In different terms, even before accession, the ECtHR has been[54] asked to indirectly review EU law in these areas via the Member States of the EU. The accession will make it possible to bring a complaint directly against the EU. Nevertheless, it will not alter the nature of the complaints. Of course (and this is something shown by Mavroidis and Hoekman, and also by Sanchez Graells), there

[54] Or could have been, as shown by Georgopoulos and especially Hoekman and Mavroidis with their Fedon case study regarding the collateral damages of the well-known saga of the dispute between the EU and the US over the import regime of bananas.

are limits to what human rights courts can do in these areas, for it is difficult for such courts to proceed with a full proportionality test over questions that imply redistribution of income across social groups—involving economics as a complement to legal analysis. Furthermore, the needs of the persons seeking protection in these areas are of a different nature, which allows Sanchez Graells to make a noteworthy normative suggestion that undertakings receive more limited protection than victims of other types of human rights violations. Finally, the chapters on trade and competition by Mavroidis and Hoekman, and Sanchez Graells respectively, offer yet another argument in favour of the idea of circularity between case studies and the theoretical perspective from which these are explored. Human rights protection in these areas gives the authors the opportunity to proceed with suggestions about policy reforms as a means to address the problems identified. In broader terms, this is also linked to the issue of the culture of human rights protection within the EU raised by Georgopoulos in his chapter.

IV. AN EPILOGUE

The TEU tells us that the EU shall accede to the ECHR. The EU now has both a competence and an obligation to proceed with accession. An introduction (especially its concluding observations) is not the place to discuss what 'shall' shall mean. Is it an obligation of means or rather of result? What is the margin of discretion enjoyed by the EU's institutions in this respect? To what extent can or should legitimate concerns, such as those raised by Protocol 8 or others not explicitly mentioned in it, be taken into account when assessing not only the content of the draft agreement, but also the EU's obligation to accede? Obviously, in answering these questions one may have to go beyond law and add political considerations to the analysis. Shall the CJEU limit its opinion to a 'test of constitutionality' of the draft accession agreement or should it rather allow itself to move beyond the concerns it has already expressed[55] and exercise 'veto' power as a means to (re)negotiate its relationship with the ECtHR? Should the *Bosphorus* presumption continue to apply? Does Strasbourg's arsenal only contain carrots or sticks as well? How will non-EU Member States react to the draft agreement? The list with the questions is rather long.

Depending on the outcome of the accession process, some of these questions may in the future find a place in the introduction of another book on the accession of the EU to the ECHR. Some other questions may be forgotten without ever being duly discussed. The process is ongoing. We only know the 'present', that is, the common tale that the two systems share to date and the actual content of the draft documents for the accession. One way or another, this tale will continue to evolve. The accession agreement is simply an instrument of international law. It will be subjected to interpretation according to the socio-political context of each case and will adapt to the evolution taking place within its social milieu. By definition, one of the two judicial instances is better positioned, as shown by its previous case law on indirect scrutiny via common Member States. However, the ECtHR and the CJEU have both proven not to lack imagination as policy makers. The(ir) tale shall go on …

[55] Discussion document of the Court of Justice of the European Union on certain aspects of the accession of the European Union to the European Convention for the Protection of Human Rights and Fundamental Freedoms, 5 May 2010, available at http://curia.europa.eu/jcms/upload/docs/application/pdf/2010-05/convention_en_2010-05-21_12-10-16_272.pdf.

Part I

Institutional Arrangements, Prior Involvement and the Autonomy of the EU

2

EU Accession to the ECHR: The Negotiation Process

ANDREW DRZEMCZEWSKI*

I. INTRODUCTION

THIS CHAPTER IS a relatively short overview of the negotiation process and is not a detailed analysis of substantive issues raised in what has turned out to be a somewhat drawn-out and complex set of negotiations. Here, I will nevertheless highlight a number of 'selected features' from the draft Accession Agreement which will, no doubt, be thoroughly scrutinised by other contributors to this book. In the concluding remarks I will do no more than identify the present state of affairs and indicate which measures must still be taken before the Accession Agreement enters into force.

II. THE NEGOTIATION PROCESS

A. General Remarks—The Context

For the first time, an entity—the EU—which is not a Member (State) of the Council of Europe is to become a party to the ECHR. While the European Court of Justice, the predecessor of the Court of Justice of the European Union (CJEU), considered, back in 1996, that there was no firm legal basis for accession in Community law at the time,[1] the situation has now been clarified. The entry into force of the Treaty of Lisbon in December 2009 and of Protocol No 14 to the ECHR in June 2010 has created the necessary legal preconditions for EU accession. Article 6(2) of the Treaty on European Union (TEU) provides an unequivocal legal basis for accession, by which all EU Member States are bound: 'The Union shall accede to the European Convention for the Protection of Human Rights and Fundamental Freedoms. Such accession shall not affect the Union's competences as defined

* Head of the Legal Affairs and Human Rights Department of the Parliamentary Assembly of the Council of Europe. I wish to thank Daniele Cangemi, the Head of the Human Rights and Policy Division, within the Council of Europe's Directorate General of Human Rights and Rule of Law, for having commented on an earlier draft of this text. Any errors are, of course, my own.

[1] Opinion 2/94 [1996] ECR I-1759 available at http://eur-lex.europa.eu/LexUriServ/LexUriServ.do?uri=CELEX:61994CV0002:EN:PDF.

in the Treaties.'[2] And Article 59 of the ECHR, as amended by Protocol No 14, specifies that: 'The European Union may accede to this Convention.'[3]

Recent interest in the 'old' idea of EU accession to the ECHR, resulting in the formal signature of the Treaty of Lisbon on 13 December 2007,[4] can probably be traced back to the impetus provided, principally by Germany in the late 1990s, to the idea of drafting a 'bill of rights' for the EU, which culminated in the adoption of the EU Charter of Fundamental Rights in 2000. Serious discussions on accession then intensified prior to and at the Laeken European Council of December 2001, which, in turn, led into the subsequently aborted attempt to draft a European Constitution in which this subject was mooted in various guises.[5] Suffice it to note in this connection—for the present purposes—that in June 2002 the Council of Europe's intergovernmental Steering Committee for Human Rights (CDDH) adopted a relatively thorough study on the legal and technical issues that would need to be addressed in the event of possible accession,[6] and that this analysis was transmitted, at the time, to the drafters of the Convention on the Future of Europe. In so doing, the CDDH advanced two principal modalities by which accession could be achieved: either by way of an amending protocol to the Convention or by means of an accession treaty to be concluded between the EU and the Council of Europe Member States.

B. The Negotiating Format

As is often the case in international negotiations, informal contacts were established between both organisations in late 2009 and early 2010—upon the entry into force of the Treaty of Lisbon—in order to determine how negotiations ought best to be structured.[7] It was, in fact, clear from the outset that accession to the Convention, as it currently stands, would not have been possible without a number of adaptations, and that an agreement

[2] That said, Article 218(6)(a)(ii) and (8) of the Treaty on the Functioning of the European Union (TFEU) stipulates that a rather heavy ratification procedure must be followed: consent by the European Parliamant is needed, as well as unanimity of the European Council, and then approval by all (now 28) EU Member States in accordance with their constitutional requirements. Details relating to the accession procedure are set out in Protocol No 8 to the Treaty of Lisbon; see also the declarations annexed to the Final Act of the Intergovernmental Conference which adopted the Treaty of Lisbon.

[3] Article 17 of Protocol No 14 to the Convention for the Protection of Human Rights and Fundamental Freedoms, amending the control system of the Convention available at http://conventions.coe.int/Treaty/en/Treaties/Html/194.htm.

[4] The Treaty of Lisbon amended the TEU and the Treaty establishing the European Community. For more details, as seen from the perspective of the Parliamentary Assembly of the Council of Europe, see, in particular, Assembly Resolution 1610 (2008) The Accession of the European Union/European Community to the European Convention on Human Rights, based on a report on this subject which was prepared by the Assembly's Committee on Legal Affairs and Human Rights, document 11533 (both available on the Assembly's website: http://assembly.coe.int).

[5] For a recent overview, see R Lawson, 'A 21st Century Procession of Echternach: The Accession of the EU to the European Convention on Human Rights' in F Dorssemont, K Lörcher and I Schömann (eds), *The European Convention on Human Rights and the Employment Relations* (Oxford, Hart Publishing, 2013) 47–59.

[6] Study of technical and legal issues of a possible EC/EU accession to the European Convention on Human Rights available at www.coe.int/t/dghl/standardsetting/hrpolicy/Accession/Working_documents/Study_accession_UE_2002_en.pdf.

[7] Although Protocol No 14 to the Convention had not yet entered into force, this did not appear to be an impediment to the commencement of serious discussions on the subject. In addition, strong indicators existed to the effect that Russia, the state that was blocking the Protocol's entry into force for reasons unconnected to the idea of accession, was about to do so.

between the 47 High Contracting Parties and the EU to that effect was required. It is understood that, initially, the legal services of the European Commission indicated a preference for 'bilateral' negotiations, with the Commission negotiating and voting on behalf of the EU and its (at the time) 27 Member States. Be that as it may, a somewhat hybrid negotiating format was finally retained, which, while negotiations were in progress, was adapted in the light of changing circumstances, ie, when—at one point—negotiations came to a standstill.

On the EU side—not long after the Treaty of Lisbon entered into force—the Commission presented to the Council a recommendation to initiate negotiations on 17 March 2010. Discussion on the definition of the negotiating directives took a relatively short time and a decision authorising the European Commission to negotiate an agreement for the EU to accede to the Convention was adopted by the Justice and Home Affairs Council in 4 June 2010.[8] The Commission, as the EU's negotiator, thereupon conducted the negotiations right up to the spring of 2013, in close consultation with the European Council's Working Party on Fundamental Rights, Citizens Rights and Free Movement of Persons (FREMP), regularly reporting to the latter.[9]

On the Council of Europe's side, the Committee of Ministers (the executive organ of the organisation) had to decide which of two approaches to the negotiations would be best. One consisted of entrusting the Secretary General, alone or with a small team, to conduct bilateral negotiations with the EU and then to submit the results thereof to the Committee of Ministers. The other option consisted of providing a mandate to an intergovernmental committee of experts within the Council of Europe, such as the CDDH, to draft the necessary legal instrument(s) in accordance with long-established procedures, with the necessary adaptations to ensure the full involvement of the EU in the process. The wish to ensure the participation and the expertise of the Convention system of representatives of the Member States of the Council of Europe that were parties to the Convention in the negotiation process probably tipped the balance in favour of the second approach,[10] which was the option that was chosen. On 26 May 2010, the Committee of Ministers then adopted ad hoc terms of reference for the CDDH to elaborate, in co-operation with representatives of the EU, a legal instrument or instruments setting out the modalities of accession of the EU to the ECHR, including its participation in the Convention system.[11]

The identification of the negotiators was, however, not sufficient, as it was necessary to identify a negotiation format that would respect the institutional prerogatives and rules of both organisations.

[8] See http://register.consilium.europa.eu/servlet/driver?ssf=DATE_DOCUMENT+DESC&srm=25&md=400&typ=Simple&cmsid=638&ff_SOUS_COTE_MATIERE=&lang=EN&fc=REGAISEN&ff_COTE_DOCUMENT=&ff_TITRE=&ff_FT_TEXT=&dd_DATE_REUNION=04%2F06%2F2010&single_comparator=%3D&single_date=04%2F06%2F2010&from_date=&to_date=&srs=26&rc=26&nr=26&page=Detail (document is not accessible without a request).

[9] Article 4(3) TEU specifies that EU Member States shall support the negotiator in carrying out tasks entrusted to it.

[10] See, in this connection, Committee of Ministers Resolution Res (2005) 47 on 'Committees and subordinate bodies, their terms of reference and working methods' as to how the Council of Europe's intergovernmental procedures function.

[11] 1085th meeting of the Ministers' Deputies: Committee of Ministers, Ad hoc terms of reference for the Steering Committee for Human Rights (CDDH) to elaborate a legal instrument setting out the modalities of accession of the European Union to the European Convention on Human Rights, 26 May 2010 available at https://wcd.coe.int/ViewDoc.jsp?Ref=CM/Del/Dec%282010%291085/4.3&Language=lanEnglish&Ver=app7&Site=CM&BackColorInternet=DBDCF2&BackColorIntranet=FDC864&BackColorLogged=FDC864.

C. The Negotiations

From a structural point of view, one can distinguish two distinct phases in the negotiations: a first 'informal', so-called '7+7' phase, where emphasis was primarily placed on technical issues and—following the 'failure' of this phase[12]— a second much more 'formal', so-called '47+1' phase.

Under this novel framework, the CDDH initially entrusted negotiations to an informal group (CDDH-UE, the '7+7 group') of 14 members (seven appointed by Member States of the EU and seven by non-Member States of the EU) chosen on the basis of their expertise and sitting in their individual capacity.[13]

Between July 2010 and June 2011, the informal working group held in total eight meetings with the European Commission. During this period it elaborated and transmitted to the CDDH a draft Accession Agreement, its Explanatory Report and a draft rule to be added to the Rules of the Committee of Ministers for the supervision of the execution of judgments and of the terms of friendly settlements.

Many of the final features of the draft Accession Agreement were already outlined—and in some cases already agreed upon—during this phase, such as the introduction of a co-respondent mechanism, the modalities of participation of the EU before the Strasbourg Court, the participation of the European Parliament in the Parliamentary Assembly's procedures in electing judges, as well as the financial arrangements. In addition, the negotiators were rather fortunate in obtaining, as it were, help from an unexpected side with respect to one rather difficult issue which was being dealt with by the negotiators.[14] In January 2011, the Presidents of both the Strasbourg and Luxembourg Courts issued a joint statement expressing their support for the idea to introduce a 'prior involvement' procedure in cases in which the EU would be a co-respondent: 'a procedure should be put in place, in connection with the accession of the EU to the Convention, which is flexible and would ensure that the CJEU may carry out an internal review before the ECHR [the Strasbourg Court] carries out external review'.[15]

In addition, a Joint Informal Body, consisting of parliamentarians from the Parliamentary Assembly and the European Parliament, had met in March and June 2011 and had worked out the modalities of the latter's 'representativity' within the Assembly when it elects judges to the Strasbourg Court.[16]

In October 2011, the CDDH held an extraordinary meeting in order to endorse the draft Accession Agreement and submit it to the Committee of Ministers. However, some EU Member States had a number of difficulties with the drafts, and therefore the EU and its Member States could not unanimously support—as required by the internal EU applicable rules—the draft texts.[17] Given the political implications of some of the pending problems, the CDDH could

[12] Negotiations were suspended for several months due to internal differences between the EU Member States.

[13] The 14 members ('7+7') were Albania (replaced by Montenegro), Armenia, Croatia, Finland, France, Germany, Latvia, the Netherlands, Norway (chairing the group), Romania, the Russian Federation, Switzerland, Turkey and the UK.

[14] As was aptly pointed out by R Lawson: see n 5.

[15] Joint communication from Presidents J-P Costa (Strasbourg Court) and V Skouris (Luxembourg Court) of 24 January 2011: (2011) 31 *Human Rights Law Journal* 236.

[16] For more detail, see my contribution in Chapter 5.

[17] CDDH, *Report to the Committee of Ministers on the elaboration of legal instruments for the accession of the European Union to the European Convention on Human Rights*, para 11, available at http://www.coe.int/t/dghl/standardsetting/hrpolicy/Accession/Meeting_reports/CDDH_2011_009_en.pdf.

therefore not adopt the texts, and transmitted them to the Committee of Ministers only as an appendix to a report on the work carried out so far, asking for further instructions.

The transmission of the drafts to the Committee of Ministers in October 2011 marked the beginning of a long phase of negotiations within the EU in order to better define the problems which had led to the impossibility of reaching a consensus and to identify possible compromise solutions acceptable to all EU Member States. Negotiations in the Council of Europe were then suspended for several months due to internal differences between the EU Member States. These discussions were held principally, but not exclusively, *in camera* within the Council's FREMP Working Party.[18] The need for unanimity led to a compromise on the minimum possible common denominator, which was eventually reached and communicated to the Council of Europe.

On the basis of this information, the second phase of negotiations could begin. On 13 June 2012, the Committee of Ministers decided to resume negotiations, and provided a new mandate to the CDDH to pursue negotiations with the EU in a newly constituted ad hoc negotiation group ('47+1'), with a view to finalising the legal instruments setting out the modalities of accession. The format chosen for this second phase was more traditional and formal, with the participation of the CDDH governmental experts representing all 47 Council of Europe Member States.

This negotiation group held in total five meetings with the European Commission. Between the fourth and the fifth meetings, an unprecedented effort of coordination between almost all the non-Member States of the EU led to the presentation of a joint negotiation paper which gave new impetus to the negotiations and helped in reaching a decisive breakthrough in the negotiations.[19] Following the fifth negotiation meeting, in which consensus was reached among the negotiating parties, the 47+1 group sent a final report to the CDDH, to which was attached a 'package' of instruments considered necessary for the EU's accession to the ECHR.[20] At its meeting in June 2013, the CDDH agreed to send the final report of the negotiation group to the Committee of Ministers for information, including the draft instruments as approved by the negotiation group.[21] This 'package' of instruments on accession consists of the draft agreement itself, a draft declaration by the EU, a draft rule to be added to the Rules of the Committee of Ministers for the supervision of the execution of the Strasbourg Court's judgments and of the terms of friendly settlements in cases to which the EU is a party, a draft model of a memorandum of understanding and a draft Explanatory Report to the Accession Agreement. In other words, the CDDH submitted an interim report—but not necessarily a final report—to the

[18] Council of the European Union, *Accession of the Union to the European Convention for the Protection of Human Rights and Fundamental Freedoms—State of Play*, 6 December 2011, paras 5–9, available at http://register.consilium.europa.eu/pdf/en/11/st18/st18117.en11.pdf.

[19] See, in particular, Working Documents 47+1 (2013) nos 3 and 6, available at http://www.coe.int/t/dghl/standardsetting/hrpolicy/Accession/Working_documents_en.asp.

[20] Fifth Negotiation Meeting between the CDDH ad hoc negotiation group and the European Commission on the accession of the European Union to the European Convention on Human Rights, *Final Report to the CDDH*, 2–3, available at www.coe.int/t/dghl/standardsetting/hrpolicy/Accession/Meeting_reports/47_1%282013%29008rev2_EN.pdf. See also Council of Europe press release, 'Milestone Reached in Negotiations on Accession of EU to the European Convention on Human Rights', 5 April 2013, available at https://wcd.coe.int/ViewDoc.jsp?Ref=DC-PR041%282013%29&Language=lanEnglish&Ver=original&BackColorInternet=F5CA75&BackColorIntranet=F5CA75&BackColorLogged=A9BACE.

[21] 78th meeting of the Steering Committee for Human Rights (CDDH), Strasbourg, 25–28 June 2013, Addendum IV: Interim report to the Committee of Ministers on the negotiations on the accession of the European Union to the European Convention on Human Rights, available at www.coe.int/t/dghl/standardsetting/cddh/CDDH-DOCUMENTS/CDDH%282013%29R78_addendum%20IV_EN.pdf.

Committee of Ministers containing this 'package' of instruments *for information*, of which the Committee of Ministers took note at its meeting on 11 September 2013.

As concerns the participation of other actors in the negotiation process, in the CDDH-UE (the 7+7 group) and in the 47 + 1 group, the participation of observers was limited to the registry of the European Court of Human Rights (ECtHR) and to the Council of Europe's Committee of Legal Advisors on Public International Law (CAHDI). That being said, consultation with civil society was ensured by inviting representatives for exchanges of views,[22] and practically all the working documents and meeting reports were made available, in both English and French, on the Council of Europe's website shortly after each meeting.[23]

III. SELECTED FEATURES OF THE DRAFT ACCESSION AGREEMENT

Negotiations revolved principally around a number of key issues which are analysed in depth by other contributors to this book: the scope of the accession (including questions related to the EU's accession to certain of the Convention's protocols); the EU's financial participation; technical adaptations needed to the Convention to take into account the specificities of the EU; the participation of the EU in Council of Europe bodies involved in the ECHR system, especially the election by the Parliamentary Assembly of an EU judge to the Strasbourg Court and the participation of the EU within the Council of Europe's Committee of Ministers, and related voting arrangements therein; the need for a co-respondent mechanism before the Strasbourg Court and arrangements of 'prior involvement', when necessary, of the CJEU in cases concerning EU law before the Strasbourg Court. These issues—at least for the present—appear to have been satisfactorily resolved in the latest draft of the Accession Agreement and of the other documents, as adopted by the 47 + 1 group in April 2013.[24]

A. The Election of an EU Judge to the Strasbourg Court

As the EU is to be a High Contracting Party to the Convention, it will be entitled to its 'national' judge, like all other High Contracting Parties. Article 6 of the draft Accession Agreement specifies that a delegation of the European Parliament is to participate, with voting rights, in sittings of the Parliamentary Assembly when the latter exercises its functions relating to the election of judges to the Court. The delegation will consist of the same number of representatives as the delegation of the Member State entitled to the highest number of representatives (currently 18).[25] Further details are to be defined by the Assembly in

[22] The informal 7+7 group held two such exchanges of views, and the 47+1 one. In addition to the availability of almost all the documents on the Council of Europe's website, most other CDDH habitual observers were made aware of developments during CDDH meetings when the latter discussed the EU's accession to the ECHR. It is in this context, as a representative of the Parliamentary Assembly, that I was able to follow proceedings and report—to the Assembly's Committee on Legal Affairs and Human Rights—on the progress being made.

[23] See generally CDDH, *Accession of the European Union to the Convention: Working Documents,* available at www.coe.int/t/dghl/standardsetting/hrpolicy/Accession/Working_documents_en.asp.

[24] As already indicated, the text of the draft Agreement is provided in the CDDH 'Interim report to the Committee of Ministers' (n 21) 5.

[25] Draft Accession Agreement, Article 6.

co-operation with the European Parliament. Some of these details, including a procedure allowing for the designation of a member of the European Parliament to sit, ex officio, on the Assembly's Sub-Committee on the Election of Judges, have already been agreed upon by the Joint Informal Body of both parliamentary institutions, of which note was duly taken by the drafters of the Accession Agreement.[26]

B. The Co-respondent Mechanism

As the first non-state party to be subject to the jurisdiction of the European Court of Human Rights and due to the specific characteristics of EU law, EU accession required the use of new procedural mechanisms to facilitate the functioning of the Convention system. Concerns existed in particular regarding the attribution of acts to either the EU and/or one or more states parties. For example, an individual could bring an application to the Strasbourg Court against his or her state when the regulation at issue was promulgated by the European Commission, obliging the national authorities to implement the EU norm whose compatibility with the ECHR is disputed by an applicant. Similarly, if an application is filed against the EU concerning a provision in EU primary law,[27] only Member States, and not EU institutions possess the authority to modify the relevant legal provision.[28] Therefore, it was in the interests of both the applicants and potential respondents (the EU and its Member States) that any accession agreement allowed for additional respondents to be joined to a case as a co-respondent if necessary.

Negotiations in this area were primarily concerned with the manner and operation of this proposed mechanism. It was initially unclear to what extent the mechanism would differ from the existing third-party intervention mechanism established under Article 36 of the Convention, which allows for written comments by third parties without providing them with the full power of a respondent to participate in the case and the hearing.[29] Further, some called for the mechanism to be compulsory if the Strasbourg Court felt its use was appropriate in order to ensure that the relevant party would be bound by the Court's decision, while others advocated for a voluntary mechanism that would not force a party to act as a co-respondent if the said party did not wish to.[30] Finally, questions remained as to how the Strasbourg Court would apportion responsibility for a violation

[26] For more detail on the procedures to be adopted to facilitate the European Parliament's participation in the election of judges, see Drzemczewski, ch 5, at pp 65–72.

[27] See the EU's website for a list of the relevant legal norms: http://europa.eu/legislation_summaries/institutional_affairs/decisionmaking_process/l14530_en.htm.

[28] See, in this connection, comments by, among others, S-Ø Johansen, *The European Union's Accession to the ECHR as Seen from Strasbourg*, University of Oslo Faculty of Law Research Paper, 6 September 2012, 47 available at http://ssrn.com/abstract=2142446.

[29] Germany proposed such a modified third-party intervention mechanism at the outset of negotiations. See X Groussot et al, 'EU Accession to the European Convention on Human Rights: A Legal Assessment of the Draft Accession Agreement of 14th October 2011', *European Issues No 218* (November 2011) 7, available at www.robert-schuman.eu/en/doc/questions-d-europe/qe-218-en.pdf.

[30] See, eg, ibid, 13 (arguing that the mechanism should be compulsory in contrast to the voluntary mechanism envisioned in the Draft Agreement). While applicants would still be free to file an application against both the EU *and* one or more states parties in the case of a voluntary mechanism, this process is more difficult than adding a party as a co-respondent, as it would require the applicant to have exhausted all domestic remedies in both the EU and national legal systems.

between respondents without interfering with the autonomy of the EU law dealing with the relative competencies of the EU and its Member States.

The draft Accession Agreement describes in detail the operations of the proposed co-respondent mechanism, largely resolving the above issues.[31] The mechanism allows for co-respondents to assume the full position of parties to the case; they are not treated simply as third-party interveners or as 'multiple respondents' for separate violations, but as fully responding, at the same time as the 'original' respondent, for the same alleged violation. This mechanism is only to come into operation after an examination of an application's admissibility, so its use is likely to be relatively infrequent, as the vast majority of applications brought before the Strasbourg Court are declared inadmissible. The mechanism is, in principle, voluntary. Potential co-respondents could apply to join a case or could be invited to join by the Court, but would not be forced to do so.[32] However, included along with the draft Accession Agreement is a draft declaration to be made by the EU stating that the EU will always request to become a co-respondent or accept the Court's invitation when the relevant conditions are met. This declaration would make the mechanism de facto compulsory in most cases involving the EU as co-respondent (but not states parties as co-respondents).[33]

The conditions under which the mechanism can be used are as follows: when the respondent is a Member State, the EU may become a co-respondent if the applicant's allegations appear to 'call … into question the compatibility with the rights at issue … of a provision of European law … notably where that violation could have been avoided only by disregarding an obligation under European Union law'; when the respondent is the EU, a Member State may become a co-respondent if the allegations appear to call into question EU primary law; when the applicant lists both the EU and one or more Member States as respondents, one of the parties may ask the Court (or be invited by it) to become a co-respondent if either of the above conditions apply (see the Appendix for a chart illustrating the co-respondent mechanism).[34]

As to attribution, the draft Agreement states that if the Strasbourg Court finds a violation, the respondent and the co-respondent will be jointly responsible except in extraordinary circumstances where the Court decides otherwise, after hearing the parties.[35] This provision reduces the risk of the Strasbourg Court being required to determine the respective competencies of the parties under EU law, preserving the autonomy of the EU legal system.

C. The Role of the CJEU in Cases Concerning EU Law

The EU Commission, EU Member States and the CJEU have raised concerns regarding the role of the CJEU as the final arbiter of EU law in the context of accession. In a post-accession

[31] See the draft Accession Agreement, Article 3. See also the Explanatory Report to the Agreement, Appendix V, paras 37–69.

[32] Ibid, Article 3(5). The rationale for this is that a High Contracting Party which has not been indicated by the applicant in the original application could not be compelled to become a party to the case against its own will.

[33] 'Draft declaration by the European Union to be made at the time of signature of the Accession Agreement': ibid, Appendix II, 14.

[34] Draft Accession Agreement, Article 3, para 5. This would be the case for the party which is not responsible for the act or omission which allegedly caused the violation, but only for the legal basis of it.

[35] Ibid, Article 3, para 7.

situation, it is possible that a case concerning the validity or compatibility of EU law with Convention standards may find its way before the Strasbourg Court *before* the Luxembourg Court has had the chance to express its view on the issue. Such a scenario is foreseeable in the event that the EU is joined to a case as a co-respondent. In such instances the applicant needs only to have exhausted all domestic remedies within the national legal system of the initial respondent, and need not have made use of the EU courts before the Strasbourg Court is entitled to hear the case. National supreme courts are able to refer questions of EU law to the CJEU; however, they are in most cases not obligated to do so.[36]

A number of proposals were discussed in the negotiating process to permit the CJEU to be seised on matters of EU law *before* the Strasbourg Court makes it decision without undue delay. These included allowing the CJEU to present an interpretation of EU law, to be submitted by the Commission in Strasbourg Court proceedings,[37] and allowing the Strasbourg Court to stay proceedings and to make a reference to the CJEU, or the Commission itself to make such a reference.[38]

Article 3 of the draft Agreement outlines a process whereby, in cases where the EU is a co-respondent and the CJEU has not yet assessed the compatibility of the relevant EU law with the Convention, 'sufficient time shall be afforded for the [CJEU] to make such an assessment, and thereafter for the parties to make observations to the Court'.[39] The Agreement stresses that such assessments be 'made quickly so that proceedings before the Court are not unduly delayed' (this process is included in the chart in the Appendix).

The exact implementation of a procedure by which the CJEU can make an assessment of a case pending before the Strasbourg Court will depend on internal EU law and procedures, which have yet to be finalised. It is important that such procedures do not confer new powers on EU bodies, such as the CJEU, beyond those granted in the EU treaties, in order to avoid the need to change EU primary law, which would be a long, cumbersome and difficult process.[40]

D. The Participation of the EU in the Meetings of the Council of Europe's Committee of Ministers

Although obviously not a Member (State) of the Council of Europe, as a contracting party to the Convention, the EU will be entitled to provide an input, plus an upgraded 'representativity' in meetings of the Committee of Ministers, when the latter deals with issues relating to the ECHR, in particular, the supervision of the execution of the Court's judgments.[41]

[36] For more information on the relationship between the CJEU and the national courts of the EU Member States, see the EU's website at http://europa.eu/legislation_summaries/institutional_affairs/decisionmaking_process/l14552_en.htm. Needless to say, a preliminary ruling by the CJEU is not a remedy at the disposal of the applicant.

[37] M Kuijer, 'The Accession of the European Union to the ECHR: A Gift for the ECHR's 60th Anniversary or an Unwelcome Intruder at the Party' (2011) 3(4) *Amsterdam Law Forum* 17, 27.

[38] Groussot et al (n 29) 15.

[39] Draft Accession Agreement, Article 3, para 6.

[40] Groussot et al (n 29) 15–16.

[41] At present, the EU, represented by the Commission/External Services, has 'Observer status' at most Committee of Ministers meetings.

Negotiations in this area dealt with the status of the EU within the Committee of Ministers post-accession, including whether the EU would have the right to vote as a Committee member, and the scope of its voting status. A concern of some non-EU Member States was the possibility of bloc voting in decisions concerning the supervision of judgments.[42] It is for this reason that the draft Agreement expresses a commitment that the exercise of voting rights by the EU will not 'prejudice the effective exercise by the Committee of Ministers of its supervisory function' and requires that the Rules of the Committee of Ministers be appropriately adapted when supervising a judgment with respect to which the EU is a party. This was felt to be most problematic in the event of a supervision of a judgment where the EU is a respondent or co-respondent, as the EU treaties would—purportedly—require EU Member States to vote in a co-ordinated manner in such circumstances.[43] For this purpose, a draft rule, 'Rule 18—Judgments and friendly settlements in cases to which the European Union is a party', amends the majority voting requirements.[44] That said, when supervising judgments where individual Member States are respondents, EU Member States would be able to vote freely as they do at present. Hence, bloc voting is less of a concern in such cases.[45]

Under the draft Agreement, the EU will be provided voting rights with respect to certain functions of the Committee of Ministers dealing with the make-up of the Strasbourg Court, advisory opinions, the supervision of judgments as well as the adoption of any future protocols to the Convention;[46] the EU must be consulted before the Committee adopts other instruments or texts relating to the Convention, the Court or the selection of candidates for the election of judges.[47]

IV. CONCLUDING REMARKS

As indicated above, negotiations pursued within the ad hoc 47+1 group under the umbrella of the CDDH resulted in an agreement at the negotiators' level on the draft texts in April 2013. The group reported to the CDDH, which, at the end of June 2013, reported on progress to the Committee of Ministers.

[42] Eg, 'the Swiss objection' to the difference of treatment by the EU of cases involving its Member States (where the EU would not vote) and non-EU Member States (where the EU could vote).

[43] Here, so it appears, the EU's argument was based on, inter alia, the need to vote as a block where there exists a so-called 'duty of loyal/sincere cooperation' and/or in foreign policy matters, as participation in the ECHR control mechanism would entail. It would be interesting to study these arguments a little more, especially the so-called notion of the 'duty of loyal/sincere cooperation', which, I suggest, is inappropriate in this context due to the specific quasi-judicial functions that the Committee of Ministers carries out by virtue of Article 46 ECHR.

[44] Under the draft rule, the majority for a decision under Rule 17 (final resolution) will be increased to four-fifths, decisions under Rules 10 (referral to the Court for interpretation of a judgment) and 11 (infringement proceedings) will require the approval of only one-quater of participants and decisions on procedural issues will require only the approval of one-fifth of participants: see 'Draft rule to be added to the Rules of the Committee of Ministers for the supervision of the execution of judgments and of the terms of friendly settlements in cases to which the European Union is a party', CDDH Interim Report, Appendix III, 15.

[45] In the case of the supervision of judgments against its Member States, according to the EU treaties, the EU would not be allowed to vote.

[46] The Committee of Ministers acts as an organ of the Convention and takes decisions under Articles 26(2), 39(4), 46(2–5) and 47. The Accession Agreement adds a specific competence for the adoption of protocols, which will appear in Article 54 of the Convention.

[47] For more details, see n 21 above: CDDH interim report to the Committee of Ministers, document CDDH (2013)R 78 Addendum IV of 28 June 2013 (especially the draft explanatory memorandum to the draft Accession Agreement, Appendix V, paras 80 and 81, which relate to EU participation as regards functions *not* explicitly foreseen in the Convention).

Adoption of the draft instrument is now subject to the completion of internal procedures by the 47 High Contracting Parties and the EU on the one hand, and the Council of Europe on the other hand.[48]

Insofar as the EU is concerned, the CJEU was seised by the European Commission, on 4 July 2013, for an Opinion on the draft Accession Agreement (and related texts).[49] Were the Luxembourg Court to find (parts of) the draft Accession Agreement incompatible with EU law, this would, in effect, block the EU and EU Member States from entering into the said Agreement. Such a ruling would almost certainly necessitate the re-opening of negotiations.

On the assumption that the CJEU does not find any of the provisions of the draft Accession Agreement as incompatible with EU law, Article 218(6)(a)(ii) and (8) of the TFEU stipulates that consent by the European Parliament is needed, as well as unanimity in the Council, before approval[50] by the (now 28) EU Member States 'in accordance with their constitutional requirements'.[51] In the meantime, the Council of the EU will need to reach at least a political agreement on the internal rules which will be necessary to implement the Accession Agreement at the EU level.[52]

Insofar as the Council of Europe is concerned, once these 'internal' steps are successfully accomplished, the Accession Agreement will have to be adopted by the Committee of Ministers and opened for signature and ratification by Member States, after having received the (formal) opinions on the text(s) from both the Strasbourg Court and the Parliamentary Assembly.

It can be assumed that the ratification procedure is likely to be straightforward for most, but probably not all, Member States of the EU (the EU and its Member States are likely to be 'bound' to sign and ratify the Accession Agreement by a decision in the Council of the EU); it remains to be seen how long it will also take the remaining 19 Council of Europe Member States, Parties to the Convention, to ratify this instrument.[53]

In short, the accession of the EU to the ECHR is a legal obligation (self-)imposed by the EU and its Member States. This process of accession has been undertaken in the form of a hybrid legal instrument in terms of traditional treaty law: the draft Accession Agreement is a text which necessitates ratification by 47 states parties to the Convention, all Member States of the Council of Europe and a non-state entity, the EU, which—when it enters into force—will in part amend the existing wording of the Convention. But some of the Agreement's provisions will also continue a 'separate life' after its entry into force. It will—as an integral part of the Convention—bind any future Contracting Parties to the Convention and its provisions will be subject to interpretation by the Strasbourg Court.

[48] As concerns procedures within the Parliamentary Assembly, see Drzemczewski, Chapter 5.

[49] See Official Journal of the EU, 2013/C 260/32 of 7 September 2013, 19, available at: http://eur-lex.europa.eu/LexUriServ/LexUriServ.do?uri=OJ:C:2013:260:0019:0020:EN:PDF.

[50] In most cases by means of a signature and subsequent ratification.

[51] OJEU C 115, 9.5.2008: Consolidated version of the Treaty on European Union. See also Protocol No 8 relating to Article 6(2) TEU on the accession of the EU to the ECHR.

[52] The Council, via FREMP, is currently in the process of drafting internal rules. These rules are likely to regulate, inter alia, the concept of 'co-respondent' and the process by which candidatures for the post of judge in Strasbourg are to be handled. Given the level of political and legal importance of these and related issues, this work could take quite some time.

[53] It may be recalled in this connection that it took the Russian Federation several years to ratify Protocol No 14 of the ECHR, an amending protocol, with ratification and entry into force eventually taking place four years after all the other states parties had ratified it.

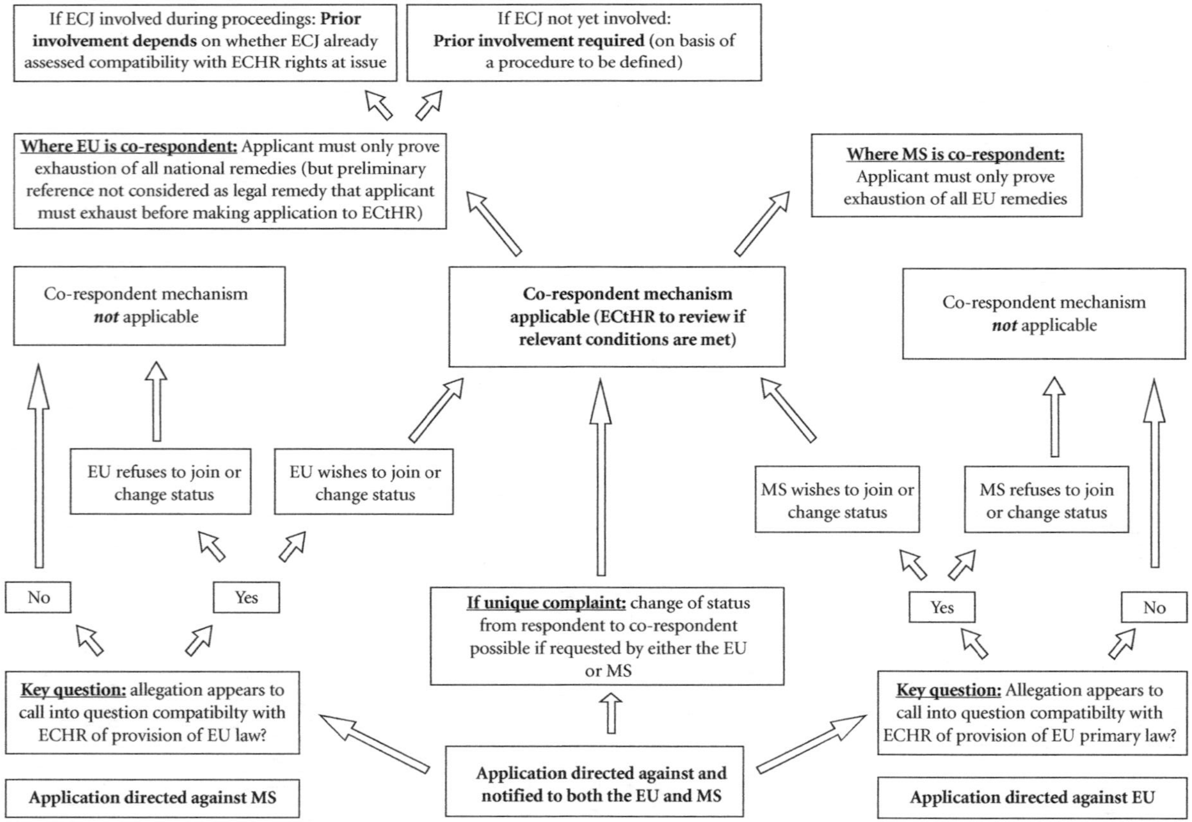

Chart illustrating the co-respondent mechanism and the role of the CJEU in cases before the European Court of Human Rights[54]

[54] Taken from Groussot et al (n 29) 11.

3

Too Many Voices? The Prior Involvement of the Court of Justice of the European Union

AIDA TORRES PÉREZ*

I. INTRODUCTION

DESPITE THE LACK of formal accession of the European Union (EU) to the European Convention on Human Rights (ECHR), the interaction between the Court of Justice of the European Union (CJEU) and the European Court of Human Rights (ECtHR) has intensified over time. Notably, the Luxembourg Court has drawn inspiration from the Convention as well as the corresponding case law to interpret EU fundamental rights. At the same time, the Strasbourg Court has also drawn on EU legal sources in order to interpret Convention rights. Mutual cross-citation has steadily increased. By quoting each other, these courts have reinforced their legitimacy and authority vis-a-vis the Member States. Thus, despite momentary tensions, a fruitful dialogue between the Luxembourg and Strasbourg Courts has developed.[1]

* Professor of Constitutional Law at Pompeu Fabra University. I thank Monica Claes, Andrew Drzemczewski, Alejandro Saiz Arnaiz, Olivier de Schutter, Bruno de Witte and the organisers of the Workshop on 'The EU Accession to the ECHR' (Brussels, 16–17 November 2012), Vicky Kosta, Nikos Skoutaris and Vassilis Tzevelekos for their illuminating comments and discussion. A previous version of this article has been published in (2013) 4 *European Journal of Human Rights. Financed by MICINN DER2011-29207-C02-01.*

[1] There is a vast literature on the interaction between the Luxembourg and Strasbourg courts. See, among others, D Spielmann, 'Human Rights Case Law in the Strasbourg and Luxembourg Courts: Conflicts, Inconsistencies and Complementarities' and B de Witte, 'The Past and Future Role of the European Court of Justice in the Protection of Human Rights' in P Alston (ed), *The EU and Human Rights* (Oxford, Oxford University Press, 1999); S Douglas-Scott, 'A Tale of Two Courts: Luxembourg, Strasbourg and the Growing European Human Rights Acquis' (2006) 43 *Common Market Law Review* 629; A Rosas, 'The European Court of Justice in Context: Forms and Patterns of Judicial Dialogue' (2007) 1 *European Journal of Legal Studies* 9; R Bustos Gisbert, 'Tribunal de Justicia y Tribunal Europeo de Derechos Humanos: una relación de enriquecimiento mutuo en la construcción de un sistema europeo para la protección de los derechos', in J García Roca and PA Fernández Sánchez (eds), *Integración europea a través de Derechos Fundamentales: de un sistema binario a otro integrado* (Madrid, CEPC, 2009); J Callewaert, 'The European Convention on Human Rights and European Union Law: A Long Way to Harmony' (2009) 6 *European Human Rights Law Review* 768; C Timmermans, 'The Relationship between the European Court of Justice and the European Court of Human Rights' in A Arnull et al (eds), *A Constitutional Order of States?* (Oxford, Hart Publishing, 2011).

In this context, the accession of the EU to the ECHR has been long awaited. Since the 1970s, European institutions[2] and scholars have advocated the EU's accession to the Convention.[3] Among the main reasons, the search for political legitimacy and coherence stands out.[4]

In addition, by granting the ECtHR jurisdiction over EU law, accession would overcome current dilemmas when complaints are directed against state action implementing EU law or concluding primary law, such as in *Bosphorus*[5] or *Matthews*.[6] Currently, by reviewing state action within the scope of EU law, the Strasbourg Court might be indirectly reviewing primary or secondary EU law without having the jurisdiction to do so.[7]

Furthermore, individuals would be allowed to sue the EU before the ECtHR. Hence, accession would provide an external check for the action of EU institutions in light of the Convention.[8] As more and more state powers in sensitive fields, such as the area of freedom, security and justice, are transferred to the EU, the EU should also be bound by the Convention.[9]

The Treaty of Lisbon has finally provided for the amendment that the CJEU Opinion 2/94 requested.[10] As such, Article 6(2) of the Treaty on European Union (TEU) sets forth that the EU shall accede to the Convention. In turn, Protocol 14 has amended Article 59 ECHR to allow the EU's accession.[11]

The path towards accession has proven to be a bumpy road. Negotiations between the European Commission and the Council of Europe started in July 2010. A year later, a draft Accession Agreement was reached and published alongside an Explanatory Report.[12] The extraordinary meeting held on 12–14 October 2011 revealed the lack of consensus among the EU Member States. The representative of the European Commission stated that there

[2] Commission of the European Communities, *Memorandum*, Brussels, 4 April 1979; Commission of the European Communities, *Communication on Community Accession to the European Convention for the Protection of Human Rights and Fundamental Freedoms and some of its Protocols*, Brussels, 19 November 1990.

[3] See, among others, I Canor, 'Primus Inter Pares. Who is the Ultimate Guardian of Fundamental Rights in Europe?' (2000) 25 *European Law Review* 3; R Harmsen, 'National Responsibility for European Community Acts under the European Convention on Human Rights: Recasting the Accession Debate' (2001) 7 *European Public Law* 625; HC Krüger and J Polakiewicz, 'Proposals for a Coherent Human Rights Protection System in Europe' (2001) 22 *Human Rights Law Journal* 1; LI Gordillo Pérez, 'Un paso más hacia la estabilización de las relaciones interordinamentales en Europa: la incorporación de la UE al CEDH' (2011) 38 *Revista Española de Derecho Europeo* 173.

[4] O De Schutter, 'L'adhésion de l'Union Européenne à la Convention Européenme des Droits de l'Homme: Feuille de Route de la Négociation' (2010) 83 *Revue Trimestrielle des Droits de l'Homme* 541.

[5] *Bosphorus Hava Yolları Turizm ve Ticaret Anonim irketi v Ireland* [GC], App No 45036/98, judgment of 30 June 2005, ECHR 2005-VI.

[6] *Matthews v UK* [GC], App No 24833/94, judgment of 18 February 1999, ECHR 1999-I.

[7] T Lock, 'The ECJ and the ECtHR: The Future Relationship between the Two European Courts' (2009) 8 *Law and Practice of International Courts and Tribunals* 375, 376–381.

[8] T Lock, 'EU Accession to the ECHR: Implications for the Judicial Review in Strasbourg' (2010) 35 *European Law Review* 777, 777–78.

[9] JP Jacqué, 'The Accession of the European Union to the European Convention on Human Rights and Fundamental Freedoms' (2011) 48 *Common Market Law Review* 995, 1001; S Sanz Caballero, 'Crónica de una adhesión anunciada: algunas notas sobre la negociación de la adhesión de la Unión Europea al Convenio Europeo de Derechos Humanos' (2011) 38 *Revista de Derecho Comunitario Europeo* 99, 125–26.

[10] Opinion 2/94, *Re Accession to the ECHR* [1996] ECR I-1759.

[11] Protocol No 14 to the Convention for the Protection of Human Rights and Fundamental Freedoms, amending the control system of the Convention, in force since 1 June 2010.

[12] 8th Working Meeting of the CDDH Informal Working Group on the Accession of the European Union to the European Convention on Human Rights (CDDH-UE) with the European Commission, *Draft legal instruments on the accession of the European Union to the European Convention on Human Rights*, Strasbourg, 19 July 2011, www.coe.int/t/dlapil/cahdi/source/Docs%202011/CDDH-UE_2011_16_final_en.pdf.

was a need for further discussion within the EU.[13] In June 2012, negotiations between the Steering Committee for Human Rights and the European Commission resumed in an ad hoc group ('47+1'). Eventually, at the fifth negotiation meeting in April 2013, an agreement was reached on the legal instruments for accession and by June 2013, the Final Report had already been published.[14]

Among the most contentious issues, one finds the 'prior involvement' of the CJEU. Even before negotiations started, the CJEU published a *Discussion document*[15] in which this Court argued that, for the sake of the principle of subsidiarity inherent in the Convention and the proper functioning of the judicial system of the EU, a mechanism must be available to ensure that the CJEU may carry out an internal review before the ECtHR carries out an external review of EU law. This claim was subsequently voiced by the *Joint communication* from Presidents JP Costa and V Skouris that was published after a meeting between both courts in January 2011.[16]

The draft revised Agreement on the Accession of the European Union to the European Convention on Human Rights (hereinafter the draft Accession Agreement)[17] has regulated the CJEU's prior involvement in Article 3(6):

> In proceedings to which the European Union is a co-respondent, if the Court of Justice of the European Union has not yet assessed the compatibility with the rights at issue defined in the Convention or in the protocols to which the European Union has acceded of the provision of European Union law as under paragraph 2 of this article, sufficient time shall be afforded for the Court of Justice of the European Union to make such an assessment, and thereafter for the parties to make observations to the Court. The European Union shall ensure that such assessment is made quickly so that the proceedings before the Court are not unduly delayed. The provisions of this paragraph shall not affect the powers of the Court.[18]

While the draft Explanatory Report to the Agreement on the Accession of the European Union to the Convention for the Protection of Human Rights and Fundamental Freedoms (hereinafter the 'Explanatory Report') provides some clues about this mechanism, further uncertainties remain. The discussion about the CJEU's prior involvement is not merely technical. Rather, this mechanism is intimately linked to the principles of autonomy, subsidiarity and, ultimately, the role of the Luxembourg Court vis-a-vis the Strasbourg Court.

[13] Steering Committee for Human Rights (CDDH), Report to the Committee of Ministers on the elaboration of legal instruments for the accession of the European Union to the European Convention on Human Rights, Strasbourg, 14 October 2011, www.coe.int/t/dghl/standardsetting/hrpolicy/Accession/Meeting_reports/CDDH_2011_009_en.pdf.

[14] www.coe.int/t/dghl/standardsetting/hrpolicy/Accession/Meeting_reports_en.asp.

[15] *Discussion document of the Court of Justice of the European Union on certain aspects of the accession of the European Union to the European Convention for the Protection of Human Rights and Fundamental Freedoms*, 5 May 2010 (hereinafter the CJEU *Discussion document*).

[16] *Accession of the European Union to the European Convention for the Protection of Human Rights and Fundamental Freedoms* (24 January 2011), curia.europa.eu/jcms/upload/docs/application/pdf/2011-02/cedh_cjue_english.pdf.

[17] *Final report to the CDHH. Fifth Negotiation meeting between the CDDH ad hoc negotiation group and the European Commission on the accession of the European Union to the European Convention on Human Rights*, Strasbourg, 10 June 2013, 74+1(2013)008rev2.

[18] Article 3 of the draft Agreement regulates the co-respondent mechanism, which is a new mechanism that allows the EU or its Member States to join the proceedings before the ECtHR when a complaint is directed against, respectively, a Member State or the EU, in the circumstances set out in the Agreement. The CJEU's prior involvement may only be activated when the EU participates in the proceedings as a co-respondent.

In the following section, the arguments allegedly justifying the prior involvement of the CJEU will be critically analysed. Next, several reasons to oppose this mechanism will be offered to conclude that it should be abandoned. Finally, since this mechanism seems to be non-negotiable, a constructive proposal that balances EU and individual interests will be advanced.

II. REASONS SUPPORTING THE CJEU'S PRIOR INVOLVEMENT

The main grounds justifying the CJEU's prior involvement are the principle of autonomy of EU law and the principle of subsidiarity of the ECtHR.

A. The Autonomy of EU Law

Protocol No 8 *Relating to Article 6(2) of the Treaty on European Union on the Accession of the Union to the European Convention on the Protection of Human Rights and Fundamental Freedoms* sets forth that the agreement relating to the accession 'shall make provision for preserving the specific characteristics of the Union and Union law' (Article 1). Even though Protocol No 8 does not elaborate on these 'specific characteristics', the principle of autonomy is paramount in the EU legal order, and a limit to international agreements concluded by the EU.[19]

In the landmark case *Costa v ENEL*,[20] the CJEU grounded the supremacy of EU law on the autonomy of the EU legal order. It put forward a view of the EU legal order as separate from both international law and state legal orders. In particular with reference to international law, it upheld the autonomy of EU law in Opinion 1/91 regarding the first draft agreement on the European Economic Area (EEA).[21]

The notion of autonomy encompasses several dimensions.[22] First, autonomy implies that the validity of EU law is not dependent on the rules of any other legal order (domestic or international). According to this notion, the validity of EU law depends solely on the Treaties, as interpreted by the CJEU.

Second, interpretive autonomy means that 'only the institutions of the particular legal order are competent to interpret the constitutional and legal rules of this order'.[23] Thus, the interpretation of EU law corresponds to EU institutions and ultimately to the CJEU.

[19] T Lock, 'Walking on a Tightrope: The Draft ECHR Accession Agreement and the Autonomy of the EU Legal Order' (2011) 48 *Common Market Law Review* 1025; X Groussot et al, 'EU Accession to the European Convention on Human Rights: A Legal Assessment of the Draft Accession Agreement of 14th October 2011' (2011) 218 *European Issues* 1, 2; Sanz Caballero (n 9) 109.

[20] Case 6/64 *Flaminio Costa v ENEL* [1964] ECR 585.

[21] Opinion 1/91, *Re Draft agreement between the Community, on the one hand, and the countries of the European Free Trade Association, on the other, relating to the creation of the European Economic Area* [1991] ECR I-6079. For an analysis of the external dimension of the principle of autonomy of the EU legal order, see Lock (n 19) 1028–32.

[22] For the notions of original, derivative and interpretive autonomy, see T Schilling, 'The Autonomy of the Community Legal Order: An Analysis of Possible Foundations' (1996) 37 *Harvard International Law Journal* 389, 389–90.

[23] Ibid, 389–90.

The prior involvement of the CJEU tends to be justified on the basis of these two notions of autonomy, which will be examined below.

The principle of autonomy also bans the modification of the Treaties by different means from the treaty amendment process.[24] Actually, as we will see later on, this notion of autonomy might work against setting up a mechanism for the CJEU's prior involvement through the Accession Agreement.

Finally, the principle of autonomy implies that the allocation of powers between the EU and its Member States cannot be determined by any court outside the EU.[25] The co-respondent mechanism, with all its complexities, partly aims at addressing this concern.[26]

i. The Validity of EU Law

The CJEU has asserted that the validity of EU law is not dependent on any other legal order.[27] Thus, the validity of secondary EU law can only be decided by reference to primary EU law. Moreover, the CJEU has exclusive jurisdiction to declare EU law invalid.[28] Protocol No 8 rules that the accession shall not affect the competences of the EU or the powers of its institutions.[29] In this context, is the prior involvement of the CJEU necessary to preserve the autonomy of EU law?

After accession, the parameter to decide upon the validity of secondary EU law will still be primary EU law. Thus, the autonomy of the EU legal order as a self-referential system will be preserved. With regard to the CJEU's monopoly on declaring EU law invalid, the CJEU *Discussion document* argued that: 'In order to preserve this characteristic of the Union's system of judicial protection, the possibility must be avoided of the European Court of Human Rights being called on to decide on the conformity of an act of the Union with the Convention without the Court of Justice first having had an opportunity to give a definitive ruling on the point' (para 9).

Nonetheless, accession would not impinge upon the monopoly of the CJEU, since the ECtHR would not rule on the validity of EU law.[30] Therefore, the prior involvement would not be warranted. The function of the ECtHR is to decide on the compatibility between EU law and the Convention. Indeed, the Strasbourg Court lacks powers to declare EU law invalid.[31] This is actually taken for granted by the Explanatory Report: 'It should also be recalled that the Court in its judgments rules on whether there has been a violation of the Convention and *not on the validity* of an act of a High Contracting Party or of the legal provisions underlying the act or omission that was the subject of the complaint.'[32]

Admittedly, in practice, if the Strasbourg Court declared an EU provision to be inconsistent with the Convention, it would be reviewing EU law, but it would be for EU authorities to decide how to enforce the judgment. In order to avoid future violations, legislative

[24] Lock (n 19) 1032.
[25] Lock (n 7) 781–82.
[26] Lock (n 19) 1038–45.
[27] Case 11/70 *Internationale Handelsgesellschaft mbH and Einfuhr- und Vorratsstelle für Getreide und Futtermitte* [1970] ECR 1125.
[28] Case 314/85 *Foto-Frost, Ammersbek and Hauptzollamt Lübeck-Ost* [1987] ECR 4199.
[29] Protocol No 8, Art 2.
[30] As is admitted in CDDH-UE (2011)02, p 3.
[31] Lock (n 8) 791.
[32] Explanatory Report, § 62 (emphasis added).

amendments might be warranted, but the ECtHR may not nullify or modify EU law. Thus, this review does not impinge upon the exclusive competence of the CJEU.

The review of internal legislation in light of the Convention is inherent to an international human rights court monitoring system. In Opinion 1/91, the CJEU declared that the Treaties did not exclude the possibility of concluding an international agreement involving the subordination to a system of judicial control.[33] Furthermore, since Article 6(2) TEU mandates accession to the ECHR, the Strasbourg Court's review is already envisaged by the Treaties.[34]

ii. Interpretive Autonomy

According to the principle of autonomy, an international court may not be given the power to issue binding interpretations of EU law.[35] Interpretive autonomy derives from Article 19(1) TEU, which sets forth that the CJEU shall 'ensure compliance with the law in the interpretation and application of the Treaties'.[36] Also, in Opinion 1/91, the CJEU held that to confer jurisdiction on a court by means of international agreement to decide on the interpretation or application of the Treaties was incompatible with EU law.[37]

Is the CJEU's prior involvement required in order to secure the interpretive autonomy of EU law? Accession to the Convention would not grant the Strasbourg Court the power to issue binding interpretations of EU law and thus autonomy would not be undermined.[38] Therefore, the answer should be in the negative.

Generally, domestic law is taken as a fact by the ECtHR. The Strasbourg Court has reiterated that it is primarily for national authorities, and notably the courts, to interpret and apply domestic law.[39] In particular, the ECtHR held that this applies also to international treaties.[40]

At the same time, the ECtHR has argued that domestic courts need to interpret and apply national provisions in the spirit of Convention rights. Failure to do so might amount to a violation of the Convention.[41] Also, in order to determine whether an interference with a Convention right was 'provided by law', the Court will examine the 'quality' of legislation, ie, whether the law was accessible and foreseeable.[42] The ECtHR might reach a different conclusion from domestic courts.[43]

In sum, in order to assess the compatibility of domestic law with the Convention, the ECtHR will rely on the interpretation given by the domestic courts. The ECtHR might reach the conclusion that the domestic interpretation is not consistent with the Convention, but it would not replace domestic courts in their function of giving meaning to domestic law.

In the same way, the ECtHR will rely on the interpretation of EU law given by the CJEU in order to assess its compatibility with the Convention. The controversial situation

[33] De Schutter (n 4) 548.
[34] Lock (n 19) 1032–33.
[35] Ibid, 1028–31; Lock (n 7) 389–90.
[36] Jacqué (n 9) 1012.
[37] Opinion 1/91, para 35.
[38] Lock (n19) 1035.
[39] *Amann v Switzerland* [GC], App No 27798/95, judgment of 16 February 2000, § 52, ECHR 2000-II.
[40] *Slivenko v Latvia* [GC], App No 48321/99, judgment of 9 October 2003, § 105, ECHR 2003-X.
[41] *Storck v Germany*, App No 61603/00, judgment of 16 June 2005, §§ 93 99, ECHR 2005-V.
[42] *Amann v Switzerland* [GC], App No 27798/95, judgment of 16 February 2000, § 55, ECHR 2000-II.
[43] See the discussion in De Schutter (n 4) 551–53.

arises when the CJEU did not have a chance to interpret EU law before the case reaches Strasbourg. As such, the meaning of EU law might not be clear, and at that point the preliminary reference would no longer be available.

Still, even if the CJEU did not intervene in this specific case, it might be that the CJEU had the chance to interpret the EU law provision at stake in the past. Also, since the prior involvement may only be activated when the EU participates in the proceedings as a co-respondent, the Commission, as the representative of the EU before the ECtHR, could also contribute to give meaning to EU law. In any event, the ECtHR would not acquire the power to issue binding interpretations of EU law, but only to declare whether EU law is compatible with the Convention.

B. The Subsidiarity of the ECtHR

Pursuant to Article 35(1) ECHR, applicants need to exhaust domestic remedies before submitting a complaint to the Strasbourg Court. The subsidiary nature of the ECtHR is premised upon the understanding that the first and utmost responsibility for rights protection lies in the States parties. Thus, state authorities need to be given the opportunity to resolve alleged violations of fundamental rights domestically. Arguably, the CJEU's prior involvement would ensure the same opportunity for this court.

The *Joint communication* distinguishes two situations: direct actions against EU law and actions against state acts implementing EU law. The mechanism for the prior involvement would only be activated regarding the latter.

EU acts in breach of fundamental rights should be challenged before EU courts by means of the existing actions. If an EU act allegedly infringed fundamental rights, individuals may bring an action of annulment before the General Court (Article 263(4) of the Treaty on the Functioning of the European Union (TFEU)).

In case of acts not addressed to them, individuals would need to show 'direct and individual concern', which has been interpreted quite restrictively by the CJEU. In particular, 'individual concern' is taken to mean that an act affects the applicants 'by reason of certain attributes which are peculiar to them or by reason of circumstances in which they are differentiated from all other persons'.[44] After Lisbon, the 'individual concern', which has always been the major obstacle for individual applicants, has been dropped regarding 'regulatory acts' that 'do not entail implementing measures'. Apparently, the impact of this amendment regarding individual access is rather insignificant.[45]

In theory, to exhaust judicial remedies, the individual should submit an action of annulment before the General Court, and in its case an appeal before the CJEU. Yet, is the action of annulment an 'effective remedy' that needs to be exhausted when the 'individual concern' is dubious?[46] According to the ECtHR case law, there is no need to make use of remedies that are not effective. Furthermore, the question might arise as to whether the EU

[44] Case 25/62 *Plaumann & Co v Commission of the European Economic Community* [1965] ECR 95; Case C-309/89 *Codorniu SA v Council of Ministers of the European Communities* [1994] ECR I-1853.

[45] In a decision of inadmissibility, the General Court defined 'regulatory acts' as acts of general application of a non-legislative nature; see Case T-18/10, *Inuit Tapiriit Kanatami et al v Parliament and Council* [2011] ECR II-5599, §§ 45–46. This case is currently on appeal (Case C-583/11P).

[46] N O'Meara, '"A More Secure Europe of Rights?" The European Court of Human Rights, the Court of Justice of the European Union and EU Accession to the ECHR' (2011) 12 *German Law Journal* 1813.

violates the Convention due to the lack of an effective remedy for the violation of fundamental rights (Articles 6 and 13 ECHR).[47]

In any event, if the action of annulment were dismissed given the lack of 'direct and individual concern' or the applicant succeeded in proving that the action of annulment is not an 'effective remedy' that needs to be exhausted, the case would reach the ECtHR without a prior internal review by the CJEU.

In this situation, the mechanism for the CJEU's prior involvement would not be available, since the EU would not be a co-respondent. The *Joint communication* assumes that regarding direct actions there will always be a prior assessment by the CJEU, but this might not be the case.

This is not to argue that the prior involvement mechanism should be extended to this kind of situation. It is within the domain of the EU legal order to provide for an effective remedy by relaxing the strained conditions allowing for individual standing. The point here is that the same reasoning could be applied to indirect actions, which will be examined next.

The actions of the EU and its Member States are closely intertwined, and individuals may challenge state acts implementing EU law for violating fundamental rights. Note that there is no judicial action available for individuals before the EU courts against state authorities. Thus, the action will need to be brought before the domestic courts, even if the violation is triggered by obligations under EU law.

In the event of doubt about the interpretation or validity of EU law, domestic courts may (or must) make a reference before the CJEU. If the preliminary reference were not made, after exhausting domestic judicial remedies, individuals could reach the Strasbourg Court without the Luxembourg Court having had the chance to rule on the validity of the EU law provisions at stake. It is for this kind of situation that the prior involvement is set up and only in cases in which the EU has the status of co-respondent.[48]

The *Joint communication* already admitted that the preliminary reference cannot be regarded as a legal remedy to be exhausted by the applicant,[49] and this is confirmed in the Explanatory Report.[50] Individuals have no way of compelling the domestic courts to make a reference.[51] At the same time, the *Joint communication* declared that 'in order that the principle of subsidiarity may be respected … a procedure should be put in place' to 'ensure that the CJEU may carry out an internal review before the ECtHR carries out external review'.

Is the prior involvement required to preserve the principle of subsidiarity in this situation? The EU would participate in the process as a co-respondent and the co-respondent position implies that the applicant does not need to exhaust internal remedies with regard to that party.[52] Thus, the principle of subsidiarity does not even apply in this situation. If the co-respondent were a Member State, domestic remedies would not need to be exhausted within the state and no prior involvement of the highest domestic courts is envisaged.

[47] Sanz Caballero (n 9) 115.
[48] Explanatory Report, § 66.
[49] *Joint communication*, § 2.
[50] Explanatory Report, § 65.
[51] Lock (n 8) 791.
[52] G Gaja, 'The Co-Respondent Mechanisms According to the Draft Agreement for the Accession of the EU to the ECHR', www.esil-sedi.eu/node/266 and ch 22 in this volume.

Finally, the principle of subsidiarity might be understood here in a broad sense.[53] Given the *sui generis* structure of the EU, in which Member States implement EU law, but there is no full-fledged 'federal-European court system' in the Member States, arguably, a mechanism should be set up to ensure that the CJEU has a chance to resolve the violation of fundamental rights by EU law.[54]

Nonetheless, a *sui generis* mechanism already exists in the EU: the preliminary reference. Courts of last instance have the obligation to make a reference if there are doubts about the validity or interpretation of EU law, except for the application of the *CILFIT* doctrine. If the CJEU were circumvented as a consequence of the failure of domestic courts to make a reference, instead of setting up a new and complex mechanism once the case reaches the ECtHR, the remedy should be sought within the EU legal framework.[55] In the end, we should remember that domestic judges are also European judges and they are bound to apply EU law and, in its case, make a reference before the CJEU.

III. REASONS TO OPPOSE THE CJEU'S PRIOR INVOLVEMENT

In the previous section, we argued that the CJEU's prior involvement is not required either by the autonomy of EU law or the subsidiarity of the ECtHR. Below, we will examine the reasons to oppose this mechanism from a technical, individual and political perspective.

A. Technical Complexities

From a technical standpoint, this mechanism raises many uncertainties. The draft Accession Agreement does not provide a full regulation and the Explanatory Report hardly adds any clues to understand it. The scarce regulation is partly due to the need to avoid interfering with EU procedural autonomy. As argued above, the principle of autonomy excludes a de facto amendment of the Treaties by means of an international agreement.[56]

Several proposals as to how this mechanism should be regulated have been advanced.[57] The two main possibilities are a sort of preliminary reference from Strasbourg to Luxembourg or a new procedural mechanism allowing the CJEU to make a prior ruling. Scholars have tended to support the latter.[58] The Explanatory Report to the draft Agreement seems to confirm this option, but many questions are left unanswered:

i) Who would be the *actors* entitled to bring the case before the Luxembourg Court? Several options have been advanced: the Commission;[59] the Commission and Member States;[60] or more broadly the Commission, the European Parliament, the Council and the Member States.[61]

[53] The Explanatory Report, § 66, indicates that this mechanism is 'inspired' by the principle of subsidiarity.

[54] *CJEU Discussion document*, §§ 5–6.

[55] Jacqué (n 9) 1010.

[56] Lock (n 19) 1048.

[57] CDDH-UE (2011)02.

[58] Lock (n 8) 793; Timmermans (n 1) 159.

[59] CJEU Judge Timmermans at the hearing organised by the European Parliament's Committee on Constitutional Affairs, 18 March 2010, § 9; Lock (n 19) 1049.

[60] Commission Working document, DS 1930/10, Brussels, 10 January 2011, § 6.

[61] Timmermans (n 1) 159.

ii) Would the CJEU's intervention be *compulsory*? Jacqué has indicated that according to the wording of Article 3(6) of the draft Accession Agreement, it seems that once the EU is recognised as a co-respondent, 'the reference to Luxembourg would be *de jure* if the Court of Justice has not intervened earlier in the case.'[62]
However, there are reasons to think that the prior involvement should not be automatic in cases in which the CJEU did not intervene. It might be that the preliminary reference was not made in that specific case, but that the CJEU had already decided in the past about the validity of the EU law provision at stake in light of fundamental rights. Thus, although the CJEU did not intervene in the specific case, it had already had the chance to assess the compatibility with fundamental rights.
On the other hand, it might be that a preliminary reference was made, but for reasons other than the compatibility with fundamental rights. Or maybe the CJEU decided on the basis of specific rights enshrined in the EU Charter of Fundamental Rights, but afterwards other rights are invoked before the Strasbourg Court.[63] Thus, although the CJEU already intervened, the prior involvement could be justified.

iii) What would be the *procedure* before the CJEU? To avoid creating a new procedure, which would require a treaty amendment, the action of annulment could provide an avenue to assess the validity of EU law in light of fundamental rights (Article 263(2) TFEU).
Nonetheless, several obstacles have been pointed out. First, the annulment action has a strict time limit of two months after the challenged provision has been enacted. Also, Article 3(6) of the draft Accession Agreement ensures the participation of the parties involved before the CJEU, and the Explanatory Report explicitly mentions the individual applicant.[64] The parties before the Strasbourg Court, however, would not automatically become parties in an annulment action before the CJEU. Still, they could participate as interveners pursuant to Article 40 of the Statute of the CJEU. This article allows the intervention of Member States, EU institutions and any other person who can establish an interest in the result of a case submitted to the Court. Nonetheless, according to Article 40, 'an application to intervene shall be limited to supporting the form of order sought by one of the parties'. Thus, the possibility for individual applicants to defend their own interests as interveners would be very much limited.
In addition, according to Appendix II (*Draft declaration by the EU to be made at the time of signature of the Accession Agreement*) to the Final Report to the CDDH,[65] the EU will ensure that non-EU Member States are entitled to submit statements of case or written observations to the CJEU under the same conditions as the Member States in a procedure under Article 267 TFEU.
This declaration adds a further difficulty, since non-EU Member States may not intervene in the annulment action. Furthermore, the reference to the preliminary ruling procedure only adds to the hybrid nature of the prior involvement mechanism.

62 Jacqué (n 9) 1021.
63 Groussot et al (n 19) 15.
64 Explanatory Report, § 66.
65 www.coe.int/t/dghl/standardsetting/hrpolicy/Accession/Meeting_reports/47_1(2013)008rev2_EN.pdf.

iv) What would be the *function* of the CJEU? The prior involvement gives the CJEU the chance to assess the 'compatibility with the Convention rights at issue of the provision of EU law' at stake.
In the meeting held in September 2012 at the initiative of the EU, a new clause was added in order to clarify the function of the CJEU: 'Assessing the compatibility shall mean to rule on the validity of a legal provision contained in acts of the European Union institutions, bodies, offices or agencies, or on the interpretation of a provision of the Treaty on European Union, the Treaty on the Functioning of the European Union or of any other provision having the same legal value pursuant to those instruments.'
According to the meeting report, the representative of the EU explained that this clarification was necessary 'since the CJEU could only invalidate EU secondary law, but not EU primary law which it could only interpret'.[66] Indeed, this is obvious. What is awkward is the possibility of activating this mechanism with regard to primary law, since the CJEU may not assess its compatibility with human rights. In this way, the prior involvement gets closer to the logic of the preliminary reference.
Eventually, this clause has been rightly eliminated from Article 3(6) in the revised agreement. Instead, a clarification has been added to the Explanatory Report[67] so that the hybrid nature of the prior involvement—an instrument to assess the validity of secondary EU law or to interpret EU primary law—is confirmed.

v) What would be the *consequences* of the CJEU's prior involvement for the process before the ECtHR? According to the Explanatory Report, the prior involvement of the CJEU will not affect the powers and jurisdiction of the Strasbourg Court and the latter will not be bound by the assessment of the former. One can imagine two scenarios:
    1) First, the EU law provision at stake is declared to be consistent with fundamental rights. Since this decision is not compulsory for the ECtHR, the case should continue before the Strasbourg Court. Indeed, the ECtHR might conclude that the EU act is not consistent with the Convention. This outcome would expose the divergence regarding the interpretation of parallel rights and the direct confrontation between these courts.
    2) Second, the EU provision at stake is declared null and void for violating fundamental rights. In this case, should the case continue before Strasbourg? The judgment of the ECtHR should not be disposed of. Even if the EU law provision has already been struck down, the Strasbourg Court could decide to grant just satisfaction. Also, it might be that the Luxembourg Court grants protection greater than the minimum standard set by the Strasbourg Court, and thus the latter could declare that the Convention has not been breached.

[66] *Second negotiation meeting between the CDDH ad hoc negotiation group and the European Commission on the accession of the European Union to the European Convention on Human Rights*, Strasbourg, 19 September 2012, 47+1(2012)R02, § 10.

[67] Explanatory Report, § 65.

B. Individual Interests

From the perspective of individual applicants, does the CJEU's prior involvement further or hinder the interest in the protection of fundamental rights? For an individual who has managed to file a complaint before the ECtHR, after several years of judicial proceedings before the state courts, the referral of the case to the CJEU would further delay the expected decision by the Strasbourg Court. Also, more time will imply greater expense.

This concern is acknowledged by Article 3(6) of the Draft Agreement, as it rules that the EU shall ensure that the CJEU's assessment shall be made quickly to avoid undue delays. The Explanatory Report adds that an accelerated procedure before the CJEU is already available, which might last around six to eight months.[68]

As mentioned before, the possibility for individuals to make observations before the CJEU will need to be ensured. The *Commission working document* insisted on the need for the applicant to be allowed to participate in the procedure before the CJEU for the sake of the equality of arms.[69] Indeed, the Explanatory Report indicates that the applicant 'will be given the possibility to obtain legal aid'.

In any event, the need to defend the case before yet another court, which is not a human rights court, amounts to an extra burden for individual applicants.[70] Since the Convention is a system for the protection of individual rights, the accession of the EU should not worsen the position of individuals.

C. Judicial Politics and Preferential Treatment

The CJEU's prior involvement has been forcefully advanced by the CJEU in its *Discussion document* and the *Joint communication*, which reveal its resistance to lose relative power and be put under the authority of the Strasbourg Court.

This mechanism would imply granting the CJEU a privileged position in comparison to domestic constitutional or supreme courts.[71] On occasions, and particularly in those systems that do not provide for an individual complaint before the constitutional court, this court, which has the monopoly on the judicial review of legislation, might not have the chance to decide on the compatibility of domestic legislation and fundamental rights.

The general principle guiding the negotiation process is that the EU should be treated in the same way as other contracting parties, as long as the 'specific characteristics' of the EU are preserved. Is there any legitimate aim that would justify a different treatment?

As argued before, the autonomy of EU law would not justify the prior involvement of the CJEU, nor would the subsidiarity principle. Indeed, the logic of the co-respondent

[68] Explanatory Report, § 66.

[69] Ibid, § 10.

[70] LFM Besselink, 'The Protection of Fundamental Rights Post-Lisbon. The Interaction between the EU Charter of Fundamental Rights, the European Convention on Human Rights (ECHR) and National Constitutions', FIDE 2012, 39, www.fide2012.eu/index.php?doc_id=94.

[71] G Gaja, 'Accession to the ECHR' in A Biondi, P Eeckhout and S Ripley (eds), *EU Law after Lisbon* (Oxford, Oxford University Press, 2012); De Schutter (n 4) 564–65; Groussot et al (n 19) 16; Besselink (n 70) 39. Several non-EU Member States stated that the prior involvement 'would constitute a privilege for one Contracting Party', see Appendix III § 3, Meeting Report, *Fourth negotiation meeting between the CDDH ad hoc negotiation group and the European Commission on the accession of the European Union to the European Convention on Human Rights*, Strasbourg, 23 January 2013, 47+1(2013)R04.

mechanism excludes the need to exhaust judicial remedies within the legal system of the co-respondent, and the prior involvement may only be activated when the EU has the status of a co-respondent.

Over time, a fruitful dialogue between the Luxembourg and Strasbourg Courts has developed, as is acknowledged by Declaration No 2 *on Article 6(2) of the Treaty on European Union*. And yet, now that the ECtHR is given the 'last word' to set a minimum standard of protection, the CJEU claims to have a 'first word' when EU law is at stake.

The CJEU's prior involvement, however, might bring too many voices to the fore and lead to undesired results. The prior involvement would increase the risk of collision between the Luxembourg and Strasbourg Courts. In the event of divergent interpretations, this mechanism would create open confrontation between the two. What is worse, the fact that the CJEU is given a 'first word' might condition the subsequent decision by the Strasbourg Court and hinder a robust review.[72]

To conclude, the CJEU's prior involvement is not justified on the basis of the principles of autonomy or subsidiarity. The prior involvement is an overly complex, time-consuming procedure that gives an unjustified privileged position to the CJEU. Hence, it is contended that it should be dropped.

IV. COMING TO TERMS WITH THE CJEU'S PRIOR INVOLVEMENT

Since the CJEU's prior involvement seemed to be non-negotiable, at least from the perspective of the EU, this section will be devoted to drafting some proposals to mitigate the foregoing shortcomings in search of a balance between the interests of the EU and individual protection.

In the context of a judicial system for the protection of human rights, the main justification for this mechanism should be to contribute to the effective protection of individuals by striking down EU legal provisions that are incompatible with fundamental rights and clarifying the allocation of responsibilities between the EU and its Member States.

First, it is contended that the *initiative* to bring the case before the CJEU should be given to any of the parties before the Strasbourg Court: the Commission, as the institution representing the EU, respondent states and individual applicants. Since it has been argued that this mechanism should be abandoned, it might seem contradictory to broaden the range of actors that may activate it. However, once this is set up, it should not be limited to the Commission. Indeed, the Commission might not be willing to activate a mechanism for reviewing legislation previously introduced by the Commission itself.[73]

The respondent states might argue that the alleged violation was triggered by the obligation to comply with EU law and that no discretion was left for implementing it, such as in *Bosphorus*. Since this is an issue related to the allocation of powers and responsibilities between the EU and its Member States, the prior decision by the CJEU could facilitate the enforcement of a potential condemnatory decision by the Strasbourg Court.

[72] O'Meara (n 46) 1828. See also the position of several non-EU Member States in Appendix III, § 3, Meeting Report, *Fourth negotiation meeting between the CDDH ad hoc negotiation group and the European Commission on the accession of the European Union to the European Convention on Human Rights*, Strasbourg, 23 January 2013, 47+1(2013)R04.

[73] Lock (n 8) 793.

In addition, individual applicants might be interested in obtaining a prior decision by the CJEU. When the EU participates in the proceedings as a co-respondent, the ECtHR may jointly condemn the EU and the respondent state. Enforcement could be further delayed if there were disagreements as to who should pay the compensation, or whether the violation was triggered by obligations under EU law.

The CJEU's prior involvement would allow this court, in its case, to strike down the EU law provision at stake. This would make it easier for the individual to ask for individual measures before the state, such as the re-opening of judicial procedures. In general, the prior intervention of the CJEU could help to indicate the allocation of responsibilities between the EU and its Member States.

Second, the activation of this mechanism should *not be compulsory*. There is no need to engage with yet another process if none of the parties believes that the CJEU's decision would be beneficial for the case before the ECtHR. As Timmermans argued, this mechanism should be reserved for 'cases where a serious question of conventionality arises'.[74]

Moreover, the ECtHR's approval should be necessary to activate this mechanism in order to avoid an abusive use by the Commission or the Member States to delay proceedings. For instance, if the CJEU already decided in the past about the interpretation or validity of the EU provision at stake, the prior involvement would not be required. Also, according to what was argued above, this mechanism is not justified to secure the interpretive autonomy of EU law or the CJEU's monopoly to review EU law.

In addition, a case should not be referred when it is clear that there is a margin of action for the Member States, such as in *MSS v Belgium and Greece*.[75] Admittedly, this kind of assessment might risk interfering with the allocation of responsibilities between the EU and its Member States. Thus, the referral may only be refused if it were clear that the Member States had discretion in implementing EU law. In any event, the EU would have the chance to defend EU law before the ECtHR since it would participate in the proceedings as co-respondent. In the end, in the event of a violation of the Convention, according to the revised Accession Agreement, the ECtHR shall declare the respondent and co-respondent jointly responsible for the violation 'unless the Court, on the basis of the reasons given by the respondent and the co-respondent, and having sought the views of the applicant, decides that only one of them be held responsible'.[76]

Third, to avoid a treaty amendment, the potentiality of the *annulment action* should be exploited. The time limit might not be an insurmountable obstacle if it can be argued that the nature and function of the procedure before the CJEU would not change.

In addition, according to this proposal, individuals should also be given the possibility of activating the prior involvement. Thus, they would confront the 'direct and individual concern' requirement. The CJEU might relax this condition when the action originated in a case before the ECtHR. Actually, it could be argued that the applicants are individually concerned 'by reason of circumstances in which they are differentiated from all other persons', ie, the process before the ECtHR.

Lastly, as to the *consequences* of the prior involvement, regardless of the outcome of the process before the CJEU, individuals should not be deprived of the chance to obtain a decision by Strasbourg. If the CJEU found no violation, the ECtHR could reach a different

[74] Timmermans (n 1) 159; Lock (n 19) argued that the Commission could perform a 'filter function'.

[75] *MSS v Belgium and Greece* [GC], App No 30696/09, judgment of 21 January 2011, ECHR 2011.

[76] Article 3(7) of the draft Accession Agreement.

outcome. And even if the CJEU declared the EU law provision null and void, the ECtHR should still decide whether just satisfaction needed to be granted.

At the same time, in order to avoid activating the prior involvement, greater pressure should be put on the domestic courts to make the *preliminary reference* in cases in which fundamental rights are involved.[77] The CJEU could be more rigorous and strengthen the obligation for courts of last instance to make a reference when the individual alleges the breach of fundamental rights.[78] The entry into force of the Charter could be an argument to justify the need to refer questions to the CJEU regarding fundamental rights.

In addition, the ECtHR might strengthen current case law according to which the arbitrary refusal to make a preliminary reference might infringe Article 6(1) ECHR.[79] It has been suggested that, as a condition of admissibility, individuals should at least have asked domestic courts to make a reference.[80] Nonetheless, individuals should not be burdened with the consequences of the failure to comply with an obligation that corresponds to courts of last instance. Yet, if they did not request the preliminary reference, individual applicants could not activate the CJEU's prior involvement later on.

In this way, a better balance of the different interests at stake would be reached. At the end, the CJEU's prior involvement should not have the effect of undermining the position of individuals before the ECtHR.

V. CONCLUDING REMARKS

The Treaty of Lisbon encapsulated the political consensus regarding the accession of the EU to the ECHR. The negotiation process, however, has revealed the reluctance of the EU to be placed under the authority of the ECtHR. In any event, accession would not introduce a hierarchical relationship between the Strasbourg and Luxembourg Courts, as this does not exist between the Strasbourg Court and the constitutional or supreme courts.[81] The Strasbourg Court will set the minimum floor of rights protection for the Member States and the EU.

Still, the CJEU aims at preserving the chance to have a prior say when EU law is at stake. While the prior involvement involves technical complexities, this mechanism responds to deeper concerns about the autonomy of EU law and the role of the CJEU within the multi-level system of rights protection in Europe.

Despite the specific characteristics of the EU legal order, the prior involvement cannot be justified on the basis of the principles of autonomy or subsidiarity. A judicial monitoring system at the international level necessarily implies reviewing the action of the EU authorities. The ECtHR, however, would not decide about the validity or binding interpretation of EU law. The preliminary reference already gives the CJEU the possibility of assessing EU provisions in light of fundamental rights. The domestic courts' failure to use this mechanism should not burden individuals before the ECtHR. Furthermore, there are

77 O'Meara (n 46) 1830–32; Sanz Caballero (n 9) 119.
78 Jacqué (n 9) 1019.
79 De Schutter (n 4) 566.
80 Ibid; Lock (n 8) 792.
81 Sanz Caballero (n 9) 109.

reasons to oppose the CJEU's prior involvement on the basis of technical complexities, the extra burden for individuals and the unjustified privileged treatment given to the CJEU.

Until now, a fruitful dialogue between the Strasbourg and Luxembourg Courts has developed. Convention and EU rights partly overlap in their scope of application to the Member States. In this context, dialogue has been a suitable avenue to search for common understandings regarding the interpretation of fundamental rights. The CJEU's prior involvement, however, might force dialogue too much. While dialogue has proven to be a useful tool for the interaction between the Strasbourg and Luxembourg Courts, the abuse of it could be exhausting and lead to undesired results. Since it is very unlikely that this mechanism will be abandoned, a constructive proposal has been advanced to strike a better balance among the different interests at stake with the aim of enhancing individual protection.

4

The Right to Extra-Judicial Redress in EU Law after the EU's Accession to the ECHR: The Legal Framework, Challenges and the Question of the Prior Involvement of the CJEU

NIKOS VOGIATZIS*

I. INTRODUCTION

THE FORTHCOMING ACCESSION of the European Union (EU) to the European Convention on Human Rights (ECHR) creates, from the point of view of EU law, a new structure in the protection of human rights. In this forthcoming institutional structure, the primary purpose of this chapter is to discuss the possible recognition of a right to extra-judicial redress in EU law. More specifically, the pursued question is whether the accession could be of any relevance vis-a-vis Jacob Söderman's idea of an autonomous right to extra-judicial redress in a chapter on available remedies at the EU and the national levels.[1] Indeed, the first European Ombudsman proposed before the Constitutional Convention that such a right be explicitly included and recognised in the Treaties; however, such a call was not eventually fulfilled.[2]

The scope of examination should be stated in advance. First, the subsequent analysis is limited to remedies available *at the national level*, in situations where *a national authority is implementing EU law*;[3] however interesting, questions that could arise concerning remedies against EU acts are not dealt with in this chapter.[4] Second, and equally important,

* Lecturer in Law, University of Liverpool. I wish to express my gratitude to Vassilis Tzevelekos for his valuable comments and support throughout the process of writing this paper. I am also grateful to Vicky Kosta for her comments on a subsequent version of this chapter, and to Michael Dougan for commenting on one of its latest versions. The usual disclaimer applies.

[1] See European Ombudsman, *Annual Report 2002*, 222–23; A Peters 'The European Ombudsman and the European Constitution' (2005) 42 *CML Rev* 708.

[2] Peters (n 1); see also J Söderman 'The Early Years of the European Ombudsman' in *The European Ombudsman: Origins, Establishment, Evolution* (Luxembourg, Official Publications of the European Communities, 2005).

[3] See Article 51(1) CFR. For a discussion on the notion of 'implementation', see K Lenaerts, 'Exploring the Limits of the EU Charter of Fundamental Rights' (2012) 8 *European Constitutional Law Review* 377–87. See also Case C-617/10 *Åklagaren v Hans Åkerberg Fransson*, not yet reported, [17] et seq.

[4] But see T Lock, 'EU Accession to the ECHR: Implications for Judicial Review in Strasbourg' (2010) 35 *EL Rev* 777–98, where this is discussed to a certain extent. See further A Arnull, 'The Principle of Effective Judicial Protection in EU law: An Unruly Horse?' (2011) 36 *EL Rev* 51–70.

the Court of Justice of the European Union (CJEU) has progressively built a jurisprudence which suggests that the principle of effective judicial protection, a general principle of EU law, should respect 'national procedural autonomy' subject to the 'principle of effectiveness' and the 'principle of equivalence'.[5] However, the primary focus of this chapter is on Article 47 of the Charter of Fundamental Rights (CFR), which of course 'reaffirms' the general principle,[6] while certain CJEU judgments on effective judicial protection will also be discussed in sections III and V. Likewise, the ongoing discussion on the relationship between Charter rights and fundamental rights as general principles of EU law will not be dealt with, although it is now generally understood that they both apply when the situation falls within the scope of EU law.[7]

In order to answer the aforementioned question, this chapter proceeds with a comparative examination of the EU (Charter) and the ECHR framework as regards the right to extra-judicial redress. It finds that the ECtHR's interpretation of Article 13 ECHR demonstrates that the Strasbourg Court will examine remedies on an ad hoc basis,[8] since the European Court of Human Rights (ECtHR) has stated in a limited number of cases that under strict circumstances, the availability of an extra-judicial remedy constitutes an effective remedy, whereas the recourse to such a remedy may equally satisfy the exhaustion of the domestic remedies rule, again under severe conditions. On the other hand, the EU's constitutional choice, reflected in Article 47 CFR, was to merge Articles 6 and 13 ECHR, thus forming the 'Right to an effective remedy and to a fair trial', which, however, restricts (or augments, depending on one's point of view, as will be shown below) the scope to an effective remedy before a *tribunal*. However, it is argued that from a constitutional perspective, the existing institutional framework of the EU enables—wisely enough—the CJEU to remedy differentiations between the two regimes. Still, the preceding comparative discussion unravels further policy-oriented and potentially legal questions that could arise after the EU's accession as regards the right to extra-judicial redress in EU law. These challenges are discussed in detail towards the end of the chapter.

There is a precondition for all the above: that, where necessary, the CJEU provides an opinion on the compatibility of national rules with the ECHR on matters that fall within

[5] See Arnull (n 4) 51–52 and case law cited therein. Arnull concludes (on p 68) that the 'general principle of effective judicial protection seems to have established itself as hierarchically superior to that of national procedural autonomy'. See also A Adinolfi, 'The "Procedural Autonomy" of Member States and the Constraints Stemming from the ECJ's Case Law: Is Judicial Activism Still Necessary?' in B de Witte and H-W Micklitz (eds), *The European Court of Justice and the Autonomy of the Member States* (Cambridge, Intersentia, 2012); M Dougan, *National Remedies before the Court of Justice: Issues of Harmonisation and Differentiation* (Oxford, Hart Publishing, 2004).

[6] See Arnull (n 4) 54; see also the explanatory text of the Charter (Section III below).

[7] See *Åkerberg Fransson* [18]–[21]. See also Lenaerts (n 3) 376–386; he adds (on p 386) that '[s]ince the material scope of the Charter is broader than that of general principles, the Charter may contribute significantly to the "discovery" of general principles'. Compare also HCH Hofmann BC Mihaescu, 'The Relation between the Charter's Fundamental Rights and the Unwritten General Principles of EU Law: Good Administration as the Test Case' (2013) 9 *European Constitutional Law Review* 73–101, rejecting a 'hierarchical approach favouring the Charter over the general principles of law' (on p 101). For a critical view on the CJEU's approach see L Pech 'Between Judicial Minimalism and Avoidance: The Court of Justice's Sidestepping of Fundamental Constitutional Issues in *Römer* and *Dominguez*' (2012) 49 *CML Rev* 1841.

[8] This was defined in *Klass* and confirmed in *Silver*; see Section IV.

the scope of EU law.[9] This will almost certainly occur through the mechanism known as the 'prior involvement of the CJEU', aiming at the preservation of the autonomy of the EU's legal order.[10] The existence of this mechanism is accepted in this chapter. However, this leads to an additional procedural question. Could an applicant who has turned to an 'effective' extra-judicial avenue without obtaining satisfactory redress 'bypass' the CJEU and obtain redress directly from Strasbourg using the envisaged mechanism? This hypothesis is discussed to a limited extent, for two reasons: first, it is a question technical in its nature; and, second, it constitutes a broader institutional question that is also applicable to the courts.

The chapter proceeds as follows. First, the proposals of the European Ombudsman at the EU's pre-Constitutional European Convention are briefly presented (section II). Next, the EU's framework is discussed, notably the scope of Article 47 CFR and the question of the CJEU's prior involvement (section III). The subsequent section (IV) examines the ECtHR's jurisprudence on Article 13 ECHR, in particular whether—and under what circumstances—non-judicial bodies could constitute effective remedies. This leads to a subsidiary (but interconnected, since it is relevant to the prior involvement question) section, which inverstigates whether recourse to effective non-judicial entities may amount to the exhaustion of domestic remedies under Article 35(1) ECHR. The chapter proceeds with a comparison of the two regimes and offers some reflections on the ad hoc approach identified by the Strasbourg Court and the possible implications of this approach on a policy-oriented and potentially legal basis as well (section V). Section VI concludes.

II. THE EUROPEAN OMBUDSMAN'S PROPOSALS AT THE EUROPEAN CONVENTION AND THE PROVISIONS OF THE CONSTITUTIONAL TREATY

The first European Ombudsman, Jacob Söderman, who was consistently supportive of the EU's accession to the ECHR—notably before the proclamation of the CFR at the EU level—was particularly concerned that, in the absence of a document similar to the ECHR, EU citizens could not comprehensively perceive the 'constitutional traditions common to the Member States'.[11] Thus, when addressing the Constitutional Convention, he proposed, inter alia, a legally binding Charter and—interestingly—'the inclusion in the Treaty of a chapter on remedies, which should clearly set out the possibilities for judicial and non-judicial redress when Community law rights, including fundamental rights, are

[9] Case C-260/89 *ERT* [1991] ECR I-2925 [42].

[10] JP Jacqué, 'The Accession of the European Union to the European Convention on Human Rights and Fundamental Freedoms' (2011) 48 *CML Rev* 995–1023; T Lock, 'Walking on a Tightrope: The Draft ECHR Accession and the Autonomy of the EU Legal Order' (2011) 48 *CML Rev* 1025–54; A Torres Pérez, 'Too Many Voices? The Prior Involvement of the Court of Justice of the European Union' (2013) *European Journal of Human Rights* 565. See also the latest version of the Accession Agreement, published on 10 June 2013: www.coe.int/t/dghl/standardsetting/hrpolicy/Accession/Meeting_reports/47_1(2013)008rev2_EN.pdf (hereinafter the 'Draft Agreement'). See in particular the explanatory text on Article 3, which refers to the co-respondent mechanism and the prior involvement: paras 37–69.

[11] Söderman (n 2) 99–100.

not respected'.[12] In particular, he viewed his idea turning into legislation (a *Chapter on remedies*) as follows:

> *General principles*
>
> 1. For the protection of his or her rights under Community law, including fundamental and human rights, everyone shall have access to the following remedies in accordance with the provisions of this Chapter:
>   — to bring proceedings in a court of competent jurisdiction
>   — to petition the European Parliament and to complain to the European Ombudsman
>   — to petition a legislative body or to complain to an ombudsman in each Member State.
>
> *Ombudsmen and bodies dealing with petitions*
>
> …
>
> 2. Any citizen of the Union and any natural or legal person residing or having its registered office in a Member State has the right to complain to an independent ombudsman or body dealing with petitions concerning instances of maladministration in the application of Community law by the public bodies of a Member State. If no ombudsman or body dealing with petitions in the Member State is competent to deal with the matter, the complaint may be addressed to the European Ombudsman.[13]

The motivations behind this ambitious proposal (summarised elsewhere by the phrase 'rights are not worth anything without effective remedies, both judicial and non-judicial'),[14] which was not eventually followed, may be found inter alia in the underlying tenet that the uniform and correct application of EU law at all levels of the supranational edifice, including the national level, should be prioritised.[15] Moreover, there is a link with legitimacy; effective remedies augment the levels of trust towards the EU.[16]

Peters criticised the Ombudsman's insistence on including a specific reference to a national ombudsman or a petitions committee, arguing that 'the Union does not possess the authority to prescribe to the Member States which concrete types of remedies they must establish in their national legal order'.[17]

In any event, the possibility for a right to extra-judicial redress merits further examination. The Constitutional Treaty and, subsequently, the Treaty of Lisbon, provides that 'Member States shall provide remedies sufficient to ensure effective legal protection in the fields covered by Union law'.[18] This provision features in the article covering the CJEU, and is arguably rather inadequate, since it is does not constitute a CFR article and therefore an explicitly guaranteed (by the Charter) right of the individual.

[12] See European Ombudsman, *Annual Report 2002*, 222–23.

[13] Contribution by Mr Jacob Söderman, European Ombudsman: 'Proposals for Treaty Changes', CONV 221/02 CONTRIB 76 Brussels, 26 July 2002; see also Peters (n 1) 708. Commenting on a similar document (CONV 221/02 CONTRIB 206), Harlow and Rawlings observed that the proposal was not met with enthusiasm due to Member States' concerns on the respect of the subsidiarity principle, but also due to the varying constitutional traditions. See C Harlow and R Rawlings, 'Promoting Accountability in Multilevel Governance: A Network Approach' (2007) 13 *European Law Journal* 559.

[14] Söderman (n 2) 100.

[15] Speech by the European Ombudsman, Mr Jacob Söderman, Round Table on the Future of Europe, Lisbon, 18 November 2002, available at www.ombudsman.europa.eu/speeches/en/2002-11-18.htm. Söderman was frequently suggesting that rights should become a 'living reality'. See Söderman (n 2) 101.

[16] Söderman (n 2) 104.

[17] Peters (n 1) 724.

[18] Art I-29 of the Constitutional Treaty, cited in Peters (n 1) 724; see also Art 19(1) of the Treaty on European Union (TEU).

III. THE EU LEGAL FRAMEWORK

A. Article 47 CFR

Article 47 CFR, entitled 'Right to an effective remedy and to a fair trial', states that: 'Everyone whose rights and freedoms guaranteed by the law of the Union are violated has the right to an effective remedy before a *tribunal* in compliance with the conditions laid down in this Article.'[19] Moreover, this right can be invoked against EU institutions and against Member States insofar as they are implementing EU law.[20]

On the other hand, Article 13 ECHR provides: 'Everyone whose rights and freedoms as set forth in this Convention are violated shall have an effective remedy before a *national authority* notwithstanding that the violation has been committed by persons acting in an official capacity.'[21] Two preliminary remarks are of relevance. First, undeniably, 'access to the courts is the fundamental remedy in a democracy governed by the rule of law'.[22] Second, the judicial avenue is not always the 'superior' mode of redress: 'justice is [also] achieved through bodies other than courts'.[23] The question whether the word 'tribunal' could encompass non-judicial redress mechanisms necessitates a (generally) negative answer.[24]

More light can be shed if one examines the explanatory text of the Convention set up to draft the CFR in 1999.[25] It was recognised therein that the first paragraph of Article 47 CFR is 'based on Article 13 of the ECHR'.[26] Nonetheless, it was added that: 'However, in Community law the protection is more *extensive* since it guarantees the right to an effective remedy before a court.'[27] I will return to the argument that the protection before the courts is necessarily more *extensive* below.[28]

Pabel accurately observed that contrary to Article 13 ECHR, which only refers to rights guaranteed by the Convention, the 'scope of application' of Article 47 CFR (then Article II-107(1) of the Constitutional Treaty) is more extensive since, beyond its application to primary EU law and the Charter, it 'is also applicable to potential infringements upon rights which derive from the remaining Union law, that is secondary law'.[29]

The explanatory text of the CFR relied on and cited previous CJEU case law. In *Johnston*, the Court stated that 'judicial control ... reflects a general principle of law which underlies

[19] Emphasis added.

[20] Art 51(1) CFR; Lenaerts (n 3).

[21] Emphasis added.

[22] Speech by the European Ombudsman, Jacob Söderman to the European Convention, 24 June 2002, available at http://european-convention.eu.int/docs/speeches/1193.pdf.

[23] P Birkinshaw, *Grievances, Remedies and the State* (London, Sweet & Maxwell, 1994) 1–4.

[24] On the prerequisites in order for a court or tribunal to submit a preliminary reference, see, for example, Case C-17/00 *De Coster* [2001] ECR I-9445 [9]–[22]. For a discussion on the competence (or lack thereof) of administrative authorities and ombudsmen to submit a preliminary reference compare M Broberg and N Fenger *Preliminary References to the European Court of Justice* (Oxford, Oxford University Press, 2014) 88–95. Compare also the explanations of the Charter (below nn 26–27).

[25] 'Text of the explanations relating to the complete text of the Charter as set out in CHARTE 4487/00 CONVENT 50' CHARTE 4473/00 CONVENT 49 (2000).

[26] Ibid, 40.

[27] Ibid, 41 (emphasis added).

[28] See section V below.

[29] K Pabel, 'The Right to an Effective Remedy Pursuant to Article II-107 Paragraph 1 of the Constitutional Treaty' (2005) 6 *German Law Journal* 1603.

the constitutional traditions common to the Member States. That principle is also laid down in Articles 6 and 13 of the ECHR'.[30] However in *Johnston*, there was an explicit provision in the pertinent Directive requiring a judicial remedy.[31] This admittedly incited the CJEU to frame the abovementioned general principle and decide that: 'By virtue of Article 6 of [the Directive], interpreted in the light of the general principle stated above, all persons have the right to obtain an effective remedy in a competent court against measures which they consider to be contrary to the principle of equal treatment for men and women laid down in the Directive.'[32] It is in *Unectef v Heylens* that we find a confirmation of the 'common constitutional traditions' thesis, with a reference to the previous case.[33]

So far, so good; it is not the purpose of this account to question the noble intentions of the Court or Advocate General Mancini at the time of this later judgment in 1987. As was also the case with the CFR drafters, the Court was clearly aiming at augmenting judicial protection at the national level. It is therefore needless to point out that especially *Johnston* was a landmark case in the safeguarding of effective judicial protection under Union law. Regardless of the time of its realisation, the EU's accession to the ECHR presents a suitable opportunity to reconceptualise the rationale behind the explanatory text (and thus the eventual formulation of Article 47 CFR), using relevant Strasbourg case law; in other words, to examine whether there are 'grounds' to Söderman's assessment in 2005 that the scope of protection offered by Article 47 CFR 'is not enough'.[34] This view appears to contradict the aforementioned rationale that the protection offered under the same Article is more *extensive*.

B. The Question of the Prior Involvement of the CJEU

The latest version of the draft agreement on the EU's accession to the ECHR provides for the prior involvement of the CJEU only in cases where the EU is a co-respondent.[35] Although the draft agreement predicts that the possibility of such activation is rare,[36] the fact remains that the EU may be a co-respondent before the Strasbourg Court. Thus, because the mechanism of prior involvement is of relevance in the case of 'actions against state acts implementing EU law',[37] it also falls within the scope of examination of this chapter, as outlined in the introduction. As has been observed, central to this debate is the preservation of the autonomy of the EU's legal order.[38] The existence of such a mechanism is taken for granted in this account. As Judge Gaja put it, it is 'pointless' to debate on something that in all probability has already been decided.[39] However, since it appears that the question has evolved into a controversial issue in academia, the debate will be succinctly summarised below.

[30] Case 222/84 *Johnston v Chief Constable of the Royal Ulster Constabulary* [1986] ECR-1651 [18].

[31] Stating that 'all persons who consider themselves wronged by discrimination must be able to pursue their claims by judicial process': ibid [9], [17].

[32] Ibid [19].

[33] See Case 222/86 *Unectef v Heylens* [1987] ECR-4097 [14].

[34] Söderman (n 2) 102.

[35] See Explanatory Report of the Draft Agreement, paras 65–66.

[36] Ibid, para 66.

[37] Torres Pérez (n 10).

[38] Jacqué (n 10); Lock (n 10).

[39] G Gaja, ch 22 in this volume.

Jacqué observes that the authoritative interpretation of EU law conferred on the CJEU stems from Article 19(1) TEU,[40] and also from Article 1 of Protocol 8 of the Treaties, which requires the Accession Agreement to respect the 'specific characteristics of the Union and Union law'.[41] Accordingly, the 'accession of the Union shall not affect the competences of the Union or the powers of its institutions',[42] including, of course, the CJEU.[43] The main line of argument *against* the prior involvement, as advanced by Lock's analysis, suggests that the prior involvement is not indispensable in order to preserve the EU's autonomy, since 'a finding by the ECtHR of a violation of the Convention would not directly lead to an invalidation of the EU act in question'.[44] The argument is accurate, but may be complemented by the observation that the autonomy of the legal order entails not only the power to annul legislation but also the power to authoritatively interpret EU law. Lock would perhaps respond, in turn, that the ECtHR's divergent interpretation would not be 'binding'.[45] Nevertheless, if one accepts that the ECtHR relies on the interpretation of domestic law by domestic courts,[46] one cannot easily identify how the CJEU's opinion is unnecessary in instances where the latter would not have interpreted EU law before a case would reach the Strasbourg Court.

Arguments implying the CJEU's involvement are also to be found in the Strasbourg principle of subsidiarity, even viewed under its broader, non-formalistic[47] sense. The ECtHR is the applicant's last resort and the exhaustion of domestic remedies is a precondition for admissibility.[48] If the EU is the intermediate level, or the ultimate 'domestic' level, in-between the Member State/contracting party and the Convention, it can hardly be justified why the CJEU should not grant an opinion on matters concerning the implementation of EU law.

At this point, a distinction may be drawn between the necessity of the prior involvement from the scope of EU law and its assessment from the point of view of the international law regime of the ECHR. As stated in the Introduction, this chapter focuses on the EU legal order. In this context, I am not convinced that, *from the perspective of EU law*, the absence of such involvement would accord with 'the specific situation of the EU as a non-State entity with an autonomous legal system',[49] and I cannot identify how 'gaps in participation, accountability and enforceability in the Convention system' could otherwise have been avoided.[50] Beyond the above argument on the authoritative interpretation of EU law, another crucial point appears to be Jacqué's concern that if the Strasbourg Court proceeds with the attribution of responsibility between the EU and the Member State concerned by the means of a control on the right choice of defendant by the applicant, it will enter into the sensitive domain of the division of competences between the EU and the Member States; and clearly, from the viewpoint of EU law, this falls upon the CJEU to define, at least in the

40 Jacqué (n 10) 1011–12.

41 Lock (n 10) 1033.

42 Art 2 of Protocol 8.

43 Conversely, it may be claimed that the prior involvement does not currently figure among the competences of the CJEU.

44 Lock (n 10) 1047, 1054.

45 Compare Lock (n 4). For a similar approach, compare also Torres Pérez (n 10).

46 Torres Pérez (n 10).

47 This is so since, as Torres Pérez explains (n 10), the principle of subsidiarity *stricto sensu* is not applicable in the context of the co-respondent mechanism, given that the applicant does not literally need to exhaust an *additional* remedy.

48 Art 35(1) ECHR; see also the Draft Agreement, para 66.

49 Draft Agreement, para 38.

50 Ibid, para 39.

first place[51] (one should note, of course, that the last word always remains with the ECtHR and one can only wait in order to identify the latter's actual stance after accession). Thus, Eckes cautiously underlines that the rationale behind the prior involvement is precisely to 'permit the ECtHR to refrain from determining who is the correct respondent or how responsibility should be apportioned as between them. Indeed, it declares the joint responsibility of the respondent and co-respondent to be the common case'.[52]

For a more complete picture, it can briefly be said that, from the perspective of the ECHR framework, it has been suggested that prior involvement grants a preferential status to the CJEU.[53] Further, regarding the issue of the delays in a sensitive area of law (human rights) caused by the mechanism of prior involvement,[54] the proposal is to include a fast-track mechanism in the event of such activation.[55]

IV. THE ECtHR JURISPRUDENCE ON NON-JUDICIAL REMEDIES

A. The interpretation of Article 13 by the ECtHR

Having rapidly discussed the landscape in the EU order and the mechanism of prior involvement aiming at addressing the 'needs' of that order for acceding to the ECHR, this chapter now moves to the question of what is, according to the ECtHR, an 'effective remedy before a national authority'.[56] As an introductory remark, let us recall that the 'procedural' notion of remedy entails 'the processes by which arguable claims of human rights violations are heard and decided, whether by courts, administrative agencies, or other competent bodies'; whereas the 'substantive' notion of remedy concerns 'the outcome of the proceedings, the relief afforded the successful claimant', often referred to as 'redress'.[57]

The pivotal question here is whether 'the national authority' may encompass avenues of extra-judicial redress as well, and if so, under what circumstances. In its well-known and praised *Golder* case,[58] where the Strasbourg Court interpreted Article 6 ECHR (right to a fair trial) as guaranteeing a right of access to courts, it also confirmed that Article 13 must be dissociated from the right to a fair trial, adding that the former Article could indeed include extra-judicial avenues. In particular, although one judge opined otherwise,[59] the majority held that the national authority 'may not be a "tribunal" or "court" within the meaning of'

[51] Jacqué (n 10) 1012 et seq.

[52] C Eckes, 'EU Accession to the ECHR: Between Autonomy and Adaptation' (2013) 76 *MLR* 267.

[53] Torres Pérez (n 10).

[54] Ibid.

[55] Draft Agreement, para 69.

[56] The selection of cases in sections IV.A and IV.B was based on the following sources: the HUDOC database: www.echr.coe.int/ECHR/EN/Header/Case-Law/Decisions+and+judgments/HUDOC+database; L Reif, *The Ombudsman, Good Governance and the International Human Rights System* (Martinus Nijhoff Publishers, 2004) 129–36; P Van Dijk et al (eds), *Theory and Practice of the European Convention on Human Rights* (Antwerp, Intersentia, 2006); RCA White and C Ovey, *The European Convention on Human Rights* (Oxford, Oxford University Press, 2010); A Mowbray, *Cases, Materials and Commentary on the European Convention on Human Rights* (Oxford, Oxford University Press, 2012).

[57] D Shelton, *Remedies in International Human Rights Law* (Oxford, Oxford University Press, 2005) 7–8.

[58] *Golder v UK*, Series A No 18 (1975).

[59] Ibid, separate Opinion of Judge Zekia: 'In my view courts come within the ambit of "national authority" mentioned in [Article 13].'

Article 6.[60] In *Klass*, the applicant submitted that a national authority should be 'a body ... at least ... composed of members who are impartial and who enjoy the safeguards of judicial independence'.[61] Germany argued that 'in contrast to [Article 6], [Article 13] does not require a legal remedy through the courts'.[62] Yet, the Strasbourg Court refrained from positioning itself as to the plurality or singularity of the members comprising the authority. Thus: 'In the Court's opinion, the authority referred to in [Article 13] may not necessarily in all instances be a judicial authority in the strict sense ... Nevertheless, the *powers* and *procedural guarantees* an authority possesses are relevant in determining whether the remedy before it is effective.'[63] This statement has been consistently used and now forms part of the general principles of the Strasbourg Court on the interpretation and the scope of Article 13.[64] Note also the pluralistic approach regarding remedies: 'although no single remedy may itself entirely satisfy the requirements of [Article 13], the aggregate of remedies provided for under domestic law may do so'.[65]

However, in *Silver*, the ECtHR found that an application to the UK Ombudsman (the Parliamentary Commissioner for Administration) did not constitute an effective remedy because the Ombudsman 'has himself no power to render a binding decision granting redress'.[66] Yet, in circumstances where the norms in question were compatible with Article 8 ECHR and the allegation concerned their misapplication, the right to petition the Home Secretary and/or the English courts could constitute an effective remedy.[67] However, given that at the time of the judgment the Human Rights Act had not been enacted, the English courts could not judge on the compatibility of the norms with Article 8 or the Convention more generally; this is why the Strasbourg Court reached the conclusion that, in the second case, contacting the courts would not satisfy the requirements of Article 13.[68]

The preceding discussion leads to an initial observation: the ECtHR proceeds with an *in concreto* examination of the available remedies, be they judicial or extra-judicial, without presupposing their effectiveness. I shall return to this point towards the end of this section.

The *Leander* case merits particular consideration.[69] It concerned a Swedish carpenter who lost his temporary position in a museum adjacent to a naval base. A personnel control was carried out on him, the outcome being the cessation of his employment, since security issues were raised as a justification. Before discussing the ECtHR's approach on Article 13, it should be noted that the applicant alleged a violation of Articles 8 and 10, but the Strasbourg Court came to the (insufficiently substantiated) conclusion that security considerations could justify the interference with his rights.[70] As to possible effective remedies, the ECtHR discussed in depth the role of the Swedish Parliamentary Ombudsman, accentuating the

[60] Ibid [33].
[61] *Klass and others v Germany*, Series A No 28 (1978) [67].
[62] Ibid.
[63] Ibid (emphasis added).
[64] See *Silver and others v UK*, Series A No 61 (1983) [113].
[65] Ibid [113]; *Leander v Sweden*, Series A No 116 (1987) [77].
[66] *Silver* [115].
[67] Ibid [116].
[68] Ibid [117]–[119].
[69] Above n 65.
[70] Ibid [47]–[75]. For a critique compare RW Davis, 'Public access to community documents: a fundamental human right?' 3 *European Integration online Papers* (1999) http://eiop.or.at/eiop/pdf/1999-008.pdf.

constitutional dimension of an office established in 1809.[71] It underlined the impact of the reports of the Ombudsman, which eventually led to changes in the practices applied in the personnel control system.[72] The Court additionally referred to the 'Parliamentary Committee on Justice', which is entitled to 'scrutinise' the personnel selection, while enjoying wide powers of investigation, notably in terms of 'access to the registers'.[73]

In more detail, the ECtHR examined the available remedies under Swedish law,[74] focusing in particular on the independence of the institutions:

> 82. The main weakness in the control afforded by the Ombudsman and the Chancellor of Justice is that both officials, apart from their competence to institute criminal and disciplinary proceedings … lack the power to render a legally binding decision. On this point, the Court, however, recalls the necessarily limited effectiveness that can be required of any remedy available to the individual concerned in a system of secret security checks. The opinions of the Parliamentary Ombudsman and the Chancellor of Justice command by tradition great respect in Swedish society and in practice are usually followed …
> 83. To these remedies, which were never exercised by Mr Leander, must be added the remedy to which he actually had recourse when he complained, in a letter … to the Government, that the National Police Board, contrary to [relevant] provisions … had omitted to invite him to comment, in writing or orally, on the information contained in the register …
> 84. Even if, taken on its own, the complaint to the Government were not considered sufficient to ensure compliance with [Article 13], the Court finds that the aggregate of the remedies set out above … satisfies the conditions of [Article 13] in the particular circumstances of the instant case.[75]

Regardless of the ECtHR's motives, it should be noted that since Sweden was the first country to establish an Ombudsman, an institution broadly respected by citizens and institutions, it was easier for the Strasbourg Court to focus on the *independence* of the office, instead of its judicial nature. The dissenting judges did not find a violation of Articles 8 and 10, but of Article 13 only. It is possible to assume that they could also have considered that Contracting Parties could 'hide' behind the *Leander* case so as to essentially justify the absence of convincing (judicial) remedies where these would be required.

Thus, as Reif explains, in the following years, the ECtHR adopted a 'stricter approach' concerning non-judicial avenues since: 'The nature of the right in question is also relevant.'[76] In *Peck*, the Court held that three media commissions lacking 'legal power … to award damages to the applicant means that those bodies could not provide an effective remedy to him'.[77] In *Keenan*, it stated that there was no effective remedy as to the right of the protection of life and to the freedom from torture and other inhuman or degrading treatment or punishment, despite the availability of an internal complaints mechanism and the Prison Ombudsman,[78] confirming that: 'The scope of the obligation under Article 13 varies depending on the nature of the applicant's complaint under the Convention.'[79]

[71] Ibid [38].
[72] Ibid [39].
[73] Ibid [40].
[74] Ibid [78].
[75] The decision was not unanimous. Three judges contested the effectiveness of non-binding redress mechanisms.
[76] Reif (n 56) 131.
[77] *Peck v UK*, ECHR 2003-I [108]–[109].
[78] *Keenan v UK*, ECHR 2001-III.
[79] Ibid [123].

A breach was also found as regards the available remedies after Keenan's death. In *Chahal*, the Court decided that, taking into account 'the importance the Court attaches to [Article 3]', neither the courts nor an advisory panel could constitute an effective remedy for the safeguard of this Article.[80] In another case, four children were found to have been seriously neglected and abused. The ECtHR held that the UK had not violated Article 6, while confirming that the critical article to be considered was Article 13.[81] In this case, the Court appeared to seriously consider the absence of legally binding decisions of non-judicial mechanisms, while reiterating that the nature of the violation also matters: 'Article 13 … guarantees the availability at the national level of a remedy to *enforce* the substance of the Convention rights and freedoms.'[82] The Court indeed found a violation of Article 13, but did not 'consider it appropriate … to make any findings as to whether only court proceedings could have furnished effective redress, though judicial remedies indeed furnish strong guarantees of independence, access for the victim and family, and enforceability of awards in compliance with the requirements of Article 13'.[83]

In *Khan*, the Police Complaints Authority was found not to satisfy the requirements of Article 13 due to its unsatisfactory degree of independence, notably vis-a-vis the Secretary of State, in particular when 'appointing, remunerating and, in certain circumstances, dismissing members of the Police Complaints Authority'.[84]

In this context, Reif argues that it is difficult for an Ombudsman[85] to qualify as an effective remedy under Article 13 because his or her decisions often lack enforceability.[86] While this is largely accurate, the above discussion has demonstrated that this qualification cannot always be excluded, whereas Reif also underlines that certain Ombudsmen in Member States benefit from 'additional powers'.[87] White and Ovey assert that the 'remedies need not be judicial, but must be effective. Ombudsman procedures and other non-judicial procedures will be included'.[88]

A justification of this viewpoint may be found in *Kudła*, which signified an 'expansion of the scope of Article 13',[89] in the sense that the ECtHR not only departed from the position that Articles 6 and 13 overlap in areas covered by the former,[90] but arguably also suggested that there might be cases where the right to an effective remedy entails an available remedy against cases where the contracting state has violated Article 6 (in this particular case by lengthy, excessive court proceedings).[91] The case was decided by the Strasbourg Court while pending before the Supreme Court of Poland.[92] Proceedings before the domestic courts had lasted for nine years overall and during considerable part of this time the applicant was detained in prison while receiving medical and psychiatric treatment.

[80] *Chahal v UK* (1996) 23 EHRR 413 [151], [153].
[81] *Z and others v UK*, ECHR 2001-V, 34 EHRR 97, in particular [96], [103].
[82] Ibid [108] (emphasis added). See further Reif (n 56) 131.
[83] Ibid [110].
[84] *Khan v UK*, ECHR 2000-V, 31 EHRR 45 [45]–[47].
[85] An Ombudsman is, of course, *one* of the means of extra-judicial redress.
[86] Reif (n 56) 132 and the additional cases cited therein.
[87] Notably the power to 'launch court actions to obtain judicial protection of individual rights and/or judgments on the constitutionality of laws'. See Reif (n 56) 132.
[88] White and Ovey (n 56) 135.
[89] Mowbray (n 56) 808.
[90] Van Dijk et al (n 56) 1019–21.
[91] *Kudła v Poland*, ECHR 2000-XI, 35 EHRR 198.
[92] Ibid [57].

The Court decided that a violation of Articles 5(3) and 6(1) ECHR had occurred. On the alleged violation of Article 13, the pertinent question was whether a violation of the right to a 'hearing within a reasonable time' should be accompanied by an effective remedy under Article 13.[93] The Polish government relied on Strasbourg case law suggesting that Article 13 is 'less strict' than Article 6 and that the requirements of Article 13 are accordingly 'absorbed' by Article 6(1).[94] The Court acknowledged that there had been cases where it did not examine the violation of Article 13, for instance, in civil rights were the 'full panoply of a judicial procedure' was available under Article 6(1) (the *lex specialis* thesis).[95] However, it found 'no overlap and hence no absorption where … the alleged Convention violation … is a violation of the right to trial within a reasonable time', since this constitutes 'a separate legal issue'.[96] The ECtHR furthermore declared that 'the time ha[d] come to review its case-law in the light of the continuing accumulation of applications before it in which the only, or principal, allegation is that of a failure to ensure a hearing within a reasonable time in breach of' Article 6(1), thus endangering the rule of law at the national level.[97] It went on to state that the safeguards of Article 6(1) 'will be less effective if there exists no opportunity to submit the Convention claim first to a national authority' and that 'nothing in the letter' or the 'drafting history' of Article 13 excludes its application vis-a-vis the 'right to a court'.[98] The Court found in this respect a violation of Article 13 as regards the aforementioned delays, in addition to a violation of Article 6(1).[99]

A similar reasoning may be observed in *Kangasluoma*,[100] where the Court found that, in addition to a violation of the 'reasonable time' of Article 6(1) ECHR, the applicant did not have at his disposal an 'effective remedy in respect of the length of the criminal investigations pending against him'. Thus, Finnish law did not provide an effective remedy both in law and in practice, which is a prerequisite for the standard of protection guaranteed by Article 13 to be achieved.[101] Accordingly, in *Stakić v Montenegro*, the Court added that: 'Where the judicial system is deficient with regard to the reasonable-time requirement', the 'best solution in absolute terms is indisputably, as in many spheres, prevention.'[102]

Overall, it is deduced that the Strasbourg case law does not preclude that recourse to a non-judicial remedy might constitute an 'effective' remedy under Article 13. One would certainly observe that the conditions for a non-judicial avenue to qualify as effective are strict, since the latter would normally be non-binding. However, the case law primarily demonstrates that each situation has to be looked at *in concreto*; in other words, that the nature of the right in question and the particular facts of the case should also be taken into consideration. Further, the aggregate of available remedies may satisfy the conditions of Article 13. One would therefore assume that for violations of rights that do not fall under Article 6 ECHR[103] (thus requiring a judicial remedy/access to courts), the Strasbourg Court has occasionally demonstrated an inclusive approach vis-a-vis non-judicial remedies.

[93] Ibid [133].
[94] Ibid [139].
[95] Ibid [146].
[96] Ibid [147].
[97] Ibid [148].
[98] Ibid [151]–[152].
[99] Ibid [159]–[160].
[100] *Kangasluoma v Finland* [2004] ECHR 29.
[101] Ibid, in particular [46]–[49].
[102] *Stakić v Montenegro,* Application 49320/07 [2013][57].
[103] For a study examining, among others, the ECtHR's case-law on the scope of 'civil rights and obligations or criminal charges' see OSCE/ODIHR, 'Legal Digest of International Fair Trial Rights' (2012, 2013).

Conversely, the *in concreto* examination of remedies by the ECtHR entails that it is not certain that for *all* rights falling under Article 6 ECHR, the ECtHR would automatically conclude, without thorough examination, that a court/tribunal is necessarily 'effective'. This point is reinforced by *Kudła* and subsequent cases, which may be translated as a message to contracting parties to guarantee judicial remedies effective *in practice*.

B. Article 35(1) ECHR and the Exhaustion of 'Domestic Remedies'

For the present purposes, consider an 'effective' national Ombudsman dealing with a case involving the implementation of EU law. Note that it was shown in section III.B above that in order for the autonomy of the EU legal order to be maintained, the CJEU should first provide its interpretation. This section therefore deals with the critical issue of how the Strasbourg Court has treated the question of the exhaustion of non-judicial domestic remedies. Besides, Articles 13 and 35(1) benefit from a 'close affinity' and they are conceptually comparable in terms of the obligations they impose upon contracting states.[104]

In *Montion*, a rural landowner was obliged under French law to allow hunting activities on his land, which in turn allegedly violated his freedom of conscience, his freedom of association and his right to property.[105] The question was whether the deadline of six months since the 'final decision' as required by Article 35(1) ECHR had elapsed. Under the old system, the Commission considered that this was indeed the case, since the French Ombudsman, who was contacted in the meantime, could not be considered as a remedy to be exhausted.[106]

In *Raninen*, however, the Court found that domestic remedies were indeed exhausted, further to the applicant's complaint to the Finnish Ombudsman.[107] The Court in particular took the Ombudsman's findings seriously[108] before deciding that it had not been 'demonstrated that either a criminal prosecution or an action for damages would in the specific circumstances of the case have offered reasonable prospects of success'.[109]

In *Lehtinen*, we had yet another jurisprudential development.[110] As a preliminary remark, the ECtHR reiterated that the rule of exhaustion apart from the 'existence of formal remedies' should also take into account 'the general legal and political context in which they operate as well as the personal circumstances of the applicants'.[111] In this case, nonetheless, the Court stated that 'as a *general rule*, a petition to the Ombudsman cannot be regarded as an effective remedy as required by Article 35'.[112] A petition to the court of first instance, instead of the Finnish Ombudsman, could be considered as a sufficient remedy to be exhausted.

104 Van Dijk et al (n 56) 1009.

105 *Montion v France*, Application 11192/84, Decision of the Commission (1987), 233.

106 Ibid, 235.

107 *Raninen v Finland* (1997) 26 EHRR 563; compare also Reif (n 56) 134–35.

108 The Ombudsman did consider that a breach of law had taken place, but found no fault or neglect from the part of the military personnel when they decided to put the applicant in handcuffs further to his objection to carrying out military duties.

109 *Raninen* [42]. Note that the government argued that whereas the Ombudsman can bring charges, this is rarely the case, since the latter will usually adopt 'less drastic measures' when he or she finds fault: ibid [38]. This approach did not convince the Court.

110 *Lehtinen v Finland*, Application 39076/97, ECHR 1999-VII (decision as to the admissibility).

111 Ibid.

112 Ibid (emphasis added).

The Court examined 'whether there were specific reasons absolving the applicant ... from exhausting [the] court remedy which was at his disposal'. By stressing the differences with *Raninen*, it found that the Ombudsman's decision 'cannot provide [such] ground':[113]

> Even assuming that the Ombudsman's above decision should be taken into account as an element in assessing the effectiveness of the court remedy in the particular case, the Court notes that the subject-matter of a petition to the national court concerning seizure is not the same as a petition to the Ombudsman.[114]

This judgment led Reif to conclude that 'in cases where a judicial remedy with reasonable prospects of success is available ... total reliance by the applicant on a complaint to the ombudsman and failure to use the court process will likely not satisfy the exhaustion of domestic remedies rule'.[115] I would subscribe to this view, noting that it actually confirms the above findings that every case has to be looked at on an ad hoc basis (taking into account the context and the particularities of the case), and also that the ECtHR has to examine whether the available judicial avenue is actually 'effective', without presupposing such an assessment and without a priori rejecting the effectiveness of an available extra-judicial avenue. Further, it cannot be excluded that there might be cases in certain constitutional settings where judicial and non-judicial avenues are equally effective concerning the alleged violation of specific Convention rights, thus leaving the choice to the applicant.

The *Egmez* case arguably confirms the above considerations.[116] The applicant was found to have been treated inhumanly by the Cypriot authorities. However, the respondent raised the preliminary objection that the domestic remedies had not been exhausted since the applicant had submitted an application to the Ombudsman and not to the courts.[117] It should be highlighted that the Strasbourg Court somewhat departed from the 'general rule' formulation in *Lehtinen*[118] and stated that 'according to the Convention organs' case-law, a complaint to the Ombudsman is not *in principle* a remedy to be exhausted under' Article 35(1).[119] However, in this case, the Court noted that the Ombudsman conducted an investigation and found ill-treatment on two occasions.[120] Since the Ombudsman lacks enforceable powers, including sanctions, the obligation to pursue the case fell upon domestic authorities, namely the Attorney General, who nonetheless remained inactive, despite the Ombudsman's findings that 'the action complained of violates the human rights of the person concerned and could constitute a criminal offence'. The Court went on to find that the respondent should have instituted 'criminal proceedings' against the persons named in the Ombudsman's report, regardless of the outcome of these proceedings. It therefore considered that 'the applicant, by lodging a complaint with the Ombudsman, discharged his duty under [Article 35(1)] ... The only way of putting matters right ... was the institution of criminal proceedings against the officers involved and ... a complaint to the Ombudsman should have normally brought about this result'.[121] Accordingly, without examining the

[113] Ibid.
[114] Ibid.
[115] Reif (n 56) 134–35.
[116] *Egmez v Cyprus*, ECHR 2000-XII, 34 EHRR 753.
[117] Ibid [59].
[118] Above n 112.
[119] *Egmez* [66] (emphasis added).
[120] Ibid [67]: 'The Court has no reason to doubt the effectiveness of the Ombudsman's investigation.'
[121] Ibid [72].

nature and prospects of judicial remedies available to the applicant, a violation of Article 13 was identified, because the Attorney General did not pursue the case further.[122] Thus, it can be argued that, indirectly, the Court recognised that complaining to the Ombudsman (with the co-operation of the Attorney General) may constitute an effective remedy, depending of course on the facts that are particular to each case.

Overall, the case law on Article 35(1) ECHR confirms the findings of section IV.A above: 'effective' judicial remedies satisfy the prerequisites of this article, but under specific circumstances a non-judicial avenue could equally lead the Strasbourg Court to decide that the exhaustion rule was observed. The ECtHR's approach in *Raninen* and *Egmez* verifies this claim.

V. BRINGING TOGETHER THE TWO REGIMES: LEGAL QUESTIONS AND POLICY-ORIENTED ASSESSMENTS

This section discusses the challenges that could arise further to the EU's accession to the ECHR. As demonstrated above, the CFR does not list a right to extra-judicial redress, but the ECtHR's principles on Article 13 suggest that under strict circumstances such an avenue might be effective. Moreover, contacting an Ombudsman might occasionally satisfy the exigencies of Article 35(1) ECHR. It has been argued that Article 8 of the Universal Declaration of Human Rights is 'potentially narrower' than Article 13 ECHR, since it refers to tribunals only.[123] The same could be claimed for Article 47 CFR when compared to Article 13 ECHR.

A. Implications Further to the CJEU's Prior Involvement

i. General Implications

The first question to be examined is whether there could be any legal implications after the accession of the EU to the ECHR, taking into consideration the CJEU's prior involvement. Let us assume that an applicant submits a complaint to an 'effective' (under the ECtHR's abovementioned standards) Ombudsman. By way of example, let us consider the Estonian Ombudsman/Chancellor of Justice, who is totally independent and has an extensive mandate covering even fundamental rights in private law.[124] He or she enjoys very wide powers,[125] appearing as the 'guardian of constitutionality' (although, according to the website, he or she clearly does not form part of the judiciary), a feature which is considered 'unique internationally'.[126] In such a hypothetical scenario, a) the complaint concerns the implementation of EU law by a national authority (thus falling under Article 47 CFR) and b)

[122] Ibid [100].

[123] White and Ovey (n 56) 131. Simultaneously it is wider, since it guarantees the individual's right by constitution or by law, according to the authors.

[124] G Kucsko-Stadlmayer (ed), *European Ombudsman-Institutions: A Comparative Legal Analysis Regarding the Multifaceted Realisation of an Idea* (Vienna, Springer Verlag, 2008) 162–64.

[125] Ibid, 167.

[126] 'Estonian Model of the Institution of the Chancellor of Justice', available at http://oiguskantsler.ee/en/estonian-model-of-the-institution-of-the-chancellor-of-justice.

the applicant alleges a violation of a Convention right, in a situation not covered by Article 6 ECHR (access to courts) or the ECtHR's interpretation of its scope of application. In our case study, let us assume that the citizen does not obtain satisfactory redress. Since Article 47 CFR refers to tribunals only, one could argue that, at least insofar as the CFR is concerned, this choice does not constitute an effective remedy at the domestic level. However, according to Strasbourg's understanding of Article 13 ECHR, it cannot be excluded that there might be no breach of the latter Article.

In addition, assuming that *somehow* the case reaches the CJEU first (I refer to this procedure below),[127] interesting questions could arise as regards the precise meaning of Article 47 CFR under Union law. Because, should the CJEU provide its views upon a request by the Strasbourg Court, would this not entail an implicit recognition that the scheme classified as 'effective' by the Strasbourg jurisprudence, actually satisfies the requirements of Article 47 CFR? The CJEU could, of course, take into consideration the aforementioned principle of national procedural autonomy.[128] Of relevance in this respect is the CJEU's decision in *Alassini*, which concerned the compatibility with the principle of effectiveness of a mandatory out-of-court settlement scheme in the telecommunications sector before the admissibility stage at the courts.[129] The CJEU stated that such a mechanism complied not only with the principle of effectiveness (national procedural autonomy), but also with the principle of effective judicial protection (Article 47 CFR), since it served inter alia the legitimate aim of 'quicker and less expensive settlement of disputes', in accordance with the proportionality principle.[130] Besides, an arbitrator in the UK satisfied the 'effectiveness' test, insofar as 'victims [were] made aware of any matter that might be used against them and [had] an opportunity to submit their comments thereon' (which was left for the national court to determine).[131]

Turning to the ECtHR, which will hear the case as the applicant's last resort, Lock has rightly pointed out that the Strasbourg Court might indeed interpret EU law when it comes to the effectiveness test of Article 13—which is one of the examples where the ECtHR may 'assess provisions of domestic law'.[132] This in turn means that because the case involves EU law, the Strasbourg Court would interpret EU law, therefore engaging in the sensitive debate on the autonomy of the EU legal order. It is unknown, of course, how exactly the ECtHR may interpret possible divergences of this kind between Article 13 ECHR and

[127] Note that, as Reif explains, an Ombudsman is generally not entitled to apply to the Strasbourg court, since he or she cannot be considered a 'victim'. See Reif (n 56) 135. Note further that in the context of the European Network of Ombudsmen, there is no institutionalised mechanism of referral from the national to the European Ombudsman. Besides, the latter's mandate does not cover national entities implementing EU law.

[128] See, for instance, the thorough examination of the ECtHR's case law on legal aid by the CJEU in Case C-279/09 *DEB v Bundesrepublik Deutschland* [2010] ECR I-13849.

[129] Joined Cases C-317/08–320/08, *Alassini* [2010] ECR I-2213 [47]–[67], cited in Adinolfi (n 5) 299. But see also C-424/99, *Commission* v *Austria* [2001] ECR I-9285, discussed by Dougan (n 5) 5–6.

[130] Compare also a discussion on the post-*DEB/Alassini* relationship between the principles of effectiveness and 'effective judicial protection' as *recognised* by Art 47 CFR in J Engström, 'The Principle of Effective Judicial Protection after the Lisbon Treaty' (2011) 4 *Review of European Administrative Law* 53. Besides, as Mak rightly points out, Art. 52(1) CFR enables 'restrictions' also to Art 47 CFR, subject to the proportionality test; see C Mak, 'Rights and Remedies: Article 47 EUCFR and Effective Judicial Protection in European Private Law Matters' (2012) Amsterdam Centre for the Study of European Contract Law Working Paper No 2012-11, available at: http://papers.ssrn.com/sol3/papers.cfm?abstract_id=2126551, p 19.

[131] C-63/01 *Evans* [2003] ECR I-14447, in particular [56]–[57].

[132] Lock (n 10) 1035. When discussing *Keenan*, White and Ovey ((n 56) 137) talk about 'a degree of encroachment on national procedural autonomy in the interpretation of Article 13'.

47 CFR.[133] It is equally unknown how the ECtHR will deal with the admissibility question of Article 35(1) ECHR, namely with the exhaustion of 'effective' domestic remedies rule, in situations where the national authority is implementing Union law.

Insofar as the CJEU is concerned, wisely, apart from the principle of national procedural autonomy,[134] the CFR enables the CJEU to remedy differentiations. Article 52(3) CFR states that: 'In so far as this Charter contains rights which correspond to rights guaranteed by the Convention for the Protection of Human Rights and Fundamental Freedoms, the meaning and scope of those rights shall be the same as those laid down by the said Convention. This provision shall not prevent Union law providing more extensive protection.' Likewise, Article 53 CFR ensures a minimum level of protection equivalent to the ECHR.[135] Similar clauses may be found in other human rights instruments as well.[136] It has been argued that the purpose of these clauses is to provide the 'utmost coherence between the different systems protecting fundamental rights in Europe'.[137] Thus, if the meaning and scope of CFR rights is the same as the ECHR, as stated in Article 52(3) CFR, in the hypothetical (and perhaps unlikely) scenario previously discussed, one would expect the CJEU to remedy differentiations, mainly relying on Article 52(3), with Article 53 being used as a reinforcing argument.[138]

ii. Could the Applicant 'Bypass' the CJEU?

As announced in the Introduction, an additional path of enquiry is to examine whether it is possible that the case does not reach the CJEU; in that event, a 'gap' would automatically be created which could entitle the complainant to 'bypass' the CJEU and to obtain redress directly from the Strasbourg Court. Indeed, a case involving the implementation of EU law by national authorities could be brought before national extra-judicial mechanisms instead of domestic courts; it should be identified whether under such a scenario, the CJEU might not have an opportunity to exercise its jurisdiction.

The brief (but by no means definitive) answer to this question should *in principle* be in the negative. After the accession of the EU to the ECHR, the applicant shall have a number of choices. The first one would be to directly complain against the Member State

[133] If the CJEU considers that a specific remedy does not satisfy the requirements of 'effectiveness', could it be excluded that the ECtHR might depart from its approach on Article 13 ECHR, and assess that EU law offers a higher standard of protection? Compare also Rozakis (ch 20 in this volume), suggesting that the EU's accession could offer the ECtHR an opportunity to augment the scope of ECHR rights, with reference to the EU CFR. He underlines that Art 47 CFR provides 'wider' protection; it remains to be seen how precisely the ECtHR will deal with these cases.

[134] The *Impact* case can tell us very little due to its particularities, including the nature of the Rights Commissioner of Ireland. See Case C-268/06 *Impact v Minister for Agriculture and Food* [2008] ECR I-2483, discussed by Arnull (n 4) 57–60. Ireland has established a Rights Commissioner and a Labour Court (as a second instance) with optional jurisdiction so as to implement the fixed-term work Directive. The Court stated that the Rights Commissioner and the Labour Court are 'a national court or tribunal' ([37]) or a 'specialised court' ([55]); accordingly, the Advocate General (points 52 and 73) opined that the Rights Commissioner may be considered as comparable with a 'publicly appointed independent arbitrator'. See further www.lrc.ie/document/More-on-the-Rights-Commission/4/745.htm.

[135] See J Bering Liisberg, 'Does the Charter of Fundamental Rights Threaten the Supremacy of Community Law?' (2001) 38 *CML Rev* 1171–99.

[136] Ibid, 1182–89.

[137] Pabel (n 29) 1604.

[138] See further on this point P Lemmens, 'The Relation between the Charter of Fundamental Rights of the European Union and the European Convention on Human Rights—Substantive Aspects' (2001) 8 *Maastricht Journal of European and Comparative Law* 52.

only. Under Article 1(4) of the Draft Accession Agreement, this must be viewed as the most logical assumption. A second path would be to direct the complaint against both the EU and the Member State concerned. In both cases, the EU would have the possibility of becoming a co-respondent,[139] and thus the prior involvement of the CJEU would be activated, allowing Luxembourg to have its say before, ultimately, Strasbourg exercises its jurisdiction. The CJEU could only be bypassed if the EU chose not to become a co-respondent. This is entirely up to the EU, since the mechanism is voluntary. Besides, it appears that the EU is considering adopting a coherent policy as regards the activation of the co-respondent option in cases where a Member State implements EU law.[140]

Third, the applicant could direct the complaint against the EU. The latter would become the *respondent*. The problem with this scenario is that, despite the general rule of shared responsibility, especially in cases stemming from the implementation of EU law by Member States, the EU does not appear, at least from what is known to date, to automatically acquire the right to become a co-respondent unless the case involves EU primary law and the Member State concerned *chooses* to become a co-respondent.[141] Only logical hypotheses can be made in that respect, implying that the ECtHR may be expected to invite the CJEU even in such a scenario to submit an opinion. This is but an estimation, albeit a logical one, because otherwise the prior involvement loses its *effet utile*[142] due to a purely technical matter. In fact, Judge Gaja recommends the extension of the prior involvement to *all* cases where the EU would be a respondent.[143] It may be reminded that the logic of the co-respondent mechanism and the CJEU's prior involvement is precisely to enable the ECtHR to prevent the applicant from choosing the respondent (so that Strasbourg does not interfere with the 'internal' EU allocation of competences).[144]

B. Further Legal and Policy-Oriented Questions Stemming from the Divergent Approaches Concerning the Right to Extra-Judicial Redress

The legal questions do not end there. While it is true that there cannot be deduced from the Strasbourg case law any tendency to insert a dimension of efficiency to the effectiveness test (namely, which entity could provide 'effective' redress faster), the ECtHR has used a convincing methodology when applying Article 13 to Article 6 ECHR in *Kudła*, stating that the former guarantees a *right* to an effective remedy *against excessive domestic judicial procedures*. Such a provision seems to be missing from the CFR, following the merger of Articles 6 and 13 ECHR. The CJEU would need to rely on the abovementioned general clauses or its jurisprudence on the 'effectiveness' of a judicial remedy.[145]

139 See in particular the explanatory text of the Draft Agreement, paras 47 and 48.

140 This stems from Appendix II of the Draft Agreement.

141 Para 49 of the Draft Agreement.

142 Which is to give the opportunity to the CJEU to interpret EU law in the absence of such interpretation and furthermore to grant the opportunity to the latter to allocate responsibility internally (ie, opine on the division of competences), at least in the first place. Compare also para 62 of the explanatory text of the Draft Agreement: 'Apportioning responsibility separately to the respondent and the co-respondent(s) on any other basis would entail the risk that the Court would assess the distribution of competences between the EU and its Member States.'

143 Gaja (n 39).

144 See Eckes (n 52).

145 Compare C-185/95 P, *Baustahlgewebe GmbH* v *Commission*, [1998] ECR I-8417, with regard to delays in a procedure before the Court of First Instance (see, in particular, [21]–[49]).

Further, it is questionable whether Article 47 CFR should be given a different interpretation from Article 19.1 TEU. If Member States are free by primary law to decide on appropriate 'effective' remedies, why is merely a right to an effective remedy before a tribunal recognised by the CFR as a right of European citizens? The effectiveness of a given remedy in a specific case is something that the Strasbourg Court will ultimately be called upon to judge. The ECtHR has decided that Article 13 does not require 'the certainty of a favourable outcome'.[146] Besides, as Kuckso-Stadlmayer observes: 'The principle of independence is the leading thought for the effectiveness of ombudsman institutions.'[147] In Europe, there are certain countries with robust, totally independent and impartial Ombudsman institutions, producing decisions that are rarely disregarded by the administration.[148]

Thus, and moving towards the boundaries of the legal and the political, it is equally questionable whether the reference to a 'tribunal' necessarily renders the protection guaranteed by Article 47 CFR more *extensive*, as the drafters of the Charter had suggested.[149] It will be usually more effective[150]—but not always. Again, the scope is certainly more extensive insofar as it refers to the 'rights and freedoms guaranteed by the law of the Union', instead of Convention rights/freedoms (Article 13 ECHR). Still, the choice of Article 47 does not appear to reflect recent developments in the constitutional and administrative law of the Member States, namely the establishment of ombudsman institutions and other extra-judicial bodies so as to complement the role of courts as the guardians of the rule of law.

Besides, the role of the Ombudsmen in 'provid[ing] effective remedies for European citizens' is discussed in Lord Woolf's report on the increasing workload of the ECtHR.[151] One of the 'key principles' recognised therein is that 'there should be increased recourse to national ombudsmen and other methods of alternative dispute resolution'.[152] It is underlined that the Council of Europe has acknowledged the contribution of non-judicial entities to the protection of human rights, whereas the 'welcome growth' of such institutions over the last 15 years is also mentioned.[153]

Finally, the EU's approach may sit uncomfortably with the Union's leading role in the protection of fundamental rights.[154] The ad hoc approach endorsed by the Strasbourg Court in the simultaneous presence of Article 6 ECHR leaves the EU in the position of excluding Charter-wise the right of citizens to extra-judicial redress in cases involving EU law. Consequently, if we consider the accession of the EU to the ECHR as a move confirming the attachment of the EU to the values defended by Strasbourg, the EU could indeed find ways to promote one's right to extra-judicial redress, in cases where such an avenue satisfies all the (high) requirements of effectiveness.

[146] White and Ovey (n 56) 135.

[147] Kucsko-Stadlmayer (n 124) 10.

[148] Nontheless, Italy does not have a national Ombudsman, but has established several regional ombudsmen. Germany has a Petitions Committee and Austria a board of three members. For details, see Kucsko-Stadlmayer (n 124).

[149] See above n 27.

[150] Primarily because the courts produce binding decisions. Compare section IV above.

[151] Lord Woolf et al, 'Review of the Working Methods of the European Court of Human Rights' (2005) 32. For further discussion see Mowbray (n 56) 61.

[152] Ibid, 4.

[153] Ibid, 31. See further ibid, 32–33, 47.

[154] Guaranteeing a protection of 'high quality', as acknowledged by the ECtHR in *Bosphorus*. See Lock (n 4) 797. See also Art 2 TEU. For a thorough discussion see G de Búrca, 'The Evolution of EU Human Rights Law' in P Craig and G de Búrca (eds), *The Evolution of EU Law* (Oxford, Oxford University Press, 2011) 465.

In sum, it is submitted that after the EU's accession to the ECHR, the merger of Articles 6 and 13 ECHR under Article 47 CFR does not entail the ideal constitutional choice vis-a-vis the protection of the individual.

VI. CONCLUSION

Undeniably, extra-judicial mechanisms will be of significance in the post-accession era too. The aim of these mechanisms is not, of course, to replace the role of courts as the guardians of the rule of law, but to serve citizens as complementary (but not necessarily substitutionary)[155] institutions. In this context, this chapter has argued that despite its good intentions, the merger of Articles 6 and 13 ECHR into Article 47 CFR does not constitute the ideal constitutional choice for the individual, especially in the light of the EU's accession to the ECHR and taking into account the prior involvement of the CJEU. The policy-oriented and potentially legal challenges may be summarised as follows. The *in concreto* approach on Article 13 by the ECtHR is not reflected in Article 47 CFR and this creates an asymmetry: even though Article 13 ECHR does not recognise a specific right to extra-judicial redress, it does not *preclude* non-judicial bodies (under strict conditions) either, whereas the ECtHR has also held that in very specific cases, recourse to a non-judicial entity might satisfy the exigencies of Article 35(1) ECHR. Since this account subscribes to the preservation of the autonomy of the EU's legal order,[156] the CJEU would need to turn to the CFR's final clauses and/or to the principle of 'effective' national procedural autonomy with a view to remedying this differentiation. Technically, the possibility of the non-activation of the prior involvement mechanism, whenever the applicant initially turns to an 'effective' extra-judicial body, may be assessed as remote, regardless of the choice of the respondent; the rationale of the mechanism is essentially to enable the CJEU to have its say in the generally limited occasions that this will be deemed necessary.

Further, the merger of Articles 6 and 13 ECHR deprives—always Charter-wise—citizens from a right to an effective remedy against excessive judicial domestic proceedings, as recognised in *Kudła*; the CJEU jurisprudence on 'effective' national remedies could provide for a suitable platform to recognise such a right in the EU framework. Moreover, it is questionable whether Article 47 CFR aligns with Article 19(1) TEU (which leaves Member States with some discretion 'to ensure effective legal protection in the fields covered by Union law'). From a policy-oriented perspective, it is therefore unclear whether the protection offered by Article 47 is necessarily more *extensive* and in line with recent developments in constitutional and administrative law, highlighted inter alia in Lord Woolf's report. Finally, it may not reflect the leading position of the EU in the protection of human rights, which should arguably include the development and explicit recognition of new rights.

For all the above reasons, the separation of Article 47 CFR into its components would be a preferable regime of protection in the EU's post-accession constitutional framework. If such a separation is not currently feasible, it is nonetheless critical that the CJEU distinguishes between these rights via its jurisprudence, taking of course into account the relevant ECtHR case law. This solution might not be exactly what Jacob Söderman had wished for, but it would certainly constitute an improvement.

[155] For an interesting study compare K Heede 'Who Litigates at Union Level, and Where?' (2001) 26 *EL Rev* 509.
[156] Jacqué (n 10) 1016 et seq.

5

Election of EU Judge onto the Strasbourg Court

ANDREW DRZEMCZEWSKI*

I. INTRODUCTION

THE ARRANGEMENTS PERTAINING to the future election of the judge in respect of the European Union (EU) are somewhat more complicated than appears at first sight. This entails the need to understand, on the one hand, the role which the drafters of the European Convention on Human Rights (ECHR) assigned to the Parliamentary Assembly, a statutory body of the Council of Europe, and, on the other hand, arrangements by which the Assembly will need to ensure the 'representativity' of the European Parliament (EP) in its election process. These arrangements can—at the outset—be conveniently summarised in three distinct yet interrelated points, which I will endeavour to explain in more detail in this chapter.

First, Article 22 of the ECHR specifies that judges to the European Court of Human Rights (hereinafter the Strasbourg Court) 'shall be elected by the Parliamentary Assembly [of the Council of Europe] with respect to each High Contracting Party by a majority of votes cast from a list of three candidates nominated by the High Contracting Party'. When the EU accedes to the Convention, the judge elected in respect of the EU will possess the same status and duties as all other judges on the Strasbourg Court and the EP will be given the right to participate in the Assembly's election process.

Second, according to the present version of the draft Accession Agreement, the EP 'shall be entitled to participate, with the right to vote, in the sittings of the Parliamentary Assembly of the Council of Europe whenever the Assembly exercises its functions related to the election of judges'.[1] While the draft instrument specifies that the 'number of representatives of the EP shall be the same as the highest number of representatives to which any State is entitled under Article 26 of the Statute of the Council of Europe [presently 18]', it leaves the details of EP participation in the Parliamentary Assembly's relevant bodies for the Assembly to determine, in cooperation with the EP.[2]

* Head of the Legal Affairs and Human Rights Department of the Parliamentary Assembly of the Council of Europe, Strasbourg, France.

[1] Full title: Draft Revised Agreement on the Accession of the European Union to the Convention for the Protection of Human Rights and Fundamental Freedoms (ECHR), appended to the 'Final report to the CDDH' (Steering Committee for Human Rights: Fifth negotiation meeting between the CDDH ad hoc Negotiation Group and the European Commission on the accession of the European Union to the European Convention on Human Rights), document 47+1 (2013)008, of 5 April 2013 Appendix I, Art 6, para 1, available at www.coe.int/t/dghl/standardsetting/hrpolicy/accession/meeting_reports_EN.asp.

[2] See draft Article 6, paras 1 and 2 (and paras 67–69 of the draft Explanatory Report).

And last, but not least, a 'Joint Informal Body', consisting of representatives of both parliamentary institutions, had a series of meetings in 2011 and 2012 in order to discuss the modalities of EP 'representativity' within the Assembly when the latter elects judges to the Strasbourg Court (Article 6 of the draft Accession Agreement). This will entail, in addition, arrangements whereby a representative of the EP will have a right to take part and vote when the election of judges to the Strasbourg Court is on the Assembly's Bureau agenda and when the Assembly's Sub-Committee on the Election of Judges to the Strasbourg Court interviews candidates.[3]

II. THE ELECTION OF JUDGES BY THE PARLIAMENTARY ASSEMBLY

A. The Institutional Framework

The Council of Europe (hereinafter 'the Council'), based in Strasbourg, was founded in 1949 with the aim of creating a democratic area throughout the continent, based on the fundamental values of human rights protection, pluralistic democracy and the rule of law. Founded by 10 countries, the Council presently has 47 Member States, with a combined population of some 800 million persons. All of the Council's Member States are parties to the ECHR and are subject to the compulsory jurisdiction of the Strasbourg Court.

The Parliamentary Assembly of the Council of Europe (hereinafter 'the Assembly') is assigned the function of 'deliberative organ' by the Statute of the Organisation.[4] In addition, it possessed the important role—within the Council—of electing judges of the Strasbourg Court, the European Commissioner for Human Rights and the Secretary General of the Organisation. The Assembly is comprised of 636 nationally elected parliamentarians (318 representatives and 318 substitutes) from the parliaments of the Member States of the Council,[5] with the balance of political parties within each national delegation reflecting the proportions of the various parties in their respective national parliaments. The vast majority of members belong to one of the Assembly's five organised political groups: the Group of the European People's Party (EPP/CD), the Socialist Group (SOC), the Alliance of Liberals and Democrats for Europe (ALDE), the European Democrat Group (EDG) and the Group of the Unified European Left (UEL).

The substantive work of the Assembly, especially the preparation of reports for adoption as 'resolutions' and/or 'recommendations' addressed to the Committee of Ministers, is in most instances carried out by the Assembly's eight permanent committees. Insofar as the election of judges to the Strasbourg Court is concerned, suffice it for the present purposes

[3] A description of the manner in which the Sub-Committee functions can be found in A Drzemczewski, 'Election of Judges to the Strasbourg Court: An Overview' (2010) 4 *European Human Rights Law Review* 377.

[4] The Assembly, alongside the Committee of Ministers, is one of two statutory organs of the Council. For details on its role and functions, see the Assembly's website at http://assembly.coe.int/DefaultE.asp. See also *Members Handbook, Parliamentary Assembly of the Council of Europe* (September 2012) at http://assembly.coe.int/AboutUs/APCE_MembersHandbookE.pdf.

[5] The number of members allocated to each national delegation is proposed by the Assembly when giving its opinion on the accession of the state to the Council, with the main criteria being population size: see Article 26 of the Statute of the Organisation (which has undergone successive modifications as additional states have become members of the Council), which can be found at http://assembly.coe.int/RulesofProcedure/Statute/Statut_CE_2008.pdf.

to note that the Committee on Legal Affairs and Human Rights (AS/Jur), one of the eight permanent committees, has a sub-committee specifically constituted for this purpose. This sub-committee, namely the Sub-Committee on the Election of Judges to the European Court of Human Rights—whose members are designated by political groups—has been mandated by the Assembly to make proposals prior to the vote in plenary, after having studied the curriculum vitae and interviewed all candidates for the post of judge (as will be explained below).[6]

B. The Normative Framework

The control mechanism of the ECHR, negotiated back in 1950 and in force since 1953, was substantially overhauled and streamlined in 1994 by Protocol No 11. In addition, since 1998 individuals, after having exhausted all domestic remedies, can seise the Strasbourg Court directly with respect to alleged violations of the ECHR and its protocols.[7]

The Strasbourg Court is made up of judges resident in Strasbourg and operating on a full-time basis. The number of judges is equal to that of the High Contracting Parties. Since the entry into force of Protocol No 14 to the ECHR in 2010, judges are elected for a single term of office of nine years and must retire when they reach the age of 70.[8] When amending Protocol No 15 enters into force, judges will, in effect, be able to stay in office until the age of 74.

Article 21(1) of the ECHR stipulates that:

> The judges shall be of high moral character and must either possess the qualifications required for appointment to high judicial office or be jurisconsults of recognised competence.

And, as already indicated, according to Article 22 of the ECHR:

> The judges shall be elected by the Parliamentary Assembly with respect to each High Contracting Party by a majority of votes cast from a list of three candidates nominated by the High Contracting Party.

Paragraph 4 of Parliamentary Assembly Resolution 1646 (2009) specifies that:

> [T]he Assembly recalls that in addition to the criteria specified in Article 21 § 1 of the Convention, as well as the gender requirement,[9] states should, when selecting and subsequently nominating candidates to the Court, comply with the following requirements:
>
> 4.1. issue public and open calls for candidatures;
>
> 4.2. when submitting the names of candidates to the Assembly, describe the manner in which they had been selected;
>
> 4.3. transmit the names of candidates to the Assembly in alphabetical order;

[6] See n 3 above. An overview of work undertaken by the AS/Jur can be found on the Assembly's portal at http://assembly.coe.int/Main.asp?link=/Committee/JUR/role_E.htm.

[7] See A Drzemczewski, 'A Major Overhaul of the ECHR Control Mechanism: Protocol No. 11' in *Collected Courses of the Academy of European Law 1995*, vol IV, Book 2 (The Hague, Martinus Nijhoff, 1997) 121–244.

[8] Article 23(1)–(3) of the Convention stipulates: '1. The judges shall be elected for a period of nine years. They may not be re-elected. 2. The terms of office of judges shall expire when they reach the age of 70. 3. The judges shall hold office until replaced. They shall, however, continue to deal with such cases as they already have under consideration.'

[9] For more details, see 'Procedure for Electing Judges to the European Court of Human Rights', document AS/Jur/Inf (2014) 03 rev 1 www.assembly.coe.int/CommitteeDocs/2014/ajinfdoc03_2014.pdf.

4.4. candidates should possess an active knowledge of one and a passive knowledge of the other official language of the Council of Europe (see model curriculum vitae appended hereto);[10] and

4.5. that, if possible, no candidate should be submitted whose election might result in the necessity to appoint an ad hoc judge.[11]

This text consolidated and reinforced recommendations made to states in 2004 when governments were asked to ensure, inter alia, 'that a call for candidatures has been issued through the specialised press' and that 'every list contains candidates of both sexes' (paragraph 19 of Assembly Recommendation 1649 (2004)). Indeed, the last two sentences in paragraph 2 of Resolution 1646 (2009) specify that:

> In the absence of a real choice among the candidates submitted by a state party to the Convention, the Assembly shall reject lists submitted to it. In addition, in the absence of a fair, transparent and consistent national selection procedure, the Assembly may reject such lists.

This Resolution is based on a report of the Committee on Legal Affairs and Human Rights (document 11767 of 2008), which emphasised the need for more fairness and transparency in national selection procedures,[12] as well as the need for candidates to possess a number of years of relevant (judicial) work experience and a knowledge of both working languages of the Council of Europe. It is also important to underline, in this context, that the Assembly will accept single-sex lists of candidates only if the sex is under-represented (less than 40 per cent of judges) or if exceptional circumstances exist to derogate from this rule.[13]

[10] The text of the model curriculum can be accessed at Resolution 1646 (2009) http://assembly.coe.int/Mainf.asp?link=/Documents/AdoptedText/ta09/ERES1646.htm. It is also available on the Assembly's website: http://assembly.coe.int/CommitteeDocs/2009/ModelCVEN.doc.

[11] The issue of ad hoc judges is not broached in this contribution, although it is (also) relevant in the context of the EU's need to provide a list of such judges to the Court: see Article 26(4) of the Convention and Assembly document 12827 issued in 2011, entitled 'Ad hoc Judges at the European Court of Human Rights', http://assembly.coe.int/ASP/Doc/XrefViewPDF.asp?FileID=13035&Language=EN. It is understood that procedures for the designation of a list of three to five ad hoc judges, as indicated in the Strasbourg Court's Rules (Rule 29), have been foreseen in the internal EU Council rules being prepared by the FREMP (Working Party on Fundamental Rights, Citizens Rights and Free Movement of Persons).

[12] Recently reinforced by Guidelines of the Committee of Ministers on the selection of candidates for the post of judge at the European Court of Human Rights, adopted on 28 March 2012. In 2010, the Committee of Ministers also set up an advisory panel of experts on candidates for election as judges to the Court. Their function is to advise states parties to the Convention—*before* the latter transmit lists of candidates to the Assembly—whether candidates for election meet the criteria stipulated in Article 21(1) of the Convention (see Resolution CM/Res(2010)26 on the establishment of an Advisory Panel of Experts on Candidates for Election as Judge to the European Court of Human Rights. The panel is composed of seven personalities: see Committee of Ministers decision of 8 December 2010). The role of this advisory panel must not be confused, as it sometimes is, with the panel set up by virtue of Article 255 of the Treaty on the Functioning of the European Union, as explained in § 11 of the AS/Jur's report on this subject (Assembly document 12391 of 7 October 2010, http://assembly.coe.int/ASP/Doc/XrefViewPDF.asp?FileID=12764&Language=EN, which led to the adoption of Resolution Assembly Resolution 1764 (2010)).

[13] See Assembly Resolution 1366 (2004), as modified by Resolutions 1426 (2005), 1627 (2008) and 1841 (2011), paras 3 and 4. In para 4 it is specified that such 'exceptional circumstances' exist 'where a Contracting Party has taken all the necessary and appropriate steps to ensure that the list contains candidates of both sexes meeting the requirements of Article 21 § 1 of the European Convention on Human Rights'. Such exceptional circumstances must be duly so determined by a two-thirds majority of the Sub-Committee on the Election of Judges, whose position subsequently needs to be endorsed by the Assembly in the framework of a Progress Report of the Assembly's Bureau. As concerns the issue of 'affirmative action' with respect to an under-represented sex, see, in particular, the Strasbourg Court's first Advisory Opinion referred to in my article cited in n 3 above.

C. The Election Procedure

As already indicated above, Article 22 of the ECHR specifies that judges are elected by the Parliamentary Assembly from a list of three candidates nominated by a High Contracting Party. To the extent possible, parties to the ECHR are allowed ample time to organise an open call for candidatures prior to the list's transmission. Upon receipt of the lists by the Assembly, the curriculum vitae of the candidates are translated, if need be, and then placed on the Assembly's portal, which can be accessed by the public at large. The Assembly sets aside for itself a certain time for its own election procedure depending on the scheduling of its plenary meetings.

To assist it in making its decision as to which candidate ought to be elected, the Assembly invites its specifically constituted—by political groups—Sub-Committee on the Election of Judges to make recommendations based on personal interviews with all the candidates and assessments of their curriculum vitae. The document containing these recommendations is made available to Assembly members in the framework of the Progress Report of the Bureau of the Assembly (since 2013 the Sub-Committee has established a practice of making public its recommendations).

The manner in which the system of interviews functions is as follows: each candidate is interviewed for 30 minutes, with the first five minutes of the interview being allotted for a short self-presentation if the candidate so wishes. The candidate is informed of the possibility of making such a presentation by the Secretariat in the letter convening him or her for interview. Members of the Sub-Committee then pose questions, in English or in French, and the candidate responds in either or both of these languages; simultaneous interpretation is provided. The interviews are carried out in the alphabetical order of the names of candidates. After all three candidates have been interviewed, the Chairperson provides Sub-Committee members with a brief summary of his or her first impressions of the candidates, after which a general discussion ensues. A vote is then taken—by secret ballot—after which the Chairperson announces the result of the vote. This procedure is confidential.

The Sub-Committee's report is then transmitted to the Bureau of the Assembly. If the report does not propose rejection of a list, the Bureau forwards copies of the said report to Assembly members in good time before voting in plenary commences. The Sub-Committee may, if it so wishes, decide to declassify such reports.[14]

On the basis of the candidatures transmitted to it, the Assembly elects the judges to the Strasbourg Court during its part-sessions in Strasbourg.[15] The candidate who has obtained an absolute majority of votes cast is declared to be elected a member of the Court. If no candidate obtains an absolute majority, a second ballot is held on the next day, after which the candidate who has obtained a relative majority of the votes cast is declared to be elected. Election results are publicly announced by the President of the Assembly during the part-session.[16]

[14] For further details, see the article I have written on this subject (n 3). It is interesting to note, in this connection, the Sub-Committee's recent practice of deciding to 'declassify' its reports (remove confidentiality) when transmitting them to the Bureau, as indicated above.

[15] Modalities for the election procedure can be found in the Appendix to Assembly Resolution 1432 (2005), reproduced in Rules of Procedure of the Assembly, Strasbourg, January 2012, at 154.

[16] See para 8 of Assembly Resolution 1726 (2010), adopted on 29 April 2010, which specifies when judges' terms of office commence. This paragraph reads: '[The Assembly] confirms its position that the nine-year term

III. THE ELECTION OF THE JUDGE IN RESPECT OF THE EU

A. The Institutional Framework

As indicated in the introduction, whereas negotiations at the intergovernmental level concerning EU accession to the ECHR have—understandably—taken a considerable time, negotiations at the Assembly-EP level, with respect to the election of a judge in respect of the EU, were concluded with remarkable speed; indeed, they may be cited as a model of excellent inter-parliamentary co-operation. A 'Joint Informal Body',[17] consisting of representatives of both parliamentary institutions, managed, after three meetings (one in Brussels on 14 March 2011 and two in Paris on 15 June 2011 and 19 June 2012) to work out the modalities of EP 'representativity' within the Parliamentary Assembly when the latter elects judges to the Strasbourg Court.[18] The draft Association Agreement has already taken these arrangements into account.

At the intergovernmental level, it was decided that Article 22 of the ECHR does not need amendment. Instead, express mention is made, in the Accession Agreement, of the fact that a delegation of the EP will participate, with a right to vote, in the sittings of the Assembly (and its relevant bodies) whenever the Assembly exercises its functions relating to the election of judges to the Strasbourg Court.

B. The Procedure Envisaged

Article 6 of the draft Accession Agreement, entitled 'Election of judges', reads:

1. A delegation of the European Parliament shall be entitled to participate, with the right to vote, in the sittings of the Parliamentary Assembly of the Council of Europe whenever the Assembly exercises its functions related to the election of judges in accordance with Article 22 of the Convention. The number of representatives of the European Parliament shall be the same as the highest number of representatives to which any State is entitled under Article 26 of the Statute of the Council of Europe.
2. The modalities of the participation of representatives of the European Parliament in the sittings of the Parliamentary Assembly of the Council of Europe and its relevant bodies shall be defined by the Parliamentary Assembly of the Council of Europe, in cooperation with the European Parliament.

of office of a judge elected by the Assembly to the Court shall commence from the date of taking up of his/her duties, and in any event no later than three months after his/her election. However, if the election takes place more than three months before the seat of the outgoing judge becomes vacant, the term of office shall commence the day the seat becomes vacant. If the election takes place less than three months before the seat of the outgoing judge becomes vacant, the elected judge shall take up his/her duties as soon as possible after the seat becomes vacant and the term of office shall commence as from then and in any event no later than three months after his/her election.'

[17] This Joint Informal Body was established upon the initiative of the EP 'in order to coordinate information sharing' (see § 34 of EP Resolution, of 19 May 2010, on the institutional aspects of the accession to the EU to the ECHR, (2009/2241 (INI)).

[18] See, in particular, the synopses of the last two meetings of the Joint Informal Body which are available on the Assembly's website at www.assembly.coe.int/committee/BUR/2011/BURJointInformalBodyE.pdf and www.assembly.coe.int/committee/BUR/2012/BURJointInformalBodyE.pdf.

When the EU accedes to the ECHR, the judge elected in respect of the EU will possess the same status and duties as all other judges on the Strasbourg Court and the EP will be given the right to participate in the Assembly's election process.[19]

The need to ensure the 'equal footing' of Parties to the ECHR has been given a broad interpretation by the Assembly (as well as those negotiating the Accession Agreement), with the result that the EU's parliamentary body (representatives of the EP) are, for the specific purpose of the election of judges, given 'equivalent' voting rights as provided to the parliamentary delegations of all the other State Parties to the ECHR. It may be recalled, in this connection, that membership of the Parliamentary Assembly is dealt with in the 1949 Statute of the Council of Europe (Articles 22–35), Article 25a of which specifies that: 'The Consultative [Parliamentary] Assembly shall consist of representatives of each member, elected by its parliament from among the members thereof, or appointed from among the members of that parliament.' In addition, Article 26 indicates the number of representatives each Member State of the Council of Europe is entitled to have in the Assembly. All expenses relating to representation in the Assembly are borne by Member States (presently 47 states; Article 38(a) of the Statute of the Council of Europe). Here, it was agreed that the EP be entitled to the same number of representatives in the Assembly as the state(s) entitled to the highest number of representatives, as specified in Article 26 of the Statute. This means that the EP delegation will consist of 18 members, as is the case at present in respect of five Council of Europe Member States, namely France, Germany, Italy, the Russian Federation and the UK. The EU will also contribute, as indicated in draft Article 8 of the Accession Agreement, 34 per cent of what the other five 'grands payeurs' contribute to the annual ordinary budget of the Council of Europe; this sum represents the expenditure taken into account which is directly related to the functioning of the ECHR.[20]

The parliamentary 'Joint Informal Body' also had to determine how best to ensure some form of EP 'representativity' within two bodies of the Assembly, namely the Sub-Committee on the Election of Judges and the Bureau, when these bodies act in the context of the Assembly's election process for judges.

As indicated in section II above, in order to make an informed choice when voting for a candidate, the Assembly invites its 17-member Sub-Committee on the Election of Judges to the European Court of Human Rights of the Committee on Legal Affairs and Human Rights (AS/Jur)[21] to make recommendations based on personal interviews with all candidates and assessments of their curriculum vitae. This Sub-Committee is specifically constituted for this purpose by the Assembly and, as already explained, its members are designated by the Assembly's five political groups from among members of the AS/Jur.[22]

To agree, in principle, to EP 'representativity' within the Sub-Committee on the Election of Judges is simple, but to determine how this ought to be envisaged is potentially problematic. The composition of the Sub-Committee is determined, on an annual basis, by the five political groups within the Assembly, with apportionment being determined mainly

[19] All documents pertaining to the negotiations are accessible online at http://www.coe.int/t/dghl/standardsetting/hrpolicy/Accession/default_en.asp (Directorate General of Human Rights and Legal Affairs, Council of Europe). See also n 1 above.

[20] For a detailed explanation, see Article 8 of the draft Accession Agreement and paras 93–99 of the draft Explanatory Report to the Accession Agreement.

[21] The Chairperson of the AS/Jur is an ex officio member of the Sub-Committee: see Rule 48.6 of the Assembly's Rules of Procedure.

[22] A list of the political groups is to be found in section I above.

but not exclusively by recourse to the so-called 'D'Hondt principle'.[23] But how could the EP, which itself possesses seven political groups, fit into this? Negotiations, on an annual basis, relating to the EP's involvement in the Assembly's internal political group arrangements could be complicated in terms of inter-institutional negotiations between (and implementation within) the two respective parliamentary bodies. Fortunately, the Joint Informal Body came up with a pragmatic solution: it was agreed that the EP would designate one member (and one alternative) to 'represent' the EP—with the right to vote—within the Sub-Committee when the latter interviews candidates. Although this solution appears to provide a 'privileged status' to a contracting party within a Sub-Committee whose composition is determined by political groups, this was the price to pay in order to find a simple, easy-to-implement solution in what might otherwise have necessitated the putting into place of an extremely complex and time-consuming procedure.

The Sub-Committee's recommendation(s), prepared by its Chairperson, are transmitted to the Bureau of the Assembly. If the report does not propose rejection of a list (which has occurred in the past when the gender requirement had not been complied with, or where there existed no real choice among candidates submitted), the Bureau forwards copies of the said report to Assembly members in good time before voting in plenary commences. That said, if a proposal is made to reject a list, this must be ratified by the Assembly in the framework of a Progress Report. Hence, so it was noted, the utility of an EP representative's presence in the Bureau when such issues are on the agenda. The Joint Informal Body therefore agreed to the proposal that an ex officio participation of a member of the EP should be ensured when the subject of the election of judges is discussed by the Bureau. The EP will therefore designate one representative to the Assembly's Bureau—with the right to vote—when the Bureau deals with the Sub-Committee's reports.

The above procedure may be summarised thus:

— Every time the plenary Assembly elects judges to the Strasbourg Court, 18 members of the EP will be entitled to take part in such elections.
— Whenever the Bureau has the subject of election of judges on its agenda, one representative of the EP, with a right to vote, will be entitled to take part in the meetings.
— One member of the EP (with an alternate) will be entitled to sit, with the right to vote, ex officio on the Assembly's Sub-Committee on the Election of Judges to the European Court of Human Rights when the Sub-Committee—whose composition is determined by the Parliamentary Assembly's political groups—interviews candidates and provides recommendations to the plenary Assembly to enable the latter to make an informed choice when it elects judges.

Once the Accession Agreement has been formally adopted, the above arrangements will need to be approved by the Parliamentary Assembly and the EP in accordance with their respective internal procedures. Insofar as the Assembly is concerned, this is likely to be done in the form of a Resolution, in which proposals to changes the Assembly's Rules of Procedure are likely to be included.

[23] This is a mathematical formula, named after a Belgian mathematician, which ensures that representation is fairly distributed in proportion to the number of seats held in the Assembly as a whole. It requires the number of seats for each political group to be divided successively by a series of divisors (1, 2, 3, 4), with seats on committees allocated successively to political groups to secure the highest resulting quotient or average. The method is also used in the parliamentary elections of certain Member States of the Council of Europe.

Part II

Allocation of Responsibility and the Co-respondent Mechanism

6

A European Law of International Responsibility?

The Articles on the Responsibility of International Organisations and the EU

JEAN D'ASPREMONT*

PRACTICE HAS BORNE witness to recurring pleas by regional economic integration organisations (REIOs)—and especially by the European Union (EU), which is the organisation most often referred to within the concept of REIOs—that the determination of their responsibility ought not to be entirely subjected to the general regime of responsibility for internationally wrongful acts. In the case of REIOs such as the EU, such pleas have mostly been voiced in relation to the question of attribution. It is well known that in the first instance, the Special Rapporteur of the International Law Commission (ILC), in the course of the preparation of the Articles on the Responsibility of International Organizations for Internationally Wrongful Acts (ARIO), shied away from accommodating such requests and expressly recognising such specificities, and the specific rules associated with them previously, before changing its position and acknowledging that such a possibility falls within the ambit of the *lex specialis* provisions.[1]

The first section of this chapter will briefly describe the plea made by the EU for recognition of special rules of responsibility for REIOs, with an emphasis on rules on attribution. Section II will then critically evaluate this claim and the way it was addressed by the ILC in its work on the ARIO. Arguing that the ARIO leaves enough room for the development of rules of international responsibility specific to REIOs, section III will then evaluate the possible source for such special rules and gauge the value of EU law for the sake of the *lex specialis* principle. Section IV will finally turn to the draft Accession Agreement of the EU to the European Convention on Human Rights (ECHR) and will reflect on

* Chair of Public International Law, University of Manchester and Professor of International Legal Theory at the University of Amsterdam. Author SSRN page: http://ssrn.com/author=736816. Many thanks to Christiane Ahlborn for her insightful comments on an earlier draft and to Madeleine Gorman for her assistance.

[1] On the concept of *lex specialis* in the context of the law of responsibility, see generally B Simma and D Pulkowski, 'Of Planets and the Universe: Self-contained Regimes in International Law' (2006) 17 *EJIL* 483; see also C Ahlborn, 'The Rules of International Organizations and the Law of International Responsibility' (2011) 8 *International Organizations Law Review* 391.

the extent to which the mechanism set up on that occasion could be conducive to the emergence of special rules of international responsibility for the EU.

I. THE PLEA FOR EUROPEAN RULES OF INTERNATIONAL RESPONSIBILITY

The claim by the European Commission that the European Community (EC), and subsequently the EU, cannot be considered as falling within the generic definition of international organisations was voiced as early as the commencement of the examination of the topic of responsibility of international organisations by the ILC.[2] Notably, the EU has repeatedly argued for the necessity of special rules of attribution of conduct for REIOs.[3] In particular, invoking some allegedly supportive practice of the World Trade Organization (WTO),[4] the EU has been advocating that the conduct of its Member States enforcing EU decisions in areas of exclusive competence—and similar situations—should be construed as conduct of the EU, for the Member States must, in these situations, be considered de facto organs.[5] This contention was underpinned by the argument that the normative control—that is, the control that originates in a conferral of power by opposition to a purely factual control—exercised by the EU over the Member States when the latter are solely implementing EU legislation should be considered, for the sake of international responsibility, as making the conduct of the Member States the conduct of the EU.[6]

The reasons for such a plea are well known. There is a general tendency for the EU—like the United Nations—to 'generously' claim responsibility for actions pertaining to its areas of competence in a way that may lead one to think that it construes responsibility with autonomous identity and independence on the international plane. In this specific case, the

[2] See Statement of the European Commission to the UNGA Sixth Committee (58th Session), 27 October 2003 (22 December 2003) UN Doc A/C.6/58/SR.14, paras 13–14; see also EU Presidency Statement on the ILC Report, 2004, New York (5 November 2004) available at www.europa-eu-un.org/articles/en/article_4020_en.htm, cited by F Hoffmeister, 'Litigating against the European Union and its Member States: Who Responds under the ILC's Draft Articles on International Responsibility of International Organizations?' (2010) 21 *EJIL* 728.

[3] See the comments by the European Commission, 'Responsibility of International Organizations, Comments and Observations Received from International Organizations' (3 May–4 June and 5 July–6 August 2004) UN Doc A/CN.4/545, 18 and (26 April–3 June and 4 July–12 August 2011) UN Doc A/CN.4/637, 7.

[4] See WTO Panel Report, European Communities ± Geographic Indications (15 March 2005) WT/DS174/R [7.98] and [7.725]; see also WTO Panel Report, European Communities ± Selected Customs Matters (16 June 2006) WT/DS315/R and WTO Appellate Body Report, European Communities—Selected Customs Matters (13 November 2006) WT/DS315/AB/R; WTO Panel Report, European Communities ± Biotech (29 September 2006) WT/DS 291/R [7.101]. For some critical remarks on the use of this case law, see F Messineo, 'Multiple Attribution of Conduct' in A Nollkaemper and I Plakokefalos (eds), *Principles of Shared Responsibility* (forthcoming), SHARES Research Paper No 2012-11, available at www.sharesproject.nl.

[5] This has usually been uncontested from the standpoint of EU law; see E Paasivirta and PJ Kuyper, 'Does One Size Fit All? The European Community and the Responsibility of International Organizations' (2005) 36 *Netherlands Yearbook of International Law*, 169, 192.

[6] S Talmon, 'Responsibility of International Organizations: Does the European Community Require Special Treatment?' in M Ragazzi (ed), *International Responsibility Today: Essays in Memory of Oscar Schachter* (Leiden, Brill, 2005) 414. The debate about normative control has mostly swirled around the situation of state organs put at the disposal of international organisations, as is envisaged in Article 7 of the ARIO. This is the so-called 'peacekeeping provision', as it mostly addresses questions of responsibility in the case of peacekeeping operations. In this respect, it is interesting to note that the UN has always claimed that wrongful conduct by peacekeepers ought to be dealt with from the vantage point of Article 6 (see UN Doc A/CN.4/637/Add.1 (2011) 15–17), whilst the Special Rapporteur claimed that this rule was a codification of UN practice.

European Commission claimed that the EU/EC constituted a REIO,[7] which could not be conflated with other international organisations and accordingly could not be submitted to the whole general regime being designed by the ILC. The specific features emphasised by the European Commission can be summarised as follows.[8] In contrast to other less integrated international organisations, the EU is said to rest on a full transfer of 'sovereign powers'[9] in certain areas where states have relinquished public power to the benefit of permanent structures at the supranational level, with a view to achieving certain common objectives.[10]

In the first instance, these contentions were largely ignored. In its 2004 Report, the ILC Special Rapporteur only envisaged the supplementary possibility of specific responsibility of the EU in the case of enforcement action by Member States, which could result in the EU's responsibility under the hypothesis of attribution of responsibility, but not from a situation of attribution of conduct. In particular, the EU could incur responsibility for an act still formally attributable to its Member States by virtue of its binding decisions.[11] As such, no special rule of attribution of conduct was designed.

Such a position met with strong criticism in the literature. It was portrayed as a 'second-best' option,[12] and called for the inclusion of a special provision for cases where Member States are the de facto organs of the EU were made.[13] Although the literature is replete with some semantic instability with respect to the distinction between de facto organs and

[7] The notion of REIOs is in substance closely associated with the conclusion of multilateral agreements that were meant to be open to the EU. The most famous examples include Article 305(1)(f) of UNCLOS; the 1995 UN Fish Stocks Agreement; the 1994 WTO Agreement; the Energy Charter Treaty (1994) (which expressly uses the term REIO); Article 13 of the 1985 Vienna Convention for the Protection of the Ozone Layer; Article 22 of the 2000 UNFCC; Article 34 of the 1992 Convention on Biological Diversity; Article 36 of the 2000 Cartagena Protocol in Biosafety; and the 2000 UN Convention Against Corruption. For further insights on this notion, see Paasivirta and Kuyper (n 5) 205–12.

[8] On the specific features of the EU justifying such a claim, see Paasivirta and Kuyper (n 5) 174–83; D Curtin, 'The Constitutional Structure of the Union: A Europe of Bits and Pieces' (1993) 30 *CMLR* 17–69; R Wessel, 'Division of International Responsibility between the EU and its Member States in the Area of Foreign, Security and Defence Policy' (2011) 3 *Amsterdam Law Forum* 42–47. See also M Cremona, 'External Relations of the EU and the Member States: Competence, Mixed Agreements, International Responsibility, and Effects of International Law' (2006) 22 *EUI Working Papers, Law* 2–25 (including the particular questions raised by mixed agreements).

[9] D Sarooshi, *International Organizations and Their Exercise of Sovereign Powers* (Oxford, Oxford University Press, 2005) 69 ff.

[10] The exclusive competences of the EU, where Member States only have enforcing responsibilities, are customs, union, competition, monetary policy, commercial policy and the conservation of marine biological resources. Matters slightly more complicated in areas of shared competence include the environment, transport, agriculture, fisheries and consumer protection. See a description of these competences and the articulation between the experience of public power by the EU and that by the Member States in Paasivirta and Kuyper (n 5) 188–92.

[11] ILC Draft Articles on the Responsibility of International Organizations (3 August 2009) A/66/10, Article 17: 'Circumvention of international obligations through decisions and authorizations addressed to members: 1. An international organisation incurs international responsibility if it circumvents one of its international obligations by adopting a decision binding Member States or international organisations to commit an act that would be internationally wrongful if committed by the former organisation. 2. An international organisation incurs international responsibility if it circumvents one of its international obligations by authorising Member States or international organisations to commit an act that would be internationally wrongful if committed by the former organisation and the act in question is committed because of that authorisation. 3. Paragraphs 1 and 2 apply whether or not the act in question is internationally wrongful for the Member States or international organisations to which the decision or authorisation is addressed.' For a discussion of the application of this provision in the case of the EU, see Wessel (n 8) 37–40.

[12] See, eg, the comments by Hoffmeister (n 2) 729; see also the criticisms of this 'second-best' option by Paasivirta and Kuyper (n 5) 217–18.

[13] Paasivirta and Kuyper advocated the inclusion of the following provision: 'Without prejudice to article 4, in the case of a REIO the conduct of its member states and their authorities shall be considered as an act of the REIO

agents,[14] others have claimed that a sister provision to Article 5 of the Articles on State Responsibility (ASR)[15] should be included so as to cover situations where a Member State acts as 'agent' of the organisation.[16] The argument was also made that normative control should be elevated into a criterion for the attribution of conduct of a Member State to the organisation.[17]

Interestingly—and irrespective of whether this should be read as a reaction to these criticisms—the ILC changed its position during its 2009 session by explicitly recognising the possibility of a special rule of attribution that could fall within the ambit of the more general Article 64 on the principle of *lex specialis*.[18] Even though such an explicit acknowledgment is not strictly necessary for a *lex specialis* to come into play, reference was thus made, for the first time, to the possible existence of special rules in connection with 'the attribution to the European Union Community of conduct of States members of the Community when they implement binding acts of the Community'.[19] This approach is the one that eventually prevailed and now informs the final version of the ARIO, and especially Article 64. Although falling short of an explicit acknowledgment of a rule of attribution of conduct for the EU, this solution does not bar the general rules of attribution from yielding to any specific rule, including one possibly pertaining to the relations between the EU and its Member States. Even though the lack of express acknowledgement that normative control exercised by the EU could generate attribution of conduct was criticised,[20] the solution eventually endorsed by the ILC was positively received, even by the EU. In this respect, it has been argued that, during the negotiations leading to the Draft Agreement on Accession of the European Union to the European Convention on Human Rights, the EU went as far as explicitly abandoning its idea that Member States can in some circumstances act as organs of the EU.[21]

under international law to the extent that such conduct falls within the competencies of the REIO as determined by the rules of that REIO.' See Paasivirta and Kuyper (n 5) 216.

[14] See the criticism by C Ahlborn, 'The Rules of International Organizations and the Law of International Responsibility', ACIL Research Paper No 2011-03 (SHARES Series) 40–41.

[15] ILC Articles on Responsibility of States for Internationally Wrongful Acts (31 May 2001) A/56/10, Article 5: 'The conduct of a person or entity which is not an organ of the State under article 4 but which is empowered by the law of that State to exercise elements of the governmental authority shall be considered an act of the State under international law, provided the person or entity is acting in that capacity in the particular instance.'

[16] Talmon (n 6) 412.

[17] See Talmon (n 6).

[18] ILC, 'Report on the Work of its Sixty-First Session, Commentary on Draft Article 63' (4 May–5 June and 6 July–7 August 2009) UN Doc A/64/10, 173. See also the remarks by Hoffmeister (n 2) 729–30.

[19] ILC Report on Draft Article 63, 176, para 2.

[20] Hoffmeister (n 12) 746–47: 'The conduct of a State that executes the law or acts under the normative control of a regional economic integration organisation may be considered an act of that organisation under international law, taking account of the nature of the organisation's external competence and its international obligations in the field where the conduct occurred.' He calls for an explicit acknowledgment rather than the implicit one in Article 64.

[21] Gaja, ch 22 in this volume. Gaja writes: 'Last September, the EU proposed "to make explicit the attribution rule whereby acts of member States are and remain only attributable to them, even if they are acts of implementation of EU law". Thus, one has to assume that, like the *Bosphorus* judgment, the Accession Agreement will start from the premise that, if an organ of one of the Member States causes a breach of an obligation under the ECHR when implementing an EU rule, the act is attributed to that State which incurs responsibility.'

II. A NEED FOR AN EXPRESS ACKNOWLEDGMENT OF A EUROPEAN LAW OF INTERNATIONAL RESPONSIBILITY?

The argument could cogently be made that the debate that unfolded in the years 2004–11 on the need to recognise specific modes of attribution of conduct for the relation between REIOs and their Member States could have been avoided simply by recognising that the situation where states act as a de facto organ of the organisation is covered by the general principle governing the attribution of conduct. Indeed, it can be argued that, even without the addition of a sister provision to Article 5 of the ASR, conduct of Member States when enforcing EU legislation in areas such as customs, competition, monetary policy, commercial policy or the conservation of marine biological resources could fall under the general rule of Article 6 of the ARIO, according to which the conduct of an organ or agent of an international organisation in the performance of functions of that organ or agent shall be considered an act of that organisation under international law, whatever position the organ or agent holds in respect of the organisation.[22] In that sense, the argument could be made that when merely implementing and enforcing EU policies, Member States disappear behind the corporate veil[23] of the organisation[24] and constitute organs of that organisation, thereby making the design of a specific rule of attribution unnecessary.[25] This idea—that Member States can be an organ of an international organisation under Article 6 when implementing EU law—had been expressly rejected by Special Rapporteur Gaja,[26] invoking the cases of *Bosphorus*[27] and *Kadi*,[28] as well as a possible contradiction with the ASR.[29] He subsequently invoked the *Kokkelvisserij* case.[30] Certainly this reading of these controversial decisions, as well as their respective authority, could be contested. Other decisions also offer support for the exact opposite understanding.[31] Likewise, it is not certain whether the characterisation of Member States as organs of the EU in this case would necessarily entail a discrepancy with the ASR.[32]

Although simpler and more satisfactory conceptual routes than tackling the specificities of REIOs could have been followed, as was discussed above,[33] it is true that Article 64 leaves space for developing rules tailored to REIOs. This is why it does not seem worth bickering

[22] The argument has been compellingly made by Ahlborn (n 14) 38–39.

[23] On this notion, see C Brölmann, *The International Institutional Veil in Public International Law: International Organisations and the Law of Treaties* (Oxford, Hart Publishing, 2007).

[24] Ahlborn (n 14) 38–39.

[25] See, however, the specific situation addressed by Article 17 mentioned above (n 11).

[26] ILC, 'Seventh Report on Responsibility of International Organizations' (27 March 2009) UN Doc A/CN.4/610, 12–13, para 33.

[27] *Bosphorus Hava Yolları Turizm ve Ticaret Anonim Şirketi v Ireland*, App No 45036/98 (2005) 42 EHRR 1 [153].

[28] Joined Cases C-402/05 P and C-415/05 P *Kadi, Al Barakaat International Foundation v Council and Commission* [2008] ECR I-6351 [313].

[29] For some critical remarks on the case law invoked by the Special Rapporteur, see Messineo (n 4).

[30] *Cooperatieve Producentenorganisatie van de Nederlandse Kokkelvisserij UA v The Netherlands*, App No 13645/05 (2009). On the invocation of this case, see ILC, 'Eighth Report on Responsibility of International Organizations' (14 March 2011) UN Doc A/CN.4/640, 37.

[31] See WTO Panel Report, 'European Communities—Protection of Trademarks and Geographical Indications for Agricultural Products and Foodstuffs—Complaints by the United States' (20 April 2005) WT/DS293/R, para 7.725, which accepted that 'the European Communities explanation of what amount to its *sui generis* domestic constitutional arrangements that Community laws are generally not executed through authorities at Community level but rather through recourse to the authorities of its Member States act as de facto as organs of the Community, for which the Community would be responsible under WTO law and international law in general'.

[32] For a criticism of the motivation of the Special Rapporteur, see Ahlborn (n 14) 39–40.

[33] EU Commission (n 3).

over the deficiencies of that approach. Whilst it is not certain that the motives invoked by the Special Rapporteur for rejecting the possibility of Member States acting as de facto organs of the organisations are entirely convincing, there seems to be no need to (re-) engage with the normative and conceptual choices which have been made in the course of the work of the ILC, especially when it comes to rules pertaining to attribution. We can take for granted that the ARIO will not be amended and that possible subsequent steps in the codification process will not bring about any change with respect to the above-mentioned question of EU specificity.[34] Even the EU seems to have capitulated and accepted that its specificities are sufficiently accommodated by the avenue opened by Article 64, which, as was explained above, expressly acknowledged the theoretical possibility of special rules of attribution. The foregoing certainly does not mean that Article 64 is a panacea. Its wording is highly problematic, especially when it comes to the understanding of the rules of the organisation.[35] Yet, it comes with the explicit recognition that special rules of international responsibility in relation to REIOs like the EU may (have) come into existence, including with respect to attribution of conduct.

III. THE SOURCES OF A EUROPEAN LAW OF INTERNATIONAL RESPONSIBILITY

As was explained above, the conceptual approach for accommodating possible special rules of international responsibility was the object of variations in the course of the ILC's work on the responsibility of international organisations. It was eventually decided to address this question through a general *lex specialis* clause. For the sake of the argument made here, once the possibility of a European law of international responsibility is established, the question of where such special European rules would come from arises. In other words, acknowledging the possibility of a special law raises the question of its sources.

Such a question can be easily addressed when special rules of responsibility—and, in particular, special rules of attribution—are the object of express provisions in the regime concerned.[36] However, it is submitted here that the EU regime does not contain express provisions that put in place special rules of international responsibility of the EU and/or the Member States. According to this position, there are no express rules of international responsibility found under EU law, which constitute a *lex specialis* for the sake of the international responsibility of the EU and/or Member States.

In order to make this point, it must be understood as a preliminary matter that the rules of an organisation pertaining to its relation with its Member States are of an internal nature and therefore cannot constitute special rules for the sake of Article 64. Indeed, these rules, albeit dealing with questions of responsibility, constitute the internal law of

[34] On the epistemological consequences thereof, see J d'Aspremont, 'The Articles on the Responsibility of International Organizations: Magnifying the Fissures in the Law of International Responsibility' (2012) 9 *International Organizations Law Review*, available at http://papers.ssrn.com/sol3/papers.cfm?abstract_id=2163427.

[35] Ahlborn (n 14).

[36] Traditional examples of a regime providing for a special rule of attribution are found in Article 3 of the 4th Hague Convention and Article 91 of the 1st Additional Protocol to the Geneva Convention, whereby every state party is responsible for the violations committed by the members of its armed forces, irrespective of the capacity in which they acted when the wrongful act was committed. On this special rule, see J d'Aspremont and J de Hemptinne, *Droit international humanitaire* (Paris, Pedone, 2012) ch 13.

the organisation. As has been convincingly argued elsewhere, such an internal law of the organisation cannot in itself constitute *lex specialis*.[37] Indeed, rules of an internal nature cannot affect the functioning of the general regime of responsibility. This point was made very clear by the ILC in its commentary to the Vienna Convention on the Representation of States in their Relations with International Organizations.[38] On that occasion, Roberto Ago also emphasised that particular rules cannot prevail over a general rule unless the two rules share membership of the same legal order.[39] The international conventional character of the framework within which such arrangements are enshrined does not alter this conclusion. As pointed out by the ILC in its commentary to the ASR, 'international law does not permit a State to escape its international responsibility by a mere process of international subdivision'.[40] There is no reason why a different conclusion would hold for a REIO, which can accordingly not be seen as being in a position to generate specific rules of responsibility applicable to relations between it or its Member States and third states.

In the case of the relations of the EU with its Member States, the foregoing means that the internal rules of the EU about the distribution of competences cannot qualify as *lex specialis*. Put differently, the rules of the EU about the distribution of competences cannot be considered to have the same status as the rules of attribution of the general regime of international responsibility and accordingly cannot be considered 'special'. These rules of the allocation of competence between the EU and its Member States cannot be considered as special rules of attribution for the sake of international responsibility. They boil down to purely internal arrangements between the EU and its Member States and are merely rules of an internal nature.[41]

Interestingly, such a contention conflicts with the current wording of Article 64, which provides that: 'Such special rules of international law may be contained in the rules of the organisation applicable to the relations between an international organisation and its members.' Unless this provision is counter-intuitively construed as a merely illustrative list, this affirmation is highly problematic—as was spotted by scholars[42] as well as a few states[43]—as it allows internal rules to be turned into international rules of international responsibility. This is a clear denial of the specific and internal nature of the rules of international organisations. It boils down to allowing any internal arrangement between an international organisation and its Member States—if it provides different solutions—to exclude the general rules. In other words, recognising a *lex specialis* status—and thus an excluding effect—of the internal rules of the organisation allows general law to be excluded on the basis of internal, or quasi-domestic, arrangements.

[37] Ahlborn (n 14) 29; see also J d'Aspremont and C Ahlborn, 'The International Law Commission Embarks on the Second Reading of Draft Articles on the Responsibility of International Organisations' (30 April 2011), available at www.ejiltalk.org/the-international-law-commission-embarks-on-the-second-reading-of-draft-articles-on-the-responsibility-of-international-organisations/#more-3326.

[38] ILC 'Commentary to the Draft Articles on the Representation of States', ILC Yearbook vol II (Part One) (1971) UN Doc A/CN.4/SER.A/1971/Add.1 (Part 1) 287–88.

[39] ILC, 'Summary records of the 20th Session', ILC Yearbook vol I (27 May—2 August 1968) UN Doc A/CN.4/SER.A/1968, 31, para 24.

[40] ILC, 'Report of the International Law Commission on the Work of its Fifty-Third Session', ILC Yearbook vol II (Part Two) (2001) UN Doc A/CN.4/SER.A/2001/Add.1 (Part2) 39, para 7.

[41] Ahlborn (n 14) 38.

[42] Ibid, 29; see also d'Aspremont and Ahlborn (n 37); d'Aspremont (n 34).

[43] See ILC (n 30) 36–37.

This is certainly not the place to ignite a new debate about the nature of the rules of international organisations and, more specifically, whether internal rules of international organisations can be recognised as *lex specialis*. However, this debate is very central when it comes to the sources of the special regime of attribution vindicated by the EU. Indeed, if they are not found in the rules of an internal character of international organisations, they must be sought elsewhere. Indeed, claiming that the rules of a purely internal character cannot constitute *lex specialis* for the sake of the international responsibility of the EU and its Member States certainly does not mean that there cannot be such rules. Rather, it is argued here that these derogations from the general regime found in the ASR and the ARIO are not the object of express provisions of EU law and must instead be sought in practices pertaining to the establishment of international responsibility of the EU and/or its Member States in relation with other states or entities—and not responsibility of a purely internal character. Because they are not expressly formulated in rules of an internal character, rules of responsibility of a special character are, instead, to be found in the practices of law-applying bodies external to the EU. The best examples of these are international judicial proceedings where either the Member States or the EU have been accused of a breach of international law and where the (co-)responsibility of the other has been invoked or established. Such judicial practice can be highly indicative of the special rules of responsibility pertaining to the EU and its Member States in their international relations with one another. The WTO and the European Court of Human Rights (ECtHR), for instance, constitute platforms where special rules of international responsibility of the EU and/or its Member States in relation to other states or entities can manifest themselves or be given insight.[44] As will be explained below, special rules that could possibly coalesce in the judicial practice within these regimes do not necessarily constitute international special rules of responsibility bearing effect beyond the regime concerned. Yet, the possibility of special rules or practices generated by (and within) a regime like the WTO or the ECtHR must be critically explored.

The following section will focus on one of these two fora: namely, the ECtHR. In doing so, it will take particular account of the impact of the new mechanism put in place on the occasion of the accession of the EU to the European Convention on Human Rights (ECHR) for the possible coalescing of special rules of international responsibility, especially in terms of attribution. The question of their effects beyond this framework will also be examined.

IV. THE EU–ECHR MECHANISM AS A SPECIAL EUROPEAN REGIME OF INTERNATIONAL RESPONSIBILITY?

Cases where the responsibility of Member States of the EU for action within the framework of the EU has been invoked are well known. *M & Co v Germany*, *Matthews*,[45] *Senator Lines*,[46]

[44] For the case of the WTO, see, eg, P Eeckhout, 'The EU and its Members States in the WTO—Issues of Responsibility' in L Bartels and F Ortino (eds), *Regional Trade Agreements and the WTO Legal System* (New York, Oxford University Press, 2006) 449–64.

[45] *Matthews v United Kingdom*, App No 24833/94 (1999) 28 EHRR 361.

[46] *Senator Lines GmbH v Austria, Belgium, Denmark, Finland, France, Germany, Greece, Ireland, Italy, Luxembourg, the Netherlands, Portugal, Spain, Sweden and the United Kingdom*, App No 56672/00 (2004).

Bosphorus,[47] *MSS*[48] or *Michaud*,[49] although concerning the responsibility of Member States, have to some extent been instrumental in the (reinforcement of the) idea of the accession of the EU to the ECHR, which has now come close to reality. Indeed, negotiations about the modalities of the accession of the EU to the ECHR started in July 2010 and ended in June 2011 with the presentation of a draft agreement that was subsequently endorsed by the Council of Europe's Steering Committee on Human Rights.[50] The agreement sets out the changes to the ECHR system of human rights protection. The Draft Agreement on Accession of the European Union to the European Convention on Human Rights has been finalised, but is not yet in force.[51] However, it is interesting to formulate some preliminary observations on the extent to which the mechanism puts in place—or has the potential to generate—special rules and practices for the sake of the international responsibility of the EU and its Member States, especially in terms of attribution. Could the practice that will emanate from such accession be conducive to the development of special rules of international responsibility for the EU? And, if so, would this practice bear any effect beyond the ECHR regime? This is the issue that these final observations will grapple with.

Yet, before investigating such a question, an important caveat must be formulated. The relevance of such special rules should certainly not be exaggerated, for their applicability would be limited to the contractual relation established under the ECHR. It is important to realise that contentious questions arising within such a contractual relationship are very unlikely to be raised before (or to fall within the jurisdiction of) courts other than the ECtHR or domestic courts acting in the framework of the ECHR. In that sense—very similar to the case of the special rules of responsibility pertaining to the contractual relations established in the WTO framework—the relevance and applicability of such potentially special rules would remain confined to their forum of origin. That being said, the limited practical impact of such rules does not, from a conceptual point of view, strip the question of the impact of the accession on the emergence of special rules of responsibility of its importance. This is why this chapter ends with a few conceptual remarks on the consequences of the accession for the autonomisation of the regime of responsibility under the ECHR.

Certainly, the accession of the EU will generate a new practice of engagement of responsibility with respect to a new form of contractual relation, ie, that between the EU and the other states parties to the ECHR. Within the framework of this contractual relation, it cannot be excluded that new rules of responsibility—and, in particular, new rules of attribution—will emerge. For instance, it cannot be excluded that for the sake of the obligations enshrined in the ECHR, the normative control exercised by the EU over its Member States will be elevated into a criterion for attribution of conduct. The co-respondent mechanism, which has now been included in the draft Agreement with a view to allowing the EU to be entitled to all the rights of a party to the proceedings in order to defend what it believes to be the proper interpretation of the relevant provisions of EU law and of the ECHR,[52] may

[47] *Bosphorus* (n 27).

[48] *MSS v Belgium and Greece*, App No 30696/09 (2011) 53 EHRR 28.

[49] *Michaud v France*, App No 12323/11 (2012).

[50] For a useful stocktaking, see T Lock, 'End of an Epic? The Draft Agreement on the EU's Accession to the ECHR' (2012) 31(1) *Yearbook of European Law* 162. See also Drzemczewski, ch 2 in this volume.

[51] The draft Agreement and its Explanatory Report can be found in the Council of Europe document 47+1 (2013) R008, available at http://www.coe.int/t/dghl/standardsetting/hrpolicy/accession/Working_documents_en.asp.

[52] On the co-respondent mechanism, see Casteleiro, ch 8 in this volume.

even constitute a procedural framework within which such a *lex specialis* could potentially be perceived (or designed by the ECtHR).[53]

Whilst it cannot be excluded that the (litigation) practice pertaining to the new contractual relation between the EU and the other signatory parties to the ECHR will pave the way for special rules of responsibility for the sake of that specific contractual relation, the accession of the EU to the ECHR may rather hamper the possibility of new special rules of responsibility when it comes to questions of responsibility of the EU and of its Member States beyond the ECHR regime. Indeed, it is argued here that accession will transform the way in which the ECtHR may potentially approach the nature of EU law—and thus of EU mechanisms of responsibility—in general and may hinder the emergence of special rules of responsibility that are not specific to the ECHR. In that sense, by formally subjecting the whole EU regime to the ECHR and the Court, the Accession Agreement will limit the space that has existed for the possible development (or discovery) of a special non-ECHR specific rule of responsibility. Such a contention can be explained as follows. By making the EU formally bound by the ECHR and justiciable before the Court, the Accession Agreement will change the nature of EU law and practices. EU law and practices before the accession, as they are now, have been of a completely external nature to the ECHR. As long as they are external to the ECHR, they can constitute the breeding ground of special rules or practices pertaining to the international responsibility of the EU in its relationship with its Member States, the unearthing of which the ECtHR could contribute to, even if only incidentally. Yet, as a result of the accession, EU law and practices will become internal to the ECHR too, and the Court will approach EU law and practices in their internal dimension: that is, as internal rules of an organisation party to the Convention. After the accession, EU law and practices will thus no longer constitute (or generate) mere external practices, which could be turned into special rules of international responsibility opposable to non-Member States or entities. In that sense, the ECtHR will be bound to approach EU law and practices as rules of the organisation of an internal nature and which, as was explained above, will be unable to qualify as (or generate) *lex specialis* for the sake of international responsibility, that is, beyond the specific framework of the ECHR. The impact of this change of vantage point is accordingly fundamental when it comes to the possibility of the ECtHR uncovering or allowing the coalescing of special rules of responsibility which are not ECHR-specific. Rather than offering a platform for the further development of special rules of responsibility, accession will restrict the contribution of the ECHR system to a European law of international responsibility.

V. CONCLUDING REMARKS

After arguing that the ARIO leaves enough room for the development of rules of international responsibility, this short study has reflected on the extent to which the mechanism set up by the Draft Agreement on Accession of the European Union to the European Convention on Human Rights could be conducive to the emergence of special rules of international responsibility for the EU. Although acknowledging that special rules

[53] As was pointed out by Giorgio Gaja, this question will arise irrespective of issues of competence, the question being whether a provision of EU law is actually at the origin of the breach. See Gaja, ch 22 in this volume.

could possibly emerge in the judicial practice of the ECtHR in connection with the draft Agreement, this chapter has argued that, as a result of the accession, EU law and practices will become internal to the ECHR too, and the ECtHR will approach EU law and practices in their internal dimension, that is, as internal rules of an organisation party to the Convention, thereby precluding the emergence of international rules of responsibility. In that sense, the Accession Agreement, rather than buoying the emergence of special rules of international responsibility, will limit the space that has existed for the possible development (or discovery) of a special non-ECHR-specific rule of responsibility. Unless one sees any value in the continuous development and specialisation of the law of international responsibility, the finding made here should not be bemoaned.

7

The EU Accession to the ECHR and the Law of International Responsibility

ARMAN SARVARIAN*

NEGOTIATIONS ON THE accession of the European Union (EU) to the European Convention on Human Rights (ECHR or 'the Convention') have been completed with a draft Accession Agreement to be submitted to the European Court of Justice (ECJ or the 'Luxembourg Court') for its opinion.[1] Although several stages lie ahead before the completion of this process, its consequences for the EU, the Member States, the European Court of Human Rights (ECtHR or the 'Strasbourg Court') and third parties are potentially profound. Analysis of the ratification process and its implications for the adjudication of claims concerning the EU before the Strasbourg Court is therefore timely.

With the increased international activity and inter-organisational cooperation of the post-Cold War period alongside the evolution and expansion of the EU and the Council of Europe, these originally parallel regimes have increasingly interfaced with one another and with the United Nations (UN) and the North Atlantic Treaty Organization (NATO) in practice. The Strasbourg Court has adjudicated several applications concerning the activities of Member States pursuant to United Nations Security Council (UNSC), NATO and/or EU mandates. This is connected to the wider phenomena of 'proliferation' and 'fragmentation' of international law by which risk of conflict amongst legal regimes increases with their number and power.[2]

The demand for regularity in the field of international responsibility and its integral importance to general international law is exemplified by the UN International Law Commission (ILC) Articles on State Responsibility for Internationally Wrongful Acts 2001[3] (ASR) and the ILC Articles on the Responsibility of International Organizations for Internationally Wrongful Acts (ARIO).[4] In 2002, the ILC commenced the drafting of principles concerning the responsibility of international organisations—a matter that had

* Lecturer in Law, University of Surrey and Director of the Surrey International Law Centre.

[1] 'Fifth Negotiation Meeting between the CDDH ad hoc Negotiation Group and the European Commission on the Accession of the European Union to the European Convention on Human Rights: Final Report to the CDDH', Council of Europe Doc 47+1(2013)008rev2 (10 June 2013). See further www.coe.int/t/dghl/standardsetting/hrpolicy/Accession/default_en.asp.

[2] See generally 'Fragmentation of International Law: Difficulties Arising from the Diversification and Expansion of International Law: Report of the Study Group of the International Law Commission', UN Doc A/CN.4/L.682 (3 April 2006), paras 5–20.

[3] UNGA Resolution 56/83 (2001).

[4] UN Doc A/66/10, *Yearbook of the International Law Commission* 2011, Vol II, Part Two.

been left open by Article 57 of the ASR. In 2011, the ILC adopted the ARIO on its second reading.

The conclusion of the ASR project by the ILC provided an influential articulation of both orthodox and progressive principles of international responsibility. The ASR, in both draft and adopted form, have been widely applied in practice by states and by international courts and tribunals.[5] Subsequently, the UN General Assembly has repeatedly delayed consideration of the adoption of the ASR as a treaty.[6] As for the ASR, the General Assembly 'took note' of the ARIO on a 'without prejudice' basis and included it in its provisional agenda for its 2015 session.[7]

This chapter examines the potential consequences of EU accession to the ECHR for the attribution of conduct to the Member States and/or international organisations under the law of international responsibility before the Strasbourg Court. In its first section, it criticises the policy of the European Commission concerning the attribution of conduct before international courts and tribunals and the ILC. In its second section, it assesses the jurisprudence of the Strasbourg Court concerning the attribution of conduct in joint operations pursuant to the EU Common Foreign and Security Policy (CFSP), UNSC resolutions and NATO resolutions.

The chapter focuses upon three areas of CFSP activity engaging human rights connected to the UN Security Council: 1) sanctions regimes, especially 'targeted sanctions' against individuals;[8] 2) peacekeeping and international governance missions; and 3) collective enforcement action.[9] Whilst the jurisprudence examined in this chapter is also relevant to EU 'autonomous sanctions'[10] and other CFSP activity unconnected to the UNSC, the chapter focuses upon EU sanctions pursuant to Security Council resolutions. Moreover, the additional complexity of the UNSC context assists in elucidating doctrinal problems in the field of international responsibility.[11] The chapter argues that the analytical approach of the Strasbourg Court has been inconsistent and confused on the attribution of conduct and that the policy of the European Commission seeking special treatment for the EU is misguided.

[5] J Crawford and S Olleson, 'The Continuing Debate on a UN Convention on State Responsibility' (2005) 54(4) *International and Comparative Law Quarterly* 959, 965–71.

[6] Most recently, the General Assembly in Resolution 65/19 (2011) provisionally included the ASR in its agenda for its sixty-eighth session to be held in 2014.

[7] International Law Commission, 'Report on the Work of its Sixty-Third Session' (2011), UN Doc A/66/10, paras 80–84; International Law Commission, 'Responsibility of International Organizations: Statement of the Chairman of the Drafting Committee' (3 June 2011) 1–2; UNGA Sixth Committee (Legal), 'Report of the ILC: Report of the Sixth Committee', UN Doc A/66/473 (15 November 2011), 'Draft Resolution III'; UNGA Resolution 66/100 (2012), OP4.

[8] See, eg, G Verdirame, *The United Nations and Human Rights: Who Guards the Guardians?* (Cambridge, Cambridge University Press, 2011); A Tzanakopoulos, *Disobeying the Security Council: Countermeasures against Wrongful Sanctions* (Oxford, Oxford University Press, 2011); A Ciampi, 'Security Council Targeted Sanctions and Human Rights' in B Fassbender (ed), *Securing Human Rights? Achievements and Challenges of the UN Security Council* (Oxford, Oxford University Press, 2011) 98–140.

[9] For background on UNSC activity engaging human rights, see B Fassbender, 'The Role for Human Rights in the Decision-Making Process' in Fassbender (n 8) 88–92.

[10] Namely, sanctions directed not towards Member States, but rather towards third parties and prompted not by the UNSC or another body, but emanating from the EU itself.

[11] Current missions include: the Military Mission in Bosnia and Herzegovina, the Rule of Law Mission in Kosovo and the Naval Mission off Somalia: 'Overview of the Missions and Operations of the European Union: September 2012', available at www.consilium.europa.eu/eeas/security-defence/eu-operations?lang=en.

An important terminological point should be noted here. Part One of both ILC texts are divided into separate chapters addressing 'attribution of conduct' (Chapter Two) and 'responsibility of an international organization in connection with the act of a State or another international organization' (Chapter Four). International responsibility is defined by Article 4 as comprising two components: 1) attribution of conduct; and 2) breach of an international obligation. The arrangement of Part One appears to be inconsistent with this definition in that Chapters Two and Four concern 'attribution', but are arranged under discrete headings and, sandwiched between the two chapters, Chapter Three is entitled 'breach of an international obligation'.

The separation of the Articles contained within Chapters Two and Four is in one sense logical: whereas Chapter Two is concerned with the 'primary' attribution of conduct, with a conceptual predisposition towards exclusivity,[12] Chapter Four addresses 'secondary' or 'ancillary' attribution. This is reflected in Article 19 within Chapter Four: 'This Chapter is without prejudice to the international responsibility of the State or international organization which commits the act in question, or of any other State or international organization.' Notwithstanding the omission of 'attribution' from Chapter Four, since they essentially concern the problem of 'attribution' rather than 'breach', the term 'attribution' is employed in this chapter when describing the operation of provisions under both Chapters Two and Four.

I. THE EUROPEAN COMMISSION AND THE ARIO[13]

There is a tension concerning the degree to which the Convention system is integrated into general international law. In the absence of express provisions on responsibility within the Convention itself, according to the law of treaties, the Strasbourg Court may even be bound to 'take into account' the general international law of responsibility in interpreting the Convention as 'relevant rules of international law applicable in the relations between the parties'.[14] The concept of 'self-contained regime' breaks down not only from the incompleteness of the Convention but also from encounters in practice with other sub-systems (eg, the EU and the UN).[15]

The need to apply the law of responsibility through Article 31(3)(c) VCLT in the absence of Convention provisions does not necessarily imply that the ILC texts ought to be applied *in toto*. Even as they continue to be assessed, they have already proved to be of considerable importance and utility in practice.[16] Provisions reflecting progressive development or compromise during the drafting process rather than articulation or endorsement of long-standing principle may not necessarily be *lex lata*.[17] Consequently, the

[12] ASR with Commentaries, Commentary to Chapter IV, paras 1, 3, 5–8. The ILC refers in the Commentary to the 'principle of independent responsibility' with the situations covered in Chapter IV comprising 'exceptions to [the principle]' (para 8). See further Dominicé, 'Attribution of Conduct to Multiple States and the Implication of a State in the Act of Another State' in Crawford et al, *The Law of International Responsibility* (2010) 281–289.

[13] See also d'Aspremont, ch 6 in this volume.

[14] Article 31(3)(c) of the Vienna Convention on the Law of Treaties 1969 (VCLT).

[15] See further the ILC Report on Fragmentation of International Law (n 2) 30–34 (paras 46–54), 65–101 (paras 123–94) and especially 74–82 (paras 138–52).

[16] Crawford and Olleson (n 5) 965–71.

[17] Ibid.

authoritativeness of individual provisions should be carefully evaluated by international courts rather than applied as part of wider texts that are erroneously assumed to comprise definitive statements of the law of international responsibility at the present time. Even after their putative adoption as treaties, the ILC texts may undergo continual refinement through practice.

To resolve normative conflicts, consistency demands a comprehensive generality that is not yet fully provided either in the jurisprudence of the Strasbourg Court or in the ARIO itself. Controversially, the ILC adopted a *lex specialis* rule in Article 64:

> These articles do not apply where and to the extent that the conditions for the existence of an internationally wrongful act or the content or implementation of the international responsibility of an international organization, or a State in connection with the conduct of an international organizations, are governed by special rules of international law. Such special rules of international law may be contained in the rules of the organization applicable to the relations between an international organization and its members.

The Commentary to Article 64 explains that this provision was specifically formulated with the EU in mind.[18] In its comments to the ILC, the European Commission suggested that such a provision was necessary due to the 'special nature' of the EU and 'other potentially similar organisations'. The Commission argued that the EU is not a 'classic' international organisation because it is not merely a forum for Member States but rather an international actor with its own legal order.[19]

However, Special Rapporteur Giorgio Gaja 'saw no need to devise special rules on attribution in order to assert the organization's responsibility in this type of case [where the authorities of the Member States act as implementing authorities in areas of Community competence]'.[20] Rather, he suggested that the responsibility of the organisation could be incurred without the attribution of conduct—a proposal seemingly inconsistent with the definition of an internationally wrongful act under Article 4. Nevertheless, the ILC adopted Article 64 providing that EU law displaces the ARIO in determining the attribution of conduct as between the EU and its Member States. This would apply not only to 'internal' disputes within the EU legal order but also to 'external' disputes involving third parties (eg, WTO or ECtHR proceedings).

Although Hoffmeister argues that the *lex specialis* provision is analytically justifiable through reference to the 'bearer of the obligation' or 'normative control' rather than the 'factual actor' for the purposes of attribution,[21] this approach does not operate in a nuanced and precise manner. As the 'ultimate control and authority' test (developed by the ECtHR in *Behrami and Saramati* discussed below) illustrates, under a 'normative' approach, the actions of multiple actors may be attributed to a remote legislator with scant involvement in the factual process that produced the outcome. It also ignores the possibility of ultra vires conduct[22] and the difficulty of attribution pursuant to norms that are themselves

[18] ARIO with Commentaries, 100–02.

[19] S Talmon, 'Responsibility of International Organizations: Does the European Community Require Special Treatment?' in M Ragazzi (ed), *International Responsibility Today: Essays in Memory of Oscar Schachter* (Leiden, Brill, 2005) 406.

[20] Ibid, 409.

[21] F Hoffmeister, 'Litigation against the European Union and its Member States—Who Responds under the ILC's Draft Articles on International Responsibility of International Organizations?' (2010) 21(3) *European Journal of International Law* 723, 746.

[22] Talmon (n 19) 409.

ambiguous (eg, 'mixed agreements' with third parties).[23] Complex cases involving multiple actors in particular require a fact-sensitive approach that separately attributes conduct according to control and causation.

Moreover, the position of the European Commission erroneously assumes that EU law operates according to distinctive principles when attributing *conduct* (as opposed to *powers*) to the EU and the Member States. Article 340 of the Treaty on the Functioning of the European Union[24] (TFEU) provides that 'in the case of non-contractual liability, the Union shall, in accordance with the general principles common to the laws of the Member States, make good any damage caused by its institutions or by its servants in the performance of their duties'. Whilst this is not as such an attribution rule but rather a reparation duty, the formula of causation by organs and servants (effectively an attribution rule) is substantively similar to Article 5(1) ARIO.[25] Thus, apart from its reparation element, the sole TFEU provision concerning the attribution of conduct is substantively identical to the ARIO.

Jurisprudence of the Court of Justice of the European Union (CJEU) suggests that Member States generally exercise discretion when implementing EU law and are obliged to respect Convention standards when doing so.[26] When Member States implement EU regulations that are binding in their entirety and are directly applicable, they may nevertheless exercise discretion in their implementation.[27] Consequently, there is no apparent inconsistency in the underlying principle of Article 340 TFEU such that would necessitate a divergence from general international law on attribution. However, the position of the European Commission is more readily explained with reference to its policy of seeking to appear as sole respondent for alleged breaches arising from actions taken pursuant to EU law in WTO, ECtHR and United Nations Convention for the Law of the Sea (UNCLOS) proceedings.[28] Its rationale is to encourage respect for the supremacy of EU law by Member States even where compliance results in breaches of other legal regimes.

The case of *Chile v European Communities*[29] before a Special Chamber of the International Tribunal for the Law of the Sea (ITLOS) is an apposite example. Chile brought proceedings against the EU[30] for failure to ensure the conservation of swordfish in the fishing activities of Spanish vessels on the high seas adjacent to its exclusive economic zone in breach of UNCLOS. Whilst the chamber did not have to address the attribution of conduct due to the settlement of the case, it is unlikely that the imputability of the EU would have been

[23] Ibid, 416–17.

[24] *OJEU* C 83/47 (30 March 2010). In French: 'En matière de responsabilité non contractuelle, l'Union doit réparer, conformément aux principes généraux communs aux droits des États membres, les dommages causés par ses institutions ou par ses agents dans l'exercice de leurs fonctions.'

[25] 'The conduct of an organ or agent of an international organization in the performance of functions of that organ or agent shall be considered as an act of that organization under international law whatever the position the organ or agent holds in respect of the organization.'

[26] C Costello, 'The *Bosphorus* Ruling of the European Court of Human Rights: Fundamental Rights and Blurred Boundaries in Europe' (2006) 6(1) *Human Rights Law Review* 87, 108–09.

[27] The implementing discretion may be scant or absent, so it will depend upon the particular regulation.

[28] Hoffmeister (n 21) 732–39.

[29] Case No 7 concerning the Conservation and Sustainable Exploitation of Swordfish Stocks in the South-Eastern Pacific (*Chile v European Union*), Order 2009/1 (16 December 2009), available at: http://www.itlos.org/index.php?id=99&L=0.

[30] Then called the European Community (EC) prior to the entry into force of the Treaty of Lisbon. For simplicity, the EU is retroactively substituted for the EC throughout this chapter.

challenged in light of the Commission's aforementioned policy based upon the exclusive competence of the EU for the conservation of maritime resources under EU law.[31]

Notwithstanding the apparent neatness of this approach from the adjudicatory standpoint, it is nevertheless problematic from a doctrinal perspective. The ostensible connection between the EU and the alleged breach was remote; no EU organ was involved in the impugned conduct by the flag state and there was not even a normative link to EU law. According to both EU law and general international law, competence is not determinative of attribution. Pursuant to both Articles 4 ASR and 6 ARIO (as well as Article 340 TFEU, were EU law applicable), the correct outcome would be the exclusive attribution of the impugned conduct to Spain for want of a factual connection to the EU.

Whilst the Commission's acceptance of responsibility with the agreement of all parties as well as the Tribunal can be viewed as an 'acknowledgement of conduct' under Article 9 ARIO, the underlying rationale of the Commission's stance is suggested to be flawed and likely to convolute attribution in future litigation. The perceived need to encourage Member States to respect the supremacy of EU law was absent, since the implementation of EU law did not feature. The exclusivity of EU competence concerning the conservation of maritime resources pertains to the power of prescription, not to the attribution of conduct.

Before the Strasbourg Court, the Commission and respondent states have consistently asserted the attribution to the EU of conduct by organs of Member States in performance of EU law. In *Matthews*,[32] the UK argued that the applicant's complaint concerned EU legislation by which it was bound and over which it had no effective control. The Strasbourg Court rejected this argument, holding that the UK remained obliged to secure Convention rights within its jurisdiction:

> The Court observes that acts of the EC as such cannot be challenged before the Court because the EC is not a Contracting Party. The Convention does not exclude the transfer of competences to international organisations provided that Convention rights continue to be 'secured'. Member States' responsibility therefore continues even after such a transfer.[33]

Implicit in this approach was the attribution of conduct by UK organs to the UK, notwithstanding its obligation to implement EU law.

In *Senator Lines*,[34] the applicant asserted that the respondents were 'individually and collectively responsible for the acts of the [EU] institutions, and that … the [EU] courts were allowing a mere administrative body to force the applicant company into liquidation, in violation of the rights to a fair hearing'.[35] The respondents' 'principal contention was that … the acts complained of did not represent an exercise by the individual States of their jurisdiction within the meaning of Art. 1 of the Convention'.[36] In support, the Commission further asserted:

> The Member States of the European Union are responsible for the procedure of the CFI and the ECJ, in the sense that they must ensure that provision is made for equivalent protection of

[31] Article 3(d) TFEU.
[32] *Matthews v UK*, App No 24833/94 (1999) 28 EHRR 361 [26]–[35].
[33] Ibid [33].
[34] *Senator Lines GmbH v 15 Member States*, App No 56672/00 (2004) 39 EHRR SE3.
[35] Ibid, 15.
[36] Ibid.

> fundamental rights in those courts. It added that, so long as such protection exists in general, the Member States are not responsible for the manner in which those courts assess and decide issues of fundamental rights in individual cases.[37]

The Strasbourg Court did not decide upon this question of attribution, dismissing the application on other grounds.

In *Bosphorus*,[38] the Commission argued that the impugned conduct was attributable to the EU as the implementing regulation and decision of the European Court of Justice (ECJ) left Ireland with no discretion concerning the impounding of the aircraft. The Commission asserted:

> The reason for initially adopting this 'equivalent protection' approach was equally, if not more, pertinent today. It was an approach which was especially important for the [EU] given its distinctive features of supranationality and the nature of [EU] law: to require a state to review for Convention compliance an act of the [EU] before implementing it would pose an incalculable threat to the very foundations of the [EU], a result not envisaged by the drafters of the Convention, supportive as they were of European co-operation and integration. Moreover, subjecting individual [EU] acts to Convention scrutiny would amount to making the [EU] a respondent in Convention proceedings without any of the procedural rights and safeguards of a Contracting State to the Convention.[39]

The Strasbourg Court's rejection of the preliminary objection based the attribution of the impoundment to Ireland upon its factual commission by state organs.[40] Whilst the Court placed greater emphasis upon the doctrine of equivalent protection rather than factual attribution,[41] the attribution of the impoundment to Ireland is nevertheless justifiable on a 'factual actor' basis pursuant to Article 4 ASR. However, it ignores the role of the ECJ judgment and the legislation of the Regulation 990/93 by EU organs (as well as the background UNSC Resolution 820) in causing the impugned breach of the Convention.

In assessing this jurisprudence, it is difficult to see how the position of the European Commission in seeking to create a double standard for the EU as opposed to other international organisations would produce more rational results in practice. Not only is Article 340 TFEU broadly consistent with the general international law approach of attributing conduct to international legal persons based upon factual control, but it also accords with the approach of the Strasbourg Court in *Bosphorus*. Following EU accession, the attribution of conduct to the executor of the impugned act rather than the legislator would become even more logical with the ability of the EU to respond to impugned EU legislation.[42]

The Commission's policy of seeking special treatment to attribute 'responsibility' to the EU on the basis of legal powers rather than factual conduct is reflected in Article 3(1)(b) of the draft Accession Agreement of the EU to the ECHR:

> The European Union or a member State of the European Union may become a co-respondent to proceedings by decision of the Court in the circumstances set out in the Agreement on the

[37] Ibid, 18–19.

[38] *Bosphorus Hava Yollari Turizm Ve Ticaret Anonim Sirketi v Ireland*, App No 45036/98 (2005) 42 EHRR 1, Judgment of 30 June 2005 [108]–[110], [122]–[125], [129]–[132].

[39] Ibid [124].

[40] Ibid [137].

[41] Ibid [149]–[158].

[42] Indeed, the ECJ has rejected the attribution of targeted sanctions to the UN through the implementation of Security Council resolutions and juxtaposed the contradictory *Bosphorus* and *Behrami* decisions of the Strasbourg Court: Joined Cases C-402/05 P and 415/05 P *Kadi and Al Barakaat International Foundation v Council and Commission* [2008] ECR I-6351 (ECJ) [312]–[314].

> Accession of the European Union to the Convention for the Protection of Human Rights and Fundamental Freedoms. A co-respondent is a party to the case. The admissibility of an application shall be assessed without regard to the participation of a co-respondent in the proceedings.[43]

The power of the Strasbourg Court to decide upon co-respondent status is a crucial improvement over earlier proposals to vest High Contracting Parties with an effective veto over their own addition as co-respondent.[44] Nevertheless, this formulation does not resolve the inconsistencies in the jurisprudence of the Strasbourg Court.[45]

Draft Article 3(2) and (3) provides that the conditions for co-respondent status for either the EU or an EU Member State is 'if it appears that such allegation calls into question the compatibility with the rights at issue defined in the Convention or in the protocols to which the European Union has acceded of a provision of the Treaty on European Union, the Treaty on the Functioning of the European Union or any other provision having the same legal value pursuant to those instruments, notably where that violation could have been avoided only by disregarding an obligation under those instruments'. This 'normative approach' focusing upon conflicts between the Convention and EU law does not exclude the EU and Member States from becoming co-respondents concerning the discrete acts of legislation versus implementation.[46]

II. THE ATTRIBUTION OF CONDUCT IN STRASBOURG JURISPRUDENCE

In recent years, the attribution of conduct has become an important and recurring issue in Strasbourg proceedings concerning multiple actors in operations pursuant to UN Security Council resolutions. There is considerable inconsistency and misapplication of the law of responsibility in the jurisprudence. Whilst the Court's analytical approach has purported to apply the ASR and the ARIO in the absence of Convention provisions on attribution, it has not done so consistently or precisely.

Article 1 ('obligation to respect human rights') pertains to responsibility: 'The High Contracting Parties shall secure to everyone within their jurisdiction the rights and freedoms defined in Section 1 of this Convention.'[47] However, Article 1 concerns the discrete issue of 'breach' rather than that of 'attribution',[48] in that it defines the scope of Convention rights and obligations, but does not stipulate when parties have committed an act or

[43] CDDH Report (n 1) 6.

[44] 'Fourth Negotiation Meeting between the DDH Ad-Hoc Negotiation Group and the European Commission on the Accession of the European Union to the European Convention on Human Rights: Common Paper of Andorra, Armenia, Azerbaijan, Bosnia-Herzegovina, Iceland, Liechtenstein, Monaco, Montenegro, Norway, Serbia, Switzerland, Russian Federation, Turkey and Ukraine on major concerns regarding the Draft revised Agreement on the Accession of the European Union to the European Convention on Human Rights' (21 January 2013), para 12: 'The [non-EU Member States] point out that, given the main purpose of accession, it would be consequent to make the [Co-Respondent Mechanism] binding in the sense that the EU and its member States have to accept the invitation of the Court. A [*sic*] optional character of the CRM might lead to gaps in participation and, consequently, to lack of accountability and enforceability in the ECHR system.'

[45] Den Heijer, 'Issues of Shared Responsibility before the European Court of Human Rights', ACIL Research Paper No 2012–04 (SHARES Series), finalised 26 January 2012, 40–43.

[46] The latest amendment proposal seemingly improves on this formulation by substituting 'or' for 'and', thus providing for the possibility of compulsory impugnability.

[47] 'Les Hautes Parties contractantes reconnaissent à toute personne relevant de leur juridiction les droits et libertés définis au titre I de la présente Convention.'

[48] Article 2 ASR and Article 4 ARIO.

omission. The Convention can also be said to indirectly address compliance with obligations in its provisions on execution with judgments (Article 46).

The scope of the key phrase 'within their jurisdiction' was considered by the Court in 2001 in *Banković*.[49] Relatives of persons killed in bombings of television and radio facilities during the NATO bombardment of Serbia and Montenegro alleged that the 16 respondents had breached the right to life of the deceased. This judgment did not address the attribution of the airstrikes to NATO versus the respondents; still less did it cite the then-draft ASR or general international law. Whilst the respondents had argued that the application was inadmissible *ratione personae* through the *Monetary Gold* principle[50] of general international law and France had asserted that the impugned conduct was attributable to NATO rather than the respondents,[51] the Court declined to address these arguments after a finding of inadmissibility *ratione loci*.[52]

Although the Court declined to address the question of attribution in *Banković*, the judgment indirectly bears upon the status of the general international law of responsibility. As the Court has done elsewhere in its jurisprudence, it purported to apply Articles 31 and 32 VCLT to interpret the Convention.[53] The lack of a textual basis in the Convention to refer to the law of treaties for its own interpretation destroys the concept of the 'self-contained regime' that is both comprehensive and exclusively self-referential. Indeed, Article 31(3)(c) VCLT provides that '[in interpreting a treaty] there shall be taken into account, together with the context ... any relevant rules of international law applicable in the relations between the parties'.[54] Thus, the general international law of responsibility may be invoked to interpret the Convention.

Although the aforementioned *Bosphorus*[55] case is best known for the '*Bosphorus* presumption',[56] it is also interesting from the perspective of attribution. The UNSC adopted Resolution 820 (1993), deciding, inter alia, that 'all States shall impound all vessels, freight vehicles, rolling stock and aircraft in their territories in which a majority or controlling interest is held by a person or undertaking in or operating from the Federal

[49] *Vlastimir and Borka Banković and others v Belgium and others*, App No 52207/99 (2007) 44 EHRR SE5, Judgment of 12 December 2001.

[50] Originating from the International Court of Justice, this doctrine provides that proceedings which engage the litigious rights of third parties that have not provided jurisdiction to the Court are inadmissible.

[51] *Banković* (n 49) paras 31–32. See also the argument of France that all of its actions were taken under the direction and control of NATO and attributable to it: *Case Concerning Legality of the Use of Force (Serbia and Montenegro v France) (Preliminary Objections), Oral Pleadings* (22 April 2004), CR/2004/12 [49]–[52]. See also *Case Concerning Legality of the Use of Force (Serbia and Montenegro v Portugal) (Preliminary Objections), Oral Pleadings* (19 April 2004), CR/2004/9 [4.8]; *Oral Pleadings* (20 April 2004), CR/2004/18 [4.1]–[4.7]. However, this argument was exceptional in that none of the other eight respondent states in the *Legality of the Use of Force* proceedings made the same argument: P Klein, 'The Attribution of Acts to International Organizations' in Crawford (n 12) 302–03 (note 30). See also T Stein, 'Kosovo and the International Community. The Attribution of Possible Internationally Wrongful Acts: Responsibility of NATO or of its Member States?' and A Pellet, 'L'imputabilité d'éventuels actes illicetes Responsabilité de l'OTAN ou des États membres' in Tomuschat (ed), *Kosovo and the International Community: A Legal Assessment* (New York, Springer, 2002).

[52] *Banković* (n 49) para. 83.

[53] *Banković* (n 49) [16]–[18]. For an assessment of the Court's treatment of general international law, see M Forowicz, *The Reception of International Law in the European Court of Human Rights* (Oxford, Oxford University Press, 2010) 352–405.

[54] For analysis, see also the ILC Report on Fragmentation of International Law (n 2) paras 410–80.

[55] *Bosphorus* (n 38) [1]–[60].

[56] See, eg, Costello (n 26) 87–130; T Lock, 'Beyond *Bosphorus*: The European Court of Human Rights' Case Law on the Responsibility of Member States of International Organisations under the European Convention on Human Rights' (2010) 10(3) *Human Rights Law Review* 529.

Republic of Yugoslavia (FRY) (Serbia and Montenegro) and that these … may be forfeit to the seizing State upon a determination that they have been in violation of resolutions 713 (1991), 757 (1992), 787 (1992) or the present resolution'.[57] The EU adopted Regulation 990/93,[58] Article 8 of which obliged Member States to impound aircraft under the same terms as Resolution 820. Irish organs subsequently impounded one of the applicant's aircraft in Ireland.

Upon judicial review of the ministerial decision to impound the aircraft, the Irish High Court held that Regulation 990/93 did not apply to the aircraft as a 'majority or controlling interest' was not held by a person operating from the FRY due to its lease to a person operating outside the FRY. On appeal by the government, the Supreme Court requested a preliminary reference from the Luxembourg Court concerning the applicability of Regulation 990/93 to the aircraft in question. The applicant argued, inter alia, that its application would breach his fundamental right to peaceful enjoyment of possessions. The ECJ ruled that Regulation 990/93 applied to the aircraft in question and that the interference with the peaceful enjoyment of possessions was justified.[59] Having noted the mandatory character of the ECJ judgment, the Irish Supreme Court allowed the appeal and the impoundment was reinstated.

On appeal to the ECtHR, Ireland argued that 'the Convention must be interpreted in such a manner as to allow State Parties to comply with international obligations so as not to thwart the current trend towards extending and strengthening international co-operation'.[60] Ireland submitted that its impugned act of impoundment was in implementation of an obligation emanating from Resolution 820 and Regulation 990/93 rather than an exercise of discretion, and that it was obliged under EU law to implement the ECJ judgment.[61] Italy, appearing as intervener, went further in asserting that the duty to comply with the Resolution, the Regulation and the ECJ judgment 'warranted a conclusion of incompatibility ratione personae'.[62] Whilst the applicant agreed that the Court lacked the competence to examine acts pursuant to international obligations, it argued that the impoundment was an exercise of discretion.[63]

Following a brief analysis, in taking Article 1 of the Convention as its starting point, the Court implicitly held that the impugned act was attributable to Ireland:

> In the present case it is not disputed that the act about which the applicant complained, the detention of the aircraft leased by it for a period of time, was implemented by the authorities of the respondent State on its territory following a decision to impound of the Irish Minister of Transport. In such circumstances the applicant company, as the addressee of the impugned act, fell within the 'jurisdiction' of the Irish State, with the consequence that its complaint about the act is compatible ratione loci, personae and materiae with the provisions of the Convention.[64]

[57] UNSC Resolution 820 (1993) OP24.

[58] Council Regulation (EEC) No 990/93 of 26 April 1993 concerning trade between the European Economic Community and the Federal Republic of Yugoslavia (Serbia and Montenegro), OJ L 102, 28 April 1993, P 0014–16.

[59] Case C-84/95 *Bosphorus Hava Yollari Turizm ve Ticaret AS v Minister for Transport, Energy and Communications and others* [1996] ECR I-03953 [21]–[27].

[60] *Bosphorus* (n 38) [108].

[61] Ibid [109]–[111].

[62] Ibid [129].

[63] Ibid [115]–[119].

[64] Ibid [137].

Whilst the ARIO was not available to the Court at the time, it is nevertheless surprising that the Court did not refer to the ASR in its terse analysis and that the intricate issue of attribution was not canvassed more thoroughly. For the reasons set out above, it is suggested that the Court's citation of Article 1 of the Convention was erroneous as Article 1 is concerned with breach rather than attribution.

Interestingly, the Court's decision exclusively emphasises the factual actor rather than the legislator of the obligation. Under Article 15 ARIO, the possibility is envisaged of secondary responsibility of an international organisation when pursuant to the latter's 'direction and control'. The Commentary explains:

> In the relations between an international organization and its member States and international organizations the concept of 'direction and control' could conceivably be extended so as to encompass cases in which an international organization takes a decision binding its members ... If one interprets the provision in light of the passages [from the Commentary to Article 17 ASR] quoted above, the adoption of a binding decision on the part of an international organization could constitute, under certain circumstances, a form of direction or control in the commission of an internationally wrongful act. The assumption is that the State or international organization which is the addressee of the decision is not given discretion to carry out conduct that, while complying with the decision, would not constitute an internationally wrongful act.[65]

According to this approach, it was arguable that the impoundment in *Bosphorus* meant that the UN and the EU incurred secondary responsibility in that both had enacted binding legislation, which left Ireland with no discretion concerning the performance of the impugned conduct.

However, this approach raises a number of problems. First, it ignores the fact that the state has consented to be bound by potentially conflicting obligations, namely, the Article 25 Charter duty to implement Security Council resolutions and the Article 4 of the Treaty on European Union (TEU)[66] duty to implement EU regulations and ECJ judgments on the one hand, and the Article 1 ECHR duty to secure Convention rights within its jurisdiction on the other. As the Court held:

> On the other hand, it has also been accepted that a Contracting Party is responsible under Art. 1 of the Convention for all acts and omissions of its organs regardless of whether the act or omission in question was a consequence of domestic law or of the necessity to comply with international legal obligations. Article 1 makes no distinction as to the type of rule or measure concerned and does not exclude any part of a Contracting Party's 'jurisdiction' from scrutiny under the Convention.[67]

It may be the case that states attempting to circumvent compliance with Convention duties may plead the duty to comply with a competing UNSC resolution to enable them to do so.[68] To attribute conduct to the UN or the EU for obliging Ireland to impound the aircraft would not reflect the practical reality of state discretion and may lead to states invoking UNSC resolutions to avoid compliance with Convention rights.

Second, the application of the 'direction and control' concept to legislative acts is imprecise. It effectively attributes to the legislator all actions or omissions causing the breach,

[65] ARIO with Commentaries, 38–39 (para 4).

[66] 'Consolidated Version of the Treaty on European Union', *OJEU* C 83/13 (30 March 2010).

[67] Ibid, para 153.

[68] See Article 61 ARIO,. By addressing the responsibility of a state within the paradigm of Article 61, it is already assumed (perhaps falsely) that the conduct in question is attributable to the organisation.

regardless of its degree of involvement. The prescription of Resolution 820 by the UNSC and of Regulation 990/93 by the EU would render all of the prescriptive, interpretive and implementation stages of those instruments attributable to the UN and the EU. This would unrealistically ignore the roles of the states parties to the Convention not only in enacting those instruments but also in implementing them within their domestic legal orders. In complex cases involving multiple actors, a more nuanced analytical approach is necessary to precisely attribute conduct.

Third, the extension of the 'direction and control' concept to normative acts was not envisaged by the ILC in Article 17 ASR upon which Article 15 ARIO is based. Rather, the direction and control envisaged in the Commentary to Article 17 involves a relationship of dependency between a dominant state and a dependent state (eg, a protectorate or military occupation).[69] The principle served is that the subservient state remains responsible for its own acts even if it is *factually* dependent upon another with respect to the specific acts. The principle of concurrent or separate responsibility is reflected, inter alia, in Articles 19 and 47 ASR (Articles 18 and 47 ARIO) concerning a plurality of responsible states. There is a real distinction between a state that has freely chosen to be bound by conflicting obligations and a state that, as a result of occupation or other dependence, is incapable of controlling its conduct.

In *Behrami and Behrami*,[70] the applicants complained on behalf of their sons who had suffered death and injury in Kosovo while playing with a cluster bomb that exploded. The bomb had been deployed during the NATO-sanctioned airstrikes upon the FRY in 1999. Following the withdrawal of the FRY from most of Kosovo, the NATO-led Kosovo Force (KFOR) and the UN Interim Administration Mission in Kosovo (UNMIK) were deployed pursuant to UNSC Resolution 1244 (1999). In the joined case of *Saramati*, the applicant complained of his arrest and detention in Kosovo on the orders of the Commander of KFOR (COMKFOR). Two admissibility issues arose in these cases: 1) the attribution of the infringements *ratione personae* to the respondents as opposed to KFOR, NATO and/or the UN; and 2) if attributable to the respondents, the applicability of the Convention *ratione loci* to their conduct in Kosovo. Ruling that it was not competent to examine the cases *ratione personae*, the Strasbourg Court did not consider it necessary to examine the admissibility objection *ratione loci*.

In *Behrami*, the Strasbourg Court held that the impugned conduct was 'in principle' attributable to the UN by virtue of the fact that NATO (through KFOR) was exercising delegated powers from the UN Security Council, which retained 'ultimate authority and control' over KFOR operations in Kosovo.[71] The Court cited Article 7 ARIO: 'The conduct of an organ of a State or an organ or agent of an international organisation that is placed at the disposal of another international organisation shall be considered under international law an act of the latter organisation if the organisation exercises effective control over that conduct.' Whilst the Court purported to apply this test of 'effective control over conduct' to the facts of the two cases before it,[72] its reasoning has been much criticised as

[69] C Dominicé, 'Attribution of Conduct to Multiple States and the Implication of a State in the Act of Another State' in Crawford (n 12) 287–88.

[70] *Behrami and Behrami v France, Saramati v France, Germany and Norway*, App No 71412/01 (2007) 45 EHRR SE10, Judgment of 2 May 2007 (admissibility) [2]–[17].

[71] Ibid [132]–[153].

[72] Ibid [30]–[31], [138].

a misapplication.[73] Sections of the Court subsequently affirmed this reasoning in the cases of *Berić*, *Gajic* and *Kasumaj*.[74]

Although not expressly referred to by the Court, its reasoning is similar to that of Article 61(1) ARIO: 'A State member of an international organization incurs international responsibility if, by taking advantage of the fact that the organization has competence in relation to the subject-matter of one of the State's international obligations, it circumvents that obligation by causing the organization to commit an act that, if committed by the State, would have constituted a breach of the obligation.' Whilst this provision is controversial due to the introduction of the element of intent, its grounding in legal powers ('competence') as opposed to factual conduct resembles the Court's approach in *Behrami*. According to this analysis, a Member State is not responsible for the breach in question (which remains attributable to the organisation), but rather is separately responsible for having *caused* the organisation to commit the breach. This makes Article 61 more of a primary than a secondary rule because it prescribes a duty not to 'abuse' membership of an organisation.

In *Saramati*, the attribution exercise was relatively simple because the deprivation of liberty involved relatively few actors and the factual control was clear. The orders for the applicant's arrest and detention were issued by COMKFOR (initially a Norwegian and later a French officer) and implemented by UNMIK police officers. COMKFOR at all times operated within the unified command structure of NATO up to its political governing body, the North Atlantic Council.[75] NATO is endowed by the North Atlantic Treaty with international legal personality and is thus capable of assuming responsibility for the impugned conduct. Effective control being a factual question concerning specified acts, the retention of national control over seconded units concerning disciplinary, financial and other administrative matters was not germane to the operational control exercised by NATO through its subsidiary organ COMKFOR over the specific act of detention.

In *Al-Jedda*,[76] the Court distinguished *Behrami* for the purpose of attribution. The UK was found to have violated the liberty of the applicant through long-term detention without trial in Iraq whilst acting pursuant to powers prescribed by UNSC Resolutions 1511 (2003) and 1546 (2004). The parties agreed that the governing principle for attribution was 'effective control' under Article 7 ARIO.[77] After noting the agreement, the Court held: 'the Court considers that the UN Security Council had neither effective control nor ultimate authority and control over the acts and omissions of troops within the Multi-National Force and that the applicant's detention was not, therefore, attributable to the United Nations'.[78] Whilst the Court seemingly edged away from its *Behrami* formula, it did not disavow it and found that Resolutions 1511 and 1546 did not oblige the UK to detain the applicant, but empowered it to do so.[79]

[73] For an extensive list of critical scholarship on the reasoning of the Court, see the ILC ARIO Commentary, 23 (note 115).

[74] *Berić v Bosnia and Herzegovina*, App No 36357/04 (2008) 46 EHRR SE06, Judgment of 21 September 2004 [26]–[30]; *Gajiv v Germany*, App No 31446/02, Judgment of 5 July 2007; *Kasumaj v Greece*, App No 6974/05, Judgment of 5 July 2007.

[75] *Behrami* (n 70) [139].

[76] *Al-Jedda v UK*, App No 27021/08 (2011) 53 EHRR 23, Judgment of 7 July 2011 [74]–[86].

[77] Ibid [18].

[78] Ibid [84].

[79] Ibid [83], [105].

In its recent judgment of *Nada*,[80] the Court again considered the attribution of conduct to the UN. The Security Council in Resolutions 1267 (1999), 1333 (2000), 1373 (2001) and 1390 (2002) created a sanctions regime targeting suspected al-Qaeda and Taliban operatives. Switzerland enacted enabling legislation and, following the listing of the applicant by the UN Sanctions Committee as a proscribed individual, denied the applicant entry into and transit through Switzerland. The applicant complained of violations to, inter alia, his liberty and privacy.

Addressing the argument of France and others that the implementing measures taken by UN Member States were attributable to the UN, the Court held:

> The Court cannot endorse that argument. It would point that it found in *Behrami and Behrami* that the impugned acts and omissions of KFOR, whose powers had been validly delegated to it by the Security Council under Chapter VII of the Charter, and those of UNMIK, a subsidiary organ of the United Nations set up under the same Chapter, were directly attributable to the United Nations, an organisation of universal jurisdiction fulfilling its imperative collective security objective (ibid., § 151). In the present case, by contrast, the relevant Security Council resolutions, especially Resolutions 1267 (1999), 1333 (2000, 1373 (2001) and 1390 (2002), required States to act in their own names and to implement them at national level.[81]

Unlike in *Al-Jedda* (where the parties had agreed on the applicability of then-Article 5 ARIO), the Court did not refer to or purport to apply the ARIO in its analysis of the attribution issue. Rather, it conceptualised the problem as falling within the scope of 'jurisdiction' under Article 1 of the Convention notwithstanding, as argued above, that this provision concerns breach rather than attribution.

As in *Behrami* and *Al-Jedda*, the Court's analysis focused upon the aims of the UNSC resolutions rather than factual control. Multiple actions caused the infringement of the applicant's liberty. First, the legislation of an obligation upon all UN Member States to 'prevent the entry into or the transit through their territories of these [listed] individuals'[82] was attributable to the UN as an act of the Security Council.[83] However, it is arguable that the conduct of the Council of Europe Member States—especially the veto-wielding Permanent Members—in voting in favour of this resolution 'knowing' that there was a risk of incompatibility with Convention rights comprised discrete acts forming part of the chain of causation.[84]

Second, the proscription of the applicant was attributable to the UN through the Sanctions Committee as a subsidiary organ of the Security Council. In this respect, an important distinction between *Nada* and the UN Human Rights Committee case of *Sayadi and Vinck*[85] is that whereas in the former the listing of the applicant by the Sanctions Committee was instigated by the US, in the latter it was prompted by the respondent

[80] *Nada v Switzerland*, App No 10593/08, Judgment of 12 September 2012 [117]–[123].

[81] Ibid [120].

[82] UNSC Resolution 1390 (2002), OP2(b).

[83] Article 6 ARIO. See also *Nada* (n 80) [76].

[84] Article 16 ASR. In particular: France, the UK, the Russian Federation, the Netherlands, Slovenia, the Ukraine, Norway and Ireland. See UNSC 4452nd Meeting (16 January 2002), UN Doc S/PV.4452; UNSC 4385th Meeting (28 September 2001), UN Doc S/PV.4385; UNSC 4251st Meeting (19 December 2000), UN Doc S/PV.4251, 9 (Canada); UNSC 4051st Meeting (15 October 1999), UN Doc S/PV.4051.

[85] *Nada* (n 80) [88]–[92].

(Belgium). As noted by the Federal Court of Switzerland, Switzerland was not authorised to list or delist the applicant *ex proprio motu*.[86]

Third, the denial of entry into Switzerland to the applicant was attributable to Switzerland pursuant to Article 4 ASR. Whilst the Court arrived at the same conclusion, its reasoning placed greater emphasis upon the terms of the Security Council resolutions rather than the fact that Swiss organs had performed the impugned conduct of denial of entry.[87] The provisions of Resolution 1390 were relevant context, yet the determinative fact was the status of the implementing authority as a state organ rather than a UN organ for that purpose. The argument of France that the effect of Article 103 of the UN Charter was to render the actions of Switzerland attributable to the UN was misconceived because Article 103 was relevant to mitigation rather than attribution. Whilst its effect was potentially to either displace the obligation or to mitigate the breach, it had no bearing upon whether it was Switzerland that factually denied entry and transit to the applicant.

However, the Court instead concluded that Switzerland had an 'admittedly limited but nevertheless real' discretion concerning implementation:

> In the present case, the applicant mainly challenged the Swiss entry and transit ban imposed on him in particular through the implementation of Resolution 1390 (2002). Whilst paragraph 2(b) of that resolution required States to take such measures, it stated that the ban did 'not apply where entry or transit [was] necessary for the fulfilment of a judicial process…' (see paragraph 74 above). In the Court's view, the term 'necessary' was to be construed on a case-by-case basis.
>
> In addition, in paragraph 8 of Resolution 1390 (2002), the Security Council '[urged] all States to take immediate steps to enforce and strengthen through legislative enactments or administrative measures, where appropriate, the measures imposed under domestic laws or regulations against their nationals and other individuals or entities operating on their territory …' (see paragraph 74 above). The wording 'where appropriate' also had the effect of affording the national authorities a certain flexibility in the mode of implementation of the resolution.
>
> Lastly, the Court would refer to the motion by which the Foreign Policy Commission of the Swiss National Council requested the Federal Council to inform the UN Security Council that it would not longer unconditionally be applying the sanctions prescribed against individuals under the counter-terrorism resolutions (see paragraph 63 above). Even though that motion was drafted in rather general terms, it can nevertheless be said that the applicant's case was one of the main reasons for its adoption. In any event, in the Court's view, the Swiss Parliament, in adopting that motion, was expressing its intention to allow a certain discretion in the application of the Security Council's counter-terrorism resolutions.
>
> In view of the foregoing, the Court finds that Switzerland enjoyed some latitude, which was admittedly limited but nevertheless real, in implementing the relevant binding resolutions of the UN Security Council.[88]

The critique of this reasoning in the Joint Concurring Opinion of Judges Bratza, Nicolaou and Yudkivska is cogent and compelling.[89] The Court's finding of a breach by Switzerland was grounded not in its implementation of Resolution 1390, but rather in its failure to take practicable steps to mitigate its effects, particularly by informing the Sanctions Committee

[86] Ibid [50], [187]–[188]. See also UNSC Resolution 1390 (2002), OP2.

[87] Ibid [120]–[121].

[88] *Nada* (n 80) [177]–[180].

[89] Ibid, Joint Concurring Opinion of Judges Bratza, Nicolaou and Yudkivska [1]–[8].

of the findings of its investigation concerning the applicant and by lobbying Italy to apply to the Committee to delist the applicant.[90] Neither the main judgment nor the Joint Concurring Opinion connected the discretion afforded to Switzerland to the question of attribution to the UN under the ARIO.

This appraisal of the recent jurisprudence of the Strasbourg Court concerning the attribution of conduct in cases involving international organisations and states acting pursuant to UN Security Council resolutions demonstrates that the Court has not applied the ASR and the ARIO consistently or precisely. Rather, despite the lack of a Convention foundation, the Court has invented an ad hoc doctrinal approach to attribution or has often misapplied the ILC texts. This has resulted in a sporadic and confused jurisprudence that is not based upon any clear rationale and analytical method. The resulting detriment is the weakening of legal predictability and coherence, which is likely to spawn needlessly repetitive admissibility objections based upon unrealistic attempts by states to attribute to international organisations or by applicants to states regardless of the facts. A more rational approach would seek to apply (and, indeed, refine and develop) the ILC texts based upon factual control in a precise and fact-sensitive manner.

III. CONCLUSIONS

This chapter has assessed the potential consequences of the accession of the EU to the ECHR for the attribution of conduct under the law of international responsibility before the Strasbourg Court. In its first section, it asserted that the policy of the European Commission, in seeking to exempt the EU from the general international law of responsibility, is misconceived both as a matter of pragmatism and EU law. In its second section, it argued that the jurisprudence of the Strasbourg Court concerning the attribution of conduct in cases involving the UN, the EU and NATO is doctrinally flawed due to its analytical inconsistency and imprecision.

It is questionable whether the accession of the EU to the Convention would substantially improve these problems. Although the availability of the EU as a respondent might be expected to prompt a more consistent and realistic approach in cases involving the implementation of EU legislation or in CFSP operations, the Commission's policy of seeking to arrogate responsibility to the EU in international litigation that even remotely engages EU law does not accord with the approach of general international law. The policy of the Commission that divisions of competence in the EU legal order be applied externally complicates an already-confused area before the Strasbourg Court, which the current formulation of the draft 'co-respondent mechanism' is also likely to exacerbate.

Moreover, the doctrinal problems in the jurisprudence of the Strasbourg Court are not principally caused by the absence of the EU as a party to the Convention. Rather, they arise from a tendency by the Court to adopt an ad hoc and factually imprecise approach in cases involving international organisations and joint operations. These include cases such as *Behrami and Saramati* or *Al-Jedda* that did not concern the EU. Whilst accession may prompt a rethink in cases involving the implementation of EU law, particularly if the

[90] Ibid [185]–[194].

EU finds itself paying substantial sums in compensation for breaches in which it scarcely played a role, it is unlikely to provide a holistic cure.

These problems could be rectified through the consistent and precise application of the control-based approach of the ILC texts and more nuanced and detailed scrutiny of the facts. Although the ILC texts are inevitably imperfect, they have not only undergone careful and thorough scrutiny in their drafting by experts in the field, but the ARIO have also been specifically designed to apply to all international organisations despite their architectural diversity. Flaws and gaps in the ILC texts (eg, 'normative control' under Article 17 ARIO) can be rectified and refined through practical application, especially since neither text has yet been enacted as a treaty. In this respect, greater development and refinement of these carefully-drafted texts would produce better results than the ad hoc invention of doctrine.

In addition, a rigorous and nuanced examination of the facts is particularly necessary in cases involving multiple actors in joint operations and sanctions within a complex legal architecture. In such cases, simplicity can be achieved by carefully identifying and separating the actions and omissions that cause the alleged breach of the Convention. Instead of artificially attributing conduct to actors (eg, the UN) that had scant involvement in the commission of the impugned conduct, parsing out according to control of *specific acts* would create more realistic and consistent results. For this purpose, greater focus upon the enactment of legislation by Member States and causation would improve the rigour of the analysis in weighing the factors that contributed to the breach. This would enable respondents to justifiably claim mitigation for remedial purposes due to the involvement of third parties, whilst ensuring that they are held responsible for their own contribution to the breach is properly acknowledged.

8

United We Stand: The EU and its Member States in the Strasbourg Court

ANDRÉS DELGADO CASTELEIRO*

I. INTRODUCTION

THE ACCESSION OF the European Union (EU) to the European Convention on Human Rights (ECHR) will mark not only the beginning of a new era in terms of the protection of Fundamental Rights in Europe, but also in terms of the EU's participation in international courts and tribunals. Up until now, the EU has never become a party to an international agreement with such a strong adjudicatory body. Therefore, it can be expected that the EU's accession to the ECHR will have important implications for the common assumptions surrounding the relationship between the EU and adjudicatory decision making of international organisations.[1] Furthermore, it cannot be excluded that the articulation of EU participation in the European Court of Human Rights (ECtHR) will not be replicated in other international agreements with an international court.

Consequently, the examination of the mechanism envisaging the EU's participation in ECtHR proceedings undoubtedly raises many interesting issues as regards the EU's external representation. There are many noteworthy questions concerning the relationship between the Court of Justice of the EU (CJEU) and the ECtHR in institutional and substantive terms. This paper focuses on an institutional matter, namely, the EU's *locus standi* in the ECtHR. More precisely, it examines how the draft Accession Agreement[2] deals with the participation of the EU in the proceedings of the ECtHR; in other words, how the co-respondent mechanism organises the participation of the EU and its Member States in ECtHR proceedings. The current institutional design of the ECHR, and more specifically the way in which the ECtHR works, leads to many problems linked with the future joint

* Lecturer in Law, University of Durham, United Kingdom. The author would like to thank Vasiliki Kosta and Vassilis Tzevelekos for their useful comments and suggestions. The usual disclaimer applies.

[1] On those views, see: J Klabbers, *The European Union in International Law* (Paris, Pedone, 2012) 69; BI Bonafé, 'Direct Effect of International Agreement in the EU Legal Order: Does it Depend on the Existence of an International Dispute Settlement Mechanism?' in E Cannizzaro, P Palcehtti and RA Wessel (eds), *International Law as the Law of the European Union* (Leiden, Martinus Nijhoff, 2012); P Eeckhout, *EU External Relations Law* (Oxford, Oxford University Press, 2011) 434; M Bronckers, 'The Relationship of the EC Courts with Other International Tribunals: Non-committal, Respectful or Submissive?' (2007) 44 *Common Market Law Review* 601; N Lavranos, *Legal Internation between Decisions of International Organizations and European Law* (Amsterdam, Europa Law, 2004).

[2] The draft Agreement and its Explanatory Report can be found in the Council of Europe Doc 47+1 (2013) R008, available at www.coe.int/t/dghl/standardsetting/hrpolicy/Accession/Meeting_reports/47_1(2013)008_final_report_EN.pdf.

participation of the EU and its Member States: the lack of legal certainty as regards the respondent and the lack of unity when pleading or issues concerning the autonomy of the EU's legal order[3] create problems in terms of the EU's *locus standi.*

As a way of dealing with these issues, the draft Agreement and more precisely its Explanatory Report enshrine the so-called co-respondent mechanism. This legal device aims at alleviating the different tensions underpinning the accession of the EU, such as the different views on the division of competences, the autonomous nature of the EU legal order and the problems of legal certainty that the EU's participation can entail. However, a closer look at the co-respondent mechanism will show that certain gaps in accountability would still remain after the EU's accession. This chapter will proceed with this examination in three parts. First, it assesses how the co-respondent mechanism deals with the main interests affecting EU participation in the ECtHR. Second, it shows how the principles that govern the relations between the EU and its Member States affect their participation in the proceedings in front of the ECtHR. More specifically, it builds on recent developments in the case law of the CJEU on the duty of cooperation. Third, it examines whether the EU's participation in other international court proceedings can give us some clues as to how the duty of cooperation might operate when pleading in Strasbourg. More precisely, the issue of joint participation in front of other international courts will undoubtedly shed some light on how the EU and its Member States will act in the Strasbourg Court. In this regard, the chapter concludes that the design of the co-respondent mechanism could pose some problems as regards the autonomy of EU Member States when pleading in front of the ECtHR. It critically concludes that, although innovative, the co-respondent mechanism can restrict the autonomy of EU Member States in front of the ECtHR.

II. THE CO-RESPONDENT MECHANISM: PROCEDURALISING THE PROBLEMS

A. Organising Principles of the Co-respondent Mechanism

The main reason behind the necessity of a special mechanism dealing with EU intervention stems from both the way in which the EU will accede to the ECHR and the *sui generis* nature of the EU. On the one hand, both the EU and its Member States will be party to the ECHR. The EU will not replace the Member States, so the division of competences and the allocation of responsibilities as regards the ECHR become blurred. This becomes especially relevant when speaking about responsibility and *locus standi.* If the division of competence is not settled, it becomes difficult to know who is going to be prima facie responsible and consequently who will plead in Strasbourg.

While formally the ECHR is not going to differ significantly from any other mixed agreement in terms of negotiation, conclusion and ratification, the institutional design of the ECHR, and more specifically the way in which the ECtHR functions, has the potential to intensify some of the problems linked to mixity.[4] The co-respondent mechanism would

[3] For an extensive discussion on the issue of the EU's autonomy and the accession to the ECHR, see A Torres Pérez, ch 3 in this edited collection.

[4] On the different issues arising from mixity, see: C-D Ehlermann, 'Mixed Agreements A List of Problems' in D O'Keeffe and HG Schermers (eds), *Mixed Agreements* (Deventer, Kluwer Law and Taxation, 1983); NA Neuwahl, *Mixed Agreements: Analysis of the Phenomenon and their Legal Significance* (Florence, European University Institute,

aim at alleviating precisely these problems. In this regard, the Explanatory Report to the draft Agreement clearly shows that the co-respondent mechanism is necessary in order to 'accommodate the specific situation of the EU as a non-State entity with an autonomous legal system that is becoming a Party to the Convention alongside its own member States'.[5] In other words, the ECHR will be a mixed agreement. Since both the EU and its Member States will be parties, the extent to which both of them are bound and responsible under the ECHR is unclear.

Moreover, the EU implements its *acquis* in quite a complicated manner, indirect administration being the most obvious example. In a nutshell, like other international organisations, the EU relies on its Member States for the application and implementation of EU law.[6] The decentralised application of EU law is guided by the principle of primacy: all organs of a Member State's administration—executive *and* judicial—must not apply conflicting national law in every individual case before them. From an institutional perspective, national administrations are not integrated into the European administrative machinery.[7] From a functional perspective, they operate as a decentralised European administration;[8] they cannot be considered EU organs.[9] Customs administration constitutes the most obvious example of the EU's executive federalism. Customs falls under the exclusive competence of the EU,[10] yet there are no EU customs administrations. Instead, there are 28 customs administrations which implement the EU customs legislation. Therefore, what happens when one of these authorities breaches a fundamental right (eg, the right to property)? Who should be responsible? Who should stand in front of the ECtHR to defend the compatibility of the action of a customs official?

Moreover, EU law nowadays operates in even more complex ways, in which the principles that govern the relations between EU law and the national realm get diluted. Examples of this could be the European Arrest Warrant, in which a framework decision[11] lays down the conditions under which a Member State has the obligation to extradite individuals to another Member State.[12] Thus, could the EU intervene in cases dealing with a European Arrest Warrant?

1988); E Neframi, 'International Responsibility of the European Community and of Member States under Mixed Agreements' in E Cannizzaro (ed), *The European Union as an Actor in International Relations* (Leiden, Kluwer Law International, 2002); C Tomuschat, 'The International Responsibility of the European Union' in E Cannizzaro (ed), *The European Union as an Actor in International Relations* (Leiden, Kluwer Law International, 2002).

[5] Explanatory Report, para 38.

[6] J Klabbers, *An Introduction to International Institutional Law* (Cambridge, Cambridge University Press, 2009) 279. HG Schermers and NM Blokker, *International Institutional Law: Unity Within Diversity* (Leiden, Martinus Nijhoff, 2003) 958.

[7] R Schütze, 'From Rome to Lisbon: "Executive Federalism" in the (New) European Union' 47 (2010) *Common Market Law Review* 1385.

[8] R Schütze, *From Dual to Cooperative Federalism: The Changing Structure of European Law* (Oxford, Oxford University Press, 2009) 57; PJ Kuijper, 'International Responsibility for EU Mixed Agreements' in C Hillion and P Koutrakos (eds), *Mixed Agreements Revisited: The EU and its Member States in the World* (Oxford, Hart Publishing, 2010).

[9] Contra: PJ Kuijper and E Paasivirta, 'Further Exploring International Responsibility: The European Community and the ILC's Project on Responsibility of International Organizations' (2004) 1 *International Organizations Law Review* 111; F Hoffmeister, 'Bosphorus Hava Yollari Turizm ve Ticaret Anonim Sirket v. Ireland' (2006) 100 *American Journal of International Law* 442.

[10] Article 3 TFEU.

[11] Council Framework Decision 2002/584 JHA of 13 June 2002 on the European Arrest Warrant and the surrender procedures between Member States, OJ 2002 L190/1.

[12] S Peers, *EU Justice and Home Affairs* (Oxford, Oxford University Press, 2011) 469.

In this regard, the Explanatory Report acknowledges the 'special feature of the EU legal system that acts adopted by its institutions may be implemented by its member States and, conversely, that provisions of the EU founding treaties agreed upon by its member States may be implemented by institutions, bodies, offices or agencies of the EU'.[13] Therefore, the issue of the implementation of the *acquis* by Member States and the role of the latter in the decision-making process of the EU will also play a relevant role in the co-respondent mechanism.

The joint participation of the EU and its Member States, added to the complexity in which EU law is implemented, could create uncertainty as to who has competence over a certain area, who would be responsible for a specific breach of the ECHR in that area and who would have standing. As a matter of practice, when dealing with complex issues linked to the division of competences in mixed agreements, the EU has tended to proceduralise the matter. Whenever there is some kind of disagreement between the diverging interests underpinning an international agreement, the EU and the other parties to the agreement tend to favour the inclusion of a procedural solution. Instead of establishing clear obligations for all parties, the agreement defers away the obligation into procedures and future decision making.[14] For instance, the EU and its Member States agree on an internal procedure, which solves the issue of competence in most of the aspects of the international agreement. The decision as to the division of competences is postponed to a later stage while assuring the other parties to the agreement that the solution to the issue of competence, responsibility or standing will be rapidly resolved once the procedure is triggered. Declarations of competence made to multilateral environmental agreements[15] or the institutional arrangement dealing with the EU´s participation in the FAO are examples of this tendency to lay down procedures dealing with the EU's participation in a mixed agreement.[16]

These concerns on the division of powers and the legal uncertainty that creates can also be found in Article 1 Protocol nº 8 of the Lisbon Treaty. The protocol, which deals with the EU accession to the ECHR, provides that:

> The agreement relating to the accession of the Union to the European Convention on the Protection of Human Rights and Fundamental Freedoms (hereinafter referred to as the 'European Convention') provided for in Article 6(2) of the Treaty on European Union shall make provision for preserving the specific characteristics of the Union and Union law, in particular with regard to:
>
> [...] (b) the mechanisms necessary to ensure that proceedings by non-Member States and individual applications are correctly addressed to Member States and/or the Union as appropriate.

The protocol and by extension EU Member States are concerned that the mixed character of the ECHR can lead to the incorrect targeting of the EU or its Member States. EU Member States would want to avoid being responsible for acts committed by the EU. In this

[13] Explanatory Report, para 38.

[14] M Koskenniemi, 'Theory: Implications for the Practioners' in British Institute of International and Comparative Law (ed), *Theory and International Law: An Introduction* (London, British Institute of International and Comparative Law, 1991) 13. In fact, as Koskenniemi points out, this trend is not exclusive from the EU. It is a common trend in international law-making and is especially present in Multilateral Environmental International Agreements.

[15] A Delgado Casteleiro, 'EU Declarations of Competence to Multilateral Agreements: A Useful Reference Base?' (2012) 17 *European Foreign Affairs Review* 4, 491–510.

[16] A Delgado Casteleiro, 'The International Responsibility of the EU: Between Pragmatism and Proceduralization' (2012–2013) *Cambridge Yearbook of European Legal Studies 15.*

regard, legal certainty works in two directions. The mechanism should give the individual bringing the claim certainty that somebody will be held responsible for the violation of the ECHR, while at the same time it gives EU Member States certainty that they will not be held liable for acts which they are not responsible. Put differently, Member States wanted to avoid similar scenarios to the *Senator Lines* case.[17] In this case, the claimant (Senator Lines) argued that a fine imposed by the European Commission, applying EU competition law violated articles 6 and 13 of the ECHR. Since the EU was not a party to the ECHR, Senator Lines brought the case against the EU Member States. Eventually, the ECtHR declared the application inadmissible, due to the fact that the European Commission had annulled the fine. After the EU's accession, a similar case would endanger the autonomy of EU Legal order. The EU Member States would be obliged to comply with a judgement that tells them to stop applying EU legislation. However since the EU would not be bound by the judgment, if the Member States comply with the ECtHR judgment they would be in breach of EU law and vice versa.[18] Furthermore, a case resembling *Senator Lines* would also create potential problems regarding the vertical division of powers. The Member States would be held responsible for an action of the European Commission. Yet, given the vertical division of powers in the EU, the Member States have no powers in this area. They cannot annul or stop complying with a decision of the Commission unless the CJEU has annulled it. Therefore, the EU Member States, after having being held responsible by the ECtHR, would need to bring either an infringement action or an annulment action against the Commission.[19] Obviously, this would put EU Member States' compliance with the ECtHR outside of their control. They cannot simply disregard the Commission decision without a prior CJEU decision, which can take years.

The co-respondent mechanism envisages a procedure which tries to deal with such issues as a lack of legal certainty on the question of who should be liable for violations of the Convention or the autonomy of the EU legal order understood both as the independent legal personality of the EU and the division of competences.[20] In this regard, Article 36(4) ECHR as modified by the draft legal instrument provides that:

> The European Union or a member State of the European Union may become a co-respondent to proceedings by decision of the Court in the circumstances set out in the Agreement on the Accession of the European Union to the Convention for the Protection of Human Rights and Fundamental Freedoms. A co-respondent is a party to the case. The admissibility of an application shall be assessed without regard to the participation of a co-respondent in the proceedings.

This provision enshrines a procedure by which the EU and the Member States will jointly participate in the proceedings brought against any of them. The aim of this procedure,

[17] *Senator Lines GmbH v Austria, Belgium, Denmark, Finland, France, Germany, Greece, Ireland, Italy, Luxembourg, the Netherlands, Portugal, Spain, Sweden and the United Kingdom*, App No 56672/00 (2004). See also, in relation to Eurocontrol, *Boivin v 34 Member States of the Council of Europe*, App No 73250/01 (2008).

[18] T Lock, 'End of an Epic? The Draft Agreement on the EU's Accession to the ECHR' (2011) 31 *Yearbook of European Law* 162; JM Cortés Martín, 'Adhesión al CEDH y Autonomía del Derecho de la Unión: Legitimación pasiva de la Unión y sus miembros y compatibilidad material' (2010) 22 *Revista General de Derecho Europeo* 53; JA Pastor Ridruejo, 'La interrelación de los sistemas de protección de los derechos fundamentales' in E Álvarez Conde and V Garrido Mayol (eds), *Comentarios a la Constitución Europea*, vol 2 (Valencia, Tirant Lo Blanch, 2005).

[19] Article 259 TFEU.

[20] In more general terms, see J Heliskoski, *Mixed Agreements as a Technique for Organising the International Relations of the European Community and its Member States* (Leiden, Kluwer Law International, 2001) 19.

as mentioned before, is to create a balance between the *sui generis* nature of the EU and legal certainty for the parties to the proceedings. As the Explanatory Report shows, the co-respondent mechanism is 'a way to avoid gaps in participation, accountability and enforceability in the Convention system'. The mixed participation of the EU and its Member States combined with the complex nature of the EU's legal system could lead to gaps in responsibility,[21] which in this context means gaps in the protection of fundamental rights in Europe. Consequently, the co-respondent mechanism establishes that the EU and/or its Member States will take part in the proceedings whenever the compatibility between an EU law instrument and a provision of the ECHR is called into question.[22]

Furthermore, the protocol expresses another concern usually linked with the mixed participation in international agreements: the encroachment of competences by the EU through practice. Article 2, Protocol No 8 provides that: 'The agreement referred to in Article 1 shall ensure that accession of the Union shall not affect the competences of the Union or the powers of its institutions.'

This kind of statement can also be found in other recent arrangements regarding the participation of the EU and its Member States in international organisations. More precisely, in a recent arrangement concerning EU statements in multilateral organisations (the arrangement), the following disclaimer was added: 'The adoption and presentation of statements does not affect the distribution of competences or the allocation of powers between the institutions under the Treaties. Moreover, it does not affect the decision-making procedures for the adoption of EU positions by the Council as provided in the Treaties.'[23]

The protocol, like the arrangement, put forward the concern of certain Member States with regard to the implications that the external representation of the EU has on the internal division of powers.[24] To deal with all these concerns, the draft Agreement establishes a new model of proceduralisation of the EU's participation in international agreements. So far, most of the procedures have been of an internal nature. They have either been internal arrangements between the different institutions of the EU or instruments with international legal effects, albeit unilateral and internal in nature.[25] As a general rule, procedures addressing the EU's participation in international agreements were not included in the body of such agreements. They were required by the agreement, but they were considered an internal matter of the EU. The co-respondent mechanism breaks with this trend to a certain extent, since it appears that further internal rules on the EU's participation in the ECtHR are being discussed in the EU Council of Ministers.[26]

Moreover, it appears that the responsibility of the EU and its Member States will be joint unless the they decide otherwise.[27] Consequently, when the co-respondent mechanism is triggered, both the EU and at least one of its Member States will stand in front of the ECtHR

[21] *Cf* R Collins and ND White, 'Moving Beyond the Autonomy-Accountability Dichotomy: Reflections on Institutional Independence in the International Legal Order' (2010) 7 *International Organizations Law Review* 1.

[22] Article 3(2) of the draft Agreement.

[23] Council Document 15901/11.

[24] See European Scrutiny Committee, *House of Commons. Fifty-fourth Report*, available at www.publications.parliament.uk/pa/cm201012/cmselect/cmeuleg/428-xlix/42802.htm. On a more general level and theoretical level, see Heliskoski (n 20).

[25] *Cf* Delgado Casteleiro (n 15) 491.

[26] Lock (n 18) 169.

[27] Article 3(7) of the draft Agreement.

to defend the compatibility of their actions with the provisions of the ECHR. In addition, depending on the nature of the EU legal act called into question, the co-respondent mechanism lays down different procedures.

B. Scenarios that Trigger the Co-respondent Mechanism

The co-respondent mechanism establishes two different procedures depending on whether the breach stems from an EU primary norm (ie, the Treaties) or from a secondary norm (ie, regulations, directives, etc.). It lays down a procedure to involve the EU or its Member States depending on the type of act which caused the violation of the ECHR. If the breach stems from an EU primary norm, a different procedure will apply than if the breach stems from an EU secondary provision. By allowing the EU and/or its Member States to act as co-respondents, the draft Agreement tries to ensure, as pointed out before, that there will not be gaps in responsibility. However, a closer look at the co-respondent mechanism shows that certain gaps in accountability would still remain after the EU's accession. This section is divided into three parts. First, it will examine how the co-respondent mechanism operates in cases in which the validity of EU primary law is put into question. The second part focuses on the validity of EU secondary norms, while the third examines other situations in which EU law can appear in an incidental manner.

i. Breach of the ECHR by Primary Law

To deal with breaches of the ECHR stemming from EU primary norms, ie, the Treaties, Article 3(3) of the draft Agreement provides that:

> Where an application is directed against the European Union, the European Union member States may become co-respondents to the proceedings in respect of an alleged violation notified by the Court if it appears that such allegation calls into question the compatibility with the Convention rights at issue of a provision of the Treaty on European Union, the Treaty on the Functioning of the European Union or any other provision having the same legal value pursuant to those instruments, notably where that violation could have been avoided only by disregarding an obligation under those instruments.

The co-respondent mechanism thus tries to deal with situations like the one that occurred in *Matthews*.[28] The co-respondent mechanism recognises that in those cases in which the breach stems from a rule enshrined in a treaty, it is necessary to hold the Member States liable. The liability of the Member States would ensure that the treaty provision would be modified following Article 48 of the Treaty on European Union (TEU).[29] However, this provision raises many questions as regards its practical application. For instance, the responsibility of the EU in this scenario, while symbolic, is not justified by a coherent legal doctrine of attribution of responsibility.[30] First, if there is an incompatibility between a provision of the ECHR and a provision of the EU Treaties, the Member States were the

[28] *Matthews v United Kingdom*, Series A 24833/94, (1999) 28 EHRR 36; Lock (n 18) 171.

[29] X Groussot, T Lock and L Pech, *Adhésion de l'Union européenne á la Conventions européenne des droits de l l'homme: analyse juridique du projet d'accord d'adhesion du 14 de octobre 2011* (Brussels, Question d'Europe, 2011) 13.

[30] Lock (n 18) 172.

ones that negotiated, agreed, signed and ratified that incompatibility in the first place. Therefore, it would make sense to hold them liable. Second, since the Member States are the driving force behind any treaty modification, to hold them responsible alongside the EU for a breach stemming from a treaty provision would be redundant. Third, the EU comprises its Member States, especially in situations in which the compatibility of EU law with international law is put into question. Article 216(2) of the Treaty on the Functioning of the European Union (TFEU) clearly recognises this when it states that agreements concluded by the EU are binding upon the institutions of the EU and on its Member States. Moreover, the CJEU has extended this provision to apply to the decisions of the bodies set by those agreements.[31]

However, it is the exact scope of EU–Member State intervention that casts doubt on the practical functioning of the co-respondent mechanism in this scenario. First, given the rationale underpinning the mechanism, it would be expected that all EU Member States would have to act as co-respondents. Even though this is not entirely clear in the draft Agreement and the Explanatory Report, it would be the only way to ensure that there were no gaps in responsibility.[32] However, as will be further explained below, the voluntary nature of the mechanism[33] does not guarantee this result. More precisely, a hypothetical judgment of the ECtHR in this scenario would most likely fall within the scope of Article 48(6) and (7) TEU. By virtue of this provision, unanimity in the European Council is a *conditio sine qua non* to reform the Treaties.[34] Thus, if a Member State does not join the proceedings, there are no assurances that the treaty reform that would lead the conflict with the ECHR being solved will take place.

By way of an example, in a situation like *Matthews*, all the Member States would be invited to join. However, there is the possibility that certain Member States might decide not to join the proceedings. For instance, in a case similar to *Matthews*, it would be rather unlikely that Spain would join the proceedings as a co-respondent. Spain already expressed its unease to the previous *Matthews* case by bringing an action to the CJEU against its implementation.[35] By not joining the other EU Member States as co-respondents, Spain would avoid being internationally bound to renegotiate a part of the EU Treaties it does not want to compromise on. Consequently, in this scenario, the co-respondent would not effectively fill the gap in responsibility because of its voluntary nature.

Second, the wording of the co-respondent mechanism as regards breaches stemming from EU primary law seems to adopt a narrow approach to the situations in which these kinds of breaches might arise. The co-respondent mechanism rightly reflects that the most likely scenario in which this kind of situation might arise will be in cases brought against the EU. However, it cannot be excluded that a breach of primary EU law might also arise in proceedings brought against EU Member States. Yet neither paragraph 2 nor paragraph 3 of Article 3 of the draft Agreement allows EU Member States to become co-respondents in actions brought against other EU Member States. So, should that claim be declared inadmissible *ratio personae*? Taking into account that the ECtHR allows individuals to

[31] Case 181/73 *Haegeman* [1974] ECR 449; Case 12/86 *Demirel* [1987] ECR 03719; Case C-192/89 *Sevince* [1990] ECR I-3461.

[32] Lock (n 18) 171.

[33] Article 3(2)–(3) of the draft Agreement.

[34] K Lenaerts and P van Nuffel, *European Union Law* (London, Sweet & Maxwell, 2011) 79.

[35] Case C-145/04 *Spain v United Kingdom* [2006] ECR I-7917.

bring cases without the need of legal counsel and how the EU's executive federalism dilutes the visibility of EU law, it would create an unfair burden on the individual if her claim is declared inadmissible and has to bring a new one. For instance, an individual could see her case declared inadmissible because it was not able to identify that her fundamental rights were violated not only by the Member State she is bringing the case against but also by a provision of the EU Treaties.

Overall, the co-respondent mechanism deals with most of the situations in which a breach of the ECHR might stem from a provision of EU primary law. However, the voluntary nature of the mechanism can create problems as regards the reparation of the wrongful act. Also, the co-respondent mechanism does not allow certain possibilities, such as permitting EU Member States to act as co-respondents in actions brought against other EU Member States, which could place an extra burden on the claimant. The narrow wording of the provision combined with the voluntary nature of the mechanism cast some shadows over the practical effectiveness of the co-respondent mechanism.

ii. Breach of the ECHR by Secondary Law

Article 3(2) of the draft Agreement enshrines the way in which the EU and its Member States will participate in those proceedings in which the compatibility of EU secondary legislation with the ECHR is called into question. The paragraph reads as follows:

> 2. Where an application is directed against one or more member States of the European Union, the European Union may become a co-respondent to the proceedings in respect of an alleged violation notified by the Court if it appears that such allegation calls into question the compatibility with the Convention rights at issue of a provision of European Union law, notably where that violation could have been avoided only by disregarding an obligation under European Union law.

The provision provides, inter alia, for the participation of the EU in proceedings brought against its Member States when they implement EU secondary legislation. In this regard, the Explanatory Report makes reference to the specific example of EU executive federalism as one of the reasons for the adoption of the co-respondent mechanism.[36] Member States implement EU regulations and directives on a daily basis. Therefore, questions on responsibility and *locus standi* in those situations are likely to appear in front of the Strasbourg Court.[37] Nevertheless, the provision is also designed to cover other situations. The use of the expression 'provision of European Union Law' also gives the EU the possibility to intervene in proceedings in which EU primary law is called into question. The Explanatory Report explicitly mentions this possibility.[38]

However, the broad scope for EU participation in these kinds of scenarios is not matched by the participation of Member States. It could be argued that the participation of EU Member States is not necessary in this case, since it is only the EU that can solve the incompatibility. In this respect, the participation of the EU is necessary in order to fill any gap in responsibility. Despite the logic underpinning the co-respondent mechanism, there are

[36] Explanatory Report, para 38.
[37] Ibid, para 50.
[38] Ibid, para 49.

some issues concerning the internal coherence of paragraph 2, especially as regards the role of the Member States. Two comments need to be made in this respect.

First, if the participation of the EU is necessary in order to solve the issue of the compatibility of an EU secondary norm and the ECHR, is the presence of the EU Member States really necessary? The co-respondent mechanism does not provide for any exit once it has been initiated.[39] Neither the Member States nor the EU can leave the proceedings once the 'correct' party has joined them. If the EU is the only one that can put an end to the breach of the ECHR, why should an EU Member State continue to be a respondent? It is submitted that this situation places the EU Member State identified in an unequal situation. Since the other EU Member States cannot join proceedings brought against other Member States,[40] why should the Member State targeted continue to be a part of the case, and not the others? Furthermore, the Explanatory Report slightly shows this inconsistency. According to the Report, Article 3(2) of the draft Agreement would apply 'if an alleged violation could only have been avoided by a member State disregarding an obligation under EU law (for example, when an EU law provision leaves no discretion to a member State as to its implementation at the national level)'.[41] Therefore, if no discretion is left to the Member States, it can be assumed that not only the Member States against which the case is being brought is violating the ECHR, but also the other 27. Hence, why this differentiated approach?

Second, the draft Agreement includes in Article 3(7) a rule concerning the responsibility under the co-respondent mechanism. The paragraph reads as follows:

> If the violation in respect of which a High Contracting Party is a co-respondent to the proceedings is established, the respondent and the co-respondent shall be jointly responsible for that violation, unless the Court, on the basis of the reasons given by the respondent and the co-respondent, and having sought the views of the applicant, decides that only one of them be held responsible.

The provision establishes the joint responsibility of the co-respondents as the general rule of responsibility. Leaving aside general considerations about joint responsibility and given the design of the co-respondent mechanism, establishing the joint responsibility of the EU and the Member State(s) which is a party to the proceedings would seem a bit uneven for two main reasons. First, joint responsibility would be non-existent if the individual would only have targeted the EU. Since EU Member States cannot join all the proceedings as co-respondents,[42] there might be a situation in which identical facts could lead to different responsibilities.[43] Identical facts could lead to either the EU's exclusive responsibility or joint responsibility of the EU and a Member State depending on who the individual initially targeted. Second, if we assume that joint responsibility is necessary to strengthen the effectiveness of the judgment, then the other Member States which are not co-respondents should also bear the responsibility. This becomes especially relevant in those situations in which there was no discretion for the EU Member States. These concerns show how joint

[39] It only provides for a change of status from respondent to co-respondent: Article 3(4) of the draft Agreement.

[40] See above, section II.B.i.

[41] Explanatory Report, para 48.

[42] They can only join those proceedings involving primary EU law: Article 3(3) of the draft Agreement.

[43] It could be argued that even though the responsibility of the other subjects has not been declared, that responsibility would still exist nevertheless. However, the precise content, limits and scope of that responsibility are left to the ECtHR to determine. On the different perspectives on the rules on responsbility, see J d'Aspremont, ch 6 in this edited collection.

responsibility within the co-respondent mechanism has no legal foundations behind it. It has been assumed to be the easy solution as regards responsibility within the ECHR, but the drafters have not really thought about its position within the overall structure of the mechanism.

Moreover, these deficiencies in the mechanism have the potential to create legal uncertainty not only for the individual affected by the breach of the ECHR but also as regards the EU Member States. Consequently the proposed internal rules should really spell out the role of the Member States in the co-respondent mechanism well.

iii. Heterodox EU Law and the Co-respondent Mechanism

The Explanatory Report explains that the reasons for the adoption of the co-respondent mechanism model are rooted in the *sui generis* nature of the EU:

> It is a special feature of the EU legal system that acts adopted by its institutions may be implemented by its member States and, conversely, that provisions of the EU founding treaties agreed upon by its member States may be implemented by institutions, bodies, offices or agencies of the EU. With the accession of the EU, there could arise the unique situation in the Convention system in which a legal act is enacted by one High Contracting Party and implemented by another.[44]

In spite of this, EU law nowadays (and especially since the Treaty of Lisbon) does not always operate on the basis of the same principles which gave the EU legal order its autonomous character. The Common Foreign and Security Policy (CFSP) would be a good example in this regard. To what extent would the actions of the EU Member States by virtue of a CFSP provision fall within the scope of the co-respondent mechanism? EU principles like primacy or direct effect seem not to apply in this part of the EU legal order.[45] Moreover, the CJEU lacks jurisdiction over this policy.[46] Therefore, it seems plausible to argue that in principle, the actions of the EU Member States falling within the CFSP would not be covered by the co-respondent mechanism. A previous version of the draft Agreement seemed to point in that direction. Article 59(bb) of the ECHR as amended by Article 1 of the draft Agreement would have read as follows:

> [A]cts and measures are not attributable to the European Union where they have been performed or adopted in the context of the provisions of the Treaty on European Union on the common foreign and security policy of the European Union, except in cases where attributability to the European Union on the basis of European Union law has been established by the Court of Justice of the European Union.[47]

This article created plenty of concerns as regards accountability and legal certainty. As a response, the European Commission assured the other parties that 'this rule would not have as effect to exclude any acts taken under the Common Foreign and Security Policy from the Court's jurisdiction but only to identify to whom the act is attributable'.[48]

[44] Explanatory Report, para 38.

[45] *Cf* Eeckhout (n 1) 478; G de Baere, *Constitutional Principles of EU External Relations* (Oxford, Oxford University Press, 2008) 201.

[46] Article 275 TFEU.

[47] This version of the agreement can be found in the Report of the Second Negotiation Meeting between the Ad hoc Negotiation Group and the European Commission on the Accession of the European Union to the European Convention on Human Rights. 47+1 (2012) R002, 15.

[48] 47+1(2012) R02, 1, para. 5.

Nevertheless, some High Contracting Parties were not convinced by the EU's statement.[49] The ECtHR's lack of jurisdiction over the CFSP would be very difficult to argue once the EU is a High Contracting Party to the ECHR. If the acts falling within the CFSP could be attributed to the EU, does it mean that these actions are attributable to its Member States? As a result, the Explanatory Report tries to clarify the situation by drawing a parallelism for the first pillar and equating the implementation of the CFSP with the implementation of EU law.[50] Therefore, by assimilating the CFSP into more orthodox EU legislation, the draft Agreement solves the question of whether the CFSP would fall within the scope of the co-respondent mechanism.

Conversely, some aspects in the area of freedom, security and justice are going to fall outside the scope of the co-respondent mechanism. More specifically, those aspects linked with mutual recognition, and judicial cooperation will not be covered by the co-respondent mechanism In these areas the EU only lays down a framework in which the Member States operate. EU Member States do not implement EU law *stricto sensu* in these areas. This is reflected in the Explanatory Report:

> It is understood that a third party intervention may often be the most appropriate way to involve the EU in a case. For instance, if an application is directed against a State associated to parts of the EU legal order through separate international agreements (for example, the 'Schengen' and 'Dublin' agreements and the agreement on the European Economic Area) concerning obligations arising from such agreements, third party intervention would be the only way for the EU to participate in the proceedings. The issue of the EU requesting leave to intervene will be dealt with in separate Memoranda of Understanding between the EU and the concerned States, upon their request.[51]

Even in these scenarios, the EU would have a say as a third party instead of as a co-respondent. Whereas there should not be a problem with leaving these areas outside the co-respondent mechanism and allowing the EU to intervene as another third party, the fact that they will also be left outside the cross-referral procedure between the ECtHR and the CJEU might be seen as problematic. The Explanatory Report links the possibility to refer an ongoing case in the ECtHR to the CJEU to those cases in which only the validity of the EU instrument is put into question.[52] Therefore, these scenarios would not be covered by the co-respondent mechanism or the cross-referral procedure, but perhaps in certain cases a potential interpretation of the CJEU might be required nonetheless.[53]

This section has shown how the draft Agreement and its Explanatory Report try to lay down a procedure to deal with the EU's participation in the ECtHR. The establishment of the co-respondent mechanism tries to ensure respect for the division of competence between the EU and its Member States while at the same time giving legal certainty to the individual involved in the proceedings. Nevertheless, the mechanism is not very successful in taking into account these two interests. On the one hand, the voluntary nature of the participation casts some doubts on the ex ante willingness of the EU and its Member

[49] Ibid.

[50] Explanatory Report, para 23.

[51] Ibid.

[52] Article 3(6) of the draft Agreement.

[53] C Eckes, 'EU External Representation in Context: Accession to the ECHR as the Final Step Towards Mutual Recognition' in S Blockmans and RA Wessel (eds), *Principles and Practices of EU External Representation* (The Hague, CLEER Working Paper 2012/5, 2012) 109.

States to assume their responsibilities under the ECHR. On the other hand, the mechanism should be more exhaustive in dealing with the different ways in which EU law could interact with the ECHR. Even though it is pointless to advance an alternative to the co-respondent mechanism,[54] it is submitted that the further developments of the mechanism either externally or through internal rules are necessary so as to provide a right balance between legal certainty and the autonomy of the EU legal order.

III. THE PRINCIPLE OF UNITY IN EXTERNAL REPRESENTATION AND THE VOLUNTARY NATURE OF THE MECHANISM

A. The Voluntary Nature of the EU's Participation in the Proceedings

As already mentioned in the previous sections, one of the main flaws of the co-respondent mechanism is its voluntary character. Article 3(2) and (3) of the draft Agreement points in this direction when using expressions like 'the European Union may become a co-respondent' and 'the European Union member States may become co-respondents'. In the same vein, Article 3(5) provides that, inter alia: 'A High Contracting Party shall become a co-respondent either by accepting an invitation by the Court or by decision of the Court upon the request of that High Contracting Party.' The wording of all these provisions denotes the idea that the High Contracting Parties have the last word as to becoming co-respondents. Regardless of whether they actually bear responsibility for the violation, the EU and/or its Member States can avoid being held responsible by simply not joining the proceedings. This is confirmed by the Explanatory Report, which clearly states that:

> No High Contracting Party may be compelled against its will to become a co-respondent. This reflects the fact that the initial application was not addressed against the potential co-respondent, and that no High Contracting Party can be forced to become a party to a case where it was not named in the original application.[55]

The voluntary nature of the co-respondent mechanism raises many concerns. On the one hand, while it preserves the autonomy of the EU legal order,[56] it can potentially create uncertainty as to who is going to intervene in the proceedings. Allowing the EU and its Member States to decide whether to join can create inconsistencies as regards their expected intervention, since they might decide that for a specific case, it is better not to intervene. Furthermore, as highlighted above, the voluntary nature of the mechanism can put its effectiveness at risk, especially in those cases in which unanimity is needed.

In a nutshell, the voluntary nature could also negatively affect the unity of the external representation of the EU and the coordination within the ECtHR. Since EU Member States are not obliged by the co-respondent mechanism, they could decide not to join the proceedings based on their own national interests. In this regard, it is argued that the duty of cooperation will play a fundamental role in the relationship between the EU and its Member States in the ECtHR.

[54] See Gaja, ch 22 in this edited collection.

[55] Explanatory Report, para 53.

[56] S Vezzani, 'L'Unione europea e i suoi Stati membri davanti ai giudici di Strasburgo: una valutazione critica del meccanismo del co-respondent', 2012, www.sidi-isil.org/wp-content/uploads/2012/10/Simone-Vezzani-LUnione-europea-e-i-suoi-Stati-membri-davanti-ai-giudici-di-Strasburgo-una-valutazione-critica.pdf.

B. The Duty of Cooperation and the Co-respondent Mechanism

Two issues will be discussed in this section: first, how the duty of cooperation would operate when the co-respondent mechanism is triggered; and, second, the implications during the proceedings. It is argued that, in the absence of any internal arrangements, the duty of cooperation has the potential to solve most of the problematic issues concerning the participation of the EU in ECtHR proceedings.

i. *Voluntary Nature as a Matter of International Law: Voluntary Nature as a Matter of EU Law?*

Whereas the voluntary nature of the co-respondent mechanism as a matter of international law is beyond doubt, as a matter of EU law, it is not that clear. Eckes rightly points out: 'what is certain is that the EU's accession to the ECHR is susceptible of entailing different and further-going duties for the Member States under EU law than the Member States' own participation entails under international law'.[57] Hence, it could be argued that the Member States would have an obligation to intervene as matter of EU law. Regardless of the voluntary nature of the mechanism, the mixed nature of the ECHR and more precisely the unity of external representation of EU could limit the extent to which EU Member States can refuse to join the mechanism. In this regard, some recent CJEU cases would support this argument. For instance, the Court of Justice held in *Etang de Berre* that:

> Since the Convention and the Protocol thus create rights and obligations in a field covered in large measure by Community legislation, there is a Community interest in compliance by both the Community and its Member States with the commitments entered into under those instruments.[58]

By assimilating a mixed agreement to a pure EU agreement,[59] the Court not only expanded its interpretative jurisdiction over areas not covered by EU competence, it also showed that in mixed agreements, the relations between the EU and its Member States are not regulated by international law, but rather by internal law.[60] Moreover, the special relation that the EU and its Member States have when implementing mixed agreements can impose stringent obligations on EU Member States that could also mean that they have to exercise their autonomous treaty-making powers. In the *Berne Convention* case,[61] the Court recognised that Ireland had failed in its obligations under EU law by not signing the Berne Convention, an agreement to which the EU was not a member due to its lack of competence on the issue.[62] In this regard, it has been argued that there is an EU interest in ensuring the implementation of mixed agreements in their entirety, regardless of the competence involved.[63]

[57] Eckes (n 53) 120.

[58] Case C-239/03 *Commission v France (Ètang de Berre)* [2004] ECR I-9325 [29].

[59] P Koutrakos, 'Intepretation of Mixed Agreements' in Hillion and Koutrakos (n 8) 123.

[60] M Cremona, 'Defending the Community Interest: The Duties of Cooperation and Compliance' in M Cremona and B de Witte (eds), *EU Foreign Relations Law: Constitutional Fundamentals* (Oxford, Hart Publishing, 2008) 148.

[61] Case C-13/00, *Ireland v Commission (Berne Convention)* [2002] ECR I-2943.

[62] Cremona (n 60) 147.

[63] E Neframi, 'The Duty of Loyalty: Rethinking its Scope Through its Application in the Field of EU External Relations' (2011) 47 *Common Market Law Review* 333.

Therefore, inter alia, it could be argued that within the framework of the ECHR and its co-respondent mechanisms, EU Member States have an obligation as a matter of EU law to intervene in the co-respondent mechanism when invited to do so by the ECtHR. In this regard, a negative response would cast some doubts over their willingness to comply with the ECHR, which would go against the interests of the EU. This would become especially relevant in those cases in which the participation of a Member State is needed, such as those in which the compatibility of the ECHR with EU primary norms is at stake. Thus, the duty of cooperation would, to a certain extent, limit Member States' autonomy in deciding whether to intervene or not in a specific case. Moreover, the Commission could bring an infringement action against EU Member States for their decision not to intervene as a co-respondent.

ii. A Single Voice in Strasbourg

Besides limiting the scope of Member States' autonomy as to their decision to join the EU as a co-respondent, the duty of cooperation would also apply when pleading in the ECtHR. The duty of cooperation would not only ensure that a Member State becomes a co-respondent, it would also limit their autonomy on what exactly to plead.

Following well-established case law,[64] the joint participation of the EU and its Member States in the ECtHR proceedings will undoubtedly require close cooperation and coordination. In this regard, this close cooperation would usually entail that EU Member States would not be allowed to deviate from the previously agreed EU position. In this particular scenario, this will entail not to argue differently from what the EU has argued. This could become a problematic issue given that the interests of the EU and its Member States could differ greatly.

IV. CONCLUDING REMARKS

This chapter has tried to show the current way in which the draft Agreement and its Explanatory Report deal with the EU's participation in the ECtHR's proceedings; it has yet to strike the right balance between the different interests involved, mainly the autonomy of the EU legal order and legal certainty. In this respect, the co-respondent mechanism aims at proceduralising the issue. This fact has two main consequences: first, it postpones the solution to the conflict between the diverging interests to a later stage; and, second, any solution to this conflict or balance would be contextualised, ie it would not be in principle possible to draw general conclusions on it. Whereas this managerial approach could be a good way to deal with mixed participation in international agreements,[65] the specific shape that it takes in the draft Agreement raises plenty of legal questions.

[64] Case C-246/07 *Commission v Sweden (PFOS)* [2010] ECR I-03317; Case C-266/03 *Commission v Luxembourg (Inland Waterways)* [2005] ECR I-06985; Case C-433/03 *Commission v Germany (Inland Waterways)* [2005] ECR I-04805; Case C-45/07 *Commission v Greece (IMO)* [2010] ECR I-00701; *Opinion 1/94 Competence of the Community to conclude international agreements concerning services and the protection of intellectual property* [1994] ECR I-05267.

[65] Heliskoski (n 20).

The co-respondent mechanism, with its voluntary nature and joint responsibility, gives pre-eminence to the concerns over the autonomy of the EU legal order and the concerns on legal certainty by the individuals suffering from human rights violations. Inasmuch as the co-respondent mechanism allows the EU and its Member States to decide whether or not to join proceedings against the other, that decision would always have to be approached on an ad hoc basis which cannot be generalised, leading to uncertainty as to whether in similar situations the outcome for the co-respondent would be the same. It is submitted that another way to strike this balance is needed. Even joint participation in all cases (which would have no legal foundations whatsoever) would seem to be a better solution than leaving the decision to intervene (and to be held responsible) to the discretion of the EU and its Member States.

This chapter has also argued that insofar as there are not yet internal arrangements on the participation in the ECtHR, the duty of cooperation would play a very big role in this. Furthermore, in the absence of internal arrangements, the duty of cooperation could solve some of the problems entailed by joint participation. However, a duty does not entail a legal obligation, so it cannot be considered the panacea to apply in the absence of clear legal rules.

Part III

Accommodating Multiple Actors: Multi-level Protection and the Role of the National Legal Orders

9

Kissing Awake a Sleeping Beauty? The Charter of Fundamental Rights in EU and Member States' Policy Practice

JOHN MORIJN*

I. THE EU CHARTER OF FUNDAMENTAL RIGHTS: THE SECOND COMPONENT OF THE EU FUNDAMENTAL RIGHTS PROTECTION ARCHITECTURE

THE TWO MAIN components of the European Union (EU) fundamental rights protection structure as envisaged by the Treaty of Lisbon are the obligation for the EU to accede to the European Convention on Human Rights and Fundamental Freedoms (ECHR) (Article 6(2) of the Treaty on Eurpopean Union (TEU)) and the elevation to legally binding status of the EU Charter of Fundamental Rights (CFR) (Article 6(1) TEU). Interestingly, these two components were initially intended as alternative ways to ensure a good level of fundamental rights protection within the EU. The first essentially envisages external judicial overview of the EU's (including the Court of Justice's) performance. In contrast, and quite differently, the second hinges on 'internalising the external' by integrating ECHR standards into the CFR and empowering the European Court of Justice to check compliance with these standards as integral part of primary EU law. The EU Treaty now tells us to pursue both visions cumulatively, ie, organising external judicial review of simultaneously formally EU internalised and EU internally judicially supervised standards. Paradoxically, part of the current sensitivities of EU accession may lie precisely in this 'Lisbon layout'. The context in which it is to be developed sets up a much clearer possibility for the collision of Strasbourg and Luxembourg judicial interpretations than each of the original alternatives. A keen awareness of this in Luxembourg may explain the Court of Justice's unprecedented pro-active stance during the negotiations.[1]

* LLM (College of Europe); PhD (EUI Law Department, 2009); senior human rights law adviser, Department of Constitutional Affairs and Legislation, Dutch Ministry of the Interior and Kingdom Relations; Assistant Professor of European Human Rights Law, Department of European Union Law, University of Groningen, the Netherlands. Useful comments by the editors and colleagues from Dutch Ministries are gratefully acknowledged. All views are personal to the author and do not in any way reflect the official position of the Dutch government.

[1] Court of Justice of the European Union, 'Discussion document on certain aspects of the accession of the European Union to the European Convention for the Protection of Human Rights and Fundamental Freedoms', 5 May 2010, available at http://curia.europa.eu/jcms/upload/docs/application/pdf/2010-05/convention_en_2010-05-21_12-10-16_272.pdf.

EU anomalies have not stopped there. In national contexts, decision making as to how to organise submission to external judicial overview will usually have *followed* the establishment of explicit internal procedures and mechanisms to ensure compliance with fundamental rights. The possible effect and impact of the external judicial review will then typically be discussed and assessed in the light of the way in which these internal procedures have functioned in practice. In the case of the EU, however, such procedures and mechanisms are inevitably still very much under development vis-a-vis the intended new lynchpin of internal fundamental rights protection—the newly legally binding CFR. In fact (again paradoxically), since the entry into force of the Treaty of Lisbon, arranging for external judicial control has taken *precedence* not only in policy debates but also in scholarly contributions. In the context of EU accession discussions, parallel comprehensive analysis of the state of the (new) EU internal system of fundamental rights protection—over which, after all, the intended external review is being established—has even been largely absent. A remarkable consequence has been that the EU accession discussions have essentially taken the *pre*-Lisbon internal EU fundamental rights protection system as a point of reference, ie, a way of protecting fundamental rights based largely on Luxembourg's inherently flexible case law on general principles rather than a written document, and limited guidance in the prior stage of policy development and law making.

The implications of the CFR as a legally binding text have of course been widely studied in their own right. Assessment of its effects has nonetheless largely mirrored discussions about EU accession, in that attention has been almost exclusively focused on the practice of the—end of pipeline—Court of Justice.[2] This does not, however, allow for a fully comprehensive analysis. *Judicial* output is only the second side of the coin. Both at the EU and the national levels of administration, its crucial flipside is to ensure—prior—CFR compliance at the policy stage, ie, during the policy development and law-making process. Incidentally, although largely below the radar,[3] both at the EU and the national levels, some significant first steps towards developing methods and procedures for that purpose have been taken. These will largely determine the shape of internal EU fundamental rights protection—and, as a consequence, the intensity and nature of future external judicial overview that is to be needed and expected.

However, the application of the CFR, including at the policy development and law-making stages, poses specific challenges. This is a consequence of the CFR's so-called horizontal clauses, particularly Articles 51–53. These provisions regulate its field of application, the scope and interpretation of the rights and principles laid down in it and the level of protection to be offered. The combination of ambiguous wording about the domestic field of application and the CFR's challenging interpretative structure may explain the slow start in its policy application.

Article 51 stipulates that the CFR's obligations are binding on all activities of EU institutions, agencies and bodies, on the one hand, but, on the other hand, on Member States

[2] For recent analyses, see A Rosas and H Kaila, 'L'application de la Charte des Droits Fondamentaux de l'Union Européenne par la Cour de Justice : un premier bilan' (2011) XVI(1) *Il Diritto dell'Unione Europea* 1; T von Danwitz and K Paraschas, 'A Fresh Start for the Charter: Fundamental Questions on the Application of the European Charter of Fundamental Rights' (2012) 35 *Fordham International Law Journal* 1396; J Morijn, 'Het Juridisch Bindende Handvest van de Grondrechten van de Europese Unie: Eerste Ervaringen en Openstaande Vragen' (2011) 36(1) *Nederlands Tijdschrift voor de Mensenrechten/NJCM-Bulletin* 45.

[3] See, however, I De Jesus Butler, 'Ensuring Compliance with the Charter of Fundamental Rights in Legislative Drafting: The Practice of the European Commission', (2012) 37(4) *EL Rev* 397 (focusing solely on EU-level activities).

'only when they are implementing Union law'. Quite when that latter scenario occurs has remained a problematic question even after some recent Luxembourg case law, paralysing domestic policy application of the CFR. There is a need for further clarification and refinement on this front.

Articles 52 and 53 CFR, as well as the 'Explanations relating to the CFR',[4] contain instructions as to how the Charter's substantive norms are to be interpreted in relation to fundamental rights norms laid down in the ECHR, the (Revised) European Social Charter (ESC), United Nations (UN) instruments and national constitutions. Article 53 CFR positions these sources as a minimum level of protection by instructing that 'nothing in this Charter shall be interpreted as restricting or adversely affecting' them. Now, paradoxically, in the practical terms of applying the CFR, this forces its interpreters to take these *other* instruments, and not the CFR itself, as a point of departure. In policy practice, things have often actually immediately ended there too. For even if one of the CFR's main aims was to offer *additional* protection 'in the light of changes in society, social progress and scientific and technological developments',[5] there is generally still little awareness of how and where the CFR goes beyond that minimum level provided in the other fundamental rights sources. Equally, here lies a specific challenge.

Against this background, this chapter will focus on the policy stage practice with regard to the CFR to date. Building on previous analysis,[6] it will first describe and assess the current policy use of the CFR both at the EU level and the national level (sections II and III). It will be argued that when it comes to truly shaping policy development and law making in line with its legal rank, at the moment the CFR cannot but be characterised as little more than a paper beauty still asleep. It will also be shown that kissing her awake may be more tedious and elaborate a prince's task than is readily apparent. In particular, the CFR's EU-level cheek may warm up to different forms of tenderness than her Member State-level cheek. In that light, some EU-level and national-level avenues will be suggested to romance our beauty out of bed and on her feet (section IV).

II. EU-LEVEL POLICY EFFORTS TO KISS AWAKE THE CFR

A. State of Affairs

The transformation of the CFR from 'new kid on the block' to 'new kit for the block' is gradually shaping up. The Court of Justice now gives it its place next to the other legal sources of fundamental rights, such as the ECHR. This judicial use has been regularly assessed.[7] What has been happening with the CFR in Brussels and the capitals[8] in the

[4] Explanations relating to the Charter of Fundamental Rights, OJ EC C303/17, 14 December 2007. By virtue of Article 6(1), third sentence TEU and Article 52(7) CFR, as well as the CFR preamble, fifth indent, this document has to be taken into account when interpreting the CFR.

[5] CFR preamble, fourth indent.

[6] PBCDF van Sasse van Ysselt and J Morijn, 'Niet-rechterlijke handhaving van het EU-Grondrechtenhandvest: een analyse van de eerste stappen' (2012) 37(3) *Nederlands Tijdschrift voor de Mensenrechten/NJCM-Bulletin* 295 and my following blog postings: 'The EU Fundamental Rights Charter, the European Commission and the Council of Ministers: Checking the "Charter Checklists"' (September 2011), and '*Akerberg* and *Melloni*: What the Court Said, Did, and May Have Left Open' (March 2013), EUtopia law, Matrix Chambers, London, both available at eutopialaw.com/tag/john-morijn.

[7] See above n 2 for up-to-date analyses.

[8] See below, section III.

stages prior to judicial review is less known.[9] Given the CFR's aforementioned complicated composite structure and complex instructions as to how to use it, it is clear that the 'new kit' does require some authoritative instructions regarding its *modes d'emploi*. This section will focus on the practice of the Commission, the Council of Ministers and the Fundamental Rights Agency (FRA).

Even before the CFR's legal upgrade, the Commission adopted four policy documents about it.[10] These were meant to announce and then to evaluate a 'methodology' to ensure CFR awareness amongst its own services. These efforts resulted most visibly in the inclusion of references to CFR articles in the preamble of legislative proposals. The Commission itself admitted[11] later that the way that this requirement operated in practice may have amounted to little more than a 'box ticking exercise'.

Since December 2009, the Commission has explicitly extended its role to the CFR as 'Guardian of the Treaties'. In February 2010, Vice-President Reding announced[12] the Commission's ambition to use the CFR as a 'compass' for designing and checking EU action. She also stated that the Commission would operate a 'zero-tolerance policy' with regard to CFR violations, including through action in infringement procedures. The Commission then launched a Strategy for the effective implementation of the Charter of Fundamental Rights.[13] In this policy paper, it announced a number of measures with a stated aim to develop a 'Charter culture' throughout its services. One particularly prominent measure was the presentation of a 'fundamental rights checklist'. The Commission later explained[14] the purpose of this checklist as a tool to reinforce the evaluation of impacts on fundamental rights of its legislative proposals. It is intended to verify that EU laws are in compliance with the CFR at each stage of the legislative process—from the preparatory work in the Commission to the adoption of draft laws by the European Parliament and the Council, as well as when Member States apply them. It reads as follows:

1. What fundamental rights are affected?
2. Are the rights in question absolute rights (which may not be subject to limitations, examples being human dignity and the ban on torture)?

[9] For a comprehensive overview, see Butler (n 3).

[10] European Commission, 'Communication on the EU Charter of Fundamental Rights', COM (2000) 559, 13 September 2000, available at http://eur-lex.europa.eu/LexUriServ/LexUriServ.do?uri=COM:2000:0559:FIN:EN:PDF; European Commission, 'Communication on the Legal Nature of the EU Charter of Fundamental Rights', COM (2000) 644, 11 October 2000, available at http://eur-lex.europa.eu/LexUriServ/LexUriServ.do?uri=COM:2000:0644:FIN:EN:PDF; European Commission, 'Communication on Compliance with the Charter of Fundamental Rights in Commission Legislative Proposals—Methodology for Systematic and Rigorous Monitoring', COM (2005) 172, 27 April 2005, available at http://eur-lex.europa.eu/LexUriServ/LexUriServ.do?uri=COM:2005:0172:FIN:EN:PDF; European Commission, 'Report on the Practical Operation of the Methodology for a Systematic and Rigorous Monitoring of Compliance with the Charter of Fundamental Rights', COM (2009) 205, 24 April 2009, available at http://eur-lex.europa.eu/LexUriServ/LexUriServ.do?uri=COM:2009:0205:FIN:EN:PDF.

[11] See European Commission, 'Report on the Practical Operation of the Methodology' (n 10).

[12] Speech of 18 March 2010, 'The EU's Accession to the European Convention on Human Rights: Towards a Stronger and More Coherent Protection of Human Rights in Europe', available at http://ec.europa.eu/commission_2010-2014/reding/pdf/speeches/speech_20100318_1_en.pdf.

[13] European Commission, 'Strategy for the Effective Implementation of the Charter of Fundamental Rights by the European Union', COM (2010) 573/4, 19 October 2010, available at http://ec.europa.eu/justice/news/intro/doc/com_2010_573_4_en.pdf (hereinafter the 'CFR Strategy').

[14] Commission Staff Working, 'Document Accompanying the 2010 Report on the Application of the EU Charter of Fundamental Rights', SEC (2011) 396, 30 March 2011, available at http://ec.europa.eu/justice/policies/rights/docs/sec_2011_396_en.pdf (at 3) (hereinafter the 'Accompanying Document 2010').

3. What is the impact of the various policy options under consideration on fundamental rights? Is the impact beneficial (promotion of fundamental rights) or negative (limitation of fundamental rights)?
4. Do the options have both a beneficial and a negative impact, depending on the fundamental rights concerned (for example, a negative impact on freedom of expression and beneficial one on intellectual property)?
5. Would any limitation of fundamental rights be formulated in a clear and predictable manner?
6. Would any limitation of fundamental rights:
   a. be necessary to achieve an objective of general interest or to protect the rights and freedoms of others (which)?
   b. be proportionate to the desired aim?
   c. preserve the essence of the fundamental rights concerned?

In its CFR Strategy, the Commission also announced that it would publish an annual report on the application of the CFR. In reality, it has begun to publish two such reports simultaneously.[15] The actual report is a concise policy-orientated report, but so far, the Commission has also each time added a more extensive and systematically structured so-called 'accompanying document' (which was, judging by its format, perhaps at some point intended to become the actual annual report). It takes the CFR's chapters as its structure and discusses developments relating to each of the rights. In fact, it is a shame that this accompanying document did not become the annual report itself, because from a substantive policy perspective, it is a much more informative read.

Finally, the Commission also issued a paper on how to take account of fundamental rights in the conduct of impact assessments.[16] A notable aspect of this is that fundamental rights are not presented as a separate category next to the existing categorisation of economic, social and environmental issues; rather, fundamental rights compliance is presented as a transversal issue, to be assessed with the help of the aforementioned checklist.[17] According to the CFR Strategy, the Impact Assessment Board is given the additional task 'systematically [to check] the fundamental rights aspects of draft impact assessments submitted to it and will issue an opinion on them where necessary'.[18]

[15] European Commission, '2010 Report on the Application of the EU Charter of Fundamental Rights', COM (2011) 160, 30 March 2011, available at http://eur-lex.europa.eu/LexUriServ/LexUriServ.do?uri=COM:2011:0160:FIN:EN:PDF (hereinafter the 'Commission 2010 Report'); Accompanying Document 2010 (n 13); European Commission, '2011 Report on the Application of the EU Charter of Fundamental Rights', COM (2012) 169, 16 April 2012, available at http://eur-lex.europa.eu/LexUriServ/LexUriServ.do?uri=COM:2012:0169:FIN:EN:PDF (hereinafter the 'Commission 2011 Report'); Commission Staff Working Document, 'Document Accompanying the 2011 Report on the Application of the EU Charter of Fundamental Rights', SWD (2012) 84, 16 April 2012, available at http://ec.europa.eu/justice/fundamental-rights/files/swd2012-84-fundamentalrights_en.pdf (hereinafter the 'Accompanying Document 2011'); European Commission, '2012 Report on the Application of the EU Charter of Fundamental Rights', COM (2013) 271, 8 May 2013, available at http://ec.europa.eu/justice/fundamental-rights/files/2012_report_application_charter_en.pdf (hereinafter the 'Commission 2012 Report'); European Commission, 'Document Accompanying the 2012 Report on the Application of the EU Charter of Fundamental Rights', SWD (2013) 172, 8 May 2013, available at http://ec.europa.eu/justice/fundamental-rights/files/swd_2013_172_en.pdf.

[16] Commission Staff Working Paper, 'Operational Guidance on Taking Account of Fundamental Rights in Commission Impact Assessments', SEC (2011) 567, 6 May 2011, available at: http://ec.europa.eu/governance/impact/key_docs/docs/sec_2011_0567_en.pdf.

[17] For a discussion on this issue, see Butler (n 3) 404–05.

[18] CFR Strategy (n 13) 7–8.

In response to the Commission's CFR Strategy and annual report(s), the Council has so far adopted four sets of conclusions.[19] It announced, inter alia, that it will aim to ensure that legislative proposals cleared by it will be worthy of a 'fundamental rights label'.[20] The Council also decided[21] to develop its own 'guidelines on methodological steps to be taken to check fundamental rights compatibility at the Council's preparatory bodies'.[22] After these were drafted, the Council praised their 'efficacy' remarkably quickly[23]—just several days after their adoption. It has recently reaffirmed the need to enhance efforts to put into practice these working methods aimed at ensuring that practical steps are taken at any level of the legislative process to ensure CFR compliance throughout the Council's internal decision-making procedures and to raise awareness of the CFR within the Council.[24] As far as relevant, these methodological guidelines read as follows:

Council guidelines on methodological steps to be taken to check fundamental rights compatibility at the Council's preparatory bodies

II. Identify the general link with fundamental rights.
    1. Check whether the proposal affects fundamental rights at all; think from a fundamental rights perspective.
    2. Check the recitals of the original proposal and the attached impact assessment.

III. Examine whether the proposal is in line with the Charter.
    1. Check the exact content of relevant fundamental rights with the help of the following methods:
        a. Check the Charter, the explanations to the Charter, the case-law of the Court of Justice of the European Union and other relevant sources for understanding the Charter …
        b. Check also thematic fundamental rights reports, publications, handbooks made by the institutions, bodies, offices and agencies of the European Union and by the Council of Europe and make use of the expertise of the European Union Agency for Fundamental Rights.
        c. Consult the Council Legal Service.

[19] Council Conclusions on the Role of the Council of the European Union in Ensuring the Effective Implementation of the Charter of Fundamental Rights of the European Union, 24–25 February 2011 (hereinafter 'Council Conclusions 2011-1'), available at http://register.consilium.europa.eu/pdf/en/11/st06/st06387.en11.pdf; Council Conclusions on the Council's Actions and Initiatives for the Implementation of the Charter of Fundamental Rights of the European Union, Doc 10139/1/11 REV 1, 20 May 2011 (hereinafter 'Council Conclusions 2011-2'), available at http://register.consilium.europa.eu/pdf/en/11/st10/st10139-re01.en11.pdf; Council Conclusions on the 2011 Report from the Commission on the Application of the EU Charter of Fundamental Rights, Doc 10935/12, 12 June 2012, available at http://register.consilium.europa.eu/pdf/en/12/st10/st10935.en12.pdf (hereinafter 'Council Conclusions 2012'); Council Conclusions on Fundamental Rights and Rule of Law and on the Commission 2012 Report on the Application of the Charter of Fundamental Rights of the European Union, Doc 10168/13, 29 May 2013, available at http://register.consilium.europa.eu/pdf/en/13/st10/st10168.en13.pdf (hereinafter 'Council Conclusions 2013').

[20] Council Conclusions 2011-1 (n 19) para 8.

[21] Ibid, paras 15–16.

[22] COREPER, 'Guidelines on Methodological Steps to be Taken to Check Fundamental Rights Compatibility at the Council's Preparatory Bodies', Council Document 10140/11, 18 May 2011 (hereinafter the 'Council Guidelines'), available at http://register.consilium.europa.eu/pdf/en/11/st10/st10140.en11.pdf. *Cf* Annex for the checklist. The Council has consistently acknowledged the importance of these Guidelines subsequently; see Council Conclusions 2012 (n 19) para 4; Council Conclusions 2013 (n 19), para 2.

[23] Council Conclusions 2011-2 (n 19) para 9.

[24] Council Conclusions 2013 (n 19) para 4.

2. Check the proposal to assess whether it limits fundamental rights and whether this limitation is in compliance with the Charter.
   a. May fundamental rights at issue be subject to limitations?
   b. Are the limitations provided by law; are they adequately accessible and foreseeable?
   c. Are the limitations necessary and proportionate to achieve an objective of general interest recognised by the Union or to protect the rights and freedoms of others?

IV. In case of doubt:
   1. Consult the Council Legal Service.
   2. Use the expertise of national experts in the capitals.
   3. Ask the [Council Working Party on Fundamental Rights, Citizens' Rights and Free Movement of Persons (FREMP)] or other preparatory bod[ies] specialising in a specific fundamental right.

Annex IV of the Council Guidelines[25] indicates that in examining limitations of CFR rights, a specific order needs to be followed. First, it needs to be assessed whether an absolute Charter right is at issue (eg, the right to life (Article 2 CFR) and the prohibition of torture (Article 4 CFR)). Limitation of this category of human rights is never permitted. According to Annex IV, Article 52 of the Charter clarifies that limitations of non-absolute rights are possible, but only if they are:

a. provided for by law,
b. respect[ing] the essence of those rights and freedoms,
c. subject to the principle of proportionality,
d. necessary, and
e. genuinely meet[ing] objectives of general interest recognised by the Union or the need to protect the rights and freedoms of others.

A final noteworthy development is that the EU FRA, the EU agency set up to provide 'assistance and expertise'[26] to EU institutions and Member States with regard to EU fundamental rights protection, has gradually started claiming its role in checking compliance with the CFR at the EU level. Generally, it refers to the relevant CFR article in each of the reports that it publishes. It has issued a number of opinions on pending legislative proposals at the request of EU institutions, in which it specifically takes the CFR as a framework for analysis.[27] The FRA has also undertaken CFR compliance-dedicated projects. In particular, it developed a helpful database, Charterpedia, in which it documents EU and national case law about the CFR on an article-by-article basis.[28] In its 2012 and 2013 conclusions, the Council expressed its appreciation for the FRA's role in raising awareness about when the CFR applies, referred to the Charterpedia database as particularly useful,[29] and mentioned it as a possible actor to increase knowledge of the CFR's application.[30] Finally, the FRA's mandate[31] also tasks it to publish an annual report on the fundamental rights situation in

[25] *Cf* Council Guidelines (n 22) 16–18.

[26] Council Regulation (EC) No 168/2007 of 15 February 2007 establishing a European Union Agency for Fundamental Rights (hereinafter the 'FRA Founding Regulation'), Article 2.

[27] The FRA opinions can be found at a dedicated section of its website: http://fra.europa.eu/en/publications-and-resources/opinions.

[28] EU Fundamental Rights Agency, Charterpedia database: http://infoportal.fra.europa.eu/InfoPortal/infobase-FrontEndCountryHome.do?btnCountryLinkHome_1.

[29] Council Conclusions 2012 (n 19) para 10.

[30] Council Conclusions 2013 (n 19) para 3.

[31] FRA Founding Regulation, Article 4(1)(d).

the EU. Like the Commission's accompanying documents, it is structured along the lines of the CFR's chapters. The FRA has presented it at the Council and the European Parliament. One notable aspect is that over the years, the FRA annual report has become increasingly voluminous.[32]

B. Assessment

On their face, these developments and measures with regard to the CFR, both individually and taken together, look impressive. Given their recent adoption, it may simply be too early to assess to what extent they have had a practical effect in terms of (changing) policy practices at the EU level. Nonetheless, there is a provisional sense that no significant transformation away from a paper reality may even be beginning to take place. For example, the Council's Guidelines do not seem to have been mentioned, let alone applied in any visible way, apart from in the annual reaction to the Commission's CFR reports. The Commission's practice of including CFR articles in the recitals of legislative instruments and the application of its checklist both seem not to have led to a noticeable substantive change of policy outcomes.[33]

An express disclaimer needs to be attached to this provisional conclusion, however. Experience at the national level suggests that part of the effectiveness of checking compliance with fundamental rights only shows, paradoxically, in terms of initiatives that eventually never leave the house. Just focusing on 'output' or 'outside mentioning' would therefore surely be misleading. Nonetheless, given this apparent state of play, the Commission and Council measures designed to ensure CFR compliance would definitely merit evaluation at some point. This should preferably be done by an independent expert outsider, for example, the FRA. The FRA would do well to report on the actual practice of the application of the CFR at the EU level on its own motion too. The Commission could itself opt to start reporting about how its own tools are being applied in practice in a section of its CFR annual report(s).

Yet, based on experience with fundamental rights proofing at the national policy level, already at this early stage, some further observations can be made with regard to the way in which the Commission and Council checklists have been drafted. In particular, these checklists seem to be problematic tools for raising awareness of and inducing compliance with the CFR. For sharply at odds with the prominence that they have been given by the Commission and the Council (at least in words), without further guidance on how to apply them, they could result in raising 'CFR alerts' in the wrong way, to the wrong people at the wrong time in the EU policy-making process. Let me explain.

To lawyers, the checklists are readily recognisable as abbreviated versions of a common fundamental rights law analysis. To non-lawyer policy makers, who will actually have to apply them, they may not. In particular, by advocating the application of the checklists at an early stage of policy development in the way that they are worded, they place

[32] See the 2010 FRA Annual Report at http://fra.europa.eu/sites/default/files/fra_uploads/917-AR_2010-conf-edition_en.pdf (175 pages), for the 2011 FRA Annual Report at http://fra.europa.eu/en/publication/2012/fundamental-rights-challenges-and-achievements-2011 (272 pages), and the 2012 FRA Annual Report at http://fra.europa.eu/sites/default/files/annual-report-2012_en.pdf (322 pages).

[33] *Cf* Butler (n 3).

non-lawyers in the position of answering questions essentially defined from a legal angle—but without substantive guidance. On the one hand, this may lead policy officers to focus unduly on questions that are, although normatively evidently important, very unlikely in practice to be relevant to their specific case, given the focus of most EU policies (eg, is an absolute right at issue?). On the other hand, and more importantly, given the apparently intended exhaustiveness of the checklists in making a CFR compliance assessment, the way in which the questions are phrased may actually result in *preventing* the full teasing out of what should become known at the early stages of policy development.

The one thing that will frequently come to lie at the heart of the effort to make EU policies consistent with the CFR is technical, statistical and other discipline-specific information about whether measures are at hand that have the same policy effect while being less intrusive to individual liberties. However, in the present checklists, *no* detailed questions are included to get this information on the table. Experience in fundamental rights proofing of (new) policy shows that this is precisely the information that non-(fundamental rights) lawyers tend to sit on—frequently without realising its relevance to a fundamental rights compliance analysis—at a stage that plans could still be easily adapted. Therefore, there is a mismatch between the much-heralded questionnaires and the information needed at the prior stage of policy development.

The resulting paradox of the current checklists is that they may make it far too easy for relevant considerations *not* to be properly weeded out at a stage at which this is still relevant. It also increases the chance of real dissatisfaction with 'those lawyers' when, on the basis of the *same* list of questions, they enter the stage late and ask for further justification and materials under the guise of 'legal' fundamental rights proofing. That is certainly not conducive to fostering a CFR culture—at least not one that is institutionally productive. In that light, it would seem advisable to amend the Commission CFR checklist, explicating aspects of the proportionality and subsidiarity test (which are now all included under question 6a). Likewise, the importance of this specific element should be much more strongly stressed in the impact assessment stage. The same goes for question III.3.c of the Council's Methodological Guidelines.

III. MEMBER STATE-LEVEL POLICY EFFORTS TO KISS AWAKE THE CFR

A. State of Affairs

The CFR is also applicable to the Member State level, but—in the words of the CFR—'only' when they are 'implementing' Union law (Article 51(1) CFR). The essential role of the Member State level in guaranteeing compliance with the CFR has been stressed by the EU institutions. In its 2011 conclusions, the Council stressed 'that Member States' administrations are the first level where compliance with obligations deriving from the Charter … should be guaranteed'[34] and that Member State-submitted amendments to legislative initiatives should be subject to a prior CFR conformity check by the Member States' services.[35]

[34] *Cf* Council Conclusions 2011-1 (n 19) para 9.
[35] *Cf* ibid, para 10.

In addition, the Commission has drawn attention to the importance of the Member State level in its 2011 and 2012 Annual Reports.[36]

Although national courts have started to refer to the CFR,[37] Member State-level *policy* activity in ensuring compliance with the CFR appears to have been far less intense than at the EU level. Yes, occasionally the CFR has started to appear in explanatory memoranda of legislative proposals, but this cannot obscure the reality that the lack of clarity so far about the applicability of the CFR to Member State actions seems to have had a strongly paralysing effect. Yet the ambiguity in the wording of Article 51(1) CFR is by no means the only element that may stand in the way of Member State-level traction when it comes to ensuring compliance with the CFR. Other characteristics inherent in the very structure of the CFR, and its existence in parallel to other fundamental rights sources, have a potential chilling effect too.

First, it appears that the ECHR is still the dominant touchstone for (the more established) fundamental rights proofing practices at the Member States level in any policy area, both within and outside the scope of EU law. This is significant because in important ways the CFR goes far beyond the ECHR in terms of rights protected, for example, by including economic and social rights. In fact, placing the discussion about the EU's accession to the ECHR somewhat into perspective, CFR rights with a ECHR equivalent form a *minority* in the CFR.[38] The extent to which there appears to be a lack of awareness about this is in policy circles—and perhaps beyond—is rather striking. There is still a widespread misconception that the CFR is simply and only an EU version of the ECHR and its protocols. Second, even if a CFR right is identified (in that case often a direct equivalent of an ECHR right), the CFR's horizontal clauses that are to help in interpreting it are often perceived by those not well-versed in EU law (and even to those who thought they were) as a discouragingly complex hall of mirrors. To give just one example, a distinction between rights and principles is introduced (Article 52(5) CFR), but then it is nowhere explained authoritatively and exhaustively which CFR provision would fall in which category, and what would be the legal or practical consequence(s) of either categorisation. As a result of these two aspects, a default position of continuing to rely on the ECHR and UN human rights norms almost exclusively—therefore substantively missing out on those aspects where the CFR provides added protection in terms of add-ons to ECHR rights and in terms of rights that are not at all present in the ECHR[39]—is a logical practical consequence.

A third characteristic of the CFR that complicates guaranteeing its application at the Member State level is the institutional arrangements that its effective application requires. In its CFR Report 2011,[40] the Commission stated that it had set up an inter-services group to deal with CFR-related issues. Such institutional anchoring appears to be equally important at the Member State level. In the Netherlands, an inter-ministerial CFR group was set

[36] *Cf* Commission 2011 Report (n 15) 9; Commission 2012 Report (n 15) 6.

[37] *Cf* Commission 2012 Report (n 15) 8–9. For a recent comprehensive overview, see the national reports prepared in the context of a CFR-dedicated seminar of the Association of the Councils of State and Supreme Administrative Jurisdictions of the European Union (ACA) in The Hague (November 2011) and Madrid (June 2012) at www.aca-europe.eu/en/colloquiums/sem_2011_theHague.html and www.juradmin.eu/en/colloquiums/colloq_en_23.html See also the Charterpedia database by the FRA (n 28), which includes a useful CFR article-by-article search function.

[38] See below, section IV.

[39] See below, section IV.

[40] *Cf* Commission 2011 Report (n 15) 3.

up, although with the immediate purpose of coordinating the position to be taken with regard to interventions at the Luxembourg Court. It was not therefore initially aimed at developing policy to ensure prior CFR compliance checking as well. In the meantime, work is underway to address these aspects too.

A specific, more substantive issue that the CFR raises, which may be self-evident to EU-level observers but can still have important practical and organisational implications at the Member State level, is that interpreting the CFR requires both traditional EU law expertise (originally focused on EC law) and traditional fundamental rights law expertise (originally focused on Council of Europe and UN human rights law, as well as national constitutional law). These fields of expertise have traditionally tended to fall under different units and/or different ministries. Ensuring policy compliance with the CFR therefore may require an (re-)organisational effort that is conscious of this.

B. Assessment

It cannot be overstated just how damaging it would be to efforts to develop measures for ensuring Member State-level compliance with the CFR if the CFR's scope of application to Member States' actions were to remain ambiguous. Given that we are dealing with a text of primary EU law aimed at guaranteeing fundamental rights, this point takes on added significance in two further ways. First, it is well known that one of the conditions for legality of infringing fundamental rights as a matter of ECHR law is that the law under scrutiny has foreseeable effects. This idea is copied in the CFR itself (Article 52(1)). Now, would it not be ironic if a fundamental rights text itself requiring that any infringement to the rights in it should be laid down in 'foreseeable' regulations binds interpretation of its *own* applicability to (an ambiguous interpretation of) ambiguous wording?[41] Second, as noted above,[42] the added value of the CFR is that in many respects, it provides for higher levels of protection than the ECHR and national constitutions.[43] This potential cannot be unlocked for the benefit of citizens at the Member State level until it is authoritatively established precisely when the CFR applies. Without clarification of the CFR's scope, it is, in some situations, simply impossible to know to which standard (the sometimes higher ones in the CFR or the often lower ones in the ECHR and national constitutions) to proof domestic legislative measures and policy choices.

Against this background, the judgment in *Åkerberg Fransson*[44] was most eagerly awaited. The case concerned a Swedish fisherman whom the Swedish tax authorities accused of incorrectly reporting his income, impacting inter alia on the assessment of Value Added Tax (VAT) due. He was given a fine for tax offences, a small part of which was a VAT offence. At a later stage, the Public Prosecutor also commenced criminal proceedings against the fisherman for tax evasion relating to the same year. In the context of the latter proceedings, the Swedish referring court wanted to know whether the duplication in administrative

[41] For an analysis of the discrepancy between the CFR text, the CFR explanations and previous Court of Justice case law, see Rosas and Kaila (n 2) 18–20 and Von Danwitz and Paraschas (n 2) 1399–409.

[42] See above, section III.A.

[43] See below, section IV.

[44] European Court of Justice (Grand Chamber), Case C-617/10, *Åklagaren v Hans Åkerberg Fransson*, 26 February 2013.

and criminal proceedings was problematic in the light of the CFR. Several Member States and the Commission argued that this situation was outside of the CFR's scope, because it was not a situation in which the Member State was clearly 'implementing Union law'. The Court disagreed, but did not actually give hands-on guidance how to assess this better in the future. In a key passage,[45] it held that Member States should uphold EU fundamental rights 'in all situations governed by European Union law, but not outside such situations … that it has no power to examine the compatibility with the [CFR] of national legislation lying outside the scope of European Union law'. It did not, however, explain in practical terms precisely what falls within and what falls outside EU law. Since this wording of the Court is purely circumscriptive, not descriptive or prescriptive, the problems from a practical policy perspective remain largely the same.

Awaiting further clarification from Luxembourg, there are things that can be done about this issue of Member State-level applicability of the CFR, both at the EU level and the Member State level. At the EU level, an elaborate indication by the European Commission, perhaps together with the Council and European Parliament (or otherwise endorsed by them), about what it/they consider(s) to fall within the category of CFR-covered Member State actions would be very helpful.[46] If Member States do not want to leave this issue fully to the Court, or if the Commission is worried that too broad a scope of the CFR with regard to Member States' actions would raise expectations as to its actions based on it, there is nothing that prevents revisiting and clarifying this issue at the political level. At the Member State level, sections in law-making manuals explaining how fundamental rights proofing in the light of international human rights norms is to be undertaken can be amended to include a reference of the CFR. However, in line with the discussion above, here the caveat of potential grey areas will have to be added. Such alterations could also be made to sections in law-making manuals where it is beyond doubt that EU law is at issue, for example, those concerning implementing Regulations and transposing Directives. It should also be explained how the checking of compliance with the CFR should be reported in explanatory memoranda of such legislative proposals.

One of many interesting substantive questions to be answered in such an exercise will be whether the CFR should altogether take the place of the ECHR in those sections of explanatory memoranda reporting about fundamental rights compliance in policy areas clearly dominated by EU law, or whether the CFR should instead continue to be mentioned side by side with the ECHR. Substantively, in situations within the scope of EU law, the ECHR is fully absorbed by the CFR. This would mean that, legally, it would no longer be necessary for the ECHR to be mentioned separately. Referring to the ECHR next to the CFR would perhaps even create confusion, as it could suggest that some parts of the national policy are outside of the scope of EU law (and therefore are not covered by the CFR). On

[45] Ibid [19].

[46] In its 2010 and 2012 CFR Reports, the Commission did dedicate brief sections to it. In its 2010 Report, it noted: 'The [CFR] applies to Member States only when they are implementing EU law … it does not apply to situations where EU law is not involved and it does not extend the powers of the Union as defined in the Treaties' (at 3). In its 2012 Report, it explained: 'The provisions of the [CFR] are addressed to the Member States only when they are implementing EU law … Where the national legislation at stake does not constitute a measure implementing EU law or is not connected in any other way with EU law, the jurisdiction of the Court is not established' (at 7). However, both these descriptions do little more than restate the problem. From a practical (national) policy perspective, the issue is in what factual situations *precisely* is the EU 'not involved' or is policy not 'implementing' or 'in any other way connected' with EU law?

the other hand, the compliance check with regard to the ECHR has been a long-standing legislative practice in many Member States. Mentioning it separately, even if it is clear that EU law is being implemented, could be justified simply by presenting it as a continuation of a legislative tradition. Another reason for perpetuating the separate check with regard to the ECHR could be that it represents a powerful reminder of the underlying importance of the ECHR even in the context of CFR-centred EU fundamental rights protection. Perhaps then that is also the background against which the accession of the EU to the ECHR should be appreciated and judged once CFR-based EU fundamental rights protection has shaped up, both at the EU and Member State levels.

IV. OUTLOOK: WHAT MORE CAN BE DONE TO AWAKEN THE CFR IN A POLICY CONTEXT?

So far, this contribution has tracked and analysed a number of EU- and Member State-level developments in shaping compliance with the CFR in policy making. This section will suggest additional ways forward to bolster and add to the policies that have already taken shape. The purpose is to help develop a (fuller) set of methods and procedures to be put in place within the foreseeable future. In this way, it will become more likely that the CFR truly becomes a touchstone in pre-judicial EU fundamental rights protection in a way that is reflective of its rank as primary EU law and its actual substantive scope of protection.

As was pointed out earlier, the CFR's complex composite structure poses specific challenges in communicating where the CFR goes *further* than fundamental rights sources that are already well known. The Commission and FRA publications structured on the basis of the CFR's own chapters paradoxically do not provide such an insight, because each of the CFR chapters contains both rights that are equal to those laid down in other sources as well as CFR rights that provide additional protection. In this way, it remains (too) vague as to why applying the CFR rather than in particular only its most dominant underlying source—the ECHR—is in fact important.

Perhaps counter-intuitively in that light, it is suggested here that a particularly useful way to promote and explain the CFR's substance, both at the EU level and at the Member State level, would be to take the familiar ECHR rights *as a starting-point*. This can be done by extrapolating from the CFR explanations[47] at Article 52 CFR, which already provides for a list of which CFR rights fully correspond to ECHR rights and which CFR rights correspond to ECHR rights, but provides additional protection, and dividing the substance of the CFR into four categories as follows:

a. CFR rights with the same meaning and scope as the corresponding ECHR rights (eg, Article 11, freedom of expression and information);
b. CFR rights with the same meaning but a wider scope compared to the corresponding ECHR rights (eg, Article 8, the right to data protection);
c. CFR rights with no corresponding ECHR right, but often corresponding ESC rights (eg, Article 34, the right to social security and social assistance);
d. CFR rights that are EU context-specific (eg, Article 39, the right to vote and stand as a candidate for European Parliament elections).

[47] See above, n 4.

Against this background, the CFR rights can be divided up as follows:

Category	A	B	C	D
CFR articles	2	8	1	12(2)
	4	9	3	39
	5	12(1)	10(2)	40
	6	14(1)	14(2)	41
	7	14(3)	15	42
	10(1)	21	16	43
	11	23	18	44
	13	47(1)	24	45
	17	47(2) and 47(3)	25	46
	19(1)	50	26	
	19(2)		27	
	20		28	
	21		29	
	23		30	
	48		31	
	49(1) (with the exception of the last sentence) and 49(2)		32	
			33	
			34	
			35	
			36	
			37	
			38	
			49(1) (last sentence) and 49(3)	

This way of presenting the substance of the CFR seems instrumental for three reasons. First, it makes it more transparent that in interpreting the CFR, the ECHR is always an essential starting point, on the one hand, but, on the other hand, that the same should be the case for lesser-known sources, such as the ESC. This also leads to the policy suggestion that in order to promote compliance with the CFR in a meaningful way, it is essential—and again this may be counter-intuitive—to build up far more detailed knowledge of ECHR and ESC case law, and present this on EU websites and in publications. This seems to be particularly relevant because the focus in EU circles is often mainly on the Luxembourg Court. Such a consciously broader focus would be incredibly helpful in truly coming to a 'fundamental rights culture' in the EU. Second, dividing up the CFR in this way makes it easier to make immediately visible what categories of CFR rights offer a higher level of protection than the ECHR (categories b and c). In fact, the *majority* of CFR rights are in this category. Policy and promotional activities to raise awareness in the area of *these* CFR rights therefore seem particularly appropriate. Third, it makes apparent that some rights are in fact EU context-specific.

Procedurally and organisationally, there are also a number of further measures that would be conducive to ensuring compliance with the CFR in the EU policy context. It may appear to be an open door, but for CFR proofing to be undertaken rigorously, it is important that there are sufficient staff working on this at each of the EU institutions, including the Commission's impact assessment units. The Council could move regularly to discuss FRA research reports and ensure follow-up on their findings, for example, in the Working Party on Fundamental Rights, Citizens' Rights and Free Movement of Persons (FREMP). It has already expressed its intentions to this effect several times,[48] but has yet to act on it in a consistent and institutionalised way. However, on the side of the FRA, this would equally require a move to formulate its recommendations in a (more) actionable, precise and measurable way.

Finally, some early practices can also be discontinued. It would appear, for example, that there is now an unnecessary overlap between the Commission's two and the FRA's one annual reports on the fundamental rights situation in the EU and the application of the CFR. As these reports seem to be aimed at a similar audience, it is important that these efforts are better coordinated so that resources are used more efficiently. If the Commission feels strongly about the necessity of issuing a report of its own, one obvious solution for it is to propose to alleviate the FRA of the task to issue such a report if and when the Commission decides to table amendments to the FRA founding regulation. This is likely to happen as a result of the evaluation of the FRA's activities that has just been finalised.[49] Another solution would be for the FRA on its own motion to considerably trim down its current approach, eating up close to five per cent of its annual budget,[50] and focus more on other ways to promote the application of the CFR.

V. CONCLUSION

The Treaty of Lisbon simultaneously laid down two ways for the EU to strengthen how it protects fundamental rights. Apart from the obligation for the EU to accede to the ECHR, it made the CFR, which takes the ECHR as a basis but offers additional protection, legally binding. Curiously, in acting upon the Lisbon mandate, arranging for the EU accession has taken precedence. But do we now have a clear idea over what internal EU fundamental rights system we are establishing external judicial overview?

This chapter has focused on this issue by analysing the practice to date with regard to the EU's internal fundamental rights protection system lynchpin-to-be: the CFR. It has particularly tracked how the CFR has been applied at the policy stage (ie, the stage of developing policy and drafting legislation) prior to judicial application. This is a relevant focus because in a well-functioning system of fundamental rights protection, dedicated

48 Council Conclusions 2011-1 (n 19) paras 19–20; Council Conclusions 2012(n 19) para 11.

49 FRA Founding Regulation, Article 30.

50 According to information available on the FRA website, its annual budget stands at around €20 million, of which around €800,000 are allocated to the production of its annual report.

methods and procedures should actually filter out the great majority of potential problems with compliance of legislative and policy measures well before they reach court. Just like ensuring independent external judicial control is fundamental to the credibility of EU fundamental rights protection efforts, so will it be crucial to put in place these internal EU- and Member State-level CFR compliance measures. In fact, the substance of the policy practice with regard to the CFR will strongly determine to what extent EU-external judicial overview by the Strasbourg Court will be required at all.[51]

This chapter first assessed the state of play with regard to how the CFR has been promoted and used at the EU level. The Commission issued several policy documents announcing an active stance in promoting the CFR. The Commission and the Council also both adopted fundamental rights checklists. Moreover, the FRA has started publishing reports taking the CFR as an explicit starting point. However, at this stage, there is a still a strong sense that below the multiple layers of policy objectives and incipient practices, pre-Lisbon business has largely continued as usual in actual policy development. It remains to be seen to what extent these various new guidelines and tools will actually help shape and—unavoidably, given the topic of fundamental rights—correct and overrule EU policy choices at the pre-judicial stage.

Then the CFR policy practice at the Member State level was assessed. Yes, national courts have started referring to the CFR in deciding national cases with a link to EU law and have also formulated questions for preliminary references relying on it. However, progress in national policy practice appears to be much slower. Lack of clarity about precisely when the CFR actually applies to Member States' actions in some *specific* situations seems to have had a serious *general* paralysing effect in relation to the national policy application of the CFR. Add to this a quite widespread unawareness about what the CFR substantively adds, particularly when it comes to social rights, as well as real difficulty in gauging the interpretational implications of the CFR's horizontal clauses (Articles 52–53). As a result, the default national policy position appears to have been largely to avoid the CFR and stick to the good old ECHR.

Finally, in analysing the CFR's use in EU and national policy making so far, various suggestions were made throughout the contribution to kiss her awake, focusing both on tools that were already developed as well as possible new avenues that could help in using the CFR's potential more fully. It was suggested that the Commission and the Council would do well to amend their CFR checklists to better spell out elements relating to the proportionality and subsidiarity test in the process of fundamental rights proofing. It was also proposed that the Commission and the FRA better synchronise their efforts in what now appear to be three very similar annual reports relating to the EU's internal fundamental rights situation. In terms of further ways to better unlock the CFR for effective application, it was proposed to sub-divide the CFR's content into four categories: 1) CFR rights with the same meaning and scope as the corresponding ECHR rights; 2) CFR rights with the same meaning but a wider scope compared to corresponding the ECHR rights; 3) CFR rights with no corresponding ECHR right (but often corresponding ESC rights); and 4) CFR rights that are EU context-specific. Such a breakdown may enable a better sense of

[51] Conversely, the envisaged accession of the EU to the ECHR has the potential to boost fundamental rights awareness within that policy practice; see V Kosta, 'Fundamental Rights in Internal Market Legislation', unpublished PhD thesis, 2013, European University Institute, ch 3 'New Mechanisms for Fundamental Rights Protection in EU legislation: Building a Fundamental Rights Culture outside the Courts', 63 et seq.

where the CFR adds value to the most familiar point of reference of fundamental rights protection in Europe: the ECHR. Finally, it was argued that better guidance on when the CFR applies to Member States' actions is required, either by the Court or by other actors.

Fleshing out further and more concrete CFR compliance policies will have to be done simultaneously with the process of further organising the EU's accession to the ECHR. It is hoped that the accession discussion will not distract from its importance, for the two components are intrinsically linked. To a large extent, the way in which the EU's internal policies with regard to the CFR develop will determine the intensity of the future control required by the Strasbourg Court. It is important not to organise accession in a way that takes yesterday's system of EU internal fundamental rights protection as a point of reference. Giving true hands and feet to the CFR at the pre-judicial stage will unavoidably force EU and national policy makers to confront some of the legal issues that were intentionally left ambiguous by the CFR's drafters—perhaps even before the Court of Justice will be able to clarify them definitely. In these cases, it is hoped that the Commission will take the initiative. For when you find yourself to be a guardian of a CFR still asleep, some prior princely kissing may be required.

10

Two Worlds (Still) Apart? ECHR and EU Law before National Judges

GIUSEPPE MARTINICO*

I. INTRODUCTION

ACCORDING TO MANY scholars, a huge distinction still exists between the European Convention on Human Rights (ECHR) and European Union (EU) law.[1] This would be a consequence of the *sui generis* nature of the EU, which would imply the impossibility of comparing EU law with other forms of public international law.[2] In other words, according to this view, EU law is provided with some structural principles which are lacking outside of the EU treaties.

In this chapter I will try to question such a view, by focusing on the—still limited—extension of the structural EU law principles (primacy and direct effect) to the ECHR. In other words, I shall investigate the similarities and differences between the national judicial treatment (ie, the application and the interpretation) of the ECHR and EU laws in the context of some selected constitutional experiences. One could argue that the EU's accession to the ECHR will render this question moot by fostering the absolute convergence in the judicial treatment of EU and ECHR laws. I am not sure about this. One should distinguish between two different issues here: that of the automatic incorporation of the international

* García Pelayo Fellow, CEPC, Madrid; Lecturer (on leave), Scuola Superiore Sant'Anna, Pisa. Many thanks to the editors of this volume and to Giuseppe Bianco and Filippo Fontanelli for their comments.

[1] This is, for instance, what Lord Hoffmann argued some years ago: 'The fact that the 10 original Member States of the Council of Europe subscribed to a statement of human rights in the same terms did not mean that they had agreed to uniformity of the application of those abstract rights in each of their countries, still less in the 47 states which now belong. The situation is quite different from that of the European Economic Community, in which the Member States agreed that it was in their economic interest to have uniform laws on particular matters which were specified as being within European competence. On such matters, the European institutions, including the Court of Justice in Luxembourg, were given a mandate to unify the laws of Europe. The Strasbourg court, on the other hand, has no mandate to unify the laws of Europe on the many subjects which may arguably touch upon human rights ... The proposition that the Convention is a "living instrument" is the banner under which the Strasbourg court has assumed power to legislate what they consider to be required by "European public order"'. Lord Hoffmann, 'The Universality of Human Rights', Judicial Studies Board Annual Lecture, London, 19 March 2009.

[2] R Schütze, *From Dual to Cooperative Federalism: The Changing Structure of European Law*, (Oxford, Oxford University Press, 2009). As the author says in the Introduction, in order to conceptualise the hybrid nature of Community law—neither international nor national law: 'European thought invented a new word—supranationalism—and proudly announced the European Union to be sui generis ... The sui generis idea is not a theory. It is an anti-theory, as it refuses to search for commonalities; yet, theory must search for what is generic ... However, this conceptualization simply can no longer explain the social and legal reality inside Europe' (at 3).

treaties concluded by the EU and that of the recognition of their direct effect. On the one hand, it is true that, according to the *Haegeman* doctrine, the agreements concluded by the European Communities' institutions (and now by the EU) benefit from a kind of 'automatic treaty incorporation'[3] into EU law, since the provisions of these agreements 'form an integral part of Community law'.[4] On the other hand, the issue of the acknowledgment of the direct effect to the international treaties should not be considered as automatically stemming from the incorporation. It is perhaps useful to recall in this sense the distinction coined by Bourgeois between 'EC law proper' and 'Community Agreements',[5] as reconceptualised by Mendez:

> [T]he Member States were implicitly striking at the very heart of a critical distinction between Community law proper and Community Agreements. The ECJ is the authoritative interpreter of the former, but at most it can only be the authoritative interpreter of the latter in the Community legal order; however, the latter, unlike the former, being international treaties, are binding on other Contracting Parties, and the ECJ is accordingly precluded from assuming the mantle of authoritative interpreter to this extent. Direct effect and supremacy were eventually accepted within a Community of states in which the central enforcement role was delegated to the national judiciary with the ECJ as the overseer keeping the construct together.[6]

This kind of national resistance led the Court of Justice of the European Union (CJEU) to reshape its original approach to public international law, and the 'WTO [World Trade Organization] exception' (WTO law's lack of direct effect) has been more recently extended to other international law treaties.[7]

There is another element that should be taken into account as well: the ECHR is a flexible instrument. This is at the heart of the margin of appreciation doctrine, for instance: the automatic extension of the direct effect to the ECHR under EU law might transform this flexible instrument into a rigid one. This is perhaps something not desired by the ECtHR itself. Moreover, even in the recent case law of the CJEU, it is possible to find a confirmation of this impression. Indeed, in the *Fransson*[8] decision, the CJEU confirmed that the domestic effects of the ECHR and the relation between the ECHR and national law are not governed by the EU Treaties. It clarified this point as follows:

> [I]t is to be remembered that whilst, as Article 6(3) TEU [Treaty on European Union] confirms, fundamental rights recognised by the ECHR constitute general principles of the European Union's law and whilst Article 52(3) of the Charter requires rights contained in the Charter which

[3] On this, see M Mendez, 'The Legal Effect of Community Agreements: Maximalist Treaty Enforcement and Judicial Avoidance Techniques' (2010) *European Journal of International Law* 83.

[4] Case C-181/73 *R & V Haegeman v Belgian State* [1974] ECR 449.

[5] J Bourgeois, 'The Effects of International Agreements in European Community Law: Are the Dice Cast?' (1984) 82 *Michigan Law Review* 1250.

[6] Mendez (n 3).

[7] See M Bronckers, 'From "Direct Effect" to "Muted Dialogue": Recent Developments in the European Courts' Case Law on the WTO and Beyond' (2004) 11 *Journal of International Economic Law* 885. Certainly, the rationale of WTO law is not that of conferring rights on individuals, so the parallelism suggested with the ECHR might seem weird. However, the parallelism with WTO law and with a case like *Mox Plant* (Case C-459/03 *European Commission v Ireland* [2006] ECR I-4635) is used in order to recall that the Court is always reluctant to give direct effect automatically under EU Law, ie, as a consequence of the incorporation of the treaty into EU law, to international treaties concluded by the EU. This is especially so when there is another interpreter that may indirectly influence its interpretative function. In this sense, the CJEU is frequently guided by reasons connected to judicial politics. See N Lavranos, *Jurisdictional Competition: Selected Cases in International and European Law* (Groningen, Europa Law Publishing, 2009).

[8] Case C-617/10, *Åkerberg Fransson*, available at www.curia.europa.eu.

> correspond to rights guaranteed by the ECHR to be given the same meaning and scope as those laid down by the ECHR, the latter does not constitute, as long as the European Union has not acceded to it, a legal instrument which has been formally incorporated into European Union law. Consequently, European Union law does not govern the relations between the ECHR and the legal systems of the Member States, nor does it determine the conclusions to be drawn by a national court in the event of conflict between the rights guaranteed by that convention and a rule of national law.[9]

By making this point, the CJEU developed what it had already said in another recent judgment (*Kamberaj*).[10] This chapter shall not deal with these recent decisions; rather, it will offer some considerations starting from the above-reported passages on the thorny issue of the domestic effects of the ECHR before national judges in the light of EU law. The *Kamberaj* case originated from a preliminary question raised by an Italian judge, the Tribunale di Bolzano, which had invoked Article 6 TEU to disapply national provisions conflicting with the ECHR by analogy with what happens with EU law. In *Kamberaj*, the CJEU concluded that:

> [T]he answer ... must therefore be that the reference made by Article 6(3) TEU to the ECHR does not require the national court, in case of conflict between a provision of national law and the ECHR, to apply the provisions of that convention directly, disapplying the provision of national law incompatible with the convention.[11]

It also clearly maintained that it will have a role in the issue of the determination of the direct effect of the ECHR by saying that:

> [P]rovision [Article 6] of the Treaty on European Union reflects the settled case-law of the Court according to which fundamental rights form an integral part of the general principles of law the observance of which the Court ensures.[12]

From the CJEU's reasoning, one infers that the Treaty of Lisbon does not automatically put the ECHR and EU law on an equal footing before national judges, and this point was also stressed, as we saw, in *Fransson*.

If this is true, it would not make sense to try to anticipate the conclusions that the CJEU will reach since they will probably also depend on the role that the CJEU will have after the accession. Instead, I will attempt to present the issue of the national judicial 'treatment' of the ECHR and EU law before national judges as a heated issue, before and probably after the accession. In order to do so, I will not deal with the accession as such; rather, I will present the situation at the national level in a retrospective manner and then seek to make some forward-looking conclusions. After a detailed analysis of national case law, I will argue that we are already (without taking into account the possible accession of the EU to the ECHR) having at least a partial convergence in the application of EU law and the ECHR's provisions. For the sake of clarity, by convergence I mean a convergence in terms of techniques used in the interpretation and application of EU law and the ECHR. This kind of convergence does not per se exclude conflicts between the ECHR and EU law in terms of different levels of protection. In this sense, the convergence I have in mind is

[9] Ibid [44].

[10] Case C-571/10, *Servet Kamberaj v Istituto per l'Edilizia Sociale della Provincia autonoma di Bolzano (IPES) and Others*, available at www.curia.europa.eu [62].

[11] Ibid [63].

[12] Ibid [61].

merely procedural (ie, it is a convergence in terms of techniques adopted when applying and interpreting these two European laws).

A different issue is given by the substance/contents of these two different sets of norms. In other words, the procedural convergence does not automatically lead to a convergence in terms of the standards of protection required by the ECHR and EU law. I am fully aware of the importance of this second kind of convergence (the substantive one), but I have decided not to deal with it given the space constraints of this chapter. In order to set out this argument, I go beyond what constitutions say about the effects of these two European laws. In this sense, I shall analyse the relevant case law of domestic judges under three aspects of potential convergence: consistent interpretation; the disapplication of national norms/provisions conflicting with European provisions (which is a sign of the direct effect of the ECHR's provisions); and the emergence of a counter-limits doctrine.

I shall approach this subject from the perspective of the EU legal order; in this sense, this chapter will not deal with possible positions in the case law of the European Court of Human Rights (ECtHR). This is a methodological choice made with a view to analyse the subject from the perspective of legal orders that define themselves as autonomous, but are influenced (either directly or indirectly) by the ECHR. Finally, in this chapter I am not going to limit myself to the analysis of the national constitutional provisions governing the effects of the ECHR and EU norms in the domestic orders; rather, I am going to focus on the law in action, paying attention to national case law.

II. BEYOND THE FORMAL PROVISIONS

The literature[13] has underscored the variety of national constitutional provisions regarding the ECHR. Indeed, looking at these provisions (and those applicable to EU law), one can notice the diversity of national approaches with respect to the domestic authority of European laws (ie, the ECHR and EU law).[14] Despite these differences, it has been noted[15] that European jurisdictions are progressively nearing the 'position' of the ECHR in the hierarchy of sources. This convergence is the final outcome of different national pathways; sometimes, national legislators must be credited, while in other circumstances, it is rather constitutional or supreme courts, or even common judges. This is irrespective of the formal position set out in the constitution or of the dualism or monism classification.[16] The ECHR is generally acknowledged to be a supra-legislative force, but its relationship with constitutional supremacy is more controversial, as will be discussed below.

A similar variety can also be found in the domestic treatment of EU law. One can identify several 'strategies' used to ensure EU law's primacy.[17] However (again), despite this

[13] G Martinico and O Pollicino (eds), *The National Judicial Treatment of the ECHR and EU Laws: A Comparative Constitutional Perspective* (Groningen, Europa Law Publishing, 2010); H Keller and A Stone Sweet (eds), *A Europe of Rights: The Impact of the ECHR on National Legal Systems* (Oxford, Oxford University Press, 2009).

[14] For an overview, see Martinico and Pollicino (n 13).

[15] H Keller and A Stone Sweet, 'Assessing the Impact of the ECHR on National Legal Systems' in Keller and Stone Sweet (n 13) 683 ff.

[16] This conclusion is also supported by ibid, 685–86.

[17] M Claes, *The National Courts' Mandate in the European Constitution* (Oxford, Hart Publishing, 2006).

variety and although there are sporadic cases of judicial resistance,[18] as has been noted,[19] EU law is applied in all jurisdictions uniformly, as primacy and direct effect are accepted by all national courts.[20]

The first common element of these two European regimes is the crucial role of national judges, who are the real 'natural judges' of both, for different reasons. They are the first guardians of the *Simmenthal* doctrine for EU law[21] and, at the same time, the first adjudicators of the ECHR in national systems, due to the principle of subsidiarity. This is a crucial point of this research, dealing with both ECHR and EU law. To provide a comparative overview, I will cover the following judicial practices:

(a) consistent interpretation (a consequence of the 'indirect effect' of supranational laws);
(b) the disapplication of domestic law (the consequence of supranational laws' direct effect/primacy);
(c) the counter-limits doctrine (setting a limit to supranational law's primacy).

A. Consistent Interpretation

A first analogy is traceable in the practices whereby judges accord an interpretive favour to the EU/ECHR norms. This can occur for reasons that are amenable to different subjects or elements of the system:

(a) constitutional provisions (Spain and Romania);
(b) legislative provisions (UK);
(c) constitutional courts' case law (Italy and Germany).

This is a reflection of the constitutional variety described above. Sometimes the language of domestic constitutions conveys a message of reaction to totalitarian experiences, eg, in the form of an increased openness to international law and the acknowledgment of peace as a fundamental constitutional principle, not simply as a strategic foreign policy option. The most important confirmation of human rights treaties' special ranking in Spain is Article 10.2 of the Constitution, which acknowledges that they provide interpretive guidance in the application of human rights-related constitutional clauses (even if the Constitutional Court specified that this does not implicate that human rights treaties have a constitutional *status*).[22] As for Portugal, the fundamental provision is Article 16 of the Constitution, which recognises that international human rights treaties have a complementary role to the Constitution. This provision accords an interpretative role to the Universal Declaration of Human Rights, seemingly excluding other conventions like the ECHR. In 1982, an attempt to insert a reference to the ECHR into the Constitution failed, but the Portuguese Constitutional Court often used the ECHR as an important auxiliary hermeneutic tool

[18] See the reaction to the *Mangold* case, for instance: R Herzog and L Gerken, 'Stop the European Court of Justice' (2008), available at http://euobserver.com/opinion/26714.
[19] Claes (n 17).
[20] Martinico and Pollicino (n 13).
[21] Claes (n 17).
[22] *Tribunal Constitucional*, Judgment 30/1991, available at http://www.tribunalconstitucional.es/en/Pages/Home.aspx.

for interpreting the Constitution, leaving the matter unresolved.[23] A similar provision is Article 20(1) of the Romanian Constitution: 'Constitutional provisions concerning the citizens' rights and liberties shall be interpreted and enforced in conformity with the Universal Declaration of Human Rights, with the covenants and other treaties Romania is a party to.' Article 5 of the Bulgarian Constitution recognises a general precedence of international law (including ECHR and EU law) over national law and also covers the duty to interpret national law in a manner that is consistent with these regimes (and the case law of their respective courts). In 1998, the Bulgarian Constitutional Court ruled that:

> The Convention constitutes a set of European common values which is of a significant importance for the legal systems of the Member States and consequently the interpretation of the constitutional provisions relating to the protection of human rights has to be made to the extent possible in accordance with the corresponding clauses of the Convention.[24]

As we can see, according to all these provisions, national law shall be interpreted in light of the ECHR (and other human rights treaties).

Consistent interpretation is a very well-known doctrine in EU law.[25] More generally, it is a typical doctrine of multilevel systems,[26] since it guarantees some flexibility in the relationship between laws of different orders and entrusts judges with the role of gatekeepers.[27] The literature described the obligation of consistent interpretation as recognition of EU law's 'indirect effect' and primacy, which is particularly convenient when the conflict between norms cannot be solved with the *Simmenthal* doctrine, because EU provisions lack a formal direct effect. As stressed by Rodin,[28] the *Simmenthal* doctrine rigidly dictates a unilateral conclusion of constitutional conflicts (ie, conflicts between constitutional supremacy and the primacy of EU law), while the consistent interpretation makes it possible to neutralise or soften constitutional conflicts, in some cases at least.

The duty to interpret national law consistently with the ECHR provisions is sometimes based on legislative provisions, like in the UK, under the Human Rights Act (HRA). In 1998, the ECHR was incorporated into the HRA, containing a selective incorporation of the ECHR's rights (the so-called 'Convention Rights'). Section 3[29] provides the necessity to interpret domestic law 'so far as is possible' in conformity with the Convention. The proposed classification—ie, the statutory source of the consistent interpretation obligation—might be contested, however, since there are some English cases where the HRA is treated as a part of the 'constitutional core'. This is precisely what happened in *Thoburn*.[30]

[23] Portuguese Constitutional Court, decision 345/99, available at www.tribunalconstitucional.pt. The episode is mentioned by F Coutinho, 'Report on Portugal' in Martinico and Pollicino (n 13) 360. On Portugal, see L Montanari, *I diritti dell'uomo nell'area europea fra fonti internazionali e fonti interne* (Turin, Giappichelli, 2002) 112.

[24] See Constitutional Court Decision no 2, of 18 February 1998: Official journal no 22, 24 February 1998. The cases reported are quoted by M Fartunova, 'Report on Bulgaria' in Martinico and Pollicino (n 13) 101.

[25] Case 14/83 *Von Colson* [1985] ECR 1891; Case C-106/89, *Marleasing* [1990] ECR I-4345.

[26] Even in the US: Charming Betsy 'canon', *Murray v The Charming Betsey*, 6 US 2 Cranch 64 64 (1804)6 US (2 Cranch) 64 (1804).

[27] See the following cases on the relationship between EU and WTO laws: Case C-53/96 *Hermès International v FHT Marketing Choice BV* [1998] ECR I-3603; Cases C-300/98 and C-302/98 *Dior and others* [2000] ECR 11307.

[28] S Rodin, 'Back to Square One. The Past, the Present and the Future of the Simmenthal Mandate', paper presented at the 8th ECLN, Madrid, 6–8 October 2010.

[29] Section 3(1): 'So far as it is possible to do so, primary legislation and subordinate legislation must be read and given effect in a way which is compatible with the Convention rights'.

[30] *Thoburn v Sunderland City Council* [2002] 1 CMLR 50.

In this judgment, Laws LJ recognised the existence of a constitutional group of statutes and acts, which included the European Communities Act 1972:

> In the present state of its maturity the common law has come to recognise that there exist rights which should properly be classified as constitutional or fundamental ... We should recognise a hierarchy of Acts of Parliament: as it were 'ordinary' statutes and 'constitutional' statutes. The two categories must be distinguished on a principled basis. In my opinion a constitutional statute is one which (a) conditions the legal relationship between citizen and State in some general, overarching manner, or (b) enlarges or diminishes the scope of what we would now regard as fundamental constitutional rights. (a) and (b) are of necessity closely related: it is difficult to think of an instance of (a) that is not also an instance of (b).[31]

The Magna Carta, the Bill of Rights of 1689, the Acts of Union of 1707, the Reform Acts, the HRA of 1998, the Scotland Act of 1998, the Government of Wales Act of 1998 and the European Communities Act of 1972 all belong to the category of 'constitutional' statutes. Looking at the judges' reasoning, it is possible to appreciate a further effort to reconcile the primacy of EU law (now vested with constitutional status) with parliamentary sovereignty. According to this judgment, in fact, the EU law's primacy is based on Parliament's self-limitation; in other words, the legal basis of the UK's relationship with the EU rests on national provisions, not on EU law.

Finally, in the absence of expressed written provisions (either constitutional or statutory), the duty to interpret national law in light of the ECHR can sometimes derive from the Constitutional Court's case law, like in Germany and Italy. In Germany, the Second Senate of the Bundesverfassungsgericht (BvG) clarified in 2004[32] the relationship between the BvG and the ECtHR, and somehow followed up on the Strasbourg Court's decision *Görgülü v Germany*.[33] As explained in the literature,[34] this judgment must be connected to another instance of judicial conflict between the two courts, the *Von Hannover v Germany* case.[35] On that occasion, the two courts had interpreted the right to privacy differently. The BvG thus in 2004 seised the occasion to bring some clarity: the ECHR and the ECtHR's case law bind the Federal Republic only as a public international law subject. The ECHR was ratified as ordinary law and therefore it can be derogated by any subsequent ordinary statute and cannot serve as a standard of constitutional review (ie, one cannot claim the violation of conventional rights before the BvG). However, the case law of the Strasbourg Court may be referred to when interpreting the Constitution if this does not entail a limitation of another constitutional right. Moreover, the BvG recalled the open character of the German Constitution (Articles 23 and 24), obliging national judges to take into account the law and case law of the European Convention and to interpret domestic norms in the light thereof, but only if this operation is possible (and providing reasons when failing to do so).

[31] Ibid [62].

[32] See order 2 BvR no 1481/04.

[33] *Görgülü v Germany*, App No 74969/01, www.echr.coe.int/echr. See A Di Martino, 'Il Tribunale costituzionale tedesco delimita gli effetti nel diritto interno delle sentenze della Corte Europea dei diritti dell'uomo' (2004), available at archivio.rivistaaic.it/.

[34] F Palermo, 'Il Bundesverfassungsgericht e la teoria selettiva dei controlimiti' (2005) *Quaderni Costituzionali* 181.

[35] *Hannover v Germany*, App No 59320/00, www.echr.coe.int/echr/.

More recently, in May 2011,[36] the BvG held preventive detention unconstitutional, basing its expansive interpretation of the *Grundgesetz* on the case law of the Strasbourg judges.[37]

In Italy, with two fundamental decisions of 2007, the Constitutional Court[38] clarified the position of the ECHR in the domestic legal system. According to the Italian Constitutional Court, the Convention has a super-primary value (ie, its normative ranking is halfway between statutes and constitutional norms). This is confirmed by the fact that, in some cases, the ECHR can serve as an 'interposed parameter' for the constitutional review of primary laws, since the conflict between them and the ECHR can entail an indirect violation of the Constitution, namely of its Article 117(1), which reads: 'Legislative power belongs to the state and the regions in accordance with the constitution and within the limits set by European Union law and international obligations.' Since Article 117 recalls international obligations, a conflict between a national piece of legislation and the ECHR can be solved by considering the ECHR as an external part of the standard employed by the Corte costituzionale to review the constitutionality of domestic norms. The constitutional favour accorded to the ECHR implies the obligation to interpret national law in light of the ECHR's norms. At the same time, this does not imply that the ECHR has a constitutional value; on the contrary, the ECHR has to respect the Constitution. As we will see when dealing with the second factor of convergence, according to the Italian Constitutional Court, the ECHR cannot be treated domestically like EU law.[39]

In the Baltic countries, the ECHR is deemed a source of inspiration for the construction[40] of national (including constitutional) law and was cited by the constitutional courts of these countries even before their accession to the ECHR.[41] This is the case in Lithuania as well as in Latvia, where the court expressly accepted to be bound by the ECtHR's case law,[42] even when it interprets its own Constitution.[43] Likewise, the Estonian Supreme Court expressly acknowledged the ECHR's priority over national law[44] and its own duty to bear in mind the ECtHR's case law.[45] The Belgian Cour constitutionnelle uses the technique of consistent interpretation, taking into account the case law of both European courts and showing its readiness even to revise its previous case law, if need be.[46] Finally, the Supreme

[36] No 2 BvR 2365/09, www.bundesverfassungsgericht.de. Federal Constitutional Court of Germany, 4 May 2011. On this case, see E Bjorge and M Andenas, 'German Federal Constitutional Court—Preventive Detention—Relationship between International and National Law—European Convention on Human Rights' (2011) *American Journal of International law* (2011) 768.

[37] For instance, *M v Germany*, App No 19359/04 (ECtHR, 17 December 2009).

[38] Corte costituzionale, judgments nos 348 and 349/2007, available at www.cortecostituzionale.it.

[39] For a detailed analysis of the judgments, see: F Biondi Dal Monte and F Fontanelli, 'The Decisions No. 348 and 349/2007 of the Italian Constitutional Court: The Efficacy of the European Convention in the Italian Legal System' (2008) 7 *German Law Journal* 889; O Pollicino, 'The Italian Constitutional Court at the Crossroads between Constitutional Parochialism and Co-operative Constitutionalism. Judgments No. 348 and 349 of 22 and 24 October 2007' (2008) 4 *European Constitutional Law Review* 363.

[40] Constitutional Court of Lithuania, Ruling of 8 May 2000. All these cases are reported by I Jarukaitis, 'Report on Estonia, Latvia and Lithuania' in Martinico and Pollicino (n 13) 167.

[41] For the Lithuanian context, see, for instance, the Ruling of 28 May 2008; the Ruling of 7 January 2008; the Ruling of 29 December 2004. For the Constitutional Court of Latvia, see the Judgment of 29 October 2009; the Judgment of 5 November 2008; the Judgment of 11 April 2006 in Case No 2005-24-01. See also Constitutional Review Chamber of the Supreme Court of Estonia, No 3-4-1-2-01 of 3 May 2001.

[42] Constitutional Court of Latvia, Judgment of 30 August 2000, No 2000-03-01.

[43] Constitutional Court of Latvia, Judgment No 2006-03-0106, adopted 23 November 2006.

[44] Supreme Court of Estonia, Judgment of 6 January 2004 in Case No 3-1-3-13-03.

[45] Judgment of the Constitutional Review Chamber of the Supreme Court of Estonia, 30 December 2008 in Case No 3-4-1-12-08.

[46] For instance, Const Court No 81/2007, 7 June 2007.

Courts of Nordic countries have acknowledged EU and ECHR law's special role.[47] They accorded to these regimes a sort of interpretative priority, and used consistent interpretation and indirect effect doctrines to avoid constitutional conflicts between national and supranational laws.

In conclusion, it emerges that the technique of consistent interpretation is applicable to both EU law and the ECHR norms, following different paths (constitutional, legislative and judicial). This does not mean that the convergence is perfect: for instance, it is not always clear whether the duty to interpret national law in light of the ECHR includes the necessity to take into account the case law of the ECtHR. In this respect, there are different answers. Formally, the mentioned constitutions are silent on this, while the UK HRA expressly provides (section 2) that: 'A court or tribunal determining a question which has arisen in connection with a Convention right must take into account any—(a) judgment, decision, declaration or advisory opinion of the ECtHR.' In Italy and Germany, as seen above, it is the Constitutional Court that gave instructions to this effect. A last word on these cases: the constitutional provisions providing for the duty of consistent interpretation do not distinguish between the ECHR and other international treaties on human rights, whereas when this doctrine is based on legislation and judicial decisions, the ECHR enjoys an ad hoc treatment.

B. The Judicial Disapplication of Domestic Law: *Simmenthal* Reloaded?

As already noted, the national judge is considered the first guarantor of EU law's primacy following the *Simmenthal* judgment of the CJEU.[48] With this judgment in mind, one can infer: a) the connection between EC (now EU) law's primacy/precedence and the duty to disapply conflicting national law; and b) the crucial role of domestic judges in ensuring the primacy.

In this section, I will show a second similitude in the national use of European laws, which is reflected in the judicial treatment of conflicts between domestic norms and EU/ECHR norms according to the *Simmenthal* doctrine and applied to ECHR law by analogy. Here again, we can find different reasons for this phenomenon.

In some countries there exist constitutional provisions empowering national judges to disapply national law that conflicts with international treaties. In France (where the Constitution stipulates the superiority of treaties), there are no specific provisions concerning human rights treaties, and all the provisions of Title VI of the Constitution—regarding the entry into force of international treaties—are applicable to the ECHR. The domestic super-legislative ranking of international treaties is inferable from Article 55, which provides that ratified treaties are superior to domestic legislation. The review of conformity of national law with international treaties (control of 'conventionnalité') is entrusted to national judges.

[47] For Denmark, see the decisions U.1979.117/2H and U.1988.454H. For Sweden, see the decision NJA 1996 s 668. Many of these cases are reported by C Lebeck, 'Report on Scandinavian Countries' in Martinico and Pollicino (n 13) 389.

[48] Case 106/77 Amministrazione delle Finanze c. *Simmenthal S.P.A.* [1978] ECR 629. On the recent developments of the *Simmenthal* doctrine, see Rodin (n 28).

Unlike France, many Eastern European countries have entrusted this control to the constitutional courts, causing a certain degree of convergence between the control of constitutionality and that of 'conventionnalité'.[49] A similar mechanism—with the important difference of the absence of the judicial review of legislation—is the Dutch model, which is based on Articles 91 and 93 of the Grondwet (the Basic Law). The clearest signal of the Dutch order's incredible openness to international law is Article 90: 'the Government shall promote the development of the international rule of law'. Grewe[50] argued that the Dutch system, recognising the prevalence of the international regime over the national one, is the only truly monist system of Europe. Another confirmation comes from Article 94 of the Grondwet: 'Statutory regulations in force within the Kingdom shall not be applicable if such application is in conflict with provisions of treaties that are binding on all persons or of resolutions by international institutions.' According to some authors,[51] this article also refers to constitutional provisions. In any case, Article 94 entitles national judges to review the conventionality of national law, even though they are not allowed to review the constitutionality of the statutory norms, under Article 120 of the Grondwet.[52]

In essence, in both France and the Netherlands, the convergence between EU and ECHR law is due to a set of constitutional instructions which do not seem to distinguish between public international law and EU law.[53]

The second case of extension of the *Simmenthal* doctrine to the ECHR—the Italian case—is completely different in terms of its scope and reasons. As widely noted,[54] Italian common (comuni) judges started disapplying domestic norms conflicting with the ECHR.[55] In 2007, the Corte costituzionale resolved to stop this trend, which constituted an undue 'constitutional exception' to the constitutional supremacy, and derogated from the centralised constitutional review. The Constitutional Court, to impede this practice and ensure at the same time the ECHR's supra-statutory status, agreed for the first time to assess the validity of national provisions using the ECHR standard. The Corte therefore, extended the doctrine of the 'interposed norm' ('norma interposta').[56] In essence, it sent

[49] On the jurisdiction of the national constitutional courts in this field, see: Bulgaria Article 149.4; Poland Article 188; Czech Republic Article 87; Slovenia Article 160. See also Montanari (n 23) 99.

[50] C Grewe, 'La question de l'effet direct de la Convention et les résistences nationales' in P Tavernier (ed), *Quelle Europe pour les droits de l'homme?* (Brussels, Bruylant, 1996) 157.

[51] P Van Dijk, 'Dutch Experience with European Convention in Domestic Law' in L Rehof and C Gulmann (eds), *Human Rights in Domestic Law and Development Assistance Policies of the Nordic Countries* (The Hague, Martinus Nijhoff, 1989), 137; Montanari (n 23) 65.

[52] Article 120: 'The constitutionality of Acts of Parliament and treaties shall not be reviewed by the courts.'

[53] G Betlem and A Nollkaemper, 'Giving Effect to Public International Law and European Community Law before Domestic Courts: A Comparative Analysis of the Practice of Consistent Interpretation' (2003) 14(3) *European Journal of International Law* 569 ff: 'there is no fundamental divide between the application of public international law and EC law'.

[54] Biondi Dal Monte and Fontanelli (n 39); Pollicino (n 39).

[55] See: Court of Pistoia on 23 March 2007: Court of Genoa, decision of 23 November, 2000; Court of Appeal of Florence decision Nos 570 of 2005 and 1403 of 2006, and the State Council (*Consiglio di Stato*), I Section, decision No 1926 of 2002: 'Some judges had already started applying this method, which comes from the judicial practice of disapplying the internal statutory norm conflicting with Community law. In some recent occasions, even the Supreme Court of Cassation (*Corte di Cassazione*) and the Supreme Administrative Court (*Consiglio di Stato*) had endorsed the use of disapplication in cases of conflict with ECHR law.' Biondi Dal Monte and Fontanelli (n 39) 891.

[56] 'Scholars have minted the wording "interposed provision" to individualize the cases in which a constitutional standard can be invoked only indirectly in a constitutional judicial proceeding, because different primary provisions are inserted between the constitutional standard and the reported provisions (suspected of being unconstitutional).' Biondi Dal Monte and Fontanelli (n 39) 897. See C Lavagna, *Problemi di giustizia costituzionale sotto il profilo della 'manifesta infondatezza'* (Milan, Giuffrè, 1957), at 28; M Siclari, *Le norme interposte nel giudizio di costituzionalità* (CEDAM, Padua, 1992).

this message to common judges: 'instead of disapplying, refer a preliminary question of constitutionality to the Constitutional Court!'

This conclusion hinged upon the distinction between ECHR and EU law:

> [A]ccording to the constitutional judges, the ECHR legal system has distinct structural and functional legal features as compared to the European legal order ... [In their view,] the EHCR is a multilateral international public law Treaty which does not entail and cannot entail any limitation on sovereignty in the terms provided by Article 11 of the Constitution.[57]

This explains the different treatment reserved to the ECHR as regards the practice of disapplication and the necessity that it be consistent with the whole Constitution, not just with the counter-limits (ie, those fundamental principles forming an untouchable constitutional core). Quite surprisingly, after the intervention of the Constitutional Court, some ordinary judges kept disapplying national provisions conflicting with the ECHR[58] for various reasons:

1. Sometimes the judges seemed not to understand the Constitutional Court's diktat or not to know the difference between the ECHR and EU law.[59]
2. In other cases, the judges duly recalled the Corte costituzionale's instructions, yet misunderstood the meaning of the new (post-Lisbon) Article 6 TEU, which paves the way for the EU's accession to the ECHR. In other words, they thought that the ECHR has (already) become part of EU law *ipso jure*, after the coming into force of the Treaty of Lisbon and therefore now has direct effect and primacy. This is perhaps the case of a judgment *Consiglio di Stato*, given in March 2010.[60]
3. Finally, there are cases of open civil disobedience of common judges who demonstrate that they know, but will not follow, the instructions of the Constitutional Court.[61]

It is possible to see the Italian case as a demonstration that a problem of application of 'external' law in the multilevel legal system might result in an 'internal' judicial conflict (the Constitutional Court versus ordinary judges).[62] The 'confrontation' between the Italian Constitutional Court and the other Italian judges (lower courts, but, to a certain extent, also supreme courts; see the mentioned case of the State Council[63]) is still live and open. In 2011 (decision 80/2011), the Corte costituzionale gave another ruling, which represents the *summa* of its view on the matter.[64] This decision is, again, based on the distinction between EU law (for which it is possible to accept those limitations to the Italian sovereignty recalled by Article 11 of the Italian Constitution) and the ECHR (for which the application

[57] Pollicino (n 39).

[58] I Carlotto, 'I giudici comuni e gli obblighi internazionali dopo le sentenze n. 348 e n. 349 del 2007 della Corte costituzionale: un'analisi sul seguito giurisprudenziale', in http://archivio.rivistaaic.it/dottrina/giustizia_costituzionale/ilaria%20carlotto%20sent.348_349_2007.pdf. E Lamarque, 'Il vincolo alle leggi statali e regionali derivante dagli obblighi internazionali nella giurisprudenza comune' (2010) http://www.cortecostituzionale.it/documenti/convegni_seminari/lamarque_definitivo_6112009.pdf.

[59] Tribunale di Livorno, Sez. Lav., ordinanza del 28 ottobre 2008. See Carlotto (n 58).

[60] Consiglio di Stato, sent 2 marzo 2010, no 1220. On this decision, see G Colavitti and C Pagotto, 'Il Consiglio di Stato applica direttamente le norme CEDU grazie al Trattato di Lisbona: l'inizio di un nuovo percorso?' (2010), www.associazionedeicostituzionalisti.it/rivista/2010/00/Colavitti-Pagotto01.pdf.

[61] Tribunale di Ravenna, 16 January 2008. On this, see Carlotto (n 58).

[62] For a wider analysis coming to this conclusion, see Carlotto (n 58): Lamarque (n 58).

[63] Consiglio di Stato, sent 2 marzo 2010, no 1220.

[64] A Ruggeri, 'La Corte fa il punto sul rilievo interno della CEDU e della Carta di Nizza-Strasburgo (a prima lettura di Corte cost. n. 80 del 2011)' (2011), www.forumcostituzionale.it/site/images/stories/pdf/documenti_forum/giurisprudenza/2011/0002_nota_80_2011_ruggeri.pdf.

of Article 11 seems to be misplaced according to the Constitutional Court).[65] In light of this confrontation, the preliminary question sent by the referring judge in *Kamberaj* acquires a very strong 'political' dimension, as we will see later.

There are other interesting (yet less clear-cut) cases: in Bulgaria, for instance, national judges are considered the first defenders of the ECHR's precedence on national law, under Article 5.4 of the Constitution. Both common judges and the Constitutional Court are seemingly entitled to carry out the 'contrôle de conventionnalité',[66] but scholars have noticed[67] a certain reluctance on the part of ordinary judges:

> The national courts prefer to decide that the case pending before them doesn't fall into a field of these two international instruments. Nevertheless, two comments should be made. First, this position does reveal a certain difficulty to solve potential conflicts between the domestic law and European instruments. Second, the national courts do still prefer to apply the relevant domestic law instead of the relevant international clauses. One of the reasons is that the judges' knowledge of these instruments is still insufficient.[68]

The Bulgarian Constitutional Court has recognised the priority of the Constitution over EU and ECHR law, but also admitted that the Constitution shall be interpreted as far as possible in light of ECHR law. This solution has been described as the paradoxical consequence[69] of the wording of Article 149 of the Constitution (namely, of the combination between paragraphs 2 and 4), which governs both the control of constitutionality (paragraph 2) and of '*conventionnalité' (paragraph 4). These kinds of review, indeed, were deemed to differ* in terms of purpose and scope.[70]

In Portugal, theoretically, it can be argued that Articles 204 and 8 of the Constitution, combined, entitle national judges to disapply national law conflicting with constitutional and international law, but scholars describe this possibility as a sort of 'sleeping giant' that has never woken up.[71]

On the domestic effects of the ECHR, another interesting provision is Article 96 of the Spanish Constitution, the meaning of which is a matter of debate: does it empower judges to disapply national legislation in conflict with ECHR provisions? Granted, according to the Constitutional Tribunal, Spanish judges may disapply national laws conflicting with international treaties,[72] although the possible disapplication of national law for conflict with human rights treaties like the ECHR appears to be more problematic, and the Constitutional Tribunal has never pronounced on this issue. Since the Constitutional Tribunal has demonstrated its willingness to take the ECHR into account—via Article 10.2 of the Constitution—scholars suggested that ordinary judges should refer a question to the

[65] Article 11 of the Italian Constitution: 'Italy rejects war as an instrument of aggression against the freedom of other peoples and as a means for the settlement of international disputes. Italy agrees, on conditions of equality with other States, to the limitations of sovereignty that may be necessary to a world order ensuring peace and justice among the Nations. Italy promotes and encourages international organizations furthering such ends.'

[66] See Article 149, paras 2 and 4 of the Constitution (Bulgaria).

[67] Fartunova (n 24) 109.

[68] Ibid, 108–09.

[69] Ibid.

[70] Ibid.

[71] 'Although authorized by the Portuguese Constitution, I could not find cases where Portuguese judges had directly invoked the ECHR to put aside conflicting national law': Coutinho (n 23) 364. See Report of the Portuguese Constitutional Court to the XII Congress of the European Constitutional Courts, 14–16 May 2002, at 53, cited by Coutinho (n 23).

[72] Tribunal Constitucional 49/1988, FJ 14; Tribunal Constitucional 180/1993.

Constitutional Tribunal when conflict arises, rather than disapplying national law.[73] This view also hinges upon the distinction between normal international treaties (Article 96) and human rights treaties (Article 10).

Finally, there are states where disapplication is forbidden: in the UK, for instance, in case of contrast between primary legislation and the ECHR, judges can only adopt a 'declaration of incompatibility',[74] which does not influence the validity and the efficacy of the domestic norm. After such a declaration, 'if a Minister of the Crown considers that there are compelling reasons for proceeding … he may by order make such amendments to the legislation as he considers necessary to remove the incompatibility'.[75]

Regardless of whether disapplication is allowed or practised to ensure the implementation of ECHR norms, in all jurisdictions the ECHR is apparently provided, at least, with a sort of 'direct effect'. In this respect, the Austrian case is significant, as Keller and Stone Sweet pointed out:

> In 1964, the political parties revised the Constitution, to confer upon the Convention constitutional status and direct effect. Today, conflicts between the Austrian Constitution and the ECHR are governed by the *lex posteriori derogat legi priori* rule, an apparently unique situation.[76]

Interestingly, even before the 1964 amendment,[77] a de facto constitutional character had been acknowledged to the ECHR, which confirms the necessity to go beyond the wording of the constitutional texts in the present investigation.

It appears that the situation has not changed much since the 1980s, when Neville Brown and McBride argued that the attribution of direct effect to the provisions of the ECHR is a matter for the national constitutions to decide on.[78] At the same time, as we saw, there are cases in which, notwithstanding the ambiguity of the national constitutions, the direct effect of the ECHR provisions is recognised: the Belgian case is emblematic, as shown in *Franco Suisse Le Ski*.[79] That is why, today, despite the literal wording of the Constitution, some scholars consider both the European laws (ie, the ECHR and EU law) as 'supranational'.[80]

[73] V Ferreres Comella, 'El juez nacional ante los derechos fundamentales europeos. Algunas reflexiones en torno a la idea de diálogo' in A Saiz Arnaiz and M Zelaia Garagarza (eds), *Integración Europea y Poder Judicial* (Oñati, Instituto Vasco de Administración Pública, 2006) 231.

[74] On this declaration, see K Ewing and J Tham, 'The Continuing Futility of the Human Rights Act' [2008] *Public Law* 668.

[75] Section 10. See also A Bradley and K Ewing, *Constitutional and Administrative Law* (London, Longman, 2007) 436.

[76] Keller and Stone Sweet (n 15) 684.

[77] P Cede, 'Report on Austria and Germany', in Martinico and Pollicino (n 13) at 63. Confirmation of the constitutional status of the ECHR is derived from the complementary nature of this document (with regard to the constitutional text). This is the real criterion to evaluate its ranking in the legal sources of the national system despite the procedure followed to incorporate them, and this explains why the ECHR had, de facto, a constitutional rank even before 1964.

[78] 'An individual could not however rely upon any provisions of the ECHR in a national court unless it was "capable of conferring rights on citizens of the Community which they can invoke before the courts". This requirement raises the question whether the ECHR's provisions are of direct effect. The only guide to this is to be found in the decisions of the courts of countries whose constitutions accord the ECHR legal effect.' L Neville Brown and J McBride, 'Observations on the Proposed Accession by the European Community to the European Convention on Human Rights' (1981) 4 *American Journal of Comparative Law* 691, 695. See also A Drzemczewski, 'The Domestic Status of the European Convention on Human Rights: New Dimensions' (1977) 1 *Legal Issues of European Integration* 1.

[79] Cass 27 May 1971, *Pas* 1971, I, 886.

[80] For instance, see P Popelier, 'Report on Belgium' in Martinico and Pollicino (n 13) 84.

Even in Luxembourg, over the years, the courts have confirmed the 'directly self-executing[81] character of many of the Convention's provisions.[82] Hence, the ECHR and its Protocols are considered to be directly applicable in the Luxembourg legal order'.[83]

C. The Limits to Primacy: The Counter-limits Doctrine

As Maduro pointed out, 'The acceptance of the supremacy of EU rules over national constitutional rules has not been unconditional, if not even, at times, resisted by national constitutional courts. This confers to EU law a kind of contested or negotiated normative authority'[84] and reveals the existence of a never-ending process of judicial bargaining between domestic courts (especially constitutional and supreme courts) and the CJEU. The conditions posed by the constitutional courts and mentioned by Maduro are represented by doctrines such as the 'counter-limits' and the *Solange* doctrines.

By 'counter-limits' ('controlimiti'),[85] I mean those national fundamental principles raised by constitutional courts—like impenetrable barriers—against the infiltration of EU law. The counter-limits are conceived as an ultimate wall to the full application of EU law. They were conceived by the Italian Constitutional Court in *Frontini*[86] and by the German BvG in *Solange I*.[87] However, many constitutional courts endorsed it later on: the French[88] and the Spanish courts did so in 2004,[89] but even earlier the English High Court had made the primacy of EU law contingent on the preservation of certain untouchable principles.[90] More recently, the decisions of the Polish[91] and German Constitutional Courts[92] (although see also the decisions of the Cypriot[93] and Czech[94] judges) have recalled the question of the

[81] Direct effect and self-executing character refer to two different notions in principle. However, the self-executing nature of a norm may be important in order to detect a precise, clear and unconditional obligation which does not need any further additional measure and is thus relevant to the direct effect analysis.

[82] For instance: Cour supérieure de justice (chambre des mises en accusation), 2 April 1980 and Cour de cassation, 17 January 1985, No 2/85.

[83] E Mak, 'Report on the Netherlands and Luxembourg' in Martinico and Pollicino (n 13) 314.

[84] M Poiares Maduro, 'Interpreting European Law: Judicial Adjudication in a Context of Constitutional Pluralism' (2007) 2 *European Journal of Legal Studies* 1.

[85] This formula has been introduced in the Italian scholarly debate by Paolo Barile: P Barile, 'Ancora su diritto comunitario e diritto interno' in G Ambrosini et al (eds), *Studi per il XX anniversario dell'Assemblea costituente*, VI (Florence, Vallecchi, 1969), 49.

[86] Corte Costituzionale, sentenza n 183/73, available at www.cortecostituzionale.it. In English see: *Frontini v Ministero delle Finanze* [1974] 2 CMLR 372.

[87] BVerfGE 37, S 271 ff, www.bundesverfassungsgericht.de/en/index.html.

[88] But see also Conseil d'Etat, dec Sarran, 30 October 1998; Cour de cassation, dec Fraisse, 2 June 2000; Conseil d'Etat, dec SNIP, 3 December 2001. In addition, see: Conseil Constitutionel 2004-496-497-498-499 DC 2004-505 DC.

[89] Tribunal Constitucional, declaracìon 1/2004.

[90] *McWhirter and Gouriet v Secretary of State for Foreign Affairs* [2003] EWCA Civ 384. On this point, see A Biondi, 'Principio di supremazia e "Costituzione" inglese. I due casi "Martiri del sistema metrico" e "McWhirter and Gouriet"' (2003) *Quaderni Costituzionali* 847.

[91] Trybunał konstytucyjny, P 1/05, www.trybunal.gov.pl/eng/index.htm.

[92] BVerfG, 2 BvR 2236/04, www.bundesverfassungsgericht.de/en/index.html.

[93] Ανώτατο Δικαστήριο, 294/2005, www.cylaw.org.

[94] Ústavní Soud, Pl. ÚS 66/04, http://www.usoud.cz/en/decisions/?tx_ttnews%5Btt_news%5D=512&cHash=94f2039f92b13843f3a3b93c6fcb237e.

ultimate barriers in the field of the European Arrest Warrant.[95] According to Panunzio,[96] the counter-limits (even in the *Solange* rendition) represent an instrument to force the courts to communicate; they are like a 'gun on the table', which induces the jurisdictional actors to confront each other.

A similar doctrine has emerged in respect of the ECHR's penetration into the domestic legal order. The most telling example is BvG's order no 1481/04,[97] mentioned above, where the Karlsruhe judges ruled that, in the case of unresolvable conflicts between the ECHR and domestic law, the latter should prevail. For the first time in its history, the BvG specified which matters are off-limits for the primacy of the ECHR: family law, immigration law and the law on protection of personality.[98] The BvG stressed the particularities of the proceeding before the ECtHR, which might lead to a different outcome in the balancing between values. The most interesting element of this decision is that the BvG made use of the selective approach also used in *Lissabon Urteil*[99] with respect to EU law.[100] In this decision the BvG made a list of sensitive areas representing the:

> [E]ssential areas of democratic formative action (citizenship, the civil and the military monopoly on the use of force, revenue and expenditure including external financing and all elements of encroachment that are decisive for the realisation of fundamental rights, above all as regards intensive encroachments on fundamental rights such as the deprivation of liberty in the administration of criminal law or the placement in an institution ... cultural issues such as the disposition of language, the shaping of circumstances concerning the family and education, the ordering of the freedom of opinion, of the press and of association and the dealing with the profession of faith or ideology).[101]

By doing so, the BvG contributed significantly to define the meaning of Article 4(2) TEU, namely elucidating the concept of 'national identity'.

Even in legal orders lacking a full-fledged constitutional text, like the UK,[102] judges limited the openness granted to the ECHR. Emblematically, in *Horncastle*, the Supreme Court[103] said that:

> There will, however, be rare occasions where this court has concerns as to whether a decision of the Strasbourg Court sufficiently appreciates or accommodates particular aspects of our domestic

[95] J Komarek, 'European Constitutionalism and the European Arrest Warrant: In Search of the Limits of Contrapunctual Principles', Jean Monnet Working Paper (2005), available at www.jeanmonnetprogram.org/papers/05/051001.html.

[96] S Panunzio, 'I diritti fondamentali e le Corti in Europa' in S Panunzio (ed), *I diritti fondamentali e le Corti in Europa* (Napoli, Editoriale Scientifica, 2005) 17 ff.

[97] 2 BvR 1481/04.

[98] On this, see F Hoffmeister, 'Germany: Status of European Convention on Human Rights in Domestic Law' (2006) 4 *International Journal of Constitutional Law* 722–31.

[99] BVerfG, cases 2 BvE 2/08 and others, 30 June 2009, available at: www.BVerfG.de/entscheidungen/es20090630_2bve000208.html.

[100] On this, see E Lanza, 'Core of State Sovereignty and Boundaries of European Union's Identity in the Lissabon–Urteil' (2010) 11 *German Law Journal* 399.

[101] BVerfG, cases 2 BvE 2/08, at para 249.

[102] See C Murphy, 'Human Rights Law and the Challenges of Explicit Judicial Dialogue', Jean Monnet Working Paper, (2011), available at http://centers.law.nyu.edu/jeanmonnet/papers/12/1210.html. See also N Bratza, 'The Relationship between the UK Courts and Strasbourg' (2011) 5 *European Human Rights Law Review* 505 ff.

[103] On the impact of the ECHR on the activity of some national supreme courts, see E Bjorge, 'National Supreme Courts and the Development of ECHR Rights' (2011) 9(1) *International Journal of Constitutional Law* 5.

> process. In such circumstances it is open to this court to decline to follow the Strasbourg decision, giving reasons for adopting this course.[104]

Even more clearly—and using a rhetoric that recalls that of continental constitutional courts—the same court said elsewhere:

> This Court is not bound to follow every decision of the [ECtHR]. Not only would it be impractical to do so: it would sometimes be inappropriate, as it would destroy the ability of the Court to engage in the constructive dialogue ... which is of value to the development of Convention law. Of course, we should usually follow a clear and constant line of decisions ... But we are not actually bound to do so or (in theory, at least) to follow a decision of the Grand Chamber ... Where, however, there is a clear and constant line of decisions whose effect is not inconsistent with some fundamental substantive or procedural aspect of our law, and whose reasoning does not appear to overlook or misunderstand some argument or point of principle, we consider that it would be wrong for this Court not to follow that line.[105]

In Austria, where the ECHR enjoys constitutional status, this Convention-friendliness cannot justify a violation of the Constitution.[106] In this sense, some authors[107] have compared the *Görgülü* judgment to the *Miltner* case,[108] where the Austrian Constitutional Court has stressed the possibility of departing from the ECtHR's case law if adherence thereto would entail a violation of the Constitution.

The Italian Constitutional Court came to a similar conclusion in 2007 (decisions 348 and 349), where it clarified that the ECHR has a privileged position, but enjoys no 'constitutional immunity'; on the contrary, it must abide by all constitutional norms. The Italian judges equated the ECHR to any source of international law and found, accordingly, that the 'constitutional tolerance' of the Italian system towards the ECHR is lower than towards EU law. This difference in degree is clearly visible: whereas the 'counter-limits' against the penetration of EU law are a subset of constitutional rights (which means that EU law prevails over non-core constitutional values), the Italian Court is stricter with the Convention, requiring its conformity with every constitutional norm:

> [T]he need for a constitutionality test on the Convention norm excludes the possibility of having a limited set of fundamental rights that could serve as a counter-limit; indeed, every norm of the Constitution shall be respected by the international norm challenged.[109]

III. INSTEAD OF A CONCLUSION: THE QUESTION OF CONVERGENCE POST-ACCESSION

This chapter has demonstrated how the treatment of EU and ECHR laws by national judges can still be considered a heated issue, even after the coming into force of the Treaty of Lisbon. Will the accession of the EU to the ECHR give a definitive answer (and this

[104] *R v Horncastle and others* [2009] UKSC 14 [11].

[105] *Manchester City Council v Pinnock* [2010] UKSC 45 [48].

[106] 'In this case, even though the Convention has constitutional rank, the contrary rule of constitutional law would have to prevail by virtue of its lex specialis character'. Cede (n 76) 70.

[107] As N Krisch says in 'The Open Architecture of European Human Rights Law' (2003) 71 *MLR* 183.

[108] Austrian Constitutional Court, Miltner, VfSlg 11500/1987, available at www.ris.bka.gv.at/vfgh.

[109] Biondi Dal Monte and Fontanelli (n 39) 915.

seems to emerge even from *Fransson*, cited at the beginning of the chapter), certainly favouring convergence? As I said, I have some doubts and *Kamberaj* seems to confirm them.

In *Kamberaj*, an Italian judge (the Tribunale di Bolzano/Bozen) sought to use a preliminary reference to the CJEU to overturn the Constitutional Court's jurisprudence on the treatment of the ECHR. Affirming that Article 6(3) TEU does not require the disapplication of domestic law conflicting with the Convention has allowed the Luxembourg Court to avoid entering a domestic war between the Italian Constitutional Court and its national judges.

The Tribunale di Bolzano/Bozen had asked:

> [W]hether, in case of conflict between the provision of domestic law and the ECHR, the reference to the latter in Article 6 TEU obliges the national court to apply the provisions of the ECHR—in the present case Article 14 ECHR and Article 1 of Protocol No 12—directly, disapplying the incompatible source of domestic law, *without having first to raise the issue of constitutionality before the Corte costituzionale* (Constitutional Court). (Emphasis added)[110]

In light of the considerations made earlier when dealing with the Italian case, the political reasons behind this preliminary question are obvious. By using the preliminary ruling in a strategic manner, the referring judge tried to obtain from the CJEU new arguments to question the case law of the Corte costituzionale and to bring its centralised control to an end. However, from a technical point of view, this use of Article 6 TEU to argue in favour of the extension of the *Simmenthal* doctrine to the ECHR makes sense. For instance, Bruno de Witte once mantained that Article 6 TEU (Lisbon version) would make the ECHR already binding, since it refers to the ECHR as part of the general principles of EU law. In his own words, 'the ECHR … is now still binding by way of its incorporation in the general principles, but … will become directly binding on the EU after the Union's accession'.[111] Now, in my view, although the wording of Article 6 is clear, it does not deprive the CJEU of having the control on the general principles. In other words, it does not prevent the Court from being the authentic interpreter of general principles, as shown in *Mangold*.[112]

Arguing the contrary might have the effect of making the ECHR too rigid an instrument, which has been known as a traditionally flexible tool (eg, by means of the margin of appreciation doctrine). A confirmation might be found by analogy with the common constitutional traditions. The fact that they are a source of inspiration for the general principles of EU law does not mean that the CJEU directly applies them or feels bound by the interpretation given by national constitutional courts (as the *Mangold*[113] example again seemingly confirms).

Finally, a case like *Kücükdeveci*[114] appears to demonstrate that even after the coming into force of the Treaty of Lisbon (with the consequent entry into force of the Charter of

[110] *Kamberaj* (n 10) [59].

[111] B de Witte, 'The Use of the ECHR and Convention Case Law by the ECJ' in P Popelier, C Van de Heyning and P Van Nuffel (eds), *Human Rights Protection in the European Legal Order: The Interaction between the European and the National Courts* (Oxford, Intersentia, 2011). The new version of Article 6 TEU reads: 'Fundamental rights, as guaranteed by the European Convention for the Protection of Human Rights and Fundamental Freedoms and as they result from the constitutional traditions common to the Member States, shall constitute general principles of the Union's law.' The previous version read: 'Article 6.2. The Union shall respect fundamental rights, as guaranteed by the European Convention for the Protection of Human Rights and Fundamental Freedoms signed in Rome on 4 November 1950 and as they result from the constitutional traditions common to the Member States, as general principles of Community law.'

[112] Case C-144/04 *Werner Mangold. v. Rüdiger Helm* [2005] ECR I-9981.

[113] Ibid.

[114] Case C-555/07 *Seda Kücükdeveci v Swedex GmbH & Co KG*. On this, see F Fontanelli, 'General Principles of the EU and a Glimpse of Solidarity in the Aftermath of Mangold and Kücükdeveci' (2011) 17 *European Public Law* 225.

Fundamental Rights), general principles of EU law (as interpreted by the CJEU) will have a crucial role in the case law of the Luxembourg Court. This is due to the fact that the CJEU has a margin in reshaping them, which is an advantage that the written wording of the principles codified in the Charter of Fundamental Rights of the EU does not offer.[115]

This point is indeed present in *Kamberaj*. It recalled that Article 6(3) TEU reproduced the approach taken by the CJEU in its jurisprudence, which considers fundamental rights as part of the general principles of law whose respect the Court ensures (paragraph 61). In this way, the CJEU confirmed having the last word on the definition of these principles. From *Kamberaj*, one can infer that the debate on the direct effect to be given to the ECHR under EU law is very far from being exhausted. Comparing the current scenario with that studied by Neville, McBride and Drzemczewski in the 1970s and 1980s, it is immediately clear that, today, the issue of the ECHR's primacy and direct effect does not depend only on what is written in the constitutions; indeed, it is something that seems to go beyond the full control of national constitutions. In this scenario, EU law has also provided national judges (the Italian case is very clear on this) with arguments for reconsidering the ECHR's force, as Keller and Stone Sweet,[116] for instance, noticed and as *Kamberaj* once again shows.

Very much will depend on the CJEU and on its position in the future system. The chapter by Torres Pérez included in this volume also shows that the final draft of the Accession Agreement presents many ambiguities in this respect, and many of them seem to be connected to questions of judicial politics. Moreover, cases like *Mox Plant*,[117] clearly reveal how the CJEU still holds the reasons connected to its interpretive monopoly dear, and bespeak its scarce tolerance for interpretive competitors. Will this be the case for the Strasbourg court too?

[115] Also, we must consider that, according to certain literature, general principles have a scope of application broader than that of the Charter. This would explain why the CJEU might still refer to them in the future, even when fundamental rights are codified by the Charter. In other words, this reference to general principles would be a way to use the principles as a Trojan horse to enlarge the scope of EU law by circumventing Article 51 of the Charter. A confirmation of this reading might be found in the approach followed by the CJEU in some cases where it adopts the general principles as a starting point of its reasoning, recalling only in a second moment that the given principle is also codified by the Charter. In this way, it might appear to recognise a mere codificatory value to the Charter. On this debate, see M Safjan, 'Areas of Application of the Charter of Fundamental Rights of the European Union: Fields of Conflict?', EUI Working Paper LAW 2012/22, available at http://cadmus.eui.eu/bitstream/handle/1814/23294/LAW-2012-22.pdf. One may argue that both the provisions of the Charter of Fundamental Rights and the general principles of EU law inspired by the ECHR de facto refer to the Convention. However, a distinction should be made in our view. While for the Charter we may encounter detailed explanations referring to specific case law on the provisions of the ECHR, Article 6 includes a more generic reference to the Convention when it mentions fundamental rights 'as guaranteed by the ECHR'. The context is also different and in my view the existence of provisions having a content not included in the ECHR might lead the two European courts to decide in a different manner. For instance, when striking the balance, the CJEU will balance these rights with other provisions of the Charter that do not have a corresponding norm in the European Convention. Yet, of course, much will depend on the law in action.

[116] 'European integration—the evolution of the EU's legal system, in particular—has shaped reception in a number of crucial ways. First, the ECJ's commitment to the doctrines of the supremacy and direct effect of Community law provoked processes that, ultimately, transformed national law and practice. Supremacy required national courts to review the legality of statutes with respect to EC law, and to give primacy to EC norms in any conflict with national norms. For judges in many EU States, the reception of supremacy meant overcoming a host of constitutional orthodoxies, including the prohibition of judicial review of statutes, the *lex posterior derogat legi priori*, and separation of powers notions. These same structural issues arose anew under the Convention': Keller and Stone Sweet (n 15) 681.

[117] Case C-459/03 *European Commission v Ireland* [2006] ECR I-4635.

11

National Courts in the New European Fundamental Rights Architecture

MONICA CLAES AND ŠEJLA IMAMOVIĆ*

I. INTRODUCTION

THE EUROPEAN HUMAN rights landscape is changing.[1] In the EU context, this can be seen, for instance, in the fact that the EU Charter of Fundamental Rights has acquired the same legal value as the EU Treaties (Article 6 of the Treaty on European Union (TEU)), and has been given centre stage in the case law of the Court of Justice of the European Union (CJEU) as well as in EU policy and law making.[2] In the context of the European Convention on Human Rights (ECHR), reform of the enforcement system has been on the agenda since the 1990s, when the number of contracting parties dramatically increased. The focus is on improving compliance with the case law of Strasbourg and on reforming the Court. In addition, several European countries have in that same period re-designed their domestic architecture of human rights protection, often in order to accommodate the new role for European rights domestically,[3] or to re-arrange responsibilities between ordinary and constitutional courts in that light.[4] Europe's complex fundamental rights landscape is evolving, and these changes occur both within each of the systems making up the complex European fundamental rights system and between them.

* Monica Claes is Professor of European and Comparative Constitutional Law at Maastricht University and Šejla Imamović is a PhD candidate at Maastricht University.

[1] In this chapter, we use the terms 'human rights' and 'fundamental rights' interchangeably.

[2] S Iglesias Sánchez, 'The Court and the Charter: The Impact of the Entry into Force of the Lisbon Treaty on the ECJ's Approach to Fundamental Rights' (2012) 49 *CML Rev* 1565; Commission Communication, Strategy for the effective implementation of the Charter of Fundamental Rights by the European Union, COM(2010)573 final of 19 October 2010; Draft Council Conclusions on the role of the Council of the European Union in ensuring the effective implementation of the Charter of Fundamental Rights of the European Union, Council Document 6387/11 of 11 February 2011.

[3] Thus, Finland has amended its constitution to introduce or extend constitutional review of statutes in order to remove the discrepancy that had arisen with the incorporation of the ECHR and the ensuing review powers of the courts. For a recent discussion, see J Lavapuro, T Ojanen, and M Scheinin, 'Rights-based Constitutionalism in Finland and the Development of Pluralist Constitutional Review' (2011) *International Journal of Constitutional Law* 505.

[4] In France, the respective roles of the ordinary and constitutional courts have been rearranged by the introduction in 2008 of the 'question prioritaire de constitutionnalité'; see, eg, F Fabbrini, 'Kelsen in Paris: France's Constitutional Reform and the Introduction of A Posteriori Constitutional Review of Legislation' (2008) 9 *German Law Journal* 1297. On the Belgian case, see J Velaers, 'The Protection of Fundamental Rights by the Belgian Constitutional Court and the *Melki-Abdelhi* Judgment of the European Court of Justice' in M Claes, M de Visser, P Popelier and C Van de Heyning (eds), *Constitutional Conversations in Europe* (Cambridge, Intersentia, 2012).

This contribution focuses on one specific reform to the overall European human rights architecture that is underway, namely the accession of the EU to the ECHR. Debated for decades, accession appears in a different light today, as it is now included in Article 6(2) TEU after the Treaty of Lisbon as an obligation rather than a choice. In principle, the accession of the EU to the ECHR concerns only the relationship between the EU and the ECHR. It is little wonder then that the focus of scholarly attention has been on the question of how this accession will affect the relations between Strasbourg and Luxembourg. Nevertheless, it is likely that the new architecture will also affect the functioning of the national courts in the context of fundamental rights protection as it will give rise to more litigation and therefore more involvement of courts at all levels in ever more cases. Accession will of course directly affect the relationship between Strasbourg and Luxembourg, and designing this relationship is one of the most delicate dossiers on the negotiating table.[5] Yet, each of these courts also has a specific relationship with the national courts. So how will accession affect the dynamics in the tri-partite relationship between national courts and each of the European courts?

This chapter is structured as follows. The next section revisits the prevailing complex and multi-sourced system of fundamental rights protection in the European space, analysing the co-existence of several layers of fundamental rights protection. Section III identifies and discusses the elements in the accession debate which may impact the national courts. Section IV then discusses these issues from the perspective of national courts.

II. A WEB OF FUNDAMENTAL RIGHTS REGIMES: A THREE-DIMENSIONAL VIEW

Fundamental rights protection and policy in the European legal space feature human rights bills originating in different regimes (national, EU and ECHR).[6] They each organise their own machinery for enforcement, whereby use may, however, also be made of actors and mechanisms belonging to another regime. Moreover, each of the regimes has its own conceptions of how legal norms belonging to the different systems relate to one another and its own rules of conflict. This section structures these various pluralities along three axes: the level of the norms, their actors and enforcement mechanisms, and the prevailing rules of conflict.

A. National Constitutions and National Fundamental Rights Policy

All Member States have their own fundamental rights catalogue, usually in constitutional form.[7] Fundamental rights legislation and policies complement the protection offered by

[5] There is a burgeoning literature on the consequences of accession for the relationships between Luxembourg and Strasbourg. See, among many others, T Lock, 'End of an Epic? The Draft Agreement on the EU's Accession to the ECHR' (2012) *Yearbook of European Law* 162; JP Jacqué, 'The Accession of the European Union to the European Convention on Human Rights and Fundamental Freedoms' (2011) 48 *CML Rev* 995.

[6] The term 'European legal space' is used to denote the complex of legal regimes applicable on the territory of the Member States of the EU, including mainly, but not only, the ECHR and EU law (in the entire space), and the national law of each of the Member States within their territory.

[7] The classic exception is the UK, for the simple reason that it lacks a constitutional document of the 'higher law' type that most Member States possess. Nevertheless, the Human Rights Act fulfils a role that is very much comparable to that played by national constitutional bills of rights.

these constitutional catalogues.[8] The enforcement mechanisms differ from one state to the next, and usually contain a mix of hard law and soft law instruments and mechanisms. In many (but not all) Member States, (constitutional) courts are involved in the process of constitutional rights protection and act as the ultimate guardians of constitutional rights.[9] In more and more Member States, moreover, the ECHR and other treaties form part of the domestic fundamental rights system. Thus, in the Netherlands, France and Belgium, for instance, all courts enforce ECHR rights even as against primary legislation, even though they are precluded from reviewing the constitutionality of such legislation. In these cases, the ECHR functions as a substitute (the Netherlands) or complementary constitution (Belgium and France). In the UK, the Human Rights Act 1998 provides that primary legislation and subordinate legislation must be read and given effect in a way which is compatible with the Convention rights, and account is given to the case law of the Strasbourg Court. Lord Bingham has even stated in *Ullah* that: 'The duty of national courts is to keep pace with the Strasbourg jurisprudence as it evolves over time: no more, but certainly no less.'[10] In other countries, the ECHR serves as an aid to interpret domestic standards, but ultimately, when there is a discrepancy between the constitution and the ECHR, priority will be awarded to the constitution.[11] The German Constitutional Court, for example, has famously held that: 'The Basic Law accords particular protection to the central stock of international human rights. This protection … is the basis for the constitutional duty to use the ECHR in its specific manifestation when applying German fundamental rights too … As long as applicable methodological standards leave scope for interpretation and weighing of interests, German courts must give precedence to interpretation in accordance with the Convention.' Yet, this means 'taking notice of the Convention provision as interpreted by the ECtHR and applying it to the case, provided the application does not violate prior-ranking law, in particular constitutional law'.[12]

With respect to EU law, the current position in many Member States today is that the primacy of EU law is accepted, even over the constitution, except in cases where certain core elements of the domestic constitution are at stake. These core elements come under different guises, such as 'les conditions essentielles de l'exercice de la souveraineté nationale' or 'l'identité constitutionnelle' (in France),[13] as 'i principi fondamentali del nostro ordinamento costituzionale, o i diritti inalienabili della persona umana' (in Italy)[14] or the 'grundgesetzlichen Identität' which may also include specific balances struck in the context

[8] This roughly coincides with the distinction between negative and positive effects of fundamental rights. We do not develop this point further here.

[9] Comparative analyses can be found in V Ferreres Comella, *Constitutional Courts and Democratic Values* (New Haven, Yale University Press, 2009); AHY Chen and MP Maduro, 'The Judiciary and Constitutional Review' in M Tushnet, T Fleiner and Ch Saunders (eds), *Routledge Handbook of Constitutional Law* (New York, Routledge, 2013), 97; M de Visser, *Constitutional Review in Europe: A Comparative Analysis* (Oxford, Hart Publishing, 2013).

[10] *R (Ullah) v Special Adjudicator* [2004] INLR 381. This mirror principle has now been challenged. See, eg, B Hale, 'Argentoratum Locutum: Is Strasbourg or the Supreme Court Supreme?' (2012) 12 *Human Rights Law Review* 65; *R v Horncastle and others* (Appellants) (on appeal from the Court of Appeal Criminal Division) [2009] UKSC 14.

[11] See, eg, for Germany, C Tomuschat, 'The Effects of the Judgments of the European Court of Human Rights According to the German Constitutional Court' (2010) 11 *German Law Journal* 513.

[12] *Bundesverfassungsgericht*, Order of the Second Senate of 14 October 2004, 2 BvR 1481/04, Görgülü.

[13] Conseil constitutionnel, Decision No 2006-540 DC of 27 July 2006 (Loi relative au droit d'auteur et aux droits voisins dans la société de l'information).

[14] Corte costituzionale, Sentenza no 183/1973, [1974] 2 CMLR 372 (*Frontini*).

of fundamental rights (in Germany).[15] Nevertheless, these so-called 'controlimiti' are reserved for exceptional cases: only in cases of manifest infringement of the constitutional standards or when it is proven that the EU system has sunk below an acceptably similar level would the constitutional courts regain control over EU law. Conversely, national courts do take account of EU fundamental rights, and the Charter plays an important role in this respect.[16]

B. The ECHR

The Strasbourg Court is the ultimate interpreter and 'the supreme guardian' of the ECHR. The protection and enforcement of the rights protected in the ECHR are of course not a matter for the Strasbourg Court alone. This is first and foremost a matter for national authorities, including the courts. Moreover, the ECHR imposes only a common minimum standard of protection and allows (wide) divergences when it comes to the protection of human rights in concrete cases. It allows a (variable) margin of appreciation to the national authorities. The Convention system does not impose specific techniques for the domestic implementation and enforcement of the ECHR: it is the end result that counts. Therefore, it does not matter whether or not the ECHR as such formally plays a role in the process or whether protection is achieved through other means, such as the national constitution. In this respect, the ECHR differs greatly from EU law.[17] Finally, Article 53 ECHR encourages Member States to go beyond the minimum standards arising out of the Convention and Strasbourg case law. Since the ECHR is an international agreement and the Strasbourg Court is an international court, it should be clear that from the perspective of the ECHR, national law should never be given precedence. The Strasbourg Court may also scrutinise national constitutional law and decisions of national constitutional courts.[18] With respect to the EU, the current conception of the relationship between the ECHR and EU law is defined by the fact that the EU is not internationally bound by the ECHR, while all its Member States are. The current state of play is well known and a mere reference to the landmark cases will suffice: *Bosphorus*, *Kokkelvisserij* and *MSS v Greece and Belgium*.[19] In short, the Member States remain bound by the ECHR when acting under EU law, but since the EU has a system of human rights protection that can be considered both substantively and procedurally to offer equivalent protection, the presumption is that a Member State has acted in accordance with the ECHR when it does no more than implement EU

[15] *Bundesverfassungsgericht*, 2 March 2010, 1 BvR 256/08, 1 BvR 263/08, 1 BvR 586/08 (*dataretention*).

[16] Examples can be found in Implementation of the Charter of Fundamental Rights of the European Union, General Report of the ACA-Europe presented at the occasion of 23rd colloquium in Madrid 25–26 June 2012, available at www.aca-europe.eu/index.php/en/colloques-top-en.

[17] Comparative analyses can be found in H Keller and A Stone Sweet (eds), *A Europe of Rights: The Impact of the ECHR on National Legal Systems* (Oxford, Oxford University Press, 2008); and G Martinico and O Pollicino (eds), *The National Judicial Treatment of the ECHR and EU Laws: A Comparative Constitutional Perspective* (Groningen, Europa Law Publishing, 2010).

[18] For example, *Caroline von Hannover v Germany*, App No 59320/00 (ECtHR, 24 June 2004).

[19] *Bosphorus Hava Yolları Turizm ve Ticaret Anonim Şirketi v Ireland*, App No 45036/98 (2005) 42 EHRR 1; *Cooperatieve Producentenorganisatie van de Nederlandse Kokkelvisserij UA v The Netherlands*, App No 13645/05 (2009); *MSS v Belgium and Greece*, App No 30696/09 (2011) 53 EHRR 28. See also the Factsheet on the European Court of Human Rights (ECtHR) case law concerning the EU, December 2012, available at http://www.echr.coe.int/Documents/FS_European_Union_ENG.pdf.

legal obligations. The presumption can however be rebutted if, in the circumstances of a particular case, it is considered that the protection of Convention rights was manifestly deficient.

C. The EU Fundamental Rights Regime

The EU regime of fundamental rights builds on the existing national and ECHR systems and taps into them. At the outset, it was particularly the common constitutional principles of the Member States that served as sources of inspiration in the formulation of the general principles of EU law.[20] Gradually, this role of prime source was taken over by the ECHR, while today, the EU Charter serves as the preferred document for the EU institutions, including the CJEU.[21] Nevertheless, the Charter does not replace the other sources, as is evident from Article 6 TEU. The EU has also adopted a substantial body of fundamental rights legislation, especially in the areas of equality and non-discrimination. In terms of enforcement, the usual mechanism, techniques and procedures apply, giving a central place to national courts, and with the European courts acting as the 'ultimate interpreter' of the EU fundamental rights.[22]

Where no harmonious interpretation can be achieved, divergences and conflicts may arise. In the EU–ECHR relationship, this should be exceptional, given the role of the ECHR in the EU system and the expressed intention to interpret the Charter in line with the ECHR. Divergences are only problematic if the EU level of protection would fall below the ECHR minimum standard. Conversely, no problem arises if the divergence results from a higher level of protection offered by the EU.

With respect to the relationship between EU fundamental rights (drawn from the various sources) on the one hand and national constitutional rights on the other, several doctrines and techniques apply.

Under *Internationale Handelsgesellschaft*, national courts are precluded from setting aside EU law with reference to national constitutional rights. This follows from the principle of primacy and has been consistently repeated since.[23] This does not mean that national constitutional rights play no role in EU law. On the contrary, *Internationale Handelsgesellschaft* came with the promise that fundamental rights would be protected in the EU *qua* general principles of EU law, and the common constitutional traditions of the Member States would play an important role in defining these.[24] In addition, EU law to some extent allows space for the protection of national fundamental rights that are not common to the Member States, or for specific national preferences with respect to the balancing in a concrete case. Several techniques are available in EU law to achieve this result: leaving

[20] The story does not need recounting here. See, eg, B de Witte, 'The Past and Future Role of the European Court of Justice in the Protection of Human Rights' in P Alston (ed), *The EU and Human Rights* (Oxford, Oxford University Press, 1999) ch 27.

[21] See S Morano-Foadi and S Andreadakis, 'Reflections on the Architecture of the EU after the Treaty of Lisbon: The European Judicial Approach to Fundamental Rights' (2011) 15 *ELJ* 595.

[22] M Dawson, E Muir and M Claes, 'Enforcing the Rights Revolution in the EU: The Case of Equality' (2012) *EHRLR* 276.

[23] Case 11/70 *Internationale Handelsgesellschaft mbH v Einfuhr- und Vorratsstelle für Getreide und Futtermittel* [1970] ECR 1125.

[24] In practice, this turns out not to be the way in which EU fundamental rights have been formulated. Much more often, the CJEU has taken recourse to the ECHR as a source (of inspiration).

the final decision and balancing to the national courts, the mechanism of derogations in internal market law or, more recently, national identity (Article 4(2) TEU).[25] However, it is important to stress that this space exists only insofar as the EU allows it, and it is patrolled and supervised by the CJEU.[26]

III. THE ACCESSION OF THE EU TO THE ECHR

The accession of the EU to the ECHR constitutes a major step in the architecture of human rights protection in Europe. It has been on the agenda for a very long time. Proponents of accession see it as a way to close gaps in legal protection[27] and to give individuals the same protection vis-a-vis the EU (acting directly or indirectly via the Member States) as they presently enjoy against Member States. It would furthermore demonstrate the commitment of the EU to human rights by submitting the EU's legal system to independent external control exercised by Strasbourg. Also, it would avoid divergences between the respective bodies of case law of both European courts on the interpretation of human rights by settling the question of final authority over the interpretation of the ECHR, and thus preventing the national courts from being caught in the middle. Finally, it would prevent the Member States from being held liable for violations of the ECHR which are in fact attributable to the EU.

The two main procedural novelties in the draft Accession Agreement are the *co-respondent mechanism* and the *procedure of prior involvement*. The co-respondent mechanism was considered necessary to accommodate the specific situation of the EU as a non-state entity with an autonomous legal system that is becoming a party to the Convention alongside its own Member States.[28] When an application is directed against one or more Member States of the EU, the EU may become a co-respondent to the proceedings if it appears that alleged violation calls into question the compatibility of EU law with the Convention rights. Likewise, the mechanism would allow the EU Member States to become co-respondents to cases in which the applicant has directed an application only against the EU.[29] In cases where alleged violations against the EU and the EU Member States are different, the co-respondent mechanism would not apply. The draft states two conditions under which the co-respondent mechanism is triggered.[30] First, in the event that one or more Member State is indicated as a respondent and not the EU, the EU may become co-respondent if the alleged violation of the Convention concerns EU primary and/or secondary law and could only have been avoided by disregarding the obligation under EU law. With respect to

[25] Case C-279/09 *DEB v Bundesrepublik Deutschland* [2010] ECR I-13849; Case C-571/10 *Kamberaj v IPES* [2012] ECR I-00000; C-36/02 *Omega v Oberbürgermeisterin der Bundesstadt Bonn* [2004] ERC I-09609.

[26] See on this M Claes, 'Negotiating Constitutional Identity or Whose Identity is it Anyway?' in M Claes, M de Visser, P Popelier and C Van De Heyning, *Constitutional Conversations in Europe: Actors, Topics and Procedures* (Cambridge, Intersentia, 2012).

[27] See, eg, *Connolly v 15 Member States of the European Union*, App No 73274/01 (ECtHR, 9 December 2008).

[28] Draft Explanatory Report to the Agreement on the Accession of the European Union to the Convention for the Protection of Human Rights and Fundamental Freedoms, Final Report to the CDDH 47+1(2013)008rev2 (Strasbourg, 10 June 2013), para 38.

[29] Ibid, para 42.

[30] Draft Revised Agreement on the Accession of the European Union to the Convention for the Protection of Human Rights and Fundamental Freedoms, Final Report to the CDDH 47+1(2013)008rev2 (Strasbourg, 10 June 2013), Article 3(2) and 3(3).

primary EU law, this is striking, as it is up to the Member States acting together to change EU primary law, while the EU itself is unable to remove such violations without the consent of the Member States.[31] Accordingly, if a violation were to be found, the EU would not be in a position to do what it takes to comply with the decision of the ECtHR. While it may seem unlikely for this ever to occur, the explicit mention of primary law is remarkable. Second, if the EU is indicated as a respondent and not one of its Member States, the Member State may become a co-respondent if the alleged violation of the Convention concerns EU primary law (ie, the treaties and other instruments having the same legal value) and, notably, could only have been avoided by disregarding an obligation under those instruments. A contracting party will become a co-respondent only at its own request and by a decision of the ECtHR. The Court will seek the views of all parties to the proceedings before assessing whether the two conditions as stated in Article 3(2) and (3) of the draft are met.

The second procedural novelty concerns the mechanism of *prior involvement*. In proceedings before the ECtHR in which the EU is a co-respondent, the CJEU will be given the opportunity to assess the compatibility of the relevant provision(s) of EU law with the Convention, if it had not already done so, before the procedure continues in Strasbourg.[32] This mechanism was proposed in order to remedy the situations where a Member State implementing EU law has been accused of violating the Convention rights, and the CJEU has not pronounced itself on the alleged violation as the case has not been brought before it. Since references for preliminary rulings in EU law are not in the hands of the applicants but in those of the national courts, the condition of 'exhaustion of domestic remedies' for admissibility in Strasbourg will not include the condition that a reference has been made.[33] Accordingly, applications may arrive in Strasbourg before Luxembourg has had a chance to look at the issue.[34] It was considered appropriate that in cases in which the EU is a co-respondent, the CJEU would not be circumvented, since EU law is at stake. The decision of the Luxembourg Court will not bind the ECtHR.

The procedure was suggested by the CJEU itself in a discussion document released shortly after the entry into force of the Treaty of Lisbon on certain aspects on the accession of the EU to the ECHR. The Court pointed out that it alone had the task of ensuring the proper interpretation and application of EU law, and jurisdiction to declare EU legislation void.[35] Furthermore, it made reference to the subsidiary character of the ECHR system.[36] Yet, ideally, this mechanism should never be used, as this would suggest that a national court has not made appropriate use of the preliminary reference procedure under Article 267 TFEU. Accordingly, and somewhat paradoxically, the proposed procedure seems to be

[31] T Lock, 'End of an Epic? The Draft Agreement on the EU's Accession to the ECHR' (2012) 31 *Yearbook of European Law* 162.

[32] Draft Revised Agreement (n 30) Article 3(6).

[33] Draft Explanatory Report (n 28) para 65.

[34] Note, however, that these situations may also occur in cases brought against Member States and not involving EU law, namely that the constitutional court has not been able to pronounce itself, for instance, because the reference was not made by the national court. No exception has ever been made in this type of cases, and the condition of prior involvement of a constitutional court is alien to the ECHR system. When a decision of a constitutional court has been handed down, this will be taken into account, but it does not 'save' the state from a possible finding of a breach. See, eg, *Von Hannover v Germany*, App No 59320/00 (2004) 43 EHRR 139.

[35] Discussion Document of the Court of Justice of the European Union on Certain Aspects of the Accession of the European Union to the European Convention for the Protection of Human Rights and Fundamental Freedoms (5 May 2010), para 8.

[36] Ibid, para 7.

aimed at assuaging the CJEU's distrust of the national courts rather than of the ECtHR. This is striking, as it seems to place the burden of a 'malfunctioning' of the internal EU system at the feet of the ECHR system of enforcement and of the applicant seeking a decision in her case.

In any case, the Strasbourg Court supported the CJEU's point of view. A joint communication of the Presidents of the ECtHR, Jean Pierre Costa and the CJEU, Vassilios Skouris, basically re-stated the position of the CJEU: a flexible procedure should be put in place allowing the CJEU to carry out an internal review before the ECtHR carries out its external review.[37] Nevertheless, the solution also carries a risk of direct conflict between the two European courts, as indicated by some delegations in the European Council.[38] Indeed, matters of interpretation in Strasbourg and Luxembourg are similar but not identical and conflicts may arise.[39] Accession should, in principle, rectify any possible inconsistencies, as the ECtHR will have the last say on the interpretation of the ECHR and the question of whether it has been violated in a given case.

IV. ACCESSION AND ITS IMPACT ON NATIONAL COURTS

So, what then will be the impact of accession on national courts and on the triangular set of relationships involving national courts, Luxembourg and Strasbourg? Of course, it is too early to give a full assessment of this impact, but it is possible to identify a number of elements that are likely to influence the dynamics in the relationship. First, the ECHR will become an integral part of EU law and will hence, within the scope of EU law, acquire all the characteristics of EU law, including primacy. Thus, within the scope of EU law, national courts will be obliged under EU law to set aside national law for breaching the ECHR. Yet, it is debatable whether this is really revolutionary, since the ECHR materially already forms part of EU law under Article 6(3) TEU. Second, accession obviously changes the design of the human rights architectures and introduces new actors and procedures. This is likely to affect the dynamics of the system as a whole and national courts may have to decide how to position themselves. Third, the closer links between the respective national, EU and ECHR catalogues, mechanisms and courts increase the likelihood of divergences in the interpretation and balancing of rights in concrete cases. While the respective catalogues are to a large extent similar and several mechanisms exist to ensure convergence, different courts have ultimate jurisdiction over different but overlapping catalogues and may arrive at different decisions. National courts may thus find themselves 'caught in the middle' between conflicting Treaty obligations. Finally, accession will require both courts and academics to reconsider the conceptualisation of the overall fundamental rights landscape and the mutual relations between the norms and actors involved. These elements will now be discussed in turn.

[37] Joint communication from Presidents Costa and Skouris, 17 January 2011, http://curia.europa.eu/jcms/upload/docs/application/pdf/2011-02/cedh_cjue_english.pdf.

[38] Council Document 10568/10 of 2 June 2010 authorising the Commission to negotiate the Accession Agreement of the European Union to the European Convention for the protection of Human Rights and Fundamental Freedoms (ECHR), 5.

[39] The traditional reference is to Joined Cases 46/87 and 227/88 *Hoechst v Commission* [1989] ECR 2859 and the subsequent judgment in *Niemietz v Germany*, App No 13710/88 (1992) 16 EHRR 97.

B. The ECHR as Part of EU Law

Upon accession, the EU will be internationally bound by the ECHR and will accordingly be subject to the Strasbourg system of supervision, making it possible for individuals to bring complaints directly against the EU, and for the ECtHR to lift the preferential treatment of the EU which it has resorted to until now under *Bosphorus.* Moreover, upon the entry into force of the Accession Agreement,[40] the ECHR, just like other treaties concluded by the EU, will be formally incorporated in EU law.[41] It will acquire the same characteristics as EU law, including primacy. National courts will thus be under an obligation, within the scope of application of EU law, to enforce the ECHR, if necessary by setting aside conflicting provisions of national law. This implies that within this scope, all national courts become human rights courts and are under an EU obligation to review national law in the light of the ECHR. While this does not change anything for the judge in, say, the Netherlands, where all courts already review all national law in the light of the ECHR in all cases, including those outside the scope of EU law, it does extend the powers and responsibilities of, say, the German, Italian and British courts, which, under the domestic system and outside the scope of EU law, must leave the review of compliance of primary legislation with human rights to the constitutional court (Italy and Germany) or to Parliament (the UK). Human rights protection and review will thus become more decentralised, and constitutional courts will also, in those systems where they have thus far retained a monopoly to review primary legislation, have to share their responsibility with the ordinary courts. The domestic application of the ECHR will thus become differentiated *within* the Member States, whether or not a case comes within the scope of application of EU law. While in the latter situation the powers and competences of the ordinary courts are defined by the national constitutional set-up, in the former case, it is a matter of EU law and all courts have review powers.

Now, while these shifts in the domestic balance between legislatures, constitutional and ordinary courts may seem revolutionary, on a closer look, it may all turn out to be less dramatic. Indeed, as has been recalled, the ECHR largely corresponds with the Charter, which already has the same legal force as primary EU law under Article 6(1) TEU. Given the substantive equivalence between the Charter and the ECHR, the duties of consistent interpretation contained in Article 52(3) of the Charter and the repeated statements of intention for consistency on the part of both European courts, a national act that allegedly infringes the ECHR will usually, for the same reasons, also allegedly infringe the Charter (and, for that matter, the national constitution). And even today, national courts must, within the scope of EU law, ensure that the Charter rights are duly respected.[42]

In fact, the same obligation to ensure compliance with EU fundamental rights in the domestic application of EU law also existed before the Charter was even adopted, through the general principles of EU law, and before that through the general principles of Community law, which are informed by the ECHR.[43]

[40] Accession requires ratification in accordance with Article 218(8) TFEU and requires ratification by all Member States in accordance with their respective constitutional requirements.

[41] Case 181/73 *Haegeman v Belgium* [1974] ECR 449; see also Case C-617/10 *Åklagaren v Åkerberg Fransson* [2013] ECR I-00000, at [44].

[42] On the scope of the Charter, see *Åklagaren v Åkerberg Fransson* (n 41). See also K Lenaerts, 'Exploring the Limits of the EU Charter of Fundamental Rights' (2012) 8 *European Constitutional Law* 375.

[43] The seminal case is Case C-260/89 *ERT v DEP* [1991] ECR I-2925; *Åklagaren v Åkerberg Fransson* (n 41).

In this light, the CJEU's remarks in the recent *Kamberaj* decision, which were repeated in *Åkerberg Fransson*, are puzzling.[44] The Italian referring court wanted to know whether in the event of a conflict between a provision of domestic law and the ECHR, the reference to the ECHR in Article 6 TEU obliged the national court to apply Articles 14 ECHR and Article 1 of Protocol No 12 directly, disapplying the incompatible source of domestic law, without first having to raise the issue of constitutionality before the national constitutional court. If the CJEU were to answer the question in the affirmative, this would have an important impact on the effect of the ECHR in certain domestic legal orders. The ECHR would then acquire the same qualities as EU law, including primacy. As a consequence, all national courts, including ordinary courts, would become 'ordinary courts of ECHR human rights', since they are 'ordinary courts of EU law'. This would be especially significant for those countries where so far the constitutional court has the monopoly on reviewing primary laws, as is the case in Italy and Germany, or where the courts do not have jurisdiction to set aside primary legislation for breaching the ECHR, such as in the UK. A clear answer affirming these implications of Article 6(3) TEU would thus lay bare the shifts in the national constitutional design. Yet, in its answer, the CJEU avoided the issue and narrowed down its answer to the effect of the ECHR *qua* ECHR, stating that Article 6(3) TEU does not govern the relationship between the ECHR and the legal systems of the Member States and does not lay down the consequences to be drawn by a national court in the event of conflict between the rights guaranteed by the ECHR and national law.

While this decision may well be legally correct (yet highly ambiguous!), the decision at the same time neglects the fact that Article 6(3) TEU does confirm that the fundamental rights as protected by the ECHR are general principles of EU law and must be complied with *as general principles of EU law*. In other cases, the CJEU has not hesitated to declare that national courts must guarantee the full effectiveness of the general principles, setting aside any provision of national law which may conflict with EU law.[45] After accession, the CJEU will no longer be able to duck this type of inquiry into the obligations which EU law imposes on national courts. It will have to give clear guidance to the national courts on their obligations as a matter of EU law. In fact, as a party to the ECHR, the EU and The CJEU will be under an ECHR obligation to ensure that within their jurisdiction, ECHR rights are protected.

If talk of a revolutionary change—accession transforms all national courts into human rights courts and accordingly extends the effect of the ECHR in domestic systems—is indeed appropriate, it has already taken place a long time ago. The obligation imposed on national courts to enforce human rights in the scope of application of EU law already exists under EU law today, without accession, and the ECHR is already crucial in defining the contours of this obligation via the interpretation of the Charter and the general principles of EU law. Any further adaptations implicated by accession concern the form rather than the substance of the duties imposed on national courts. The fact that the ECHR will become effective in a more overt manner without first being transformed into general principles may matter a great deal psychologically, given the current political sensitivity of European human rights protection and the attacks on the legitimacy of the ECtHR, but essentially, this rather seems like a case of old wine and new bottles.

[44] *Kamberaj v IPES* (n 25).

[45] Case C-144/04 *Werner Mangold v Rüdiger Helm* [2005] ECR I-9981.

B. Adding to the Institutional Complexity

Accession will add to the overall system the external supervision of the EU by the Strasbourg machinery. It will allow individuals to bring complaints directly against the EU rather than having to follow indirect routes via the Member States who co-author or implement EU law. Accession thus makes a significant change to the overall architecture, adding a new actor and opening up new procedural avenues for the protection of fundamental rights. Politically and symbolically, accession is highly significant: it completes the ECHR system of protection and fills the gaps that had been created when Member States transferred sovereignty to the EU.

In substance, though, there is much continuity, and accession confirms at the international level the commitment of the EU to the values and rights protected under the ECHR, which is already contained in Article 6 TEU. Moreover, while at first sight accession may seem to complete the European system of fundamental rights protection, the Accession Agreement does not solve questions of hierarchy and authority between the actors involved and the rights protected. Bringing in new players and new procedural relationships may affect the dynamics of the system as a whole, and thus also national courts. It further increases the already-existing complexity, which can in itself be detrimental for the enjoyment of rights and for their judicial enforcement. In the end, there may be financial as well as legitimacy costs to all of this, both for individual litigants and for society as a whole: procedures will become even more protracted and it will take even more time to achieve closure in concrete cases.[46] At the end of the day, the human rights case law of both European courts has to be absorbed into the domestic legal systems, where it is likely to give rise to an ever-larger caseload.[47]

National courts will be confronted with procedural issues, procedural economy and judicial strategy. We will restrict our discussion here to the situation where national authorities implement EU law—in other words, to 'situations governed by EU law' or falling 'in the scope of EU law'.[48] When individuals make a serious claim before the national court that their fundamental rights have been infringed, the court will have to make a decision whether or not to make a reference for a preliminary ruling to Luxembourg. This decision will have to be taken in a different setting after accession. If no preliminary reference is made, this may trigger the prior involvement procedure at a later stage if the applicant brings her case to Strasbourg. Whether or not a reference is made at this stage, the procedure is likely to build in a very lengthy litigation involving three systems of courts, with ensuing financial implications, and at the cost of justice being delayed. National courts as well as the litigants before them will have to make their decisions whilst taking account of a number of concerns, including time, the need for closure, financial costs etc. National courts may have an institutional interest in having the case off their dockets as fast as possible, passing it on to

[46] This has also been pointed out by non-governmental organisations (NGOs), who have made their views known in the course of the negotiations; see the submissions of Amnesty International, the International Court of Justice and the Aire Centre on EU accession to ECHR, available at: www.coe.int/t/dghl/standardsetting/hrpolicy/accession/Working_documents/NGO_submissions_EU_accession_5Nov2012.pdf, at point 19.

[47] This concern has recently been voiced by Lady Arden, who raised the question of how the (domestic) judiciary should react to the (European) case law on a collective basis. See Rt Hon Lady Justice Arden DBE, 'Peaceful or Problematic? The Relationship between National Supreme Courts and Supranational Courts in Europe' (2010) 29 *Yearbook of European Law* 3.

[48] To use the phrasing of the CJEU in *Åklagaren v Åkerberg Fransson* (n 41).

a higher or non-national court (albeit that in the case of Luxembourg it will return!). They will have to calculate the pros and cons of involving Luxembourg and of opening up the state to applications in Strasbourg. This must also be seen in the context of the national settings in which these national courts are operating, and their relationship with political actors and the public at large. 'Partnering' with Luxembourg (or Strasbourg) may be part of a wider strategy to borrow the legitimacy of these European courts or, conversely, to outsource controversies which the domestic courts cannot settle at home.[49]

The sheer complexity of the overall system and the volume of the fundamental rights case law will complicate the work of all national courts, both ordinary courts and constitutional courts which deal with fundamental rights cases on a daily basis. Keeping up with both the Strasbourg and the Luxembourg case law will become even more of a challenge than it is today. One of the main difficulties that national judges have to deal with already today is when to apply which catalogue, which test and with what consequences. [50] They sometimes struggle with the combined application of overlapping catalogues where two or more apply, and how to decide whether infringements are justified in a particular case. In itself, this is not a novel phenomenon that is created by accession: the simultaneous application of fundamental rights instruments is fairly common, and courts have thus far coped rather well. They usually take recourse to methods of consistent interpretation[51] and apply the conditions for justified restrictions to fundamental rights cumulatively.[52]

Yet, there will be instances in which the various sources and systems strike different balances and arrive at different outcomes, or where different competing rights may also be at stake. In such cases, simply lumping together the various sources will no longer be possible.

C. Diverging Standards

The further development of a multi-level system of fundamental rights increases the risk of diverging interpretations of fundamental rights between the respective national and international systems. Even if both the Charter and the draft Accession Agreement, as well as the practice of the European courts and most if not all national courts, seek to avoid cases of divergent interpretation, experience shows that it is difficult to avoid contradictions where two differently worded texts on the same subject matter are interpreted by

[49] The term is borrowed from W Sadurski, 'Partnering with Strasbourg: Constitutionalization of the European Court of Human Rights, the Accession of Central and East European States to the Council of Europe, and the Idea of Pilot Judgments', available at: http://ssrn.com/abstract=1295652. Examples of such cases in which domestic battles are outsourced to Luxembourg include the references of the Belgian Constitutional Court in Case C-212/06 *Government of the French Community and Wallon Government v Flemish Government* [2008] ECR I-01683 and the Czech Supreme Administrative Court in Case C-399/09 *Landtová v Česká správa socialního zabezpečení* [2011] ECR I-05573.

[50] See, for instance, the 23rd colloquium organised by the Association of Council of State and Supreme Jurisdictions of the European Union, Madrid, 25–26 June 2012.

[51] Examples include Article 10(2) of the Spanish Constitution, which obliges state organs to construe provisions relating to the fundamental rights and liberties recognised by the Constitution to be in conformity with the Universal Declaration of Human Rights and international treaties and agreements thereon ratified by Spain.

[52] This is the practice of, eg, the Belgian Constitutional Court, which 'maximises' protection by opting for the highest level of all applicable standards; see M Bossuyt and W Verrijdt, 'The Full Effect of EU Law and of Constitutional Review in Belgium and France after the *Melki* Judgment' (2011) 7 *European Constitutional Law* 355.

different courts.[53] In addition, as conceptions over the actual content of rights and the justification for interferences also reflect specific historical conditions and societal choices, and since national constitutions, the EU Charter and the ECHR and their respective courts cater for different contexts, it should come as no surprise that these courts may at times arrive at different conclusions. Divergences in conceptions on the level of protection of fundamental rights between national courts, the CJEU and the ECHR will in fact arise more and more often, with EU law expanding into more sensitive areas, with the Charter coming into force and the CJEU developing more into a human rights court, and litigants beginning to find their way to Luxembourg to have their fundamental rights protected. Also, such divergences will increasingly be the result merely of different ways to strike a balance between conflicting rights, or a clash of fundamental rights with other social values or general interests. In other words, it will matter a great deal who gets to decide.

Divergences are usually solved between courts by reference to rules of construction (eg, conform interpretation) or avoidance techniques (eg, the margin of appreciation). Yet even if they can be *legally* solved in this way, diverging standards can be problematic in another respect as well. Following a decision adopted by one or both of the European courts may force the national courts to hand down decisions which may carry lower social legitimacy and societal acceptance at home. Think for instance of the commotion in the UK concerning voting rights for prisoners since *Hirst* or the debate in many countries on the implications of *Salduz.* Legally, there is no question that these decisions are binding and thus have to be complied with, but the increased involvement of both European courts in sensitive matters which fundamental rights cases often entail does call for sensitivity and caution on their part, since not only their own legitimacy but also that of national courts and human rights *tout court* may be at stake. These concerns would endorse a search for a consistent interpretation and harmonious application of the various sources.

However, there is also a downside to the search for coherence, and coherence must not become an aim in itself at the cost of fundamental rights protection. Although it may be confusing for citizens to see different courts arrive at different conclusions on the basis of the same or similar provisions, the overall system is such that it allows for such divergences. This is obvious in the relationship between national law and the ECHR (subsidiary system, margin of appreciation and minimum standard) and is not uncommon in the relationship between national law and the EU (justified restrictions, decision for national court, national identity). The search for coherence and harmony expressed in the various documents, in the case law of the respective courts and the extra-judicial comments of their members should not have a chilling effect on the protection of rights. Minimum standards should not be mistaken for general standards. Examples of such 'stiffening effects' already exist. Thus, in the UK and the Netherlands, the level of protection offered by the ECHR is adopted as the national standard, as was expressed by Lord Bingham in *Ullah*: 'to keep pace with Strasbourg jurisprudence as it evolves over time: no more, but certainly no less'.[54] Not only is such a position not called for under Article 53 ECHR, it may also prevent further

[53] On divergent interpretations see J Callewaert, 'The European Convention on Human Rights and European Union Law: a long way to harmony' (2009) 6 *EHRLR* 768; RA Lawson and CJ Van de Heyning, 'The EU as a party to the European Convention on Human Rights; EU law and the European Court of Justice case law as inspiration and challenge to the European Court of Human Rights Jurisprudence' in P Popelier, P Van Nuffel and CJ Van de Heyning (eds), *Human Rights Protection in the European Legal Order: the Interaction Between the European and the National Courts* (Cambridge, Intersentia, 2011) 35–64.

[54] *R (Ullah) v Special Adjudicator* [2004] 2 AC 323 at [20]. The stance has since been relaxed; see Hale (n 10); and *R v Horncastle and others* (n 10). On the argument in the Netherlands, see JH Gerards, 'Samenloop

evolution and emulation, not only at the national level, but also at the European level. As was recently recalled by the British judge in the ECHR, it is healthy that national courts should feel free to criticise Strasbourg judgments where those judgments have applied principles which are unclear or inconsistent or where they have misunderstood national law or practices.[55] European human rights protection does not and ought not to seek harmonisation of human rights protection as an aim in itself: it should only be a means to the end of better protection.

When it comes to divergences between EU law and ECHR law, or between the CJEU and the ECtHR, they are only really problematic for national courts in one particular constellation of treaty conflicts, namely when the respective standards are impossible to apply simultaneously, and complying with one treaty obligation would necessarily lead to a violation of the other. Since the ECHR sets only minimum standards, national courts should comply with the EU standard when it is higher, as this allows them to comply with both. When the protection offered by EU law should fall below the ECHR minimum standard, then the national courts are caught in the middle. Thus far, these cases appear to have been very rare and concerned situations where the standard offered by the EU was later corrected to comply with the ECHR.

So, does accession 'solve' the problem of divergence? Does it create a correction mechanism so that national courts should no longer be faced with possible divergences? In a way, it does: in the event that the EU, with the approval of the CJEU, infringes the ECHR as interpreted by the ECtHR and thus forces national courts to co-operate with a breach of the ECHR, the victim can lodge a complaint before the Strasbourg Court, which can then declare that there has been such a violation. Since the Strasbourg Court has the ultimate say over the interpretation of the ECHR, the CJEU will be bound by this decision and will also have to accept that the Member States and their courts comply with the decision. However, this does make for an extremely long and arduous process, and can hardly be seen as the most appropriate mechanism for such a situation, both for the individual involved and for the national judge who finds herself confronted with conflicting treaty obligations.

A Strasbourg finding of a violation by the EU or the EU and one or more Member States will call for action by the EU and/or its Member States to comply with the decision. This may involve legislative, administrative and judicial action at both the EU and the national level, depending on the facts of the case and the legal background. There may be cases in which a national court would then be confronted with EU law which has been found to violate the ECHR, but which has not yet been amended accordingly. In such a case, could the national court set aside EU law? Certainly, under EU law, it could not, but one can imagine that national courts may be tempted in such a case to omit the reference to Luxembourg and draw their own conclusions following the decision of the ECtHR.

But the more challenging situations will occur before the case is decided by Strasbourg, when for instance the CJEU misreads the Strasbourg case law[56] and declares an EU measure compatible with fundamental rights as protected by the ECHR, while national courts have a different reading of the case law of the ECtHR. Should a national (constitutional)

van nationale en Europese grondrechtenbepalingen—hoe moet de rechter daarmee omgaan?' (2010) 1 *Tijdschrift voor Constitutioneel Recht* 224.

[55] N Bratza, 'The Relationship between the UK Courts and Strasbourg' (2011) 5 *EHRLR* 505.

[56] The CJEU is under an obligation to follow the case law of the Strasbourg Court, both under the Charter and, after accession, as a matter of ECHR law as well.

court in such a case comply with the CJEU? Or would it be legitimate even under EU law and more precisely Article 52(3) of the Charter to disregard the decision of the CJEU?

D. Conceptualising the Relationship between Courts and Rights Regimes

Academics and increasingly also members of both European courts and constitutional courts have become accustomed to describe the relationships between the relevant systems and courts in terms of 'Verfassungsgerichtsverbund',[57] 'constitutional pluralism', 'multi-level constitutionalism' and in terms of networks. Such a spirit of co-operation, dialogue, equilibrium and avoidance of conflict is certainly welcome, but it should not obscure the fact that after accession, there will be a formal relationship between the ECtHR and the CJEU, with the ECtHR more clearly than before supervising compliance with the ECHR by the EU and its Member States acting as agents. Similarly, talk of pluralism, networks and the absence of a clear hierarchy should not detract from the fact that national courts are also bound by the EU fundamental rights and the case law of the CJEU, and cannot let their constitutional rights prevail without infringing their obligations under EU law. Nevertheless, for the system to function well, courts should all be aware of the concerns and preoccupations of the other orders. Accession will provide the answer to the question of ultimate authority when it comes to ECHR rights and will resolve the problem of co-existence of norms when the case law of the European courts diverges. For the national courts, things may therefore appear in a different light after accession. But all courts involved, irrespective of the legal and institutional hierarchies, would be well advised to take serious account of the considerations of the others involved in this *Verfassungsgerichtsverbund*. Creating mutual trust will be essential and will require all courts involved to participate in the European constitutional discourse on fundamental rights.

V. CONCLUSION

This chapter has sought to identify and discuss the position of national courts in the multi-sourced European legal space involving the EU, the ECHR and national law. Our expectation is that the national courts are likely to face significant challenges in the fundamental rights area in the years to come. The implications of the binding character of the EU Charter as well as the accession of the EU to the ECHR will not only considerably affect the relationship between the CJEU and the ECtHR but also their relationships with the national courts. The position of national courts is the most difficult one since they are at the crossroads of three legal systems: as state organs, they ensure compliance of their state with the ECHR, but they must at the same time uphold their national Constitution, and comply with EU law and EU fundamental rights.

One of the concerns indicated here is that of competing and conflicting obligations for the protection of fundamental rights, since different catalogues of fundamental rights may

[57] A Voßkuhle, 'Multilevel Cooperation of the European Constitutional Courts: Der Europäische Verfassungsgerichtsverbund' (2010) 6 *European Constitutional Law* 175.

not require the same level of protection and are interpreted by different highest courts, while clear and generally accepted rules governing their mutual relationship are lacking. The challenges posed by overlapping protection systems are described in Advocate General Maduro's opinion in the *Elfagaji* case:

> [T]he protection of fundamental rights in the Community legal order exists alongside other European systems of protection of fundamental rights. These include both systems developed within the national legal systems and those stemming from the ECHR. Each of those protection mechanisms certainly pursues objectives which are specific to it and the mechanisms are certainly constructed from legal instruments particular to them, but sometimes they apply none the less to the same facts. In such a context, it is important, for each existing protection system, while maintaining its independence, to seek to understand how the other systems interpret and develop those same fundamental rights in order not only to minimise the risk of conflicts, but also to begin a process of informal construction of a European area of protection of fundamental rights. The European area thus created will, largely, be the product of the various individual contributions from the different protection systems existing at [the] European level.[58]

Another related problem for national judges is that they find themselves in an ever more complex institutional and procedural environment. As pointed out earlier, this complexity may become a threat in itself, for the individual applicant seeking to her rights, for the judges operating it and for the system as a whole. Each existing protection system will have to find a way to understand how fundamental rights are interpreted and developed by other systems in order to minimise the risk of conflicts and ensure the optimal protection for the individual. But this is easier said than done. There is a mighty task ahead for national courts.

[58] Case C-465/07 *Elgafaji v Staatssecretaris van Justitie* [2009] ERC I-00921, Opinion of AG Maduro [22].

Part IV

Pluralism within the New Order

12

Bosphorus *Post-Accession: Redefining the Relationships between the European Court of Human Rights and the Parties to the Convention*

OLIVIER DE SCHUTTER*

IN THE 2005 *Bosphorus* case,[1] the European Court of Human Rights (ECtHR) innovated. It shaped a doctrine expressing its trust in the fact that the EU guarantees a level of protection of fundamental rights equivalent to what the European Convention on Human Rights (ECHR) provides itself, and that it, the Court, could therefore presume that any measure adopted by an EU Member State in fulfilment of its obligations under EU law, under the supervision of the Court of Justice of the European Union (CJEU), is compatible with the Convention's requirements unless a 'manifest deficiency' is apparent. At the time it was developed, the doctrine was well suited to the need to organise the co-existence of two jurisdictions, the ECtHR and the European Court of Justice, both ensuring respect for Convention rights, but without a hierarchical link or coordination between one another.

This chapter argues that there will be no argument to justify the survival of the doctrine in its current form following the accession of the EU to the ECHR, as this would establish the EU in an unduly privileged position vis-a-vis the other parties to the Convention. But if it is to die in its current incarnation, the *Bosphorus* presumption-of-compliance doctrine may re-emerge in an expanded and different guise. Reborn and generalised, it may guide the future relationships between the ECtHR and the domestic courts of the parties to the ECHR. This would transform such relationships from their current hierarchical and vertical mode to a more dialogical and horizontal mode. In this new understanding, in order to deserve the trust they claim for themselves, domestic courts will be expected to provide

* Professor of Law, University of Louvain (UCL) and College of Europe, Visiting Professor at Columbia University, member of the Scientific Committee of the EU Fundamental Rights Agency. The author would like to thank the participants in the Workshop on 'The EU Accession to the ECHR' held in Brussels on 16–17 November 2012 for their illuminating comments and discussions. He is grateful in particular to Andrew Drzemczewski, Bruno de Witte, Robert Harmsen, Giorgio Gaja, Christos Rozakis, Christiaan Timmermans and to the organizers of the conference, Vicky Kosta, Nikos Skoutaris and Vassilis Tzevelekos. The usual disclaimer applies. A longer version of this chapter was published as O De Schutter, 'The Two Lives of *Bosphorus*: Redefining the Relationships between the European Court of Human Rights and the Parties to the Convention' (2013) *European Journal of Human Rights* 4, 584–624.

[1] *Bosphorus Hava Yolları Turizm ve Ticaret Anonim Şirketi v Ireland*, App No 45036/98 (2005) 42 EHRR 1 (hereinafter referred to as '*Bosphorus*').

a solidly argued reasoning for the outcomes that they reach which takes into account the framework set out in the existing case law of the ECtHR. According to this model, the conclusions that domestic courts reach may differ from those that the ECtHR would have arrived at itself—that is left open. But the reason why they are to be trusted in reaching such outcomes is because of the tools they use in doing so, meeting a burden of justification that is defined by the jurisprudence of the ECtHR.

This chapter proceeds as follows. The following section briefly recalls the circumstances in which the *Bosphorus* doctrine emerged, as well as its content. Section II then explores three scenarios following the accession of the EU to the ECHR. The third scenario is one in which the *Bosphorus* presumption of compatibility, under certain conditions that it would be for the ECtHR to define, extends to all parties to the Convention that directly apply the Convention rights, with the interpretation authoritatively given to those rights by that Court. Section III briefly discusses the significance of the transformation in the relationship between the ECtHR and the domestic courts that such an approach would entail. The shift that would occur under this scenario would *not* mean that the level of scrutiny exercised by the ECtHR on states parties would be lowered. Rather, the nature of its scrutiny would be transformed: it would be procedural more than substantive, focused on the means through which protection of Convention rights is ensured at a domestic level rather than on the outcome in each individual case. This would result in a horizontal and dialogical type of relationship between the European Court and national courts, rather than a vertical and hierarchical relationship. The chapter describes what this 'second life' of the *Bosphorus* doctrine could look like and how it could in fact strengthen the architecture of the European system of human rights protection. Section IV offers a brief conclusion.

I. THE *BOSPHORUS* DOCTRINE

The ECtHR has always sought not to obstruct the establishment of international organisations or other forms of international cooperation by the states parties to the ECHR, while at the same time ensuring that the progress of such cooperation does not result in states evading their obligations under the Convention. The need for a compromise between these two potentially conflicting objectives is at the heart of the *Bosphorus* line of case law.

The Convention, the Court has consistently held, 'does not exclude the transfer of competences to international organisations provided that Convention rights continue to be "secured". Member States' responsibility therefore continues even after such a transfer'.[2] In order to ensure that human rights continue to be secured even as international organisations are attributed larger competences in areas that might affect the enjoyment of human rights, the Court had to develop a doctrine that would accommodate both the need to allow certain transfers of powers, including transfers through which the Member States of the organisation renounce any possibility to veto decisions adopted by that organisation, and the need to ensure that they do not thereby 'circumvent' their pre-existing human rights obligations.[3] In order to do so, the Court proposed to provide a reading of the

[2] *Matthews v United Kingdom*, App No 24833/94 (1999) 28 EHRR 361 [32].

[3] The notion of 'circumvention' is of course borrowed from the final version of the Draft Articles on the Responsibility of International Organizations, adopted by the International Law Commission (ILC) at its sixty-thrid session in 2011 and presented to the sixty-sixth session of the General Assembly (A/66/10, para 87).

requirements of the ECHR that could accommodate other obligations states may have incurred by joining an international organisation.[4] It announced that it would presume the compatibility with the ECHR of acts adopted by states in fulfilment of the obligations imposed on them as members of an international organisation, to the extent that these acts may be adequately reviewed for their compatibility with fundamental rights in the system set up within that organisation itself. That, in essence, is the doctrine established in the 2005 *Bosphorus* case, where the Court announced that:

> State action taken in compliance with such legal obligations [deriving from commitments of a state party to the Convention under a treaty concluded subsequently to their accession to the Convention] is justified as long as the relevant organization [set up by such subsequent treaty] is considered to protect fundamental rights, as regards both the substantive guarantees offered and the mechanisms controlling their observance, in a manner which can be considered at least equivalent to that for which the Convention provides ... By 'equivalent' the Court means 'comparable': any requirement that the organization's protection be 'identical' could run counter to the interest of international co-operation pursued.[5]

Under the *Bosphorus* doctrine, measures that a state has adopted in the implementation of obligations imposed on it as a member of an international organisation it has joined after acceding to the ECHR will be presumed to be compatible with the Convention if the said organisation protects human rights in a way that could be considered as 'equivalent' to their guarantee under the Convention: 'If such equivalent protection is considered to be provided by the organisation, the presumption will be that a State has not departed from the requirements of the Convention when it does no more than implement legal obligations flowing from its membership of the organisation'[6]—that is, when the state is deprived of any margin of appreciation in the implementation of those obligations.

Such a presumption may not be absolute, however. The Court reiterates its view according to which 'absolving Contracting States completely from their Convention responsibility in the areas covered by such a transfer would be incompatible with the purpose and object of the Convention: the guarantees of the Convention could be limited or excluded at will thereby depriving it of its peremptory character and undermining the practical and effective nature of its safeguards'. It follows not only that the state 'is considered to retain Convention liability in respect of treaty commitments subsequent to the entry into force of the Convention',[7] but also that the presumption of compatibility as defined above 'can be rebutted if, in the circumstances of a particular case, it is considered that the protection of Convention rights was manifestly deficient. In such cases, the interest of international

According to Article 61 of the Draft Articles, entitled 'Circumvention of international obligations of a State member of an international organization': 'A State member of an international organization incurs international responsibility if, by taking advantage of the fact that the organization has competence is relation to the subject-matter of one of the State's international obligations, it circumvents that obligation by causing the organization to commit an act that, if committed by the State, would have constituted a breach of the obligation.' The General Assembly commended the ILC for having completed its work on this topic (Res 66/98, 'Report of the International Law Commission on the work of its sixty-third session', para 4).

[4] The Court has sought to read the Convention, to the fullest extent possible, in the light of any relevant rules and principles of international law applicable in relations between the contracting parties, in conformity with Article 31 § 3(c) of the Vienna Convention on the Law of Treaties of 23 May 1969: see *Al-Adsani v United Kingdom*, App No 35763/97 (2001) 34 EHRR 273 [55].

[5] *Bosphorus* (n 1) [155].

[6] Ibid [156].

[7] Ibid [154].

co-operation would be outweighed by the Convention's role as a "constitutional instrument of European public order" in the field of human rights'.[8]

In essence, the *Bosphorus* doctrine transforms the obligations of the states parties to the ECHR, when they transfer certain powers to an international organisation, into a due diligence obligation to ensure that Convention rights will be protected through mechanisms internal to that organisation.[9] The doctrine is enunciated in general terms by the Court and it is therefore not necessarily limited to the EU.[10] But it did emerge in a highly specific context: one in which a number of states parties bound by the ECHR decided to establish the European Communities, now absorbed by the EU, joining a new 'legal order' within which a judicial control of compliance with fundamental rights has emerged since the late 1960s.[11] Indeed, the approach of the Court was clearly inspired by the attitude of the German Federal Constitutional Court (*Bundesverfassungsgericht*) towards what was then European Community law. Only after it surmounted its initial hesitations and was convinced that fundamental rights were adequately protected in the legal order of the Community did the German Federal Constitutional Court agree to recognise the supremacy of European Community law without a scrutiny of its compatibility with the fundamental rights protected under the German Basic Law (*Grundgesetz*).[12]

Nor is this cooptation of the '*Solange*-in-reverse' doctrine of the German Federal Constitutional Court by the supervisory bodies of the ECHR unprecedented. It is already that attitude of the *Bundesverfassungsgericht* which had led the European Commission of Human Rights in 1990—at the instigation of Henry Schermers and Hans-Christian Krüger, respectively one of its members and its Secretary—to develop the doctrine of an 'equivalent protection', according to which the monitoring bodies set up by the ECHR should not control acts adopted by states parties as Member States of the European Community in fulfilment of their Community obligations insofar as the legal order of the Community provides for its own system of protection of fundamental rights which can be considered to be generally satisfactory.[13] The doctrine has also been relied upon implicitly in later cases by the ECtHR, even before its spectacular reaffirmation in *Bosphorus*.[14]

[8] Ibid [156].

[9] See J Callewaert, 'The European Convention on Human Rights and European Union Law: A Long Way to Harmony' (2009) 6 *European Human Rights Law Review* 768, 771–74.

[10] See, for instance, *Gasparini v Italy and Belgium*, App No 10750/03 (2009) (concerning an employment dispute within the North Atlantic Treaty Organization (NATO)).

[11] Case 29/69 *Stauder v City of Ulm* [1969] ECR 419; Case 11/70 *Internationale Handelsgesellschaft v Einfuhr- und Vorratsstelle Getreide* [1970] ECR 1125; Case 4/73 *Nold v Commission* [1974] ECR 491. The Court recognises not only that the EU institutions are bound to comply with fundamental rights, but in addition that the EU Member States may invoke the need to protect fundamental rights as general principles of law, even where this may lead them to derogate from their obligations under EU Law (see, eg, Case C-368/95 *Familiapress* [1997] ECR I-3689 [24]; Case C-112/00 *Schmidberger* [2003] ECR I-5659 [81]). This is crucial, since it makes it unlikely, if not impossible, for a situation where a state might have to forego its human rights obligations in order to comply with its obligations under EU law to occur.

[12] For the current position of the Bundesverfassungsgericht, see 2 BvL 1/97, EuGRZ 2000, 328 (333) (concerning the market organisation for bananas); and for a doctrinal summary, J Limbach, 'La coopération des juridictions dans la future architecture européenne des droits fondamentaux. Contribution à la redéfinition des rapports entre la Cour constitutionnelle fédérale allemande, la Cour de justice des Communautés européennes et la Cour européenne des droits de l'homme' (2000) 12 *Revue universelle des droits de l'homme* 369.

[13] Eur Comm HR, *M & Co v Germany*, App No 13258/87, decision of 9 February 1990, *Decisions and Reports*, vol 64, 138; and see also, inter alia, Eur Comm HR, *Heinz v The Contracting Parties Also Parties to the European Patent Convention*, App No 21090/92, decision of 10 January 1994, *Decisions and Reports*, vol 76-A, 125.

[14] *Beer and Regan v Germany*, App No 28934/95 (1999) [53]; *Waite and Kennedy v Germany*, App No 26083/94 (1999) [63] (recognising that the setting-up of remedies within the internal structures of the European Space

The case law of the ECtHR leading to the *Bosphorus* judgment seeks to ensure that the Convention will not constitute an obstacle to further European integration by the creation among the Member States of the EU of a supranational organisation—a development which, as the representatives of the European Commission argued in their submissions to the Court in that case, would be seriously impeded if the Member States were obliged to verify the compatibility with the ECHR of the acts of EU law before agreeing to apply them, even in situations where they have no discretion to exercise at the implementation level. The Court stops short of stating that, as the Member States have transferred certain powers to a supranational organisation (the EU), their international responsibility could not be engaged for situations resulting directly from the application of European Community acts. The Convention remains applicable to such situations and the states parties remain fully answerable to the supervisory bodies it sets up. But the nature of the inquiry of the ECtHR will be quite decisively influenced by the circumstance that the alleged violation has its source in the application of an act adopted within the EU. The Court considers that, insofar as the legal order of the EU ensures an adequate level of protection of fundamental rights and unless it is confronted with a 'dysfunction of the mechanisms of control of the observance of Convention rights' or with a 'manifest deficiency',[15] it may be allowed to presume that, by complying with the legal obligations under this legal order, the EU Member States are not violating their obligations under the ECHR.

Though certainly not immune from critique, the *Bosphorus* doctrine played a useful role in defining the modalities of the cooperation between the CJEU and the ECtHR. The CJEU is tasked with preserving fundamental rights in the EU legal order: as long as it does so, upholding the Convention rights while taking into account the interpretation given to those rights by the ECtHR, its findings will be trusted; only where 'manifest deficiencies' appear—or, of course, where the CJEU has not been able to exercise its control—will such findings be questioned. At times, the presumption does appear to enlarge the margin of appreciation of the CJEU, which seems to be recognised a freedom to adapt the requirements of the ECHR to the specific exigencies of EU law, beyond what would be tolerated from even the highest domestic courts.[16] But it also has a disciplining function: in order to deserve this trust, the CJEU must be irreproachable. Indeed, it is likely that it has been a particularly diligent student of the jurisprudence of the ECtHR, not *despite* of, but rather *because* of the division of labour established by the *Bosphorus* doctrine.

II. THE FUTURE OF THE *BOSPHORUS* DOCTRINE: THREE POST-ACCESSION SCENARIOS

Will the *Bosphorus* doctrine survive the accession of the EU to the ECHR? It will continue to apply, in principle, to international organisations other than the EU, which some states parties to the Convention have joined. With respect to these organisations, the ECtHR will

Agency (ESA) could ensure compatibility with the requirements of Article 6 § 1 of the Convention, although the immunity of jurisdiction of the ESA implied that it could not by sued before the domestic courts of Germany in employment disputes).

[15] *Bosphorus* (n 1) [166].

[16] See, eg, *Cooperatieve Producentenorganisatie van de Nederlandse Kokkelvisserij UA v The* Netherlands, App No 13645/05 (2009).

in future continue to distinguish, as it currently does, between: (i) the acts adopted by the international organisation itself, for which the Member States incur no responsibility and which, as the organisation is not a party to the ECHR, the ECtHR considers to fall outside its jurisdiction *ratione personae*;[17] and (ii) the acts adopted by the states parties to the Convention, particularly as they establish the international organisation or transfer certain powers to be exercised by the organisation. Such acts remain subject to the supervision of the ECtHR, which will examine, in particular, whether in establishing the organisation, the states concerned have been acting 'in good faith' or instead have 'circumvented' their pre-existing international obligations.

The more delicate question, however, is whether the *Bosphorus* doctrine will continue to apply for the benefit of the EU itself once the EU has acceded to the ECHR. In theory, three scenarios are possible.

A. Scenario 1: The EU Loses its Privileged Position

A first possibility is that the presumption established by *Bosphorus* will be abandoned. After all, the presumption aimed to ensure a harmonious co-existence between the requirements imposed under EU law and the requirements imposed under the ECHR *in a context in which the European Union was not bound to comply with the Convention*: the doctrine therefore appeared necessary in order to avoid a situation where the EU Member State concerned would be facing inconsistent international obligations, stemming respectively from EU law and from the ECHR. Following the EU's accession to the ECHR, this justification will lose much of its weight: since the EU will have become a party to the ECHR, any inconsistency between the obligations following for the EU Member States from their membership in the EU and the requirements of the Convention will have to be resolved in favour of the latter, and in principle there should be no reason to grant the EU a treatment more favourable than that granted to any other party to the Convention. The first scenario is therefore one of normalisation: though with some minor institutional adjustments, the EU will simply appear as one more party to the Convention—the 48th—without any difference in the nature of the supervision exercised.[18]

[17] See, eg, *Boivin v France and Belgium, and 32 other Member States of the Council of* Europe, App No 73250/01 (2008) (inadmissibility of an application filed against the states parties to the 1960 International Convention relating to Co-operation for the Safety of Air Navigation establishing Eurocontrol, for a decision of that organisation validated by the Administrative Tribunal of the International Labour Organisation); *Gasparini v Italy and Belgium* (n 10); *Galić v The Netherlands*, App No 22617/07 (2009); *Blagojević v The Netherlands*, App No 49032/07 (2009); *Beygo v 46 Member States of the Council of Europe*, App No 36099/06 (2009); and *cf Chapman v United Kingdom*, App No 27238/95 (2001) 33 EHRR 399 (where the domestic courts of the defending state had applied the doctrine of immunity of jurisdiction in a case concerning an employee of the NATO). I return to this situation below, when exploring the second 'post-accession' scenario: see text corresponding to notes 22–26.

[18] Paul Mahoney has sought to defend the current, pre-accession, deference to the assessments made by the CJEU as one that should be maintained post-accession, on the basis that 'the EU, as an international organisation, will not lose its specificity in relation to the ECHR Contracting States and so will never be in a position where it can be assimilated, purely and simply, to a Contracting State … The EU pursues a general aim broadly comparable to that assigned to the ECHR by the Council of Europe, namely to create a European, supranational "space" governed by political democracy and the rule of law. By reason of those parallel supranational tasks, there exists a certain overlapping of competence vis-a-vis the States between the EU and the ECHR, which in itself creates a relationship different from that between the ECHR and the States. This different relationship must have some incidence on the nature of the external control that the Strasbourg Court will be called on to exercise over the legal acts of the EU after the latter's accession to the ECHR' (P Mahoney, 'From Strasbourg to Luxembourg and

Under this scenario, in a situation such as that presented in *Matthews* or *Bosphorus*, it will be the EU itself and its Member States (it being left to the EU and its Member States to allocate responsibilities in this regard), not the EU Member State implementing EU law by adopting measures that are the immediate cause of the violation, that will in fact have to adopt the measures required to avoid the repetition of such a violation. The EU will be treated by the ECtHR the same as any other party to the Convention: the acts adopted *by the EU* would be subject to the same level of scrutiny as the acts adopted by any other party to the ECHR. Since the sole purpose of the doctrine of 'equivalent protection'—requiring that a lower level of scrutiny be applied—is to facilitate the compliance *by states* with commitments they have made in the context of a supranational organisation such as the EU, without setting aside their responsibilities under the Convention, there would be no reason either to extend that privilege *to the EU itself*, or even to maintain that privilege for the benefit of the Member States following accession.[19]

Though plausible in theory, this scenario is not very likely in practice. It would certainly not seem to be the expectation of the CJEU. Indeed, soon after the entry into force of the Treaty of Lisbon, which finally provided an indisputable legal basis for the accession of the EU to the ECHR, the CJEU insisted on the need to ensure that it should be provided an opportunity to intervene, prior to the ECtHR having to decide whether a particular application of EU law is in violation of the Convention, in order to allow it to pronounce itself on any alleged incompatibility with the Convention, where such decision concerns the application or implementation of EU law.[20]

Neither the argument based on the subsidiarity of the international judicial control exercised by the ECtHR nor arguments based on the logic of EU law itself—including the monopoly of the Court of Justice on findings of validity of EU law—fully explain the insistence of the CJEU that it have a say on the alleged incompatibility of the measure adopted by the EU with the requirements of the ECHR prior to any involvement of the ECtHR.[21] The motives of the CJEU probably reside elsewhere: in its hope, or its anticipation, that once it will have made its own determination, the ECtHR will simply defer to that assessment, consistent with the *Bosphorus* doctrine described above. If this is indeed

Back: Speculating about Human Rights Protection in the European Union after the Treaty of Lisbon' (2011) 31 *Human Rights Law Journal* 73, 79). The argument remains a circular one: in essence, it states that the EU deserves a specific treatment due to it being an specific international organisation, rather than a state.

[19] It is clear that this is the sole reason for the development by the ECtHR of the doctrine of 'equivalent protection'. This is consistent with the approach of the Court, which is to read the requirements of the Convention within the broader framework of public international law and to seek, to the fullest extent possible, to avoid imposing on states conflicting international obligations (see, for instance, the *Bosphorus* judgment at [148]: 'The Court has also long recognised the growing importance of international co-operation and of the consequent need to secure the proper functioning of international organisations ... Such considerations are critical for a supranational organisation such as the EC. This Court has accordingly accepted that compliance with EC law by a Contracting Party constitutes a legitimate general interest objective within the meaning of Article 1 of Protocol No. 1'). Such a rationale disappears once the EU itself has become a party to the Convention. No risk of the EU Member States being faced with conflicting international obligations will then exist, since EU law itself will have to comply with the Convention, not out of its own volition, but as a matter of international law.

[20] Discussion document of the Court of Justice of the European Union on certain aspects of the accession of the European Union to the European Convention for the Protection of Human Rights and Fundamental Freedoms, Luxembourg, 5 May 2010.

[21] For a more detailed critique, see O De Schutter, 'L'adhésion de l'Union européenne à la Convention européenne des droits de l'homme: feuille de route de la négociation' (2010) *Revue trimestrielle des droits de l'homme* 535.

its expectation, it becomes highly unlikely that the first scenario—that of 'normalisation', in which the doctrine would be simply abandoned—will materialise. In such circumstances, judicial realpolitik generally trumps arguments of principle. Indeed, we may expect the opinion that the Court of Justice will deliver on the draft Agreement providing for the EU's accession to the ECHR to reflect its understanding that the *Bosphorus* doctrine will be maintained: the doctrine may be seen as part of the implicit package deal that allowed the negotiations to be finalised.

B. Scenario 2: The Preservation of the *Status Quo*

If the conclusion above is correct, the reason why the CJEU has insisted on being given a chance to review the compatibility with Convention rights of an act adopted in the field of application of EU law before such an assessment is made by the ECHR is because it expects that, as regards the relationship between the EU legal order and the ECHR, nothing of importance will change. The CJEU places its hopes in what is our second scenario: the doctrine of 'equivalent protection' will continue to be relied upon by the ECtHR when examining the compatibility of measures adopted by the EU with the ECHR—whether these have their source in primary or secondary EU law.

While this second scenario is not implausible, it would be both legally unjustified and politically inopportune. Indeed, once the EU shall have acceded to the Convention, the need to reconcile potentially conflicting international obligations of the EU Member States (as having to comply both with EU law and with their obligations under the Convention) will have disappeared. In addition, while the doctrine may have been useful until now for evaluating the obligations of the *EU Member States* under the Convention, its rationale cannot plausibly be extended to evaluating the obligations of *the EU itself*—for there are no potentially conflicting obligations that the EU is imposed that might represent an obstacle to its full implementation of the Convention rights. This scenario would also be politically inopportune. Since it would not align the status of the EU with that of the other parties to the Convention, it would be sending the wrong signal to the public opinion and it would only partly address the problems justifying the accession of the EU to the Convention in the first place.

There are two versions of this second scenario. According to the 'weak' version, the presumption of compatibility established under *Bosphorus* would benefit the EU Member States, thus ensuring that their national courts will not be obliged either to depart from the interpretation of EU law imposed by the CJEU or to prioritise the obligations imposed under the ECHR. According to the 'strong' version, the presumption would extend also to acts adopted by the institutions of the EU in which the EU Member States have taken no part—such as decisions or regulations adopted by the European Commission. This scenario deserves a word of explanation.[22]

Currently, acts that are adopted by an international organisation without any implication of the states parties to the Convention are considered by the ECtHR to lie outside its jurisdiction: where applications are filed against specific decisions of organs of international

[22] See further X Groussot and L Pech, 'La protection des droits fondamentaux dans l'Union européenne après le traité de Lisbonne', *Questions d'Europe* no 173, Fondation Robert Schuman, 14 June 2010; and Florence Benoît-Rohmer, 'Bienvenue aux enfants de Bosphorus' (2010) 21(81) *Revue trimestrielle des droits de l'homme*. 19.

organisations in the adoption of which the Member States have played no role (as opposed to applications alleging a 'structural deficiency', which the states having established the organisation should have prevented), the Court simply treats them as incompatible *ratione personae* with the Convention. In other words, such applications are in reality challenging a conduct adopted not by the states parties to the Convention that have joined the organisation but by a distinct international legal subject, the international organisation, that is not itself a party to the Convention.

The case of *Boivin* provides an illustration of this.[23] In this case, the applicant was challenging a decision of its employer, the European Organisation for the Safety of Air Navigation ('Eurocontrol'), to cancel his appointment to a post within the organisation and then to deny him an appointment, after his name was not included on the list of qualified candidates drawn up by a selection board. He took his case to the International Labour Organisation Administrative Tribunal (ILOAT), the sole body having competence to settle disputes between Eurocontrol and its staff according to Article 5 § 2 of Eurocontrol's Statute, challenging the cancellation of his appointment and seeking compensation for the injury caused to him. Though he did obtain some compensation, he failed to obtain the annulment of the impunged decision concerning the appointment. He then applied to the ECtHR, alleging that the ILOAT had violated a number of procedural rights guaranteed by the ECHR.

The Court found that the application was incompatible *ratione personae* with the provisions of the Convention. It reasoned that Eurocontrol has a legal personality separate from that of its Member States and is not a party to the Convention: neither Belgium nor France played any role in the adoption of the decision that allegedly caused the violation. The Court analogised the situation of Mr Boivin to that of the applicants in the 2007 cases of *Behrami* and *Saramati*,[24] where, distinguishing *Bosphorus* and *Matthews*, the Court took the view that the respondent states' responsibility could not be engaged on account of the impugned acts and omissions of NATO troops deployed in Kosovo or of the UN mission to Kosovo (KFOR and UNMIK), as such acts were 'directly attributable to the United Nations, an organisation of universal jurisdiction fulfilling its imperative collective security objective'. The Court considered that Boivin was in a similar situation: the acts he was challenging were not those of the Member States of Eurocontrol, because these acts did not reveal a 'structural deficiency' these states should have prevented—they were, rather, discrete acts adopted by the (ILOAT), without any implication of its Member States. In reality, said the Court, 'the applicant's complaints were directed essentially against the relevant judgment of the ILOAT concerning his individual labour dispute with Eurocontrol'. It continued:

> The Court would point out that the impugned decision thus emanated from an international tribunal outside the jurisdiction of the respondent States, in the context of a labour dispute that lay entirely within the internal legal order of Eurocontrol, an international organisation that has a legal personality separate from that of its member States. At no time did France or Belgium intervene directly or indirectly in the dispute, and no act or omission of those States or their authorities can be considered to engage their responsibility under the Convention. In this respect the instant case is to be distinguished from previous cases where the international responsibility of the respondent States has been in issue, for example that of the United Kingdom in the

[23] *Boivin v France and Belgium and 32 Other Member States of the Council of Europe*, App No 73250/01 (2008).

[24] *Behrami and Behrami v France* and *Saramati v France, Germany and Norway*, App Nos 71412/01 and 78166/01 (2007).

> *Matthews* case (18 February 1999, no. 24833/94—decision not to register the applicant as a voter on the basis of an EC treaty), that of France in the *Cantoni* case (15 November 1996, *Reports of Judgments and Decisions* 1996-V—enforcement against the applicant of a French law implementing an EC Directive), that of Germany in the *Beer and Regan* and *Waite and Kennedy* cases ([GC], nos. 28934/95 and 26083/94, 18 February 1999—denial of access to the German courts) or that of Ireland in the above-mentioned *Bosphorus* case. Unlike in those cases, in all of which the State or States concerned had been involved directly or indirectly, in the present case the applicant cannot be said to have been 'within the jurisdiction' of the respondent States for the purposes of Article 1 of the Convention.

The Court concluded on these grounds that the violations of the Convention alleged by Boivin therefore could not be attributed to France and Belgium. As to the possibility of finding Eurocontrol itself to be responsible, the suggestion was given short shrift by the Court: 'since this international organisation is not a party to the Convention, its responsibility cannot be engaged under the Convention'.

The Court currently takes the same position where the acts allegedly resulting in a violation of Convention rights are adopted by organs of the EU, through procedures in which the Member States play no role. In *Connolly*, the applicant was a public servant of the European Commission who had been subjected to disciplinary proceedings for having published a book denouncing certain practices within the EU institutions while on short leave from his institution.[25] He was dismissed as a result. He challenged that decision before what was then the Court of First Instance of the European Communities (CFI), and later, in cassation proceedings after the CFI rejected his action for annulment, the European Court of Justice. His requests to be given an opportunity to respond to the views expressed in the opinion presented to the European Court of Justice by the Advocate General were rejected by the Court. Connolly then turned to the ECtHR, alleging violations both of freedom of expression and of his right to a fair trial, as guaranteed under Article 6(1) of the ECHR. He considered that he had not been given a fair opportunity to challenge the reasoning of the Advocate General, since the AG's opinion is presented after the proceedings are closed. The Court considered that the situation was similar to that in *Boivin.* Noting that the impunged measures were adopted by bodies of the EU rather than by the EU Member States as states parties to the Convention, it concluded that the application was incompatible *ratione personae* with the provisions of the Convention.

In clear contrast to the *Boivin* and *Connolly* line of cases are cases where the applicant challenges not the decision adopted by the international organisation itself, but a structural feature of the procedures through which human rights are protected within the organisation and for which the Member States—who have established the organisation and are its 'fathers'—may be held responsible. Thus, in the case of *Gasparini*, the applicant had sought to rely on the internal procedures established within NATO to challenge the consequences of a decision by the North Atlantic Council concerning the prorata of wages that would go to paying pensions. After he failed in his attempt, he turned to the ECtHR, challenging the compatibility with the procedural rights guaranteed under the Convention of the procedures themselves. This, the Court noted, concerned an alleged 'structural deficiency' of NATO's internal procedures: as such procedures are defined by the North Atlantic Council in which the NATO Member States' representatives are sitting,

[25] *Connolly v 15 Member States of the European Union*, App No 73274/01 (2008).

the Member States themselves may be held responsible for such a deficiency.[26] It matters not that the application failed: what is striking is that the Court examined the substance of the application filed by Gasparini, asking specifically whether the NATO Member States had acted in good faith or whether instead they should have suspected that the system they were establishing within the organisation was not sufficiently 'rights-proofed'.

Following the accession by the EU to the ECHR, in cases such as *Connolly*, it would fall upon the ECtHR to examine whether the EU has been acting in accordance with the requirements of the Convention. There is no logical reason why the presumption of compatibility with these requirements, as established by *Bosphorus*, should apply to such cases: there is no risk here of the addressee, the EU, having conflicting international obligations imposed on it or being able to comply with the ECHR only at the expense of deepening the process of integration—especially not since all the EU Member States are also parties to the ECHR. And just like the fact that there is no reason to apply the presumption to the EU itself, there is no reason to apply it to the EU Member States implementing EU law, even in circumstances where they have no margin of appreciation, because the very possibility of EU law having to be implemented despite its incompatibility with Convention rights is excluded in principle as a result of the EU having become a party to the Convention. This is why the second scenario, the closest to the *status quo*, should be avoided: it would confirm the current privileged position of the EU Member States when they act in accordance with obligations imposed under EU law and under the supervision of the CJEU, when the current justification for this privilege will have disappeared. The real problem with this scenario, however, is not that it allows the ECtHR to rely on a presumption of compatibility with the Convention in certain circumstances; it is that these circumstances are reserved to some parties and denied to others, when there is no principled justification for this difference in treatment. The next scenario is one in which the doctrine is maintained, but the differential treatment is removed.

C. Scenario 3: *Bosphorus* Generalised

Our third and final scenario is that the doctrine of 'equivalent protection' will expand further: the privilege which is currently granted to the EU Member States when they act in the implementation of requirements of EU and under the supervision of the CJEU would not be denied to them; rather, it would be extended to all situations which comply with the same set of (strictly defined) conditions. As noted by six judges of the ECtHR who filed a joint concurring opinion in *Bosphorus*, the 'general abstract review of the Community system' to which the Court proceeds in that case (which leads it to conclude that the EU offers a protection of fundamental rights 'equivalent' to that of the system of the ECHR) is one 'to which all the Contracting Parties to the ECHR could in a way lay claim'.[27] In this separate concurring opinion, the argument is put forward to question the attitude of the ECtHR towards situations where states are merely fulfilling obligations incurred under EU law, under the supervision of the European Court of Justice. But it could also be invoked to justify an *extension* of the *Bosphorus* doctrine beyond its current scope of application,

[26] *Gasparini v Italy and Belgium* (n 10; decision only available in French).

[27] Joint concurring opinion of Judges Rozakis, Tulkens, Traja, Botoucharova, Zagrebalsky and Garlicki, to the *Bosphorus* judgment of 30 June 2005 (n 1) [3].

under certain well-specified conditions. The third scenario would establish a *Bosphorus*-like presumption in any situation where, at the national level, a protection 'equivalent' to that provided by the ECHR system is ensured.

The conditions for such 'equivalence' would have to be clarified by the Court, but one could easily think of a set of requirements including, at a minimum, the direct application of the Convention rights by the domestic courts before which a claim was filed by the alleged victim, an interpretation of the Convention systematically based on the case law of the ECtHR, or the adoption of appropriate measures to ensure that claims based on Convention rights are processed without unreasonable delays. Other requirements could be included beyond these elementary conditions. The could concern, for instance, the relationship between substantive rules applied by domestic courts and the procedural requirements that define the scope of their powers; or they could relate to measures ensuring that the ECHR is taken into account preventively, in the formulation of generally applicable regulations (rather than merely on an individual and *ad hoc* basis, at the request of aggrieved litigants).[28]

This new and strengthened version of the doctrine would clearly manifest the principle of subsidiarity in the system of the ECHR—ie, the principle according to which the protection of the rights and freedoms of the Convention must primarily take place at the national level, the intervention of the ECtHR being only justified where those internal mechanisms have failed to prevent violations from occuring or, if they do occur, from being remedied.[29] The principle of subsidiarity, it is worth emphasising, does not assert that the ECtHR should somehow renounce fully exercising its role in scrutinising measures adopted at the domestic level. Rather, it insists on the domestic authorities having to play their part in strengthening the protection of individual rights: though the principle of subsidiarity does not, as such, require a direct application of the Convention in the domestic legal order, its aim is to ensure that the individual will not have to wait to file a claim at the international level in order to be able to denounce a violation of the Convention.

Similarly, in line with the principle of subsidiarity thus understood, this third scenario would allow the ECtHR to develop a case law providing strong incentives to the states parties to the Convention to *strengthen* the protection of Convention rights within their domestic legal order. It could do so, inter alia, by enhancing the status of the ECHR at the national level. Today, all Member States of the Council of Europe allow their courts to directly apply the ECHR in the disputes in which they are asked to adjudicate.[30] But the modalities can vary significantly from state to state.[31] For instance, courts in different states may or may

[28] Some of these conditions could be set seeking inspiration from Recommendation Rec(2004)6 of the Committee of Ministers to Member States on the improvement of domestic remedies (adopted by the Committee of Ministers on 12 May 2004, at its 114th session). In any event, the *Bosphorus* doctrine in its new incarnation would only apply to situations that have been reviewed by domestic courts on the basis of the requirements of the ECHR, as interpreted by the Strasbourg Court.

[29] For an in-depth discussion of the principle of subsidiarity under the ECHR, see O De Schutter, 'La subsidiarité dans la Convention européenne des droits de l'homme: la dimension procédurale' in M Verdussen (ed), *L'Europe de la subsidiarité* (Brussels, Bruylant, 2000).

[30] For studies comparing the status of the ECHR in different national legal orders, see R Blackburn and J Polakiewicz (eds), *Fundamental Rights in Europe: The ECHR and its Member States, 1950–2000* (Oxford, Oxford University Press, 2001); H Keller and A Stone Sweet (eds), *A Europe of Rights: The Impact of the ECHR on National Legal Systems* (Oxford, Oxford University Press, 2008).

[31] For a comparative overview, see G Martinico and O Pollicino, *The National Judicial Treatment of the ECHR and EU Laws: A Constitutional Comparative Perspective* (Amsterdam, Europa Law Publishing, 2010).

not accept that, in cases of conflict with the national constitution, the Convention rights will prevail; they may be authorised to disapply even clear legislative mandates in order to apply provisions of the Convention or they may be prohibited from doing so;[32] they may be under a duty to raise *ex officio* the issue of compatibility with Convention rights in legal proceedings, or provide that this question shall only be raised at the initiative of the parties;[33] they may or may not apply the provisions of the Convention, or all of them, to relationships between private parties where protecting the rights of one of the parties would imply imposing correlative obligations on other parties.[34] Moreover, even where its provisions are directly applied, the Convention can only be invoked before national courts in accordance with the procedural requirements imposed, for instance, under statutes of limitations defining the maximum time that may have elapsed between the moment when the alleged violation took place and the commencement of legal proceedings based on that event, under rules of evidence or under other rules defining the conditions of access to court—only a small portion of which will be included among the minimum requirements imposed as part of the right to an effective remedy under Article 13 of the Convention.[35] Finally, moving beyond the role of courts in enforcing Convention rights and to other actors within the domestic legal system, the attention paid to the requirements of the Convention by parliamentary committees or by the Executive differs widely from state to state: human rights proofing of legislation or policies remains the exception rather than the rule, and the inclusion of human rights in impact assessments, even when such assessments are performed, is variable.[36] Not all pieces of legislation or policy frameworks that could impact human rights are preceded by a consultation of stakeholders and not all Council of

[32] In the UK, for instance, the Human Rights Act 1998 has allowed the domestic courts since 2 October 2000 to apply Articles 2–12 and 14 of the Convention, as well as Articles 1–3 of the (First) Additional Protocol, and (since the Human Rights Act 1998 (Amendment) Order 2004 (SI 2004/1574)) Article 1 of the Thirteenth Protocol, together with Articles 16 and 18 of the Convention. But where an Act of Parliament cannot be interpreted in order to ensure compliance with the Convention, the courts can only make a declaration of incompatibility, without being authorised either to strike down the legislative provision found to be incompatible or to disapply such provision; the principle of parliamentary sovereignty remains unaffected. See, inter alia, D Hoffman and J Rowe, *Human Rights in the UK: An Introduction to the Human Rights Act 1998* (Harlow, Longman, 2006) 64–65.

[33] In the 1996 case of *Ahmet Sadik v Greece*, Judge SK Martens famously stated that 'in those cases where domestic courts, under their national law, are in a position to apply the Convention ex officio, those courts must do so under the Convention. That is an obvious demand of the effectiveness both of the Convention as a constitutional instrument of European public order (ordre public) and of the "national human right systems"' (*Ahmet Sadik v Greece*, App No 18877/91 (1996), partly dissenting opinion of Judge Martens, joined by Judge Foighel at [11]). He was not followed on this point by his fellow judges.

[34] It is notable that, while, as seen above, the Committee of Ministers of the Council of Europe has sought to encourage the Member States to improve the effectiveness of the remedies available, at the domestic level, to the alleged victims of violations of the Convention (Recommendation Rec(2004)6 of the Committee of Ministers to member states on the improvement of domestic remedies (adopted by the Committee of Ministers on 12 May 2004, at its 114th Session)), its recommendations have addressed none of these points. Here, the principle of procedural autonomy of the states seems to prevail.

[35] It is of course telling that Article 13 ECHR is not listed among the provisions of the Convention listed by the Human Rights Act 1998 as provisions that the UK courts may rely on in their development of the common law or in their interpretation of legislation: thus, they will not be tempted to expand their powers in order to ensure that aggrieved individuals turning to the courts have access to effective remedies.

[36] See Committee of Ministers of the Council of Europe, Recommendation Rec(2004)5 to member states on the verification of the compatibility of draft laws, existing laws and administrative practice with the standards laid down in the European Convention on Human *Rights* (adopted by the Committee of Ministers on 12 May 2004 at its 114th Session) (identifying a range of good practices to ensure that 'there are appropriate and effective mechanisms for systematically verifying the compatibility of draft laws with the Convention in the light of the case law of the [European Court of Human Rights]'; that 'there are such mechanisms for verifying, whenever necessary, the compatibility of existing laws and administrative practice, including as expressed in regulations,

Europe Member States have an independent national human rights institution, while even the practice of the existing institutions is highly uneven.

The list could be made longer and each of its items could be discussed at length. But the point made is a simple one: were the *Bosphorus* presumption-of-compatibility doctrine to be expanded into a rule applicable across the full range of situations covered by the Convention, the Court could seize upon this opportunity to impose strict conditions on the Parties who claim to be worthy of benefiting from the doctrine—or, more likely, for an equivalent doctrine, inspired by *Bosphorus* without replicating it exactly.

That is clearly the direction encouraged by the Brighton Declaration adopted at the 19–20 April 2012 High-Level Conference on the Future of the European Court of Human Rights. Reiterating concerns already expressed by similar conferences in the past,[37] the Brighton Declaration addressed a number of recommendations to the Member States of the Council of Europe in order to ensure the 'full implementation of the Convention at the national level', including the establishment of national human rights institutions; the adoption of 'practical measures to ensure that policies and legislation comply fully with the Convention, including by offering to national parliaments information on the compatibility with the Convention of draft primary legislation proposed by the Government'; 'the introduction of necessary of new domestic legal remedies, whether of a specific or general nature, for alleged violations of the rights and freedoms under the Convention'; or providing information and training on Convention rights to judges and lawyers, and to public officials.[38] The Declaration also emphasised that, according to the principle of subsidiarity, it is first and foremost up to the national authorities to ensure that the Convention is complied with: 'the Convention system is subsidiary to the safeguarding of human rights at national level and … national authorities are in principle better placed than an international court to evaluate local needs and conditions'.[39] It suggested inserting a reference to the principle of subsidiarity and the doctrine of the margin of appreciation as developed in the Court's case law in the Preamble of the Convention, as well as the possibility of providing the Court with a competence to deliver 'advisory opinions upon request on the interpretation of the Convention in the context of a specific case at domestic level'.[40]

Most importantly for our purposes, however, the Declaration recommended a stricter application of the existing criteria that determine whether an application will or will not be considered admissible and examined on the merits, and even an amendment to Article 35(3) of the Convention in order to strengthen the conditions of admissibility of individual applications. It 'affirms' that 'an application should be regarded as manifestly ill-founded … inter alia, to the extent that the Court considers that the application raises a complaint that has been duly considered by a domestic court applying the rights guaranteed by the

orders and circulars'; and ensuring 'the adaptation, as quickly as possible, of laws and administrative practice in order to prevent violations of the Convention').

[37] Particularly the High-Level Conferences convened at Interlaken on 19 February 2010 and at Izmir on 27 April 2011.

[38] See High-Level Conference on the Future of the European Court of Human Rights, Brighton Declaration, 19–20 April 2012, para 9.

[39] Ibid, para 11.

[40] Ibid, para 12(d). See now Protocol (No 16) to the Convention for the Protection of Human Rights and Fundamental Freedoms, adopted on 2 October 2013, providing for this possibility; the Protocol shall enter into force three months after the tenth ratification is received. The reference to the principle of subsidiarity has been inserted into the Preamble of the Convention by Protocol (No 15) Amending the Convention for the protection of Human Rights and Fundamental Freedoms, adopted on 24 June 2013.

Convention in light of well-established case law of the Court including on the margin of appreciation as appropriate, unless the Court finds that the application raises a serious question affecting the interpretation or application of the Convention; and encourages the Court to have regard to the need to take a strict and consistent approach in declaring such applications inadmissible, clarifying its case law to this effect as necessary'.[41]

This is a plea to the Court to consider that an application will not be examined on its merits if the alleged violation has already been duly examined at the domestic level by a court applying the provisions of the Convention and taking into account the case law of the Court, unless there is a need for the Court to intervene ('the application raises a serious question affecting the interpretation or application of the Convention'). In practice, following this suggestion implies a shift in the nature of the control exercised by the ECtHR: instead of examining each application on its merits, essentially re-examining how the various rights and interests were balanced by the domestic court, the European Court should consider whether the domestic court applied the rights stipulated by the Convention, accompanied by the interpretation authoritatively provided to these rights by the European Court. The control would be less substantive and more procedural; it would liken the role of the ECtHR more to a court of cassation, limited to ensuring that the law is correctly applied, but leaving it to the domestic court itself to assess the facts and to decide the outcome of the balancing act that human rights courts are commonly required to perform.

However, it is striking that, in contrast to the third scenario explored here, nothing of significance is said about the conditions that the domestic judicial proceedings should comply with for such proceedings to be trusted. In other words, the Brighton Declaration takes the view that, provided the individual has access to effective remedies in the domestic legal order and provided the domestic courts faithfully apply the case law developed by the ECtHR, it would be unnecessary to superimpose a review at the international level to the judicial review that took place at the national level. In contrast, the suggestion here is that, whereas a shift in the nature of the control to be exercised by the ECtHR may be justified provided a set of conditions are fulfilled, this should not result in a lower level of scrutiny, potentially at the expense of the protection of the rights of the individual. It is rather the opposite: because remedies at the national level are more accessible to the individual and can provide more immediate protection, insisting on such remedies being strengthened as a condition for the ECtHR to trust that the protection of individual rights is ensured within the national legal order may in fact improve the level of such protection rather than undermine it.

III. THE SECOND LIFE OF *BOSPHORUS*

In fact, though it would be made more explicit if a new version of the *Bosphorus* doctrine were to expand in the future, this evolution would simply deepen what largely corresponds to the current approach of the ECtHR. The nature of the scrutiny exercised by the Court already depends, to a significant extent, on how the domestic courts have reached their decision in the particular case that it is presented with: the 'how' matters as much, it might

[41] Ibid, para 15(d). The Declaration also 'concludes' that 'Article 35(3)(b) should be amended to remove the words "and provided that no case may be rejected on this ground which has not been duly considered by a domestic tribunal" and invites the Committee of Ministers to adopt the necessary amending instrument by the end of 2013' (para 15(c)). See now Art 5 of Protocol (No 15), referred to above (n 40), inserting this change into Article 35 ECHR.

be argued, as 'what' outcome has been reached. It is important to note, however, that once the procedures followed at the domestic level are assessed, it is less the *degree* of scrutiny exercised by the European Court that evolves (for example, from a 'strict' scrutiny to an 'intermediate' level of scrutiny or to a mere 'rationality review', to borrow from the categories of Equality Clause jurisprudence in American constitutional law) than the *kind* of scrutiny that is exercised: instead of the Court performing anew the balancing act that will lead it to arrive at its own conclusions as to the existence of a violation, essentially replicating what the domestic jurisdictions have done, the European Court will examine whether the arguments put forward by the domestic court are consistent with its case law and with the nature of the claims put forward. The focus is on the quality of the arguments offered rather than on the conclusions reached.

The result is that the relationship between the domestic courts and the ECtHR is more dialogical and horizontal than based on judicial fiat and vertical.[42] There follows a strong incentive for domestic courts to provide consistent and substantive reasons for the conclusions they reach in order to convince the ECtHR that they have considered all the dimensions of the case, without neglecting any major aspect, and have provided the kind of detailed response to each of the arguments presented by the alleged victim of a violation, commensurate with the quality of these arguments themselves. This new approach, based on mutual trust between the ECtHR and national jurisdictions of the parties to the Convention, would present three defining characteristics. First, it would lead to an emphasis on compliance with certain procedural rules that national authorities, including courts, would have to comply with as a condition for the trust they would claim to deserve. Second, it would redefine the ECtHR as a standard-setter, defining the parameters that should be taken into account by the domestic courts applying the Convention, but leaving it to these courts to apply those standards to the specific facts they are presented with. Third, it would encourage collective learning, and the rapid adoption of best practices, provided the justifications required from national courts are understood to include what other national authorities have done when confronted with similar problems, if the solutions they arrived at have ensured a better preservation of the rights at stake. The following sections describe the approach proposed and highlight the key advantages that can be expected from this shift in perspective.

A. The Procedural Turn

At present, there is already a strongly dialogical dimension to the relationship between the ECtHR and the domestic courts of the states parties to the Convention. This dimension enters the case law most explicitly through the channel of the margin of appreciation doctrine.[43] In the Court's summary of this doctrine: 'by reason of their direct and continuous

[42] This approach is expounded and richly illustrated in CF Sabel and O Gerstenberg, 'Constitutionalising an Overlapping Consensus: The ECJ and the Emergence of a Coordinate Constitutional Order' (2010) 16 *European Law Journal* 511.

[43] The literature on this point is overwhelming. We owe much to the most extensive studies of the subject by HC Yourow, *The Margin of Appreciation Doctrine in the Dynamics of European Human Rights Jurisprudence* (The Hague, Martinus Nijhoff, 1996); JGC Schokkenbroek, *Toetsing aan de vrijheidsrechten van het Europees Verdrag tot bescherming van de Rechten van de Mens*, (Zwolle, WEJ Tjeenk Willink, 1996) 11–241; and E Kastanas, *Unité et diversité. Notions autonomes et marge d'appréciation des Etats dans la jurisprudence de la Cour européenne des*

contact with the vital forces of their countries, the national authorities are in principle better placed than an international court to evaluate local needs and conditions'.[44] Although it is often misunderstood, the doctrine is *not* a blank authorisation given to national authorities, including courts, to do as they please, in areas that are particularly sensitive and in which, therefore, great weight should be attached to domestic public opinion.[45] The doctrine of the margin of appreciation simply recognises that national authorities may be better placed to make certain *factual assessments*, including those that enter into play in balancing of interests analysis, but *using the framework of analysis that the case law of the ECtHR provides*. Indeed, whenever the Court invokes the doctrine, it hastily adds that the choices made at the national level remain to be monitored for their compliance with the Convention at the international level. By relying on this doctrine, the Court does not abdicate its role. Instead, as already suggested above,[46] the doctrine is a mechanism for the allocation of decision making between the international level and the national level. In matters pertaining to the Convention, the assessments made by the national authorities will be deferred to, to the extent that the procedures followed at the national level may be presumed to ensure an adequate compliance with the Convention.

Thus understood, the doctrine of the national margin of appreciation could create an incentive for legislative and executive authorities to better take the Convention into account in their law- and policy-making procedures, and for the domestic courts to pay greater attention to the requirements of the Convention and the evolving international case law, providing it with an authoritative interpretation. In accordance with the principle of subsidiarity of international judicial supervision, the 'wide margin of appreciation' could benefit national authorities where, for instance, human rights impact assessments have been performed prior to the adoption of legislation or the implementation of certain policies, or where decisions were preceded by consultations of stakeholders; or where the Convention is directly applied by national jurisdictions, taking into account the relevant case law of the ECtHR. Far from deferring to the evaluations of the domestic authorities, the Court would thus put more pressure on those authorities to implement fully the requirements of the Convention in the decisions they adopt.

Consider, for instance, the case of *Hatton and others v United Kingdom*. There, the applicants challenged before the ECtHR the implementation in 1993 of a new scheme for regulating night flights at Heathrow. The scheme replaced the earlier system of movement limitations with a regime which gave aircraft operators a choice, through a quota count, as

droits de l'homme (Brussels, Bruylant, 1996). See also the special issue dedicated to this issue by the *Human Rights Law Journal* in 1998 under the title 'The Doctrine of the Margin of Appreciation under the European Convention on Human Rights: Its Legitimacy in Theory and Application in Practice'; Y Arai, 'The Margin of Appreciation Doctrine in the Jurisprudence of Article 8 of the European Convention on Human Rights' (1998) *Netherlands Quarterly of Human Rights* 41; E Brems, 'The Margin of Appreciation Doctrine in the Case Law of the European Court of Human Rights' (1996) 56 *Zeitschrift für ausländisches öffentliches Recht und Völkerrecht* 240; TH Jones, 'The Devaluation of Human Rights under the European Convention' [1995] *Public Law* 430; P Mahoney, 'Universality versus Subsidiarity in the Strasbourg Case Law on Free Speech: Explaining Some Recent Judgments' (1997) 4 *EHRLR* 364; J Callewaert, 'Quel avenir pour la marge d'appréciation?' in P Mahoney, H Petzold, F Matscher and L Wildhaber (eds), *Protection des droits de l'homme: la perspective européenne. Mélanges en hommage à R. Ryssdal* (Cologne, Carl Heymanns, 2000).

44 *Buckley v United Kingdom*, App No 20348/92 (1996) 23 EHRR 101 [75].

45 For a more detailed analysis of this point, see O De Schutter and F Tulkens, 'The European Court of Human Rights as a Pragmatic Institution' in E Brems (ed), *Conflicts between Fundamental Rights* (Antwerp, Intersentia, 2008).

46 See above, text corresponding to notes 28–36.

to whether to fly fewer noisier aircraft or more, less noisy types. The 1993 scheme accepted the conclusions of the 1992 sleep study, which found that, for the large majority of people living near airports, there was no risk of substantial sleep disturbance due to aircraft noise and that only a small percentage of individuals (some 2–3 per cent) were more sensitive than others. On this basis, disturbances caused by aircraft noise were regarded as negligible in relation to overall normal disturbance rates. It was agreed, nevertheless, that the new scheme was susceptible to adversely affecting the quality of the applicants' private life and the scope for their enjoying the amenities of their respective homes, and thus their rights protected by Article 8 of the Convention. The Court noted that it was faced with two versions of the extent to which the margin of appreciation doctrine should apply: 'on the one hand, the Government claim a wide margin on the ground that the case concerns matters of general policy, and, on the other hand, the applicants' claim that where the ability to sleep is affected, the margin is narrow because of the "intimate" nature of the right protected'.[47] In effect, the Court chose to define whether the government has overstepped its margin of appreciation by examining the decision-making procedure that was followed, asking in particular which procedural safeguards had been included allowing various stakeholders to have their views heard. It found that the decision concerning the new schemes for night flights at Heathrow was based on various studies and studies allowing ample room for participation for the communities, and was grounded on solid evidence. It concluded that it was unable to 'find that, in substance, the authorities overstepped their margin of appreciation by failing to strike a fair balance between the right of the individuals affected by those regulations to respect for their private life and home and the conflicting interests of others and of the community as a whole', or that there were 'fundamental procedural flaws in the preparation of the 1993 regulations on limitations for night flights'.[48] This example is not isolated: the case law of the Court offers other examples of situations where the procedural safeguards built into decision-making processes were determinative of the question of whether the authorities had overstepped their margin of appreciation.[49]

A first characteristic of the approach proposed here is therefore that it would lead to impose on domestic authorities that they comply with a number of safeguards, ensuring that the trust in the decisions that they adopt is not blind, but instead is grounded on these authorities complying with a number of conditions of a procedural nature—related to *how* the decision was reached rather than to the *outcome* of domestic decision-making processes.[50] This may in fact strengthen rather than weaken the protection of human rights at the level of each state.

[47] *Hatton v United Kingdom*, App No 36022/97 (2003) 37 EHRR 611 [103].

[48] Ibid [129].

[49] See, eg, *Chapman v United Kingdom* (n 17) [114].

[50] See also the contribution of Robert Harmsen in ch 13 in this volume (noting the potential 'jurisprudential reorientation in which the ECtHR shows more explicit awareness and places greater weight on the 'deliberative quality' of national decision-making', in essence shifting 'to a role in which it scrutinised decision-making procedures more closely, while variably calibrating the scope and intensity of its substantive determinations in function of the extent to which questions of the balancing of fundamental rights had appropriately figured in prior national deliberations').

B. The Division of Labour between International and National Courts

A second characteristic is that the ECtHR would remain in charge of shaping the normative framework, establishing the standards that the national authorities should take into account in making their assessments. Here again, the existing doctrine on the margin of appreciation may serve as a departure point. Though the doctrine is often misunderstood, it is relevant to note that its use is limited to the evaluation of facts (of what is required in a particular situation); it does not extend to the interpretation of the requirements of the Convention (which it is the role of the ECtHR to supervise).[51] Rather, it is when the national courts appear to have faithfully applied the case law of the ECtHR that they are 'trusted' in assessing particular factual situations within the margin of appreciation that is left to them.

Importantly, however, it is not enough for national courts to re-state the well-established case law of the ECtHR in order for their appreciation of the consequences to be drawn in particular factual settings to be deferred to. Consider, for instance, the case of *Schüth v Germany*.[52] The applicant in this case was complaining that he had been dismissed from his job as an organist and choirmaster by his employer, the Catholic parish church, after having left his wife to live with another woman, for breach of his duty of loyalty under the church regulations. Asked to decide whether this resulted in a violation of the right to respect for private life as guaranteed under Article 8 ECHR, the ECtHR first recalled that the question of whether church-based organisations could require from their employees that they comply with certain duties of loyalty, as a condition for their employment, had been addressed by the Federal Constitutional Court in 1985. The Federal Constitutional Court had essentially upheld the validity of the 'loyalty clauses' in such employment relationships on the basis of the right of religious societies to manage their affairs autonomously within the limit of the general law, the *Selbstbestimmungsrecht* enshrined in Article 137 § 3 of the Weimar Constitution, a provision that the Basic Law (Grundgesetz) of 1949 had maintained in force.[53] A few years later, when asked whether this position was compatible with the ECHR, the European Commission on Human Rights answered in the affirmative.[54] Thus, when in 2010, the question again arose in *Schüth v Germany*, the ECtHR could 'observe ... that the Federal Employment Tribunal, in its judgment of 12 August 1999, referred extensively to the principles established by the Federal Constitutional Court in its judgment of 4 June 1985'.[55] However, the Court added 'that the Employment Appeal Tribunal merely stated that it did not disregard the consequences of dismissal for the applicant', but that it 'failed, however, to explain the factors it had taken into consideration in that connection when weighing up the interests involved', although in the Court's opinion, 'the fact that an employee who has been dismissed by a Church has limited opportunities of finding another job is of particular importance'.[56] It concluded that the dismissal of the

[51] See in particular Callewaert (n 43).

[52] *Schüth v Germany*, App No 1620/03 (2010) 52 EHRR 981.

[53] 2 BvR 1703/83, 1718/83 and 856/84, judgment published in the Reports of Judgments and Decisions of the Federal Constitutional Court, volume 70, 138–73.

[54] Eur Comm HR, *Rommelfanger v Germany*, App No 12242/86, decision of 6 September 1989, Decisions and Reports, vol 62, 151 (the case concerned a medical doctor employed in a hospital depending on the Catholic Church who had made declarations in favour of the freedom of women to choose abortion).

[55] *Schüth v Germany* (n 52) [60].

[56] Ibid [73].

applicant resulted in a violation of the right to respect for private life, because of its disproportionate consequences, as the domestic courts had not passed the test of deliberative justification required in this architecture:

> The Court is therefore of the view that the employment tribunals did not sufficiently explain the reasons why, according to the findings of the Employment Appeal Tribunal, the interests of the Church far outweighed those of the applicant, and that they failed to weigh the rights of the applicant against those of the employing Church in a manner compatible with the Convention.[57]

The wording used here suggests the nature of the control exercised by the ECtHR. It is not substituting its own judgment for that of the German courts, nor is it repeating the weighing of the interests performed by these courts. Rather, the European Court examines whether the domestic courts have appropriately justified, in the light of the guidelines that can be derived from the existing case law, the conclusion that they have reached: the finding of a violation follows from the finding that, in some important respects, the arguments put forward have been found lacking. The ECtHR expresses its disagreement not with the outcome per se, about which it may be said to be agnostic, but with the method by which the outcome was reached.

Such an approach may represent a significant gain in legitimacy in the implementation of the standards of the ECHR. This is both because of the active role that the actors most immediately concerned will have played in its adoption (if, among the said conditions, there are procedural conditions related to whether the decision was reached by national authorities taking into account all relevant viewpoints) and because it will be a decision better informed by the realities of the circumstances in which the alleged violation occurred—the unique constellation of facts that no predefined grid could have anticipated. Both input legitimacy (the perception that the procedure has been fair to all participants) and output legitimacy (the acceptability of the result) are strengthened. This in turn may improve the enforcement of the decision, both because, as co-authors of the solution that is reached, all the participants involved may perceive that they have an interest in the implementation and because the decision will not be seen as 'foreign' or imposed from above.

C. The 'Deliberative Polyarchic' Element

There is finally a third characteristic to this new approach that may make it particularly attractive. This characteristic, however, does not simply aim to make explicit what is already implicit in the case law of the ECtHR. It goes beyond the current approach. It does so by seeing the establishment of a more dialogical relationship between courts as an opportunity to encourage the national authorities to develop innovative solutions to questions raised by the application of the Convention for which the Member States of the Council of Europe have not defined a common solution. Indeed, one of the main justifications of the doctrine of the 'margin of appreciation' today is that it avoids imposing uniform solutions throughout the Member States, at least where no single solution is imposed by the requirements of the Convention.[58] The doctrine may therefore both promote diversity and encourage the search

[57] Ibid [74].

[58] See the references cited in this respect by S Van Drooghenbroeck, *La proportionnalité dans le droit de la Convention européenne des droits de l'homme. Prendre l'idée simple au sérieux* (Brussels, FUSL/Bruylant, 2001) 497–503.

for the best techniques through which to reconcile conflicting claims made on the national authorities. By deferring to the appreciation of the national authorities about what responses are required by the situations they are confronted with, the reliance by the Court on the 'margin of appreciation' may favour the search for solutions which, once they are identified and found to be compatible with the requirements of the Convention, may benefit other states, who may seek inspiration from local experiments. We enter into an architecture that Cohen and Sabel have labelled 'deliberative polyarchy', in which 'the very different circumstances in which problems arise suggest a need for differences in solution, while the commonality of problems indicates a need to discipline local solutions against those adopted elsewhere: the aim is not to achieve uniformity, but to pool information, identify best practices, and compare solutions across locations'.[59] It is the contention of this chapter that courts may participate in what is, in essence, a joint and co-ordinated search that will not necessarily lead to common or uniform solutions, but will increase the burden weighing on each jurisdiction to justify the solutions it prefers in the light of other, alternative solutions developed by other jurisdictions facing similar circumstances.

This greater 'freedom' left to the national authorities thus comes at a price, and it is not unconditional. The choices that they are allowed to make depend upon these choices being justified, and it will be for the European Court to assess whether the justifications provided are sufficiently convincing. Not taking into account solutions developed by other jurisdictions that achieve a better conciliation between the requirements of fundamental rights and the public policy objectives that lead to certain restrictions being imposed could be seen as a deficiency that is 'manifest' enough to trigger the intervention of the ECtHR. This would imply, for instance, a doctrine of proportionality according to which domestic courts would assess the restrictions imposed on human rights, not only based on the classical test (asking in essence whether the legitimate aim could be achieved by less restrictive means), but also taking into account solutions developed elsewhere (and therefore asking the author of the challenged measure whether such solutions have been considered and, if they have not been adopted, why).

Thus, one specific justification that could be required from the national courts claiming the benefit of trust is that when confronted with an allegation of violation of Convention rights resulting from the adoption of a particular measure by national authorities, they examine whether the same objective could have been achieved at a lesser cost to the rights concerned—ie, with less severe limitations being imposed on the said rights—*by examining how other states have been addressing the same issue*. The greater diversity of solutions adopted across the Council of Europe Member States could then be transformed into an asset: far from constituting an obstacle to the adoption of uniform solutions, it would become a condition for collective learning to take place. This is what Cohen and Sabel call 'deliberative coordination', which they describe as 'deliberation among units of decision-making directed both to learning jointly from their several experiences and improving the institutional possibilities of such learning—a system with continuous discussion across separate units about current best practice and better ways of ascertaining it'.[60]

[59] J Cohen and CF Sabel, 'Global Democracy?' (2005) 37 *New York University Journal of International Law and Politics* 763, 781.
[60] Ibid.

IV. CONCLUSION

There is an analogy between the shift proposed here in the nature of the control exercised by the ECtHR and a similar shift proposed a generation ago in the debates concerning judicial review in domestic constitutional law. We now understand better that judicial control exercised on the basis of certain constitutional norms is not necessarily opposed to democratic self-determination founded on the principle of majoritarian decision making: 'representation-reinforcing' theories of judicial review and the New Public Law Movement have shown since the 1980s that this opposition was in many cases a false one, based both (as public choice theory was emphasising at the same time in political science) on an idealisation of the democratic process and on a misunderstanding of the reasons, resulting from democratic failure, why the intervention of courts might be required to uphold the social compact.[61] For very similar reasons, we now must acknowledge that there is no necessary trade-off between a strong monitoring role of the ECtHR and a greater space for deliberation at the domestic level, based on the comparison of the best practices developed in the full range of Council of Europe Member States.

It would be neither legally justified nor politically opportune to maintain the *Bosphorus* doctrine in its current form as a doctrine that places the EU in a privileged position and that, instead of treating the CJEU as a constitutional court comparable to any other, somehow inexplicably defers to its assessments more generously than to similar assessments made by its national counterparts. But if, for obvious political reasons, *Bosphorus* must have a second life, then it is time perhaps to transform it into something that would be both more promising and more theoretically sound. It can become a doctrine by which the ECtHR expresses its confidence in the decisions reached by independent courts established within the different legal orders that it supervises, provided that certain procedural conditions are met and that these courts faithfully base their decisions on the body of jurisprudence gradually developed by the European Court itself, and meet the test of justifying their decisions, taking into account the best practices available across all parties to the Convention. If this is what the second life of *Bosphorus* looks like in a few years time, the accession of the EU to the ECHR will appear, in retrospect, as having accelerated a shift towards a new relationship between the ECtHR and the domestic courts: one that is more respectful of decision making at the national level, that strengthens the legitimacy of international judicial control of human rights and that leads to a richer and more deliberative breed of case law. The wide diversity across the Member States of the Council of Europe will then appear not as a liablity, but as an asset; the principle of subsidiarity will be seen as a tool to strengthen rights rather than used as a pretext to weaken them; and the doctrine of the margin of appreciation will be considered as a first but still under-theorised attempt to build an architecture in which courts do not compete against one another, but instead enter into a dialogue with one another based on a sound division of labour between them. It is a future such as this that this chapter has outlined.

[61] See JH Ely, *Democracy and Distrust: A Theory of Judicial Review* (Cambridge, MA, Harvard University Press, 1980); and, for major contributions to drawing the implications from public choice theory on constitutional law, the review by DA Farber and PP Frickey, 'The Jurisprudence of Public Choice' (1987) 65 *California Law Review* 873 and the follow-up volume by the same authors, *Law and Public Choice: A Critical Introduction* (Chicago, University of Chicago Press, 1991); as well as WN Eskridge and G Peller, 'The New Public Law Movement: Moderation as a Postmodern Cultural Form' (1991) 89 *Michigan Law Review* 707.

13

The (Geo-)Politics of the EU Accession to the ECHR: Democracy and Distrust in the Wider Europe

ROBERT HARMSEN*

I. INTRODUCTION

AS THE PRESENT volume attests, a burgeoning legal literature is continuing to develop around the possible accession of the European Union (EU) to the European Convention on Human Rights (ECHR). This literature has extensively explored such themes as the highly complex issues surrounding the relationship between the European Court of Human Rights (ECtHR) and the Court of Justice of the European Union (CJEU), the potential impact of accession on different areas of law and the positioning of national courts relative to their European counterparts. Yet, this substantial body of scholarship and commentary has largely neglected the wider politico-legal contexts within which accession would have to take place. Ultimately, the question of the accession of the EU to the ECHR cannot simply be reduced to a series of comparatively technical questions concerned with inter-court relationships, but must also engage the wider set of political relationships which bind (or not) 'the Europe of the 28' and the 'Europe of the 47'. Moreover, accession cannot be divorced from a concern with the wider dynamics of human rights protection in Europe and the manner in which the specific terms of any accession arrangement might—or might not—enhance such protection in the round.

This chapter provides a modest initial attempt to address this important gap in the literature, probing the wider (geo-)political questions raised by accession. It does so, in the first instance, with reference to the conceptual registers surrounding the idea of 'constitutional pluralism' as initially developed in the EU law literature and as latterly extended to wider spheres of public international law.[1] Constitutional pluralism—or, more exactly, its constituent parts—are presently used as a convenient heuristic device, allowing for relatively sharp portraits of underlying system dynamics to be quickly drawn. As such, it should be

* Professor of Political Science, University of Luxembourg.

[1] For an excellent recent survey of the constitutional pluralism literature as regards both the EU and wider arenas, see M Avbelj and J Komárek (eds), *Constitutional Pluralism in the European Union and Beyond* (Oxford, Hart Publishing, 2012).

explicitly acknowledged that this chapter is not intended to be a contribution to the rich debates surrounding the idea of constitutional pluralism itself.[2]

More specifically, the chapter takes a simple dichotomy between 'pluralism' and 'constitutionalism' as its starting point—opting for comparatively broad-brush understandings of both terms in line with its heuristic intent. 'Pluralism' is thus taken to refer to situations of heterarchy, in which no final arbitral authority is recognised. The overall politico-legal order, in situations of pluralism, is consequently deemed to function (or not) on the basis of strategies of reciprocal accommodation by comparably placed actors who retain their autonomy as regards one another. 'Constitutionalism', by way of contrast, is taken to be defined by a recognition of hierarchy. In a constitutional order, an ultimate arbitral authority is recognised as the basis of the system, though this need not imply a traditional state structure. Indeed, a concept of 'primacy'—limitatively vesting interpretive authority to the extent necessary for the maintenance of system integrity—better captures the essence of constitutionalism as presently used than more traditional, expansively defined notions of hierarchy.

Relative to this simple dichotomy, the next two sections of this chapter successively underline the limits of a pluralist analysis for understanding the operation of the Convention system and the wider relationships between the EU and ECHR politico-legal orders.[3] The Strasbourg Court's role as the 'constitutional guarantor' of the European human rights system is correspondingly (re-)affirmed, grounded particularly in relation to the scope and severity of the human rights challenges found across the full pan-European community of participating states. Having established this constitutional logic, section IV then moves to a consideration of what this might imply for the future institutional development of the ECtHR, linking the accession debate to ongoing debates concerned with the reform of the ECHR system. This final move introduces a strong concern with 'dialogue' as a cornerstone of the functioning of the ECHR system, suggesting a redefinition of the Court's contemporary role more in keeping with its initial mission as a guarantor of liberal democracy. The conclusion brings together the different elements of the analysis, emphasising both the opportunities and the risks of accession when seen in its wider (geo-) political context.

II. THE LIMITS OF PLURALISM I: THE ECHR SYSTEM

In this first stage of the argument, attention is focused on the politico-legal system surrounding the ECHR. The geographical enlargement of the Convention community is shown to have taken it beyond the bounds of what a pluralist understanding may

[2] In particular, it should be noted that the present chapter, focused on patterns of institutional relationships, does not engage with the questions raised by more radical or 'epistemic' forms of pluralism (to use Walker's term) concerned with claims over the underlying incommensurability of different politico-legal orders. See N Walker, 'The Idea of Constitutional Pluralism', (2002) 65 *MLR* 317. See also further Lucas Lixinski's contribution in ch 14 to this volume.

[3] For reasons of space, this chapter does not address the question of the applicability of pluralist analyses in the context of EU law. Logically, if both of the limbs of the present argument hold—demonstrating the need for a constitutional grounding of the ECHR system and of its extension to the EU—then the question of the nature of EU law is largely immaterial as regards the overall architecture of the system. A full picture would, nonetheless, require that this intra-EU dynamic also be appropriately explored.

reasonably bear, pointing to the need for the Strasbourg Court's role to be conceived in constitutional terms if the system as a whole is to sustain an intrinsic legitimacy.

The starting point for the present analysis is Nico Krisch's seminal pluralist analysis of the Convention system, first published as a 2008 article[4] and latterly reprised in his 2010 monograph *Beyond Constitutionalism*.[5] Krisch's account of the Strasbourg system combines substantial empirical/pragmatic and normative/prescriptive elements. On the one hand, pointing to a number of key instances of national court dissonance, Krisch makes the case that the development and 'success' of the ECHR—in contrast to a prevailing constitutionalist narrative—is better understood in pluralist terms. For him, it is the give and take between national courts and the ECtHR, including the latter's ability to accommodate these differences, which accounts for the comparatively wide acceptance of the system. From this, he goes on to draw a further prescriptive lesson—underlining the beneficial effects of this flexibility, in contrast to the stronger political reactions which a more rigid constitutional positioning would risk engendering.

Krisch's questioning of a certain 'Strasbourg orthodoxy' unquestionably allows for a degree of new insight. His work stands alongside a limited but growing body of scholarship which highlights often overlooked instances of national dissonance—or markedly differentiated understandings of the Convention[6]—which must be better incorporated into our overall analysis of the functioning of the ECHR system and its limits. Equally, Krisch's work allows for a commendably well-grounded contextualisation of the developmental dynamics of the Strasbourg system relative to a wider pluralist reading of the evolution of selected areas of public international law.

Nevertheless, Krisch's analysis of the system also suffers from a number of shortcomings. He appears to under-estimate the importance of key specificities of the Convention system. Notably, little attention is paid to its essentially 'subsidiary' character—and attendant focus on the maintenance of a *minimum* standard of human rights protection, rather than a full-fledged 'harmonisation of law'. This leads to something of a misinterpretation of the role and place of 'flexibility' within the system. Much of that which Krisch sees as a pluralist accommodation of national differences by the Strasbourg authorities may equally—if not more—plausibly be read in constitutionalist terms. The (admittedly contested) concept of the margin of appreciation is, at the end of the day, a *constitutional* principle—recognising the need for a balance to be struck between a respect for national diversity and the protection of European standards, and crucially vesting the striking of this balance with the ECtHR. As appositely argued by the former ECtHR registrar and current judge Paul Mahoney, the margin of appreciation derives from the inherent logic of the Convention system and represents 'the theory of constitutional review which the Strasbourg bodies have developed to delineate the boundaries of their proper area of concern in discharge of their international adjudicative function'.[7]

[4] N Krisch, 'The Open Architecture of European Human Rights Law' (2008) 71 *MLR* 183.

[5] N Krisch, *Beyond Constitutionalism: The Pluralist Structure of Postnational Law* (Oxford, Oxford University Press, 2010).

[6] See S Hennette-Vauchez, 'Constitutional v International? When Unified Reformatory Rationales Mistmatch the Plural Paths of Legitimacy of ECHR Law' in J Christoffersen and M Rask Madsen (eds), *The European Court of Human Rights between Law and Politics* (Oxford, Oxford University Press, 2011).

[7] P Mahoney, 'Marvellous Richness of Diversity or Invidious Cultural Relativism?' (1998) 19 *Human Rights Law Journal* 1, 6.

The central shortcoming of Krisch's analysis, however, stems from his failure to deal with the dramatically transformed post-enlargement reality of the Convention system.[8] The national cases studied are all West European. Moreover, he himself notes that the 'success' of the regime that he describes may largely be attributed to 'favourable political circumstances', going on to comment: 'The ECHR benefited much from the geopolitical environment, as it allowed West European democracies to demonstrate their commitment to human rights in the face of the Soviet challenge.'[9] Yet, clearly, this geopolitical environment has fundamentally changed—and the 'fair weather' Convention system, which took root within it, no longer exists in those terms. Following successive enlargements of the Council of Europe, the balance of the system has decisively tipped. Cases from the 'old' West European democracies now make up only about 20 per cent of the Court's docket.[10] Moreover, a small minority of contracting parties now routinely account for the vast bulk of the Court's caseload. In 2013, five countries alone (Russia, Italy, Ukraine, Turkey and Serbia) were responsible for two-thirds of the petitions referred to a judicial formation.

Faced with this very different reality, it is correspondingly necessary to rethink the scope and limits of the possibilities for dialogue at the heart of a pluralist analysis. One must account for the diversity of human rights situations in the contemporary Convention community—recognising the different roles that the Strasbourg institutions are called upon to play in relation to different national contexts and the implications of this for the position of the Court in the wider (constitutional) architecture of the system. Here, drawing on an earlier publication, I would suggest that this diversity may be understood in terms of a broad tri-partite categorisation, distinguishing between established democracies, post-transition democracies and states exhibiting serious structural difficulties.[11]

In the case of the more established democracies, a pluralist reading of the Convention system could still broadly hold. In these cases, without wishing to diminish the always-present possibility of substantial difficulties arising (particularly in the context of the post-9/11 'security state'), the main role of the Strasbourg Court is likely to continue being that of an evolutive standard setter. Consistent with the pre-1989 development of the system, the core dynamic here is that of comparatively open dialogues progressively allowing for the adaptation of Convention rights to evolving national practice—in the broad if by no means unproblematic sense of a 'progress of human rights'.[12]

Post-transition democracies offer a somewhat different picture. In these cases, the fundamentals of liberal democracy appear firmly secured, but in a situation where aspects of institutional structures or practices do not (yet) fully comply with established European norms. In this situation, the role of the Strasbourg Court is twofold. On the one hand,

[8] Strikingly, the only reference to the more serious instances of systemic dysfunction which the Convention system has faced is buried in a footnote where the author makes brief reference to the cases of Greece (under the colonels), Turkey and Russia. See Krisch (n 5) 144n.

[9] Ibid 143.

[10] Figures taken from R Harmsen, 'The Transformation of the ECHR Legal Order and the Post-Enlargement Challenges Facing the European Court of Human Rights', in G Martinico and O Pollicino (eds), *The National Judicial Treatment of the ECHR and EU Laws: A Comparative Constitutional Perspective* (Groningen, Europe Law Publishing, 2010) 30–32.

[11] Ibid.

[12] The potential perils of conceiving of 'evolutive interpretation' only in terms of a 'one-way street' have been revealingly probed in a number of publications by Luzius Wildhaber since his retirement from the Court. See, for example, L Wildhaber, 'Rethinking the European Court of Human Rights' in Christoffersen and Madsen (n 6) 213–16.

it has significantly acted as a buttress of democratic transition—in particular, crafting a jurisprudence which has proven singularly supportive of national constitutional courts in transitional situations as they sought to anchor both their own role and the wider frameworks of constitutional governance.[13] On the other hand, the Court has also acted as an adjudicator of transition. In this vein, the question is essentially that of the extent to which a state may provisionally be accorded a wider margin of appreciation as regards the restriction of particular rights in light of the specific exigencies of the process of democratic transition itself.[14] The logics of these roles are not obviously pluralist in the same way as may be argued in the case of more established democracies. In essence, while dialogues are possible as regards the mode or speed of attaining particular standards, the standards themselves are not an object of discussion in this view. Nevertheless, one must acknowledge the substantial scope for constructive dialogue and accommodation between the Strasbourg institutions and their national counterparts in these cases—arguably pointing to something of a pluralist ethos, as well as underlining the (often under-estimated) role of the Council of Europe in processes of democratic transition.

The limits of a pluralist interpretation are, nevertheless, clearly exceeded in the case of those situations falling in the third category: states exhibiting serious structural difficulties. At the extreme, this includes situations of armed conflict or where there has been a complete breakdown of effective political or legal order. More typically, such situations encompass instances of fundamental political or legal dysfunction—cases where processes of democratic transition have stalled or failed, or in which a functioning independent judiciary does not exist. If varying in severity, such cases nonetheless share the defining property of there being an *im*possibility of meaningful dialogue between the Strasbourg authorities and their national counterparts in the terms demanded by a pluralist account. In some instances, the egregiousness of the violations themselves, including acts of mass violence or torture, precludes the possibility of a dialogue—there being no margin of appreciation under the logic of the Convention system nor a basis in human rights law for a court to do anything other than establish (often-contested) facts and apportion responsibility.[15] The cases of fundamental political or legal dysfunction pose a different problem, which is essentially that of the paradox of externally driven judicial reform. Basically, the object of the reform (the judiciary) is also the necessary instrument of its realisation—creating the (interim) difficulty of finding effective national relays for the anchoring of European/international norms.[16] In the present context, this more specifically points to the absence, in a number of national cases, of viable national judicial interlocutors for the Strasbourg Court. For a pluralist order to function, national judiciaries must possess the independence and the capacity to engage in meaningful dialogue on the basis

[13] See W Sadurski, *Constitutionalism and the Enlargement of Europe* (Oxford, Oxford University Press, 2012). Sadurski interestingly contrasts the strongly positive reception of the Convention by newly (re-)established constitutional courts in the region with the more contentious patterns which have emerged as regards national judicial acceptance of the supremacy of EU law.

[14] See M Varju, 'Transition as a Concept of European Human Rights Law' (2009) *European Human Rights Law Review* 170.

[15] Questions do nonetheless arise, well beyond the limited scope of the present chapter, concerned with the relationship of human rights law to both humanitarian law on the one hand and concepts of transitional justice on the other. See further J Sweeney, *The European Court of Human Rights in the Post-Cold War Era: Universality in Transition* (London, Routledge, 2012).

[16] See, for example, M Mendelski, 'EU-Driven Reforms in Romania: A Success Story?' (2012) 28 *East European Politics* 23.

of an autonomous assessment of the cases before them. If this is not the case, an appeal to pluralism risks simply becoming a bid to legitimate human rights abuses by courts which remain subservient to other national authorities in non-democratic contexts.

This also, then, returns us to the discussion of the need for the European Court of Human Rights to be able to exercise a constitutional authority so as to secure the overall legitimacy of the system. The Strasbourg Court must be able to act as a guarantor of minimum absolute standards of human rights protection (particularly but not exclusively as regards Articles 2–4 ECHR), as well as in wider terms of the possibility of dialogue itself. In other words, the European Court must be able to adjudicate whether its interlocutors enjoy the conditions necessary to participate freely in a dialogue with it, which implies a logically prior standard that cannot itself be subject to a pluralist logic without potentially undermining the overall credibility of the system.

This perhaps rather bald assertion may be concretely teased out with reference to the *Görgülü* controversy that Krisch takes as the starting point of his analysis. In *Görgülü*, the German Federal Constitutional Court explicitly set out the limits of the Convention's binding effect within the domestic legal order.[17] At one and the same time, the Karlsruhe judges stressed that Convention compliance should be regarded as the norm, while qualifying this by equally holding that such compliance remained subject to the consistency of Strasbourg Court decisions with any supervening provisions of the domestic order. In effect, the Court affirmed that the final balancing of competing rights, as a dimension of the 'Kompetenz-Kompetenz', must remain in national hands. The decision, unsurprisingly, generated relatively sharp criticism from Strasbourg—though in terms which were perhaps not fully appreciated. Much of the criticism directed at the Karlsruhe Court related not to the application of the Convention in Germany (where the generalised norm of Convention compliance offered a practicable, if perhaps not ideal modus vivendi), but rather with the possible wider negative consequences which such a precedent might have elsewhere. Noting how the decision might be seized upon in other countries, the then Court President Luzius Wildhaber pointedly expressed his wish that the German Constitutional Court would develop 'a more European sense of responsibility'.[18] Again, it is the maintenance of the overall legitimacy of the European human rights system that points to the need for a constitutional understanding of the Strasbourg Court's role. This rationale also comes to the fore, as discussed in the following section, in understanding the articulation of the relationship between the EU and ECHR legal orders.

III. THE LIMITS OF PLURALISM II: THE RELATIONSHIP OF THE EU AND ECHR POLITICO-LEGAL ORDERS

This stage of the argument shifts from a consideration of the Convention system alone to an examination of the relationship between the ECHR and EU politico-legal orders, with pluralist models again deployed as instruments to understand underlying political dynamics. Here, a very similar pattern emerges to that seen in the previous section. In essence, while pluralist accounts are seen as providing a potentially well-grounded framework for conceiving of the relationship between the two European courts, such accounts

[17] BVerfGE 111, 307, 2 BvR 1481/01, 14.10.2004.

[18] 'Das tut mir weh', interview with *Der Spiegel* (15 November 2004) 54.

do not fare as well when taken beyond the limited confines of Luxembourg and Strasbourg. The relationship of the wider politico-legal orders is seen again to point to the need for a guarantor of the (pre-)conditions of constitutional order itself, re-establishing the case in much the same terms for a (certain) primacy to be accorded to the ECtHR.

Turning again to the relevant literature for an appropriate starting point, the case for a pluralist reading of the EU/ECHR relationship is well made by Charles Sabel and Oliver Gerstenberg. In a 2010 article, they paint a detailed portrait of an emerging 'coordinate constitutional order' in which the CJEU, the ECtHR and the national courts are engaged in an ongoing dialogue bounded by the terms of a Rawlsian 'overlapping consensus'.[19] Within this scenario, courts are seen to display a mutual respect for one another's decisions insofar as these do not violate the core principles of the constitutional identity of the receiving order. A working modus vivendi may thus be sustained in the absence of an overarching agreement or hierarchical enforcement mechanism, which may further—through dialogical enrichment—prove to be rights enhancing in the round.

As noted at the outset, such a pluralist logic may readily provide a means for conceiving of the relationship between the Strasbourg and Luxembourg Courts. There is a broad overlapping consensus as regards fundamental rights between the two courts. Equally, a culture of judicial co-operation or comity has (imperfectly) developed over time, with the two courts showing a degree of empathetic awareness of one another's jurisprudence and the systemic conditions under which judgments are made. This remains, of course, subject to necessarily variable patterns of politico-institutional interaction; a degree of 'diplomacy' is demanded on both sides, which may be punctuated by instances of 'brittleness' or periods of 'fragility'.[20] Nevertheless, the relationship between the two courts should, a priori, be manageable within a pluralist framework, and if well managed has a strong potential for mutual enrichment.

This picture, however, fundamentally changes when one moves to a consideration of the relationship between the wider EU and ECHR politico-legal orders. It is evident across the full pan-European spectrum of contracting parties that an overlapping consensus does not securely exist. As discussed in the previous section, the Convention community encompasses a significant number of members where the fundamentals of democratic governance have not (as yet) been firmly anchored. As also discussed above, this demands that the Strasbourg institutions be able to act unambiguously as guarantors of those democratic fundamentals as well as of a minimum standard of human rights protection. Correspondingly, the terms of the accession of the EU to the ECHR must not be conceived in such a way as to undermine this systemic integrity. This entails, in the first instance, that the principle of the essential equality of all contracting parties not be breached through the acceptance of an unwarranted 'exceptional' status for the EU within the Convention system. The principle of the equal treatment of the contracting parties clearly established, there must further be a comparably clear understanding of the primacy of the Strasbourg Court within this arrangement. Each of these principles is dealt with in turn below.

[19] CF Sabel and O Gerstenberg, 'Constitutionalising an Overlapping Consensus: The ECJ and the Emergence of an Overlapping Constitutional Order', (2010) 16 *European Law Journal* 511.

[20] See L Scheeck, 'Diplomatic Intrusions, Dialogues and Fragile Equilibriums: The European Court as a Constitutional Actor of the European Union' in Christoffersen and Madsen (n 6).

A. The Principle of Equal Treatment

The issue of the equality of treatment of the contracting parties has figured prominently in the accession negotiations, as the non-EU Member States of the Council of Europe have raised concerns as regards some of the demands being made by the EU, notably as driven by the Court of Justice. The Russian Federation, for example, issued a statement at the time of the June 2012 negotiation meeting emphasising that any agreement must ensure that: 'All member states are equal parties to the Convention after [the] accession of the EU, and all parties will remain in [an] equal situation with respect to all aspects of the functioning of the Convention.'[21] Much the same point was again made by a group of 16 non-EU Member States—the self-designated 'NEUMS'—who presented a common paper to the January 2013 negotiation meeting.[22] Here again it was stressed that: 'Accession should, to the largest extent possible, be based on the principle of equal footing between the EU and the 47 HCP [High Contracting Parties]'. Furthermore: 'Differences between States which are members of the EU and States which are not members of the EU should be avoided.' While much of this discussion concerns comparatively technical issues, these issues cannot be divorced from core questions of the functioning of the post-accession politico-legal order. As Aida Torres Pérez rightly stresses in her contribution in chapter three to the present volume, which critically analyses the Court of Justice's apparently incontrovertible demand for a 'prior involvement' mechanism, 'this mechanism is intimately linked to the principles of autonomy, subsidiarity and, ultimately, the role of the Luxembourg Court vis-a-vis the Strasbourg Court'.[23]

The question of equal treatment also presently arises in Olivier De Schutter's analysis of the possible fate of the Strasbourg Court's *Bosphorus*[24] jurisprudence in a post-accession scenario. De Schutter joins with other commentators in arguing that the maintenance of *Bosphorus* after accession would be 'legally unjustified and politically inopportune'.[25] As he convincingly makes the case, both the 'weak' option of maintaining the existing presumption of equivalent protection as regards the non-discretionary implementation of EU secondary law by Member States and a fortiori the 'strong' option of extending this presumption to acts of the EU institutions would appear to run contrary to the very purpose

[21] Second Meeting between the CDDH Ad Hoc Negotiation Group and the European Commission on the Accession of the European Union to the European Convention on Human Rights, Relevant Excerpts from the Report of the 75th Meeting of the CDDH, 4 July 2012, 47+1(2012)002, Appendix VI. Available at: www.coe.int/t/dghl/standardsetting/hrpolicy/accession/Working_documents/47_1(2012)02_Extracts_CDDH_Report_EN.pdf.

[22] Fourth Meeting between the CDDH Ad Hoc Negotiation Group and the European Commission on the Accession of the European Union to the European Convention on Human Rights, Meeting Report, 23 January 2013, 47+1(2013)R04, Appendix III. Available at: www.coe.int/t/dghl/standardsetting/hrpolicy/accession/Meeting_reports/Web_47_1(2013)R04_EN_final.pdf.

[23] Torres Pérez, ch 3 in the present volume.

[24] ECtHR, *Bosphorus Hava Yollari Turizm ve Ticaret Anonim Şirkett v Ireland*, App No 45036/98 (2005) 42 EHRR 1. As discussed in detail elsewhere in this volume, the Court essentially held that the non-discretionary implementation of an international obligation would be deemed as Convention compliant insofar as the international organisation in question (presently the EU) provided for an 'equivalent protection' of fundamental rights as regards both the substantive guarantees offered and the mechanisms of control. Once made, this presumption could be rebutted in a particular case only if a 'manifest deficiency' were to come to light.

[25] De Schutter, ch 12 in the present volume. See further T Lock, 'EU Accession to the ECHR: Implications for Judicial Review in Strasbourg' (2010) 35 *European Law Review* 777 at 797–98; and P De Hert and F Korenica, 'The Doctrine of Equivalent Protection: Its Life and Legitimacy before and after the European Union's Accession to the European Convention on Human Rights' (2012) 13 *German Law Journal* 874 (arguing, in a somewhat different vein, that the doctrine may persist *rationae materiae* even if formally abandoned).

of accession, in effect perpetuating a situation in which differential treatment is accorded in the absence of a principled justification.

De Schutter further pushes beyond much of the existing debate with his comparatively radical suggestion that this problem of differential treatment be resolved not by a reversal of *Bosphorus*, but rather by its generalisation—allowing other contracting parties, where merited, to benefit from a presumption of equivalent protection which would also diminish the need or at least the intensity of scrutiny by the Strasbourg Court. This latter proposition potentially opens up a further issue of equal treatment, which goes to the heart of the Court's legitimacy. One could certainly envisage a version of De Schutter's proposition predicated on a *situational* logic—ie, that the Court would exercise different degrees of control or engage in different forms of dialogue in light of the different situations which variably present themselves across the Member States. This, indeed, represents something of a 'retour aux sources' to the original rationale of the Convention and the argument for a more 'formative' jurisprudence developed in the following section of this chapter. Such situational variations should not, however, be confused with a *categorical* logic, in which different categories of Member States/contracting parties are identified, through either judicial or political processes, with the Court then differentially treating cases according to the category of member from which they originate.[26] This latter manner of proceeding would breach the principle of equality, potentially calling into question the legitimacy and cohesiveness of the system. Individual states would risk being stigmatised. Moreover, governments already known to be unsympathetic to the Convention system could politically exploit such categorisations as evidence of 'unfair treatment' before domestic audiences, sapping support for the system and effectively demobilising individual claimants. Conversely, at the same time, instances of serious problems in states given a 'certificate of good conduct' would also risk escaping control. A creeping inequity—perceived or real—could only have a corrosive effect on the overall system.

B. The Primacy of the ECtHR

The second core principle of the post-accession dispensation must be that of the primacy of the Strasbourg Court, leading us back to our initial interrogation of the wider limits of applicability of a pluralist model. This may presently be explicated in relation to a critical application of Mattias Kumm's conception of 'cosmopolitan constitutionalism', which provides an interesting example of a pluralist frame of analysis first developed in the context of EU law[27] now more widely applied to the development (and limits) of different forms of

[26] A system predicated on such formal differentiation has been proposed by Rusen Ergec, who argues for a generalisation of the Court's *Bosphorus* jurisprudence through the adoption of a 'dual supervision system' in which states deemed to meet an equivalent protection test would largely escape Strasbourg scrutiny. Ergec suggests that such a system might be operationalised through a two-stage procedure involving either the Court or a 'panel of Wise Persons' together with the Council of Europe's Parliamentary Assembly. While having the merit of both decisional clarity and an engagement with the wider Council of Europe system, it is nonetheless difficult to see how Professor Ergec's proposal would escape the difficulties outlined above. See R Ergec, 'The European Court of Human Rights: Quo Vadis?', available at: http://papers.ssrn.com/sol3/papers.cfm?abstract_id=2254186. A version is also to be published in the Mélanges Marc Bossuyt.

[27] M Kumm, 'The Jurisprudence of Constitutional Conflict: Constitutional Supremacy in Europe before and after the Constitutional Treaty' (2005) 11 *European Law Journal* 262.

international legal order.[28] As regards this wider international application, Kumm himself succinctly presents the core precepts of his conception of a pluralist legal order in the following terms:

> The refusal of a legal order to recognize itself as hierarchically integrated into a more comprehensive legal order is justified, if that more comprehensive order suffers from structural legitimacy deficits that the less comprehensive order does not suffer from. The concrete norms governing the management of the interface between legal orders are justified, if they are designed to ensure that the legal conditions for liberal-democratic governance are secured. In practice that means that there are functional considerations that generally establish a presumption in favour of applying the law of the more extensive legal order over the law of the more parochial one, unless there are countervailing concerns of sufficient weight that suggest otherwise.[29]

These terms bear unpacking. On the one hand, the inspiration of the model is broadly Kantian. It is predicated on the existence supervening principles of democracy and the rule of law (the 'legal conditions for liberal-democratic governance') whose more extensive international expressions are normally to be accorded priority by other jurisdictions. On the other hand, the model also incorporates a type of 'democratic localism', in which it is ultimately lower-level (national) authorities which act as a check on the international level, having a recognised right of dissent where they hold that the higher-level suffers from deficiencies sufficient to impugn the legitimacy of its decisions. Although the architecture of the system appears based on a presumption in favour of the international level, the final locus of decisional authority thus nonetheless remains nationally rooted. In terms of its institutional consequences, the framework essentially recasts in somewhat more abstract terms an established pattern of municipal court practice regarding forms of European or international law, most prominently identified with the *Solange* and *Görgülü* jurisprudence of the German Constitutional Court or the *Kadi* decision (on a 'rights-based' reading)[30] of the CJEU.

Kumm himself explicitly recognises the limitations of the model. He acknowledges that 'constitutional pluralism is no panacea and is not always attractive', going on to stress in terms consonant with the present argument that 'any pluralism described in *constitutionalist* terms presupposes a shared commitment to constitutionalist principles'.[31] In more general terms, he also comments that 'constitutional pluralism is not inherently superior to hierarchical constitutionalism'[32]—seeing this as an essentially context-dependent determination.

This then returns us to our more immediate context. It is clear, first, that the necessary constitutionalist consensus does not exist across the full range of contracting parties in a manner which would allow for the unfettered operation of a pluralist principle of organisation in the terms described by Kumm. That which is intended as a democratic localism risks, in effect, becoming a form of nullification doctrine where, at the limit, the principles

[28] M Kumm, 'Rethinking Constitutional Authority: On the Structure and Limits of Constitutional Pluralism' in Avbelj and Komárek (n 1).

[29] Ibid 43 and 63.

[30] See G Anthony, 'EU Law's Fundamental Rights Regime and Post-National Constitutionalism: *Kadi*'s Global Setting' in P Birkinshaw and M Varney (eds), *The European Union Legal Order after Lisbon* (Alphen aan den Rijn, Kluwer, 2010).

[31] Kumm (n 28) 65, emphasis in original.

[32] Ibid.

of liberal democratic governance are themselves challenged. Second, it is then in relation to this that the contextual argument is made for a form of hierarchical constitutionalism—presently vesting in the higher level the institutional locus of decisional authority as regards the permissible limits of any derogation from established standards. This concretely implies the primacy of the Strasbourg Court and its jurisprudence within the overall post-accession architecture of the human rights system. It should not, however, be read as necessarily implying a simple transposition of existing practice to any new dispensation. As discussed in the following section, the accession debate offers a distinctive opportunity to engage with wider debates concerning the reform of the Convention system, rethinking the role of the Strasbourg Court in relation to evolving circumstances and underlying precepts of judicial legitimacy.

IV. (RE-)POSITIONING THE STRASBOURG COURT

Debates concerning the accession of the EU to the ECHR have thus far remained surprisingly isolated from the wider, ongoing discussions concerning the reform of the Convention system.[33] Yet, the two discussions necessarily intersect—and point in much the same direction as regards the longer term (re-)positioning of the Strasbourg Court.[34] The contours of both reform processes suggest the need to rethink the role of the ECtHR in more 'modest' terms, re-centring its activities on the protection and development of the core principles of liberal democratic governance. In effect, the touchstone of reform becomes something of a 'retour aux sources', in which the initial purpose of the Convention—to act as a guarantor of European democracy—is returned to the foreground.[35] The implications of such a re-orientation are sketched out below—broadly (re-)integrating a pluralist emphasis on dialogue into a constitutionally grounded framework.

More specifically, the re-orientation of the Court is first explicated in this section relative to wider models of judicial review. This analysis draws particularly on a number of seminal contributions to established North American debates that seek to ground the legitimacy of judicial intervention within wider conceptions of the functioning of the democratic process. In the following section, attention is then focused more directly on contemporary discussions of the reform of the Convention system, with particular reference to the 2012 Brighton Declaration. Throughout, the portrait emerges of the Court as a more 'democratic' institution, in which a renewed emphasis on dialogue and deliberation is seen as a means to ground its legitimacy as the central institution of the European human rights regime, while shifting the primary responsibility for enforcement back to a necessarily national locus.[36]

[33] On the longer-term trajectory of the reform discussions surrounding the Convention system, see R Harmsen, 'The Reform of the Convention System: Institutional Restructuring and the (Geo-)Politics of Human Rights' in Christoffersen and Madsen (n 6).

[34] See also De Schutter's contribution in ch 12 to this volume.

[35] On the 'democratic' origins of the Convention, see E Bates, *The Evolution of the European Convention of Human Rights: From its Inception to the Creation of a Permanent Court of Human Rights* (Oxford, Oxford University Press, 2010) 44–76; and A Moravcsik, 'The Origins of Human Rights Regimes: Democratic Delegation in Postwar Europe' (2000) 54 *International Organization* 217.

[36] This logic of (re-)balancing has been innovatively analysed by Jonas Christoffersen relative to what he terms a logic of 'primarity'. See J Christoffersen, *Fair Balance: A Study of Proportionality, Subsidiarity and Primarity in the European Convention on Human Rights* (Leiden, Martinus Nijhoff, 2009).

A. The Judicial Role in Fostering Democratic Dialogue

This 'democratic turn' in the position of the Strasbourg Court is perhaps most readily suggestive of an increased emphasis on process-based forms of review. The logic here would largely be consonant with that famously outlined by John Hart Ely in his 1980 study of the judicial review in the US, *Democracy and Distrust*.[37] Navigating between the shoals of the 'interpretivist' and 'non-interprevist' positions which have long structured (and polarised) US debates on judicial review, Ely put forward the case for something of a modest middle ground in which judicial interventions in the political process would essentially be limited to those instances where they were necessary to maintain the integrity and fairness of the process itself. His theory of judicial review is thus essentially 'representation reinforcing', with the courts broadly called upon to act so as to 'police the process of political representation', 'clear the channels of political change' and 'facilitate the representation of minorities'. If the specific terms of Ely's model are rooted in American constitutional history, a broad transposition to the European context is nonetheless easily imaginable. The lesson in Convention terms points to a more robust development by the Strasbourg Court of Article 3, Protocol 1 guaranteeing 'free elections'. The Court has historically shown itself to be rather timid in the application of this article, according states a wide margin of appreciation in deference to their differing histories, traditions and values. Yet, while a degree of deference is undeniably appropriate as regards the specific *forms* assumed by democratic electoral systems, a blanket claim of diversity should not be allowed to cloak measures which potentially call into question the fundamental principles of equitable representation. Where there is evidence that the democratic process itself has been seriously impaired, the Court must venture more boldly into this highly sensitive political terrain if is fully to assume its responsibilities.[38]

A more 'democratic' conception of the Strasbourg Court's role cannot, however, be reduced only to a renewed emphasis on process-based judicial review. It should entail a more fundamental rethinking of the judicial role in relation to the wider institutional functioning of liberal democratic governance. In particular, it implies a move away from a simply 'corrective' view of the role of courts towards one which is more broadly 'formative'. Following this logic, the role of courts is principally seen as that of ensuring that the legislature and the executive have fully and openly weighed questions of fundamental rights in arriving at their policy decisions. The emphasis is thus placed on an ongoing dialogue between the judicial branch and the political branches in a dynamic intended to enhance the overall quality of democratic deliberation over time and to ensure that routine decision making becomes deeply embedded in a culture well attuned to fundamental rights considerations. The role of the court becomes less one of sanctioning violations and more one of facilitating debate. In (over-)simplistic terms, the constitutional role of the judiciary is focused on ensuring that 'good' decisions are reached through reasoned and

[37] JH Ely, *Democracy and Distrust* (Cambridge, MA, Harvard University Press, 1980).

[38] The Court has shown itself willing to sanction voting irregularities. See, for example, *Kovach v Ukraine*, App No 39424/02 (2008); and *Namat Aliyev v Azerbaijan*, App No 18705/06 (2010). Nevertheless, it has been markedly more reticent to engage with difficulties which stem from the choice of electoral system or the structure of the electoral process itself. Most notably, in *Yumak and Sadak v Turkey*, App No 10226/03 (2008), the Court found no violation of Protocol 1, Article 3 in the case of Turkey's 10 per cent electoral threshold, although it noted that it appeared 'excessive' and should (in line with Council of Europe recommendations) be lowered. See further Harmsen (n 10) 41–44.

open argument rather than through seeking to impose the 'right' decision on the basis of authoritative legal interpretation.

This view of the judicial role has been prominently developed in North American debates. Writing extra-judicially, US Supreme Court Associate Justice Stephen Breyer has in this vein developed a conception of what he terms 'active liberty'.[39] The term explicitly harkens back to the writings of the nineteenth-century French political philosopher Benjamin Constant, who classically distinguished between the 'liberty of the ancients' (concerned with active participation in civic life) and the 'liberty of the moderns' (focused on the protection of individual rights from state interference). Breyer argues that the 'theme' of this earlier form of liberty—'active liberty'—should be brought more to the forefront in American constitutional interpretation (and wider democratic practice). He thus calls for a corresponding 'judicial modesty', which shows due deference to the sovereign will of the people and encourages the emergence of a self-critical deliberative process. As Breyer summarises his central thesis:

> [W]hile conscious of the importance of modern liberty, I seek to call attention to the combination's other half. I focus primarily upon the active liberty of the ancients, what Constant called the people's right to 'an active and constant participation in political power'. My thesis is that courts should take greater account of the Constitution's democratic nature when they interpret constitutional and statutory texts. That thesis encompasses well-known arguments for judicial modesty: The judge, relative to the legislator, lacks the relevant experience. The 'people' must develop 'the political experience' and they must obtain 'the moral education and stimulus that come from … correcting their own errors'.[40]

A similar conceptualisation of judicial review has emerged in Canada in the form of the 'Charter dialogue' approach. In an influential 1997 article, Peter Hogg and Allison Bushell rebutted critics of the Canadian Supreme Court who had argued that the Court's expansive interpretation of the 1982 Charter of Rights had moved in an 'undemocratic' direction, showing a marked propensity to overrule the decisions of elected legislators.[41] The authors, systematically examining the legislative follow-up to Supreme Court Charter decisions, argued that the Court has rarely blocked legislators from achieving their intended objectives. Rather, the role of the Court appears to be more one of prompting a (re-)consideration of the balances of rights and limitations struck, inducing the legislator to attain their desired objectives in a manner more consistent with the values embodied in the Charter. For Hogg and Bushell, the Court's engagement is thus best conceived as a 'dialogue', in which the judicial role is generally one of ensuring a proper calibration of means rather than one of imposing ends. One may well question if the Canadian Court's jurisprudence fits the dialogical model to the extent argued by the authors. Critics have, in this respect, pointed to possible empirical shortcomings in their analysis, as well as re-engaging the initial normative debate by highlighting what they regard as instances of 'policy distortion' produced by judicial intervention.[42] Beyond the detailed complexities of the Canadian case,

[39] S Breyer, *Active Liberty: Interpreting Our Democratic Constitution* (New York, Alfred A Knopf, 2007); and S Breyer, *Active Liberty: Interpreting a Democratic Constitution* (Oxford, Oxford University Press, 2008).

[40] S Breyer, *Active Liberty: Interpreting Our Democratic Constitution* (n 39) 5. The quotations in the quotation, taken from Benjamin Constant and Chief Justice John Marshall, are as reproduced by Breyer.

[41] PW Hogg and AA Bushell, 'The Charter Dialogue between Courts and Legislators' (1997) 35 *Osgoode Hall Law Journal* 75.

[42] See CP Manfredi and JB Kelly, 'Six Degrees of Dialogue: A Response to Hogg and Bushell' (1999) 37 *Osgoode Hall Law Journal* 513, as well as PW Hogg and AA Thornton, 'Reply to "Six Degrees of Dialogue"' (1999)

however, the ideal type of 'Charter dialogue' nonetheless retains its interest in the present context—providing a further example of a formative model of judicial review.

A transposition of these North American models to the European human rights system is suggestive of a potential re-orientation of the Strasbourg Court towards a more 'dialogical' role—(re-)incorporating, as noted earlier, central elements of the pluralist conversation into a constitutional framework. This, of course, most immediately implies a renewed emphasis on the quality of its dialogues with national courts and national authorities—both directly and, in the latter case, as they are engaged through the Committee of Ministers and the wider Council of Europe system.[43] More specifically, however, this also points to a jurisprudential re-orientation in which the ECtHR shows more explicit awareness and places greater weight on the 'deliberative quality' of national decision making. In essence, the Strasbourg Court would shift to a role in which it scrutinised decision-making procedures more closely, while variably calibrating the scope and intensity of its substantive determinations according to the extent to which questions of the balancing of fundamental rights had appropriately figured in prior national deliberations.

Typically, in the case of the Convention community's more established democracies, the role of the Court might often be one of seeking to prompt a fuller (re-)consideration of the human rights implications of particular policy decisions in the light of evolving standards, without necessarily moving immediately to a—perhaps precipitate—finding of a direct Convention violation. The interest of such a more deliberative or formative approach may be illustrated with reference to what might reasonably be regarded as the shortcomings of the Court's recent jurisprudence in the area of prisoners' voting rights. As is (perhaps too) well known, the Court ventured onto this terrain with its 2005 majority decision in the case of *Hirst (No 2)*, which found the UK in violation of the Convention for its 'blanket ban' on convicted prisoners in detention voting in elections.[44] The decision has proven a highly controversial one domestically, with successive British governments having now failed to give effect to the Court's decision,[45] producing over 2,500 further complaints to Strasbourg. The controversy in itself is, of course, not necessarily a sign of a problematic jurisprudence. Nevertheless, one cannot escape the sense of this having been a somewhat ill-considered decision when seen in the light of the Court's somewhat less than clear or consistent subsequent jurisprudence in the area.

Since *Hirst*, the 2010 chamber decision in *Frodl* first appeared to set out considerably more stringent conditions, holding that 'besides ruling out automatic and blanket restrictions it is essential that the decision on disenfranchisement be taken by a judge'.[46] This expansion of the *Hirst* criteria was not, however, to stand. In the 2012 *Scoppola* case, the Grand Chamber characterised the *Frodl* approach as taking 'a broad view' which it 'does not fully share', going on to specify that the intervention of a judge could not be read as a

37 *Osgoode Hall Law Journal* 529. See also C Manfredi and M Rush, *Judging Democracy* (Peterborough, ON, Broadview Press, 2008) 17–48 for a critical survey of the American and Canadian judicial dialogue debates and their points of intersection.

[43] The importance of the Court's connections to the wider Council of Europe system is further developed in Harmsen (n 33) 132–40.

[44] *Hirst v United Kingdom (No 2)*, App No 74025/01 (2005) 42 EHRR 849.

[45] This remains the case despite the Court having explicitly held, in a 2010 'pilot judgment', that the UK must introduce remedial legislation within a period not to exceed six months from the definitive entry into force of the judgment. See ECtHR, *Greens and MT v United Kingdom*, App Nos 60041/08 and 60054/08 (2010).

[46] *Frodl v Austria*, App No 20201/04 (2010) 52 EHRR 267 [34].

necessary limb of the *Hirst* test.[47] In *Scoppola*, moreover, the Grand Chamber went on to overturn the earlier chamber finding of a violation, holding that the Italian legislation in question did not constitute an indiscriminate or blanket provision such as that found in the British case, even though its operation in practice included elements of more extensive disenfranchisement (notably providing for a revocable post-incarceration continuation of the voting ban for more serious offenders).

The overall line of jurisprudence which has thus emerged does not appear entirely satisfactory. Although the finding of a violation as regards a 'blanket ban' has been a constant,[48] subsequent decisions have not been a model of clarity or consistency. In particular, having adopted a corrective approach, the Court has not provided clear gauges as to the boundaries of Convention compatibility relative to what it has acknowledged to be a justifiable public interest in imposing some form of disenfranchisement. Furthermore, the Court has moved onto this terrain despite, as the minority stressed in *Hirst*,[49] the absence of a clear consensus of practice across the Member States. Moreover, it is common ground that no wider impairment of the democratic process is at issue.[50] It is thus in this light that a more formative or dialogical approach would have been desirable—inviting a reconsideration of national legislation in light of (tentatively) evolving opinion, without rushing to a direct finding of a violation (see the discussion of *Ždanoka* below). The objective in so doing, it should be underlined, is not that of 'avoiding controversy', but rather that of assuming a rights-enhancing position as part of a wider democratic dialogue. Such an approach might plausibly have focused attention on the issue of the terms and limits of exclusion from the democratic process in a rights-sensitive manner, rather than triggering a more polarised political debate (inevitably) focused on the remit, if not the legitimacy of the Court itself.[51]

A more formative or deliberative approach may also usefully be invoked in situations of democratic transition. Here, the quality of democratic deliberation at the national level as regards any transitory measures adopted would figure prominently. Beyond any immediate and provisional qualification of a particular right, such a focus would in itself be an external stimulus for the internal development of more robust participatory structures of political debate. The Court's 2006 decision in the *Ždanoka* case concerning Latvia offers an interesting exemplar in this respect.[52] The case concerned a ban on standing for office imposed on those who had been members of the Communist Party of Latvia in 1991 at

[47] *Scoppola v Italy (No 3)*, App No 126/05 (2012) [99].

[48] See further *Anchugov and Gladkov v Russia*, App No 1157/04 (2013).

[49] *Hirst (No 2)* (n 44) joint dissenting opinion of Judges Wildhaber, Costa, Lorensen, Kovler and Jebens at [5].

[50] See n 38 above on the more general tenor of the Court's jurisprudence concerning Protocol 1, Article 3.

[51] Interestingly, the relevant jurisprudence of the Supreme Court of Canada which formed part of the background to *Hirst* has met with similar criticisms, suggesting that the Court clearly and worryingly departed from the 'Charter dialogue' paradigm discussed above (see n 41). In *Attorney-General of Canada v Sauvé* [1993] 2 SCR 438, the Court had struck down a 'blanket' disenfranchisement of serving prisoners as a violation of the Canadian Charter of Rights and Freedoms. The federal government correspondingly amended the impugned legislation to provide that only prisoners serving sentences of two years or more would be subject to disenfranchisement. Although upheld by the Federal Court of Appeal as a reasonable limit within the context of the Charter, the Supreme Court nonetheless struck down the federal legislation for a second time in *Sauvé v Canada* [2002] 3 SCR 519—in effect, directly overriding parliament's explicit reconsideration of the legislation in light of the Court's first judgment. It is with reference to this jurisprudence that C Manfredi and M Rush conclude their comparative study *Judging Democracy* (n 42) with the trenchant observation that 'the Canadian Court's impatience with the deliberative legislative process presents in some cases an ominous threat to the democratic dialogue envisioned by the Charter' (133).

[52] *Ždanoka v Latvia*, App No 58278/00 (2006).

the time of the attempted re-imposition of Soviet authority. Although noting the passage of time and the evolution of circumstances, the Court nonetheless upheld the ban, noting both a 2000 majority decision of the Latvian Constitutional Court and the periodic reconsideration of the ban by the national parliament. Considerable weight was thus attached to the quality of national democratic deliberation. The Court nonetheless also insisted that the question be kept under review, noting that the failure to adapt legislation to a changing (and democratically stabilised) situation 'may result in a different finding' at a later date.[53] It had consequently positioned itself as a catalyst in relation to the evolution of the domestic debate, seeking to move the conversation in a more rights-sensitive direction without immediately imposing a decision in a highly sensitive area of national life.

Finally, turning to states exhibiting serious structural problems, it is evident that in the most egregious cases of human rights violations, a meaningful dialogue may not be possible. Some types of structural problem may nonetheless lend themselves to forms of dialogue as regards the adoption of appropriate systemic reforms. For example, in the *Burdov (No 2)* case, the Court was confronted with the problem of the systematic non-implementation of judicial decisions in Russia.[54] While requiring the shorter-term introduction of a remedial procedure (providing for 'adequate and sufficient redress for non-enforcement or delayed enforcement of judgments'), it nevertheless recognised that the wider structural problems demanded a commensurately wider political dialogue—and correspondingly called on the Committee of Ministers to engage with the Russian authorities so as to deal effectively with the underlying dysfunction of the judicial system. The judicial role, in this respect, emerges as one of channelling political dialogue.[55]

Overall, the concept of a 'democratic dialogue' may thus be seen as providing both a normatively grounded narrative of the Court's role and a more practical instrument allowing for a variable calibration of its interventions in different national situations. It does so, moreover, largely by bringing to the foreground an existing arsenal of jurisprudential techniques, which emphasise constructive engagements with national politico-legal systems rather than a more abstract 'judicial law-making' role. Through variably and appropriately assuming both formative and corrective roles, the Court may effectively deal with the diversity of situations which confront it and may do so in a manner which may further allow it to address growing criticisms suggesting a certain disconnection with national realities on the ground.[56]

B. The Reform of the ECHR System: Brighton and Beyond

Such a jurisprudential re-orientation would furthermore correspond to the central thrust of current discussions concerning the reform of the ECHR system. Most obviously,

[53] Ibid [135].

[54] *Burdov v Russia (No 2)*, App No 33509/04 (2009) 49 EHRR 22. See further Harmsen (n 33) 138–40.

[55] The Court adopted essentially the same jurisprudential architecture in two subsequent decisions treating comparable dysfunctions as regards the Moldovan and Ukrainian judiciaries. See *Olaru and others v Moldova*, App Nos 476/07, 22539/05, 17911/08 and 1313607 (2009); and *Yuriy Nikolayevich Ivanov v Ukraine*, App No 40450/04 (2009).

[56] The wider critiques of the Strasbourg Court, together with rebuttals and remedies, are well surveyed in S Flogatis, T Zwart and J Fraser (eds), *The European Court of Human Rights and its Discontents: Turning Criticism into Strength* (Cheltenham, Edward Elgar, 2013).

the vision of the system's overarching architecture articulated in the 2012 Brighton Declaration[57] directly fits with the conception of a robust but modest judicial role presently articulated. If much of the commentary surrounding Brighton inevitably focused on proposed further reforms to admissibility criteria and the Court's working practices, subsidiarity nonetheless emerges as one of the watchwords of the Declaration. The Declaration early on contains a strong reaffirmation of the shared responsibility of the states parties and the Court for the effective implementation of the Convention, 'underpinned by the fundamental principle of subsidiarity'.[58] This is then fleshed out in two substantive sections of the text, cataloguing an extensive series of measures to be adopted at the national level in order to ensure better Convention compliance and further making a series of proposals as regards 'the interaction between the Court and national authorities'.[59] As regards this latter dimension, the signatories—with considerable political symbolism if perhaps doubtful legal consequence—called for the drafting of an amending instrument so as to explicitly incorporate both the margin of appreciation and subsidiarity as principles of interpretation in the Preamble to the Convention.[60] Somewhat more concretely, the Declaration 'welcomes and encourages dialogues between the Court and the State Parties', noting the importance of such dialogues as concerns respectively the highest courts in each national system, the Committee of Ministers and government agents/legal experts involved in the Council of Europe system.[61] In terms of enhancing dialogue, the Declaration further called for the drafting and discussion of an optional advisory opinion mechanism—which, if brought to fruition, would allow for national requests to the Strasbourg Court for a non-binding interpretation of the relevant Convention provision(s) in the context of specific cases.[62] These proposed reforms should, moreover, be understood relative to a vision of the evolution of the system in which 'it may be necessary to evaluate the fundamental role and nature of the Court'[63]—particularly so as to 'permit the Court in the longer-term to take on a more focussed and targeted role',[64] buttressed by the effective discharge by national authorities of their 'primary responsibility' for the enforcement of Convention rights.

The balance struck at Brighton should be understood in appropriately nuanced terms. Sadly typical paroxysms of Euroscepticism in sections of the British Conservative Party, relayed by the press, tended to convey the impression of an exercise essentially concerned with 'clipping the Court's wings'.[65] The final text does not conform to this insular picture.[66]

[57] High Level Conference on the Future of the European Convention of Human Right, Brighton Declaration, 19–20 April 2012. Text consulted on the Council of Europe website: http://hub.coe.int/20120419-brighton-declaration.

[58] Ibid, para 3.

[59] Ibid, section B.

[60] Ibid, para 12b. This has since taken more concrete shape in the form of Protocol no 15 to the ECHR. This amending protocol, opened for ratification in June 2013, provides for explicit reference to the two principles in the preamble.

[61] Ibid, para 12c.

[62] Ibid, para 12d. Protocol no 16 to the ECHR, opened for ratification in October 2013, makes provision for national high courts to request advisory opinions from the ECtHR. This additional protocol will enter into force for ratifying parties once a threshold of ten ratifications has been attained.

[63] Ibid, para 31.

[64] Ibid, para 32.

[65] This notably prompted a strong public defence of the ECHR system's achievements by the Court's then British President, Sir Nicholas Bratza. See 'Britain Should Be Defending European Justice, Not Attacking it' *The Independent* (24 January 2012).

[66] See, for example, Joshua Rozenberg, 'Draft Brighton Declaration is a Breath of Fresh Air', *The Guardian* (19 April 2012).

Rather, it moves towards articulating a different vision of the Court's role in relation to an evolving pan-European reality. This vision is neither inherently more 'activist' nor more 'restrained' than its current role. As outlined above, it is indeed suggestive of both a more intrusive role in some circumstances and a more deferential one in others. The intention, instead, is to position the Court more effectively relative to the diverse challenges which confront it. Faced with both a quantitatively exploding caseload and a qualitatively broadened spectrum of serious violations, it is evident that the position of the Strasbourg Court must be fundamentally reconceived. A 'democratic dialogue' approach is one potential instrument with which to do this. Yet, whether through this framework or another, the debate must focus more on squaring the institutional circle at the heart of the Convention reform process—finding the means to maintain the Strasbourg Court's central place in the architecture of the European human rights system, while simultaneously recognising that it may assume only a necessarily subsidiary role as regards the protection of human rights on the ground.

V. CONCLUSION

The present analysis has proceeded by three principal moves. First, the limits of a pluralist model for understanding the operation of the contemporary Convention system were demonstrated. This demonstration served particularly to highlight the diversity of human rights challenges which now confront the Strasbourg institutions. Second, the limits of pluralism were then also demonstrated as regards the wider pattern of relationships between the EU and ECHR politico-legal orders. As within the context of the Convention system alone, the maintenance of the legitimacy and integrity of a pan-European system of human rights protection was seen to necessitate the recognition that the Strasbourg Court must be accorded a constitutional primacy as the ultimate guarantor of that system. The final section then turned attention to a fuller discussion of what that constitutional role might entail in the context of a reformed Convention system. Here, the pluralist concern with dialogue was (re-)incorporated into a constitutionally grounded order, with a more 'modest' but central role sketched out for the Strasbourg Court. This redefined role, consonant with the broad thrust of current reform debates, would place much greater emphasis on the fostering of democratic debate and the deepening of processes of democratisation.

As underlined at the outset, the present use of pluralist and constitutional referents has not been centrally concerned with seeking to 'prove' the superiority of one or the other position—which, it should be clear from the above analysis, remain (as Kumm appositely stresses) contextually dependent. Rather, the referents have been used as convenient heuristics to move the accession debate towards a more explicit consideration of the (geo-)political contexts within which the European human rights system operates. Doing so opens up important new horizons—suggesting both under-appreciated opportunities and under-estimated risks.

Seen in terms of the wider (geo-)politics of the European human rights regime, EU accession to the ECHR clearly offers a considerable opportunity not only to reinforce human rights protection through technically better co-ordination, but also to seize the moment for a wider redefinition of key elements of that system. In particular, as highlighted above, EU accession should not be seen in isolation from wider contemporary reform debates concerning the Strasbourg system, but rather incorporated as an integral part of those discussions. Accession, in these terms, may form part of a 'constitutional moment', allowing for a better overall articulation of a Convention system that otherwise seems to be near its breaking point. The discussion of a more 'democratic' view of the Strasbourg Court's role developed above may hopefully serve as a small prompt to move discussions more resolutely in this direction.

Yet, at the same time, accession also carries largely neglected risks for the wider European human rights system. Most obviously, were accession ultimately to be agreed on terms which appear to accord the CJEU—or, even more, EU Member States as a group—some form of 'privileged' status, this would have potentially corrosive effects for the Convention system as a whole.[67] Any agreement must preserve the essential equality of all contracting parties, with a view to maintaining overall system cohesiveness and legitimacy. Negotiators must keep an eye on these systemic considerations—and not allow a sort of 'engrenage technique' to force through an agreement which may privilege legitimate concerns over the autonomy of the EU legal order at the expense of the viability of the wider human rights system. In the final analysis, accession must not be treated as a goal in itself, but rather as an instrument to be adopted only if and to the extent that it enhances the overall protection of human rights. In this, the final political lesson to be drawn is one of a rather sanguine realism—if the right balance cannot be struck, there are agreements better left on the table.

[67] Beyond the ECHR, this also has implications for the wider pattern relationships between the EU and the Council of Europe as regards the maintenance, development and enforcement of human rights standards. See O De Schutter, 'The Two Europes of Human Rights: The Emerging Division of Tasks between the Council of Europe and the European Union in Promoting Human Rights in Europe' (2008) 14 *Columbia Journal of European Law* 509.

14

Taming the Fragmentation Monster through Human Rights?

International Constitutionalism, 'Pluralism Lite' and the Common Territory of the Two European Legal Orders

LUCAS LIXINSKI*

I. INTRODUCTION

THE RELATIONSHIP BETWEEN the European Union (EU) and the European Convention on Human Rights (ECHR) goes back several decades. Relatively early on in the economic integration process of (then) Western Europe, it was realised that, as integration progressed and more harmonisation came about, fundamental rights were affected by what was only meant to be economics, trade and customs. Faced with this challenge, judicial bodies of the integration process were in dire need of a source for fundamental rights in order to make sure that these would be protected by the integration process itself, as denying such protection would jeopardise the trust deposited in the European Communities (EC) and ultimately put the entire integrationist enterprise at risk. The first source that occurred to these judicial bodies was the 'constitutional traditions' common to the Member States, and that seemed to take care of the problem at first.[1]

Parallel to this development in regional economics, the Council of Europe forged ahead with its mandate to 'achieve a greater unity between its members for the purposes of safeguarding and realising the ideals and principles which are their common heritage' through 'the maintenance and further realisation of human rights and fundamental freedoms'.[2] A big chunk of this mandate being human rights, the European Convention on Human Rights (ECHR) kept on evolving into a common denominator for human rights across the Council of Europe's Member States. From the moment that the Member States of the European Communities also all became parties to the ECHR, it was clear that the

* Lecturer, Faculty of Law, UNSW Australia; PhD in Law, European University Institute (Florence, Italy). I am thankful to Marija Bartl and Angelos Dimopoulos for their comments to a previous draft, and to Michael Liu for his research assistance. All errors remain my own.

[1] Case 11/70 *Internationale Handelsgesellschaft mbH v Einfuhr- und Vorratsstelle für Getreide und Futtermittel* [1970] ECR 1125 [3]–[4].

[2] Statute of the Council of Europe, Article 1(a)–(b).

Convention was an ideal source for the fundamental rights common to the traditions of all the Communities' Member States. With that in mind, the Communities' courts went from 'constitutional traditions' to 'constitutional traditions and the ECHR',[3] and then to the ECHR alone.[4]

So, it seemed like all was OK in this domain: the ECHR provided the source for human rights that the Communities needed to make sure economic integration did not go too far, and the ECHR was legitimised, however informally, by an organisation of partly overlapping geographical scope. However, the big problem is that, for both the integration process and the ECHR, it was only states who were bound by these obligations: no direct accountability mechanism was available to the EU when it came to its own human rights performance.

A series of cases, including the famous *Bosphorus* case,[5] suggested that, because EC/EU Member States implemented and applied Community/Union law, they could be held to account for violations of the ECHR by the European Court of Human Rights (ECtHR), to the extent that Community/Union law formed part of their law.[6] While at the end of the day the practical effect of this solution still gave victims an adequate remedy, it was considered to be too tortuous a way for victims. Plus, it essentially left the EC/EU unscathed, because it was never to account for anything, and the burden of EC/EU infringing on human rights was still to be borne by the Member States, not the organisation directly.

This state of affairs gave rise to discussions about the relationship between the two systems (the ECHR on the one hand and the EC/EU on the other), and the idea of 'legal pluralism' seemed to be an ideal candidate to articulate and mediate these tensions. According to this doctrine, which became enmeshed with constitutional debates (after all, the ECHR was already considered to be 'a constitutional instrument of European public order (*ordre public*)')[7] and thus became 'constitutional pluralism', the two legal orders, alongside domestic legal orders, would all co-exist in a plural environment. While domestic law would always be subordinate to both the ECHR and EC/EU law, the two international or supranational orders would co-exist in a spirit of co-operation, being heterarchical rather than hierarchical. While this solution is sufficient from a pluralist standpoint, it is fundamentally at odds with the constitutional aspirations of the EU, since it calls into question the very idea of EU law as a superior legal order hovering above all other law. To that effect, negotiations restarted in earnest to find a way to allow the European Communities/Union to accede to the ECHR.

Protocol No 14 to the ECHR created the entry point[8] and, after six years in the lead-up to ratification by all ECHR parties, it entered into force on 1 June 2010. After the entry into

[3] Case 4/73 *J Nold, Kohlen- und Baustoffgroßhandlung v Commission of the European Communities* [1974] ECR 491 [12]; and Case 44/79 *Liselotte Hauer v Land Rheinland-Pfalz* [1979] ECR 3727 [16].

[4] Case 36/75 *Roland Rutili v Ministre de l'intérieur* [1975] ECR 1219 [32].

[5] *Bosphorus Hava Yollari Turizm v Ireland* (2006) 42 EHRR 1.

[6] For an explanation of the evolution of this line of cases, see P De Hert and F Korenica, 'The Doctrine of Equivalent Protection: Its Life and Legitimacy before and after the European Union's Accession to the European Convention on Human Rights' (2012) 13(7) *German Law Journal* 874.

[7] *Loizidou v Turkey* (1997) 23 EHRR 513 [75].

[8] Protocol No 14 to the Convention for the Protection of Human Rights and Fundamental Freedoms, amending the control system of the Convention. Opened for signatures on 13 May 2004. Entry into force: 1 June 2010. 'Article 17: Article 59 of the Convention shall be amended as follows: 1. A new paragraph 2 shall be inserted which shall read as follows: "2. The European Union may accede to this Convention." 2. Paragraphs 2, 3 and 4 shall become paragraphs 3, 4 and 5 respectively.'

force of this instrument on the Council of Europe's side, it became the EU's turn. And at present an Accession Agreement is being negotiated by the EU and the Council of Europe, under the latter's auspices. The Agreement covers essentially the relationship between the EU and the ECtHR. And, while that is an important part of the accession process, and definitely one of the most contentious points in the relationship between the ECHR and EU systems, is that all there is? In other words, should the unprecedented accession of the EU, an economic integration organisation, to one of the most effective international human rights systems in the world centre only on its judicial aspects? Is there not more to international human rights protection than courts and judges?

This contribution argues that the focus on the judicial mechanisms alone may be a missed opportunity on the part of both organisations and of Europe in general (citizens, governments and regional bodies) to strengthen and widen the mandate of the EU in the human rights field, as judicial mechanisms reflect what can be brought before them via jurisdictional thresholds established at some point in the past rather than the entirety of issues on the ground. I will pursue this proposition by suggesting that this focus on judicialisation can be attributed to the notion of 'constitutional pluralism' in the EU, which, by merging the discourses of pluralism and constitutionalisation, foregrounds institutional issues to the detriment of deeper substantive ones, such as legitimacy and entrenchment of human rights standards. In other words, 'pluralism lite' under the EU in fact only serves to reinforce the constitutionalist project and its hegemonic risks.

In order to substantiate my arguments, I will first explore both constitutionalisation and pluralism as master narratives of the international legal order, with particular regard to how they apply in the EU. The broader international perspective will act as a counterpoint to the versions prevailing in European legal circles, as a means to demonstrate the limitations of what European lawyers usually seem to perceive as 'pluralism'. After that discussion, I will focus more on the critique of the Draft Accession Agreement,[9] highlighting some of its blind spots and missed opportunities. I will then make some concluding remarks.

II. FROM CONSTITUTIONALISM TO PLURALISM AND BACK

This section will examine the debates within European legal circles surrounding the ideas of international constitutionalism, pluralism and constitutional pluralism. From the outset, it must be stated that I come to this debate from the perspective of an international law scholar, not an EU law expert. This bias means that I will be more critical of certain assumptions about the role of constitutionalism and the way in which plurality is understood in Europe. As far as I am concerned, '*unitas in diversitas*' is a good (and fairly poetic) idea, but not a motto that influences the way I read and understand the law in this specific context. Also underlying my discussion to a certain extent is the idea that: 'Unity and fragmentation are matters of narrative perspective. What from one angle looks like a terribly distorted and chaotic image of something, may from another appear just as a finely nuanced and sophisticated reflection of a deeper unity.'[10]

[9] In the latest (10 June 2013) iteration at the time of writing.

[10] M Koskenniemi, 'Global Legal Pluralism: Multiple Regimes and Multiple Modes of Thought' (2005), available at www.helsinki.fi/eci/Publications/Koskenniemi/MKPluralism-Harvard-05d[1].pdf.

The discussion I want to undertake here aims at providing the foundation for my critique of the accession process. With that in mind, this section begins by introducing the constitutionalisation debate both as an international legal project and the way it has played out in the specific EU context. This discussion will compare and contrast the assumptions about the possibilities of constitutionalism beyond nation-states and the extent to which supranationality makes EU constitutionalism 'thicker'. The following subsection (II.B) will focus on international legal pluralism as a project for the creation and negotiation of alterity, while in the EU pluralism has been merged into the constitutionalisation rhetoric under the label of 'constitutional pluralism' (section II.C). An exploration of constitutional pluralism follows, including a discussion of some of its dark sides (section II.D), with a view of setting up the stage for the specific discussion of the process to enable the accession of the EU to the ECHR.

A. The Constitutionalisation Narrative and the EU

The constitutionalisation narrative often conceptualises the international legal order as being in constant entrenchment and with increasing autonomy and legitimacy, in an attempt to give it a rational and justifiable shape.[11] A constitutionalising narrative may or may not require the existence of a fundamental norm (Grundnorm). The latter is most often related to a rather thick version of constitutionalism.[12] A thinner version of constitutionalism still probably requires a Grundnorm, but in a lesser, even minor, configuration. A common feature of works examining international constitutionalism is to try to compare international constitutionalism with state constitutionalism. As Tsagourias properly points out, though, the state should not be the standard for comparison, as the dynamics of post-state spaces are very different, and even state-based accounts of constitutionalism are often based on abstract and unreal models.[13] Furthermore, 'the international has no "demos" in the sense of a body-politic that can bind its members' and 'in a polyvalent order such as the international, constitutionalism may be more about normative neutrality and accommodation of differences than about the projection of a common value system'.[14]

The constitutionalisation narrative is predicated on trying to move past the voluntary or contractual nature of international law and to conceive of international legal instruments as law-making instruments more than contracts.[15] This idea has to do with eroding the concept of sovereignty, which is one of the main foundations for the project of constitutionalisation of international law. As the Westphalian concept of sovereignty is overcome, or at least re-invented, one can inquire into the possibility of establishing one universal state.

Constitutionalisation is often hailed as the solution to the fragmentation of international law (or the narrative to which fragmentation is the counter-narrative).[16] The

[11] JL Dunoff, 'International Law in Perplexing Times' (2010) 25 *Maryland Journal of International Law* 11, 23.

[12] N Tsagourias, 'Introduction—Constitutionalism: A Theoretical Roadmap' in N Tsaugourias (ed), *Transnational Constitutionalism: International and European Models* (Cambridge, Cambridge University Press, 2007) 1, 2–3.

[13] Ibid 4–5.

[14] Ibid 6.

[15] See, eg, P Capps, 'The Rejection of the Universal State', in ibid 17.

[16] B Fassbender, 'The Meaning of International Constitutional Law' in ibid 307, 311.

constitutionalisation narrative is often associated with monism;[17] Hans Kelsen's old idea of how the international and domestic legal orders are one and the same, with international law at the top of the pyramid.[18] That it is associated with monism is very telling of two important characteristics of the constitutionalisation narrative that expose it to criticism: its hegemonic tendencies and its existence as a European project.

With respect to the hegemonic tendencies of the constitutionalisation narrative, the issue seems to be that a choice for a constitution implies to be a choice in favour of a certain political project and, in an unequal society, the choice would necessarily be made by those in a position of power at the expense of weaker members of the 'international society', perpetuating the unequal power relations by legitimising them through the use of the constitutional language. After all, unity is necessarily a hegemonic project.[19]

Second, and relatedly, the constitutionalisation narrative is often perceived as an exclusively European project. If it is a European project, it is bound to not only give preference to European understandings of what international law is and what it is for, but, by doing so, to also perpetuate European (colonial) structures of international law.[20]

This connection between the constitutionalisation narrative and Europe is particularly relevant when it comes to thinking of European integration as a constitutional process, at least to the extent that, in its origins, EC law was perceived as part of international law (and has later evolved into a *sui generis* regime). It has been argued that both the EU and the international legal order possess 'constitutional mindsets', but to different degrees.[21] Perhaps the key difference between the EU and the international system is that, while the international system is usually political and security-oriented, the EU is based on economic links and is market-oriented, which 'arm[s] the regime with strong auto-constitutional structures'.[22] Therefore, international economic integration regimes are presumably stronger in relation to other regimes that are based solely on norms of international legal co-operation and existence.[23]

This strength of EU constitutionalism, however, is often over-estimated. The failure of the 2004 'Constitutional Treaty' is the prime example of how the language of constitutionalism does not fly outside of legal circles (and these legal circles being formed by EU believers). The Treaty of Lisbon, which removed all constitutional language, was eventually approved, although not without difficulties. After the passage of the Lisbon Treaty, the big question for the EU constitutionalist narrative was whether it was still alive and, if so, in what form. The Court of First Instance's and the ECtHR's judgments in *Kadi* seemed to be clear shouts in favour of hard constitutionalism or monism, at least with respect to the idea of the relationship between the EU and the rest of the international community.[24]

[17] G de Búrca, 'The European Court of Justice and the International Legal Order after *Kadi*' (2010) 51 *Harvard International Law Journal* 1, 31.

[18] H Kelsen, 'Les rapports de système entre le droit interne et le droit international public' (1926) 14 *Recueil des Cours de l'Académie de Droit International* 227.

[19] Koskenniemi (n 10).

[20] Ibid.

[21] N Tsagourias, 'The Constitutional Role of General Principles of Law in International and European Jurisprudence' in Tsagourias (n 12) 71, 103.

[22] A Skordas, 'Self-determination of Peoples and Transnational Regimes: A Foundational Principle of Global Governance' in Tsagourias (n 12) 207, 243.

[23] Ibid.

[24] De Búrca (n 17) 31.

As *Kadi* was revised by the European Court of Justice (ECJ), however, constitutional pluralism seemed to be the better answer. What is constitutional pluralism, though? In order to understand this concept, it is necessary to first understand international legal pluralism in general.

B. International Legal Pluralism and the Creation of the International 'Other'

'Looking to the "dark side" of the majestic rule of law, legal pluralism rediscovers the subversive power of suppressed discourses.'[25] This statement by Gunther Teubner highlights the main perceived purpose of legal pluralism. International legal pluralism largely challenges the constitutionalist project, offering a counterpoint to it. And it is a very natural response to the dangers of constitutionalism, but also to those of fragmentation: it is something of a positive spin on fragmentation focusing on the potential of a diverging legal order, as opposed to its apparent chaos. While fragmentation undermines international law, pluralism strengthens it.[26]

International legal pluralism generally lacks an overarching hierarchical structure, favouring the openness of different legal systems. Unlike constitutionalism's search for a Grundnorm, pluralism accepts the notion that there is no such common point of reference.[27]

Despite a fair amount of criticism against defining legal pluralism (because of its reifying effect over both law and pluralism),[28] many definitions have been attempted, each highlighting some elements of it over others.[29] And, even though I personally share these criticisms, a definition of legal pluralism offers an important starting point for the debate if it is treated as such (a starting point), instead of the canon of an extremely rich and diverse body of literature. One definition of legal pluralism, for instance, characterises it as 'the coexisting structure of different legal systems under the identity postulate of a legal culture in which three combinations of official law and unofficial law, indigenous law and transplanted law, and legal rules and legal postulates are conglomerated into a whole by the choice of a socio-legal entity'.[30] From this definition we can draw two of the key tensions relevant for our exercise.

The first one is the tension between official and unofficial law, also dubbed as a public/private distinction. This tension suggests that, in a legally pluralistic environment, the law comes from both official and unofficial sources, and that non-state actors are given increasing voice in law-making processes. And the second important tension for our purposes highlighted in this definition is that between indigenous and transplanted law, or between domestic and international law. International law in this instance is the law imposed from

[25] G Teubner, 'The Two Faces of Janus: Rethinking Legal Pluralism', (1991–92) 13 *Cardozo Law Review* 1443.

[26] WW Burke-White, 'International Legal Pluralism' (2003–04) 25 *Michigan Journal of International Law* 963.

[27] See, eg, N Krisch, *Beyond Constitutionalism: The Pluralist Structure of Postnational Law* (Oxford, Oxford University Press, 2010) 5–6.

[28] See, eg, F von Benda-Beckmann, 'Legal Pluralism and Social Justice in Economic and Political Development' (2001) 32(1) *IDS Bulletin* 46, 49; and Brian Z Tamanaha, 'A Non-Essentialist Version of Legal Pluralism' (2000) 27(2) *Journal of Law and Society* 296.

[29] For a history of legal pluralism, see BZ Tamanaha, 'Understanding Legal Pluralism: Past to Present, Local to Global' (2008) 30 *Sydney Law Review* 375; and L Benton, 'Historical Perspectives on Legal Pluralism' (2011) 3(1) *Hague Journal on the Rule of Law* 57.

[30] M Chiba, 'Other Phases of Legal Pluralism in the Contemporary World' (1998) 11(3) *Ratio Juris* 228, 242.

the outside, often from the European hegemon or coloniser, as opposed to the diverse and context-sensitive domestic law. Pluralism accommodates both types of law and mediates the conversation between them, instead of simply dictating the primacy of international over the domestic (as thicker readings of the constitutionalist project do).

Because of this mediation between domestic and international, pluralism has been associated with Kelsen's dualism,[31] or the idea of the domestic and international legal orders constituting separate legal orders. What is new compared to Kelsen's dualism is that in this instance, the two legal orders are separated by a very porous membrane and engage in a dialogue in which not only the international informs the domestic (something that Kelsen had already admitted), but the domestic also informs the international. In that sense, this permeability of legal pluralism facilitates the creation of the international 'other',[32] of states of alterity that are not rebuked by the international order in principle, but rather engaged with, creating the possibility for dissent and subversion that constitutionalist readings of the international legal order do not allow for.

One of the big risks associated with pluralism is the tendency to focus on the 'exotic other', while pluralism must rather be seen as a means to comprehend the existence of the other in every social relationship.[33] To exoticise alterity would be to marginalise the pluralist effort and essentially play into the constitutionalisation narrative's hegemonic rhetoric. According to this account, pluralism must turn from groups to discourses.[34]

Pluralism can be either institutional or systemic. Systemic pluralism is the quintessential form of pluralism, where different norms created and operated under different institutional arrangements co-exist. Institutional pluralism, on the other hand, has to do with plural legal orders operating under a common institutional framework. The latter is what Nico Krisch labels 'pluralism lite', within which the constitutionalist project lies.[35] And it is the type of constitutionalist prevailing in the EU. It is also what William Burke-White refers to in his seminal paper on international legal pluralism. Burke-White poses seven trends that should be taken into account when 'asking whether international law is undergoing a fragmentation'. These are:

> (1) [T]he diversification of tribunals applying international law; (2) the growth and potential conflict of legal norms; (3) the increased access by non-state-actors to international legal adjudication fora; (4) the distinction between jurisdiction and applicable law in international tribunals; (5) the rapid expansion of inter-judicial dialogue; (6) the merging of procedure and tradition across courts and legal systems; and (7) the development of hybrid courts incorporating national and international elements.

As can be seen, all of these elements are very court-centric, thus making Burke-White's account of pluralism an institutional one, which, although not without its merits, tends to assume the possibility that the institutionalised order can successfully account for difference and divergence, and that there are no parties entirely excluded from the legal process.

[31] Kelsen (n 18); and de Búrca (n 17) 31.

[32] For a collection of essays on the international 'other', see A Orford (ed), *International Law and its Others* (Cambridge, Cambridge University Press, 2006).

[33] Teubner (n 25) 1457.

[34] G Teubner, 'Global Bukowina: Legal Pluralism in the World Society' in G Teubner (ed), *Global Law without a State* (Dartmouth 1997) 3, 4.

[35] Krisch (n 27) 77.

Systemic pluralism rejects this premise[36] or, if it does assume that there is no exclusion from legal processes, it does so by expanding the concept of law. In that sense, institutional and systemic pluralism are fundamentally different, the former being more limited than the latter in its possibility to actually challenge the established legal order.[37] Burke-White posits that the 'respect for *legitimate* difference inherent in such a pluralist conception may actually enhance the effectiveness of international law by increasing the legitimacy and political acceptability of international legal rules' (emphasis added). The problem with his vision is precisely the qualification of difference: difference has to be *legitimate*, which is reminiscent of what Elizabeth Povinelli, in the indigenous legal pluralism context, has named 'the invisible asterisk', or the idea of the existence of 'an invisible asterisk, a proviso, [which] hovers above every enunciation of indigenous customary law: "(provided [they] … are not so repugnant)"'.[38] In other words, it seems that institutional pluralism, at least in Burke-White's reading, is not really pluralism; rather, it is institutionalised conformity (with some accommodation) passing as pluralism. It is very reminiscent of the EU take on pluralism (which is explored in more detail below).

But systemic pluralism both accounts for better social practice and is normatively preferable because it strikes a balance between law's inclusive (or hegemonic, if you will) tendencies and group self-determination that differentiates from universal norms. David Kennedy has suggested that legal pluralism 'can be good for your professional moral health'.[39] He suggests that legal pluralism is first and foremost a perspective issue, meaning that the 'struggle against legal pluralism is a professional retreat, a denial of agency, and an apology for rulership denied—a professional will to irresponsible marginality in a world we have come to rule'.[40] As such, pluralism is to be embraced and seen as a 'professional opportunity',[41] unless one conceives of pluralism as merely the plurality of opinions about methods endogenous to the discipline, as opposed to the plurality of tools to address social, economic and political problems.[42]

However appealing to an international lawyer, Kennedy's version of pluralism is unworkable in the EU context. To the extent that pluralism represents a re-opening of fundamental questions, bringing with it a lack of direction, order and coherence, it is incompatible with the EU context precisely because it will not serve *integration*, the main goal of the EU as an economic *integration* process. So, how has the EU incorporated pluralism in its rhetoric and what does it mean exactly?

[36] Ibid.

[37] Burke-White (n 26) 964.

[38] EA Povinelli, *The Cunning of Recognition: Indigenous Alterities and the Making of Australian Multiculturalism* 12 (Durham, NC, Duke University Press, 2002). Cited in K Engle, *The Elusive Promise of Indigenous Development: Rights, Culture, Strategy* (Durham, NC, Duke University Press, 2010) 133. There is a case to be made that this notion does not apply to the European context because of the similarity of values across Member States. One has only to remember the existence of indigenous (eg, Saami) and minority (eg, Roma) populations across Europe to envision the potentials of extending this critique to the European context.

[39] D Kennedy, 'One, Two, Three, Many Legal Orders: Legal Pluralism and the Cosmopolitan Dream' (2006–07) 31 *New York University Review of Law & Social Change* 641.

[40] Ibid 646.

[41] Ibid.

[42] Ibid 652.

C. Constitutional Pluralism in the EU: 'Pluralism Lite'?

The EU has long translated pluralism within the EU under the idea of 'constitutional pluralism'. The very notion of 'constitutional pluralism' comes across almost as an oxymoron if one agrees with the idea of pluralism offering a counter-narrative to constitutionalisation. Nevertheless, it is what the EU has been allegedly engaging in. In all fairness, it has been said that: 'Constitutionalism and pluralism are generalising doctrines whose political significance is ambivalent. Each may be used to support as well as to challenge the existing state of affairs. Together they provide a mapping, alternative orientations to deal with, and to reduce complexity.'[43] According to this suggestion, in other words, 'constitutional pluralism' is not an oxymoron, it is actually closer to a redundancy. And this redundancy, I argue, is exactly what the EU has been doing with its use of the 'constitutional pluralism' terminology.

The constitutional narrative in the EU goes at least as far back as the 1980s, when it came about primarily as a means to enable the further institutionalisation of European integration.[44] While constitutional terminology was in fact used between the 1960s and 1980s, it was still used somewhat tentatively, and the common perception of the integration process as a 'constitutional entity' had not emerged yet, with the supranational narrative predominantly being used instead.[45]

Classic constitutionalism is the first phase of the constitutional narrative in the EU, marked by scholarly and judicial enthusiasm with integration, and the principles of direct effect and supremacy.[46] In the early 1990s, with the Treaty on European Union's creation of the EU and its three-pillared structure, classic constitutionalism started fading away, giving way to plural understandings of constitutionalism (even if classic constitutionalism attempted a revival, in particular through the failed 2004 Constitutional Treaty).[47]

There is in the evolution of scholarly accounts of constitutionalism in the EU a general trend towards pluralist constitutionalism, even if 'many revised constitutionalisms have been, admittedly, pluralist only in their name. Their endorsement of pluralism has been in many instances much more, if not exclusively, rhetorical rather than genuine'.[48] These debates help clarify the stakes of pluralism, but, most importantly, they underline the lack of a coherent discourse around pluralism as a concept within EU legal circles, which seems to be even deeper than the one at the international level more generally.

In addition to debates around versions of EU constitutionalism, another debate has to do with the levels of pluralism. On the one hand, there is the discussion of the relationship between EU law and international law more generally (external pluralism) and, on the other hand, the relationship between EU law and domestic law (internal pluralism). The latter seems to be the main object of at least early versions of EU constitutionalism and of multi-level classical constitutionalism, whereas the former, the one that is of most interest

[43] Koskenniemi (n10).

[44] M Avbelj, 'Questioning EU Constitutionalism' (2008) 9 *German Law Journal* 1.

[45] Ibid 3.

[46] Case 294/83 *Parti écologiste 'Les Verts' v European Parliament (Les Verts I)* [1986] ECR 1339 [23]; JHH Weiler, 'Federalism without Constitutionalism: Europe's Sonderweg', in K Nicolaidis and R Howse (eds), *The Federal Vision, Legitimacy and Levels of Governance in the United States and the European Union* 56 (Oxford, Oxford University Press 2001).

[47] Avbelj (n 44) 9–10.

[48] Ibid 23.

for the present purposes, seems to be folded in these debates almost automatically, even if it is a late arrival to the debates.

As far as internal pluralism goes, Maduro identified four sources of it: (1) the plurality of constitutional sources (European and national); (2) the fact that the acceptance of the supremacy of EU rules over national constitutional rules is not unconditional (that is, it is resisted by national constitutional courts); (3) that new forms of power have challenged the public/private distinction at the EU level, bringing with them different accountability mechanisms; and (4) the EU's political pluralism, which 'can assume a rather radical form since the conflicting political claims are often supported by corresponding claims of polity authority'.[49] According to him, this kind of pluralism 'may promote a virtuous cycle whereby both Community and national constitutional law are improved even from their internal perception'.[50] And that is in fact a virtuous goal, except that it seems to be blissfully unaware of the unintended consequences of its court-centrism. Even though Maduro acknowledges political pluralism as part of the formula, little to no attention is actually paid to it, and it seems like the potentials of direct political challenges to EU uniformity do not in fact exist (or have little to no noticeable impact) at the law-making and law-enforcing level.

These two levels (EU versus national and EU versus international) seem to be joined under the same banner, which has recently been referred to as 'interordinal' constitutionalism.[51] This notion resonates from a strictly EU-centric perspective because it conveniently puts the EU at the centre of debates, almost as a mediator between the international and the domestic, which reinforces the role of the EU and advances the constitutionalist narrative within the EU. After all, if the EU is the necessary middle between the purely domestic and the purely international, it certainly must be very important and very central to all of law; therefore, it is constitutional. However, this confusion misses important differences between the two relationships:[52] for one, the EU was established as superior by the individual Member States, but their power is only to determine the status of the EU towards their own national orders. The EU was created as an international law creature and it has subsequently focused its own scope and drifted away. But it is by no means superior to international law (rather, it is equal, at least when it comes to EU primary law), nor is there much to suggest that the peculiar nature of the EU would justify prima facie its law being applied over general international law on the basis of the *lex specialis* principle. To imply so would be to violate other international legal obligations undertaken by the EU Member States. From a pluralist perspective, though, this move makes perfect sense, as it creates the option for the EU to make sure its own voice comes through internationally as well and is a distinctive voice through which specific European values can be enforced. The fact that these values are woven into a constitutional narrative once the option for alterity is accepted seems to be unimportant, and in fact it should be unimportant. After all, if the international community is really open to pluralism, it should be willing to accept

[49] MP Maduro, 'Interpreting European Law—Judicial Adjudication in a Context of Constitutional Pluralism' (2008) Working Paper IE Law School WPLS08-02, 1.

[50] MP Maduro, 'The Heteronyms of European Law' (1999) 5(2) *European Law Journal* 160, 168.

[51] LI Gordillo, *Interlocking Constitutions: Towards an Interordinal Theory of National, European and UN Law* (Oxford, Hart Publishing, 2012).

[52] Also highlighting the inadequacy of this equivalence; see S Besson, 'European Legal Pluralism after Kadi' (2009) 5 *European Constitutional Law Review* 237, 261–62.

regional propositions that deeply entrench different takes on international legal rules and obligations.

The problem with this narrative, from my perspective, is that pluralism is used as a discourse both ways. Because the levels of the narrative (EU versus international and EU versus domestic) are confused or merged in the constitutional pluralism story, there is a perception that what the EU does internally is also pluralist, whereas in fact it is closer to a constitutional model (or the principle of integrity, as Samantha Besson put it).[53] Even if presented as a pluralist discourse, at the end of the day, this version of pluralism has a constitutional vision inherent to it and a hierarchy.[54]

D. The Dark Sides of EU Pluralism

Perhaps the most fundamental problem associated with the EU version of pluralism is the idea that plurality so easily becomes 'a surface underneath which the invisible hand [of the market] will reproduce the conditions of bourgeois accumulation'.[55] In other words, pluralism in the EU seems to pacify the critics of the constitutionalist narrative by merely being brandished, while no one really seems to care about examining what lies beneath the surface of this alleged pluralism. Especially in the specific context of an economic integration process such as the EU, the fact that pluralism disguises the continuation of unequal economics, as opposed to creating the political conditions leading up to redistribution, while at the same time claiming to be doing precisely that is especially worrying.

Another dark side of EU pluralism is that it largely disregards the blurring of the public/private divide, which is normally seen as an element of legal pluralism, as discussed above. To be more specific, it privileges certain (economically powerful—after all, the EU is an economic integration process that favours market rationality above all else) private actors at the expense of the public, still relying on the public/private divide to cloak those circumstances in secrecy (the private). Because this divide is kept intact at the EU level, non-state actors without significant economic power are not really given a voice, and instead the focus is entirely on official legal (primarily judicial) structures, which are seen as apolitical and thus technical-factual-normalised. The negative consequence of this selective blurring of the divide lies mainly in the creation of the appearance that the divide is indeed successfully and indiscriminately blurred. The EU has long been accused of a 'democratic deficit', of not taking non-state actors more seriously into account, of failing to connect with the people (as opposed to governments and bureaucrats). By employing the pluralism rhetoric, it may give the erroneous impression that it is in fact going through the effort of bridging the democratic gap, while in fact it is not, paying a disservice both to itself and to pluralism, which ends up gaining a bad reputation because of the way it is employed by the EU.

EU constitutional pluralism is very court-centric, as nearly all accounts of pluralism in the EU context refer to the activities of the CJEU, either with respect to national courts, to other international courts (mainly the ECtHR, but also others) or both.[56] The unintended

[53] S Besson, 'From European Integration to European Integrity: Should European Law Speak with Just One Voice?' (2004) 10(3) *European Law Journal* 257.

[54] Krisch (n 27) 235.

[55] Koskenniemi (n 10).

[56] See, eg, Gordillo (n 51); De Hert and Korenica (n 6).

consequence of that is missing out on what happens outside of courts, and missing out on the actual relationship between law and the polities it addresses. One account of pluralism suggests that this might simply be the natural progression of things and the EU would be merely skipping a step. According to Lauren Benton's historical account of pluralism, there is a tendency in imperial legal pluralism that the subjects of empire will tend 'to adopt both rhetoric and strategies referencing the law of the imperial centre'.[57] Further, it seems that legal actors historically tend to privilege adjudication over other forms of law making because of the enforceability of results.[58] So, taking Lauren Benton's account to heart, it would mean that the EU pluralism is a replication of what pluralism has historically been, without all the debate about pluralism beyond (and outside of) courts. But my contention is that pluralism must take place outside of courts too, and that structures that warranted the preference of court-centred approaches to pluralism are the colonial structures of international law that must be avoided by pluralism and that fall in line with the criticism of constitutionalism as a hegemonic project. After all, legal pluralism has an important effect in entrenching law and creating the 'rule of law' (whatever that is).[59]

This court-centrism has to do with the fact that institutional pluralism (discussed above) is the preferred form of pluralism in EU legal circles. One EU law scholar has even stated that 'the institutional dimension is one of constitutional pluralism's principal virtues'.[60] This focus is understandable, seeing as how institutional pluralism in fact serves the constitutional narrative.[61]

III. THE DRAFT ACCESSION AGREEMENT: BLIND SPOTS AND MISSED OPPORTUNITIES

For a long time, as outlined in the introduction, there has been a tension in the EU with respect to its human rights mandate: if, on the one hand, it has been called upon to protect human rights more extensively, on the other hand, there has always been a concern with not overstepping into the mandate of the Council of Europe, which advances human rights protection through the ECHR and the ECtHR.[62] This is one of the main reasons why the EC/EU has sought accession to the ECHR to begin with: so it would be able to expand its mandate in the area of human rights and subject itself to external human rights scrutiny as a means of enhancing its legitimacy in this area. Of course, there are some who state that accession is not needed at all because 'there are no normative conflicts of fundamental rights in Europe and no need for any judicial dialogue'.[63]

Olivier De Schutter has argued as early as 2008 that 'in the current stage of integration within the EU, it is only by doing more, not less, to protect and promote human rights,

[57] Benton (n 29) 58.

[58] Ibid.

[59] Ibid 67.

[60] J Komárek, 'Institutional Dimensions of Constitutional Pluralism' (2010) Eric Stein Working Paper No 3/2010 1.

[61] Krisch (n 27) 77.

[62] O De Schutter, 'The Two Europes of Human Rights: The Emerging Division of Tasks between the Council of Europe and the European Union in Promoting Human Rights in Europe' (2008) 14(3) *Columbia Journal of European Law* 509, 511.

[63] G Letsas, 'Harmonic Law: The Case Against Pluralism and Dialogue' (2011), available at http://papers.ssrn.com/sol3/papers.cfm?abstract_id=1872366.

that the EU can alleviate the suspicion with which its interventions are sometimes met'.[64] According to De Schutter, there are two ways of looking at the relationship between the EU and the Council of Europe: one of equality and one that takes into account the supranational character of the EU. Even though De Schutter indicates that the former seems to be the prevailing view, he makes an argument for the latter position. More specifically, he highlights the exceptionalism of the EU among other international organisations, calling attention to its constitutional features (and seemingly adopting a harmonious discursive constitutionalist approach, as he stresses the role of non-state actors). But it is here that the EU falls prey to its own exceptionalism, because De Schutter concludes that the constitutional aspirations of the EU make it subordinate to the classic public international law nature of the ECHR and thus determine that the EU court (presently, the CJEU) is to be treated just like a national constitutional court, and EU institutions as if they were national human rights bodies instead of Council of Europe 'competitors'.[65] Also, De Schutter says that the EU's constitutionalist posture makes it subordinate to the ECHR in its entirety, not only with respect to its courts. And the constitutional pluralist flag that the EU waves on its own behalf requires that a plurality of actors and voices be taken into account.[66] It is questionable, however, whether the current accession process is in a position to fulfil this ambitious promise.

Gráinne de Búrca has argued that the EU follows 'in political terms a multilateralist approach and in juridical terms a constitutionalist approach'.[67] This notion can lead to the suggestion that the political organs of the EU, because they are treated on a different (actually plural) level, are fundamentally incompatible with the constitutionalist approach adopted by the EU courts, and therefore an accession agreement that attempted to set the terms of the broader relationship between the EU and the ECHR would be doomed to fail. In this sense, a narrower accession agreement focusing only on the relationship between the CJEU and the ECtHR would be more likely to succeed. And that seems to be precisely what the draft agreements currently being negotiated do, as opposed to a situation where all EU action (and not only that of the CJEU) can be scrutinised by the ECtHR.

The draft Agreement involves topics such as a co-respondent mechanism for the EU to appear alongside ECHR parties in cases that involve the implementation of EU law,[68] the election of an EU judge to the ECtHR[69] and other issues. It does not make a great deal of substantive references to the obligations of the EU or its bodies with respect to the ECHR, but one of the exceptions is quite remarkable. Article 1(3) of the Draft Instruments specifies that: 'Accession to the Convention and the Protocols thereto shall impose on the European Union obligations with regard only to acts, measures or omissions of its institutions, bodies, offices or agencies, or of persons acting on their behalf. Nothing in the Convention or the Protocols thereto shall require the European Union to perform an act or adopt a measure for which it has no competence under European Union law.' This article, if approved, would largely fulfil De Schutter's suggestion that the EU will be simply another

[64] De Schutter (n 62) 512.

[65] Ibid 560–61.

[66] Ibid 561.

[67] De Búrca (n 17) 6.

[68] Article 3 of the latest (10 June 2013) draft of the accession instruments. For more details, see the contributions by Delgado Casteleiro and De Schutter in chs 8 and 12 this volume.

[69] Article 6 of the Draft Instrument. For more details, see the contribution by Andrew Drzemczewski (ch 5) in this volume.

party and subject to the ultimate authority of the ECtHR. The Explanatory Report to the Draft Instruments largely supports this view by stating that:

> Article 1, paragraph 3, of the Accession Agreement reflects the requirement under Article 2 of Protocol No. 8 to the Treaty of Lisbon that the accession of the EU shall not affect its competences or the powers of its institutions. This provision also makes it clear that accession to the Convention imposes on the EU obligations with regard to acts, measures or omissions of its institutions, bodies, offices or agencies, or of persons acting on their behalf ... It should also be noted that, since the Court under the Convention has jurisdiction to settle disputes between individuals and the High Contracting Parties (as well as between High Contracting Parties) and therefore to interpret the provisions of the Convention, the decisions of the Court in cases to which the EU is party will be binding on EU institutions, including the CJEU.[70]

Despite this provision, the relationship between the EU and the ECHR described in the draft Accession Agreement focuses primarily on the judicial aspects of it. This court-centric approach is by no means pluralist—rather, it is constitutionalist—and it leaves out the possibility for true contestation because the structures within which this 'pluralism' operates are left largely uncontested. Instead, the discussion is deferred to the ECtHR, which will set the rhythm of pluralism in the EU by oscillating between pluralism or 'margin of appreciation' when there is no European consensus, or imposing common European standards when it favours a constitutionalist approach. There is no mention of opening EU spaces for contestation by human rights advocates other than through the ECtHR. In other words, the ECtHR becomes practically the sole arbiter of EU compliance with human rights, and no EU structures will be adjusted for compliance with human rights law unless by force of an ECtHR judgment. This possibly stems from a presumption that the EU already complies with all of the human rights protected by the ECHR and, while that may well be some people's perception, the fact of the matter is that citizens are largely excluded from this human rights process, which ends up missing an opportunity for enhancing EU transparency and bridging some of its democratic deficit in a cause that is so close to the hearts of large EU constituencies.

IV. CONCLUDING REMARKS

Maybe this draft Accession Agreement is just a first step? It is, after all, only several decades after the relationship between the EU and the ECHR started that this problem is being addressed, and perhaps it is the best that can be achieved for now. But it also seems that it is a great opportunity going to waste, one in which it could have been possible to more fully scrutinise the EU's mandate with respect to human rights, and the way in which an economic integration organisation can serve international human rights law and potentially be re-structured around it. However, the fact that the EU is being treated like just another party to the ECHR means that the door is open for enhanced scrutiny by the ECtHR.

The constitutional pluralism advocated by the EU is not really pluralist, after all, and this can have a negative impact on how the EU protects, for instance, the rights of minorities

[70] Draft Explanatory Report to the Agreement on the Accession of the European Union to the Convention for the Protection of Human Rights and Fundamental Freedoms, paras 22 and 26. This paragraph also refers to Court of Justice of the European Communities, Opinion 1/91 of 14 December 1991 and Opinion 1/92 of 10 April 1992 as supporting authorities.

in its space. But, as long as the Strasbourg Court is in a position to spring into action and the EU is committed to enforcing the judgments of the ECtHR, there is some room for perhaps turning the pluralism lite of the EU into actual pluralism, for the sake of European citizens and even of the 'others' who come to inhabit Europe and who should find outlets to make their voices heard and have an impact on policies that affect their lives. Perhaps, after all, accession to the ECHR might be just what the EU needed to address its democratic deficit gaps.

Part V

Integration in Human Rights: Towards a Common *Espace Juridique* and its Expansion in Areas of Economic Activity

15

Luxembourg or Strasbourg: Improving the Distributional Impacts of Trade Conflicts

BERNARD M HOEKMAN AND PETROS C MAVROIDIS*

I. INTRODUCTION

IN 1998, AS part of a long-running dispute between the US (as well as several banana producers in Latin America) and the EU, the Appellate Body (AB) of the World Trade Organziation (WTO) found that the EU policy regime for imports of bananas was inconsistent with various provisions of the WTO dealing with trade and goods and services (*EC–Bananas III*).[1] After the expiry of the reasonable period of time for implementing the AB ruling, the US requested authorisation to retaliate against products originating in the EU, given that the EU had failed to comply.[2] Counter-measures in the WTO to date have taken only one form: suspension of concessions in WTO legalese, whereby the injured state imposes a cost equivalent to that created by the WTO-violating measure(s) put in place by the author of the illegal act. Usually this is done by increasing tariffs on imports of products originating in the trade partner, although concessions in other areas (trade in services and trade in intellectual property rights) can also conceivably be withdrawn.

In the absence of agreement between the EU and the US on the appropriate level of counter-measures, this matter was submitted to arbitrators.[3] Based on a decision by the arbitrators, the WTO (through the Dispute Settlement Body (DSB)) authorised the US to impose annual retaliation in the amount of US$191.4 million against products originating in the EU. The list of products on which tariffs were raised by the US included products

* Bernard M Hoekman is Director of the Global Economics Program at the Robert Schuman Centre for Advanced Studies, Centre for Economic Policy Research, European University Institute and Petros C Mavroidis is Professor of Law, European University Institute. We are indebted to Jean-François Bellis, Jagdish Bhagwati, Chad Bown, Carlo-Maria Cantore, Claus-Dieter Ehlermann, Giuseppe Martinico, Andrea Mastromatteo, Luca 'Rubentus' Rubini, Kamal Saggi, André Sapir and especially Vassilis 'Tzeve' Tzevelekos for helpful discussions and useful comments, as well as to the participants at conferences and seminars at the European University Institute, Maastricht University, Columbia Law School and SciencesPo, where previous drafts of this chapter were presented.

[1] WTO Appellate Body Report, *European Communities—Regime for the Importation, Sale and Distribution of Bananas [EC–Bananas III]*, DS27.

[2] See B Hoekman and M Kostecki, *The Political Economy of the World Trading System* (Oxford, Oxford University Press, 2009) for a summary of the long saga of the bananas dispute in the WTO. The retaliation that is the focus of this chapter was linked to the third time that a formal dispute had been brought to the General Agreement on Tariffs and Trade (GATT)/WTO. E Guth, 'The End of the Bananas Saga' (2012) 46 *Journal of World Trade* 1, 32 recounts the end of the bananas saga and the eventual resolution of the dispute between the EU and the complainants.

[3] As per Article 22.6 of the WTO Dispute Settlement Understanding (DSU).

made by Fedon, an Italian company manufacturing articles of a kind normally carried in the pocket or in the handbag, with an outer surface of sheeting of plastic, of reinforced or laminated plastics (ie, cases for eyewear). In April 1999 the US imposed duties of 100 per cent ad valorem on imports of Fedon products,[4] leading to an extra duty of 95.4 per cent on Fedon products.[5] Fedon suffered considerable damage as a result of the US measures[6] and, through its request to the Court of First Instance (CFI)[7] (and the Court of Justice of the European Union (CJEU) on appeal later), sought to be reimbursed for the damage suffered.[8]

The rest of the chapter is organised as follows. In section II we present and analyse the judgment, and explain why, in our view, the Court got it wrong. In section III we briefly recap the consequences of the judgment and discuss how similar decisions may affect the incentives of EU firms to invest in export markets. In section IV we explore whether *Fedon* could have been brought to the European Court of Human Rights (ECtHR), and conclude that in light of the strategy followed, such recourse was probably not on the cards. Finally, in section V, we present a proposal to establish a fund that would compensate innocent bystanders that are injured as a result of EU decisions not to abide by its international trade obligations. Our main conclusions follow in section VI.

II. ANALYSIS OF THE JUDGMENT

A. The Claims

The plaintiff raised two claims before the CFI:

(a) even assuming that the EU authorities had not acted illegally, Fedon should still be compensated for the damage suffered since, under EU law, the EU organs can be held responsible if damage results from their legal actions;
(b) that the EU had acted illegally (by practising a WTO-inconsistent bananas import regime) which provoked the US counter-measures and, as a result, Fedon suffered trade damage.

Both the CFI and the CJEU rejected both claims, albeit on different grounds.

B. Responsibility from Legal Actions

The CFI first noted that, for the EU to be held responsible, the damage must be unusual and special. In the case at hand, the CFI held that the damage suffered by Fedon was not unusual; hence, its claim should be rejected. The CFI first explained[9] that, as constant case

[4] See Case T-135/01 *Giorgio Fedon & Figli SpA v Council and Commission* [2005] ECR II-29.
[5] Ibid [34].
[6] Ibid [46].
[7] The CFI was subsequently re-named the General Court. The CFI decision in *Fedon* is discussed in PC Mavroidis, 'It's Alright Ma, I'm Only Bleeding' in A Epiney, M Haag and A Heinemann (eds), *Challenging Boundaries, Festschrift für Roland Bieber* (Baden, Nomos Verlag, 2007).
[8] The damage to *Fedon* was €2,289,242, including interest (*Fedon* (n 4) [56]).
[9] Ibid [153].

law had made clear, the EU could be held responsible for legal actions if three conditions were cumulatively satisfied:[10]

(a) a damage exists;
(b) a causal link between the damage and actions by the EC institutions has been demonstrated; and
(c) the damage is unusual and special.

The discussion in *Fedon* hinges on the interpretation of the term 'unusual', since the CFI satisfied itself that a damage indeed existed[11] and that there was a causal link between the damage and the EU bananas import regime.[12] The CFI found that the damage suffered by Fedon was not unusual and for this reason rejected the claim of the plaintiff. Because of this finding, it did not proceed to establish whether the damage was special.[13]

Damage is unusual, in the CFI's evaluation, if foreseeing it lies beyond the bounds of the economic risks that are inherent in the sector concerned.[14] In this case, the damage was deemed not unusual because Fedon could have foreseen that it could be exposed to the risk of confronting retaliation if it exported its products to the US market.[15] Why is this the case? Simply because, so the CFI argued, there is an inherent vicissitude in the WTO system, which allows for countries to take counter-measures when they are facing illegality under the WTO.[16] Since counter-measures could hit anyone, they could hit Fedon as well, so the argument of the CFI goes. Consequently, Fedon, in the CFI's view, when deciding to export its product to the US market, should have taken into account that:

(a) the EU would adopt the bananas regime it ended up putting in place;
(b) that this would damage US interests;
(c) that the US would decide to challenge the EU regime before the GATT;
(d) that the GATT would find against the EU;
(e) that the EU would not comply, but would modify its regime instead;
(f) that the US would challenge the EU regime again, before the WTO this time;
(g) that the new EU regime would have been found to be inconsistent with the WTO;
(h) that the EU would once again decide not to comply;
(i) that the US would take counter-measures pending compliance; and
(j) that the US counter-measures would hit Fedon products.

Fedon should also have factored in that bananas distributors are a more powerful lobby in the EU than the industries and producers that would be selected for counter-measures by the US, since, otherwise, the EU would have decided to comply. Hence, Fedon should have anticipated not only that it would be hit by the US counter-measures, but also that the identity of all other EU producers that would have been hit. Clearly it is ludicrous to expect any entrepreneur to foresee all the contingencies mentioned above. Even assuming that they can and do, what is the remedy? Stop exporting? But this would go against the

[10] Case C-237/98 *Dorsch Consult v Council and Commission* [2000] ECR I-4549 [19].
[11] *Fedon* (n 4) [162].
[12] Ibid [183].
[13] Ibid [200].
[14] Ibid [191].
[15] Ibid [198].
[16] Ibid [194]–[197].

very purpose of the WTO: to liberalise international exchange, which presumably is why the EU participates in it.

Even if one uses a much lower threshold for what can be expected of EU firms when planning export investments—such as the incorporation of a probability that the EU might violate its commitments and thus that EU exports might be retaliated against and that this might affect the firm in the future—it is unreasonable to expect this to be factored into any investment decision. In practice, retaliation is very rare—in the 1990s (before the Bananas retaliation) less than 0.0002 per cent of US imports had been subjected to retaliatory counter-measures directed at the EU.[17] The EU has a strong reputation among international business as a law-abiding trading power that has consistently called for a stronger rules-based multilateral trade regime and that has a long track record of abiding by its international trade commitments. Including a non-zero probability of the EU not abiding by its WTO commitments cannot reasonably be expected to have entered into any investment decision-making process.

In the event, this finding by the CFI was overturned. The CJEU, hearing this case on appeal, held that EU law, at its current stage of maturity, could not accommodate this type of claim. It did so against the elaborate opinion of the Advocate General, who had taken the position in favour of acknowledging EU responsibility stemming from a legal act:

> The Court has held that Community law as it currently stands does not provide for a regime enabling the liability of the Community for its legislative conduct to found an action in a situation where any failure of such conduct to comply with the WTO agreements cannot be relied upon before the Community courts. The claims for compensation by the applicants sought in particular to put in issue the liability of the Community for such conduct. Accordingly, the Court of First Instance could only dismiss those claims, whatever the arguments put forward by the applicants to support them.[18]

Had the Court stopped here, one might have had little to add to the analysis. The soundness of the arguments presented by the Advocate General notwithstanding, it is at the end of the day the privilege of the CJEU to decide on the ambit of EU law: it is the final authority on how to interpret the policy space that has been ceded to the EU by the Member States. The Court, however, attempted to justify its position by offering a quasi-moral explanation of why it had to be this way. In para 183 of the judgment it held:

> With regard, more specifically, to the right to property and the freedom to pursue a trade or profession, the Court has long recognised that they are general principles of Community law, while pointing out however that they do not constitute absolute prerogatives, but must be viewed in relation to their social function. It has thus held that, while the exercise of the right to property and to pursue a trade or profession freely may be restricted, particularly in the context of a common organisation of the market, that is on condition that those restrictions in fact correspond to objectives of general interest pursued by the Community and that they do not constitute, with regard to the aim pursued, a disproportionate and intolerable interference which infringes upon the very substance of the rights guaranteed.

This paragraph is difficult to understand. How can it be that general interest of the EU is to protect banana distributors whose practices are violating the EU's commitments under

[17] US retaliation in the Hormones case was some $120 million per year, compared to total US imports that averaged $750 billion during the 1990s.

[18] *Fedon* (n 4) [135], [169]–[172] and especially [188].

the WTO (thus opening the way for the US to retaliate), while punishing Fedon and other firms that played by the rules all along? This raises the question as to what the benchmark is for evaluating the general EU interest. Should Fedon understand that the social function of its property rights is to subsidise the income of bananas distributors? The Court can of course hide behind the case law that the general EU interest is not justiciable. But is this practice consistent with the idea of the rule of law and the 'Rechtsstaat' that the EU supposedly is pursuing, especially since we are not dealing with a legislative action proscribing the irrelevance of WTO law, but with judge-made law only? We will revert to this matter in what follows.

C. Responsibility for Committing an Illegality

The CFI had held that the EU institutions did not commit an illegality in violating its WTO commitments and that, consequently, the EU had no obligation to compensate Fedon.[19] Three conditions (commission of an illegal act, damage and a causal link between the two) must be cumulatively met for compensation to be due. One of these (commission of the illegal act) was missing in this case, as in the CFI's view, WTO law is not a valid benchmark against which the legality of EU law will be measured.[20] The CFI argued that it would only be a valid benchmark if:

(a) the EU intended to execute a particular obligation assumed at the WTO level; or
(b) EU legislation explicitly refers to WTO law.[21]

The CFI observed that neither of these limiting conditions was present in this case and therefore it concluded that *Fedon* could not invoke WTO law to establish the EU's responsibility.[22] The CJEU upheld this finding of the CFI as well as its rationale. The key paragraphs in the CJEU decision are reproduced below:

> 111 As regards, more specifically, the WTO agreements, it is settled case-law that, given their nature and structure, those agreements are not in principle among the rules in the light of which the Court is to review the legality of measures adopted by the Community institutions (see, in particular, *Portugal v Council*, paragraph 47; *Biret International v Council*, paragraph 52; and *Van Parys*, paragraph 39).
> 112 It is only where the Community has intended to implement a particular obligation assumed in the context of the WTO, or where the Community measure refers expressly to the precise provisions of the WTO agreements, that it is for the Court to review the legality of the Community measure in question in the light of the WTO rules (see *Biret International v Council*, paragraph 53, and *Van Parys*, paragraph 40 and the case-law cited).
> 115 The Court also held in that judgment that, by undertaking after the adoption of the DSB's decision of 25 September 1997 to comply with the WTO rules and, in particular, with Articles I(1) and XIII of the GATT 1994, the Community did not intend to assume a particular obligation in the context of the WTO, capable of justifying an exception to the principle that WTO rules cannot be relied upon before the Community courts and enabling the Community courts to review the

[19] Ibid [142].
[20] Ibid [103].
[21] Ibid [107].
[22] Ibid [135].

legality of Regulation No 1637/98 and the regulations adopted to implement it in the light of those rules (see, to this effect, *Van Parys*, paragraphs 41 and 52).

116 It should be remembered that the decisive factor here is that the resolution of disputes concerning WTO law is based, in part, on negotiations between the contracting parties. Withdrawal of unlawful measures is admittedly the solution recommended by WTO law, but other solutions are also authorised (*Omega Air and Others*, paragraph 89).

119 The Court also pointed out that to accept that the Community courts have the direct responsibility for ensuring that Community law complies with the WTO rules would effectively deprive the Community's legislative or executive organs of the scope for manoeuvre enjoyed by their counterparts in the Community's trading partners. It is not in dispute that some of the contracting parties, including the Community's most important trading partners, have concluded from the subject-matter and purpose of the WTO agreements that they are not among the rules applicable by their courts when reviewing the legality of their rules of domestic law. Such lack of reciprocity, if accepted, would risk introducing an imbalance in the application of the WTO rules (*Van Parys*, paragraph 53).

129 A recommendation or a ruling of the DSB finding that the substantive rules contained in the WTO agreements have not been complied with is, whatever the precise legal effect attaching to such a recommendation or ruling, no more capable than those rules of conferring upon individuals a right to rely thereon before the Community courts for the purpose of having the legality of the conduct of the Community institutions reviewed.

In what follows, we take each of these grounds for rejecting Fedon's claim in turn and question their validity.[23] We should state at the outset that the Court did not have to go to such great pains to reach its conclusion; it could, for example, have mentioned only the first of the grounds for rejecting Fedon's request, ie, that the WTO law is not a benchmark on which to evaluate the legality of EU actions in the field of international trade policy except for the two instances mentioned above, neither of which was present in the instant dispute. Why spend time and effort mentioning the other grounds as well?

i. WTO Law is a Benchmark in Only Two Cases

No express reference to WTO law: The CJEU found nowhere in the relevant EU documents an explicit reference to WTO law, so the conclusion in the eyes of the judges was inescapable. But is this construction not tantamount to stating that the performance of international obligations will be decided on the basis of domestic law? Such an attitude is clearly in contradiction with customary international law rule enshrined in Article 27 of the Vienna Convention on the Law of Treaties (VCLT): 'A party may not invoke the provisions of its internal law as justification for its failure to perform a treaty.' It is true that this provision does not address the issue of private parties' rights, but simply addresses the international responsibility of the EU. Nevertheless, the CJEU did not make a qualified judgment here: it stated clearly that an absence of reference to WTO law leads to its irrelevance in the EU legal order. As such, this statement runs afoul of Article 27 VCLT.

[23] A Alemanno, 'At the End of the Tunnel There is ... Darkness: The European Court of Justice Denies EC Liability for WTO Non-compliance' (2008) 10 *European Law Reporter* 347; A Arcuri and P Poli, 'What Price for Community Enforcement of WTO Law?' (2010) 1 EUI—Department of Law Working Paper; and M Dani, 'Remedying European Legal Pluralism: The FIAMM and Fedon Litigation and the Judicial Protection of International Trade Bystanders' (2010) 21 *European Journal of International Law* 303, 34 have all offered critical comment on the *Fedon* judgment.

The EU did not intend to abide by the DSB decision: The DSB decision reflects the adoption of the WTO AB report condemning the EU practices (the *EC–Bananas III* report). In the CJEU's view, there is an inherent vicissitude in WTO law which distinguishes it from other legal systems: once inconsistency has been established, the author of the illegal act does not have to implement its obligations; instead, it can negotiate some form of compensation. The EU did not intend to assume a particular obligation when the DSB decision fell; were the CJEU to grant Fedon compensation, so the argument goes, it would have had ipso facto deprived the EU executive of the opportunity to negotiate a deal with its trading partners.

From a practical perspective, a CJEU decision in favour of the plaintiff does not have any effect on the EU's discretion to negotiate a deal with its trading partners: Fedon requested compensation for costs it has already incurred (the extra tariffs it has been forced to pay and the lost sales that result from a 100 per cent tariff). The EU could have compensated Fedon while looking for a negotiated settlement with the US. Because of the de facto absence of the retroactivity of WTO remedies, there is no risk of paying twice. Actually, the EU is paying the US less—substantially less in this case—than the damage it has caused: the damage starts from the date the illegality occurred and the obligation to compensate kicks in, by WTO case law construction, at the end of the reasonable period of time within which the EU should have complied with the adverse ruling.[24]

More importantly, it is very disturbing to hear from the CJEU that an international treaty will be the benchmark if, and only if, the EU intended this to be the case. The message sent to the EU's trading partners is that when the EU signs international treaties, sometimes it might and sometimes it might not intend to abide by it. Our judges should think about the incentives they create for our (trading) partners through similar case law.

ii. Flexibility of the WTO Contract

The CJEU, when arguing that the EU's options will be constrained if compensation were paid to Fedon, mischaracterises the WTO by describing it as a totally flexible instrument when it comes to compliance. As a matter of principle, Article 22 DSU[25] reveals a clear preference in favour of 'property rules' (specific performance of the contract); 'liability rules' (suspension of concessions) in the WTO are an interim solution that are only available until compliance has been achieved, and are aimed at inducing compliance. The obligation imposed on the EU by virtue of the DSB decision is to remove the illegal practice; in the meantime, until the moment when compliance has occurred, the EU could be paying compensation. In this respect, there is no difference between WTO and EU law; indeed, the latter also, on occasion, provides for a payment of fines until compliance has been achieved. Neither legal order can prejudge when compliance will occur, and many factors (which we could encompass in the term 'opportunity cost of non-compliance') can affect whether and when compliance will occur. It follows that from a compliance perspective, being subjected to counter-measures is not a solution equivalent to specific performance of the obligations assumed. If the CJEU aims to suggest that all systems with interim liability rules are,

[24] PC Mavroidis, 'Remedies in the WTO Legal System: Between a Rock and a Hard Place' (2000) 11 *European Journal of International Law* 763, 813 discusses the de facto absence of retroactivity of WTO remedies.

[25] DSU stands for Dispute Settlement Understanding, the WTO Agreement regulating dispute settlement.

because of this idiosyncratic element, systems that do not require specific performance, it will have to consider the implications of this statement for the EU legal order as well.

What about the payment of compensation, which is also envisaged in Article 22 DSU? Payment of compensation is also an interim solution until compliance has been achieved. Hence, being subjected to compensation does not amount to compliance. The function of compensation is thus identical to that of suspension of concessions, and the differences between the two instruments are that the former is a negotiated settlement between the author of the illegal act and the injured party, whereas retaliation could[26] be the outcome of arbitration. Retaliation always takes the form of the suspension of concessions or other obligations, while the form compensation can take is not statutorily prescribed. In practice, compensation has been paid only twice since the establishment of the WTO in 1995.[27]

iii. Reciprocity Considerations

The CJEU pays attention to the fact that other WTO members do not allow private parties to claim compensation before domestic courts for violations of the WTO contract. However, the Court fails to explain why this is a legally relevant consideration. It could be a policy-relevant consideration, but making policy is not the mandate of the CJEU. The conditions under which private parties can invoke any law before the CJEU should be defined using as its benchmark one body of law only: EU law. Standing should be conferred using domestic, not foreign, law as a benchmark.

iv. Absence of Direct Effect of WTO Law

The *Fedon* case is not about direct effect. Fedon did not argue that by virtue of a WTO provision, it was entitled to a sum of money; it argued that because of illegal actions by the EU (in principle, irrespective of whether these were in breach of its international obligations or not), it suffered trade damage. The source of its claim is not WTO law, but EU actions. The legal point here is that using the WTO law as a benchmark for testing the legality of EU actions is completely dissociated from direct effect. In fact, the Court seems to conflate two distinct questions, namely:

(a) is the WTO law, as interpreted by the WTO courts, a legal benchmark to evaluate the consistency of EU actions/omissions with its international obligations?;
(b) who can invoke WTO law, as interpreted by the WTO courts, before the CJEU?

The Court has on a number of occasions dealt with this question. In *Racke*,[28] it entertained the complaint by an individual against an EU regulation that had suspended the concessions granted under an international trade agreement to Yugoslavia. Racke, the individual,

[26] We say 'could' because it could also be the case that the two parties agree on the list of suspension of concessions as presented by the injured party. In this case, there is no need to have recourse to arbitration under Article 22 DSU.

[27] Both times involving payment by the US: once in a dispute on cotton with Brazil and once in a dispute on copyright with the EU. The latter is analysed in G Grossman and PC Mavroidis, 'United States—Section 110(5) of the US Copyright Act, Recourse to Arbitration under Article 25 of the DSU: Would've or Should've? Impaired Benefits Due to Copyright Infringement?' (2003) 2 *World Trade Review* 233, 49. We will return to these instances below.

[28] Case C-162/96 *Racke GmbH & Co v Hauptzollamt Mainz* [1998] ECR I-3655.

was arguing that the EU action was tantamount to a violation of the basic legal maxim *pacta sunt servanda*. In para 51 of its judgment the Court held:

> In those circumstances, an individual relying in legal proceedings on rights which he derives directly from an agreement with a non-member country may not be denied the possibility of challenging the validity of a regulation which, by suspending the trade concessions granted by that agreement, prevents him from relying on it, and of invoking, in order to challenge the validity of the suspending regulation, obligations deriving from rules of customary international law which govern the termination and suspension of treaty relations.

Years later, the same court in *ATAA*[29] was entertaining a claim by private operators (aviation companies) to the effect that the extension of the EU emissions trading scheme (limiting pollution by planes) to foreign carriers was not consistent with the EU obligations under customary international law. In para 110 it held:

> However, since a principle of customary international law does not have the same degree of precision as a provision of an international agreement, judicial review must necessarily be limited to the question whether, in adopting the act in question, the institutions of the European Union made manifest errors of assessment concerning the conditions for applying those principles.[30]

In none of these cases did the international law invoked by the complainants confer rights to individuals, and yet the Court did not reject the claims submitted arguing absence of direct effect. What then is so special about WTO law? In fact, we think that *Fedon* was an opportunity for the Court to draw an analogy with its *Kraaijeveld* jurisprudence,[31] where it moved away from direct effect-type considerations to evaluate the legality of Dutch law. *Fedon* could have been the *Kraaijeveld* equivalent for using international law to evaluate the legality of EU law. The CJEU failed to do this. This attitude, however, can only incite similar reactions by others and ultimately may have detrimental impacts on international co-operation.

To avoid any misunderstandings, we are not advocating the direct effect of WTO law here.[32] We are simply advocating that the WTO should be recognised as the benchmark to discuss the legality of EU actions. What we are advocating is quite straightforward and in line with the case law of the CJEU in other areas: direct effect should be one of the avenues at the disposal of interested parties to invoke international law as the benchmark to evaluate actions by EU organs; it should not be 'passage obligé' for this endeavour.[33]

[29] Case C-366/10 *Air Transport Association of America and others v Secretary of State for Energy and Climate Change* [2011] ECR I-000.

[30] See, to this effect, *Racke* (n 28) [52].

[31] S Prechal, 'Direct Effect, Reconsidered, Redefined and Rejected' in JM Prinssen and A Schrauwen (eds), *Direct Effect: Rethinking a Classic of EC Legal Doctrine* (Amsterdam, Europa Publishing, 2002) at 17 ff. There is extensive case law where the Court dissociated the question of direct effect from that of the consistency of EU law with public international law. Somehow, WTO-related case law is the one area where this is not the case.

[32] A society has to weigh how it treats the right to property against its own incentives to comply with international obligations it has freely incurred. The whole idea of direct effect (ie, that a private party can invoke a provision of the EU treaty before a court) underlying the landmark 1962 *Van Gend en Loos* decision was to ensure that private parties also derive rights from the EU construct and that this does not remain an isolated institution/document tucked away from reality. Direct effect should lead to more challenges and more testing of EU law by widening the basis of those who can invoke it (including private parties rather than just states as was the case before *Van Gend en Loos*). Now the Court has turned this on its head: private parties cannot invoke it, while states cannot invoke WTO law.

[33] Compare the thoughts of P Eeckhout, 'The Domestic Legal Status of the WTO Agreements: Interconnecting Legal Systems' (1997) 34 *Common Market Law Review* 11, 58; T Cottier, 'Theory of Direct Effect in Global Law'

On the other hand, it should not be forgotten that it is, after all, the EU that insisted on Article 23.2 DSU, which confers exclusive jurisdiction on WTO courts to interpret the covered agreements.[34] One might argue that the EU did not contest the exclusive authority of the WTO adjudicating bodies to interpret the WTO; this is a meritorious point, since nowhere does the judgment question the right of WTO panels to do so. And yet, it denied a WTO decision of its 'effet utile' by deciding that the WTO is no benchmark to evaluate the legality of actions by the EU Commission. What is the purpose of acknowledging exclusive authority to interpret WTO law to panels and the AB if their reports are then judged irrelevant for the purposes of measuring the legality of actions of WTO members?

Now, a few years later, it is the same EU that denies the WTO courts' authority to do so. It seems that the EU courts have adopted an attitude identical to that of US courts. In *Corus Staal*,[35] the Court of Appeals for the Federal Circuit (CAFC) effectively held that the *Charming Betsy* doctrine,[36] according to which courts should interpret US law whenever possible in a manner consistent with international obligations, does not apply to WTO dispute settlement decisions which are not binding on the US. The implication is that reciprocity considerations seem to matter a lot.

No one is denying that private interests could be hurt as a result of pursuit of trade policies that are deemed to be in the general interest. Trade liberalisation is, in general, welfare-enhancing, but this does not mean that there are no losers in national markets. Levy and Srinivasan[37] show why it can make good sense to assign the responsibility to decide on questions such as the one at issue here (whether to comply) to the central government. Assigning the responsibility to a government guarantees that the society as a whole will profit from opening up the market (assuming the government acts to increase social welfare, a strong assumption, alas, on this occasion at least). It is then up to the government to decide whether to compensate losers. The questions for the EU should be: is the exercise of our trade policy in the general interest? And, if so, what should the EU be doing to compensate those who end up losing in the name of the general interest?

In the present case, the response to the first question by most economists (and consumers) is likely to be a resounding 'no'. Of greater significance is the second question: whether to compensate. The answer of the Court (and other European institutions) is

in A von Bogdandy, PC Mavroidis and Y Meny (eds), *European Integration and International Coordination* (Amsterdam, Kluwer, 2002); and M Mendez, 'The Impact of WTO Rulings in the Community Legal Order' (2004) 29 *European Law Review* 517, 529 on this score. Outside of direct effect, there is an additional potential cost that some of the analysis of Tzevelekos points to with regard to the *Kadi* saga: interpreting EU law in 'autarky', that is, without regard to international law, it is the EU law that might suffer as well since it will not be profiting from arguments that could enrich its understanding and open its order to the broader international system. Among others, see V Tzevelekos, 'When Elephants Fight, it is the Grass that Suffers: "Hegemonic Struggle" in Europe and its Side-Effects for International Law' in K Dzehtsiarou, T Konstadinides, T Lock and N O'Meara (eds), *Human Rights Law in Europe: The Influence, Overlaps and Contradictions of the EU and the ECHR* (London, Routledge, 2013) and the authors he is referring to.

[34] T Stewart, *The GATT Uruguay Round: A Negotiating History (1986–1994), vol IV: The End Game (Part 1)* (Amsterdam, Kluwer International, 1999) contains all proposals submitted during the negotiations of the Uruguay round concerning Article 23.2 DSU, which reflects the obligation to submit disputes regarding the operation of the various WTO agreements exclusively to the procedures established under the DSU.

[35] CAFC, *Corus Staal BV and Corus Steel USA Inc v Department of Commerce*, 395 F 3rd 1334 (Fed Cir 2005).

[36] US Supreme Court, *Murray v The Schooner Charming Betsy*, 6 US (2 Cranch) 64, 118 (1804).

[37] P Levy and TN Srinivasan, 'Regionalism and the (Dis-)advantages of Dispute Settlement Access' (1996) 86 *American Economic Review* 93, 101.

'no' again. In our view, refusing to compensate those who through their own industry are able to penetrate foreign markets and are subsequently excluded through no fault of their own is not satisfactory. It is this dimension of the case at hand that provides a rationale for compensation. We are not making a general argument that all losers from EU trade policy should have a legitimate claim for compensation. This would not only be unworkable but inappropriate as well. Trade policy in any democratic polity is made through a process in which competing and conflicting interests lobby for the policies that are most advantageous to them. The outcome of this policy-formation process is endogenous, but presumably reflects a 'political economy equilibrium' that is deemed to be what 'society wants'. In this process there will be winners and losers, but the losers will have had a shot at influencing the outcome. This outcome includes the various commitments that the EU negotiates in the WTO. The situation in the case at hand is very different: the outcome that reflects the political economy equilibrium is altered as a result of an action by a trading partner to defend its negotiated WTO rights that responds to an EU decision not to abide by its commitments.

III. BITE THE BULLET, *FEDON* (SO SAYS YOUR COURT)

By keeping the WTO illegality in place, the EU is essentially engaging in a redistributive policy: the bananas importers (those selling ACP bananas) were not exposed to a greater level of international competition as they would have been if the WTO ruling was implemented and thus benefited from higher profits. Fedon and other EU firms hit by the US counter-measures saw the return on the successful investments they made in penetrating the US market greatly reduced: they must bite the bullet.

The Court is there to test the legality of the actions of the agents of the European peoples, the EU institutions. It has established through its case law an elaborate system to test the legality of the activity of these institutions. Illegality can occur because either domestic or international law is breached. The EU has signed an agreement whereby it has accepted that WTO adjudicating bodies have a monopoly in determining the legality of actions by all trading partners (Article 23.2 DSU). This is a contractual promise made by the EU to the rest of the world. Now that the WTO adjudicating bodies have made such a determination, the CJEU turns around and says that a wrong in the eyes of the WTO is not a wrong in the eyes of the EU institutions because the EU action (or rather non-action) is in the general interest.

IV. ANOTHER CITY, ANOTHER COURT: *FEDON* IN STRASBOURG?

One might legitimately wonder whether the strategy adopted was the optimal strategy: arguably, *Fedon* could have also litigated before the ECtHR. To this effect, the lawyers of Fedon would have to persuade the Court in Strasbourg that their case comes under its competence (according to Article 1, Protocol 1, the Court is competent to adjudicate disputes regarding interventions to private property).

Had it submitted a similar complaint, one can only speculate as to the eventual outcome. There are several legal as well as policy factors that cast doubt to the feasibility of similar action.

A. Are the Incentives Present?

First, Fedon would have to act against an EU institution before a court lying outside the EU institutional architecture and for this reason alone, it might think twice before doing so: it is one thing to clean dirty laundry in one's own house (Luxembourg) and quite different to do so abroad. One could very well imagine scenarios why Italy, whose nationality Fedon bears, might try to dissuade one of its 'citizens' from entering this avenue. To be sure, Fedon does not need the approval of Italy to lodge its complaint. If at all this would be a concern of 'political order', not a legal compulsion at all. Political order concerns matter, though, especially when what is at stake is the legality of actions in an area of genuine exclusive EU competence. But assuming any such diffidence had been overcome, Fedon would have to face a series of legal impediments that it would probably find it hard to overcome.

If Fedon were to pursue its dispute before the Strasbourg Court, then there would be no issue regarding the competence of the Court to hear its case; as argued above, the Court is competent to adjudicate disputes regarding interventions to private property and it has also developed a quite rich case law, holding that states can be responsible for human rights breaches linked to their membership to an international organisation, especially when they enjoy discretion[38] as to whether to comply with obligations stemming from their membership to an international organisation that raises issues of compatibility with their commitments under the European Convention on Human Rights (ECHR). In principle, the Court—especially before its famous *Bosphorus* presumption[39] concerning the high standards of equivalent to the ECHR protection the EU is offering—could have had exercised competence in a case like *Fedon*. The question is what the response of the Court would be. In what immediately follows, we speculate about the response.

B. Will Strasbourg Say 'Yes, You are Right'?

The Court would have to ponder on various issues. First, there is the issue of causality: unless Fedon could show a causal link,[40] in the legal sense of the term, between the EU decision to not comply with its obligations under the WTO and the damage inflicted to it, then its claim would not have succeeded in Strasbourg either. Now the response to this question is far from obvious: logically, there is rational connection between the two, in the sense that had the EU complied with its obligations, then no damage could have ever resulted for Fedon. Rational connection is a looser test than causality, though. The Court could, for example, have taken the view that between the EU decision to not comply and the damage suffered by Fedon, the causal 'chain' is interrupted since the discretion of the US government enters the picture. In other words, since the US could have chosen a different target, the damage suffered by Fedon is not the direct result of the EU decision to not comply, but of the exercise of discretion by the US government.

In short, the response to this question is far from clear: a strict causality test would lead the Court to a negative response, whereas a more nuanced rational connection test would

[38] *Michaud v France*, App No 12323/11 (2012).

[39] *Bosphorus Hava Yollari Turizm v Ireland*, App No 45036/98 (2005) 1 EHRR 42.

[40] Among other cases, see *Önyeryildiz v Turkey*, App No 48939/99 (2004) 41 EHRR 325 [135]; and *Varnima Corporation International SA v Greece* App No 48906/66 (2009) [41].

lead the Court to respond affirmatively to Fedon's challenge. The case law so far suggests that a response along the lines of the former test is more probable.

But even if the Strasbourg Court takes the view that a causal link is established in the present case, the EU could always respond that its actions were dictated by the pursuance of the general EU interest and that they were proportional to the objective pursued. It would take a very courageous court indeed to second-guess the EU in this respect, and we have no tangible reason to invest in this perspective. For this reason, we believe that a similar claim in Strasbourg would not end up the way Fedon would have wished it to: to be clear on this point, we would find it hard to see how any non-EU court would be prepared to interpret 'EU interest' for the EU. This is an area which is best left to the EU institutions, the only institutions that can legitimately discuss it anyway.

Fedon could also face arguments regarding, for example, exhaustion of local remedies: it had not argued interventions to its private property before EU courts, and the doctrine of exhaustion of local remedies espoused by the ECHR could present yet another obstacle for the lawyers of Fedon. This is less of an issue though, since, although technically Fedon had not explicitly argued this point, de facto it did: the basis for its complaint to the Court is of course the impact on its property.

Finally, under its *Bosphorus* case law,[41] the ECtHR has accepted the principle of equivalent protection between the EU and the ECHR legal order. In this vein, the Court in Strasbourg might now find it hard to decide against the level of protection afforded to *Fedon* by the Luxembourg court, even though the principle mentioned here simply creates a rebuttable and not an irrebuttable presumption. Under the circumstances one can only conclude that a challenge before the ECHR was unlikely to succeed.[42]

C. Independent versus Sequential Litigation

Would the response have been the same had Fedon litigated only before Strasbourg? As things stand, the lawyers for Fedon argued in Luxembourg that the EU had violated WTO law, and as a result, Fedon had lost export income in the US. The CJEU rejected the claim that WTO law is the benchmark to evaluate the legality of acts of the Commission and also stated (as obiter dictum) that the negative welfare implications for Fedon were proportional: the general EU interest dictated this approach.

However, what if Fedon had not submitted the dispute to Luxembourg? What if it had initiated only one complaint in Strasbourg? In this case, the Strasbourg Court would have no claim before it that the attack on Fedon's property was proportional in light of the (undefined) wider EU general interest that had to be served. Unless, of course, the EU were to appear before the Strasbourg Court and argue its case this way, which is after all the purpose of the co-respondent mechanism that will apply after the EU's accession to the ECHR.

[41] *Bosphorus* (n 39).

[42] Nevertheless, this conclusion should be taken with a pinch of salt. We can only state this in a definitive manner in the presence of case law to this effect. There is none. As a result, it is probably advisable (assuming manageable opportunity cost) to pursue a similar avenue in the future, the low likelihood of succeeding notwithstanding.

D. Should the Road to Strasbourg Remain Closed?

Our discussion above is, of course, case-specific. It is not meant to address the wider issue of whether challenges, like the one by Fedon discussed here, should be exclusively submitted to Luxembourg's jurisdiction. In fact, very good arguments could be made in favour of using both avenues simultaneously.

Besides technical issues regarding the competence of Strasbourg and Luxembourg respectively, it is the multifaceted subject matter of similar cases that would allow the two courts to deal comfortably with essentially the same case without stepping on each other's toes.[43] Take the facts in *Fedon*: the question before the Luxembourg Court would be the strict question of consistency of EU actions with WTO law, while the question before the Strasbourg Court would be the legality of the (negative) welfare implications suffered by Fedon as a result of the US counter-measures. Technically, the two questions could, in principle, live side by side without the response to one prejudging the status of the response to the other.

V. A WAY OUT OF THE CURRENT MESS

In effect, what we have in the case at hand is an example of a 'regulatory taking'. Fedon is not able to contest it because the action is deemed to be in the interest of the EU as a whole, but clearly it has suffered a loss as a direct result of the EU decision not to comply with the WTO ruling. The fact that the US imposes the harm is irrelevant, except insofar as the motivation underlying the counter-measures is to induce the EU to comply. The US action is costly, both to itself (US consumers of the imported products pay higher prices and/or are induced to switch to less desirable varieties) and to the affected EU producers, their workers and their communities. Indeed, the costs of retaliation may be increased by the fact that the US uses a so-called carousel approach—it changes the list of products to retaliate on periodically, in the process creating uncertainty regarding the conditions of market access that will prevail for a larger set of EU exporters than those subject to retaliation at any given point in time.[44]

Action by the EU to compensate Fedon (and, by implication, all the other EU firms hit by the US retaliation) would alter the incidence of the costs of counter-measures. Instead of telling some firms to bite the bullet and 'take one for the team', it would appear much more logical—given the presumption that the EU decision is in the general interest—that the cost of the retaliation be spread across the EU population. Offering financial compensation for trade losses incurred by the targeted EU firms would achieve this, as the compensation would have to be paid for. If it comes from general taxpayer-funded sources, the costs of the

[43] Among others, see Tzevelekos (n 33), who discusses the relevant case law and critically evaluates the *Bosphorus* presumption. See also in the present collection the contribution by O De Schutter in ch 12, who presents a number of scenarios about the future of *Bosphorus* after the accession.

[44] The incentive effects of pursuing carousel retaliation are ambiguous. A greater number of EU firms will need to factor in the probability of being hit—which can be expected to increase the number of firms and industries that will push for the EU to bring its trade policy into compliance with its WTO obligations—but carousel retaliation also reduces the cost of retaliation for EU firms that are hit, as this will at least be time-bound. Whatever the net impact on compliance incentives and the total welfare cost of retaliation/non-compliance, how retaliation is put into effect has no implications for the argument for compensation.

EU policy would be spread widely, as is appropriate given that the general interest is served by the EU's trade policy. This could also improve allocative efficiency and reduce the real resource costs associated with carousel retaliation—while firms would still be hit by higher tariffs if they are targeted, they can decide to pass on the compensation to their importers to allow them to offset the effect of the tariff.

A legal issue which might arise were such a solution to be adopted is that the EU could be accused before the WTO of subsidising its domestic producers. Recall that by virtue of Articles 1 and 2 of the WTO Agreement on Subsidies and Countervailing Measures (SCM), a scheme is considered to be a subsidy if a financial contribution confers a benefit to specific recipients. Two types of instruments (export subsidies and local content incentives) are illegal under the WTO; all other instruments that qualify as subsidies can be counteracted. A WTO member can either impose countervailing duties (CVDs) against exports of companies that have benefitted from subsidies or can challenge their consistency before the WTO and request that they be adjusted (or even withdrawn). The question that arises here is whether the EU risks being accused of subsidisation in the event that it compensates innocent bystanders like *Fedon* who have been hurt by WTO legal counter-measures.[45]

The first criterion, namely, financial contribution, is of course satisfied in our scheme.[46] There is doubt, however, that a benefit is conferred: were a panel to take the view that a narrow set of facts is properly before it, that is, the provision of a financial contribution to operators, then undoubtedly the second criterion is met as well. However, if a panel were to take the view that it has the mandate to inquire into the rationale for procuring a benefit, then the opposite should be true, since, at the end of the day, economic operators will not be receiving anything beyond what they would have received from the market (assuming the compensation is limited to lost trade). Unfortunately there is no case law suggesting that an inquiry into the rationale for subsidisation is appropriate when deciding whether a benefit has been conferred. Indeed, this was the reason for including Article 8 in the SCM Agreement, a provision that exonerated from liability three forms of subsidies aiming at providing (more or less) public goods. Article 8 of the SCM Agreement lapsed in 2000, however, and to date no WTO panel has ever pronounced on similar grounds: a benefit has been bestowed, according to standard case law, if an individual receives from the government what he or she could not receive from the market with no additional inquiry into the rationale for subsidisation full stop.

We are thus left with the last element: specificity. The case law[47] has consistently held that both de jure (eg, by statutory language the list of beneficiaries is limited to a few operators) and de facto (eg, in the absence of similar statutory language, the measure operates so as to limit the list of beneficiaries to a few operators) schemes are covered, Adopting a law that would provide for compensation of innocent bystanders would fall, if at all, under the latter category. But then it would be impossible to demonstrate that the EU would know ex ante the identity of the firms that eventually would be compensated (subsidised). There is an

[45] We should note at the outset that if the response is affirmative, then the US in our example would have even more of an incentive to choose those targets that will make more noise through their lobbying efforts in Brussels, since the only way to make them stop making noise would be for the EU to comply with its obligations.

[46] This is not compensation in the sense of Article 22 DSU, since the beneficiary is not a third state, but EU economic operators.

[47] For an overview of the case law in this respect, see L Rubini, *The Definition of Subsidy and State Aid Law: WTO and EC Law in Comparative Perspective* (Oxford, Oxford University Press, 2009); see also PC Mavroidis, P Messerlin and JM Wauters, *The Law and Economics of Contingent Protection* (Cheltenham, Elgar Publishing, 2008).

analogy to free (but non-compulsory) education: a state provides it without knowing who will make use of it, let alone intending for specific beneficiaries. The identity of beneficiaries will depend on the action not of the subsidiser, but of a third entity, in our example, the US. For these reasons, we believe that the better arguments lie with the view that similar schemes should not be considered specific.

An even better solution to the problem of addressing the specific costs to targeted firms from non-compliance by the EU is one where EU exporters are not retaliated against in the first place. Firms would then not confront the costs associated with reallocating output etc. Economists and lawyers have long advocated greater use of direct compensation of the negatively affected trading partner in cases like the one at hand.[48] The EU could have simply transferred the value of the lost trade volume as determined by the WTO arbitrators to the US, ie, some US$200 million a year.

As noted above, there is precedent for financial compensation to be used in instances where a WTO member is not in a position to comply with a WTO ruling. In *US—Section 110(5) Copyright Act*,[49] a dispute brought by the EU in which the WTO ruled against the US, the US was not able to revise its legislation within the reasonable period of time established by the WTO. Arbitration determined that the loss incurred by the EU as a result of the illegal US action amounted to 1,219,900 per year. As part of the Wartime Supplemental Appropriations Act, signed into law on 16 April 2003, the US Congress approved a $3.3 million appropriation—to cover three years of payments—which was subsequently paid to the European Grouping of Societies of Authors and Composers at the request of the European Commission.[50] There is no legal or technical impediment to the European Commission undertaking a similar initiative in the case at hand.

A solution along these lines was also adopted in *US-Upland Cotton*.[51] In this case, Brail won its claim that the US government had been subsidising the production of upland cotton, and the two governments concluded a 'Framework for a Mutually Agreed Solution to the Cotton Dispute in the WTO'. According to the agreed framework, the US government agreed to transfer funds to an entity designated by Brazil. The Brazilian government would in turn use this money for technical assistance and capacity-building activities such as the promotion of the use of cotton, natural resources management and conservation, application of post-harvest technology etc.[52] All such activities, of course, could be characterised as subsidies, but no one mounted a challenge against Brazil for disbursing funds in this way.

In these two examples, the legal question remains the same: are we in the presence of a subsidy? The difference between these two instances where compensation was paid and the

[48] See, for example, R Hudec, 'The Adequacy of WTO Dispute Settlement Remedies for Developing Country Complainants' in B Hoekman, A Mattoo and P English (eds), *Development, Trade and the WTO: A Handbook* (Washington DC, World Bank 2002); and M Bronckers, and N van den Broek, 'Financial Compensation in the WTO' (2005) 8 *Journal of International Economic Law* 101, 126. N Limão and K Saggi, 'Tariff Retaliation versus Financial Compensation in the Enforcement of International Trade Agreements' (2008) 76 *Journal of International Economics* 48, 60 show that a system of monetary fines that is supported by the threat of tariff retaliation is more efficient than one based on retaliation alone.

[49] Panel Report, *United States—Section 110(5) Copyright Act* [US—Section 110(5) Copyright Act], DS160.

[50] The funds were used for combating piracy on the Internet and supporting actions to strengthen copyright enforcement in Europe and the US. See Hoekman and Kostecki (n 2). The details of the arbitration award are discussed in Grossman and Mavroidis (n 27).

[51] Appellate Body Report, *United States—Subsidies on Upland Cotton* [US—Upland Cotton], DS267.

[52] WTO Doc WT/DS267/45 of 31 August 2010. See also US Department of State, International Agreements Other than Treaties Transmitted in Accordance with the Provisions of 1 USC 112b as amended.

solution we advocate to the innocent bystander problem from a purely legal perspective is that it could be the US that is accused of subsidisation. This is not compelling. While it is probably too early to speak of acquiescence, one case of compensation is an accident, but two cases start taking us down the continuum towards the direction of 'practice'. It seems that WTO members are willing to accept that payments of this sort should not enter the framework of the SCM Agreement either because they do not consider them to confer a benefit or because they fail the specificity requirement.

While a shift towards the use of financial compensation would help solve one problem, it may give rise to another. From a systemic, WTO compliance perspective, such a move could reduce compliance incentives, as the individual (per EU household) cost of compensating the affected European firms will be (very) small—just a few euros a year. At the same time, the evidence suggests that while firms like Fedon incur high costs and as a result have big incentives to lobby for policy reform (and to litigate), it is not very effective in inducing compliance. The illegal Banana policy lasted for many years. Complaints by negatively affected firms such as Fedon do not appear to have played any role in the eventual reform of EU policy.

There is a broader point here. At present, retaliation by one WTO member randomly (at least from the perspective of the targeted firms) imposes excess costs on the affected exporters in the WTO member maintaining illegal policies. But the same would happen if the latter was to renegotiate the terms of the WTO contract with the former. Thus, if the EU were to take the position that it is not in its interest to comply with a WTO ruling, it can offer the US other trade concessions. This would give rise to the same sort of effects as selective US retaliation: some industries and firms would be negatively affected on a rather arbitrary basis and this would therefore result in 'inequitable' outcomes. This suggests that there is a case for a general rule to be proposed: either offer financial compensation during the period in which there is non-compliance with a WTO ruling or compensate all the exporters targeted by retaliation, in both instances shifting the cost to taxpayers. This leaves it to the US to continue to make the case in the WTO for compliance. If it becomes clear that there is not going to be compliance, the EU has the choice of either continuing to pay compensation indefinitely or to engage in renegotiations with the US. The latter is the primary mechanism foreseen in the GATT/WTO to address matters of this type and there is a long history of successful renegotiation of tariff commitments. We would argue that such renegotiations should be pursued in a way that affects all import-competing industries in the EU proportionately so as to maintain the initial structure of relative protection that presumably reflected the political economy equilibrium that prevailed at the time the EU engaged in the original exchange of market access concessions with the US (and other WTO members if this exchange took place in a multilateral round of trade negotiations).[53]

An implication of our suggestion is that policy is moved towards improving economic welfare by lowering trade barriers. This is also a key dimension of the approach proposed by Lawrence,[54] who calls on WTO members when negotiating market access liberalisation to identify ex ante which tariffs/sectors would be targeted for additional liberalisation in

[53] In practice, a uniform tariff reduction strategy is unlikely to be feasible because there is another party at the table with export interests in specific industries. Thus, reductions may need to be limited to a sub-set of sectors. But the principle of 'spreading the pain' as equitably as possible across EU industries should continue to apply.

[54] R Lawrence, *Crimes and Punishment: Retaliation under the WTO* (Washington DC, Institute for International Economics, 2003).

cases such as the one discussed in this chapter. In practice, governments have not shown any interest in pursuing this idea, but the ex post approach sketched out above would be a feasible path to move from retaliation and the associated welfare costs towards a system where the remedy involves trade liberalisation. Moving towards greater neutrality in the incidence of the adjustment costs associated with non-compliance/renegotiation would both safeguard the implicit property rights of EU firms and do more to protect the general interest—if defined as the overall economic welfare of the EU.

VI. CONCLUDING REMARKS

The CJEU, in its *Fedon* judgment, confused two issues: the issue of the relevance of WTO law (as a benchmark to evaluate the consistency of EU actions with the international obligations assumed by the EU by virtue of its adherence to the WTO) and the issue of *locus standi*, eg, who can legitimately claim a breach of WTO obligations by the EU before the Luxembourg Courts. In doing so, it condoned a practice of redistribution of wealth across segments of the EU society in the name of the 'general' EU interest. This is wrong. While we believe that there is no place for the direct effect of WTO law in the EU legal order, we have argued why the EU should compensate losers like Fedon who play the game by the rules. Taking one for the team is commendable when it is the team and not another individual player that profits. We have pointed to avenues that the EU institutions could explore in order to avoid repetition of the unfortunate Fedon experience in the future. Otherwise, the EU might find its responsibility engaged for a breach of the ECHR in the same way and for the same legal reasons that the responsibility of its Member States could be—under certain conditions that have been highlighted in this chapter—engaged (should the Strasbourg Court decide to set aside its *Bosphorus* case law) for what this chapter has described as a regulatory taking. In that vein, we have also discussed the possibility of submitting disputes of this sort to the Strasbourg Court. In our view, this possibility should be encouraged and probably privileged, in case the CJEU continues to construe EU law in clinical isolation of WTO law.

16

The EU's Accession to the ECHR and Due Process Rights in EU Competition Law Matters: Nothing New under the Sun?

ALBERT SANCHEZ GRAELLS*

I. INTRODUCTION

THE FORESEEABLE ACCESSION of the European Union (EU) to the European Convention on Human Rights (ECHR)[1] (as per Article 6(2) of the Treaty on European Union (TEU))[2] raises important questions regarding the extent to which amendments to the current EU competition law enforcement system are required.[3] In view of the future (clearer) possibility of bringing challenges against judgments of the Court of Justice of the European Union (CJEU) before the European Court of Human Rights (ECtHR)—not least, in view of the envisaged co-respondent mechanism discussed in detail in other chapters of this book—or, at least, the (clearer) mandate for the CJEU to apply the ECHR in full in all its jurisdictional activities,[4] an analysis of the current enforcement mechanisms in that light seems particularly relevant and has triggered substantial attention from academics and practitioners alike.

* Senior Lecturer in Commercial Law, School of Law, University of Leicester, LE1 7RX, UK. Presented at the conference on 'Accession of the EU to the ECHR', held in the Brussels campus of the University of Maastricht on 16–17 November 2012, where a lively discussion with participants helped the author gather some interesting insights. I am also grateful to my colleagues Vassilis Tzevelekos, Francisco Marcos, Nikos Vogiatzis, Vicky Kosta and Nikos Skoutaris for their comments to earlier drafts. The usual disclaimer applies.

[1] European Convention for the Protection of Human Rights and Fundamental Freedoms as amended by Protocols Nos 11 and 14 as from its entry into force on 1 June 2010.

[2] [2010] OJ C83/13.

[3] See I Forrester, 'Due Process in EC Competition Cases: A Distinguished Institution with Flawed Procedures' (2009) 34(6) *European Law Review* 817; I Forrester, 'Judicial Review and Competition Law: An Overview of EU and National Case Law' (April 2011) *e-Competitions*, No 35611; I Forrester, 'A Bush in Need of Pruning: The Luxuriant Growth of Light Judicial Review' in CD Ehlermann and M Marquis (eds), *European Competition Law Annual 2009: The Evaluation of Evidence and its Judicial Review in Competition Cases* (Oxford, Hart Publishing, 2011); and C Bellamy, 'ECHR and Competition Law Post-Menarini: An Overview of EU and National Case Law' (July 2012) *e-Competitions*, No 47946.

[4] Until now, the ECtHR was only reviewing EU law and its application indirectly. After accession, the ECtHR's review of EU law and the judgments of the CJEU will be direct and, possibly, more intense. For discussion and a critical appraisal of the interaction between both courts, among others, see V Tzevelekos, 'When Elephants Fight, it is the Grass that Suffers: "Hegemonic Struggle" in Europe and its Side-Effects for International Law' in K Dzehtsiarou, T Konstadinides, T Lock and N O'Meara (eds), *Human Rights Law in Europe: The Influence, Overlaps and Contradictions of the EU and the ECHR* (London, Routledge, 2013).

In my opinion, the most hotly disputed issue concerns whether due process rights are sufficiently protected through the review mechanisms in place for decisions of the European Commission in EU competition law matters.[5] Therefore, this chapter will focus on an analysis of the EU competition law enforcement system under Article 6(1) ECHR and, to the extent necessary, the corresponding Article 47 of the Charter of Fundamental Rights of the European Union (EUCFR).[6]

In order to 'set the scene' for the analysis of this research question, an outline of the ongoing discussion about the compatibility of the current EU competition enforcement system with Article 6(1) ECHR will be provided (section II). Then, this chapter will aim to contribute to such debate in a threefold manner by: (i) sketching the peculiarities of the enforcement of EU competition law, which basically derive from the complex and data intensive economic assessments required in most cases (section III); (ii) critically appraising the requirements of Article 6(1) ECHR in the field of EU competition law in view of those peculiarities (section IV); and (iii) assessing the impact of those requirements in terms of the potentially necessary amendments to the EU competition law enforcement system upon the EU's accession to the ECHR (section V). Some brief conclusions will close the chapter (section VI).

Suffice it to anticipate here that the basic contention of the chapter is that, given the specific architecture of the EU competition law enforcement system under Regulation 1/2003[7] and as long as an effective (arguably, soft or marginal) judicial review mechanism is already available to the undertakings affected by sanctions derived from EU competition law infringements, no significant changes are required in order to make the system comply with Articles 6(1) ECHR and 47 EUCFR.[8] This position will be further supported by the express normative assumption that undertakings (or companies) deserve a relatively more limited protection than individuals under the ECHR and, more specifically, under Article 6(1) ECHR—at least as regards non-core due process guarantees, such as the standard of review applicable to the revision of competition law decisions (as opposed to 'core' due process guarantees such as the presumption of innocence, the principle of equality of arms, the right to have full access to the evidence, or the right not to suffer undue delays, which, due to space constraints, will not be discussed in full; see below, section IV.B).

II. COMPETITION LAW ENFORCEMENT AND COMPLIANCE WITH ARTICLE 6(1) ECHR

Given the (apparently) increasingly heftier fines imposed by the European Commission[9] on the basis of Articles 101 and 102 of the Treaty on the Functioning of the European Union

[5] In similar terms, see AE Beumer, 'The Interplay between Article 6 ECHR & Article 47 Charter and the EU Competition Enforcement System—Is There a Need of 'Reviewing' the Standard of Review?', Working Paper presented at the 'A Europe of Rights: the EU and the ECHR' Workshop, University of Surrey (8–9 June 2012).

[6] [2000] OJ C364/1.

[7] Council Regulation (EC) No 1/2003 of 16 December 2002 on the implementation of the rules on competition laid down in Articles [101] and [102] of the Treaty [2003] OJ L1/1.

[8] Similarly, A Scordamaglia, 'Cartel Proof, Imputation and Sanctioning in European Competition Law: Reconciling Effective Enforcement and Adequate Protection of Procedural Guarantees' (2010) 7(1) *Competition Law Review* 5, 51. Contra, see Forrester, 'Due Process' (n 3) 832.

[9] See WPJ Wils, 'The Increased Level of EU Antitrust Fines, Judicial Review, and the European Convention on Human Rights' (2010) 33(1) *World Competition* 5; FR Agerbeek, 'EU Antitrust Fines and ECHR Fair Trial Rights' (2010), available at http://echrblog.blogspot.co.uk/2010/05/eu-antitrust-fines-and-echr-fair-trial.html.

(TFEU),[10] there is no doubt that allegations of competition law infringements must be considered 'criminal charges' of sorts for the purposes of the ECHR—which, in principle, triggers the application of the due process guarantees envisaged in Article 6(1) ECHR.[11] However, the situation is not that simple since, as hinted by the ECtHR in *Jussila*,

> [T]he evolution of the notion of a 'criminal charge' has underpinned a gradual broadening of the criminal head to cases not strictly belonging to the traditional categories of the criminal law, for example ... competition law ... [which] differ from the hard core of criminal law [so that] the criminal-head guarantees will not necessarily apply with their full stringency.[12]

Therefore, there is an open question concerning the intensity and extent to which due process rights must be guaranteed in EU competition law enforcement (ie, whether only paragraph 1 or also paragraphs 2 and 3 of Article 6(1) ECHR are applicable in these cases and, if applicable, to which extent), and whether the current enforcement system complies with the 'less than fully stringent' requirements of Article 6(1) ECHR in 'non-hard core criminal cases'.[13]

This has generated a wave of scrutiny and criticism of the enforcement and review mechanisms available at the EU level in view of the institutional architecture of the European Commission and the possibilities for the review of its decisions before the General Court (GC) and the CJEU.[14] Indeed, given the institutional design and the concurrent powers of investigation and decision making of the European Commission in competition law matters (most notably under Regulation 1/2003),[15] it must be configured as a body not meeting the requirements of Article 6(1) ECHR for a 'fair and public hearing within a reasonable time by an independent and impartial tribunal established by law'.[16] From the perspective of the ECHR and its interpretation by the ECtHR, there is no question about it and, however less than 'fully stringent' the requirements of Article 6(1) ECHR in the competition law field are, the system would not be compliant.

However, it is also acknowledged that this must not be automatically seen as a sufficient justification for any major changes in the enforcement system of EU competition law. According to the majority interpretation of Article 6(1) ECHR, the requirement for a 'fair and public hearing within a reasonable time by an independent and impartial tribunal established by law' must not necessarily be met at first instance when an administrative body reaches an initial decision imposing fines (even if they qualify as 'criminal

[10] [2010] OJ C83/47.

[11] This was first declared in *Société Stenuit v France*, Series A No 232 (1992) 14 EHRR 509. Generally, see D Harris, M O'Boyle and C Warbrick, *Law of the European Convention on Human Rights*, 2nd edn (Oxford, Oxford University Press, 2009) 201–99.

[12] *Jussila v Finland*, App No 73053/01 (2006). *Cf* M Bronckers and A Vallery, 'Business as Usual after Menarini?' (2012) 3(1) *MLex Ab Extra* 44.

[13] For the purposes of our discussion, this chapter will only be looking at Article 6(1) ECHR *as such* and, more specifically, at the issue of the standard of judicial review required in EU competition law cases. Other issues, such as the right to a trial without unjustified delays or the role and application of the presumption of innocence, will not be discussed more than in passing.

[14] For general discussion, see D Slater et al, 'Competition Law Proceedings before the European Commission and the Right to a Fair Trial: No Need for Reform?' (2008) GCLC Working Paper 04/08, www.coleurope.eu/content/gclc/documents/GCLC%20WP%2004-08.pdf, as well as the special issue of the *Competition Law Review* available at www.clasf.org/CompLRev/Issues/CompLRevVol7Issue1.pdf.

[15] See A Andreangeli et al, 'Enforcement by the Commission: The Decisional and Enforcement Structure in Antitrust Cases and the Commission's Fining System' in M Merola and D Waelbroeck (eds), *Towards an Optimal Enforcement of Competition Rules in Europe: Time for a Review of Regulation 1/2003?* (Brussels, Bruylant, 2010).

[16] L Ortiz Blanco, *European Community Competition Procedure* (Oxford, Oxford University Press, 2006) 159.

charges' under the ECHR). The guarantees mandated by Article 6(1) ECHR will be (if not absolutely sufficiently) upheld if such initial 'conviction' can be challenged before a body meeting the requirements of Article 6(1) ECHR that can review it on the merits, both in facts and in points of law[17] (see below, section IV.A). In my view, this is also in compliance with Article 13 ECHR, given that access to judicial review serves the purposes of being an effective remedy against any potential breaches of the fundamental rights of the undertakings involved in Commission-led investigations.[18]

Hence, the discussion turns towards the actual possibilities to challenge decisions adopted by the European Commission before the GC and the CJEU and, more specifically, criticises the (potential) limitations imposed by Article 263 TFEU on the scope of review of the Commission's Decisions in competition law matters, since the GC and the CJEU have jurisdiction for the following grounds for review: 'lack of competence, infringement of an essential procedural requirement, infringement of the Treaties or of any rule of law relating to their application, or misuse of powers' (which, in its literal tenor, does not include a full review on the facts). However, it should also be taken into consideration that, according to Article 31 of Regulation 1/2003, the European courts have 'unlimited jurisdiction to review decisions whereby the Commission has fixed a fine or periodic penalty payment [and] may cancel, reduce or increase the fine or periodic penalty payment'.[19]

At this point, the assessment of whether or not Articles 263 TFEU and 31 of Regulation 1/2003 (and the practice developed by the GC and the CJEU on their basis) is sufficient to comply with the requirements of Article 6(1) ECHR becomes crucial. So far, this question has been brushed aside relatively easily by the CJEU while, even if it has not been expressly tackled by the ECtHR, there are doubts that the Strasbourg Court will be equally supportive of EU competition law enforcement—particularly in terms of the *scope and intensity of the judicial review* available for challengers of Commission Decisions enforcing Articles 101 and 102 TFEU.

Indeed, according to the incipient CJEU case law in *KME Germany v Commission*[20] and *Chalkor v Commission*,[21] the question of whether any reforms to the review of EU competition law enforcement decisions are necessary in view of Article 6(1) ECHR has been (tentatively) answered in negative terms. In the CJEU's view, the protection conferred by Article 47 EUCFR 'implements in European Union law the protection afforded by Article 6(1) of the ECHR' and 'it is necessary, therefore, to refer only to Article 47 [EUCFR]'.[22] In doing so, the CJEU concluded that the EU competition law system is compliant and that there is no infringement of the principle of effective judicial protection laid down in Article 47 EUCFR, since the review process before the EU Courts *in fact* involves review of both the law and the facts, and means that they have the power to assess the evidence, to annul the contested

[17] *A Menarini Diagnostics Srl v Italy*, App No 43509/08 (2011) [59]. See, along the same lines, Bellamy (n 3) 2; and Beumer (n 5) 12–13.

[18] Indeed, the procedures before the GC and the CJEU do not make it excessively difficult or unreasonable to defend those rights. See *Kudła v Poland*, App No 30210/96 (ECtHR, 26 October 2000).

[19] On the standard for review, see the key contribution by M Jaeger, 'The Standard of Review in Competition Cases Involving Complex Economic Assessments: Towards the Marginalisation of Marginal Review?' (2011) 2(4) *Journal of European Competition Law & Practice* 295. See also F Cengiz, 'Judicial Review and the Rule of Law in the EU Competition Law Regime after *Alrosa*' (2011) 7(1) *European Competition Journal* 127.

[20] Case C-389/10 P *KME Germany AG, KME France SAS and KME Italy SpA v European Commission* [2011] nyr.

[21] Case C-386/10 P *Chalkor AE Epexergasias Metallon v European Commission* [2011] nyr.

[22] C-389/10 P *KME v Commission* [2011] nyr, [51] and [52]. See Wils (n 9) 13.

decision and to alter the amount of fines.[23] Hence, the current system sufficiently guarantees the due process rights of undertakings involved in competition law investigations and/or having been found in breach of EU competition rules and, consequently, there is no need to promote a more protective system. Whether the CJEU has or not reached such a conclusion (implicitly) taking into account a 'reduced' set of fair trial requirements in view of the 'non-hard core' nature of competition law as a 'criminal charge' remains unclear. But the legal position is that, in general terms, the current system for the enforcement of EU competition rules and its review uphold the required due process rights of the undertakings involved and, more specifically, that there is no insufficiency in the scope or intensity of judicial review in EU competition law cases.

On its part, the ECtHR has so far not been expressly and directly confronted with the issue of compliance of the EU competition law enforcement system with Article 6(1) ECHR,[24] but it has already analysed the Italian system of competition law enforcement in *Menarini*.[25] Given the shared elements in the Italian and EU enforcement systems, the findings of the ECtHR in *Menarini* are considered highly relevant to the appraisal of the EU situation. Even if the majority decision in *Menarini* found that, in the case at hand, there had been no breach of due process rights under Article 6(1) ECHR because the initial 'conviction' had de facto been fully reviewed on appeal (again, despite a language similar to that of Article 263 TFEU, imposing judicial deference towards the exercise of administrative discretion by the Italian competition authority), the dissenting opinion by Judge Pinto De Albuquerque openly questioned that such degree of judicial deference towards administrative decisions based on complex economic assessments[26] allows appellants to benefit from sufficient scrutiny of 'the core of the reasoning of the administrative decision of conviction, namely the technical evaluation of the charges against the applicant'. Indeed, the dissenting opinion in *Menarini* reads Article 6(1) ECHR as requiring a full (hard) substantive judicial review of the core of the technical evaluations conducted in competition law procedures and clearly points to the need for an independent, specific and detailed evaluation of the illegality and culpability of the challenger's behaviour by the review tribunal[27]—hence excluding any possible judicial deference or marginal review of the decision adopted by the competition authority (or, by implication or extension, the European Commission).

In this regard, the application of the test advanced by the *Menarini* dissenting opinion has been considered to leave some doubts in the air, since the (literal) wording of Articles 263 TFEU and 31 of Regulation 1/2003 may fall short of ensuring a full scrutiny of 'the core of the reasoning of the administrative decision of conviction, namely the technical evaluation

[23] Summary of the *KME v Commission and Chalkor v Commission* cases by the Legal Service of the European Commission, http://ec.europa.eu/dgs/legal_service/arrets/09c272_en.pdf.

[24] Although this issue was due to be considered by the ECtHR in *Senator Lines*, App No 56672/00 (2004), the hearing of which was cancelled in light of the judgment of the Court of First Instance (now the GC) setting aside the fine imposed by the European Commission. N Colneric, 'Protection of Fundamental Rights through the Court of Justice of the European Communities', http://denning.law.ox.ac.uk/iecl/pdfs/working2colneric.pdf.

[25] Prior decisions were reached in relation to the French enforcement system, but in those cases, they concerned the review available against an interlocutory decision, ie, a challenge of a warrant authorising a raid of the premises of suspected cartelists; see *Canal Plus v France*, App No 29408/08 (ECtHR, 21 December 2010) and *Primagaz v France*, App No 29613/08 (ECtHR, 21 December 2010). See also Beumer (n 5) 14.

[26] Which is the general rule in the system of EU competition law enforcement (both at the EU and the decentralised levels); see R Thompson QC, 'Judicial Review and the European Courts: Working with Our Partners. Part 1' (24 July 2012), http://eutopialaw.com/2012/07/24/judicial-review-and-the-european-courts-working-with-our-partners-part-1.

[27] *Menarini Diagnostics* (n 17) dissenting opinion [7].

of the charges against the applicant'—regardless of whether *in fact* such full review is conducted by the European courts, as clearly found by the CJEU in *KME Germany v Commission* and *Chalkor v Commission*. Such doubts will be dispelled in this chapter, which broadly sides with the position of the CJEU and will aim to show that the peculiarities and strengths of the current system of enforcement of EU competition law suffice to meet the standards of Article 6(1) ECHR—and, consequently, that there is no need for reform (either immediately or upon the accession of the EU to the ECHR).

In any case, it is worth stressing that, following the reported academic debate, a judicial debate between the CJEU and the ECtHR is served regarding the extension of the requirements of Article 6(1) ECHR after the EU's foreseeable accession to the ECHR and, additionally, concerning the extent of the duty of consistent interpretation of Article 47 EUCFR in its light—particularly in view of the 'less than fully stringent' requirements of Article 6(1) ECHR in 'non-hard core criminal cases' such as competition law cases.[28] All in all, and depending on the result of such debate, there seems to be room for a potential 're-reading' (ie, restriction) of the requirements of Article 6(1) ECHR in the field of EU competition law, particularly as regards the *scope and intensity of the judicial review* available for challengers of Decisions of the European Commission enforcing Articles 101 and 102 TFEU, in view of a joint construction based on *Jussila* and *Menarini*. This constitutes the focus of what will be attempted in the remainder of this chapter.

III. SOME PECULIARITIES OF COMPETITION LAW ENFORCEMENT

In order to further contextualize the discussion on due process and the implications of Article 6(1) ECHR in the field of competition law, particularly as regards the scope and intensity of the judicial review of administrative decisions, it is worth stressing some of the peculiarities of the EU competition law enforcement system. As shall be discussed in further detail (see below, section IV.A), the ECtHR is prepared to allow for relatively limited judicial review when the initial administrative procedure is robust—and, consequently, having a bird's eye view on some features of the system of EU competition law enforcement can be helpful.

First of all, it should be taken into consideration that the Directorate General for Competition (DG COMP) of the European Commission is probably among the most sophisticated enforcement bodies and far exceeds the level of resources and technical knowledge of most of its potential benchmarking counterparts. Therefore, if administrative bodies could be ranked by expertise and existing enforcement capacity, without doubt, the European Commission is one of the top competition law enforcement agencies worldwide. This is not to say that it is too big or too sophisticated to be subjected to effective judicial review, but I think that the existing level of enforcement capacity (even if always improvable, subject to resources availability) should be taken into consideration as a positive factor in favour of a relatively lenient approach towards the scrutiny of the system.[29]

[28] Scordamaglia (n 8) 52.

[29] This perception is shared by most practitioners, although not all of them consider that these characteristics and the ensuing 'good institutional reputation' should in any way alleviate the requirements of the ECHR in the field of EU competition law enforcement; see Forrester, 'Judicial Review and Competition Law: An Overview' (n 3).

Second, the European Commission and the National Competition Authorities of the EU Member States (NCAs) are integrated in the European Competition Network (ECN), which serves both purposes of coordination and cooperation, and facilitates the exchange of information and best practices that contribute to the further refinement of enforcement mechanisms and operations.[30] In that regard, there is a certain level of peer review in the enforcement activities of the European Commission, which can even trigger the attention of the competition authorities of other jurisdictions (notably the US) in high-profile cases. Such scrutiny beyond the EU jurisdiction is further promoted by the International Competition Network (ICN) and the active participation in this forum of the main competition authorities worldwide. All this is to indicate that the European Commission's enforcement activities are subject to a degree of (restricted) transparency and potential peer review that seem to work as an effective check and balance of the administrative discretion it exercises.

Third, it should also be stressed that the community of EU competition law practitioners has grown significantly in recent years and that companies involved in competition law investigations tend to be represented by skilled and highly qualified teams of lawyers (and economists) that defend their interests effectively before the European Commission—that is, that competition law enforcement tends to involve lawyers from the very beginning of the investigative procedure and not only at the judicial stage, which is not always the case in other areas of economic regulation (of a 'criminal' nature for the purposes of the ECHR, such as the conduct of disciplinary proceedings by professional bodies or the development of tax investigations and audits). Moreover, in many instances, it is not rare to see the enforcement team outnumbered by the group of lawyers and consultants engaged by the undertakings under investigation or challenging an infringement decision before the relevant courts (either individually or in the aggregate, particularly in cases with multiple defendants such as cartel cases). In that regard, it is hard to think of instances where the undertakings under investigation are not given a full, proper opportunity to present their case and defend against the charges eventually pressed by the European Commission. Again, this is not to say that the burden of ensuring fair trial rights can be discharged by the mere participation of lawyers in the procedure. However, this is to dispel the possible view of 'inferiority' of competition law defendants vis-a-vis the almighty competition authorities. In competition law procedures, the effective 'strength' of the parties tends to be much more balanced and, in the end, this should be taken into account in the analysis of the need for effective protection under Article 6(1) ECHR (see below, section IV.B).

Fourth, and with potentially far-reaching consequences, I think that it must be stressed that competition law enforcement is not a neutral exercise of economic regulation, but a policy oriented one that rests on incomplete and broad rules.[31] At the very end, the final

[30] However, it should be stressed that the European Commission does not oversee the enforcement activities of the NCAs. Indeed, as indicated in the Joint Statement of the Council and the Commission on the Functioning of the Network of Competition Authorities: 'All competition authorities within the Network are independent from one another. Cooperation between NCAs and with the Commission takes place on the basis of equality, respect and solidarity': http://ec.europa.eu/competition/ecn/joint_statement_en.pdf. Consequently, the European Commission assumes no responsibility for the NCA's enforcement decisions. See also Commission Notice on cooperation within the Network of Competition Authorities [2004] OJ C101/43.

[31] A Marra and A Sarra, 'Incomplete Antitrust Laws and Private Actions for Damages' (2010) 30 *European Journal of Law & Economics* 111; DA Crane, 'Rules versus Standards in Antitrust Adjudication' (2007) 64 *Washington & Lee Law Review* 49.

decision to be reached will be (strongly) conditioned by the ultimate goal that the competition authority wants to achieve.[32] However standard or 'textbook' a case may be, it must be borne in mind that competition law is inherently subject to the underlying microeconomic theories and other insights derived from industrial economics and, consequently, subject to change and to policy drivers.[33] Therefore, the complex economic assessments on which competition law enforcement unavoidably rests are not only complicated, but are also not (policy) neutral.[34] Moreover, given that enforcement resources are always limited, all competition authorities need to set their enforcement priorities and most of them also routinely disclose documents where they not only communicate such enforcement priorities, but also make public their theories of economic harm and their interpretation of the existing law (in the form of 'soft law'). Such publication of *soft law* documents not only contributes to the knowledge of the applicable laws, but also tends to bind the corresponding authorities in the conduct of their enforcement activities on the basis of general principles of legitimate expectations and estoppel.[35] Therefore, there is a high degree of transparency and some increased foreseeability of the enforcement activities to be conducted by most advanced competition authorities.

Finally, it should also be taken into consideration that the enforcement procedures followed at the EU level offer several opportunities for undertakings to challenge the views of the European Commission, including the conduct of hearings (which, however, tend not to be public due to confidentiality issues and basically in protection of the business interests of the investigated parties) and that they are designed on the blueprint of generally accepted administrative sanctioning procedures and their ensuing guarantees.[36] These procedures are overseen by a Hearing Officer who acts as an independent arbiter where a dispute on the effective exercise of procedural rights between parties and the European Commission's Directorate General for Competition arises in antitrust proceedings.[37] Ultimately, procedural flaws can also be reported to the European Ombudsman, who can open an investigation against the European Commission on the basis of the complaints raised by the undertakings concerned.[38] Therefore, even if the enforcement of competition law has some peculiarities, from a procedural point of view, it is hard to see why or how the same or very similar rules on administrative sanctioning procedures would be valid in other areas of law enforcement (particularly at the national level, such as securities regulation, taxation or money laundering supervision), but not acceptable when it comes to EU competition law. In my view, as a matter of general appraisal, it should be considered that the administrative

[32] RH Bork, *The Antitrust Paradox. A Policy at War with Itself*, 2nd edn (New York, Free Press, 1993) 50.

[33] For some authors, this should justify the complete abolition of competition laws. See, remarkably, the works of DT Armentano, *Antitrust Policy. The Case for Repeal* (Washington, CATO Institute, 1986) or ES Rockefeller, *The Antitrust Religion* (Washington, Cato Institute, 2007). However, failing a complete dismantling of the competition rules, the intrinsic policy element must be emphasised and put in perspective.

[34] DA Crane, 'Technocracy and Antitrust' (2008) 86(6) *Texas Law Review* 1159.

[35] For further discussion and references, see O Stefan, *Soft Law in Court. Competition Law, State Aid and the Court of Justice of the European Union* (The Hague, Wolters Kluwer Law & Business, 2012). See also A Sanchez Graells, 'Soft Law and the Private Enforcement of the EU Competition Rules' in JL Velasco San Pedro (ed), *Private Enforcement of Competition Law* (Valladolid, Lex Nova, 2011).

[36] Similarly, see Beumer (n 5) 26–27.

[37] Decision 2011/695/EU of the President of the European Commission of 13 October 2011 on the function and terms of reference of the hearing officer in certain competition proceedings [2011] OJ L275/29.

[38] European Parliament Decision 94/262/ECSC, EC, Euratom of 9 March 1994 on the regulations and general conditions governing the performance of the Ombudsman's duties [1994] OJ L113/15, as amended by Decision 2002/262/EC, ECSC, Euratom [2002] OJ L92/13 and Decision 2008/587/EC, Euratom [2008] OJ L189/25.

sanctioning procedures followed by the European Commission are sound and already offer a very advanced degree of procedural guarantees to the undertakings under investigation. Moreover, and in any case, the decisions of the European Commission are subjected to appeals procedures and, therefore, compliance with the right to a fair trial under Article 6(1) ECHR should be evaluated at this second stage, as discussed below.

IV. THE REQUIREMENTS OF ARTICLE 6(1) ECHR IN THE FIELD OF EU COMPETITION LAW ENFORCEMENT, WITH A FOCUS ON THE FACT THAT MOST DEFENDANTS ARE CORPORATIONS

As mentioned before (section II), the ECtHR clearly indicated in *Jussila* that the criminal-head guarantees will not necessarily apply with their full stringency to competition law cases, since they do not belong to the hard core of criminal charges covered by the ECHR. This section aims to re-assess such requirements in the field of competition law enforcement, taking into consideration the peculiarities just discussed (section III) and the fact that most competition law defendants are corporate entities.

A. What Requirements of Judicial Review Should be Derived from Article 6(1) ECHR in Non-hardcore Criminal Cases such as Competition Law Investigations?

In my view, the ECtHR recognised in *Jussila* that a full transfer of the guarantees developed under Article 6(1) ECHR for 'pure' criminal proceedings to the field of competition law cases would be an excess in the interpretation and application of the Convention.[39] Following that (implicit) recognition of a risk of excessive extension of the guarantees recognised in Article 6(1) ECHR, it seems appropriate to reconsider the extent and intensity of protection in competition law cases.[40] My proposal is to re-read the requirements of Article 6(1) ECHR to depart from the stringent position concerning hardcore criminal cases and to get closer to the requirements of Article 6(1) ECHR regarding administrative procedures (however less developed or consolidated they may be at this point in time). In my view, what is required in this area is, simply put, that *decisions adopted in the application of EU competition law are open to sufficient judicial review by a body that complies with Article 6(1) ECHR and that has jurisdiction to quash the decision in case it identifies material errors in fact or law*[41]—ie, the standard applicable to administrative decisions.

A limitation on the viability of this 'light(er) judicial review' approach may be found in the fact that the ECtHR declared that 'on an application for judicial review, the courts do not review the merits of the decision but confine themselves to ensuring, in brief, that the authority did not act illegally, unreasonably or unfairly'.[42] Indeed, in this same line of argument, it should be taken into consideration that as a matter of general requirements of

[39] Contra, see Bellamy (n 3) 9.

[40] For discussion, see A Andreangeli, 'Between Economic Freedom and Effective Competition Enforcement: The Impact of Antitrust Remedies Provided by the Modernisation Regulation on Investigated Parties' Freedom to Contract and to Enjoy Property' (2010) 6(2) *Competition Law Review* 225, 233–34.

[41] Similarly, see Harris, O'Boyle and Warbrick (n 11) 228–29.

[42] *Weeks v UK*, Series A No 114 (1987) 10 EHRR 293.

Article 6(1) ECHR, the reviewing tribunal must have 'jurisdiction to examine all questions of fact and law relevant to the dispute before it'.[43] However, in my view, such a restrictive approach would disregard the indications of the ECtHR itself in *Jussila* and would imply a full extrapolation of the guarantees developed under Article 6(1) ECHR for 'pure' criminal proceedings in their full stringency to this type of non-hardcore criminal cases.

On the contrary, I think that the case law of the ECtHR offers support for such a 'light(er) judicial review' approach in the field of administrative decisions. It is worth stressing that the ECtHR has found that, where: (i) the administrative body adopting the initial decision follows a procedure that sufficiently complies with Article 6 ECHR;[44] and (ii) the decision involves a 'classic exercise of administrative discretion' or, in other words 'the issues to be determined [require] a measure of professional knowledge or experience and the exercise of administrative discretion pursuant to wider policy aims',[45] (mere) judicial review of the legality of the decision suffices and a (full) right of appeal on the merits is not necessary[46]—always provided that the reviewing tribunal can effectively grant a remedy to the appellant if successful,[47] which includes the possibility of quashing the decision and remitting the case for a new decision.[48]

With all these considerations in mind, it seems difficult to contend that the current mechanisms for the review of enforcement decisions in the field of EU competition law are not only compliant with but already exceed the requirements of Article 6(1) ECHR when administrative decisions are concerned.

B. Should Corporate Defendants in Competition Law Cases Obtain Full Protection under Article 6(1) ECHR or are Some Limitations Justifiable?

On top of the former considerations, I think that in determining the extent and intensity of human rights protection in the enforcement of EU competition law, it should also be taken into consideration that, in my opinion, there is an inherently limited applicability of the ECHR to companies[49] (and, more generally, to legal entities).[50] Even if it has been submitted that 'Some rights have always and without discussion been regarded as applicable to

[43] *Terra Woningen v The Netherlands* (1996) 24 EHRR 456 [53].

[44] *Bryan v UK*, Series A No 335 (1995); 21 EHRR 342 [47].

[45] *Tsfayo v UK*, App No 60860/00 (ECtHR, 14 November 2006) [46]; see Wils (n 9), 23–24; and Beumer (n 5) 13–14 and 24–25.

[46] *Zumtobel v Austria*, Series A No 268 (1993); 17 EHRR 116 [32].

[47] *Kingsley v UK* (2002) 33 EHRR 13.

[48] For further details on these issues and the balance between full rights of appeal and limited judicial review in the analysis of Article 6 guarantees in the area of challenges against administrative decisions, see Harris, O'Boyle and Warbrick (n 11) 229–32.

[49] Generally, on the applicability of Article 6 ECHR to the rights of companies in antitrust proceedings, see TK Giannakopoulos, *Safeguarding Companies' Rights in Competition and Anti-dumping/Anti-subsidies Proceedings* (The Hague, Kluwer Law International, 2011) 16–27.

[50] Harris, O'Boyle and Warbrick (n 11) 795–96. For a general review of the applicability of the ECHR to companies, see M Emberland, *The Human Rights of Companies: Exploring the Structure of ECHR Protection* (Oxford, Oxford University Press, 2006) 26–64; PHMC van Kempen, 'Human Rights and Criminal Justice Applied to Legal Persons. Protection and Liability of Private and Public Juristic Entities under the ICCPR, ECHR, ACHR and AfChHPR' (2010) 14(3) *Electronic Journal of Comparative Law* 14–17, www.ejcl.org/143/art143-20.pdf; and A Austin, 'Commerce and the European Convention on Human Rights' (2004) 11 *Commercial Law Practitioner* 223.

companies, including the right to enjoyment of the procedural guarantees in Art 6(1)',[51] in my view, this maximalist position requires further scrutiny in light of the potential de facto configuration of the ECtHR as a third appellate instance in EU competition law cases.[52] Should the standard for review applied by the GC and the CJEU be deemed insufficient, all EU competition law cases would immediately be susceptible to be brought before the ECtHR (under Article 6(1) ECHR and, potentially, Article 13 ECHR as well). If it then applied the standard of review indicated in the *Menarini* dissenting opinion, it would indeed be reviewing the substance of the case—which surely cannot be an outcome desirably derived from the guarantees built in Article 6(1) ECHR.

As a preliminary observation, it should be made clear that, in my opinion, not all fair trial or due process-related guarantees in Article 6 ECHR (even within Article 6(1) ECHR) carry the same weight and relevance. In this regard, the standard of review applied in the appeal of preliminary decisions adopted by a robust administrative body *is a 'non-core' due process guarantee* (since a relaxation of its requirements has already been accepted by the ECtHR; see above, section IV.A), as opposed to 'core' due process guarantees such as the presumption of innocence, the principle of equality of arms, the right to have full access to the evidence[53] or the right not to suffer undue delays.[54] Admittedly, corporate defendants deserve the proper protection of their core due process guarantees, as any other potential victim of (blatant or, at least, material) breaches of due process requirements. However, at least in the area of non-core guarantees, my view is that corporate defendants can see the scope of protection reduced under the ECHR and that such limitation of (full, non-core) protections would not significantly diminish their (effective) legal position or substantially affect their possibilities to (actually) defend their legal interests. And this should not be seen as a discrimination against corporate entities as compared to individuals (ie, natural persons) or other types of associations, since their effective or actual need of protection is lower and, in any case, the scope of this protection through non-core due process guarantees needs balancing against the potential risks for strategic abuse.

Indeed, given the sophistication of legal counsel that competition law defendants usually enjoy (see above, section III), it is not hard to see that there is an actual risk of the ECtHR becoming a sort of third appellate instance for competition law infringers whose challenges to the Commission's infringement decisions have already been dismissed by the GC and the CJEU. If the standard of review imposed was too stringent and the ECtHR took on the task of enforcing it to its full and ultimate consequences, it would actually assume the task of re-opening the case on its substance (which is questionably the purpose of Article 6(1) ECHR protections), it would need to reappraise the case in full and it would make itself into a 'competition law court' (ie, effectively, a third appellate instance in EU competition law cases—without it being clear that the ECtHR is in a good position to carry out such

[51] Emberland (n 50) 110. Further than that, Article 6(1) is considered amongst a group of ECHR 'provisions that apply ipso facto to corporate entities pursuing economic goals because they by their nature have collective aspects, economic facets, and/or are more or less objectively construed': ibid 63.

[52] Which would very likely be the case if the ECtHR were to follow the recently identified trend of an extension of its jurisdiction by an expansive teleological interpretation of the ECHR; ibid 201.

[53] This was analysed by the ECtHR specifically as concerns competition law enforcement in France and in terms of the general principle of equality of arms, and a violation of Article 6(1) ECHR was found where the corporate defendant was not given access to certain parts of the legal reports issued throughout the appeals process; see *Lilly France v France*, App No 53892/00 (ECtHR, 14 October 2003).

[54] *Cf* van Kempen (n 50) 17, who considers that the position of companies is more limited than that of individuals, in view of the different ways in which legal persons and stakeholders are affected.

an undertaking without major changes and investments, particularly in terms of expertise or human capital; see below, section V). Other remedies, basically limited to a monetary compensation to the undertakings, would be equally unsatisfactory unless they covered the whole or part of the fines imposed—which the ECtHR should in any case not determine without a full reappraisal of the case. All in all, the system seems fundamentally incapable of satisfactorily addressing these situations.

In this regard, I think that it is necessary to draw a line between situations where there is an actual need to protect a legitimate corporate interest derived from its due process rights (ie, situations where corporate entities are true victims of an infringement of fundamental rights by an ECHR Member State, such as cases of flagrant expropriation or other instances of breaches of 'core' due process rights) and other situations (such as relatively theoretical discussions on the intensity of the standard of judicial review) where the system may be too openly exposed to abuse if corporations are fully equated to individuals (which affected rights, such as personal freedom, do deserve more demanding standards of protection). In my view, *this justifies a restriction on the requirements concerning the scope and intensity of judicial review of competition enforcement decisions since the situation could otherwise become unmanageable*[55]—and such a restriction of non-core due process guarantees should not be seen as disproportionate, given the general level of protection of due process rights in EU competition law enforcement (see above, section III).

In the absence of other (material) breaches of 'core' due process rights (the protection of which may be subject to more stringent, almost absolute requirements), I think that it is worth taking into consideration that the ECHR 'is intended to guarantee not rights that are theoretical or illusory but rights that are practical and effective'[56] and that this is particularly true in the case of non-core due process-related guarantees. Therefore, the mere (theoretical) expectation of a corporation to have a given competition enforcement decision against it reviewed in potentially more detail on factual grounds by the GC falls short from constituting a practical and effective ('core', but possibly even 'non-core') due process right and in (almost) all instances will merely be a theoretical or illusory construct aimed at deferring (or, ideally, striking out) the effects of the adverse enforcement decision (already subjected to generally robust administrative and judicial review procedures). Therefore, there seems to be no good justification for the extension of this possibility of challenge before the ECtHR of a decision enforcing EU competition law rules *solely on the basis that the judicial scrutiny conducted by the GC and the CJEU may have been excessively limited.*

[55] A similar approach was favoured by Advocate General Ruiz-Jarabo in his Opinion in Case C-338/00 P *Volkswagen v European Commission* [2003] ECR I-9189 [66]. See WPJ Wils, 'EU Antitrust Enforcement Powers and Procedural Rights and Guarantees: The Interplay between EU Law, National Law, the Charter of Fundamental Rights of the EU and the European Convention on Human Rights' (2011) 34(2) *World Competition* 189. *Cf* C Leskinen, 'An Evaluation of the Rights of Defense During Antitrust Inspections in the Light of the Case Law of the ECTHR: Would the Accession of the European Union to the ECHR Bring About a Significant Change?' (29 April 2010) Instituto de Empresa Business School Working Paper No 10-04, http://ssrn.com/abstract=1616521.

[56] *Artico v Italy*, Series A No 37 (1980) 3 EHRR 1 [33]; Harris, O'Boyle and Warbrick (n 11) 15.

V. ANY NEED FOR CHANGE IN EU COMPETITION LAW ENFORCEMENT AS PER ARTICLE 6(1) ECHR?

As just discussed—given the potential risk of the ECtHR becoming a sort of third appellate instance and the feebleness of the expectations of corporations to achieve an even higher degree of (factual) scrutiny of the adverse decision at stake—in the absence of other (material) breaches of due process rights, *it is hard to see an advantage derived from opening or extending the possibilities to challenge competition enforcement decisions before the ECtHR on the sole basis that the judicial scrutiny conducted by the GC and the CJEU could have been more intense.* Therefore, I consider it both legally consistent and normatively desirable to adopt a restrictive approach towards the assessment of any need for the introduction of changes in the system for the enforcement of EU competition rules and the revision of such enforcement decisions on the basis of Article 6(1) ECHR (*if it ain't broke, don't fix it*). This is so for many reasons.

A. Sufficiency of the Actual Scope and Intensity of Judicial Review

First and foremost—regardless of the literal drafting of Articles 263 TFEU and 31 of Regulation 1/2003,[57] and the eventual mentions of the European courts to the 'discretion', the 'substantial margin of discretion' or the 'wide discretion' of the Commission in their judgments—it has been made abundantly clear that the European courts do *in fact* subject the European Commission's decisions in competition law cases to very high standards of review, both in law and in the factual situation concerned.[58] And, in my view, this is perfectly in line with the requirements of the ECtHR in *Menarini*.[59]

Only adopting the very demanding test advanced in the *Menarini* dissenting opinion that 'the core of the reasoning of the administrative decision of conviction, namely the technical evaluation of the charges against the applicant' is subjected to 'an autonomous, specific and detailed evaluation' by the review body, the current EU review system would show a deficiency[60]—since the EU courts do not engage of their own in a full (re)assessment of the evidence available to the European Commission throughout the competition investigation.[61] Indeed, the CJEU has been clear in determining that it is 'required not to

[57] This approach is supported by the concurring opinion of Judge Sajo in *Menarini Diagnostics* (n 17). See also Bellamy (n 3) 5, who stresses that the same anti-formalistic approach was favoured by Advocate General Sharpston in her Opinion in Case C-389/10 P *KME v Commission* [2011] nyr, [73] and [83].

[58] As expressly indicated by the CJEU in Case C-389/10 P *KME v Commission* [2011] nyr, [121] and [131]. The same conclusion was reached in Case C 386/10 P *Chalkor v Commission* [2011] nyr, [82]. Along the same lines, see Jaeger (n 19) *in totum*; H Schweitzer, 'The European Competition Law Enforcement System and the Evolution of Judicial Review' in Ehlermann and Marquis (n 3) 87; A Andreangeli, *EU Competition Enforcement and Human Rights* (Cheltenham, Edward Elgar, 2008) 165; B Vesterdorf, 'Judicial Review in EC Competition Law: Reflections on the Role of the Community Courts in the EC System of Competition Law Enforcement' (2005) 1 *Global Competition Policy* 1; and Beumer (n 5) 18. *Cf* N Zingales, 'The Hearing Officer in EU Competition Law Proceedings: Ensuring Full Respect for the Right to Be Heard?' (2010) 7(1) *Competition Law Review* 129, 136.

[59] *Menarini Diagnostics* (n 17) [63]–[64].

[60] Bellamy (n 3) 9.

[61] But *cf* KPE Lasok, 'Judicial Review of Issues of Fact' (1983) 4 *European Competition Law Review* 85; and Beumer (n 5) 17.

carry out of its own motion a full review of the judgment under appeal, but to respond to the grounds of appeal raised by the appellant'.[62]

However, in my view, requiring the European courts (ie, the CJEU and the GC) to conduct full reviews of their own motion would be excessive and disproportionate to the (marginal if not negligible) possibility that the standard of review applied (upon proper and sufficient allegations by the appellant) is insufficient to detect an instance of insufficient or defective assessment of the evidence available to the European Commission in the conduct of the competition investigations. On the other hand, if the potential discrepancy between the courts and the competition authorities was on the 'policy' elements embedded in EU competition rules (see above, section III), then deference to proper 'classical exercises of administrative discretion' should be found to fully meet the requirements of Article 6(1) ECHR as per the standard doctrine of the ECtHR (see above, section IV.A).[63]

Notwithstanding the above, and as already mentioned, my personal position goes one step further and I submit that even a judicial review standard that fell short of the requirements indicated by the majority in *Menarini* should suffice,[64] given that we are in the area of decisions that involve a certain degree of 'classic exercise of administrative discretion'.[65]

B. Avoidance of Strategic Abuse of Due Process Guarantees by Applicants

Second, there seems to be no good reason to alter the current rules and promote a permissive rule on access to the ECtHR solely on the basis of the standard of review used in competition law cases because undertakings having been fined for breaches of competition law will always have a very strong (financial) incentive to challenge them before the ECtHR or, at least, to win some time by resorting to this additional review procedure. Therefore, there are strong incentives for an excessive recourse to (if not an abuse of) the procedure for human rights protection on the basis of spurious claims of insufficient review of Commission competition decisions before the European courts. As a matter of system design, then, such a restriction on the chance to bring an action before the ECtHR (ie, denying challenges solely or primarily based on the standard of review applied by the GC and the CJEU) seems a proportionate and desirable counterbalance to such perverse incentives.[66]

[62] Case C-386/10 P *Chalkor v Commission* [2011] nyr, [49]. See also C-389/10 P *KME v Commission* [2011] nyr, [131]. For discussion on whether this meets the requirements of Article 6(1) ECHR, see Beumer (n 5) 21–22.

[63] Discussing this possibility, and mostly in favour, see Beumer (n 5) 23–24 and 27. Contra, see Forrester, 'Due Process' (n 3) 819.

[64] This is in line with the position of the European Commission; see *Chalkor v Commission* (n 62) [43].

[65] In very clear terms, see J Joshua, 'The Right to Be Heard in EEC Competition Proceedings' (1991) 15 *Fordham International Law Journal* 16, 39. In more moderate terms, see J Flattery, 'Balancing Efficiency and Justice in EU Competition Law: Elements of Procedural Fairness and their Impact on the Right to a Fair Hearing' (2010) 7(1) *Competition Law Review* 53, 77.

[66] For general discussion, see S Shavell, *Foundations of Economic Analysis of Law* (Cambridge, MA, Harvard University Press, 2004) 400–01.

C. Case Load Management and Protection of the Effective Functioning of the ECtHR

Third, in that regard, the ECtHR should be aware of the potentially significant impact of those cases on its workload and the significant amount of resources needed to deal with such complex cases. Furthermore, it would need to significantly expand its expertise in the area of competition law (and, more generally, of economic regulation) in order to properly appraise the applications submitted for its protection under the ECHR—and this could be disproportionate to protect 'theoretical' due process rights of corporate defendants[67] (see above, section IV.B).

And finally, there seems to be no need to set a very stringent standard of judicial review of competition law cases because changes at the EU level would be extremely difficult to implement (a renegotiation of the EU Treaties is certainly not an easy endeavour) and some basic functional considerations require a restriction of the scope of the ECtHR activities and to keep them focused on their core functions (in this case, enforcement of Article 6(1) in hard-core criminal cases against individuals) if it is to remain effective and do its job.[68] Otherwise, the ECtHR could end up trapped in a situation governed by an hypertrophy of Article 6(1) ECHR in connection with EU competition law cases and could find itself flooded with a significant number of difficult-to-manage cases that would drain its resources and diminish the overall effectiveness of its policing of the respect of effective and practical human rights in Europe.

VI. CONCLUSION

Throughout this chapter, it has been emphasised that there is a significant risk of hypertrophy of Article 6(1) ECHR if an excessively demanding standard for judicial review is imposed. First, this is because the discussion on the actual standard of review applied by the European courts in the review of the European Commission's decision in competition law cases is to a large extent excessively formal and theoretical—which renders the discussion, to a certain extent, moot and devoid of practical effects. Both the ECtHR and the CJEU have already found that de facto there is full review of EU competition law enforcement decisions and, consequently, it can hardly be sustained that there is an actual (material) lack of due process guarantees in the enforcement of EU competition law by the European Commission and the NCAs. This, probably, should suffice to put an end to the discussion.

However, from a less pragmatic approach and considering that the delineation of the scope and intensity of judicial review requirements in the field of EU competition law can have an intrinsic value (at least in terms of legal certainty), the discussion developed in this chapter has in my view shown that there is no need for any significant change in the EU

[67] Most of the claims for a stricter standard of judicial review seem to a large extent purely theoretical or, sometimes, even grammatical. See, for instance, Forrester, 'Judicial Review and Competition Law' (n 3) 3–4. This is indicated by Bellamy (n 3) 3. In similar terms, see Beumer (n 5) 16–17; Schweitzer (n 58) 100; and D Geradin and N Petit, 'Judicial Review in European Union Competition Law: A Quantitative and Qualitative Assessment' (2010) Tilburg Law School Legal Studies Research Paper 01/2011, 23, http://ssrn.com/abstract=1698342.

[68] For an interesting warning on rights inflation, see G Letsas, *A Theory of Interpretation of the European Convention on Human Rights* (Oxford, Oxford University Press, 2007) 126–30.

competition law enforcement system to make it comply with Article 6(1) ECHR *as such*, given that: (i) competition law does not belong to the 'core' of criminal offences foreseen in Article 6(1) ECHR (section II above); (ii) at least arguably, the standard (ie, scope and intensity) for judicial review is a non-core due process guarantee (section IV.B above) that has already been limited by the ECtHR in cases where an administrative body, following robust (sanctioning) administrative procedures, adopts a decision that represents a 'classic exercise of administrative discretion' (section IV.A above); (iii) there are significant peculiarities in the enforcement of EU competition law that tend to diminish the effective/actual need for 'non-core' due process guarantees (section III above), particularly in the case of corporate defendants (section IV.B above); and last, but not least, (iv) there is a significant risk of transforming the ECtHR in a third appellate instance in EU competition law cases (sections IV.B and V above), without it being justified or proportional in light of the actual need of protection and that, on the contrary, would generate a risk of strategic abuse and, ultimately, of diminishing the effectiveness of the protection of human rights in Europe more generally (given the significant resources required for such a task).

All in all, I think that there are more than good arguments in favour of not introducing any changes to the current EU competition law enforcement system as far as the *scope and intensity of the judicial review* available for challengers of Decisions of the European Commission enforcing Articles 101 and 102 TFEU is concerned, since it is not required by Article 6(1) ECHR and, more generally and from a normative perspective, is a less than desirable legal reform. In my opinion, the future accession of the EU to the ECHR does not alter this conclusion.

17

The EU Accession to the ECHR: An Attempt to Explore Possible Implications in the Area of Public Procurement

ARIS GEORGOPOULOS*

I. INTRODUCTION

THE FIELD OF public procurement has witnessed a remarkable surge of regulatory activity at the European Union (EU) level and consequently at the national level over the last two decades. The practical consequence of this development together with the fact that public procurement is associated with significant amounts of public spending currently estimated at around 19 per cent of the EU's Gross Domestic Product (GDP)[1] meant that the latter has become a niche area that has attracted the focused attention of academic researchers and practitioners alike.

The impression that public procurement constitutes a 'self-contained' field of both legal scholarship and practice has been supported not only by a series of regulatory instruments establishing detailed substantive rules but also by a tailor-made system of administrative and judicial remedies adopted at the EU level and transposed in the various national jurisdictions (the latter being the main tangible regulatory departure from the sacrosanct principle of national procedural autonomy). However, in contrast with other niche areas of economic law such as competition law,[2] the issue of the interaction between public procurement and the area of human rights has attracted much less attention both in academia and in practice. In this context, it is worthwhile wondering how the EU's accession to the European Convention on Human Rights (ECHR) could affect this prima facie 'self-contained' field.

The aim of this chapter is twofold. First, it tries to map out the areas of potential interplay/interaction between public procurement and human rights. Second, it explores

* Lecturer in European and Public Law, University of Nottingham School of Law. The author would like to thank the book editors and particularly Vassilis Tzevelekos for their very pertinent and helpful comments on earlier drafts of the present piece. The usual disclaimer applies.

[1] In 2011 the total expenditure of government at the central, regional and local levels, the service providers of the wider public and utility sectors on works, goods and services was estimated at €2,405.89 billion (namely 19.0 per cent of EU GDP); see 'Public Procurement Indicators 2011', Brussels, 5 December 2012, 1 and 9, available at http://ec.europa.eu/internal_market/publicprocurement/docs/modernising_rules/public-procurement-indicators-2011_en.pdf.

[2] Regarding the impact the accession of the EU to the ECHR may have in that area, see the contribution by Dr Sanchez Graells in ch 16 in the present volume.

whether the prospective accession of the EU to the ECHR will have concrete consequences in the area of public procurement regulation and practice by creating new pathways/areas of intersections/interaction and/or strengthen existing ones, thus rendering them more attractive. Finally, it will argue that the EU's accession might have a qualitative impact by assisting the shift in the balance between market freedoms and human rights that began with the coming into force of the Treaty of Lisbon and the European Charter of Fundamental Rights.

Section II proceeds with the necessary definitions and delimitations, and attempts to conceptualise the relationship between the notion of procurement and human rights—understood as policy tools, objectives and the ensemble of specific rights in the context of a given legal order—arguing that the latter sets the limits of the first, but also that the former may constitute one of the means that are available to states for the promotion of human rights policies and objectives. Section III attempts to explain why, to date, the interaction between the two regimes has only been limited as opposed to other areas of economic law; for that reason, it proceeds with a brief comparison between procurement and competition law. Furthermore, it provides a number of examples about how human rights and procurement may intersect within the European context. Section IV contains the core argument of the chapter. After highlighting the fact that, even without the EU's accession to the ECHR, much of what is discussed in the chapter can be claimed before the European Court of Human Rights (ECtHR) in an oblique way—by lodging applications against EU Member States for issues involving EU law—the chapter focuses on the impact that the accession may have on the protection of human rights in the area of procurement law. In that respect, it distinguishes between direct, or tangible impact, on the one hand, and the subtler version of influence the accession will potentially have, consisting in the emergence of a certain human rights 'ethos' in the way procurement performs, on the other hand. Section V sums up the argument and presents some conclusive thoughts.

II. PUBLIC PROCUREMENT AND HUMAN RIGHTS: PRELIMINARY CLARIFICATIONS REGARDING NOMENCLATURE

Although there is no official definition of the term 'public procurement', it is generally understood as the process through which the various entities[3] in the public sector[4] acquire the goods, services or works they need in order to perform their duties and fulfil their

[3] The EU rules on public procurement use the term 'contracting authorities' to refer collectively to these entities. The term 'contracting authorities' covers the state, regional and local authorities, and the so-called bodies governed by public law, which are bodies that enjoy a special link with the public sector either in the way they are financed, the way their management is appointed or because of the general control that the public sector exercise upon them, or associations formed by one or several of these entities. See Article 1(9) of Directive 2004/18/EC of the European Parliament and of the Council of 31 March 2004 on the coordination of procedures for the award of public works contracts, public supply contracts and public service contracts [2004] OJ L134/114 (the Public Sector Procurement Directive). The notion of contracting authorities essentially defines the personal scope of the field of application of the EU public procurement directives.

[4] It should be mentioned that in the field of utilities (water, energy, transport and postal services), the notion of contracting entities also includes private entities that operate on the basis of special or exclusive rights. See Article 2(2)(b) of Directive 2004/17/EC of the European Parliament and of the Council of 31 March 2004 coordinating the procurement procedures of entities operating in the water, energy, transport and postal services sectors [2004] OJ L134/1 (the Utilities Procurement Directive).

roles.[5] By and large, public procurement rules are applicable when public authorities resort to the market for finding the solution to their needs.[6] Public procurement could be further distinguished in public procurement in the narrow sense (*stricto sensu*) and public procurement *lato sensu*. The first refers to the process that normally starts with the publication of a contract opportunity and finishes with the award of the contract to a specific economic operator. It is this process that constitutes the focus of the harmonised regime of the European Public Procurement Directives.[7] Public procurement in the wider sense is synonymous with the notion of 'contracting out'. In other words it not only covers the process that leads to the award of the contract but also includes the stages that follow the award, namely the various stages of contract execution and project management.

Likewise, the concept of human rights can be understood narrowly or widely, at least in the area of legal and judicial practice as well as policy making, depending on the enumeration of specific rights protected at the national,[8] supranational[9] and international[10] levels, the policy choices of the government and equally—if not more—importantly on the intensity of interpretation of these rights by the relevant judge. In this way we have a wide spectrum of rights that stretches from rights that are linked with core issues (namely, issues that attract wide—if not universal—consensus) such as the right to life and the prohibition of torture, to other important areas such as social justice, sustainability and the protection of the environment, where support and policy choices vary amongst jurisdictions. Moreover, since all these rights are subject to judicial interpretation, this fact adds a further parameter that affects the intensity of their protection through the establishment of a number of obligations on state authorities reflecting the triptych classification that distinguishes between respect (negative in nature), protection (positive in nature, linked with the idea of due diligence as well as the so-called indirect horizontal effect[11] (*Drittwirkung*) of human rights) and fulfilment (reflecting the idea of progressive realisation).

Following the aforementioned observations, it can be argued that the interplay between public procurement and human rights is more evident when the concepts of public procurement and human rights are understood more widely. In particular, when the concept of human rights also refers to general policy choices and priorities set by governments in order to improve or adhere to higher standards linked with the promotion of human welfare (understood under the terms of general or public interest), then the interplay with public procurement is clearer. Human rights are destined to impose limits on the conduct

[5] For example, they buy stationery and IT equipment for fulfilling their administrative duties, they build bridges and motorways, and they acquire cleaning and security services for their premises.

[6] Public authorities are not obliged to resort to the market for the goods and services they need if they choose to provide them relying on internal resources.

[7] Public Sector Procurement Directive 2004/18/EC (n 3), Utilities Procurement Directive 2004/17/EC (n 4). These two directives are currently subject to a process of amendment. At the time of writing, the 'trialogue' negotiations between the EU Parliament, the Council and the Commission had reached an agreement. The reform proposals also include another substantive legislative instrument, a Directive in the field of concessions. See also Directive 2009/81/EC of the European Parliament and of the Council of 13 July 2009 on the coordination of procedures for the award of certain works contracts, supply contracts and service contracts by contracting authorities or entities in the fields of defence and security, and amending Directives 2004/17/EC and 2004/18/EC [2009] OJ L216/76 (the Defence and Security Procurement Directive).

[8] For example, the Human Rights Act 1998 (Chapter 42) Schedule 1.

[9] For example, the European Charter of Fundamental Rights in the EU legal order.

[10] For example, the Universal Declaration of Human Rights or the ECHR.

[11] For a discussion, see P van Dijk and GJH van Hoof, *Theory and Practice of the European Convention on Human Rights* (The Hague, Martinus Nijhoff, 1998) 22 et seq.

of public authorities. However, outside this obvious dimension, it could also be argued that, in a sense, public procurement can be a vehicle through which the government may facilitate the fulfilment of human rights. In this regard, there are instances where public procurement has been used as an instrument to promote equality and social inclusion, and to correct injustices of the past by reintegrating segregated sections of the society.

For example, the legislation in South Africa uses a preferential system of procurement with the clear aim of reintegrating into society and the mainstream economy large parts of the population that have been subject to unfair racial discrimination during the apartheid era.[12] Similarly, in Malaysia the public procurement system[13] has put in place a number of measures of positive discrimination (preferences and set aside mechanisms)[14] that aim to raise the economic position of the ethnic Malay part of the population.[15] Another example is the use of procurement in Northern Ireland as a tool to promote the policy of prohibition of discrimination on the basis of religious and political grounds, and to ensure equal opportunities for all communities by employing the threat of exclusion from public procurement opportunities for economic operators who did not comply with the anti-discrimination rules.[16] Even at the EU level, the rules on public procurement (which, as mentioned earlier, correspond to the notion of procurement *stricto sensu*) contain provisions whose objectives are linked with wider human rights considerations such as the integration of people with disabilities to the labour market.[17]

III. PUBLIC PROCUREMENT AND HUMAN RIGHTS IN THE EUROPEAN CONTEXT: LIMITED BUT POSSIBLE INTERACTION

When public procurement and human rights are considered in their narrower sense and in the European context by reference to their respective regulatory frameworks, namely on the one hand the EU public procurement rules—including implementing national legislations—and the EU Charter of Fundamental Rights together with the ECHR on the other, it is observed that, by contrast to other niche areas of economic law, for example, competition

[12] Preferential Procurement Policy Framework Act 5 of 2000 and Preferential Procurement Policy Framework Regulations of 2011. P Bolton, 'The Regulatory Framework for Public Procurement in South Africa' in G Quinot and S Arrowsmith (eds), *Public Procurement Regulation in Africa* (Cambridge, Cambridge University Press, 2013); P Bolton, 'An Analysis of the Preferential Procurement Legislation of South Africa' (2007) 16(1) *Public Procurement Law Review* 36; G Quinot and P Bolton, 'Social Policies in Procurement and the Government Procurement Agreement: A Perspective from South Africa' in S Arrowsmith and R Anderson (eds), *The WTO Regime on Government Procurement: Recent Developments and Challenges Ahead* (Cambridge, Cambridge University Press, 2011); D Letchmiah, 'The Process of Public Sector Procurement in South Africa' (1999) 8(1) *Public Procurement Law Review* 15.

[13] C McCrudden and S Gross, 'WTO Government Procurement Rules and the Local Dynamics of Procurement Policies: A Malaysian Case Study' (2006) 17(1) *European Journal of International Law* 155, 168 et seq.

[14] Set aside mechanisms effectively reserve certain public procurement contracts—often identified by value thresholds—for a specifically designated group or groups of people.

[15] Malaysia has three main ethnic groups: Malay, Chinese and Indian. The Malay ethnic group is the majority, but in the years before independence was the poorest of the three. The policy of positive discrimination in favour of the Malay majority has its origin post-independence in Article 153 of the Federal Constitution of Malaysia.

[16] Fair Employment and Treatment Order 1998, Order 3162 (NI 21). For an analysis of the regime, see C McCrudden, *Buying Social Justice: Equality, Government Procurement, and Legal Change* (Oxford, Oxford University Press, 2007) 305 et seq.

[17] See Article 19 and recital 28 of the Public Sector Procurement Directive.

law,[18] the interaction both at the level of legal practice and academic study has been more scarce. Why is that?

It is argued that, although the EU competition rules and EU public procurement rules share the same ultimate goals, namely the attainment and preservation of the internal market, in the case of EU competition law, the focus of the rules and in particular the architecture of enforcement is substantially different from the rules in EU public procurement law.

First, in the case of competition law, the focus of the regulatory framework falls by and large on the conduct of private natural or legal persons. In other words, the main provisions of EU competition law, namely Articles 101[19] and 102[20] of the Treaty on the Functioning of the European Union (TFEU) were included in primary EU law precisely because the European legislator believed that the so-called four freedom provisions[21]—whose main focus is the prohibition of measures that are likely to create obstacles or distortions in the internal market as a result of state actions—was not sufficient to deal with the risk of fragmentation of the internal market posed by the conduct of private actors. On the other hand, the public procurement legal framework can trace its origins to the fundamental economic freedom provisions, which, as mentioned above, are concerned primarily with obstacles to trade in the internal market linked with the conduct of public/state actors (contracting authorities more specifically in this case) when they establish specific obligations on contracting authorities and corresponding rights for economic operators participating in public procurement.

In addition, the architecture of enforcement of EU competition law is characterised by the dominant role of centralised enforcement carried out by the European Commission and the National Competition Authorities of the EU Member States (NCAs)[22] who have wide investigatory[23] and adjudicative powers that can encroach upon the rights enshrined in the European Convention on Human Rights (ECHR) (for example, Article 6).[24] In this

[18] See, for example, *Compagnie des Gaz de Pétrole Primagaz v France*, App No 29613/08 (2010); *Canal Plus v France*, App No 29408/08 (2010); *A Menarini Diagnostics SRL v Italy*, App No 43509/08 (2011); Case 374/87 *Orkem v Commission* [1989] ECR 3283; Case C-46/87 *Hoechst AG and others v Commission* [1989] ECR 2859. See also indicatively W Wils, 'The Increased Level of EU Antitrust Fines, Judicial Review, and the European Convention on Human Rights' (2010) 33(1) *World Competition* 5; OB Vincents, 'The Application of EC Competition Law and the European Convention on Human Rights' (2006) 12 *European Competition Law Review* 693; E Ameye, 'The Interplay between Human Rights and Competition Law in the EU' (2004) 25(6) *European Competition Law Review*, 332–41.

[19] Prohibiting agreements between undertakings, decisions by associations of undertakings and concerted practices which may affect intra-EU trade and have as their object or effect the prevention, restriction or distortion of competition in the internal market. The focus of the provision is on the conduct of two or more undertakings/actors.

[20] Prohibiting undertakings from abusing their dominant position in a given market. The focus of the provision is on the unilateral conduct of the dominant undertaking.

[21] Articles 34 (free movement of goods), 45 and 49 (free movement of people), 56 (free movement of services) and 63 (free movement of capital) TFEU.

[22] This trait of the system has not been changed by the decentralisation effected by the 'Modernisation Regulation' (Council Regulation 1/2003/EC of 16 December 2002 on the implementation of the rules on competition laid down in Articles 81 and 82 of the Treaty [2003] OJ L 1), in the sense that the same 'centralised' architecture of enforcement is also replicated at the national level.

[23] Including wide powers of inspection of office and even of private premises (Articles 20 and 21 Regulation 1/2003).

[24] *Senator Lines GmbH v Austria, Belgium, Denmark, Finland, France, Germany, Greece, Ireland, Italy, Luxembourg, the Netherlands, Portugal, Spain, Sweden and the United Kingdom*, App No 56672/00 (2004). See also, in relation to Eurocontrol, *Bovin v 34 Member States of the Council of Europe*, App No 73250/01 (2008).

regard, the arsenal of the enforcement of competition law includes fines of a punitive nature[25] and increasingly significant criminal sanctions for natural persons.[26]

However, in the case of the EU public procurement enforcement system, the dynamics are quite different. It could be argued that this is due to the development of a detailed and sophisticated system of judicial remedies[27] established at the EU level but implemented at the national level. This means that a lot of the enforcement takes place in a diffused, decentralised manner mainly as a result of the initiative of the aggrieved economic operator before national courts without raising the (same type of) concerns observed in the context of EU competition law enforcement. The Commission may also have a role through the general procedure of Article 258 TFEU, but this is clearly secondary since the Commission uses it mainly in order to address systemic failures in the application of public procurement rules in a Member State rather than as a means to provide relief to an aggrieved contractor. Moreover, in this type of intervention, the Commission has a very specific role, namely that of the pursuer, whereas the adjudicative role is entrusted to the Court of Justice of the European Union (CJEU). This is a completely different set-up from the one in the case of competition law where the Commission acts—at a first level at least—as investigator, prosecutor and judge.

Nevertheless, despite the previous observations, it is argued that there are conceivable situations or instances where the regimes of procurement law and human rights may intersect in the European context. In other words, it is possible for human rights, including, more specifically, the ECHR, to provide a pathway for the protection of an individual's rights in the field of public procurement. For example, it is possible in some jurisdictions that economic operators who bid for procurement contracts whose value is below the procurement thresholds—and as a result is not subject to either the substantive or remedy rules of EU public procurement—to have virtually no remedy to challenge the decisions of the contracting authority. Moreover, in such situations, even if EU rights are at stake,[28] because the usefulness of the mechanism of preliminary reference relies in practice on the willingness of the national courts to make use of it (de facto lack of automaticity in the reference process despite the legal obligation stipulated in Article 267 (3) TFEU), and because there are occasions where the national courts demonstrate reluctance to make preliminary

[25] Regarding the punitive nature of such measures, see by analogy *Engel and others v The Netherlands*, Judgment of 8 June 1976 [81]. Article 23(2) of Regulation 1/2003/EC provides that the Commission may impose fines up to 10 per cent of the total annual turnover of the undertaking.

[26] Not at the EU level yet, but in a number of EU Member States. See, for example, s 188 of the Enterprise Act 2002 establishing a cartel offence (as amended by s 47 of the Enterprise and Regulatory Reform Act of 2013) and s 190 of the Enterprise Act 2002 establishing a penalty of imprisonment for those guilty of the aforementioned offence.

[27] Council Directive 89/665/EEC of 21 December 1989 on the coordination of the laws, regulations and administrative provisions relating to the application of review procedures to the award of public supply and public works contracts [1989] OJ L 395 (the Remedies Directive) and Council Directive 92/13/EC of 25 February 1992 coordinating the laws, regulations and administrative provisions relating to the application of Community rules on the procurement procedures of entities operating in the water, energy, transport and telecommunications sectors [1992] OJ L 76 (the Utilities Remedies Directive) as amended by Directive 2007/66/EC of the European Parliament and of the Council of 11 December 2007 amending Council Directives 89/665/EEC and 92/13/EEC with regard to improving the effectiveness of review procedures concerning the award of public contracts [2007] OJ L 335.

[28] In principle, contracts below the EU procurement thresholds which may be of 'cross-border' interest are subject to the general principles of EU law (non-discimination, equal treatment, transparency) even if they fall outside the field of application of the EU public procurement directives. See in particular Advocate General Sharpston's Opinion in Case C-195/04 *Commission* v *Finland* [2007] ECR I-3353.

reference to the CJEU,[29] the ECtHR could provide a parallel pathway for the protection for aggrieved parties. This possibility could also extend post-accession, either against the EU directly or before it, indirectly, by requesting that an EU Member State be held accountable for a situation linked with powers it has transferred[30] to the EU.

Another example could refer to a case where an economic operator is excluded by a procurement procedure pursuant to Article 45 of the Public Sector Directive because he or she has been convicted in another country by a judgment which has the force of *res judicata* for an offence concerning his or her professional conduct, but he or she argues that the standard of due process—in the jurisdiction where he or she was convicted—had been disregarded.

Likewise, it is possible in the context of a procurement process for issues of intellectual property to arise. This is common in the case of procurements that are complex, for example, when the drafting of specifications is rather difficult or when there are no existing solutions in the market. This is the case in the context of procurement procedures—like the 'competitive dialogue[31] or the 'negotiated procedures'—that allow some level of interaction between the contracting authorities and the economic operators during the procurement process. This means that the final new solution may have elements stemming from the ideas of different candidates.[32] In such a case, the ECtHR could also provide a pathway for the protection of intellectual property rights under the ambit of Article 1 of Protocol 1 of the ECHR.[33] By the same token, the ECHR could protect the legitimate expectations[34] of a contractor whose procurement contract has been (unlawfully) cancelled by the contracting authority.

The proposition that the ECtHR could provide an additional—or rather parallel—pathway for the protection of aggrieved parties in the context of public procurement is supported by the fact that there have been cases in the area of public procurement that reached the Strasbourg Court, such as *Tinnelly & Sons Ltd and others v United Kingdom*[35] and *ITC v Malta*.[36] The rather old *Tinnelly* case raises issues of access to justice as well as of denial of the opportunity for the applicants to bid for a contract on discriminatory grounds related to their religious beliefs. The case is interesting not only as a specimen that prima facie confirms the possibility of using the ECHR as a pathway to protection in the context of public procurement, but also because it perhaps provides an indication as to why that pathway has not been used more widely. *Tinnnelly* used the domestic remedies that were available before the establishment of the comprehensive remedies system introduced with

[29] It should be remembered that the preliminary reference procedure aims to provide assistance to the national judge in the interpretation of EU law. This means that even if the parties in a dispute before the national court make suggestions for the need of a preliminary reference, the national judge is not bound in any way to act.

[30] *M&Co v Germany*, App No 13258/87 (admissibility) EComHR, 9 February 1990.

[31] P Telles, 'Competitive Dialogue: Should the Rules be Fine-Tuned to Facilitate Innovation?' in C Risvig Hansen, C Tvarnø and G Skovgaard Ølykke (eds), *EU Procurement Directives: Modernisation, Growth and Innovation: Discussions on the 2011 Proposals for Public Procurement Directives* (Copenhagen, Djøf Forlag, 2012).

[32] The opportunity for intellectual property issues to arise is expected to increase with the proposal of the *innovation partnership* procedure. Article 29 of the Proposal for a Directive of the European Council and of the Council on Public Procurement COM (2011) 896 final, 2011/0438 (COD), Brussels, 20 December 2011.

[33] For example, see *AD v The Netherlands*, App No 21962/93 (1994) (admissibility decision); *Melnychuk v Ukraine*, App No 28743/03 (2005) (admissibility decision).

[34] *Maltzan and others v Germany*, App Nos 71916/01, 71917/01 and 10260/02 (2005) (admissibility decision).

[35] *Tinnelly & Sons Ltd and others and McElduff and others v United Kingdom*, App No 20390/92 (1998) 27 EHRR 249.

[36] *ITC Ltd v Malta*, App No 2629/06 (2007).

the Remedies Directive[37] In other words, this case took place in a considerably weaker environment of judicial protection.[38] These observations are further supported by the case of *ITC*, which, likewise, was brought before the ECtHR in a domestic regulatory environment before Malta's accession to the EU and thus before the creation of a comprehensive system of procurement remedies in Malta.[39]

The above analysis shows that even without looking at the prospective accession of the EU to the ECHR, the Strasbourg pathway for the protection of individual's rights in the context of public procurement has been pertinent, but under-used. Then how and to what extent—if at all—will this 'self-contained' field of economic law and policy be affected by a future accession of the EU to the ECHR? We will attempt to address this question in the next section.

IV. PUBLIC PROCUREMENT AND HUMAN RIGHTS AFTER THE EU'S ACCESSION TO THE ECHR

It is beyond any doubt that the accession of the EU to the ECHR will not simply be an event of great symbolic importance, but it will also pose certain challenging questions regarding the de jure constitutional co-habitation of the two judicial powerhouses in Europe. Although the existing de facto relationship is characterised by an element of comity on the basis of the criteria set by the *Bosphorus*[40] jurisprudence, and although it is difficult to imagine a post-accession order where the CJEU would not be, formally at least,[41] subordinated to Strasbourg, it is argued that the last two observations do not prejudge either the

[37] The transposition of the Remedies Directive in this case (works) took effect on 21 December 1991. *Tinnelly* has begun the process of complaints at the national level in 1985 and the final national decision was issued on 3 December 1991. It should be remembered that the procurement remedies are only available for public procurement contracts that fall under the field of application of the substantive procurement directives (namely provided that they are above the applicable value thresholds). It is not clear if the contract in *Tinnelly* was above those thresholds. However, even if we assume that the contract opportunity was below these thresholds, the judicial protection of *Tinnelly* at the national level would have been enhanced because of the 'spillover' effect that the establishment of a specialised system of procurement rules (including the remedies system) had in the application of what could be called traditional pre-existing remedies. See also the next footnote.

[38] The UK until the transposition of the Remedies Directives did not have any special remedies in the area of public procurement. In fact, public procurement disputes were considered not to demonstrate any 'public' features that warranted the availability of judicial review proceedings, but rather were considered to be part of private law—a view whose validity was contested in the literature at the time; see in particular S Arrowsmith, 'Enforcing the EC Public Procurement Rules: The Remedies System in England and Wales' (1992) 2 *Public Procurement Law Review* 92; S Arrowsmith, 'Judicial Review and the Contractual Power of Public Authorities' (1990) 106 *Law Quarterly Review* 277.

[39] Interestingly, *ITC v Malta* on the one hand strengthens the argument that the ECHR pathway is stronger as an option in the event of a lack of EU rules on remedies, but on the other hand the lack of substantive rules on procurement limits the usefulness of the ECHR pathway, because as the ECtHR stated in the same decision, 'Article 6(1) of the Convention is not aimed at creating new substantive rights without a legal basis in the Contracting State, but at providing procedural protection of rights already recognised in domestic law'.

[40] *Bosphorus Hava Yolları Turizm ve Ticaret Anonim irketi v Ireland*, App No 45036/98 (2005) 42 EHRR 1. This judgment established the presumption that the EU offers equivalent standards of protection to those of the ECHR and, for that reason, the Strasbourg Court refrained from reviewing the compatibility of EU law with the ECHR.

[41] Regarding the future of the *Bosphorus* presumption, see the contribution by O De Schutter in ch 12 of the present volume.

real type[42] or the intensity[43] of the relationship post-accession. With this in mind, one can hypothesise that the new institutional, vertical structure and also the dynamics that will be created may lead to a recalibration of the institutional balance.

On that basis, it is argued that the accession of the EU to the ECHR may indeed have a bearing on the area of public procurement and in fact in two possible ways: one tangible and one subtler. Yet, before exploring these two ways further, it is important to clarify that, theoretically, the ECHR could have played and may still play a role in EU public procurement before the EU's accession. This could apply not only against the conduct of EU Member States stemming from purely national legislation and practices, but also for Member State conduct that originates in and gives effect to rules and practices established at the EU level. In other words, Member States are responsible for the conduct of/linked to the participation to international organisations in which they are members, including the EU. This was the case in *Matthews*,[44] for instance, concerning EU primary law, but also in a number of other cases stemming from the implementation of EU law at the national level, such as the aforementioned *Bosphorus* case or more recently the *Michaud* jurisprudence.[45] That said, the argument could be that, substance-wise, no major change will be brought about by the EU accession to the ECHR. If there is an important change, this is that individuals will be allowed to bring their claim directly against the EU (and its Member States), whereas now they can only accuse it in an oblique way, via its Member States—and this is only if the *Bosphorus* presumption is not satisfied or the state is found to exercise discretion[46] in the way in which it will implement EU law in its domestic system. Yet this is mainly a question of allocation of responsibility (although such allocation will be hindered by the co-respondent mechanism) and accountability *ratione personae*. The substance of the claims shall be the same both before and after the accession.

Returning to the ways in which the EU's accession to the ECHR may be relevant to EU public procurement, it is submitted that first of all, this may happen in cases where the EU acts as the contracting authority (through its institutions or agencies). This is what we called earlier as the more obvious/tangible area of accession impact. We can illustrate this by making reference to few scenarios/examples.

A. Potential for Tangible Impact

First, we can refer to the example where the EU acting in the area of Common Security and Defence Policy is involved in a peacekeeping mission outside the EU's geographical area and uses the services of a Private Military and Security Company (PMSC) after a procurement process. The use of PMSCs for the discharge of police and security services in the context of peace-making, peacekeeping missions[47] is a growing trend that raises a number

[42] Parity between the two courts or subordination of the CJEU to the jurisdiction of the ECtHR.

[43] Intensive review or deference (including the degree and conditionalities of deference) of the ECtHR towards the CJEU.

[44] *Matthews v United Kingdom*, Series A 24833/94 (1999) 28 EHRR 36.

[45] *Michaud v France*, App No 12323/11 (2012).

[46] *Bosphorus* (n 40) [147]–[148]; and *Michaud* (n 46) [103].

[47] In fact, in almost all the range of the missions foreseen in Article 43 TEU: 'joint disarmament operations, humanitarian and rescue tasks, military advice and assistance tasks, conflict prevention and peace-keeping tasks, tasks of combat forces in crisis management, including peace-making and post-conflict stabilisation'.

of important questions such as the human rights obligations of the contractor, as well as the responsibility of the contracting authority.[48] The same is true when the EU directly or through the Member States uses PMSCs for the discharge of illegal immigration detention facilities within the EU's geographical area. It is submitted that the accession of the EU to the ECHR will potentially open the pathway of the ECtHR to victims and other aggrieved parties from actions or omissions of the contractor against the EU itself,[49] which is an issue that of course raises technical questions of attribution, extraterritoriality and the obligation to demonstrate diligence that do not fall within the limited scope of the present study.

Second, one can contemplate situations where the relevant EU body that carries out the procurement is not subject to the full jurisdiction of the EU courts. This may be the case, for example, where the EU body or agency is established under Title V of the Treaty on European Union (TEU) regarding the Common Foreign and Security Policy. According to Article 24(1)(2) TEU and Article 275 TFEU, the CJEU does not have jurisdiction with respect to provisions of the CFSP in principle. It can only review the legality of decisions providing for 'restrictive measures' against natural or legal persons adopted by the Council under the CFSP framework. According to Article 215(1) TFEU, the concept of 'restrictive measures' covers measures that relate to the 'interruption or reduction, in part or completely, of economic and financial relations'. Procurement decisions do not seem to fall under the notion of 'restrictive measures' and therefore it seems that these do not fall under the jurisdiction of the EU courts.

For example, the European Defence Agency (EDA) has been established under the CFSP[50] provisions of the TEU. The EDA is subject to the authority of the Council of the EU and, according to Article 42(3)(2) TEU, is active in the field of defence capabilities development, research, acquisition and armaments. One may think of a situation where the EDA acts on behalf of the EU as contracting authority for the development or the acquisition of common defence assets for use in EU defence and security operations.[51] Based on the above analysis, the procurement decisions of the EDA will not be subject to the review of EU courts[52] and therefore potential aggrieved economic operators will in effect be deprived

[48] For an analysis of these issues, see the Priv-War report, 'Priv-War Recommendations for EU Regulatory Action in the Field of Private Military and Security Companies and their Services', submitted before the EU Commission in spring 2011, available at http://priv-war.eu/wordpress/wp-content/uploads/2013/03/Priv-War_Recommendations-FINAL-.pdf.

[49] The issue of human rights obligations of economic operators in the context of public service outsourcing has arisen at the national level. For example, in *Y v Birmingham City Council* [2007] UKHL 27, the UK Supreme Court examined whether a private care home when providing accommodation and care to a resident, pursuant to arrangements made with a local authority, is performing 'functions of a public nature' and as a result is subject to the application of the ECHR through the Human Rights Act. The Court answered this by majority of 3:2 negatively. The UK Parliament responded with a statutory measure that restored the balance by extending the application of the Human Rights Act to private entities engaged in the delivery of care home services. It is argued that had the UK Parliament not intervened, the matter could have reached the ECtHR.

[50] Council Joint Decision 2004/551/CFSP of 12 July 2004 on the establishment of the European Defence Agency [2004] OJ L 245/17.

[51] See the initiative to promote the European defence industrial base as a necessary component of the CFSP, Commission Communication COM(2013) 542 final, 'Towards a more competitive and efficient defence and security sector'.

[52] For a detailed analysis of the procurement rules of the EDA, see B Heuninckx, 'The Law of Collaborative Defence Procurement Through International Organisations in the European Union', PhD Thesis (University of Nottingham, 2011) 177 et seq; A Georgopoulos, 'The New European Defence Agency: Major Development or Fig Leaf' (2005) 14(2) *Public Procurement Law Review* 103; A Georgopoulos, 'The European Defence Agency's Code of Conduct for Armament Acquisitions: A Case of Paramnesia?' (2006) 15(2) *Public Procurement Law Review* 55.

of access to justice or an effective remedy. Although today this scenario could theoretically trigger an indirect pathway to Strasbourg for the aggrieved economic operators through the responsibility of Member States for the conduct of the international organisation to which they belong (here the EU), post-accession, a direct route to the ECtHR against the EU itself could be established.

This would also be the case if the procurement of the common defence assets is entrusted to another international organisation that also has limited or no review mechanisms. This is not simply a hypothesis since the other major international organisation in the field of collaborative defence procurement and project management in Europe is the Organisation for Joint Armament Cooperation (better known by its French acronym 'OCCAR'), which has been established by six EU Member States.[53] Although it has a distinct international legal personality from the EU, because of its expertise and European character, OCCAR has been deemed even by the European legislator as a plausible candidate for acting as an agent in the procurement of collaborative projects in the EU.[54] However, it becomes clear by looking at OCCAR's rules that the procurement decisions are only subject to an internal two-stage review.[55] In particular, the complaints of aggrieved economic operators are heard at a first instance by the Director of the OCCAR Executive Administration (OCCAR-EA) and, if need be, by the OCCAR's Board of Supervisors (BoS) at a second instance.[56] Neither the decision of the Director OCCAR-EA or that of the BoS is subject to judicial review.[57] It is self-evident that this wholly internal complaint process lacks the necessary guarantees of independence and impartiality and therefore falls short of the standards required by the ECHR. Although, as such, the EU is not a member of OCCAR, in the post-accession environment, the EU's failure to ensure that the decisions of the international organisation entrusted (on the basis of contractual links established in the sphere of international law) with the procurement of the common EU defence assets are subject to an independent and impartial review could pave the way to Strasbourg. An oblique avenue already exists, since one could accuse the common Member States of the EU and OCCAR that have transferred powers to the latter organisation. Furthermore, although this may raise delicate questions of attribution, one could envisage that the same indirect scheme will also apply for holding the EU accountable when it is contracting out to OCCAR. Any other conclusion would lead to an unacceptably convenient way for the EU to limit its responsibility under the ECHR by 'delegating' tasks to international organisations who are not signatories to the ECHR.

Third, it can be observed that even in the case of institutions, agencies or other bodies of the EU whose procurement decisions in principle fall under the jurisdiction of the EU courts, the EU's accession to the ECHR might have an impact.[58] If one examines the juris-

[53] OCCAR was initially established by France, Germany, Italy and the UK. Belgium and Spain joined later. However, there are more Member States and third countries that participate in one or more of the OCCAR-run collaborative programmes.

[54] See, for example, Article 25(2) of Council Joint Decision 2004/551/CFSP.

[55] OCCAR Management Procedures 5 Annex I, available at www.occar.int/media/raw/OMP5_Contract_Placement_Issue3_170609new.pdf.

[56] The BoS is an an organ composed of representatives of OCCAR's signatory Member States.

[57] Heuninckx (n 52) 232 et seq.

[58] It should be mentioned at this point that the procurement process for bodies or agencies that are financed by the EU budget follow the rules contained in the Regulation (EU, EURATOM) No 966/2012 of the European Council and of the Council on the Financial Rules applicable to the general budget of the Union and repealing Council Regulation (EC, EURATOM) 1605/2002. It is submitted that the procurement rules contained in this Regulation (Tile V) are largely based on the rules of the EU Procurement Directives.

prudence of the General Court (GC, the competent EU court to hear actions of natural or legal persons against acts of EU bodies) and that of the CJEU (which provides the appeal jurisdiction against GC judgments) with regard to the liability of EU bodies in the context of procurement, it becomes clear that the EU courts seem to adopt a very lenient approach.

For example, in *Alfastar Benelux v Council*,[59] the applicant successfully challenged an award decision on the basis of inadequate reasoning in the relevant decision. *Alfastar Benelux* then claimed damages for the loss of the public contract. The GC rejected the claim because of what, in its eyes, constituted an apparent lack of a causal link between the unlawful conduct (in this case the inadequate reasoning of the award decision) and the alleged damage (in this case the loss of the contract). Furthermore, the GC ruled that it could not examine the pleas for manifest error of assessment based on the available evidence (which the GC found to be inadequate).[60] Although the rejection of the claim of damages in this case referred to loss of chance, it is not clear whether the Court would have reached a different conclusion had the applicant also claimed damages for the costs of participating in the process. In any case, it is obvious that a number of interesting questions are raised that concern loss of property, *manque à gagner* (loss of prospective economic gain), as well as the issue of causality[61] between unlawful conduct and property rights, which are central to the jurisprudence of the ECtHR—that could be called upon to exercise jurisdiction.

The picture of the GC's lenient approach towards EU bodies to the detriment of the rights of economic operators is further elucidated by *Evropaiki Dynamiki v European Investment Bank (EIB)*.[62] In this case the applicant successfully sought the annulment of the EIB's award decision and also supplemented its action with a claim for damages. Interesting contextual points in this case are the fact that the contract was to be completed before or soon after the decision of the GC, which meant that the annulment of the award decision would constitute a moral victory for the applicant, but not much else. Moreover, the applicant explicitly mentioned—as a general comment about its previous experience of the effectiveness of judicial protection against the actions of EU bodies in the field of procurement that also highlights the importance of the claim for damages in this case—that successful annulment actions that it had lodged in the past against procurement decisions of EU institutions were not followed up in a satisfactory manner by the relevant EU bodies,[63] which apparently raises an issue of effectiveness in terms of judicial protection and implementation of case law by the administration, falling under Article 6 ECHR.[64] Despite all this, the GC rejected the claim for damages because, according to the latter, the applicant did not manage to establish a causal link between the contested (unlawful) decision and the damage.[65] More alarmingly, the GC stated in effect that it would have been impossible

[59] Case T-57/09 *Alfastar Benelux v Council of the European Union* [2011] ECR II-368.

[60] Ibid [51].

[61] See, for instance, *Önyeryildiz v Turkey*, App No 48939/99 (2004) 41 EHRR 325 [135]; and *Varnima Corporation International SA v Greece*, App No 48906/66 (2009) [41].

[62] Case T-461/08 *Evropaiki Dynamiki* v *European Investment Bank (EIB)* [2011] ECR II-6367.

[63] Ibid [61].

[64] *Hornsby v Greece*, App No 18357/91 (1998) [40]–[45].

[65] Ibid [212].

anyway to establish the causal link because the EIB did not have any obligation to sign the contract with the winning bidder.[66]

It is submitted that the impact of the decision in this case—given that due to the factual background of the case, the only 'effective' remedy in this case was the action for damages, but also due to the aforementioned parts of the reasoning which seem extremely problematic—raises questions as to whether in cases like this one there is in fact access to justice and whether the available remedies are indeed effective. Furthermore, it is argued that the duty of compliance with a set of procedural rules—which can be quite prescriptive at times—on the part of the contracting authority gives rise to legitimate expectations of participating economic operators not only regarding compliance but also vis-a-vis the expected logical outcome/result of this procedural compliance. Furthermore, it should be pointed out that this decision provides a very problematic message to EU bodies that leads directly to what could be considered a systemic 'moral hazard'. Although the analysis of all the aspects of the case fall beyond the purposes of this chapter, it suffices to note that the EIB infringed most of the fundamental rules of the procurement process, yet this epitome of flagrant violation of procurement rules attracted merely the proverbial slap on the wrist by the GC, which of course could de facto incentivise EU bodies to continue to disregard procurement rules.[67]

Of course, the ECtHR cannot act as a fourth degree jurisdiction and rule on the legality in terms of procurement law of the relevant practice of the EU and its Member States. Nor is its role or its jurisdiction to remove the discrepancies that appear to exist between the level of judicial protection that economic operators are afforded depending on whether their procurement law rights are infringed by national or by EU contracting authorities. Instead, the ECtHR has jurisdiction to review whether there is in fact access to justice, whether effective remedies are available and whether the standards of fairness are met, as well as whether state and EU authorities comply with judicial decisions. In this regard, it can be observed that the ECtHR tends to adopt a deferential approach in the intensity of the review of proportionality of national rules and practices—provided that certain minimum standards are observed—in the sense that it does not try to superimpose a higher standard, but rather it uses the national standards that exist in the given legal order as a point of reference.

With this in mind, it is argued that the expected standards of protection of the procurement law rights of economic operators in the EU legal order are expressed by the European legislator in the tailor-made system of procurement remedies that was created with the enactment of the Remedies Directives.[68] The fact that these Directives are addressed to

[66] Ibid [211]: 'in any event, even if it were to be accepted that the applicant's tender ought to have been placed first and that the applicant should therefore have been awarded the contract, that would not have obliged the EIB to sign the framework contract with the applicant. Indeed, there is no principle or rule applicable to the EIB's tendering procedures which requires it to sign the relevant contract with the person designated as the contractor at the conclusion of the tendering procedure'.

[67] Moreover, the judgment runs contrary to the logic of the principle of effectiveness in judicial protection of EU rights in the European legal order. It is reminded that in *Factortame* (Case C-213/89 *R v Secretary of State for Transport ex parte Factortame Ltd and others* [1990] ECR I-2433), the prospect of a meaningless victory—comparable in principle with the empty victory of *Evropaiki Dynamiki*—in the main proceedings led the CJEU to demand the setting aside of a rule of constitutional significance in the UK—namely the lack of the possibility to orderinterim relief against the Crown.

[68] See in this regard recital 7 of Directive 89/665/EC: 'Whereas in certain Member States the absence of effective remedies or inadequacy of existing remedies deter Community undertakings from submitting tenders in

the Member States and not the EU institutions and agencies is of no consequence for the identification of the appropriate EU standards by the ECtHR, particularly in the context of the professed unity of the EU legal order after the Treaty of Lisbon. The EU legislator established this tailor-made regime as a response to the poor standard of judicial protection witnessed in comparable cases such as *Evropaiki Dynamiki v EIB* at the national level. Thus, it can be argued that the Remedies Directives constitutes a statement of the expected standards for the protection of economic operators involved in procurement processes in the EU. There is no logical explanation as to why the rights of the same economic operators should be subject to lower standards of protection when procurement rule violations are committed by EU bodies. This argument is supported by the fact that the substantive procurement rules of the Financial Regulation 966/2012/EU, EURATOM—the instrument that governs the procurement of EU institutions and agencies financed by the EU budget—correspond largely to those of the EU public procurement Directives. Thus, after the EU accession to the ECHR, the Strasbourg pathway will be open for economic operators in such cases. Furthermore, it is believed that the mere availability of this option may function as the Sword of Damocles over the shoulders of the EU courts, which might feel compelled to correct the discrepancy on their own motion.

In addition, a more recent case of the CJEU revealed another instance where the involvement of the ECtHR could be contemplated. In *Commission v Systran SA*,[69] the CJEU reversed, on appeal, the decision of the GC[70] which ordered the Commission to pay to Systran lump-sum damages for infringement of copyright and disclosure of know-how following an invitation to tender. According to the CJEU, the GC had concluded erroneously that the dispute was of a non-contractual nature and as a result infringed the rules that demarcate its jurisdiction (negative jurisdiction).[71] The case raises a number of interesting issues regarding the delimitation of EU courts' jurisdiction vis-a-vis their national counterparts in the area of the contractual liability of the EU. However, for the purposes of this chapter, it also highlights the risk that economic operators face in such a case, namely to be left without any judicial protection if all the courts that potentially could be involved issue negative jurisdiction rulings, thus leaving economic operators in a judicial limbo. It should be remembered that the CJEU's judgment in the present case was binding on the GC, but it was not binding on the national courts in Luxembourg, which had jurisdiction to hear disputes arising from the relevant contract.[72] Although in principle situations like this should be resolved within the EU legal order on the basis of sincere cooperation between

the Member State in which the contracting authority is established'; see also recital 3 of Directive 2007/66/EC: 'Consultations of the interested parties … have revealed a certain number of weaknesses in the review mechanisms in the Member States … As a result of these weaknesses, the [review] mechanisms … do not always make it possible to ensure compliance with Community law, especially at a time when infringements can still be corrected. Consequently, the guarantees of transparency and non-discrimination … should be strengthened to ensure that the Community as a whole fully benefit from the positive effects of the modernisation and simplification of the rules on public procurement … [the rules] should therefore be amended by adding the essential clarifications which will allow the results intended by the Community legislature to be attained.'

[69] Case C-103/11 P *Commission v Systran SA and Systran Luxembourg*, Judgment of 18 April 2013 (not yet reported).

[70] Case T-19/07 *Systran SA and Systran Luxembourg v Commission* [2010] ECR II-6083.

[71] In particular Articles 256(1), 268 and 274 TFEU.

[72] *Systran* (n 69) [12].

all the actors involved[73]—in this case the national and EU courts—if economic operators are found in such a limbo of lack of effective remedy and access to justice, they may seek the ECtHR's protection. Before the accession of the EU to the ECHR, such recourse could be limited against Member States directly (insofar as their failure to provide remedies at the national level is concerned) and indirectly (as members of the EU for the failures of the latter to provide an effective remedy at the EU level). However, post-accession to the ECHR, economic operators could be in a position to lodge an application against the EU directly, which, under certain conditions, may be placed in the position of a co-respondent together with its Member States.

B. Potential for Subtle Impact

Finally, apart from the instances mentioned above, where the EU accession to the ECHR could potentially have a tangible impact in the area of public procurement, there are also other cases where accession may have a subtler impact.

One such example refers to the use of fair trade standards by the contracting authorities. It is important to remember that EU Member States have a positive obligation to respect, protect and fulfil the right enshrined under Article 4 ECHR, namely the prohibition of slavery and forced labour.[74] This area is of particular importance in the context of the globalised market economy and has continued to attract attention, not least because of reports revealing the appalling conditions that employees, sometimes children, have to endure in the so-called 'sweatshops' around the world. Although Member States are in a position to respect and protect human rights in their own territories, arguably they may also be under due diligence obligations not to condone practices violating these rights that take place outside their territory.[75] The examination of the existence of the due diligence obligation and the limit of the latter, especially in the case of extraterritoriality, is beyond the scope of the present chapter.[76] However, it suffices to note that due diligence is an obligation of means in the sense that Member States have discretion in choosing the relevant methods/means to achieve the intended objective, ie, the protection of human rights. One of these possible means is the adoption of fair trade policies/preferences in the context

[73] See Article 4(3) TFEU; Case 294/83 *Les Verts v Parliament* [1986] ECR 1339 [23]; Case C-50/00 P *Unión de Pequeños Agricultores v Council of the European Union* [2002] ECR 6677 [62].

[74] The ECHR does not contain a definition of the term 'forced or compulsory labour'. Instead, it uses as a working definition, the one stipulated in Article 2 of the ILO Convention 29 concerning forced or compulsory labour. Article 2 reads: 'forced or compulsory labour shall mean all work or service which is exacted from any person under the menace of any penalty and for which the said person has not offered himself voluntarily'. Furthermore, the ECtHR adopts a wide interpretation of the both the notion of forced or compulsory labour. See *Van der Mussele v Belgium*, Series A No 70 (1983); *Graziani-Weiss v Austria*, App No 31950/06 (2011); *Stummer v Austria*, App No 37452/02 (2011) 54 EHRR 369; *CN and V v France*, App No 67724/09 (2012); *Siliadin v France*, App No 73316/01 (2005) 43 EHRR 287.

[75] The possibility of using procurement by states as a means to achieve results beyond their own jurisdiction is termed by McCrudden as *outward links* of procurement. These outward links are of particular importance in the era of globalised markets. See McCrudden (n 16) 93 et seq.

[76] In that respect, see the paper by V Tzevelekos, examining how due diligence imposes an obligation for states to exercise jurisdiction over their own nationals when they operate abroad and break human rights, but also, more generally, how states are obliged to demonstrate diligence every time they are effectively linked to a situation raising issues of human rights protection. V Tzevelekos, 'In Search of Alternative Solutions: Can the State of Origin be Held Internationally Responsible for Investors' Human Rights Abuses which are Not Attributable to it?' (2010) 35 *Brooklyn Journal of International Law* 155.

of public procurement. For example, public procurement authorities could require[77] economic operators to abide by certain standards regarding the employment conditions of the workforce that will be involved in the delivery of the procured goods or services. This requirement for compliance could be set as a condition for participation in the procurement process—as part of the so-called 'selection criteria' in the sense that economic operators who do not comply with these standards cannot participate in the procurement process—or as part of the 'contract award criteria'—namely the criteria used to identify the winning tender—or as part of the 'contractual conditions'—the conditions that concern the performance of the contract. It could also be included as a ground for exclusion if, for example, a contractor has been convicted of or has been involved in[78] using forced labour.

Looking at the aforementioned options, it should be noted that they may have a different impact in the procurement process. In particular, the first option, namely the inclusion of the fair trade conditionality at the stage of selection, is connected with the 'general conduct' of the economic operator in the sense that it requires these standards to be followed by the latter in general, ie, in all its economic operations. The same is true for option four, namely the exclusion of the economic operator in the event of previous conviction/involvement. By contrast, the second and third options focus on the conduct of the economic co-operator in the delivery of the specific procurement contract. Consequently, an economic operator who normally does not comply with these standards can decide to do so in the case of a specific procurement opportunity in order to participate in a specific procurement process. Therefore, one key difference between options one and four on the one hand and options two and three on the other is that the use of the former may lead to a reduction of the number of eligible economic operators—and equally to a reduction of competition. By contrast, options two and three do not lead a priori to a reduction of competition in the procurement process. However, as we will see later, options one and four may be arguably more successful in effecting the due diligence obligation by creating more powerful incentives for economic operators to comply with the intended standards.

When Member States consider the options/means that they have at their disposal in order to protect and implement the rights enshrined in the ECHR, they also have to consider the extent to which these are compatible with other obligations that arise under EU law. These policy decisions are subject to the scrutiny of the CJEU, which is competent to review whether the consequences of the latter disproportionately encroach on EU obligations. Looking at the case of the use of procurement as a means to offer protection under Article 4 ECHR, the question that arises is whether this is allowed as a matter of principle and, if so, to what extent. The answer has been provided recently by the CJEU in *Commission v The Netherlands.*[79] The case involved the supply and management of dispensing machines for hot drinks (and the supply of other relevant products such as coffee, tea etc). One of the main points of the action of the European Commission was that a requirement imposed by the contracting authority (The province of North Holland) for the use of fair trade criteria constituted a violation of the EU procurement rules. The CJEU accepted the possibility of the use of fair trade criteria in public procurement, but subject to certain conditions. In particular, these fair trade considerations can be used as part of the award criteria provided that they are clear, precise and unequivocal, and are linked with

[77] This could reflect wider governmental policies or be based on the initiative of the public authority.
[78] The proving the involvement in ways other than a prior conviction will raise significant evidentiary issues.
[79] Case C-368/10 *Commission v The Netherlands*, Judgment of 10 May 2012 (not yet reported).

the subject matter of the contract at hand.[80] This means that these fair trade considerations cannot refer to the tenderer's general purchasing policy or other matters of corporate social responsibility in general as part of the assessment of the technical capacity of the tenderer; in other words, the CJEU seems to limit the possibility of fair trade considerations as part of the 'selection criteria'.

It is submitted that the CJEU seems to have adopted a position that is based on a balance of proportionality in the sense that it tried to accommodate fair trade-related considerations within the EU public procurement framework of rules and obligations. However, it suffices to note at this point that an alternative approach in striking this balance could also be envisaged. If measures that try to facilitate a response against forced labour can only be used as award criteria, this means that the use of these below-par practices become simply a consideration in the process of a cost and benefit analysis. Tenderers will continue to use them whenever it is beneficial for them from an economic point of view.

To be more precise, let us imagine that in a contract award, the criterion of price of the product corresponds to 70 per cent of the overall weighting and the criterion for the use of fair trade practices in the delivery of the product amounts to 15 per cent of the overall weighting.[81] Let us also imagine that there are two tenderers: one that abides by high labour standards and one that uses forced labour abroad. The latter will be penalised in effect by 15 per cent in the overall weighting because it does not fulfil the fair trade award criterion. However, if the use of forced labour abroad means that the production costs will be significantly lower, enabling the tenderer to submit a much more competitive price, then there seems to be an incentive for the tenderer to continue—or even to increase—the use of these practices. In this case, the dissuasive power of the de facto penalisation of 15 per cent through the award criteria is minimal. Of course, the balance could be tipped if the contracting authority would assign a greater weighting to the fair trade award criterion. Furthermore, it is obvious that the inclusion of these fair trade considerations in the 'selection criteria' would carry a much stronger moral message to tenderers and would immediately change the cost and benefit analysis; those who do not abide to higher standards would not be able to participate in the procurement. However, as we saw before, the CJEU seems not to allow the use of these criteria at the selection stage because this approach could have the impact of limiting competition in the procurement market.

In the pre-accession environment, it would be possible for sufferers of forced labour to bring an action against an EU Member State for its failure to comply with its obligation under the ECHR to demonstrate due diligence (aiming at the prevention of wrongfulness taking place outside its territory),[82] while complying with its EU obligations in the field of procurement, although, as already mentioned, due the *Bosphorus* jurisprudence, this might have limited chances of success unless it could be shown that the state enjoyed discretion in the way it implemented EU law. By contrast, in the post-accession environment, it would be theoretically possible for the same victims to also bring an action against the EU itself for failure to comply with its due diligence obligations as a result of legislative (content of the substantive rules on procurement that introduce limits) or judicial action (interpretation of these rules by the CJEU), hindering the use of an effective and available positive measure (fair trade policy as a precondition in procurement) against forced labour.

[80] Ibid [91] and [92].

[81] Let us assume that the remaining 15 per cent is linked with other award criteria such as time delivery etc.

[82] *Ilaşcu and others v Moldova and Russia*, App No 48787 (2004) 40 EHRR 1030 [331].

However, even if this pathway seems indirect or far-fetched because the CJEU's position could stand the scrutiny by Strasbourg since it allows in principle the use of fair trade criteria in procurement subject to what seems to be a 'reasonable' balance of proportionality, it is argued nevertheless that the accession of the EU to the ECHR may contribute to the strengthening of what could be termed as the process of 'moral subordination' of the rules of the internal market to those of human rights. It is exactly at this point where the accession of the EU to the ECHR may produce the more subtle effect, because it might assist the transformation of the hermeneutic paradigm that the CJEU uses when human rights are at stake. At present, the hermeneutic paradigm has as a starting point the protection of market freedoms[83]—based on the assumption that the role of the CJEU is primarily their protection—and human rights are seen as factors that could justify measures that prima facie constitute trade barriers. Despite the often deferential approach that the CJEU follows when human rights clash with economic freedoms, through a fairly flexible proportionality test, human rights considerations seem to be an 'add-on' in this hermeneutic paradigm.[84] Although it is doubtful whether post-accession the new hermeneutic paradigm would entail a repositioning of human rights as the point of departure in the CJEU's evaluation (this will very much depend on the type of cases that would reach the CJEU), it can be argued that the function of the CJEU as a 'human rights court' would not be simply a welcome surprise, but an expectation. For example, in the field of procurement as in other areas of the internal market, the CJEU would perhaps be more susceptible to allow even more discretion to Member States to assess the effectiveness of the means they use to comply with their human rights obligations (including due diligence obligations). This could take place during the CJEU's assessment of the means used by Member States in the context of the examination of proportionality. Besides, post-accession, the subtle effect of this 'moral subordination'[85] could be manifested in the area of procurement not only at the judicial level but also at the legislative level.[86]

V. CONCLUSIONS

The present chapter set out to answer the following questions; first, whether there are any points of intersection between the field of public procurement and of human rights in general; second, whether such intersections exist between the European public procurement regulatory framework and that of the ECHR in particular; and, third, if a future EU

[83] As well as related rights deriving from secondary EU law such as those established in the area of public procurement.

[84] See, for example, Case C-438/05 *International Transport Workers' Federation v Viking Line ABP* [2007] ECR I-10779; Case C-341/05 *Laval un Patneri* v *Svenska Byggnadsarbetareförbundet* [2007] ECR I-11767.

[85] The term 'moral subordination' does not necessarily insinuate a position of higher authority for human rights in the hierarchy of norms within the EU legal order. Instead, it refers to a qualitative change in the ethos of the EU—a process that started with the EU Charter of Fundamental Rights—as manifested in the workings of the EU courts and the EU legislator.

[86] For example, the proposal for the new public procurement Directive submitted by the European Commission contains in Article 55(3) a possible—but not compulsory—ground for exclusion of an economic operator for the infringement of the ILO Convention 29 concerning forced or compulsory labour. However, it seems that the final text after the 'trialogue' negotiation between the EU Parliament, the Council and the Commission may include some provisions against forced labour in the compulsory exclusions of Article 55(1).

accession to the ECHR is likely to have any impact in the law and practice of EU public procurement.

First of all, the chapter demonstrated that despite there being a prima facie disjuncture between public procurement and human rights, there have been instances of interrelation between these two fields of law and policy for some time now. This interrelation is stronger when the notions of public procurement and human rights are understood widely, but it also exists even when these notions are perceived more narrowly. Furthermore, the chapter tried to explain why in the European context, the area of public procurement appears to be more disconnected from human rights in comparison to other areas of economic law—for example, competition law—both at the level of legal scholarship and at the level of legal practice. It argued in particular that this seems to be attributable to the fact that the EU has an elaborate legal framework of substantive rules governing public procurement supported by a sophisticated system of judicial remedies. Using the field of EU competition law as a point of comparison, the chapter observed that the architecture and the dynamics of the public procurement enforcement system create different types of concerns from those detected in the context of EU competition law enforcement, thus leading to a more 'self-contained' legal framework.

The chapter then elucidated that certain, albeit indirect, pathways for interaction between the two legal frameworks already exist. However, these pathways—particularly in the form of protection of individual rights before the ECtHR—have not been used so far at least to a meaningful degree. The chapter then argued that the EU's accession to the ECHR is likely to create new pathways of interaction between public procurement and human rights and may even strengthen existing ones by rendering them more appealing. This development could be effected through the recalibration, as a result of the accession, of the vertical institutional structure at the apex of which the ECtHR will be positioned—even if this does not lead to a substantial change to the existing relation of 'working parity' that exists between the courts in Luxembourg and Strasbourg—but most importantly through a change of ethos within the EU legal order.

In particular, the chapter concluded that the accession could have two types of impact on the interaction between these two areas of law and policy: a direct, tangible one and a more indirect, subtler one. The tangible impact is linked with the new pathway of judicial protection that would allow individuals to bring complaints against the EU directly—in addition to the existing possibility of bringing claims against the Member States for conduct that originates in and gives effect to rules and practices established at the EU level, in cases where the *Bosphorus* presumption is not satisfied or where Member States have discretion in the implementation of EU policies.

On the other hand, the subtler impact of accession relates to the overall strengthening of the process of 'moral subordination' of the rules of economic freedoms to those of human rights. This change of ethos would first of all complete the transformation of the CJEU into a 'human rights court'. This process has already started through the jurisprudence of the CJEU and more recently through the entry into force of the Charter of Fundamental Rights of the EU, but it can be argued that, due to the limits and conditions of the scope of application of the latter, the aforementioned process of transformation is to a certain degree incomplete. The EU's accession to the ECHR would 'superimpose' the Convention rights as a legal but also as a moral comparator/point of reference in a more complete, holistic manner. This transformation would not leave the field of EU public procurement unaffected. Instead, the chapter considered that this change could be manifested in the field of procurement first of all at the judicial level through a possible transformation of the hermeneutic paradigm employed by the CJEU—that could perhaps allow more discretion to Member States when they choose the means for effecting their human rights obligations—and also at the legislative level by strengthening the role human rights considerations as a significant parameter that the European legislator ought to take into account.

18

The EU Accession to the ECHR as an Opportunity for Conceptual Clarity in European Equality Law: The New European Paradigm of Full Equality

PANOS KAPOTAS*

I. INTRODUCTION

IN THE LAST few decades, European equality law seems to have entered a coming-of-age stage. The principle of equal treatment in its various forms and guises, refined through legislative developments and judicial interpretation by the Court of Justice of the European Union (CJEU)and the European Court of Human Rights (ECtHR), has become a core element of the European normative sphere, both as an individual non-discrimination right under the European Convention on Human Rights (ECHR) and as a foundational component of European Union (EU) law and policy. Arguably the most significant feature of this transformative process is the gradual repositioning of the meaning of equality towards more substantive lines. The reference to *full equality* in Protocol 12 of the ECHR and Article 157 of the Treaty on the Functioning of the European Union (TFEU) is an eloquent, albeit tacit, admission that existing inequalities cannot be adequately redressed through a formulaic and neutral principle[1] that creates primarily negative and minimally positive obligations.[2]

* Lecturer in Law, University of Portsmouth. The author wishes to thank Vassilis Tzevelekos, Hugh Collins, Lizzie Barmes, Mark Bell and the participants in the November 2012 workshop on the EU Accession to the ECHR (University of Maastricht) for valuable comments on various iterations of this chapter. The usual disclaimer applies.

[1] On the relationship between formal equality and state neutrality, see A Gutman, *Liberal Equality* (Cambridge, Cambridge University Press, 1980); M Sandell, *Liberalism and the Limits of Justice* (Cambridge, Cambridge University Press, 1982).

[2] Under the Convention system, Article 14 has been associated with positive obligations for the first time at the dawn of the new century in the case of *Thlimmenos v Greece* (2001) 31 EHRR 411 (see below, section III.B). In the subsequent case of *Stec* (*Stec and others v UK*, Grand Chamber, 12 April 2006, ECHR 2006-VI) the ECtHR explicitly acknowledged that 'in certain circumstances a failure to attempt to correct inequality through different treatment may in itself give rise to a breach of the article' ([51]). A similar development has taken place within the framework of EU law, with 'fourth generation' equality duties introduced through secondary law instruments based on what was then Article 13 TEC in the Treaty of Amsterdam (now Article 19 TFEU). See B Hepple, M Coussey, and T Choudhury, *Equality: A New Framework: Report of the Independent Review of the Enforcement of UK Anti-Discrimination Legislation* (Oxford, Hart Publishing, 2000); S Fredman, 'Equality: A New Generation?' (2001) 30 *Industrial Law Journal* 145, 163 et seq.

Despite these developments, the discourse on equality remains convoluted and fraught with doctrinal inconsistencies.[3] Formal equality continues to cast its shadow over anti-discrimination mechanisms designed to achieve concrete results, and terms like positive action, reasonable accommodation and special treatment are often seen as interchangeable exceptions to equal treatment. The accession of the EU to the ECHR provides a unique opportunity to rethink the concept of equality and its modus operandi in the European normative space and to identify a singular, coherent and philosophically robust general legal principle of equal treatment for the whole *Civis Europeus*.[4] With the ambition to make a small contribution to the wider debate, this chapter will attempt to shed some light on facets of the equality discourse that lack analytical clarity.

Instead of adopting the orthodox approach that views equality as oscillating between competing models, the analysis will challenge the philosophical integrity of formal equality as a distinct category of normative significance. Section II of this chapter, then, will endeavour to deconstruct formal equality, explain why it is an unfit philosophical premise for European anti-discrimination law and identify the 'substantive' turn in the case law of the two European courts. It will be argued that, despite the tentative emergence of a new paradigm of *full equality*, conceptual confusion continues to be part of the picture, especially insofar as the relationship between positive action and equal treatment is concerned. Section III therefore will discuss positive action as a key index of full equality and will use it as the backdrop against which to clarify the place of reasonable accommodation and forms of special treatment to vulnerable social groups. Section IV will turn to assess the possible impact of EU accession to the Convention on European equality law. Although EU equality law is obviously broader in scope and inevitably more sophisticated than a system built around a single Convention Article, accession can still become the driver for greater conceptual clarity and interpretative convergence. Section V concludes.

A final note on methodological choices is in order. Despite the fact that the discussion is not confined to any one protected ground or human characteristic, several arguments are designed to target gender equality in particular. This emphasis on gender is the most suitable means of exploring the differences between positive action, reasonable accommodation and special treatment. A similar caveat applies to the almost exclusive focus of that part of the enquiry on EU law, as the relevant mechanisms have drawn less attention within the context of the Convention. This notwithstanding, the claims advanced here are intended to cover the whole spectrum of European equality law in its broadest sense, with gender equality used as a proxy to develop a more general analytical framework.

[3] On the conceptual complexity underlying European equality and non-discrimination law in general, see C McCrudden and S Prechal, *The Concepts of Equality and Non-discrimination in Europe: A Practical Approach*, Report by the European Network of Legal Experts in the Field of Gender Equality (European Commission, Directorate-General for Employment, Social Affairs and Equal Opportunities, November 2009). For remarkable attempts to work through the doctrinal inconsistencies, see C McCrudden and H Kountouros, 'Human Rights and European Equality Law' in H Meenan (ed), *Equality Law in an Enlarged European Union: Understanding the Article 13 Directives* (Cambridge, Cambridge University Press, 2007); O De Schutter, 'Three Models of Equality and European Anti-discrimination Law' (2006) 57 *Northern Ireland Legal Quarterly* 1.

[4] Joined Cases C-132/91, C-138/91 and C-139/91 *Katsikas v Konstantinidis* [1992] ECR I-06577, Opinion of AG Jacobs [46].

II. THE MAGICAL (SUR)REALISM OF FORMAL EQUALITY[5]

Formal equality is one of the most cited and, arguably, ill-treated terms in the equality discourse. Liberal moral and political philosophy has claimed paternity of the term early on, attributing it to Aristotle, who is, in turn, often labelled an *ex post facto* unsuspecting recruit to the liberal cause.[6] The famous 'treating likes alike' maxim[7] has consistently been thought to constitute a foundational principle of liberal justice, underpinning the general legal principle of equal treatment in its various national constitutional endorsements.[8] It is no surprise that this particular notion of equality remains at the epicentre of liberal thinking, as it is a good fit for a normative framework predicated on state neutrality[9] and the primacy of the individual.[10] Classical formal equality therefore usually translates into a general prohibition of discrimination involving primarily negative obligations, which may be coupled with minimal regulatory intervention horizontally when necessary to ensure a degree of gender neutrality in the private sphere.

This line of analysis was long thought to be mirrored by the rationale underpinning the prohibition of discrimination under the ECHR system, with the state obligation stemming from Article 14 ECHR accordingly understood as primarily a *negative* one. For quite some time, part of the theory asserted that Strasbourg case law was[11] reflective of 'a clear preference for formal equality',[12] in line with the 'treating likes alike' Aristotelian maxim.[13] In this context, Article 14 of the Convention was used as a tool to ensure that individuals in *similar* situations received the *same* treatment by the respondent state.[14] In recent years, however, a number of commentators have identified a shift in the Strasbourg Court's conceptualisation of equality under the Convention[15] from a *formal* to a more *substantive*

[5] On magic realism as an artistic category and a literary genre, see W Spindler, 'Magic Realism: A Typology' (1993) 22 *Forum for Modern Language Studies* 75. As will hopefully become apparent in the course of this section, formal equality shares a conceptual affinity with magic realism in that it introduces surreal elements—namely the assumption that individuals or groups can be treated as starting from the same position—in an otherwise realistic normative environment.

[6] SG Salkever, *Finding the Mean: Theory and Practice in Aristotelian Political Philosophy* (Princeton, Princeton University Press, 1990).

[7] Aristotle, *Nicomachean Ethics* (Athens, Papyrus, 1975) V.3. 1131a10–b15; Aristotle, *Politics* (Athens, Papyrus, 1975) III.9.1280 a8–15, III. 12. 1282b18–23.

[8] Most post-Renaissance national constitutions include some form of a general equality clause among their provisions. The same is true of most international legal texts on the protection of human rights, in which case, however, the provision often appears in the form of a general non-discrimination clause.

[9] See, for instance, A Gutman, *Liberal Equality* (Cambridge, Cambridge University Press, 1980); M Sandell, *Liberalism and the Limits of Justice* (Cambridge, Cambridge University Press, 1982).

[10] See, among others, W Kymlicka, *Contemporary Political Philosophy* (Oxford, Clarendon Press, 1990).

[11] At least up until the late 1990s. See K Henrard, *Devising an Adequate System of Minority Protection: Individual Human Rights, Minority Rights and the Right to Self-Determination* (The Hague, Martinus Nijhoff, 2000) 59 and 76.

[12] G Tarr, RF Williams and J Marco (eds), *Federalism, Subnational Constitutions and Minority Rights* (Westport, Praeger, 2004) 31.

[13] OM Arnardóttir, *Equality and Non-discrimination under the European Convention on Human Rights* (Leiden, Martinus Nijhoff, 2002) 10; T Loenen, 'Rethinking Sex Equality as a Human Right' (1994) 12 *Netherlands Quarterly of Human Rights* 253.

[14] *Fredin v Sweden (No 1)*, Series A No 192 (1991) [60]; *Salgueiro da Silva Mouta v Portugal* (1999) 31 EHRR 47 [26]; *Edoardo Palumbo v Italy*, App No 15919/89 (ECtHR, 30 November 2000) [51].

[15] Part of the literature has identified a similar shift from formal to substantive equality in the positive action case law of the CJEU, which will be explored in more detail later on.

notion.[16] Accepting *difference* as an intrinsic element of the equal treatment rationale is thought to be the key in this alleged reconceptualisation, with the Court's ruling in the seemingly inconspicuous case of *Thlimmenos v Greece*[17] often viewed as a turning point. In *Thlimmenos*, the Court, for the first time in almost half a century's worth of judgments, moves to explicitly suggest that: 'The right not to be discriminated against in the enjoyment of the rights guaranteed under the Convention is also *violated when States* without an objective and reasonable justification *fail to treat differently persons whose situations are significantly different.*'[18]

Despite what may appear to some as a revolutionary change of tack in Strasbourg's approach to equality, the *Thlimmenos* ruling does not constitute a theoretical leap away from formal equality. A closer look at *Nicomachean Ethics* should be more than enough to shatter such simplistic assumptions. The laconic maxim 'treating likes alike' only tells half of the story on equality as Aristotle intended it. If similar situations are to be treated according to the same norm, it is only logical that, by extrapolation, *different* situations call for *different* normative treatment. This is nothing more than a concrete expression of a general rule of rationality,[19] although it is not always clear that 'equality as rationality'[20] is understood as including an obligation for differentiated treatment.[21] In Aristotle's own words, 'this is the origin of quarrels and complaints—when either equals have or are awarded unequal shares, or unequals equal shares' because if two persons are not equals, 'they should not be entitled to enjoy equal shares'.[22] Similarity and difference, then, are complementary criteria in determining the appropriate normative content of equal treatment and the CJEU has been quicker than its Strasbourg counterpart in explicitly recognising this as the correct interpretation of EU gender equality legislation.[23]

Reasonable as it may sound, such an interpretation of formal equality leaves a lot to be desired in terms of conceptual integrity and theoretical robustness. Accepting difference as an intrinsic element of formal equality blurs the conceptual boundaries between formal and substantive equality insofar as the former is traditionally understood as a strict principle of consistency in the treatment of similar cases[24] embodying a notion of procedural justice.[25] In other words, by removing absolute gender neutrality[26] from the definitional content of formal equality, gender is no longer automatically classified as a

[16] S Spiliopoulou-Akerman, 'The Limits of Pluralism—Recent Jurisprudence of the European Court of Human Rights with Regard to Minorities: Does the Prohibition of Discrimination Add Anything?' (2002) 3 *Journal of Ethnopolitics and Minority Issues in Europe* 5; R O'Connell, 'Commentary—Substantive Equality in the European Court of Human Rights?' (2009) *Michigan Law Review First Impressions* 107, 129.

[17] *Thlimmenos v Greece* (2001) 31 EHRR 411.

[18] Ibid [44], emphasis added.

[19] I Berlin, 'Equality as an Ideal' in FA Olafson (ed), *Justice and Social Policy: A Collection of Essays* (Englewood Cliffs, Prentice Hall, 1961).

[20] C McCrudden, 'Chapter 11: Equality and Non-discrimination' in D Feldman (ed), *English Public Law* (Oxford, Oxford University Press, 2004) 581, 582.

[21] From the point of view of English public law, for instance, McCrudden's analysis (ibid 614) seems to implicitly accept that equality as rationality entails both types of obligation, but he nonetheless refrains from exploring the nature, scope and limits of the obligation for differentiated treatment in any detail.

[22] Aristotle *Nicomachean Ethics* (n 7).

[23] Case 106/83 *Sermide SpA v Cassa Conguaglio Zucchero* [1984] ECR 4209 [28]; Opinion of AG Van Gerven, 15 September 1993, Case C-146/91 *Koinopraxia Enoseon Georgikon Synetairismon Diacheiriseos Enchorion Proionton Syn PE (KYPED) v Commission* [1994] ECR I-4199.

[24] C Barnard and B Hepple, 'Substantive Equality' (2000) 59 *Cambridge Law Journal* 562.

[25] Ibid 563.

[26] Or neutrality on any other protected ground for that matter.

morally irrelevant characteristic[27] and it is therefore possible to suggest that the conceptual distance between formal and substantive conceptions of equality is significantly diminished. Effectively, then, the legitimacy of differentiated treatment under such a conception of formal equality would inevitably move from a normative to a *factual* level of enquiry, with a view to determining whether gender in that particular context is a factor that places men and women in relatively different situations. What counts as a normatively significant factual difference will remain, of course, a matter of interpretation and, arguably, considerable disagreement. The same is true a fortiori with regard to the actual content of the treatment afforded to individuals or groups in different positions, as factual differences per se will not automatically justify *every* deviation from the 'standard'. The point, however, is that such a conception of formal equality is not incompatible in principle and by default with *any* form of differentiated or even special treatment, up to and including positive action, as long as it can be justified in concreto.

The lack of conceptual clarity that is associated with formal equality has often led to terminological discrepancies and analytical confusion in the field of EU equality law. One of the most famous examples is to be found in the reactions to the CJEU's early ruling on positive action in the *Kalanke* case.[28] Although *Kalanke* is, indeed, a rather weak specimen of legal reasoning and rightfully attracted fierce academic criticism at the time,[29] there is no consensus in the literature on whether the fault lies in the CJEU's commitment to formal equality[30] or in its 'narrow and procedural approach to equality of opportunities',[31] which is generally considered to fall within the broad spectrum of substantive equality.[32] It is quite telling that this interpretative divergence exists even though EU gender equality law was, in theory, explicitly predicated on a conception of *equality of opportunities* rather than formal equality ever since the adoption of the original Equal Treatment Directive.[33]

Far from indulging purely philosophical musings on the meaning of equality, this line of enquiry is laden with practical normative significance. It begs the question whether there is any room left within the combined normative framework of EU law and the ECHR for a conception of formal equality in the classical liberal sense, which may resonate with the ensuing state obligations and still be sufficiently distinguishable from rival notions of equality. In other words, is it possible to conceive of formal equality as a sufficiently defined self-standing notion that does not collapse into a 'less substantive' variant of substantive equality? Although any answer would not be fully convincing outside the framework of a

[27] J Nickel, 'Discrimination and Morally Relevant Characteristics' (1972) 32 *Analysis* 113.

[28] Case C-450/93 *Kalanke v Freie Hansestadt Bremen* [1995] ECR I-3051.

[29] A Peters, 'The Many Meanings of Equality and Positive Action in Favour of Women under European Community Law—A Conceptual Analysis' (1996) 2 *European Law Journal* 177; S Prechal, 'Case C-450/93, Kalanke v Freie Hansestadt Bremen, [1995] ECR I-3051' (1996) 33 *Common Market Law Review* 1245; E Szyszczak, 'Positive Action after Kalanke' (1996) 59 *MLR* 876.

[30] See, among others, M De Vos, 'Beyond Formal Equality: Positive Action under Directives 2000/43 EC and 2000/78 EC' (2007) *European Commission, Directorate-General for Employment, Social Affairs and Equal Opportunities* 22.

[31] Barnard and Hepple (n 24) 577.

[32] S Fredman, *A Critical Review of the Concept of Equality in UK Anti-discrimination Law: Independent Review of the Enforcement of UK Anti-discrimination Legislation* (Cambridge, Cambridge Centre for Public Law and Judge Institute of Management Studies, 1999) Working Paper No 3, para 3.12.

[33] Council Directive 76/207/EEC of 9 February 1976 on the implementation of the principle of equal treatment for men and women as regards access to employment, vocational training and promotion, and working conditions.

robust European theory of equality,[34] it is possible to offer some preliminary suggestions in this direction. If disengaged from its alleged intellectual progeny, a liberal conception of formal equality can still make sense in a *non-comparative* context.[35] If one accepts that the allocation and enjoyment of certain rights is entirely independent of situational differences, it seems reasonable to suggest that the distinction between morally relevant and morally irrelevant characteristics is not applicable and, consequently, equal protection of the law in this context renders interpersonal comparisons redundant, if not outright unlawful.

The natural normative environment wherein such a conception of equality—tentatively termed here *non-comparative formal equality*—is intuitively resonant is the realm of *absolute rights*. Take, for instance, the right not to be tortured or subjected to inhuman or degrading treatment.[36] This is generally accepted as a 'peremptory norm of jus cogens'[37] in international law—and recognised as such under the ECHR[38]—which is not subject to degrees, limitations or restrictions of any kind. Over the years, Strasbourg has been careful to safeguard the absolute nature of the prohibition by firmly denying the legitimacy of all attempts to justify state policies and practices through reference to elements of comparison in any shape or form. Torture is prohibited irrespective of the circumstances of the victim's conduct[39] and it does not lend itself to a balancing act between competing rights[40] or between the risk of harm to the victim and the danger he poses to the state.[41]

One might be tempted to extrapolate and suggest that, in the case of absolute rights, equal treatment is automatically tantamount to (gender) neutrality. Even if that were correct,[42] however, the category of non-comparative formal equality would continue to suffer from the philosophical thinness attributed to its traditional liberal version. If the obligation to treat equally is exhausted by treating everyone *identically* solely by virtue of our shared 'humanity',[43] then equality becomes a normatively redundant concept[44] as it collapses into nothing more than a prohibition of direct discrimination.[45] In fact, according to part of the literature, it would make more sense to remove equality and discrimination altogether

[34] Which, inevitably, goes far beyond the limited scope and ambitions of the present enquiry.

[35] It is often suggested that the first part of the Aristotelian maxim corresponds to formal equality, whereas its second part is reflective of substantive equality. See L Waddington and A Hendriks, 'The Expanding Concept of Employment and Discrimination in Europe: From Direct and Indirect Discrimination to Reasonable Accommodation Discrimination' (2002) 18 *International Journal of Comparative Labour Law and Industrial Relations* 403, 2.1. This line of argument, however, is premised on the traditional but erroneous assumption that it is possible to conceptually decouple formal from substantive equality simply by reference to the similarity/difference dichotomy.

[36] Article 3 ECHR.

[37] *Prosecutor v Furundzija* (10 December 1998), ICTY, Case No IT-95-17/I-T (1999) 38 International Legal Materials 317 [144].

[38] *Al-Adsani v United Kingdom*, ECHR 2001-XI (2001) [61].

[39] *Lorse v The Netherlands*, App No 52750/99 (ECtHR, 4 February 2003).

[40] *Chahal v United Kingdom*, EHRR 1996-V (1996).

[41] *Saadi v Italy*, App No 37201/06 (ECtHR, 28 February 2008).

[42] Which is not necessarily the case, as the lack of consensus on the matter indicates.

[43] B Williams, 'The Idea of Equality' in P Laslett and WG Runciman (eds), *Philosophy, Politics and Society* (Oxford, Blackwell, 1962).

[44] P Westen, 'The Empty Idea of Equality' (1982) 95 *Harvard Law Review* 537.

[45] It goes without saying that any conception of equality that fails to recognise *indirect discrimination* as an intrinsic definitional element of the prohibition of discrimination is by default too narrow to encapsulate the current normative framework of European equality law. See, among others, E Ellis, *EU Anti-Discrimination Law* (Oxford, Oxford University Press, 2005); S Besson, 'Evolutions on Non-discrimination Law within the ECHR and ESC Systems: It Takes Two to Tango in the Council of Europe' (2012) 60 *American Journal of Comparative Law* 147.

from this kind of normative equation,[46] as the morally reprehensible and legally prohibited act par excellence in this case is the violation of the absolute right itself. Simply put, when torture is at issue, the gender of the victim[47] should be morally and legally irrelevant.

This line of argument may be correct in exposing the logical incoherence of formal equality in any of its conceptual guises, but it fails to capture the essence of the philosophical problem and is clearly at odds with the normative reality of European equality law. The Strasbourg Court has often considered the merits of complaints alleging a violation of Article 3 in conjunction with Article 14 of the Convention, where torture was thought to be the *result of discrimination*.[48] In its reasoning, the Court identified that racially motivated torture was 'a *particular* affront to human dignity'.[49] The corresponding state obligation, then, is interpreted as requiring 'authorities [to] use all available means to combat racism and racist violence, thereby reinforcing democracy's vision of a society in which diversity is not perceived as a threat but as a source of its enrichment'.[50] Transposed into the context of gender, this echoes feminist critiques of *jus cogens* as being reflective of a male perspective that permeates international human rights law[51] and uses the public/private dichotomy[52] as a mechanism to obfuscate the role that gender equality should play in the relevant philosophical discourse and corresponding normative framework.[53]

With the Strasbourg Court apparently in tune with those arguing in favour of the need to incorporate an equality dimension even in the interpretation of absolute rights, it seems that there is hardly any room left for a conception of formal equality predicated on absolute neutrality. This rings even more true in the context of EU law, where gender mainstreaming has been introduced with the explicit aim of rendering gender equality an integral consideration across the spectrum of the whole normative agenda since the late 1990s.[54] The 'symmetrical' approach that formal equality is seen as encapsulating[55] may have enjoyed some currency in the not-so-distant past, but it is losing its legal and political lustre in the European normative space.

This notwithstanding, the relevant discourse continues to oscillate between the 'formal' and the 'substantive' that are seen as occupying opposite ends of the equality spectrum. It is the dichotomy itself, then, that lies at the heart of the philosophical problem. The mistake of recognising formal equality as the conceptual *altera pars* of substantive equality is not rectified by accepting the latter as the preferred interpretation of equal treatment. The

[46] J Raz, *The Morality of Freedom* (Oxford, Clarendon Press, 1986) ch 9.

[47] Or any other characteristic that may constitute a ground for discrimination.

[48] *Nachova and others v Bulgaria* (2005) ECHR 2005-VII; *Bekos and Koutropoulos v Greece* (2005) ECHR 2005-XIII; *Stoica v Romania*, App No 42722/02 (ECtHR, 4 March 2008); *Virabyan v Armenia*, App No 40094/05 (ECtHR, 2 October 2012). All these cases involve an allegation of torture as a result of *racial* rather than gender discrimination, but the argument regarding the relationship between equal treatment and absolute rights holds true vis-a-vis all grounds of discrimination.

[49] *Virabyan v Armenia* (n 48) [199], emphasis added.

[50] Ibid.

[51] H Charlesworth and C Chinkin, 'The Gender of Jus Cogens' (1993) 15 *Human Rights Quarterly* 63, 67.

[52] Ibid 72.

[53] H Charlesworth, C Chinkin and C Wright, 'Feminist Approaches to International Law' (1991) 85 *American Journal of International Law* 613, 624.

[54] C Boothand and C Bennett, 'Gender Mainstreaming in the European Union' (2002) 9 *European Journal of Women's Studies* 430; MA Pollack and E Hafner-Burton, 'Mainstreaming Gender in the European Union' (2000) 7 *Journal of European Public Policy* 432.

[55] S Fredman, 'After Kalanke and Marschall: Affirming Affirmative Action' (1999) 1 *Cambridge Yearbook of European Legal Studies* 199, 200.

thrust of the analytical claim advanced here is that the concept of equality is *singular* and should not be fragmented into binary schemas. Simply put, the modus operandi of equal treatment as a general legal principle requires that *personal circumstances* are *always* a core element of the reasoning, even if only to ascertain the absence of any normatively significant differences. As explained earlier, if this is true even for absolute rights, then it should be true a fortiori with regard to every other type of right. If this line of analysis is correct, it begs the question whether the notion of formal equality should be abandoned altogether.

Part of the theory has attempted to offer a less radical solution by striking a conceptual compromise. Besson, for instance, explains that the different dimensions of equality may give rise to multiple binary dichotomies, such as between symmetrical and asymmetrical equality and between formal and material equality.[56] According to this schema, symmetrical equality amounts to both treating comparable situations similarly and different situations differently, with asymmetrical equality covering cases where special treatment is required.[57] Besson seems to argue that both symmetrical and asymmetrical equality can be accommodated under a conception of formal equality, but then goes on to acknowledge that the latter does not always amount to material equality due to the effects of past discrimination. In these cases, positive action becomes a legitimate means to bridge the gap between formal and material equality.[58]

Although this approach leaves a lot to be desired in terms of conceptual clarity, it does help identify a significant problem with the equality discourse. This is none other than the conflation between special treatment and positive action, which are often seen both in the EU and in the ECHR contexts as interchangeable deviations from the norm of formal equality. Besson's analysis offers some useful insights into why only special treatment should be regarded as asymmetrical, but rests firmly rooted in the assumption that formal equality is the norm. It follows that any move towards a substantive paradigm of equality is virtually impossible without a clearer image of where special treatment and positive action fit into the normative picture.

III. CONCEPTS AND CONCEPTUAL BOUNDARIES: POSITIVE ACTION, REASONABLE ACCOMMODATION, SPECIAL TREATMENT AND SUBSTANTIVE EQUALITY

A. Clarifying the Concept: A Typology of Positive Action and the Interpretative Status Quo in EU Law

According to a moderate, comprehensive and relatively non-controversial definition, positive action denotes the deliberate use of race or gender-conscious criteria for the specific purpose of benefiting a group that has previously been disadvantaged or excluded from important areas of the public sphere on the grounds of race or gender respectively.[59] Two important points regarding the notion of group employed here become immediately

[56] S Besson, 'Gender Discrimination under EU and ECHR Law: Never Shall the Twain Meet?' (2008) 8 *Human Rights Law Review* 647, 673.

[57] Ibid 674–75.

[58] Ibid 675–76.

[59] S Fredman, *Discrimination Law* (Oxford, Oxford University Press, 2002) 126.

obvious. First, any category of persons that have been or are being discriminated against on grounds of a shared characteristic should, in principle, be entitled to claim the status of a social group for the purposes of positive action.[60] In other words, there appears to be nothing in the definition of positive action to suggest that its use should be limited to particular social groups.[61] Second, the benefiting groups may be either disadvantaged or under-represented as a result of the invidious use of the shared characteristic. The relationship, however, between disadvantage and under-representation is severely under-theorised, which undermines doctrinal clarity and threatens normative consistency.

In the EU law jargon, positive action is an 'umbrella' term that is understood in a deliberately open-ended manner, so that it can potentially encompass a wide range of equality and non-discrimination policies and practices. Although there is no terminological consensus in the literature,[62] the view that positive action can take a number of different shapes or forms became the default position early on.[63] It is obvious that this lack of conceptual specificity obfuscates the relevant discourse and creates unnecessary confusion. Distinguishing, then, between different types of positive action should be an analytical priority in order to lay down success standards and accurately assess the effectiveness of such measures in achieving the aim of 'full equality in practice'.[64]

The most successful recent attempt to provide a comprehensive typology of positive action in employment has been undertaken by De Schutter,[65] Who identifies six types of positive measures in employment:[66]

— 'Monitoring the composition of the workforce in order to identify instances of under-representation and, possibly, to encourage the adoption of action plans and the setting of targets' (type 1).
— 'Redefining the standard criterion on the basis of which employment or promotion are allocated (in general, merit)' (type 2).
— 'Outreach measures, consisting in general measures targeting underrepresented groups, such as the provision of training aimed at members of the underrepresented groups or job announcements encouraging members of such groups to apply' (type 3).
— 'Outreach measures, consisting in individual measures such as the guarantee to members of underrepresented groups that they will be interviewed if they possess the relevant qualifications' (type 4).
— 'Preferential treatment of equally qualified members of the underrepresented group, with or without exemption clause (also referred to as "flexible quotas")' (type 5).
— 'Strict quotas, linked or not to objective factors beyond the representation of the target group in the general active population' (type 6).

60 On a very significant discussion on the normative construction of the concept of social group, see IM Young, *Justice and the Politics of Difference* (Princeton, Princeton University Press, 1990) 42–48; IM Young, 'Polity and Group Difference: A Critique of the Ideal of Universal Citizenship' (1989) 99 *Ethics* 250.

61 This is, indeed, the rationale behind the ongoing expansion of the scope of anti-discrimination law towards a more inclusive approach. Besides race and gender, other human characteristics, such as age, ethnicity, disability and sexual orientation, have been gradually added to the list of protected grounds of discrimination. Note, for instance, the phrasing of Article 14 ECHR and of Article 1 of Protocol 12 to the Convention.

62 See Fredman (n 59) 125–36.

63 See, among others, C McCrudden, 'Rethinking Positive Action' (1986) 15 *Industrial Law Journal* 219.

64 Article 157(4) TFEU.

65 O De Schutter, 'Positive Action' in D Schiek, L Waddington and M Bell (eds), *Cases, Materials and Text on National, Supranational and International Non-discrimination Law* (Oxford, Hart Publishing, 2007).

66 Ibid 762.

De Schutter's typology is meticulous and covers a wide range of measures and schemes. In essence, though, it is premised upon a simpler binary distinction. On the one hand, there are 'true positive measures' that involve some form of preferential treatment to members of the disadvantaged groups and, on the other hand, 'outreach measures' that aim primarily at improving the competitiveness of the group in the labour market without granting preferential treatment. According to this criterion,[67] measures of types 4, 5 and 6 fall under the former category, while measures of types 1, 2 and 3 fall under the latter.[68]

Turning from theory to practice—and bearing in mind that a detailed examination of the CJEU case law on positive action lies beyond the limited scope of the present enquiry—it can be safely argued that the legitimacy of soft measures under EU law is currently beyond doubt. The legality of strict measures, on the other hand, depends on whether they satisfy the test the CJEU laid down in its *Badeck* ruling.[69] According to the three-pronged *Badeck* test, the measure must:

— be designed to address a de facto *inequality* between men and women in employment;
— be *flexible* with regard to the achievement of desired results, so that the allocation of the benefit is *not automatic*;
— contain a *saving clause*, so that the allocation of the benefit is *not unconditional.*

The Court explicitly or implicitly refers to each of these criteria in all of the judgments[70] and all three must be satisfied if the measure is to pass the Court's scrutiny successfully.

A final note on the position of the CJEU on positive action is necessary here. Although *Badeck* provoked a surge of enthusiasm at the time from pro-equality lawyers and theorists who regarded it as evidence of a shift from formal to substantive equality,[71] its alleged radicalism has been significantly overplayed. The Court in *Badeck* refined the test that was already introduced in its previous *Marschall* ruling[72] in order to adapt it to the requirements of former Article 141(4) (now Article 157(2) TFEU),[73] but, in reality, the link from the severely criticised *Kalanke* to *Marschall* to *Badeck* remained unbroken.[74] *Badeck* confirms that 'soft' quotas are permissible in principle and maybe proved that Member States could feel confident that carefully designed positive action schemes will survive the scrutiny of the Court. Nevertheless, the Court was not really faced with a hard case: if positive

[67] De Schutter argues that there is a second criterion according to which positive measures can be classified into two categories, namely whether they require that the beneficiary is a *member of the* (disadvantaged) *target group*. Although it is true that, in certain cases, non-members can take advantage of a programme designed primarily for the benefit of a specific group, it is submitted that this is a direct consequence of the principle of equal treatment understood as full and effective equality.

[68] De Schutter (n 65) 762.

[69] Case C-158/97 *Badeck v Landesanwalt beim Staatsgerichtshof des Landes Hessen* [1999] ECR I-1875.

[70] Case C-366/99 *Griesmar v Ministre de l'Economie* [2001] ECR I-9383; Case C-476/99 *Lommers v Minister van Landbouw, Natuurbeheer en Visserij* [2002] ECR I-2891; Case C-319/03 *Briheche (Serge) v Ministère de l'intérieur, de la securité intérieure et des libertés locales* [2004] ECR I-8807. Specifically, on the first criterion, see para 46 in *Griesmar*, para 41 in *Lommers* and para 22 in *Briheche*; on the second criterion, see para 56 in *Griesmar*, para 43 in *Lommers* and para 23 in *Briheche*; and on the third criterion, see para 57 in *Griesmar*, para 45 in *Lommers* and para 23 in *Briheche.*

[71] N Burrows and M Robinson, 'Positive Action for Women in Employment: Time to Align with Europe?' (2006) 33 *Journal of Law and Society* 24.

[72] Case C-409/95 *Marschall v Land Nordrhein Westfalen* [1997] ECR I-6363.

[73] The *Marschall* test was tailored to the original Equal Treatment Directive.

[74] This link is cleverly characterised by Fredman as an 'individualistic straitjacket'. See Fredman (n 55) 390.

action is a contentious issue that calls for elaborate theoretical exercises in legal reasoning, *Badeck* was a let-off.[75] As with *Marschall*, the *Badeck* quota would pass the threshold of legality even against the theoretical backdrop of a *less substantive* notion of *equality*.

The explicit reference to substantive equality, then, as a legitimate state objective may be welcome, but its implications are symbolic rather than normative. Accepting the legitimacy of selection criteria that 'are manifestly intended to lead to an equality which is substantive rather than formal'[76] is not enough to guarantee anything more than the abandonment of strict or non-comparative formal equality. This, however, begs the question whether *Badeck* had anything to add to our existing understanding of the concepts involved, given that the rejection of 'strict' formal equality can be directly inferred from Article 157(4) TFEU without the need to engage in a rigorous interpretative process. Even more significantly, the formal/substantive equality dichotomy continues to underpin the legal reasoning, which in itself undermines the robustness of the concept of equality at play.

B. Clarifying Conceptual Boundaries (I): Positive Action v Reasonable Accommodation

Disability discrimination in employment is one of the most rapidly developing areas of anti-discrimination law in Europe. This is in no small part due to the Framework Equality Directive[77] that imposed on Member States an obligation to implement anti-discrimination measures for the protection of disabled persons in employment.[78] In Article 5 the Directive introduces the notion of *reasonable accommodation*, which is intended to occupy centre-stage in eliminating discrimination on grounds of disability. The positive duty[79] of reasonable accommodation entails that employers should take ad hoc measures 'to enable a person with a disability to have access to, participate in, or advance in employment, or to undergo training'.[80] The Directive, then, purports to achieve a double aim: first, to establish

[75] The *Badeck* scheme involved public service rules that gave priority to women in promotions, access to training and recruitment. Such priority, however, was neither *automatic* nor *unconditional*: it was only allowed in sectors of the public service where women were under-represented, when the female candidate was equally qualified to her male counterpart and only if no reasons 'of greater legal weight' that might tilt the balance in favour of the male candidate were put forward. According to the German government, these reasons 'of greater legal weight' concerned 'various rules of law ... which make no reference to sex and are often described as social aspects' (*Badeck* (n 69) [34]). The *Badeck* positive action system amounted to what is usually described as a 'flexible result quota'. In para 28 of the ruling, the Court itself attributed two main characteristics to this system: it does not 'determine quotas uniformly for all the sectors and departments concerned' and it 'does not necessarily determine from the outset—automatically—that the outcome of each selection procedure must, in a stalemate situation where the candidates have equal qualifications, necessarily favour the woman candidate'.

[76] *Badeck* (n 69) [32].

[77] Directive 2000/78/EC.

[78] A Lawson and C Gooding, 'Introduction' in A Lawson and C Gooding (eds), *Disability Rights in Europe: From Theory to Practice* (Oxford, Hart Publishing, 2005) 1.

[79] Fredman (n 59) 59.

[80] Article 5 of Directive 2000/78/EC reads as follows: 'In order to guarantee compliance with the principle of equal treatment in relation to persons with disabilities, reasonable accommodation shall be provided. This means that employers shall take appropriate measures, where needed in a particular case, to enable a person with a disability to have access to, participate in, or advance in employment, or to undergo training, unless such measures would impose a disproportionate burden on the employer. This burden shall not be disproportionate when it is sufficiently remedied by measures existing within the framework of the disability policy of the Member State concerned.'

reasonable accommodation as a *general norm* that applies to all employers in the public and private sectors; and, second, to affirm that the *absence* of it amounts in and of itself to discrimination.[81]

Domestic legislation in most Member States has also adopted the approach taken in the Directive. A characteristic example is the UK Disability Discrimination Act 1995, as amended in 2005, which introduces the term 'reasonable adjustments' as equivalent to reasonable accommodation.[82] As Fredman points out, through the notion of reasonable adjustments, the Act does not simply require employers to conform to the 'able-bodied norm', but to modify that norm with a view to 'afford[ing] genuine equality to disabled persons'.[83] The language of the Directive and of the domestic implementing provisions echoes the traditional formal/substantive equality dichotomy, with commentators keen to suggest that the obligations in question are clearly inspired by a conception of substantive equality.

It is exactly this perceived adherence to substantive equality that led some commentators to regard reasonable accommodation as a form of positive action,[84] although not necessarily as 'reverse or positive discrimination'.[85] Such an interpretation, however, is erroneous and has been rightfully contested,[86] as it confuses two substantively and procedurally distinct normative techniques.[87] Reasonable accommodation should be conceived of as 'a particular kind of non-discrimination legislative provision, related to, but not synonymous with, the established forms of *direct* and *indirect discrimination*'.[88] It is thus an instrument designed according to the 'difference model of discrimination', which is in turn premised on an 'asymmetric notion' of equality.[89] In other words, the recognition that disabled persons are in a substantially different situation from able-bodied persons entails that the equal treatment principle in this case requires *different* treatment of the respective groups.

From this point of view, it is evident why reasonable accommodation does not amount to positive action. Whether or not disabled persons can be classified as a disadvantaged or under-represented group in particular employment cadres is *irrelevant*. Reasonable accommodation is thus understood as possessing an 'individualised character',[90] contrary

[81] United Nations Ad Hoc Committee on a Comprehensive and Integral International Convention on the Protection and Promotion of the Rights and Dignity of Persons with Disabilities, 'The Concept of Reasonable Accommodation in Selected National Disability Legislation', 2005, available at www.un.org/esa/socdev/enable/rights/ahc7bkgrndra.htm.

[82] For a more detailed analysis of the UK Disability Discrimination Act and its interpretation by national courts, see C Gooding, 'Disability Discrimination Act: From Statute to Practice'(2000) *Critical Social Policy* 533.

[83] Fredman (n 59) 59.

[84] See, for instance, H Fenwick, *Civil Liberties and Human Rights* (London, Cavendish Publishing, 2002) 1043.

[85] B Doyle, 'Enabling Legislation or Dissembling Law? The Disability Discrimination Act 1995' (1997) 60 *MLR* 64, 74. In the US context, see BP Tucker, 'The ADA's Revolving Door: Inherent Flaws in the Civil Rights Paradigm'(2001) 62 *Ohio State Law Journal* 335, 365.

[86] And not only in the European discourse. For a discussion of the matter from a US point of view, see C Jolls, 'Antidiscrimination and Accommodation' (2001) 115 *Harvard Law Review* 642.

[87] L Waddington, 'Reasonable Accommodation' in D Schiek, L Waddington and M Bell (eds), *Cases, Materials and Text on National, Supranational and International Non-discrimination Law* (Oxford, Hart Publishing, 2007) 745.

[88] DG Employment, Social Affairs and Equal Opportunities, *International Perspectives on Positive Action Measures: A Comparative Analysis in the European Union, Canada, the United States and South Africa* (European Commission Publications Office, 2009) 27, emphasis added.

[89] Ibid. See also Fredman (n 59) 126–30, especially 128–29.

[90] DG Employment, Social Affairs and Equal Opportunities (n 88) 28.

to the group approach that is instrumental in the conceptualisation and operation of positive action. Admittedly, the boundaries between the two are not always clear in practice. Systems that introduce a *disability quota*, requiring that a minimum percentage of the workforce should consist of disabled persons, as is the case in France, Austria and Sweden,[91] go beyond reasonable accommodation and into the realm of positive action. This, however, does not undermine the doctrinal distinctiveness of the two concepts.

Although the Commission's interpretation of reasonable accommodation is generally correct, one cannot help but notice the echoes of the traditional formal/substantive equality dichotomy. Insofar as the official language of equality remains entrapped in this parochial analytical schema, a return to a formalistic conception of equality as nothing more than due process remains theoretically possible, even if unlikely.

C. Clarifying Conceptual Boundaries (II): Gender Equality between Disadvantage and Vulnerability

The practical impact of EU gender equality law has been seriously contested from a feminist perspective both at the early stages of its development[92] and even after the recent additions to the normative framework.[93] Most commentators recognise the contributions of new legislation and of the policy and governance tools that have been employed, such as gender mainstreaming,[94] in improving the socio-economic status of European women, especially during the last decade.[95] Significant gender inequalities across the spectrum, however, continue to exist despite the efforts of European institutions and national legislators.

For some, this is the inevitable result of a general institutional mentality that 'condemns' EU social policy to the back seat in a primarily market-oriented policy agenda.[96] In feminist writings, however, the problem lies primarily with the conception of equality at play, which fails to recognise and adequately structural disadvantage.[97] This is particularly evident in the case of *pregnancy* and the way in which the CJEU has interpreted the relevant legal provisions.

McGlynn, for instance, accuses the Court for adopting the 'dominant ideology of motherhood'[98] across its case law on gender equality. Although its motives may be benign, the aim of addressing structural discrimination against women is only superficially served. If traditional assumptions about the socially constructed role of women are not

[91] Ibid 29.

[92] S Fredman, 'European Community Discrimination Law: A Critique' (1992) 21 *Industrial Law Journal* 119.

[93] A Masselot, 'The State of Gender Equality Law in the European Union' (2007) 13 *European Law Journal* 152.

[94] F Beveridge, 'Building against the Past: The Impact of Mainstreaming on EU Gender Law and Policy' (2007) 32 *European Law Review* 193; J Shaw, 'Mainstreaming Equality and Diversity in European Union Law and Policy' (2005) 58 *Current Legal Problems* 255. See, however, a more sceptical view in F Beveridge and S Nott, 'Mainstreaming: A Case for Optimism and Cynicism' (2002) 10 *Feminist Legal Studies* 299.

[95] For an overview of the disadvantaged status of women across the EU at the end of the twentieth century, see A Glasner, 'Gender and Europe: Cultural and Structural Impediments to Change' in J Bailey (ed), *Social Europe* (London, Longman, 1998).

[96] S Prechal, 'Equality of Treatment, Non-discrimination and Social Policy: Achievements in Three Themes' (2004) 41 *Common Market Law Review* 533, 533.

[97] Fredman (n 92) 134.

[98] C McGlynn, 'Ideologies of Motherhood in European Community Sex Equality Law' (2000) 6 *European Law Journal* 29, 31–32.

shattered, then under-representation of women in positions of power near the top of the socio-political hierarchy will continue to mar any superficial success of equality strategies.[99]

But what McGlynn goes on to suggest is far more radical than that. In her view, the underlying problem is that EU gender equality law revolves around a 'paternalistic "protection" principle'[100] that overrides equal treatment. In other words, the 'rhetoric of protection'[101] that presents women as a *vulnerable* social group is itself at fault for the perpetuation of vulnerability.[102] If this is true for pregnancy-related legislation,[103] then it is true a fortiori for positive action. The echoes of the typical social stigma argument are loud and clear.[104] It would be redundant to rehearse the full set of counter-arguments, especially in view of the fact that the real point here seems to be more refined compared to its classical formulation in the US literature.

To do justice to this critique, one needs to move beyond the feminist reluctance of labelling women as vulnerable and understand the thrust of the argument in the following terms: women should be treated as a vulnerable group in need of *special protection* only when they are *actually vulnerable* because of attributes specific to their gender.[105] When they are *disadvantaged* because of their gender, on the other hand—that is, because of the simple fact that they are women—the matter should be dealt with as a case of direct or indirect *gender discrimination*. Eradicating disadvantage that stems from discrimination or from gender-biased normative perceptions does *not* qualify as special protection, even though it may require 'asymmetric' legal tools such as positive action.

Distinguishing between *vulnerable groups* and *disadvantaged groups* is no easy task in practice, but it is normatively significant. It is a necessary condition to understand positive action as an *expression of equal treatment* and *not* as a form of *special treatment* as in its classical conception. Disadvantaged groups, then, are entitled to positive action,[106] whereas vulnerable groups are entitled to the special benefits provided for in general policies that promote *social inclusion*,[107] according to the basic ideals of the welfare state.

This latter dichotomy between positive action and general welfarist or social inclusion policies is clearly and coherently presented in the recent Report on Positive Action of the European Commission.[108] Drawing insights from the Report, one can also make sense of the further distinction between disadvantaged and vulnerable groups introduced here. *Children*, for instance, constitute an emblematic and arguably uncontested case of a

[99] On the normative attitudes towards women, see generally Fredman (n 32).

[100] McGlynn (n 98) 35.

[101] Ibid.

[102] The argument here is not a distinctly feminist one, in the sense that it applies equally to other disadvantaged or under-represented social groups.

[103] J Conaghan, 'Pregnancy and the Workplace: A Question of Strategy?' (1993) 20 *Journal of Law and Society* 71, 82–83.

[104] For a recent empirical analysis of the argument in its racial dimension, see A Onwuachi-Willig, E Houh and M Campbell, 'Cracking the Egg: Which Came First—Stigma or Affirmative Action?' (2008) 96 *California Law Review* 1299.

[105] These attributes are not necessarily—if at all—biological. The argument here refers primarily to *social attributes* that may render women a vulnerable group in a specific social context. Women of a particular ethnic or religious background, for instance, may be subjected to cultural or religious rituals, without their consent, as a matter of custom or religious doctrine. In this case the *external* perception of gender imposes additional burdens on women that need to be taken into account when allocating legal protection.

[106] Or, in any case, can become legitimate target groups for positive action programmes.

[107] On social inclusion as the principal goal of anti-discrimination law, see H Collins, 'Discrimination, Equality, and Social Inclusion' (2003) 66 *MLR* 16.

[108] DG Employment, Social Affairs and Equal Opportunities (n 88) 28.

vulnerable social group. They are thus allocated special protection exactly because of their perceived vulnerability, without this violating the general principle of equal treatment.[109] Free education for young persons is a good example of such special protection.[110] As cogently pointed out in the Report, the fact that free education is only available for this particular age group does not entail that the education system is 'an age-related form of positive action'.[111]

Admittedly in some cases there will be inevitable overlap, as disadvantage and vulnerability may appear as concomitant elements of the social condition of the same group. *Ethnic minority children*, for instance, are not simply a vulnerable group but may additionally suffer from disadvantage related to their ethnic origin. In this case, it may be necessary to supplement the 'standard' protection reserved for children in general with positive measures specifically designed to cancel out the effects of the additional disadvantage this particular group of children is burdened with.

IV. TOWARDS A COMMON EUROPEAN CONCEPTION OF FULL EQUALITY: EU ACCESSION TO THE ECHR AS AN OPPORTUNITY?

It would be premature, if not outright erroneous, to suggest that the EU's accession to the Convention would have an automatic impact on the conceptualisation of equal treatment in general and of gender equality in particular. After all, the act of accession in and of itself is, in actual fact, little more than an official proclamation of an already-acknowledged symbiotic relationship between the two systems. It is, however, reasonable to predict that such a move is likely to produce effects that go above and beyond mere institutional symbolism. Although Luxembourg and Strasbourg are generally keen to avoid a head-on conflict, the convergence in their interpretations of equal treatment is neither absolute nor always consistent.[112] Part of the problem lies with the apparent reluctance of the two European courts to provide a systematic theoretical account of their respective anti-discrimination regimes,[113] which, admittedly, would be a rather difficult task without an underlying theoretical account of equality. The EU's accession to the Convention may, indeed, provide the opportunity for an alignment of both normative theory and judicial practice with the emerging European paradigm of *full equality*.[114]

By the same token, however, accession in and of itself is extremely unlikely to resolve the conceptual inconsistencies identified throughout this analysis. Despite the fact that both European courts appear to be moving away from strict formal equality, EU equality law is considerably more developed and sophisticated than the Convention system in this regard. All three substantive dimensions of equal treatment—positive action, reasonable accommodation and special treatment—have a concrete textual basis in secondary EU law, coupled with the interpretative scrutiny of the CJEU. The ECtHR, on the other hand, may have found it more difficult to translate the non-discrimination guarantee of Article 14

[109] It is interesting to note that this is true under *any* conception of equal treatment, even under the formal/substantive dichotomy.

[110] DG Employment, Social Affairs and Equal Opportunities (n 88) 28.

[111] Ibid.

[112] Besson (n 56).

[113] Ibid 651.

[114] According to the Preamble to Protocol 12 ECHR and to the equivalent phrasing of Article 157(4) TFEU.

and Protocol 12 into a coherent and full-fledged principle of full equality, but it also seems more willing to make a tentative leap in that direction.

In *Runkee*,[115] for instance, the ECtHR opens up a new path to full equality, but seems reluctant to follow it through. The Court indirectly confirms that positive action can be a legitimate means to redress factual inequalities insofar as the specific measures are proportionate[116] and finds that reserving the widowers' benefits to female widows until 2001 could be objectively and reasonably justified.[117] More importantly, it goes so far as to suggest that 'in certain circumstances a failure to attempt to correct inequality through different treatment may in itself give rise to a breach of the article'.[118] Hinting that signatory parties may be under a *positive obligation* to introduce positive action is a far more progressive stance on equality than the CJEU has ever attempted to entertain and fits well with the full equality paradigm. At the same time, however, the Court does not appear to have any problem with the UK government's policy choice 'to bring about equality through "levelling down"'.[119] Combined with a wide margin of appreciation 'usually allowed under the Convention when it comes to general measures of economic or social strategy',[120] this approach effectively eliminates the possibility of imposing any meaningful positive obligation on national legislators. Once again then, the problem seems to lie first and foremost in the lack of conceptual integrity that makes it impossible to gauge what the true meaning of full equality is.

A relatively more coherent attitude emerges in *Konstantin Markin*, where the Grand Chamber chastises the Russian government for misconceiving positive action,[121] despite failing to explain that the misconception lies in the conflation of positive action and special treatment. The case involved a national rule stipulating that only female military personnel would be entitled to three years of parental leave. Although the Court is correct to dismiss the 'special biological link' argument[122] as inapplicable to the three-year period following childbirth,[123] it still goes on to consider the possibility that women have a 'special role' in bringing up children.[124] Distinguishing between childbirth and upbringing echoes the CJEU's approach in *Griesmar*[125] and also reflects the way in which positive action and special treatment are distinct equality mechanisms. Reserving parental leave for female personnel only is not intended to correct the disadvantaged position of women in that employment area and, as such, it cannot qualify as a positive action measure.[126] On the other hand, Strasbourg observes that 'contemporary European societies have moved towards a more equal sharing between men and women of responsibility for the upbringing of their children'.[127] This emerging European consensus makes it difficult to justify

[115] *Runkee and White v United Kingdom*, App No 42949/98 and 53134/99 (ECtHR, 10 May 2007).
[116] Ibid [35].
[117] Ibid [40].
[118] Ibid [35].
[119] Ibid [41].
[120] Ibid [36].
[121] *Konstantin Markin v Russia*, App No 30078/06 (ECtHR, 22 March 2012) [141].
[122] Ibid [116].
[123] Ibid [132].
[124] Ibid [139]–[140].
[125] *Griesmar v Ministre de l'Economie*. In *Konstantin Markin*, the ECtHR examined *Griesmar* in detail in [65]–[66].
[126] *Konstantin Markin v Russia* (n 121) [141].
[127] Ibid [140].

the national rule in question as special treatment, especially since it seems to perpetuate stereotypes about traditional gender roles.[128]

Although the Court's reasoning in *Konstantin Markin* is generally beyond reproach, the thrust of the matter remains that this 'clean' picture of the Convention system has little, if anything, to contribute to current EU equality law. The latter is broader, more sophisticated and nuanced to the extent that one would naturally expect Strasbourg to be mostly at the receiving end of any fruitful judicial dialogue. The only meaningful effect of EU accession would be to produce a direct link between the notion of full equality and a positive obligation to address existing gender inequalities through any means available, including positive action. Strasbourg is better placed to entrench and defend such a substantive conception of equality, as it claims to maintain the coveted position of a neutral arbiter that moves forward only after European consensus has been achieved. The CJEU, on the other hand, is bound to tread more lightly in view of its limited human rights mandate and in the face of a precarious political balance within the EU. As things stand at the moment, however, there is little evidence that Strasbourg is willing to take the pole position in this respect and dictate the terms of a genuinely common European paradigm of full equality.

V. CONCLUSION

The story of European equality law so far is one of continuous evolution and qualified success. It is impossible to deny that a number of equality indexes have noticeably improved across European societies in the last few decades. The lion's share of the credit rightfully belongs to Strasbourg and Luxembourg for gradually developing a mature understanding of equal treatment that goes beyond the narrow confines of formalism. This is also reflected in a tentative shift in the law towards an emerging paradigm of *full equality*, intended to reconcile normative intentions with social reality. At the heart of this transformative process is the recognition that formal equality fails to account for and redress endemic inequalities stemming from past and present discrimination. Such recognition, however, remains partial and half-hearted. Despite rhetorical declarations to the contrary, the two European courts seem generally reluctant to commit to the new equality paradigm unequivocally and pursue its legal consequences to their full extent. Formal equality continues to be treated not as a dead concept, but rather as a valid—albeit not always preferred—alternative interpretation of equality. On the same token, the blurred conceptual boundaries between distinct anti-discrimination mechanisms and the conflation between positive action and special treatment make it difficult to envisage what the proper meaning of a common European conception of equality really is.

The possible accession of the EU to the Convention system may provide the impetus to instil much-needed clarity into the normative picture. The first step in this direction will be an explicit abandonment of formalism that eschews normatively significant situational differences between individuals or groups and makes unrealistic assumptions about past and present social realities. The combined interpretative efforts of the two European courts, coupled with academic scholarship, can translate the European vision for full equality into a coherent analytical framework, wherein positive action, reasonable accommodation and

[128] Ibid [127], [139], [142] and [143].

special protection of vulnerable groups will feature as affirmations of genuine equality of treatment. The second and more decisive step, however, will depend on the willingness of Strasbourg to use the language of positive obligations in its Article 14 and Protocol 12 jurisprudence. If the paradigm of full equality is to have any substantial impact on policy making, it must be seen as generating concrete state responsibilities. There is hardly anything novel, let alone revolutionary, about the suggestion that European states have an obligation, both under the Convention and as a matter of EU law, to address social inequalities through appropriate means. Holding states liable for failure to act upon positive equality obligations is clearly within Strasbourg's mandate, but it is admittedly a precarious political move, likely to attract severe criticisms of unwarranted judicial activism on the part of the ECtHR. Post-accession, however, the reinforced position of the Strasbourg Court, with the support of its Luxembourg counterpart, should be enough to guarantee that the leap towards full equality has every chance of succeeding.

19

European Consensus and the EU Accession to the ECHR

KANSTANTSIN DZEHTSIAROU AND PAVEL REPYEUSKI*

I. INTRODUCTION

THE EUROPEAN UNION (EU) occupies new territories. It developed from an organisation with a predominantly economic agenda to a gigantic creature having an impact in many spheres of the political and social life of its Member States. Human rights obligations of the EU Member States, including obligations under the European Convention on Human Rights (ECHR), have also been affected by laws generated by the EU.[1] After the Treaty of Lisbon and Protocol 14 to the ECHR came into force, it became mandatory for the EU to accede to the ECHR. This accession has not yet occurred due to complicated and lengthy negotiation which should take into account the *sui generis* nature of the new 48th contracting party to the ECHR: the EU.

The possibility of the EU's accession to the ECHR has generated an increased academic interest in EU–ECHR relations. The majority of commentators, however, focus on the technical aspects of the EU's accession to the ECHR and their institutional interaction.[2] Some commentators have discussed the aims and outcomes of the accession.[3] Almost nothing has been said about how the EU's accession may affect the reasoning of the European Court of Human Rights (ECtHR).[4]

* Dr Kanstantsin Dzehtsiarou is Lecturer in Law at the University of Surrey. Dr Pavel Repyeuski is Senior Lecturer in Law at the Leeds Metropolitan University. The authors would like to express their gratitude to Dr Filippo Fontanelli, Dr Giuseppe Martinico and Dr Tobias Lock for their comments. We would also like to thank the participants and the organisers of the workshop 'The EU Accession to the ECHR' which took place in Brussels on 16–17 November 2012, where this chapter was presented. The usual disclaimers apply.

[1] See *Bosphorus Hava Yolları Turizm ve Ticaret Anonim Şirketi v Ireland*, App No 45036/98 (2005) 42 EHRR 1.

[2] See N O'Meara, '"A More Secure Europe of Rights?" The European Court of Human Rights, the Court of Justice of the European Union and EU Accession to the ECHR' (2011) 12 *German Law Journal* 1813; T Lock, 'Walking on a Tightrope: The Draft Accession Agreement and the Autonomy of the EU Legal Order' (2011) 48 *Common Market Law Review* 1025; T Lock, 'EU Accession to the ECHR: Implications for the Judicial Review in Strasbourg' (2010) 35 *European Law Review* 777; T Lock, 'The ECJ and the ECtHR: The Future Relationship between the Two European Courts' (2009) 8 *Law and Practice of International Courts and Tribunals* 375.

[3] See T Pavone, 'The Past and Future Relationship of the European Court of Justice and the European Court of Human Rights: A Functional Analysis', available at www.ssrn.com/abstract=2042867.

[4] For instance, a recent paper on the topic scrutinises 'the implications of the EU's accession both for the Union and for its Member States', but does not talk about its influence on the decision making of the ECtHR. See C Eckes, 'EU Accession to the ECHR: Between Autonomy and Adaptation' (2013) 76 *MLR* 254, 255.

In this chapter it is argued that the EU's accession to the ECHR will have a considerable effect on the reasoning of the ECtHR, facilitated by the European consensus, provided that the tendencies identified in this chapter will continue to exist. Therefore, this chapter will first examine the nature and definition of the European consensus, which is more than just post factum rationalisation of the decision[5] and is taken seriously by the ECtHR.

The European consensus has been deployed by the ECtHR in a relatively high number of important cases. The ECtHR would normally accept that there is the European consensus if a significant number of the contracting parties to the ECHR adopt similar legislation or follow similar legal practices. If the European consensus is identified by the ECtHR, it is highly likely that the Court will hold that the contested law or legal practice, which differs from the European consensus, violates the ECHR. In order to establish the European consensus, the ECtHR compares laws and practices of the contracting parties, including their obligations under international treaties.

This chapter will then identify three tendencies in the areas of the ECtHR case law and EU–ECHR relations. These tendencies illustrate a possible influence of the EU's accession to the ECHR on the decision making of the ECtHR. The first tendency emerges against the background of the expansion of the human rights agenda of the EU and the ECHR. It is argued here that increasing EU activity in the area of human rights protection and expanding scope of the ECHR through evolutive interpretation of its provisions created a continuously growing overlap.

The second tendency emphasises the importance of the EU's accession to the ECHR. It is argued here that the accession will change the nature of EU law within the Convention system from international to national (domestic). This development is not merely symbolic: the consensus, which is established on the basis of national laws or practices, is more legitimate than 'international consensus'. Therefore, once EU law is transformed from international to national, the Court's reliance on it in establishing the European consensus can be perceived by the stakeholders as legitimate.

Related to the first two tendencies, the final tendency reveals an increasingly mathematical and rigorous approach of the ECtHR to the European consensus. If this tendency continues to exist, the 28 Member States[6] of the EU plus the EU itself as contracting parties to the Convention will create a critical mass necessary to establish consensus. The second and third tendencies combined will signal that the EU will become a key player in European human rights law after its accession.

II. THE EUROPEAN CONSENSUS AND ITS IMPACT ON THE DECISION MAKING OF THE COURT

This section briefly outlines how the European consensus operates in the ECtHR's reasoning. The European consensus establishes a presumption in favour of the solution adopted in the majority of the Member States. This presumption can be rebutted[7] if the respondent

[5] Stijn Smet, '*X. and Others v Austria* (Part II): A Narrow Ruling on a Narrow Issue', available at http://strasbourgobservers.com/2013/03/06/x-and-others-v-austria-part-ii-a-narrow-ruling-on-a-narrow-issue/#comments.

[6] If one takes into account the members of the EEA, which are also bound by the EU rules, EU law creates a clearly dominant consensus once certain regulation is adopted.

[7] E Brems, *Human Rights: Universality and Diversity* (The Hague, Martinus Nijhoff, 2001) 420.

state's justification for diversion from the solution, supported by the majority, is accepted by the ECtHR. While some inconsistencies in the application of consensus are evident in the case law of the ECtHR,[8] it is argued here that the European consensus is more than just a *post factum* rationalisation of the judgment, as is sometimes suggested.[9] The ECtHR judges admit and the case law of the ECtHR shows that the European consensus influences the outcome of the case.

Dzehtsiarou conducted interviews with 25 judges of the ECtHR[10] and most of them[11] admitted that they are likely to follow what the European consensus provides if it is clearly established.[12] That said, the European consensus does not normally act as a sole reason for a particular outcome of the case. Judge Rozakis, for instance, acknowledged the importance of the European consensus, but explained that, in his view, the Court uses a hierarchy of sources approach. He maintains that the Convention is at the top, followed by the case law, and if both of these sources are unclear, the Court can then resort to consensus.[13] At the same time, if the consensus is overwhelming, the reasons not to follow it need to be particularly compelling.

The European consensus is based on the Court's comparative analysis of laws and legal practices of the contracting parties. Such research can lead the ECtHR to three possible conclusions: (i) there is a lack of European consensus; (ii) the European consensus is established and the law, judicial decision or administrative practice at hand, is a part of it; (iii) the European consensus is established and the law at hand contradicts it.

First, the ECtHR can reach the conclusion that there is no European consensus regarding the issue in question.[14] In this situation the Court normally confirms that the issue falls within the state's wider margin of appreciation. For example, in *Evans v United Kingdom*,

[8] See, for example, *Christine Goodwin v United Kingdom*, App No 28957/95 (2002) 35 EHRR 18; *A, B and C v Ireland*, App No 25579/05 (2011) 53 EHRR 13. For discussion of trumping internal consensus, see F de Londras and K Dzehtsiarou, 'Grand Chamber of the European Court of Human Rights, *A, B and C v Ireland*, Decision of 17 December 2010' (2013) 62 *International & Comparative Law Quarterly* 250. See also LR Helfer, 'Consensus, Coherence and the European Convention on Human Rights' (1993) 23 *Cornell International Law Journal* 133; C McCrudden, 'A Common Law of Human Rights?: Transnational Judicial Conversations on Constitutional Rights' (2000) 4 *Oxford Journal of Legal Studies* 499; A McHarg, 'Reconciling Human Rights and the Public Interest: Conceptual Problems and Doctrinal Uncertainty in the Jurisprudence of the European Court of Human Rights' (1999) 62 *MLR* 671, 691.

[9] Smet (n 5).

[10] Between 2008 and 2013, K Dzehtsiarou interviewed former judges and currently sitting judges. These judges were selected to ensure wide geographical representation. The following judges were interviewed (in alphabetical order): Bîrsan (Romania), Caflisch (former judge from Lichtenstein), De Gaetano (Malta), Garlicki (former judge from Poland), Gritco (Moldova), Hirvelä (Finland), Jaeger (former judge from Germany), Kalaydjieva (Bulgaria), Kovler (former judge from Russia), Laffranque (Estonia), Lemmans (Belgium), Malinverni (former judge from Switzerland), Myjer (former judge from the Netherlands), Møse (Norway), Nussberger (Germany), Poalelungi (former judge from Moldova), Popovič (Serbia), Raimondi (Italy), Rozakis (former judge from Greece), Šikuta (Slovakia), Spielmann (Luxembourg), Trajkovska-Lazarova (Macedonia), Tulkens (Belgium), Ziemele (Latvia) and Zupančič (Slovenia).

[11] The judges could disagree in relation to the methodology of European consensus identification, but all, except judge Zupančič, agreed that European consensus influences their decisions. For more details on judge Zupančič's position see K Dzehtsiarou, 'European Consensus and the Evolutive Interpretation of the European Convention on Human Rights' (2011) 12 *German Law Journal* 1730.

[12] For a brief overview of some interviews see K Dzehtsiarou, 'Consensus from Within the Palace Walls' (2010), available at http://papers.ssrn.com/sol3/papers.cfm?abstract_id=1678424.

[13] K Dzehtsiarou, interview with Judge Christos Rozakis (ECtHR), 12 June 2010.

[14] See, for example, *Lautsi and others v Italy*, App No 30814/06 (2012) 54 EHRR 3 [70]; *Dickson v United Kingdom*, App No 44362/04 (2007) 46 EHRR 927 [78]; *Sheffield and Horsham v United Kingdom*, App Nos 22985/93 and 23390/94 (1999) 27 EHRR 163 [55].

the Court stated: 'Where ... there is no consensus within the Member States of the Council of Europe, either as to the relative importance of the interest at stake or as to the best means of protecting it, particularly where the case raises sensitive moral or ethical issues, the margin will be wider.'[15] A wide margin of appreciation usually means that the Court will not find the law or practice of the Member State to be in breach of the Convention and that 'the Court would generally respect the legislature's policy choice unless it is manifestly without reasonable foundation'.[16] Therefore, lack of consensus does not automatically leave the issue within the area of state discretion. The ECtHR can further examine the law to determine whether it is manifestly unreasonable[17] and appropriate to allow a wide margin of appreciation.

Second, the Court can identify whether the European consensus exists and whether the law under scrutiny is in line with the consensus. This is an unusual situation, because if a legal provision or an administrative practice is clearly in line with the European consensus, such a case will likely be declared inadmissible as manifestly ill-founded. Having said that, sometimes that Court can establish that the law under question is in line with the European consensus, but its application might be disproportionate. For example, in *Stoll v Switzerland*, the applicant argued that the state had breached its Convention obligation under Article 10 (freedom of expression) by imposing a criminal sanction for disclosure of confidential information. The Court stated that 'a consensus appears to exist among the Member States of the Council of Europe on the need for appropriate criminal sanctions to prevent the disclosure of certain confidential items of information'.[18] After stating that the Swiss law was similar to the laws in the majority of European states, the ECtHR considered whether the fine for the disclosure of information was proportionate. The fine was found to be proportionate in this case and the Court found no violation of Article 10. Thus, if a scrutinised law is in line with the European consensus, it is highly likely that the Court will agree that this law is in compliance with the ECHR.[19]

The third situation emerges when the state's legislation contradicts the European consensus. The existence of an identified European consensus does not decisively determine the outcome of a case. Rather, the Court can confirm an outcome supported by the European consensus if no strong justification for an alternative solution is provided. It can disregard the consensus and take other relevant considerations into account, such as the moral views of the majority within the contracting party[20] or specificities of political and historical development within the Member States.[21]

The European consensus indubitably plays a significant role in the case law of the ECtHR. It is unlikely that the predominant view of the majority of the Member States

[15] *Evans v United Kingdom*, App No 6339/05 (2008) 46 EHRR 34 [77].

[16] *Dickson v United Kingdom*, App No 44362/04 (2007) 46 EHRR 927 [78].

[17] In *James and others v United Kingdom*, the ECtHR has stated that: 'The Court, finding it natural that the margin of appreciation available to the legislature in implementing social and economic policies should be a wide one, will respect the legislature's judgment as to what is "in the public interest" unless that judgment be manifestly without reasonable foundation.' *James and others v United Kingdom*, Series A No 98, 21 February 1986 [46].

[18] *Stoll v Switzerland*, App No 69698/01 (2008) 47 EHRR 59 [155].

[19] Dzehtsiarou (n 12).

[20] *A, B and C v Ireland* (n 8).

[21] *Republican Party of Russia v Russia*, App No 12976/07 HUDOC; *Tănase v Moldova*, App No 7/08, 29 BHRC 209.

can be easily disregarded by the Court.[22] Therefore, an entity that can effectively form a European consensus can significantly influence the decision making of the ECtHR. This chapter argues that the EU after its accession to the ECHR might become such an entity.

III. TENDENCIES

A. Tendency 1: The Growing Overlap between the ECHR and the Human Rights Activities of the EU

The first tendency illustrates the growing overlap in the areas of activity between the EU and the ECtHR. To substantiate this claim, one needs to prove that despite being initially designed as an organisation for predominantly economic cooperation, the EU is becoming increasingly proactive in the area of human rights protection. At the same time, the definition and coverage of the ECHR is also increasing through the means of evolutive interpretation and by adding new protocols to the Convention. As a result, the exponential growth of the EU competence in the area of human rights and the expanding scope of human rights as understood by the ECtHR increase the overlap between the two.

i. The EU and Human Rights

Aiming at the creation of a common market[23] between the six founding Member States, the European Economic Community[24] did not initially undertake a role of fundamental rights protection. However, due to the creation of the principles of the supremacy[25] and direct effect[26] of EU law, there was a growing concern that the protection of citizens' rights at the European level may be threatened by the lack of binding human rights standards applicable to the EU institutions.[27] Even though the EU was capable of setting the human rights standards through interpretation of the human rights provisions as part of the general principles of law,[28] it is submitted that after the Charter of Fundamental Rights (CFR) of the EU became legally binding,[29] the EU's activity in the human rights area showed a tendency to increase significantly.

Even before the Charter, the EU had already taken into account the ECHR as a special source in applying and developing the human rights standards.[30] In the absence of a legally

[22] K Dzehtsiarou, 'Does Consensus Matter? Legitimacy of European Consensus in the Case Law of the European Court of Human Rights' (2011) *Public Law* 534.

[23] See Article 3(2) TEU and Article 26(2) TFEU—the internal market shall comprise an area without internal frontiers in which the free movement of goods, persons, services and capital is ensured.

[24] Now the EU.

[25] See Case 6/64 *Flaminio Costa v ENEL* [1964] ECR 585.

[26] Case 26/62 *NV Algemene Transport- en Expeditie Onderneming van Gend & Loos v Netherlands Inland Revenue Administration* [1963] ECR 3.

[27] L Besselink, 'The EU and the European Convention of Human Rights after Lisbon: From "Bosphorus" Sovereign Immunity to Full Scrutiny?' (2008) SSRN Working Papers Series. Available at http://dx.doi.org/10.2139/ssrn.1132788.

[28] See Case C-4/73 *J Nold, Kohlen- und Baustoffgroßhandlung v Commission of the European Communities* [1974] ECR 491.

[29] By the Treaty of Lisbon on 1 December 2009.

[30] Case C-413/99 *Baumbast and R v Secretary of State for the Home Department* [2002] ECR I-7091 at 72; Case C-60/00 *Mary Carpenter v Secretary of State for the Home Department* [2002] ECR I-6279 at 41-42; Case C-200/02

binding bill of rights of its own, the CFR was used by the EU courts as an important reference document long before the Treaty of Lisbon: Advocate Generals were the first to invoke the Charter in proceedings before the European Court of Justice (ECJ) (now the Court of Justice of the European Union (CJEU)),[31] followed by the Court of First Instance[32] and then the ECJ itself.[33]

After the Treaty of Lisbon made the Charter legally binding, there is a clear trend of enhancing judicial activity in the area of human rights by the EU courts, with the impact of the Charter on the judiciary (both at the national and at the EU levels) being very visible. According to the statistics provided by the European Commission in 2011,[34] the number of CJEU decisions quoting the Charter in its reasoning rose by more than 50 per cent as compared to 2010, from 27 to 42. National courts, when addressing questions to the Court of Justice (preliminary rulings), have also increasingly referred to the Charter: in 2011, such references rose by 50 per cent as compared to 2010, from 18 to 27. This supports the conclusion that the application rate of the CFR by the EU courts in the post-Lisbon era has grown significantly and is likely to grow even further.

As to the Convention, the CJEU has confirmed that, as long as the EU has not acceded to it, the ECHR does not constitute a legal instrument which has been formally incorporated into EU law and that, consequently, EU law does not govern the relations between the ECHR and the legal systems of the Member States.[35] Despite the fact that the application of the CFR is to be limited to the area of EU law,[36] the 28 EU Member States count for more than half of the ECHR signatories, which makes it difficult, if not impossible, for the ECtHR to ignore the decisions of the CJEU setting human rights standards.

This brief overview shows that the EU is rapidly becoming a standard-setting organisation in the area of human rights protection. This role was first assumed by the CJEU as it accepted the idea that the EU should respect fundamental rights and referred to the ECHR in its case law. This tendency became even clearer with the adoption of the CFR. It is submitted that with the increase of the EU institutional activity in decision making in the area of human rights, its role in shaping the European consensus will also become more important. This should be looked at in close relation to another aspect of this tendency: the expanding scope of the ECHR and an increasing area of application of human rights norms in Europe, which is considered below.

ii. The Expanding Scope of the ECtHR

The tendency to expand the scope of human rights by the ECtHR is reflected in the doctrine of evolutive interpretation developed by the Court,[37] which is fundamental

Kunqian Catherine Zhu and Man Lavette Chen v Secretary of State for the Home Department [2004] ECR I-9925 at 16. See also Eckes (n 4) 258.

[31] See, for example, the Opinion of AG Jacobs in Case C-112/00 *Eugen Schmidberger, Internationale Transporte und Planzüge v Republik Österreich* [2003] ECR I-5659.

[32] Now the General Court.

[33] Case C-540/03 *Parliament v Council* [2006] ECR I-5769.

[34] European Commission, 2011 Report on the Application of the EU Charter on Fundamental Rights COM (2012) 169, 6.

[35] Case C-617/10 *Re Hans Åkerberg Fransson* [2013] ECR I-0000 [44].

[36] A Ciuca, 'On the Charter of Fundamental Rights of the European Union and the EU Accession to the European Convention on Human Rights', 22 June 2012, available at www.ssrn.com/abstract=2089502.

[37] K Dzehtsiarou, 'European Consensus and the Evolutive Interpretation of the European Convention on Human Rights' (2011) 12 *German Law Journal* 1730.

to the effectiveness of the Convention system and the ECtHR's authority.[38] Evolutive interpretation means that the Convention is a 'living instrument' and its interpretation can be altered if relevant circumstances have changed. There is a link between evolutive interpretation and the European consensus;[39] the emerging European consensus can be an indication for the ECtHR to trigger evolutive interpretation.[40] In other words, the Court can choose to interpret the Convention evolutively when it is in a position to establish a European consensus.

The ECtHR applied evolutive interpretation in relation to various articles of the Convention. For example, such rights as the right to access to court,[41] the right to legal aid in certain civil cases,[42] prisoners' voting rights[43] and certain environmental rights[44] were integrated into the ECtHR case law by means of evolutive interpretation.

The scope of the ECHR was also expanded by means of adding protocols to the ECHR some of which contain substantive rights. For example, Protocol 1 enshrines rights to free elections,[45] protection of private property[46] and a right to education. Protocols 4 and 7 also add certain rights to the catalogue of the ECHR, while Protocols 6, 12 and 13 amend some procedural provisions of the ECHR.

After the EU accedes to the ECHR, the tendency of expanding the scope of human rights will, arguably, have two related consequences. First, this tendency will increase the human rights presence in the decision making of the EU institutions even further. It means that more of the activities of the EU will be subject to review by Strasbourg. For instance, environmental rights were not anticipated by the drafters of the Convention and therefore any activities of the EU in this area were not previously subject to the supervision of the ECtHR. However, in *López Ostra v Spain*,[47] the ECtHR accepted that rights to a good environment fall within the ambit of Article 8 of the Convention—the right to private life. Therefore, the ever-expanding scope of human rights law increasingly makes more areas of EU activities subject to human rights review.

Having said that, another consequence would be that the EU institutions will be able to influence the interpretation of human rights by creating a new European consensus that can trigger the evolutive interpretation of the ECHR. This second consequence of the tendency has already expressed itself in cases such as *Micallef v Malta*,[48] where Article 6 (the right to a fair trial) guarantees were extended to the pre-trial injunctions in civil cases. If the tendency of expanding the scope of the ECHR and EU activities in the area of human rights continues, the overlap between these activities will keep growing further.

[38] L Wildhaber, 'European Court of Human Rights' in Donald M McRae (ed), *Canadian Yearbook of International Law*, vol 40 (UBC Press, Vancouver, 2002), 310.

[39] Dzehtsiarou (n 37).

[40] F de Londras, 'International Human Rights Law and Constitutional Rights: In Favour of Synergy' (2009) 9 *International Review of Constitutionalism* 307.

[41] *Golder v United Kingdom*, App No 4451/70 (1975) 1 EHRR 524.

[42] *Airey v Ireland*, App No 6289/73 (1979) 2 EHRR 305.

[43] *Hirst v United Kingdom (No 2)*, App No 74025/01 (2005) 42 EHRR 849.

[44] *López Ostra v Spain*, App No 16798/90 (1995) 20 EHRR 277.

[45] Article 3 of Protocol 1.

[46] Article 1 of Protocol 1.

[47] *López Ostra v Spain* (n 44). The ECtHR has reiterated that rights to a good environment fall under Article 8 in its more recent cases such as *Fadeyeva v* Russia, App No 55723/00 ECHR 2005-IV; and *Tătar v Romania*, App No. 67021/01, 27 January 2009.

[48] *Micallef v Malta*, App No 17056/06 (2010) 50 EHRR 37.

B. Tendency 2: ECtHR's perception of EU Law: from International to National

Despite a long history of communication between the Council of Europe and the EU in the field of human rights protection,[49] it was in the Constitutional Treaty where the idea that the EU should formally accede to the ECHR first found unanimous support amongst the EU heads of state. And even though the Constitutional Treaty itself has never materialized, the obligation to accede was codified in the Treaty of Lisbon.[50]

Even prior to accession, the ECtHR has often taken EU law into account in identifying consensus in Europe. Various sources of EU law were quoted by the ECtHR in its case law, including the CFR, directives of the European Parliament and of the Council,[51] Council Regulations and Decisions,[52] resolutions of the European Parliament,[53] framework decisions,[54] treaties and agreements concluded by the EU[55] and CJEU judgments.[56] One can argue that the EU can already demonstrate consensus in Europe, for instance, in the area of non-discrimination, where EU law is much more developed than the case law of the ECtHR.[57]

In the past, the ECtHR has sometimes used EU law as a sign of European consensus. The ECtHR was, however, more prepared to accept that the judgments of the CJEU and legally binding EU provisions can form a consensus. For example, in *Micallef v Malta*, the ECtHR considered the judgment of the Court of Justice of the EU in identifying consensus. In this case the ECtHR had to decide whether Article 6 of the Convention (the right to a fair trial) should cover pre-trial stages of proceeding. The ECtHR established that there is a consensus among the Member States to guarantee the right to fair trial on the pre-trial stage:

> Article 47 of the Charter of Fundamental Rights of the European Union (EU) guarantees the right to a fair trial. Unlike the Convention's art. 6, the provision of the Charter does not confine this right to disputes relating to 'civil rights and obligations' or to 'any criminal charge' and does not refer to the 'determination' of such. In *Denilauler v Couchet Frères* the European Court of Justice (ECJ) held that provisional measures given *ex parte* without hearing the defendant could not be recognised according to its case law. This implies that such safeguards should apply also outside the context of final decisions.[58]

The Charter was not binding when *Micallef* was decided; however, it was already clear in October 2009 that it would become binding and the argument of the ECtHR was also confirmed by the CJEU case law.

The Court has also heavily relied on the CFR after it became legally binding in establishing consensus in the case of *Bayatyan v Armenia* concerning conscientious objections. In

[49] See, for example, Accession of the Communities to the European Convention on Human Rights: Commission Memorandum, Bulletin of the European Communities, Supplement 2/79, COM (79) final.

[50] Article 6 TEU.

[51] *SH and others v Austria*, App No 57813/00 (2011) ECHR 2011 [44].

[52] *Hirsi Jamaa and others v Italy*, App No 27765/09 (2012) 55 EHRR 21 [141].

[53] *Bayatyan v Armenia*, App No 23459/03 (2012) 54 EHRR 15 [56].

[54] *Rantsev v Cyprus and Russia*, App No. 25965/04 (2010) 51 EHRR 1 [156].

[55] *Saadi v Italy*, App No 37201/06 (2009) 49 EHRR 30 [62].

[56] *Sergey Zolotukhin v Russia*, App No 14939/03 (2009) 26 BHRC 485 [35].

[57] See 'Handbook on European Non-discrimination Law', available at http://fra.europa.eu/sites/default/files/fra_uploads/1510-FRA-CASE-LAW-HANDBOOK_EN.pdf.

[58] *Micallef v Malta* (n 48) [32].

this case the Court established that there is consensus in Europe and used the CFR to back up this finding. It stated:

> While the first paragraph of Article 10 of the Charter reproduces Article 9 § 1 of the Convention almost literally, its second paragraph explicitly states that '[t]he right to conscientious objection is recognised, in accordance with the national laws governing the exercise of this right'. Such explicit addition is no doubt deliberate and reflects the unanimous recognition of the right to conscientious objection by the member States of the European Union, as well as the weight attached to that right in modern European society.[59]

If, however, the EU explicitly grants its Member States wide discretion or the legal instrument is not itself binding, then the ECtHR is unlikely to come to the conclusion that there is a consensus on the basis of such provisions. In *SH and others v Austria*, the applicants argued that the prohibition of sperm and ova donation for in vitro fertilisation violated their right to respect for family life. The ECtHR quoted the EU directive on the setting of standards of quality and safety for the donation, procurement, testing, processing, preservation, storage and distribution of human tissues and cells,[60] but then pointed out that according to EU law, the Member States are not obliged to legalise ova donation. The mentioned directive itself provided that it 'should not interfere with the decisions made by Member States concerning the use of or non-use of any specific type of human cells, including germ cells and embryonic stem cells'.[61] The ECtHR did not find a violation in this case.

One has to point out that consensus identification is not an exact science and sometimes it is argued that a certain degree of flexibility is necessary.[62] Having said that, the Court cannot ignore an overwhelming, in the words of the deputy registrar of the ECtHR, 'crushing',[63] majority of the contracting parties which adopted similar rules or regulations. We argue here that it is possible that the EU will become a driving force for such a 'crushing majority'. As soon as the EU accedes to the ECHR, EU law will change its status from being adopted by a supranational institution 'foreign' to the ECHR to law of one of the contracting parties. It seems that the ECtHR has already taken careful consideration of binding EU legal provisions and one can argue that accession will reinforce this tendency. This reinforcement will have two consequences: normative, meaning that the reliance on EU law will be grounded in legitimacy enhancement potential of the European consensus,[64] and technical, namely, that the ECtHR will be more inclined to include EU law in its comparative studies as EU law will achieve a status of law of one of the contracting parties.

As already stated, EU law is currently treated by the ECtHR as international law: it is placed in the international law section in the judgments and it is sometimes perceived as law foreign to the domestic laws of the contracting parties. The ECtHR also refers to EU law as to a sign of an international, not European consensus. For instance, in *Neulinger and Shuruk v Switzerland*, the Court stated:

> The Court notes that there is currently a broad consensus—including in international law—in support of the idea that in all decisions concerning children, their best interests must be paramount

[59] *Bayatyan v Armenia* (n 53) [106].
[60] *SH and others v Austria* (n 51) 44.
[61] Ibid [107].
[62] A Legg, *The Margin of Appreciation in International Human Rights Law* (Oxford, Oxford University Press, 2012) 127–29.
[63] K Dzehtsiarou, interview with Michael O'Boyle (European Court of Human Rights, 2009).
[64] Dzehtsiarou (n 22).

> (see the numerous references in paragraphs 49–56 above, and in particular Article 24 § 2 of the European Union's Charter of Fundamental Rights). As indicated, for example, in the Charter, '[e]very child shall have the right to maintain on a regular basis a personal relationship and direct contact with both his or her parents, unless that is contrary to his or her interests'.

In this case the Court mentioned the CFR in order to prove the existence of consensus in international law. Dzehtsiarou has previously distinguished European consensus from international consensus as they are deployed in the ECtHR reasoning.[65] European consensus has, arguably, higher legitimacy in comparison to the international one. Therefore, the EU's accession is liable to increase the legitimacy of consensus triggered by EU law.

The legitimacy of European consensus is based on two main arguments: first, European consensus can be understood as an implicit consent of the contracting parties to an evolutive interpretation of the Convention in the case at hand.[66] If the Court has based its decision on laws which are international and not part of national legal orders, it means that the implicit consent justification for legitimacy of consensus is not applicable anymore.[67] Arguably, EU law should not be placed in the international law basket in the first place due to its direct effect on the significant number of the contracting parties to the ECHR. However, the ECtHR does that quite persistently.[68]

Second, European consensus intensifies synergistic relations between the ECtHR and the contracting parties and provides for the embeddedness of the Convention in the national legal orders.[69] In practice it is argued that the European consensus is a medium for a dialogue between the ECtHR and the contracting parties.[70] Therefore, since the EU is not a contracting party to the Convention, it is not the primary function of the Court to establish dialogical relations with the EU institutions.

Having established the higher legitimising potential of domestic laws in comparison with international law, it is submitted that the EU's accession to the ECHR might trigger a change in how the Court perceives EU law. Decision making by the EU in the area of human rights will now affect 29 contracting parties to the Convention (including the EU itself) out of 48 contracting parties, which accounts for more than half of the signatories (over 60 per cent). Moreover, if previously EU judgments were not directly considered as national law by the ECtHR, after the accession, the chances are that the Court will be treating the EU not merely as another Member State, but as an influential and powerful player capable of shaping the European consensus.

[65] Ibid.

[66] Dzehtsiarou (n 37).

[67] This, arguably, happened in *Christine Goodwin v United Kingdom*. The ECtHR was criticised for how the European consensus was deployed in this case. See, for example, JL Murray, 'Consensus: Concordance, or Hegemony of Majority' (2008) *Dialogues between Judges* 57; JA Brauch, 'The Margin of Appreciation and the Jurisprudence of the European Court of Human Rights: Threat to the Rule of Law' (2004) 11 *Columbia Journal of European Law* 113, 145; R Sandland, 'Crossing and Not Crossing: Gender, Sexuality and Melancholy in the European Court of Human Rights; *Christine Goodwin v United Kingdom*' (2003) 11 *Feminist Legal Studies* 191, 199.

[68] See also recently *SH and others v Austria* (n 51) [44].

[69] De Londras (n 40).

[70] Sauvé, the Vice-President of the French Conseil d'Etat, points out that 'it is indeed the search for a consensus through a dialogue between cultures and legal systems which makes the Convention a "living instrument" that requires an evolutive interpretation in the light of "present-day conditions" and "commonly accepted standards"'. J-M Sauvé, 'Solemn Hearing on the Occasion of the Opening of the Judicial Year' (2010) *Dialogues between Judges* 42.

It is too early to conclusively assess what effect the transformation of EU law from international to domestic will have in the ECtHR case law. In the past, the Court has often quoted legal provisions enshrined in various international treaties[71] as well as laws and judicial decisions of the states outside the Council of Europe.[72] However, consensual reasoning is more defensible if the laws and practices of the Council of Europe Member States, rather than 'foreign' states or international organisations, are used for the identification of a consensus.

There is, of course, a risk that the increased legitimacy of EU law as a sign of consensus will marginalise the importance of laws and practices of those Council of Europe Member States which are not members of the EU. Even before the EU's accession, the rules adopted by the EU and implemented by the EU Member States had considerable impact on the judgments adopted by the ECtHR. The Grand Chamber judgment in *Konstantin Markin v Russia* can illustrate this point.[73] The ECtHR had to decide whether the refusal of military authorities to grant the applicant—an army serviceman—parental leave amounted to discrimination on the grounds of sex. It should be noted that servicewomen in the Russian army are entitled to parental leave. In this case the Court conducted a detailed comparative survey which revealed a clear basis for allowing parental leave for servicemen in EU law and the laws of the EU Member States. The outcome is totally different in the non-EU contracting parties. Of the 33 states compared, 11 were not EU Member States at the material time.[74] A total of nine out of these 11 either had no option for parental leave for servicemen or provided it only under exceptional circumstances.[75] These countries share a consensus against allowing servicemen to take parental leave. At the same time, EU law[76] and national laws of the EU Member States clearly favoured equal treatment of servicemen and servicewomen with regard to parental leave.[77] The Court found a violation of the Convention in this case, disregarding the 'non-EU consensus' against this outcome. One can argue that post-accession, the Court will have to take an even closer look at the EU which can further marginalise the joint legal traditions of the non-EU contracting parties. After the EU's accession to the ECHR, such dominance will gain more ground because the EU is no longer an outsider but a party to the Convention, which has subscribed to share common values. Having said that, the Court has to take the laws of the non-EU contracting parties into account and not follow the EU standards blindly.

This brief analysis shows that after accession, reliance on EU law will become a more attractive and legitimate argument deployed by the ECtHR because it will be relying on the legal provisions of one of the contracting parties to the Convention rather than following an example set outside the Convention system.

[71] See, for example, *Marckx v Belgium*, Series A No 31 (1979–80) 2 EHRR 330 [41].

[72] See, for example, *Christine Goodwin v United Kingdom* (n 8).

[73] *Konstantin Markin v Russia*, App No 30078/06 (2012) 56 EHRR 8.

[74] Albania, Armenia, Azerbaijan, Bosnia and Herzegovina, Croatia, the Former Yugoslav Republic of Macedonia, Georgia, Moldova, Serbia, Switzerland and Turkey.

[75] *Konstantin Markin v Russia* (n 73) [74].

[76] Ibid [63]–[70].

[77] Ibid [75].

C. Tendency 3: European Consensus—From Flexibility to Formality

The EU will represent a significant proportion of the contracting parties to the ECHR capable of forming a consensus, especially in the circumstances when the Court commits itself to a more rigorous comparative methodology. If such a methodology is not applied, then the Court's claims as to the existence of a consensus become arbitrary and does not amount to a legal standard.[78] Over the years, the Court's approach to the identification of a European consensus has changed considerably. As pointed out by Judge Garlicki,[79] in early cases (before the Research Division of the Court was established), the ECtHR could reach a conclusion about European consensus in a particular case based on the general knowledge of the judges in relation to a particular issue[80] or *amicus curiae* briefs submitted by NGOs,[81] and only in rare occasions on the basis of research. In more recent cases the Court based such conclusions on the in-house prepared research reports, which are often extensively quoted in its reasoning.[82]

The flexibility of the Court's approach to identification of the European consensus has been widely criticised by academic commentators. Arai-Takahashi, for example, stated that vague references to emerging national standards, which are not empirically verifiable, undermine their credibility and sow the seeds of suspicion that they are engaged in unfounded judicial activism.[83] Martens is more specific in his critique, arguing that:

> Sometimes the Court finds that ... a consensus exists and approves it, which might give the impression that its task is simply to endorse the choices made at State level. At other times it finds that no such consensus exists and respects the right of States to be different, as though abandoning the idea of building a democratic European society. At other times it seems indifferent to whether there is a consensus or not being anxious to develop a European public order that transcends national particularities.[84]

Helfer has also requested that the Court use more rigorous methodology in the identification of a European consensus.[85] Zwart has called on the judges of the ECtHR not only to use a rigorous methodology of consensus identification but also to 'commit themselves to the outcomes of the consensus research no matter what'.[86]

[78] Brauch (n 67) 137.

[79] K Dzehtsiarou, interview with Judge Lech Garlicki of the ECtHR (European Court of Human Rights, Strasbourg, 1 July 2009).

[80] *Dudgeon v United Kingdom*, Series A No 45 (1982) 4 EHRR 149. Such a situation can also be explained by the much smaller number of the contracting parties and the fact that all judges of the Court were sitting in every case.

[81] *Sheffield and Horsham v United Kingdom* (n 14).

[82] See, for example, *A, B and C v Ireland* (n 8) [100]–[112].

[83] Y Arai-Takahashi, The Margin of Appreciation Doctrine and the Principle of Proportionality in the Jurisprudence of the ECHR' (Intersentia, Antwerpen, Oxford, New York, 2002) 192–93. See also P Mahoney, 'The Comparative Method in Judgments of the European Court of Human Rights: Reference Back to National Law' in G Canivet, M Andenas and D Fairgrieve (eds), *Comparative Law before the Courts* (British Institute of International and Comparative Law, London, 2005) 149; HC Yourow, *The Margin of Appreciation Doctrine in the Dynamics of European Human Rights Jurisprudence* (Martinus Nijhoff Publishers, Dordrecht, 1995) 195.

[84] P Martens, 'Perplexity of the National Judge Faced with the Vagaries of European Consensus' (2008) *Dialogues between Judges* 79.

[85] LR Helfer, 'Consensus, Coherence and the European Convention on Human Rights' (1993) 23 *Cornell International Law Journal* 133, 138–41.

[86] T Zwart, 'More Human Rights than Court: Why the Legitimacy of the European Court of Human Rights is in Need of Repair and How it Can Be Done' in Spyridon Flogaitis, Tom Zwart and Julie Fraser (eds), *The European Court of Human Rights and Its Discontents* (Cheltenham, Edward Elgar, 2013) 93.

The ECtHR took criticism of its methodology of consensus identification seriously and more scholarly comparative research is now conducted by the Court. This point can be substantiated, first, by references to the establishment of the Research Division which is a part of the Registry of the Court and, second, by the fact that the Court includes comprehensive comparative surveys in its judgments and relies on them in these judgments.

The Research Division of the Court, among other tasks, was set up to compile comparative reports. The Division was established in the early 2000s as a part of the Court's Registry.[87] If a Judge-Rapporteur[88] considers it necessary, he or she requests the Research Division of the Court to produce comparative research. Dzehtsiarou and Lukashevich describe the modus operandi of this procedure in the following terms:

> The *Judge-Rapporteur* frames the questions and the questions are then forwarded by the Research Division to national lawyers working at the Court, who each prepare a report summarising the law and practice in their respective countries. Each national report is then signed by the judge of the ECtHR elected in respect of the country concerned. Afterwards, the national reports are compiled by the Research Division in a composite report which is then sent to the *Judge-Rapporteur* and other judges of the Chamber or Grand Chamber respectively. These reports are confidential and not accessible to the general public.[89]

A summary of this research is included in the judgment and is entitled 'law in Contracting States',[90] 'comparative and international law'[91] or 'relevant comparative law and material'.[92]

The Court not only has detailed comparative data at its disposal, but it also reproduces the summary of this data in its judgments. In 2012 the ECtHR included a section on comparative law in 23 judgments. Of course, this number is very low, especially compared to the overall number of judgments that the ECtHR delivers every year.[93] Having said that, the Court includes comparative law provisions only in the judgments concerned with legal questions which have not been dealt with by it before or there is a chance that its case law can be changed. These comparative law materials are almost always referred to in the reasoning of the Court.[94] Moreover, the majority of judges interviewed by Dzehtsiarou confirmed that they take comparative materials into account in their decision making.[95] Therefore, we argue that the Court tends to treat comparative law seriously and base its

[87] The date of creation of the Research Division of the Court is not mentioned in open sources of the ECtHR. The current head of the Research Division, Montserrat Enrich-Mas, informed K Dzehtsiarou that 'it is not easy to trace the exact date of the formation of the Division, since the research function was in the Court yet in the old Commission days. However, until about year 2000 this function was vested in an employee, rather than a division, since there was much less work to do. From about the year 2000 the need to form a separate division emerged'. The Research Division is designed to prepare comparative law reports which contain relevant laws of the contracting parties and other relevant information.

[88] A Judge-Rapporteur is a judge appointed by the Section President according to Rule 49, which provides that where an application is made under Article 34 of the Convention and its examination by a Chamber or a Committee seems justified, the President of the Section to which the case has been assigned shall designate a judge as Judge-Rapporteur, who shall examine the application.

[89] K Dzehtsiarou and V Lukashevich, 'Informed Decision-Making: The Comparative Endeavours of the Strasbourg Court' (2012) 30(3) *Netherlands Quarterly of Human Rights* 272, 273–74.

[90] *A, B and C v Ireland* (n 8) [112].

[91] *Stoll v Switzerland* (n 18) [44].

[92] *Burden v United Kingdom*, App No 13378/05 (2008) 47 EHRR 38 [25]–[26].

[93] For instance, in 2012 the ECtHR delivered 1,678 judgments. 'Analysis of Statistics 2012', Strasbourg, 2013, available at www.echr.coe.int/Documents/Stats_analysis_2012_ENG.pdf.

[94] For analysis of situations in which comparative law is included in the text and then is not mentioned in the reasoning, see Dzehtsiarou and Lukashevich (n 89) 273–74.

[95] See Dzehtsiarou (n 12).

decisions on verified comparative analysis. A more detailed study has to be conducted on how these surveys affect the outcome of the case, but even without this study, one can argue that this increase of attention to comparative law at the ECtHR is a clear manifestation of the third tendency.

The argument that the Court has begun using a more rigorous 'statistical' approach to comparative law and clearly identified consensus is not universally accepted. Letsas argues that:

> [T]he new Court has moved away from placing decisive weight on the absence of consensus amongst contracting states and from treating it as the ultimate limit on how far it can evolve the meaning and scope of Convention rights. The new Court treats the ECHR as a living instrument by looking for common values and emerging consensus in international law. In doing so, it often raises the human rights standard above what most contracting states currently offer.[96]

This argument is, undoubtedly, an interesting and provocative one, but unfortunately it does not find much support in the ECtHR's case law. Letsas aims to substantiate his claim by referring to five cases.[97] Some of these cases, for example, *Christine Goodwin v United Kingdom*, were often considered unusual by the Convention commentators and were criticised for an inconsistent application of consensus.[98] In some other cases mentioned by Letsas, the Court did not even mention a European consensus[99] and it is hard to agree that it had to be mentioned. In the judgment of *Hirst v United Kingdom*,[100] the European consensus was not used consistently with the previous case law and that was also one of the reasons why this judgment was so fiercely criticised.[101] It seems that it is slightly premature to claim that the idea of a European consensus is abandoned by the Court in favour of an unclear principle of 'common values'.

It is true that the ECtHR has never been too concerned with the formal legal nature of a particular legal trend, which was used to prove the existence of a European consensus, but looked more for the reality of such a trend. Nowadays such reality must be clearly substantiated by some traceable developments in the Member States. It means that the accession of the EU and a more rigorous approach in relation to the identification of a European consensus will turn the EU into a significant player, capable of changing the architecture of commonly accepted standards in Europe.

[96] G Letsas, 'The ECHR as a Living Instrument: Its Meaning and Legitimacy' in A Follesdal, B Peters and G Ulfstein (eds), *Constituting Europe: The European Court of Human Rights in a National, European and Global Context* (Cambridge, Cambridge University Press, 2013) 122–23.

[97] *Hirst v United Kingdom* (n 43); *Christine Goodwin v the United Kingdom* (n 8); *EB v France*, App No 43546/02 (2008) 47 EHRR 21; *Demir and Baykara v Turkey*, App No 34503/97 (2009) 48 EHRR 54; *Rantsev v Cyprus and Russia* (n 54).

[98] See Sandland (n 67) 199; Brauch (n 67) 145. Murray mentions *Christine Goodwin v United Kingdom* as an example of multiple approaches of the ECtHR to European consensus. He concludes that: 'These differences in the approach of the Court to the determinative value of consensus and the somewhat lax approach to the objective indicia used to determine consensus'. Murray (n 67) 57.

[99] *Rantsev v Cyprus and Russia* (n 54).

[100] Zwart (n 86) 79.

[101] See, for example, the Backbench Parliamentary Debates, 'Prisoners' Right to Vote', available at www.publications.parliament.uk/pa/cm201011/cmhansrd/cm110210/debtext/110210-0002.htm.

IV. CONCLUSION

The EU's accession to the ECHR is now legally possible and it is likely to take place in the next couple of years. Now is a good time to discuss what the EU will bring to the ECHR and how the ECHR will affect the EU. The impact of the EU's accession on the reasoning of the ECtHR remains overshadowed by the institutional organisation of the accession, power sharing and other more technical details of the accession. It is, however, important to look at the possible transformation that the decision-making process of the ECtHR will undergo after the EU's accession. European consensus can become a medium of such transformation, because domestic laws of the contracting parties to the ECHR are taken into account by the ECtHR when the level of European consensus is considered. This chapter submits that the possible influence of the EU's accession on the decision making of the ECtHR should be assessed by analysing and comparing three tendencies: the increasing competence of the EU and broader definition of human rights as understood by the ECtHR; the transformation of EU law from international into domestic; and a more formal approach to consensus identification exercised by the ECtHR. These tendencies can increase the role of the EU in the formation of human rights standards and subsequently its influence on the decision making of the ECtHR.

V CONCLUSION

Part VI

Instead of a Conclusion

20

The Accession of the EU to the ECHR and the Charter of Fundamental Rights: Enlarging the Field of Protection of Human Rights in Europe

CHRISTOS L ROZAKIS*

IN LISBON SEVEN years ago (in 2007) the then 27 members of the European Union (EU) took two significant decisions for the future of the protection of human rights in Europe: they attributed legally binding force to the EU Charter of Fundamental Rights (hereinafter 'the Charter')[1] and, at the same time, they decided on the accession of the EU to the European Convention on Human Rights (ECHR).[2]

For an outside observer, these parallel decisions may seem to create complex and, to some degree, contradictory results. This is because these decisions introduce two instruments of protection in the same legal order, covering, in part, the same rights. Indeed, in the field of applicability of the two instruments, that of the EU institutions and that of its Member States, when (according to Article 51 of the Charter) they implement EU law, both instruments are applicable *at the same time.* This parallel, simultaneous applicability justifies the fears of an outside observer that a situation of conflict may arise in certain circumstances when the same rules, provided by two different instruments, are applied by different authorities (national or European) to the detriment of the much-desired homogeneity of protection of human rights in our continent. A homogeneity which was undoubtedly the intention of those who decided in Lisbon to adopt the decisions concerning the Charter and the ECHR.

It is undeniable that in the minds of the Lisbon decision makers, both the binding force of the Charter and the accession to the ECHR are serving the need to fill the lacunae that had existed before the taking of these decisions in the European system of protection of human rights. Indeed, there had been an obvious absence of rules protecting individuals and legal persons from acts or omissions of the EU that could violate human rights. Although the EU has developed, and is still developing, activities that affect sensitive issues of human rights, possible violations occurring in this respect have remained without

* Emeritus Professor of Public International Law, University of Athens; President, Administrative Tribunal of the Council of Europe; Member, Institut de droit international.

[1] Charter of Fundamental Rights of the European Union [2009] OJ C 83/392.

[2] Convention for the Protection of Human Rights and Fundamental Freedoms (as amended) (1950) ETS No 5.

effective remedy. The EU did not have its own instrument of protection and the ECHR was inapplicable, because, as the European Court of Human Rights (ECtHR) has repeatedly stated, the judicial organ of the ECHR did not have jurisdiction to entertain disputes where the defendant party was the EU, since the latter was not a party to the ECHR. It is true that recent case law of the ECtHR has reluctantly opened the door for an indirect control of the EU acts and activities by dealing with cases against states parties to the ECHR, and, at the same time Member States of the EU, when they applied, in their internal order, laws, regulations or decisions of the EU, which allegedly violated a protected human right.[3] It goes without saying that in these circumstances, it was not the EU that was responsible for an alleged violation, but the state itself through the implementation within its internal order and by acts or omissions of its own agencies of the EU commands.

It clearly results from the above brief analysis that the need for filling the lacunae by producing rules for protection of human rights covering the field of EU activities is more than obvious. Although, admittedly, the Court of Justice of the European Union (CJEU) has repeatedly decided on human rights issues by successfully using the rules prescribed by the national constitutions of the Member States and the case law of the ECtHR, still this technique, although aptly used by the CJEU, could not suffice to cover all instances of potential violations of human rights stemming from the EU legal order. Under the regime before the Charter, the CJEU (and the then Court of First Instance) did not have an autonomous competence to deal with a human rights issue and an invocation of protection could only be raised peripherally, ie, in a situation where the court had jurisdiction to deal with a case in which a question of human rights also—but not exclusively—arose. This phenomenon, which is of course history now, ran against the very idea and ideals of the founding fathers of the post-Second World War European organization, who had seen the protection of human rights at a pan-European level as a powerful tool of integration of the continent and aspired as a consequence to an incremental homogeneity of protection of human rights as one of the tools to achieve the desired integration.

Seen from this angle, the Lisbon decisions to give binding force to the Charter and to provide for the accession of the EU to the ECHR serve the goal of European integration by covering the pre-existing lacunae, which by itself was an impediment to the harmonisation of protection in the European continent. Still the question that remains and that requires an answer refers to the possible overlap of the two instruments when implemented in the EU legal order and the method applicable in order to avoid, in these circumstances, a fragmentation of protection instead of the much-needed homogeneity.

In dealing with the method of avoidance of a possible fragmentation, I must clarify that an overlap may occur only in certain circumstances, namely in situations where both instruments provide protection of the same rights. It is well known that the Charter is a legal document, which also protects rights that are not protected by the ECHR, and in this respect no problem of a possible overlap arises. It should also be stated that no overlap may occur where the field of applicability of the two instruments differs: the ECHR has a wider field of applicability than the Charter, since it applies to 47 States, both members and non-members of the EU, while the Charter is only applicable to the EU institutions and its members when they apply EU law.

[3] See, inter alia, the landmark judgment in the case of *Bosphorus Hava Yolları Turizm ve Ticaret Anonim Şirketi v Ireland*, App No 45036/98 (2005) 42 EHRR 1.

With regard to the avoidance of fragmentation of protection, when both instruments apply and are interpreted by different organs, the Charter itself offers a prima facie solution by stipulating that whenever an issue of interpretation of the provisions of the Charter arises, the guiding tool for the interpretation must be the ECHR and its case law as it has been developed by the decisions of its judicial organ.[4] In consequence, and at least theoretically, no issue of conflict and of a divergence of interpretation may arise, since whenever the Charter applies, there must be compliance of its interpretation with the precepts of the case law of the ECtHR.

Yet, this obligation stemming from the very text of the Charter has its limits, for at least two reasons: first, the text of the Charter provides for a number of rights (civil or political) whose content differs from the content of the corresponding rights contained in the ECHR, in the sense that they offer wider protection.[5] Second, the Charter, while professing respect to the ECHR, contains a sentence in Article 52 which clearly allows an interpretation of its provisions going beyond the constraints of the ECHR, permitting a wider content to be given to the relevant rules than the one offered by the ECHR's case law, which, as is well known, offers only a *minimum* protection. The end result is that the EU authorities, and also the national authorities of the Member States of the EU, have the right to depart from the ECHR's established case law and determine their own preferences of interpretation. In these circumstances, as is easily understandable, the homogeneity of European protection can be threatened and its beneficial role in European integration seriously affected.

I think that the answer to this problem can be given by the accession of the EU to the ECHR in the sense that the ECHR will not only become a binding instrument for the EU—which, as such, does not settle the issue of a possible fragmentation of protection,—but will also make the ECtHR the ultimate organ of control of the compatibility of EU acts with the European system of human rights protection.

Indeed, the EU accession to the ECHR means, in effect, that any issue of human rights protected by the ECHR and resulting from acts or omissions of the EU or its Member States when they apply EU law within their domestic order can end up before the ECtHR, regardless of whether the EU institutions or the Member States applied the Convention or the Charter when they dealt with the issue. An individual or a legal person can, in this respect, ask for protection after having of course exhausted all remedies provided by the domestic and the EU orders. The ECtHR can then entertain the unsettled dispute, provided of course that the right on which an application to the ECtHR is based is a right contained in the ECHR and that this right had also been previously invoked *in substance* in the EU order. The ECtHR, by acquiring the power through the accession to become the ultimate recourse for an adjudication of human rights disputes, becomes the best antidote to a possible fragmentation of protection in the European legal order and a guarantee of the continuation of the harmonisation process in a gradually integrating Europe.

Still, problems remain with regard to this new duty of the ECtHR to settle disputes between the EU institutions, its Member States and individual applicants. To my mind, the main issue requiring a solution is the extent of the protection, as a result of the fact that the Charter in certain cases offers a wider level of protection than that offered by the case law of the ECHR. Admittedly, the ECtHR, when dealing with a case before it, applies

[4] The ECtHR, as per Article 52 of the Charter.

[5] For instance, the right to a fair trial under Article 47 and the right to marriage under Article 9.

solely the ECHR, and any other source of obligation outside its text is a *res inter alios acta*. Yet, one should not forget that a case concerning the EU legal order has the peculiarity of coming from a system of protection which, as I have already indicated, is in certain aspects more advanced than the ECHR system, mainly because of the Charter, but also because of the existence of other judicial organs (national or European) which will be called upon to interpret it. The ECtHR should therefore take this peculiarity into account whenever it has to deal with a case referring to rules of protection contained in both instruments, but having a wider purview (through the very text of the Charter or through an interpretation already given by the EU authorities) than the one offered by its case law. In other words, if the ECtHR is faced with a case where the Charter or its interpretation by the EU goes beyond the boundaries of the already-existing ECtHR interpretation, then it should adapt its case law to the wider protection offered by them. Otherwise, its role as a guardian of homogeneity of protection could be compromised. An interpretation of the ECHR clauses that is more restrictive than the content of a Charter's rule, or the interpretation given to it by the EU order, cannot be easily reconciled with the intentions of the Members States of the EU when they decided in Lisbon to propose a parallel application of the two instruments in the same legal order.

The transformation of the ECHR from an instrument offering a *minimum* standard of protection to an instrument offering in certain, concrete circumstances (depending upon the Charter and its interpretation) a wider protection may present problems when it requires a change in its case law or novel approaches not acceptable by ECHR parties, who are non-members of the EU. Technically speaking, this is not an insurmountable problem since a wider protection can theoretically be limited to cases concerning the EU legal order, leaving untouched a parallel case law for cases concerning states that are not members of the EU.

Although this possibility exists, still it seems that it is not consonant with the role of the ECtHR to achieve, through its judgments, the harmonisation of protection of human rights in Europe. It seems to me, as I have already argued, that it is not easily sustainable that the ECtHR will continue to apply its past case law in all cases, regardless of the new schemes engineered by the Treaty of Lisbon.

Hence, the proper solution would be a homogeneous application of a more advanced case law in the concrete circumstances to which I have already referred, applicable to both EU and to non-EU cases. This homogeneity could be achieved by the mere invocation of two concepts, which traditionally apply in the ECtHR case law: that of the 'living instrument', and that of 'consensus'. The traditional approach of the ECtHR that the ECHR is a 'living instrument' always adapted to present-day conditions could easily serve as the systemic basis for the enlargement of the content of a protected right. The technique which is usually followed in this respect for a change of the ECtHR's case law or for the development of a new one is the invocation of the existence of a European consensus to that effect. If the ECtHR realises that the social, economic or political circumstances which supported its case law in a certain aspect of protection have changed, through the development of new attitudes among the States-parties of the ECHR, then it usually proceeds to align it to the new conditions, based on the consensus of its parties, presumed by the changes of their attitudes. This path of consensus could also apply in the process of an alignment of the ECtHR's case law with a more advanced practice of protection followed in the EU's legal order. Although, admittedly, some states parties to the ECHR may protest against a generalisation of a more advanced protection, dictated by forces alien to them, still a powerful argument against them would be the existence of a European consensus in the circumstances of a specific case. Indeed, the path followed by the ECtHR in detecting the existence of a European consensus with regard to the content of a protective rule is a search into their practice concerning the limits of protection of a certain rule. What is required, in order for the ECtHR to consider that the continent is ripe to admit a more advanced protection (or not ripe yet), is the existence of clear evidence that a substantial number of states parties to the ECHR have accepted within their domestic order or through other manifestations of their consent the novelty proposed to be adopted by the ECtHR—or, at least that there exists a clear trend to that effect. If this evidence can be substantiated, then the ECtHR can safely proceed to an adoption of the novel approach.

It is undeniable that evidence of the existence of a European consensus in situations where an advanced protection is offered by the EU legal order is easily detectable. The Charter is an instrument adopted by the vast majority of the EU Member States, which, at the same time, are parties to the ECHR. Since they are bound to apply it, they will, of course, develop practices of protection consonant to their obligations. The evidence that the EU Member States consent to an advanced protection suffices, I think, to prove the existence of a European consensus since the Member States of the EU constitute the majority of the states parties to the ECHR, and given that the real meaning of consensus is not identical to a unanimous consent of all states participating in the ECHR system.

To conclude: I do not under-estimate the difficulties that may arise with regard to the implementation of the regime dictated by the Treaty of Lisbon. Yet, those who undertake the task to apply it could rely on, and have as their driving force, the clear intention of its architects to continue and complete the harmonisation of the European protection of human rights and, through that, to further enhance the process of European integration.

21

Some Personal Comments on the Accession of the EU to the ECHR

CHRISTIAAN TIMMERMANS*

EVEN TO ATTEMPT drawing conclusions from the rich material presented and discussions held during the workshop would be presumptuous. Allow me to limit myself to a few more personal comments.

I. A MECHANISM ALLOWING PRIOR INVOLVEMENT OF THE CJEU?

My first comment concerns the issue of the prior involvement of the Court of Justice of the EU (CJEU) in cases brought before the European Court of Human Rights (ECtHR), which put into question the conventionality of EU law without the CJEU having had the opportunity to address the issue. The expediency and the necessity of such a procedure of prior involvement, as is now being provided for in Article 3(6) of the draft Accession Agreement,[1] has already been extensively discussed in legal writing.[2] Opinions are

* Former judge, Court of Justice of the European Union.

[1] See draft revised agreement annexed to *Council of Europe, Fifth Negotiation Meeting between the CDDH ad hoc Negotiation Group and the European Commission on the Accession of the European Union to the European Convention on Human Rights: Final Report to the CDDH* (10 June 2013) Doc 47+1(2013)008rev2.

[2] See X Groussot, T Lock, and L Pech, 'EU Accession to the European Convention on Human Rights: A Legal Assessment of the Draft Accession Agreement of 14th October 2011' *Fondation Robert Schuman, European Issues* No 28, 7 November 2011; M Kuijer, 'The Accession of the European Union to the ECHR: A Gift for the ECHR's 60th Anniversary or an Unwelcome Intruder at the Party?' (2011) 3 *Amsterdam Law Forum* 17; C Ladenburger, 'Vers l'adhésion de l'Union Européenne à la Convention européenne des droits de l'homme' (2011) 47 *Revue trimestrielle de droit européen* 21; T Lock, 'Walking on a Tightrope: The Draft ECHR Accession Agreement and the Autonomy of the EU Legal Order' (2011) 48 *Common Market Law Review* 1025; N O'Meara, 'A More Secure Europe of Rights? The European Court of Human Rights, the Court of Justice of the European Union and EU Accession to the ECHR' (2011) 12 *German Law Journal* 1813; A Tizzano, 'Quelques reflexions sur les rapports entre les cours européennes dans la perspective de l'adhésion de l'Union à la Convention' (2011) 47 *Revue trimestrielle de droit européen* 10; F Tulkens, 'La protection des droits fondamentaux en Europe et l'adhésion de l'Union européenne à la Convention européenne des droits de l'homme' (2012) *Critical Quarterly for Legislation and Law* 14; D von Arnim, 'The Accession of the European Union to the European Convention on Human Rights' (2012) *Critical Quarterly for Legislation and Law* 37. See more generally on the subject of accession: G Gaja, 'Accession to the ECHR' in A Biondi, P Eeckhout and S Ripley (eds), *EU Law after Lisbon* (Oxford, Oxford University Press, 2012) 180; J-P Jacqué, 'The Accession of the European Union to the European Convention on Human Rights and Fundamental Freedoms' (2011) 48 *Common Market Law Review* 995; O Mader, 'Beitritt der EU zum Europarat? Institutionelle Aspekte der Entwicklung des europaïschen Grundrechtsschutzes nach Lissabon' (2011) 49 *Archiv des Völkerrechts* 435; V Skouris, 'First Thoughts on the Forthcoming Accession of the European Union to the European Convention on Human Rights' in D Spielman, M Tsirli and P Voyatzis (eds), *The European Convention on Human Rights, a Living Instrument: Essays in Honour of Christos L Rozakis* (Brussels,

divided.[3] During our workshop I have heard only negative comments expressed on the need for such a procedure.

The only really convincing argument in favour of this procedure, it seems to me, is that of subsidiarity, the exhaustion of legal remedies principle as imposed by the European Convention on Human Rights (ECHR). To get access to the Strasbourg Court, a complainant must first have brought his case before the national courts if he has a remedy and in principle up to the highest court. This is not only a matter of efficiency, of allowing cases to be solved so as to diminish the workload of the Strasbourg Court. The national legal system should first be given the possibility to correct the human rights problem, if there is any, the national courts being responsible in the first place for providing the necessary legal protection, including the protection of fundamental rights. Now precisely in that regard, the EU legal system is more complex because of the dual nature of its system of legal protection. EU law will normally affect citizens only indirectly through national implementing legislation and measures taken by the national administration. As a consequence of this decentralised system of administration, legal protection is also largely decentralised: it must be obtained through the national courts, where necessary in cooperation with the CJEU through the preliminary ruling procedure. The possibility for private parties to have direct access to the EU courts is the exception. Since the Treaty of Lisbon, this dual nature of the system of legal protection against unlawful EU acts (and national acts incompatible with EU rules) is explicitly recognised by the Treaty on European Union (TEU) (Article 19(1)).

Now, what is the problem one could ask? If legal protection must be obtained on the national level, the complainant, as always, has first to pass through the national courts to get access to the Strasbourg Court. Well, the problem is that this access could then be obtained without the Luxembourg Court having had the opportunity to address the issue. It seems difficult to accept and at the same time hardly compatible with the rationale of the exhaustion of legal remedies principle that the Strasbourg Court could be asked to adjudicate, either directly or indirectly, on the conformity of a EU act with the Convention without the CJEU having first been able to examine the issue. Indeed, it is the Luxembourg Court that has the jurisdiction and the responsibility to ensure respect of fundamental rights within the legal system from which the act emanates. The Member States' courts, as far as the validity of EU acts is concerned, do not have that jurisdiction.[4]

But what about the preliminary ruling procedure? This procedure is indeed the only way to involve the CJEU before the case is brought to the Strasbourg Court. However, this procedure is not in the hands of the parties—it is not a remedy but a prerogative of the national court. A last instance court is of course in principle obliged to refer, but only if that court detects a question of interpretation or validity of EU law which must be answered to solve the case and without prejudice to the exceptions of 'acte clair' and 'acte éclairé'. It cannot be excluded that a case brought before the Strasbourg Court appears at that stage

Bruylant, 2011) 556; B Smulders, 'De drie-pijler structuur van de grondrechtenbescherming in de EU: Enkele institutioneelrechtelijke overwegingen omtrent de groeiende complexiteit van deze bescherming na Lissabon', in T Baumé et al (eds), *Today's Multi-layered Legal Order: Current Issues and Perspectives, Liber Amicorum in Honour of Arjen WH Meij* (Zutphen, Paris Legal Publishers, 2011) 325.

[3] Those who are critical of the need for such a procedure include: Groussot, Lock and Pech (n 2) 236; and T Lock, 'EU Accession to the ECHR: Implications for Judicial Review in Strasbourg' (2010) 35 *European Law Review* 777, 793.

[4] Case 314/85 *Foto-Frost v Hauptzollamt Lübeck-Ost* [1987] ECR 4199.

to raise serious questions about the conformity of an EU act with the Convention without the CJEU having been involved and even without the national court of last instance having necessarily infringed its obligation to refer.

In my view, once the EU is a party to the Convention, the principle of exhaustion of legal remedies must be applied in such a way that, even when an action of the EU can only be challenged indirectly through the national courts, in principle where serious questions of validity of an EU act are involved, the CJEU must first have been able to examine this question before the Strasbourg Court judges the case. It would seem to me difficult to accept, to give an example, that questions of respect of fundamental rights of such importance as raised in cases like *Bosphorus*[5], *Kadi*[6] or *Advocaten voor de Wereld*[7] would be decided by the Strasbourg Court without the CJEU, which has the competence to examine the validity of the EU act in question, having had the opportunity to address these questions first.

Another argument sometimes invoked to justify the introduction of a procedure of prior involvement relates to the monopoly of the CJEU to assess the validity of EU acts. I agree with those who consider this argument as not being really convincing. Indeed, a decision of the Strasbourg Court will not interfere with that monopoly. The Strasbourg Court will not judge the validity of EU acts, just as it does not do so with regard to national acts. Were that Court to judge an EU act to be incompatible with the Convention, the interpretation of that act would remain the sole competence of the Luxembourg Court and the validity of that act would not be directly affected. It might even be the case that the CJEU could interpret the incompatibility away by proceeding to a consistent interpretation.

I have read in some of the papers and heard during the discussions at the workshop at least three objections against introducing a procedure of prior involvement.

A first objection is one of unequal treatment. It also happens, and not infrequently, that complaints are declared admissible by the Strasbourg Court without a national constitutional or supreme court having first been addressed. This is certainly true. However, normally in such a situation at least a lower court of that state will have given judgment in the case. And that is precisely the difference: without prior involvement, none of the competent EU courts would be addressed.

A second objection is based on the argument that the insistence by the CJEU on the need for a mechanism of prior involvement is to be explained by its reluctance to accept the jurisdiction of the Strasbourg Court as the last instance court on fundamental rights issues. I would call this the bad faith scenario. Professor de Schutter has even quoted Tomasi di Lampedusa to illustrate this reluctance ('Il faut que tout change pour que rien ne change'). This makes good reading, but the objection seems to me totally unfounded. Of course, the CJEU will accept the final authority of the Strasbourg Court after accession; this is the whole purpose of accession.

In fact, the CJEU already accepts this now by fully recognising in its most recent case law the consequences of Article 52(3) of the EU Charter. According to this Article, the Member States have unilaterally agreed the obligation for the EU to respect Convention rights corresponding to Charter rights as a minimum level of protection. The Charter being part of

[5] Case C-84/95 *Bosphorus Hava Yollari Turizm ve Ticaret AS v Minister for Transport, Energy and Communications and others* [1996] ECR I-3953.

[6] Cases C-402/05P and C-415/05P *Kadi (Spain, interveners) Al Barakaat International Foundation v EU Council* [2008] ECR I-6351.

[7] Case C-303/05 *Advocaten voor de Wereld VZW v Leden van de Ministerraad* [2007] ECR I-3633.

treaty law, this obligation is situated on the level of primary law. This includes the interpretation of those corresponding Convention rights given by the Strasbourg Court. The Luxembourg Court has fully accepted this in its judgments in the cases of *McB*,[8] *DEB*[9] and *Dereci*.[10]

If this bad faith scenario is true, one wonders how the President of the Strasbourg Court could have endorsed the need for a mechanism of prior involvement by subscribing on behalf of his Court to the Joint Communication of 17 January 2011 with the President of the Luxembourg Court (and how, for that matter, the drafters of the draft Explanatory Report to the draft Accession Treaty could have written: 'The Joint Declaration by the Presidents of the two European courts ... provided a valuable reference and guidance for the negotiation').[11]

And finally, would the prior involvement of the Luxembourg Court indeed risk, so to speak, pre-empting the decision of the Strasbourg Court? The ultimate decision will entirely remain in the hands of the latter court. Personally, I have no doubt that after accession, the relationship between the two courts could not be qualified in terms of constitutional or multilevel pluralism: the Strasbourg Court will have the final say and thus be superior to the Luxembourg Court. But, of course, the existing co-operation and dialogue between both courts, including through their case law, should be continued or even increased after accession to avoid unnecessary conflicts. This is also the message given by the drafters of the Treaty of Lisbon (Declaration No 2 on Article 6(2) TEU).

A third objection is to argue that if the dual system of legal protection in the EU is creating problems for the application of the subsidiarity principle under the Convention, this is an internal problem for the EU and should be solved by the EU itself instead of burdening the Convention system with providing for a solution. Let the EU first put its own house in order before accession. I do not deny there is merit in this argument. However, one of the conditions for accession on the side of the EU as expressed in Protocol No 8 is precisely that the Accession Agreement 'shall make provision for preserving the specific characteristics of the Union and Union law'. If the non-EU contracting parties of the Convention were unwilling to accept this condition, there would be a major problem. Fortunately, this appears not to be the case, or at least not now. Moreover, what should an internal EU solution to the problem have to imply? Strengthen the obligation of last instance courts to refer by amending Article 267 of the Treaty on the Functioning of the European Union (TFEU) or providing for a remedy in the TFEU allowing private parties to bring a case before the CJEU in the absence of a preliminary reference by a last instance court? Neither would in my view be desirable, nor would it be realistic to open a debate about treaty amendments.

[8] Case C-400/10 PPU *McB v E* [2010] ECR I- 8965 [53].

[9] Case C-279/09 *DEB Deutsche Energiehandels- und Beratungsgesellschaft mbH v Bundesrepublik Deutschland* [2010] ECR I-13849 [35].

[10] Case C-256/11 *Dereci v Bundesministerium für Inneres*, judgment of 15 November 2011 [70] (not yet reported).

[11] See *Council of Europe* (n 1) para 14.

II. WHAT ABOUT *BOSPHORUS*?

After, and because of accession, the EU will become subject to the jurisdiction of the Strasbourg Court. That will also imply that the CJEU becomes subordinated to that jurisdiction. This would seem to be in line with the case law of the Court on the relationship between EU law and international law. The CJEU has in principle accepted in its first EEA Opinion[12] that the EU legal order can be made subject to the jurisdiction of an international court. The Treaty of Lisbon has now removed the hurdle erected by Opinion 2/94 for the accession of the EU to the ECHR.[13]

If the CJEU becomes subject to the jurisdiction of the Strasbourg Court, does that necessarily imply that the cooperation between both courts, as it has developed until now, will change? To be more precise, would that mean the end of the *Bosphorus* case law?[14] Most commentators regard this as a logical consequence of accession.[15] Because the EU will accede to the Convention, as a matter of principle, on an equal footing with the other contracting parties,[16] there would no longer be any justification to grant the CJEU better treatment than a supreme court of a contracting party.

This sounds convincing, but in my view the question is more complex. Prima facie, it would seem rather paradoxical if the presumption of good behaviour accepted before accession would have to be abandoned because of accession. That good behaviour has certainly continued since the *Bosphorus* judgment was rendered, and has even been improved. Convention rights insofar as they correspond to Charter rights now form part of primary EU law (Article 52(3) of the Charter), including their interpretation by the Strasbourg Court. And one should also take into consideration the practice of the CJEU to refer extensively to the Strasbourg case law. More generally, it seems at least a matter for discussion whether the CJEU, as an international court with jurisdiction covering 28 Member States and in view of its close co-operative relationship with the Strasbourg Court, can be considered to be in a similar position to a supreme court of a Member State.

On the other hand, the Strasbourg Court has accepted the *Bosphorus* standard of limited control only with regard to a situation in which a Member State's action is not the result of an exercise of discretion, but the consequence of the need to comply with legal obligations flowing from EU law. Moreover, the Court took note of the fact that the international organisation from which the relevant act emanated could itself not be held

[12] Opinion 1/91 *Draft Agreement between the Community, on the one hand, and the Countries of the European Free Trade Association, on the other, Relating to the Creation of the European Economic Area* [1991] ECR I-6079 [39] and [40].

[13] Opinion 2/94 *Accession by the Community to the European Convention for the Protection of Human Rights and Fundamental Freedoms* [1996] ECR I-1759.

[14] *Bosphorus Hava Yolları Turizm ve Ticaret Anonim Şirketi v Ireland*, App No 45036/98 (2005) 42 EHRR 1. This decision accepts the protection granted by the CJEU as being in principle equivalent to the protection ensured under the Convention as interpreted by the Strasbourg Court, justifying a more remote or subsidiary control by that Court as to the respect of fundamental rights by the EU. However, the decision of 6 December 2012 in *Michaud v France*, App No 12323/11 (ECtHR) seems to limit the applicability of the *Bosphorus* presumption to cases in which the CJEU has in fact been able to exercise its control. This decision has not been referred to the Grand Chamber of the ECtHR.

[15] See Kuijer (n 2) 21; FG Jacobs, 'The Lisbon Treaty and the Court of Justice' in Biondi, Eeckhout and Ripley (n 2) 205; Lock (n 3) 797–98; O'Meara (n 2) 1828.

[16] *Council of Europe, Steering Committee for Human Rights (CDDH), Report to the Committee of Ministers on the Elaboration of Legal Instruments for the Accession of the European Union to the European Convention on Human Rights* (14 October 2011) Doc CDDH(2011)009, para 8.

liable under the Convention. So, there also appears in the *Bosphorus* judgment an element of trying to accommodate respect of obligations under the Convention with the necessity for a Member State to honour its EU obligations in order to alleviate the possible tension between these two sets of obligations, which the Strasbourg Court could not solve. Accession will of course fundamentally change this uncomfortable situation.

On balance, I would not exclude that the *Bosphorus* standard could survive accession, possibly in a more mitigated form. In that regard, I think that the suggestions made during the Workshop by Olivier De Schutter for a more remote control, but then also applying to the supreme courts of the contracting parties, and also those of Robert Harmsen pleading for a more process-based review deserve further reflection and discussion.

In any event, at least in my view, it would be in the interest of both courts, and more generally of the EU and the Convention regime, if the existing co-operation between both courts would be continued and also possibly further developed after the EU's accession to the Convention. I might refer again to Declaration No 2 on Article 6(2) TEU. But the final say on these matters, including the fate of the *Bosphorus* case law, belongs to the Strasbourg Court.

III. THE NEED TO CLARIFY THE SCOPE OF APPLICATION OF THE EU CHARTER VIS-A-VIS THE MEMBER STATES

Various voices have pleaded for an urgent clarification in this regard. One could not agree more. However, the suggestion, which has been made, to achieve that clarification by a joint statement of Council and Commission will not really help. Even if such a statement could be agreed, which would seem doubtful, it would not be legally binding. Only the Luxembourg Court could give a legally binding interpretation. Cases are pending. Indeed, it is obvious that such interpretation is urgently needed, particularly in view of the differences of drafting between the text of Article 51(1) of the Charter and the Explanations of that Article.

Early this week, during a seminar at the Court in Luxembourg, participants were confronted with a telling example. The Brussels II Regulation concerning jurisdiction, recognition and enforcement of judgments in matrimonial matters and matters of parental responsibility[17] does not allow for any exception with regard to the recognition of an enforceable foreign judgment requiring the return of a child. The question was discussed whether, nevertheless, the receiving court might not invoke a manifest problem of fundamental rights protection to refuse recognition of the judgment. Could the EU Charter be invoked to that effect? Some argued that there could be no question in this context of an implementation of EU law in the meaning of Article 51(1) of the Charter because there has been no EU harmonisation whatsoever of national substantive family law on this issue. Others forcefully argued the contrary, because the regulation imposing recognition of such judgments could be regarded as establishing a sufficient link with EU law to admit the applicability of the Charter.

[17] Council Regulation (EC) No 2201/2003 of 27 November 2003 concerning jurisdiction and the recognition and enforcement of judgments in matrimonial matters and the matters of parental responsibility [2003] OJ L 338/1.

In the meantime, the CJEU has delivered the *Åkerberg Fransson* judgment in which it has given a first interpretation of how to understand this wording of Article 51(1) of the Charter.[18] When may Member States be considered to be implementing EU law? Understandably, the Court has refrained from defining clear, general criteria to determine the kind of situation to be so considered. Its interpretation is focused on the legal context of the case (VAT rules) and is therefore fairly casuistic. Nevertheless, one might at least conclude that the Court is intending to uphold its earlier case law with regard to situations in which Member States have to respect EU fundamental rights (and I would be inclined to add the general principles of EU law).

IV. THE NEED OF AN EFFECTIVE, PRIOR COMPLIANCE CONTROL WITH REGARD TO RESPECT OF THE EU CHARTER

I much appreciated the contribution to the Workshop by John Morijn for having drawn our attention to the importance of organising an effective compliance policy with regard to the Charter. Academic debate on the Charter is intensive and often theoretically fascinating. But one should not forget the importance of organising adequate procedures within both the EU institutions and Member States' administrations in order to scrutinise and ensure respect of Charter rights with regard to draft legislation and policy measures. Also, prevention is better than having to attempt *ex post* to obtain redress through the courts.

Allow me a more general remark in this context. More attention should also be given by academics when researching these issues of compliance or quality of legislation to the role played by legal services in the administration both at the EU level and the Member State level. Generally, legal services within the EU institutions occupy a rather strong position in internal decision-making processes. So, for instance, the legal service of the European Commission must be consulted on each legal act or legislative proposal to be decided by the College of Commissioners. Negative legal advice has important procedural consequences: the decision cannot be taken by written procedure, as is the usual practice, but can only be adopted by oral procedure, that is, by the Commission in its weekly meeting. The director general of the legal service attends these meetings and will have the possibility to explain the legal objections. Services will normally prefer to settle the legal issues during the drafting process, which strengthens the position of the legal service. A different example is given by an incident some years ago in the Netherlands. The position of legal services in the Ministry for Foreign Affairs was so weak at the time that a negative legal opinion on the legitimacy under international law of Dutch military participation in occupying military forces in Iraq never reached the minister. It was considered inopportune at the highest administrative level and put aside. Fortunately, procedures have now been changed.[19]

[18] Case C-617/10 *Åklagaren v Hans Åkerberg Fransson*, judgment of 26 February 2013 (not yet reported).

[19] See Commissie Davids, *Rapport Commissie van onderzoek besluitvorming Irak* (Amsterdam, Boom, 2010), available at www.rijksoverheid.nl/bestanden/documenten-en-publicaties/rapporten/2010/01/12/rapport-commissie-davids/rapport-commissie-irak.pdf, 250, 251, 273.

22

The 'Co-respondent Mechanisms' According to the Draft Agreement for the Accession of the EU to the ECHR

GIORGIO GAJA*

I. INTRODUCTION

MY ANALYSIS WILL consider questions of attribution of responsibility from the perspective of the Accession Agreement when an alleged breach of the European Convention on Human Rights (ECHR) involves both the European Union (EU) and one or more Member States.

Normally, this issue will arise when an application to the European Court of Human Rights (ECtHR) is directed against a Member State whose conduct implements a provision of EU law and this provision is to some extent at the origin of the alleged breach. As is well known, for this type of situation, the draft Accession Agreement[1] has provided the EU with the opportunity of becoming a party to the proceedings alongside the respondent state as a co-respondent. A similar opportunity has also been envisaged in certain cases for Member States when an application is brought against the EU. These provisions are designed to implement Article I(b) of Protocol No 8 to the EU Treaties, which calls for 'the mechanisms necessary to ensure that proceedings by non-Member States and individual applications are correctly addressed to the Member States and/or the Union as appropriate'.

It would be pointless, at the advanced stage of negotiations concerning the Accession Agreement, to propose that a different approach should be taken. My aim is necessarily more limited: to analyse the 'mechanisms' which have been devised and which by and large have already been agreed upon.

II. THE QUESTION OF ATTRIBUTION OF CONDUCT

Before examining these 'mechanisms', it is useful to consider briefly the approach taken by the ECtHR in addressing the issue of attribution of conduct and of responsibility when an

* Judge at the ICJ.

[1] The latest text at the time of writing is dated 5 April 2013. It may be found in *Council of Europe, Fifth Negotiation Meeting between the CDDH ad hoc Negotiation Group and the European Commission on the Accession of the European Union to the European Convention on Human Rights: Final Report to the CDDH* (10 June 2013) Doc 47+1(2013)008rev2.

alleged breach of an obligation under the ECHR finds its origin in a provision of EU law. So far, the issue can only be raised when an application is brought to the ECtHR against one or more Member States, and the ECtHR can only assess the Member States' responsibility. The clearest dictum of the ECtHR may be found in paragraph 153 of the *Bosphorus* judgment, given by the Grand Chamber in 2005.[2] It reads as follows:

> [A] Convention Party is responsible under Article 1 of the Convention for all acts and omissions of its organs regardless of whether the act or omission in question was a consequence of domestic law or of the necessity to comply with international legal obligations [in the case in hand, obligations under EU law].

Thus, a Member State is considered to incur responsibility when the conduct of one of its organs is in breach of the ECHR, irrespective of the possibility that the state organ was complying with an obligation under an instrument other than the ECHR. This view is consistent with the general rule on attribution set forth in Article 4(1) of the International Law Commission (ILC) Articles on Responsibility of States, according to which:

> The conduct of any State organ shall be considered an act of that State under international law, whether the organ exercises legislative, executive, judicial or any other functions.[3]

Although the ILC commentary on state responsibility does not expressly address the issue, it is implied that the fact that the state organ implements an obligation under international law or under EU law does not affect the attribution of conduct to that state. Moreover, according to the Articles on Responsibility of States, when a state's conduct is in breach of an obligation under a treaty such as the ECHR, it incurs responsibility unless it can invoke a circumstance precluding wrongfulness.

During the discussions leading to the adoption by the ILC of its articles on the responsibility of international organizations, the European Commission took a different view on the attribution of conduct implementing obligations under EU law. It sometimes referred to Regional Economic Integration Organizations (REIOs), a wider category which allows the EU to be less in evidence. According to this view, state organs act as quasi-organs of the EU when they implement an obligation under EU law which leaves them with no discretion.[4] Responsibility for their conduct would have to be attributed only to the EU, which, unlike other international organizations, does not shy away from international responsibility. The commentary on Article 64 of the ILC articles on the responsibility of international

[2] Judgment of 30 June 2005, *Bosphorus Hava Yolları Turizm ve Ticaret Anonim Şirketi v Ireland*, App No 45036/98 (2005) 42 EHRR 1, 107, 157. See also Grand Chamber, judgment of 12 September 2012, *Nada v Switzerland*, App No 10593/08 (2012) [168].

[3] *Yearbook of the International Law Commission* (2001) Vol II, Part Two, 40.

[4] See in particular Doc A/C.6/56/SR.21, para 18. The same view was expounded in the following: PJ Kuijper and E Paasivirta, 'Further Exploring International Responsibility: The European Community and the ILC's Project on Responsibility of International Organizations' (2004) 1 *International Organizations Law Review* 111, 127; S Talmon, 'Responsibility of International Organizations: Does the European Community Require Special Treatment?' in M Ragazzi (ed), *International Responsibility Today: Essays in Memory of Oscar Schachter* (Leiden, Martinus Nijhoff, 2005) 412–14; F Hoffmeister, 'Litigating against the European Union and its Member States: Who Responds under the ILC's Draft Articles on International Responsibility of International Organizations?' (2010) 21 *European Journal of International Law* 723. Three of these four authors were attached to the Legal Service of the European Commission.

organizations took account of this view and considered that there might be a special rule of international law for the attribution of conduct to the EU.[5]

However, a new approach has been taken by the EU in the negotiations concerning the draft Accession Agreement. In September 2012, the representative of the EU proposed to insert in the draft Agreement a sub-paragraph in order 'to make explicit the attribution rule whereby acts of Member States are and remain only attributable to them, even if they are acts of implementation of EU law'.[6] A provision of the draft Accession Agreement accordingly states that: 'For the purposes of the Convention, of the Protocols thereto and of this Agreement, an act, measure or omission of organs or agents of a Member State of the European Union or of persons acting on its behalf shall be attributable to that State, even if such act, measure or omission occurs when the State implements the law of the European Union.'[7] Thus, one has to assume that, like the *Bosphorus* judgment, the draft Accession Agreement starts from the premise that if an organ of one of the Member States causes a breach of an obligation under the ECHR when implementing an EU rule, the act is attributed to that state, which would then incur responsibility.

The Accession Agreement could have provided otherwise and established a special rule for the purposes of the ECHR, to the effect that the EU be considered responsible instead of its Member States when a breach finds its origin in a provision of EU law and not in the Member State's use of its discretion. This solution would have had the advantage of ensuring that, in the event of a breach, the responsible entity would have been able to provide the required remedies, for instance, by modifying a directive so as to make it consistent with the ECHR. However, since this possibility has been discarded in the negotiations, according to my self-imposed mandate, I shall not defend this solution here.[8]

III. THE 'CO-RESPONDENT MECHANISM' WHEN AN APPLICATION IS DIRECTED AGAINST A MEMBER STATE

The key aspect of the devised 'mechanisms' is that the EU may, at its request with the approval of the ECtHR or by accepting an invitation by the latter, become co-respondent with the Member State or States against whom an application is directed. The EU would thus enjoy the prerogatives of being a party to the proceedings.

One important point is that, even if the proceedings may lead to asserting the responsibility of the EU, the fact of adding the EU as a co-respondent does not affect the admissibility of the application. The last sentence of the proposed new Article 36(4) of the ECHR reads: 'The admissibility of an application shall be assessed without regard to the participation of a co-respondent in the proceedings.'[9] This seems to imply that the admissibility

[5] *Report of the International Law Commission, Sixty-third session (26 April 3 June and 1 July 12 August 2011)*, Doc A/66/10, 168–69.

[6] *Council of Europe, Third Negotiation Meeting between the CDDH ad hoc Negotiation Group and the European Commission on the Accession of the European Union to the European Convention on Human Rights: Meeting Report* (9 November 2012) Doc. 47+1(2012)R02, 2, para 4.

[7] See *Council of Europe* (n 1) 5 (Article 1(4)).

[8] I had advocated this solution in 'Accession to the ECHR' in A Biondi and P Eeckhout with S Ripley (eds), *EU Law After Lisbon* (Oxford, Oxford University Press, 2012) 190. For a similar suggestion, see B Conforti, 'L'adhésion de l'Union Européenne à la Convention Européenne des Droits de l'Homme' in *Mélanges en hommage à Albert Weitzel, L'Europe des droits fondamentaux* (Paris, Pedone, 2013) 21.

[9] *Council of Europe* (n 1) 7 (Article 2(1)).

has only to be ascertained with reference to the entity against which the application was originally directed.

Thus, when the EU is only a co-respondent, an application could be declared admissible even if the local remedies have not been exhausted within the EU legal system. This looks odd, but may find a justification in the fact that the addition of the EU as a co-respondent depends on the EU's consent, which may be taken as a waiver of any objection to the admissibility of the application concerning the EU which might otherwise have been raised.

According to the draft Accession Agreement, the EU may be invited by the ECtHR to become a co-respondent or may make a request to that effect in relation to an alleged violation of the ECHR 'if it appears that such allegation calls into question the compatibility with the Convention rights at issue of a provision of European Union law, including decisions taken under the TEU and under the TFEU, notably where that violation could have been avoided only by disregarding an obligation under European Union law'.[10]

The main purpose of the EU becoming a co-respondent is to allow the EU to enjoy all the rights of a party to the proceedings in order to defend what it considers to be the proper interpretation of the relevant provisions of EU law and of the ECHR.

IV. 'PRIOR INVOLVEMENT' OF THE COURT OF JUSTICE

In the proceedings before the ECtHR, the EU's line of defence would have to take into account the views of the Court of Justice of the European Union (CJEU), should this Court take up a position on the question of compatibility of the provision of EU law with the Convention. The role of the CJEU has been enhanced by a paragraph in the draft Accession Agreement which envisages that, in 'proceedings to which the European Union is a co-respondent', before the decision of the ECtHR, the CJEU may provide an 'assessment' of 'the compatibility with the Convention rights at issue of the provision of European Union law' in question.[11] The draft Explanatory Report states that: 'Assessing the compatibility with the Convention shall mean to rule on the validity of a legal provision contained in acts of the EU institutions, bodies, offices or agencies, or on the interpretation of a provision of the Treaty on European Union (TEU), the Treaty on the Functioning of the European Union (TFEU) or of any other provision having the same legal value pursuant to those instruments.'[12] It is clear that, when considering the validity of a provision of EU law, the CJEU will have to give an interpretation of that provision. This might lead the CJEU to conclude that the provision in question is consistent with the Convention.

The relevant procedure—the so-called procedure of 'prior involvement' of the CJEU—is still undefined. This procedure has not been outlined in the draft Accession Agreement, but will be left to provisions of EU law. This is an understandable choice that would, however, entail the need for a revision of the TFEU through one of the procedures envisaged in Article 48 TEU. Moreover, it is not clear who will be able to start the relevant proceedings and who will be entitled to be a party, nor is it easy to imagine what effects the Court's

[10] Ibid 7 (Article 3(2)).
[11] Ibid 7 (Article 3(6)).
[12] Ibid 26 (para 66).

assessment will have, both on the provision of EU law and on the legal position of the applicant.[13]

The idea of giving the CJEU the opportunity of making an assessment on compatibility with the ECHR when the EU is a co-respondent has been criticised because of the privileged position that the Accession Agreement would give this Court in relation to all the supreme courts of the states parties to the Convention. It may also be expected that the ECtHR will not lightly contradict an assessment specifically made by the CJEU. Since the members of the CJEU have clearly expressed their strong wish that the procedure of 'prior involvement' be introduced,[14] and, moreover, the same Court is likely to be requested to give an opinion on the Accession Agreement under Article 218(11) TFEU, I shall refrain from making any suggestion concerning the presence of this part of the mechanisms. However, it may be argued that if the procedure of 'prior involvement' of the CJEU will be maintained, it would be logical to extend its application.

V. ALLOCATION OF RESPONSIBILITY BY THE ECtHR

Traditionally, one matter of major concern from the EU's point of view, reflected in Opinion 1/91 of the CJEU,[15] is that no court or tribunal other than the CJEU should take a decision on the respective competences of the EU and its Member States. This issue is viewed as a delicate internal matter, which should be dealt with in the EU 'cuisine', whether it is to be settled by the CJEU or by an agreement between the EU and the relevant Member States.[16]

This concern has led the negotiators to omit in the draft Accession Agreement any indication of the criteria that the ECtHR should use in order to allocate responsibility between the EU and its Member States in case of an assessed breach. With regard to the EU being a co-respondent, the following text was added in November 2012 as Article 3(7):

> If the violation in respect of which a High Contracting Party is a co-respondent to the proceedings is established, the respondent and the co-respondent shall be jointly responsible for that violation, unless the Court, on the basis of the reasons given by the respondent and the co-respondent, and having sought the views of the applicant, decides that only one of them be held responsible.[17]

[13] It is difficult to imagine that a possible consequence of an assessment may be, as suggested by C Ladenburger, 'Vers l'adhésion de l'Union européenne à la Convention européenne des droits de l'homme' (2011) 47 *Revue trimestrielle de droit européen* 20, 25, that the CJEU 'constaterait l'invalidité de l'acte de l'Union qui disparaîtrait dès lors de l'ordre juridique de celle-ci'.

[14] See 'Discussion Document of the Court of Justice of the European Union on Certain Aspects of the Accession of the European Union to the European Convention for the Protection of Human Rights and Fundamental Freedoms', 5 May 2010, http://curia.europa.eu/jcms/upload/docs/application/pdf/2010-05/convention_en.pdf, according to which 'a mechanism must be available which is capable of ensuring that the question of the validity of a Union act can be brought effectively before the Court of Justice before the European Court of Human Rights rules on the compatibility of that act with the Convention'.

[15] Opinion 1/91 *Draft Agreement between the Community, on the one hand, and the Countries of the European Free Trade Association, on the other, Relating to the Creation of the European Economic Area* [1991] ECR I-6079 at I-6104-5, [33]–[36].

[16] One example of an elaborate text designed to prevent a court or tribunal other than the CJEU from addressing the question of the respective competences of the EU and its Member States is given by Annex IX of the United Nations Convention on the Law of the Sea.

[17] *Council of Europe* (n 1) 7. The view that 'it would be wiser to retain joint responsibility in all cases where co-respondents are involved' was expressed by JP Jacqué, 'The Accession of the European Union to the European Convention on Human Rights and Fundamental Freedoms' (2012) 48 *Common Market Law Review* 995, 1016.

The draft Explanatory Report states that: 'Apportioning responsibility separately to the respondent and the co-respondent(s) on any other basis would entail the risk that the Court would assess the distribution of competences between the EU and its member States.'[18]

The solution endorsed in these texts is not convincing. In most cases in which the EU would be a co-respondent, no issue of competence will arise. The question of competence may be relevant when a breach derives from an omission,[19] supposing that the procedure of co-respondent is also applicable in that case. This will be a rare occurrence. What the ECtHR would normally have to decide is whether, apart from the responsibility of the Member State against whom the application is directed, the EU would also be responsible for its contribution to the wrongful act of the Member State. The question is *not about who is competent, but whether the provision of EU law is actually at the origin of the breach.*

For instance, if a breach depended on the implementation of a directive, the question would be whether the breach is due to the use by the Member State of its discretion or whether the breach depends on the mandatory content of the directive. In the latter case, the EU would also be regarded as responsible.

It is true that, in deciding on the responsibility of the EU, the ECtHR would then have to examine some provisions of EU law and the way they relate to rules of municipal law. This is nothing new in terms of the ECtHR's jurisprudence: one may refer as an example to the 1996 judgment in *Cantoni v France*.[20] Moreover, how can one expect an external control over compliance by the EU with its obligations under the Convention if the ECtHR was prevented from interpreting the content of provisions of EU law? The concern that matters relating to EU law should be left to be resolved by the EU and its Member States cannot be carried too far.

Letting the ECtHR decide when the EU is responsible would be more consistent with what is required by Protocol No 8 to the Treaties than what is suggested in Article 3(7) of the draft Accession Agreement. The relevant text of the Protocol, which I quote again, requires the Agreement to provide for 'the mechanisms necessary to ensure that … individual applications are correctly addressed to Member States and/or the Union, as appropriate'. This requirement does not imply, but rather seems to exclude, that a mechanism be established according to which the EU be considered as a rule jointly responsible when, as in the example of a breach committed through the implementation of a directive, the application has been correctly addressed against a Member State which breached its obligations under the ECHR in the exercise of its discretion in the implementation of the directive. This would also correspond to the position that the EU may have taken as co-respondent in the case.

[18] *Council of Europe* (n 1) 26 (para 62).

[19] The question of omissions was specifically discussed by T Lock, 'Accession of the EU to the ECHR: Who Would Be Responsible in Strasbourg?' in D Ashiagbor, N Countouris and I Lianos (eds), *The European Union after the Treaty of Lisbon* (Cambridge, Cambridge University Press, 2012) 129–34. He observed that 'a solution anchored to the division of competences is not acceptable for the EU when it comes to individual complaints regarding omissions'.

[20] Judgment of 15 November 1996, *Cantoni v France*, App No 17862/91, ECHR Reports, 1996-V, 1614 at 1626–29.

VI. THE 'CO-RESPONDENT MECHANISM' WHEN AN APPLICATION IS DIRECTED AGAINST THE EU

As I mentioned at the beginning, the 'mechanism' of adding a co-respondent is also intended to apply when an application is directed against the EU. According to Article 3(3) of the draft Accession Agreement, Member States may, when invited by the ECtHR or at their request subject to the Court's approval:

> [B]ecome co-respondents to the proceedings in respect of an alleged violation ... if it appears that such allegation calls into question the compatibility with the Convention rights at issue of a provision of the TEU, the TFEU or any other provision having the same legal value pursuant to those instruments, notably where that violation could have been avoided only by disregarding an obligation under those instruments.[21]

This provision is intended to reflect the fact that Member States are required to express their consent when one of the Treaties has to be revised. The paragraph in question gives Member States the opportunity of making their views known before the ECtHR even when the applicant is not one of their nationals. Moreover, they would be entitled to do so with the rights belonging to a party to the proceedings. However, since the Treaties are part of EU law and the interpretation that the CJEU may have given of the relevant Treaty provisions is authoritative for the Member States, there is little that a Member State could contribute by becoming a co-respondent.

VII. THE POSSIBILITY FOR A RESPONDENT TO CHANGE STATUS

Article 3(4) of the draft Accession Agreement also envisages that: 'Where an application is directed against and notified to both the European Union and one or more of its Member States, the status of any respondent may be changed to that of a co-respondent' if the conditions set out in the previous paragraphs are met.[22] It is difficult to understand the practical meaning of this provision. The ECtHR could at any event find that a co-respondent incurs international responsibility. With regard to a co-respondent, admissibility of the application would not have to be assessed, but this would hardly correspond to an interest of the entity (EU or Member State) accepting the ECtHR's invitation or requesting that Court to become a co-respondent.

Under the draft Accession Agreement, another consequence of there being a co-respondent is that it becomes possible to trigger the procedure for 'prior involvement' of the CJEU. However, there is little reason why this procedure should not also be applicable when the EU is a respondent. It would be even more logical to make it applicable in all the instances in which a question of compatibility of a provision of EU law with the ECHR arises.

[21] *Council of Europe* (n 1) 7.

[22] Ibid.

23

Beyond the Accession Agreement: Five Items for the European Union's Human Rights Agenda

BRUNO DE WITTE*

ONCE THE ACCESSION Agreement of the EU to the ECHR is signed, the complex process of ratification by the EU itself, and by all the current contracting parties of the Convention, will start. In the meantime, the EU will continue to develop its own human rights agenda. In this short chapter, we highlight five issues that will—or should be—high on this agenda. Some of them are directly linked to the pending accession to the ECHR and others indirectly so.

I. IMPLEMENTING THE ACCESSION AGREEMENT

A number of elements included in the Accession Agreement will need to be worked out in greater detail by the EU institutions. Those elements include the practical arrangements—on the EU side—for the operation of the co-respondent mechanism,[1] for the election of the future EU judge in the Strasbourg Court[2] and for other forms of EU participation in the institutional life of the Convention.

The trickiest question, in legal terms, seems to be the implementation of the prior involvement mechanism. The mechanism itself remains very controversial,[3] but it is now clear that it will form part of the final Accession Agreement. From the perspective of EU law, the question arises how this task of the Court of Justice of the European Union (CJEU) can be fitted within its existing constitutional mandate. Like all EU institutions, the CJEU is subject to the principle of conferred powers laid down in Article 5 of the Treaty on European Union (TEU). Its powers are defined by the TEU and the Treaty on the Functioning of the European Union (TFEU) by means of a set of specific procedures.

In addition to the specific procedures, however, we also find an open-ended clause in Article 273 TFEU allowing the Member States to submit to the Court 'under a special

* Professor of European Law, Maastricht University & European University Institute, Florence.

1 On which, see Delgado Casteleiro, ch 8 and Gaja, ch 22 in this volume.

2 See Drzemczewski, chapter 5.

3 See, for example, the contrasting views of the mechanism presented by Timmermans, ch 21 and Torres Pérez, ch 3 in this volume; and also R Baratta, 'Accession of the EU to the ECHR: The Rationale for the ECJ's Prior Involvement Mechanism' (2013) 50 *Common Market Law Review* 1305.

agreement between the parties … any dispute between Member States which relates to the subject matter of the Treaties'. This clause was recently used in the Treaty establishing the European Stability Mechanism and in the Treaty on Stability, Coordination and Governance in the Economic and Monetary Union (also known as 'Fiscal Compact'), both of which are extra-EU agreements between a set of EU Member States, in which the CJEU was given a (limited) jurisdictional role in addition to its normal powers under the TEU and the TFEU.[4]

However, this 'flexibility clause' cannot be used as a basis for the prior involvement mechanism, since cases pending before the ECtHR are not 'disputes between Member States' in the sense of Article 273 TFEU. It is equally clear that the prior involvement cannot be considered as falling within the scope of the preliminary ruling mechanism of Article 267 TFEU, since that mechanism organises references from the national courts of the EU Member States and therefore cannot accommodate 'references' of cases pending before the Strasbourg Court. Thus, strictly speaking, none of the existing heads of jurisdiction of the CJEU can accommodate the prior involvement mechanism, so that an amendment of the TFEU would seem necessary to create this new power for the CJEU.

And yet, in view of the cumbersome nature of European treaty revisions and the lack of appetite of governments for engaging in them if they are not absolutely necessary, one may expect the European Commission and the European Council to concoct an ingenious plan that would allow for the prior involvement mechanism to be created without prior EU treaty amendment. The basis could be found in the CJEU's recent ruling in *Pringle*. In that case, the Court was asked whether the Treaty establishing the European Stability Mechanism (which, as mentioned above, is a separate international agreement between the 17 Eurozone states, outside the EU legal framework) could lawfully entrust certain tasks to the Commission and the European Central Bank. The Court of Justice approved this on condition that those extra tasks—not foreseen in the TEU or TFEU—do not 'alter the essential character of the powers conferred on those institutions by the EU and FEU Treaties'.[5] This formula stems from some Opinions given by the Court in the context of the conclusion of international agreements by the EC, in which it had emphasised, by the use of that same formula, that such agreements should not alter the institutional identity of the EU.[6] Applying this doctrine to the prior involvement mechanism, one could envisage an international agreement concluded between all EU Member States that would attribute this new task to the CJEU, and this agreement could be submitted for ratification in each Member State together with the Accession Agreement to the ECHR.

II. REVISITING THE IMPACT OF THE ECHR IN THE EU LEGAL ORDER

The formal incorporation of the ECHR into the EU legal order following accession raises the question whether this will have implications for the way in which the *national* courts

[4] See S Peers, 'Towards a New Form of EU Law? The Use of EU Institutions Outside the EU Legal Framework' (2013) 9 *European Constitutional Law Review* 37.

[5] Case C-370/12 *Thomas Pringle v Government of Ireland, Ireland, The Attorney General*, Judgment of the Court of Justice of 27 November 2012 [158].

[6] Opinions 1/92, 1/00 and 1/09, referred to by the Court in [158] of the *Pringle* judgment. See also Baratta (n 3) 1329–30, who argues that the prior involvement mechanism would not require a TFEU amendment.

of EU Member States should treat the ECHR. As we know, there is currently a wide variety in terms of the way national legal systems give effect to the Convention.

This question has already arisen prior to accession. In the *Kamberaj* case, a local Italian court had asked the CJEU whether the fact that Article 6 TEU refers to the ECHR (as a source of EU general principles) implies that the ECHR has direct effect and that national courts of the EU Member States should disapply their national laws when they are incompatible with the ECHR. The CJEU answered that: 'Article 6(3) TEU does not govern the relationship between the ECHR and the legal systems of the Member States and nor does it lay down the consequences to be drawn by a national court in case of conflict between the rights guaranteed by that convention and a provision of national law.'[7] This position was repeated later on in the *Åkerberg Fransson* judgment.[8] This statement by the Court was, at the very least, misleading, since it hid the fact that, in practice, the ECHR indeed benefits from the primacy of EU law over national law to the extent that its content is incorporated into the general principles of EU law and in the EU Charter of Rights.[9] This situation will become clearer after accession. Since the ECHR will then become a separate source of EU law, it will benefit from the special legal force of EU law within the national legal orders, so that the current divergence in the domestic effect of the ECHR will have to disappear in all cases coming within the scope of EU law. But if the national courts of, say, Sweden, Italy and Germany will have to recognise the primacy of the ECHR over national legislation in EU-related cases, they may well be led to also extend that same primacy to 'purely national' (ie, not EU-related) cases in which the ECHR will be invoked.

III. ALLOCATING RESPONSIBILITY IN THE EU'S MULTILEVEL GOVERNANCE SYSTEM

The creation of the co-respondent mechanism by Article 3 of the draft Accession Agreement is a consequence of the fact that EU policies are mostly implemented by means of legal acts adopted by the EU Member States. When questions arise about the ECHR compatibility of such national measures, it may not always be clear whether the responsibility for the alleged human rights violation lies with the national authority that has adopted the measure or with the underlying EU legal instrument which the national authority faithfully applied. The co-respondent mechanism is a procedural device allowing this problem to be 'papered over' when a case is pending before the Strasbourg Court, but the underlying problem is not solved by this mechanism. Therefore, there is a special post-accession task for the CJEU to define more rigorously the criteria for allocating the responsibility for fundamental rights violations between the EU and its Member States.

When implementing EU law, the parliaments and governments of Member States often enact legal norms which are not strictly required by the EU directive or regulation in question. EU law may leave to the Member States the discretion to adopt certain measures or not, or to choose between different legal solutions (the *discretionary choice* hypothesis);

[7] Case C-571/10 *Servet Kamberaj v Istituto per l'Edilizia sociale della Provincia autonoma di Bolzano and others*, Judgment of 24 April 2012 [62]. On the Italian constitutional law background against which this preliminary question was formulated, see Martinico, ch 10 in this volume.

[8] Case C-617/10 *Åklagaren v Hans Åkerberg Fransson*, Judgment of 26 February 2013 [44].

[9] See Claes and Imamovič, ch 11 in this volume.

alternatively, it may expressly allow the Member States to adopt more far-reaching norms to protect certain interests such as consumer rights or rights relating to the environment (the *minimum harmonisation* hypothesis); moreover, the EU act may simply not deal at all with certain connected questions, which are therefore left for the Member States to regulate or not (the *incomplete harmonisation* hypothesis). In all three situations, the national measure is not directly determined by EU law. To what extent is the EU nevertheless responsible if a violation of the ECHR (or, indeed, of the EU Charter of Rights) occurs?[10] More specifically, the question will be whether the (possible) violation is committed by the EU legislator when adopting a directive or regulation or by the Member State when using its policy discretion in implementing the directive or regulation.

For the national court faced with a dispute, the reply to this question will make a huge difference: if the EU is responsible for the alleged breach of the Charter or the ECHR, the national court will have to ask the CJEU whether the act is invalid as a matter of EU law. However, if the Member State is responsible, then the national court can decide the case itself or, if necessary, ask a preliminary question to the CJEU about the interpretation of the Charter.

The difficulty of this allocation of responsibility can be illustrated by what happened with the implementation of the Data Retention Directive of 2006.[11] At least three constitutional courts, those of Germany, Romania and the Czech Republic, held that the national laws implementing this directive infringed the right of privacy protected by their respective national constitutions. None of them referred a question on the validity of the underlying EU Directive, although it has been argued that, at least in the case of the Romanian judgment, the criticism by the constitutional court was, in reality, directed not only at the implementing law but also at the content of the Directive itself, and that the Romanian court should have referred a question of validity to the CJEU.[12] The Irish High Court and the Austrian Constitutional Court, on the other hand, when faced with a legal action against the implementation of the same Directive in their countries, had doubts as to whether the Directive *itself* was compatible with the right to privacy as protected by the EU Charter and put this question to the CJEU, where the two cases are now pending.[13]

In the past, the CJEU has had the tendency in such cases to 'save' the EU legislative act by adding an interpretative gloss to it, thereby putting the burden on the Member States when implementing the EU act to do so in accordance with the rights guidance offered by the

[10] This question mirrors another question, namely that of knowing when Member States are acting within the scope of EU law and are therefore bound by EU fundamental rights. The latter question is hotly debated in EU law scholarship. For a recent analysis, see D Sarmiento, 'Who's Afraid of the Charter? The Court of Justice, National Courts and the New Framework of Fundamental Rights Protection in Europe' (2013) 50 *Common Market Law Review* 1267.

[11] Directive 2006/24 of 15 March 2006 on the retention of data generated or processed in connection with the provision of publicly available electronic communications services or of public communication networks, OJEU 2006, L 105/54.

[12] C Murphy, 'Romanian Constitutional Court, Decision No 1258 of 8 October 2009' (2010) 47 *Common Market Law Review* 933. For a comment on the Czech case, see P Molek, 'Czech Constitutional Court Unconstitutionality of the Czech Implementation of the Data Retention Directive; Decision of 22 March 2011, Pl. ÚS 24/10' (2012) 8 *European Constitutional Law Review* 338; and on the German case, see A-B Kaiser, 'German Federal Constitutional Court: German Data Retention Provisions Unconstitutional in their Present Form; Decision of 2 March 2010, *NJW* 2010, p. 833' (2010) 6 *European Constitutional Law Review* 503.

[13] Case C-293/12 *Digital Rights Ireland Ltd v Minister for Communications et al*, preliminary reference by the High Court of Ireland of 11 June 2012, pending; Case C-594/12 *Kärtner Landesregierung, Michael Seitlinger et al*, preliminary reference by the Austrian Constitutional Court of 19 December 2012, pending.

CJEU.[14] One may wonder, though, whether the Court should not lay more responsibility for human rights compliance at the doorstep of the European legislator rather than 'outsourcing' it to national authorities. In future ECHR cases, and particularly in the context of the co-respondent mechanism, such multilevel allocation issues are likely to arise more frequently and more visibly than before.

IV. ENGAGING WITH OTHER INTERNATIONAL HUMAN RIGHTS INITIATIVES

Once the EU has strengthened its special bond with the ECHR by means of the Accession Agreement, it will face the question of how it should relate to the other parts of the international human rights universe. One may argue that the EU should beware of moving to a position of splendid isolation in the human rights field; rather, it should encourage and embrace the evolution of human rights at the broader regional and universal levels.[15]

The EU has recently become involved in human rights standard setting on the international scene. The European Community (EC) had, in its final years, started to participate in the adoption of multilateral human rights treaties and one may expect its successor the EU to continue to do so when the occasion arises. Its participation in multilateral human rights conventions requires those conventions to have a clause allowing for accession not only by states but also by 'regional integration organisations' or similar expressions. The classical international human rights conventions (such as the ECHR prior to its recent amendment) do not have such clauses, but when new initiatives are taken, the EU is able to appear on the negotiation scene and try to insist on their inclusion. Thus, the EC helped to negotiate and signed the UN Convention on the Rights of Persons with Disabilities, which was adopted by the United Nations General Assembly on 13 December 2006. This Convention does indeed contain a 'regional integration organisations' clause. The competence of the EC to sign the Convention was based, by the Commission, on Articles 13 and 95 of the EC Treaty, thus connecting the Convention to both the anti-discrimination and internal market competences of the EC.[16] The EU has decided to ratify this Convention without waiting for most or all of its Member States to take that step.[17] Ratification not only entails the binding effect of this Convention for the EU institutions, and possibly its direct effect

[14] The *Family Reunification* judgment of 2006 (Case C-540/03 *Parliament v Council*) and the *Dublin Regulation* judgment of 2011 (Case C-411/10 *NS v Secretary of State for the Home Department*) are cases in point; see the discussion by E Muir, 'The Court of Justice: A Fundamental Rights Institution among Others' in M Dawson, B de Witte and E Muir (eds), *Judicial Activism at the European Court of Justice* (Cheltenham, Edward Elgar, 2013) 76, 94–96.

[15] This outward-looking human rights policy agenda is strongly advocated by I de Jesus Butler and O De Schutter, 'Binding the EU to International Human Rights Law' 27 (2008) *Yearbook of European Law* 277. For a similar argument in relation to the interpretative practice of the CJEU, see also G de Búrca, 'After the EU Charter of Fundamental Rights: The Court of Justice as a Human Rights Adjudicator?' 20 (2013) *Maastricht Journal of European and Comparative Law* 168.

[16] Proposal for a Council Decision on the signing, on behalf of the European Community, of the United Nations Convention on the Rights of Persons with Disabilities and its Optional Protocol, COM(2007)77 of 27 February 2007.

[17] For a discussion of the role of the EC in the negotiation of the Convention and its possible impact on EU law after its ratification, see L Waddington, 'Breaking New Ground: The Implications of Ratification of the UN Convention on the Rights of Persons with Disabilities for the European Community' in OM Arnardottir and G Quinn, (eds), *The UN Convention on the Rights of Persons with Disabilities: European and Scandinavian Perspectives* (Leiden, Martinus Nijhoff, 2009) 111.

in the EU and national legal orders, but also the submission by the EU to the international monitoring mechanism set in place by the Convention.

The Disability Convention is hailed as the first human rights convention ever concluded by either the EU or the EC. But there are other, less straightforward examples, such as the Council of Europe Convention on the Protection of Children against Sexual Exploitation and Sexual Abuse,[18] whose Article 45(1) specifies clearly that it is open for signature by the EC (now the EU) alongside its Member States. One may expect to see further examples in the future. This development is linked to the extension of the EU's internal competences way beyond economic life into human rights-sensitive policy areas. The existence and use of internal EU competences in fields such as non-discrimination, employment and social policy, immigration and asylum is likely to raise the question sooner or later of whether the EU should adhere to existing human rights instruments related to those policy fields or should participate in new drafting initiatives. For example, both the United Nations and the Council of Europe have adopted conventions for the protection of the rights of migrant workers. These conventions suffer from a lack of ratification by immigration countries.[19] One may wonder whether the EU, if it takes its commitment to guarantee the fundamental rights of all persons seriously and in view of its growing body of migration law, should seek to become a party to one or both of those conventions or, if this is difficult in practice, to require all its Member States to ratify them.

It is still somewhat uncertain whether, from an internal competence perspective, the EU could also become a party to the European Social Charter, which, in human rights policy matters, would seem an obvious companion initiative to the projected accession to the ECHR.[20]

V. PROTECTING FUNDAMENTAL RIGHTS THROUGH POSITIVE MEASURES

As for all other contracting parties, the ECHR will also act as a minimum standard of protection for the EU, but will not prevent the EU from giving more protection to Convention rights under its own fundamental rights regime. This additional protection may result from a rights-friendly interpretation given by the CJEU to the EU Charter provisions which correspond to Convention rights, but it is more likely to result from the action of the EU legislator to give concrete effect to EU Charter rights by means of 'positive measures'.

As long as fundamental rights had the status of unwritten general principles of Community law, they were prominent in the judicial discourse of the CJEU, but remained relatively invisible in the law-making and executive activities of the EC and the EU. This has changed quite noticeably after the adoption of the EU Charter of Rights and Freedoms, and

[18] Convention adopted in Lanzarote on 25 October 2007, *Council of Europe Treaty Series* No 201.

[19] The International Convention on the Protection of the Rights of All Migrant Workers and Members of their Families of 18 December 1990 has 42 contracting parties, among which there is not a single EU Member State. The European Convention on the Legal Status of Migrant Workers, adopted on 24 November 1977 (CETS No 93), has only been ratified by seven EU Member States so far: France, Italy, the Netherlands, Norway, Portugal, Spain and Sweden.

[20] For a powerful argument (written in pre-Lisbon times) that the EU should accede to the European Social Charter and has the legal competence to do so, see O De Schutter, 'Anchoring the European Union to the European Social Charter: The Case for Accession' in G de Búrca and B de Witte (eds), *Social Rights in Europe* (Oxford, Oxford University Press, 2005) 111.

even more so after the Charter acquired binding force as primary EU law. In fact, the EU institutions have put in place new mechanisms to check whether their activities (especially when adopting new EU laws) comply with Charter rights.[21] The Commission also produces an annual report on the Charter, in which it gives a detailed overview of the action taken by the EU's political institutions to protect and promote the exercise of Charter rights.[22]

It is true that the Charter, according to its Article 51(2), does not 'establish any new power or task for the Union, or modify powers and tasks as defined in the Treaties'. The intention of the drafters of the Charter was clearly to avoid that the mere enumeration of a fundamental right would create a competence for the European institutions to act for the protection of that right. The scope of the rights follows existing EU competences rather than the other way round. However, even though this intention is clear, the actual wording of the clause is misleading by its use of the word 'tasks'. Whereas it makes legal sense to affirm that the Charter does not extend the powers of the EU, if one takes 'powers' as meaning 'legal competences', it does not make sense to state that the Charter will not extend the tasks of the EU. Indeed, the very purpose of adopting a Charter of Rights was to make it a task for the European institutions to apply the Charter rights in their various activities. The first paragraph of the same Article 51 of the Charter imposes an obligation on the Member States and the EU to 'promote the application' of the rights contained within it. Many Charter rights require positive action for 'the progressive achievement of their full realization' (to use the words of the UN Social Covenant), so that the right only becomes meaningful when seen in conjunction with the legislative and executive measures taken for its effective enjoyment.

Thus, the question is not so much whether the EU might gain *extra* legislative powers under the Charter for the promotion of human rights (they do not), but whether the *existing* legislative and other powers of the EU will be re-oriented and infused with a range of different values and policy considerations after the enactment of the Charter. So far, the action taken by the EU is very piecemeal: it has adopted or is discussing legal measures to strengthen the right to data protection, the right to non-discrimination, the rights of children and the rights of the accused in criminal proceedings. But so far, it has not adopted an overall strategy defining the positive measures that need to be taken for the entire range of rights and principles contained in the EU Charter. In particular, the social rights listed in the solidarity chapter of the EU Charter have been entirely neglected so far. The danger exists that accession to the ECHR will tend to focus the attention of the EU institutions even more on those rights that are contained in the ECHR (and for which the EU may be called to account before the Strasbourg Court), whilst forgetting about the equally important parts of the EU's own 'bill of rights' which reach beyond the ECHR—in particular, the social rights.

[21] On those initiatives, see Morijn, ch 9 in this volume; and I de Jesus Butler, 'Ensuring Compliance with the Charter of Fundamental Rights in Legislative Drafting: The Practice of the European Commission' (2012) 37 *European Law Review* 397.

[22] The latest such report is the *2011 Report on the Application of the EU Charter of Fundamental Rights*, COM (2012) 169.

Index